Macroeconomics in Context

Macroeconomics in Context lays out the principles of macroeconomics in a manner that is thorough, up to date, and relevant to students. Like its counterpart, *Microeconomics in Context,* the book is uniquely attuned to economic, social, and environmental realities. The "In Context" books offer engaging coverage of current topics including policy responses to recession and inflation, inequality, deficits and government debt, economic impacts of the COVID-19 pandemic, and the economics of environmental sustainability.

This fourth edition includes:

- Improved and concise discussions of introductory topics, especially on key economic activities, macroeconomic goals, and economic models

- Further emphasis on inequality, environmental sustainability, financialization, the changing nature of work, and international developments such as the role of transnational corporations and supply chain issues

- Discussion of the impacts of the COVID-19 pandemic on macroeconomic factors like well-being, inequality, and labor markets

- Presentation of policy issues in historical, environmental, institutional, social, political, and ethical contexts, including an updated discussion of fiscal policy in relation to the Biden administration's infrastructure and social investment spending

- Clear explanations of basic economic concepts alongside more in-depth analysis of macroeconomics models and economic activity

This book combines real-world relevance with a thorough grounding in multiple economic paradigms. It is the ideal textbook for modern introductory courses in macroeconomics. The book's companion website is available at: http://www.bu.edu/eci/macro

Neva Goodwin is a Distinguished Fellow at the Economics in Context Initiative at Boston University's Global Development Policy Center and Co-Director of the Global Development and Environment Institute (GDAE) at Tufts University. Her current interests focus on ecological restoration and its potential for improving human health and helping to mitigate climate change.

Jonathan M. Harris is Visiting Scholar at the Global Development and Environment Institute at Tufts University and Senior Research Fellow at the Economics in Context Initiative at Boston University's Global Development Policy Center. His current research focuses on the implications of large-scale environmental problems, especially global climate change, for macroeconomic theory and policy.

Julie A. Nelson is Emeritus Professor of Economics at the University of Massachusetts Boston and Senior Research Fellow at the Global Development and Environment Institute at Tufts University. Many of her books and articles critique economic methodology from a feminist perspective. She has published in journals ranging from *Econometrica* and the *Journal of Political Economy* to *Hypatia: Journal of Feminist Philosophy* and *Ecological Economics*.

Pratistha Joshi Rajkarnikar is Assistant Director of the Economics in Context Initiative at Boston University's Global Development Policy Center and a lecturer at Boston University and Brandeis University. Her research covers topics on women's empowerment, economic development, and the impacts of globalization on developing economies.

Brian Roach is Director of the Theory and Education Program at the Tufts University Global Development and Environment Institute and a Senior Research Fellow at the Economics in Context Initiative at Boston University. He is a lecturer at Tufts University and has taught at Brandeis University, Brown University, and the University of Maine. He specializes in environmental economics and is a co-author (with Jonathan Harris) of *Environmental and Natural Resource Economics: A Contemporary Approach*.

Mariano Torras teaches Economics at Adelphi University in Garden City, New York, and is Chair of the Department of Finance and Economics. A heterodox economist with a background in ecological and development economics, his recent research has been in the areas of institutional economics, climate change, and financialization.

Macroeconomics in Context

Fourth Edition

Neva Goodwin,
Jonathan M. Harris,
Julie A. Nelson,
Pratistha Joshi Rajkarnikar,
Brian Roach, and
Mariano Torras

Routledge
Taylor & Francis Group

NEW YORK AND LONDON

Cover image: © Getty Images

Fourth edition published 2023
by Routledge
605 Third Avenue, New York, NY 10158

and by Routledge
4 Park Square, Milton Park, Abingdon, Oxon, OX14 4RN

Routledge is an imprint of the Taylor & Francis Group, an informa business

© 2023 Neva Goodwin, Jonathan M. Harris, Julie A. Nelson, Pratistha Joshi Rajkarnikar, Brian Roach, and Mariano Torras

The right of Neva Goodwin, Jonathan M. Harris, Julie A. Nelson, Pratistha Joshi Rajkarnikar, Brian Roach, and Mariano Torras to be identified as authors of this work has been asserted in accordance with sections 77 and 78 of the Copyright, Designs and Patents Act 1988.

First edition published by M. E. Sharpe 2008
Third edition published by Routledge 2019

ISBN: 978-1-032-17039-8 (hbk)
ISBN: 978-1-032-17037-4 (pbk)
ISBN: 978-1-003-25152-1 (ebk)

DOI: 10.4324/9781003251521

Typeset in Times New Roman
by codeMantra

Access the Support Material: http://www.bu.edu/eci/macro

Contents

Figures

Tables

TABLES

Preface

For students taking an introductory macroeconomics course, *Macro-economics in Context* lays out the principles of macroeconomics in a manner that is thorough, up to date, and highly readable. Whether students take this class simply to gain some understanding of how economics can be useful to them or go on to further studies in economics or business, this book will equip them with the critical understanding that they need to succeed. It introduces students both to the standard topics and tools taught in most introductory courses and to a broader and richer set of topics and analyses to deepen comprehension of the economic realities of the twenty-first century.

The study of macroeconomics should not be highly abstract, but closely related to real-world events. *Macroeconomics in Context* addresses this challenge by keeping the theoretical exposition close to the actual experience of economic events. The authors believe that students will achieve a deeper and more memorable understanding of economic theory if they can relate it to contemporary issues of interest and importance.

This textbook is written to encourage engaged and critical thinking about topics in economics. While demonstrating the uses of economic theory, it also provides a variety of viewpoints. Differing economic perspectives—including not only classical and Keynesian, but also monetarist, classical-Keynesian synthesis, and new classical and post-Keynesian approaches—are presented. Woven throughout the book are themes of great importance in everyday life as well as for an understanding of the economy. Within the broad themes of social and environmental well-being and sustainability, attention is given to issues of inequality, globalization, unpaid work, technology, and the environment as well as the financialization of the economy. A specific focus in this edition is on the economic and social impacts of the pandemic. These elements are integrated within discussions of historical, institutional, political, and social factors that affect, and are affected by, the economy.

Macroeconomics in Context is the companion textbook to *Microeconomics in Context* (5th ed.), also published by Routledge.

CONTENT AND ORGANIZATION

NOTE TO INSTRUCTORS: To present a more compact introduction, Part 1 has three chapters, rather than four chapters as in the 3rd edition; instructors who have used the 3rd edition should note that all following chapter numbers are adjusted accordingly; the chapter number is now one less than in the 3rd edition in all chapters from the former Chapter 4, now Chapter 3, up to the final chapter on Growth and Sustainability, now Chapter 17. In addition, the material on Financial Instability has been moved from the former Chapter 15, "Financial Instability and Economic Inequality" to Chapter 10, "Money, Banking and Finance" to allow for a full focus on inequality in Chapter 14, "Inequality: Economic and Social Perspectives."

Although this textbook takes a broader approach to economic analysis, it fits this within a familiar overall organizational strategy. The Sample Course Outlines on pp. xxxvii–xl provide guidance for instructors seeking to present a particular focus within the wide range of topics covered.

■ Part I, "The Context for Economic Analysis," presents the themes of the book and the major actors in the economy. Students are introduced to a range of macroeconomic questions and goals, to basic empirical and theoretical tools, and to the essential activities and institutions of a modern economy. This section concludes with an overview of supply-and-demand analysis and elasticity.
■ Part II, "Macroeconomic Basics," introduces basic macroeconomic definitions and accounting methods, including gross domestic product (GDP), inflation, aggregate demand, and unemployment. These are supplemented with an overview of critiques of GDP, and a discussion of how new accounting systems are being developed to measure the economic contributions of the natural environment, unpaid household labor, and other previously uncounted factors. The second half of Part II brings these abstractions down to earth with a description of the structure of the U.S. macroeconomy and a discussion of the labor market and unemployment.
■ Part III, "Macroeconomic Theory and Policy," explores macroeconomic analysis, including Keynesian and classical theories of economic fluctuations and a full presentation of fiscal and monetary policies. This section also develops an *AS/AD* model of output and inflation, with inflation rather than price level on the vertical axis, and extensive examples of real-world applications. Part III concludes with a chapter discussing macroeconomic issues in the global economy.

■ Part IV, "Macroeconomic Issues and Applications," addresses the contemporary issues of inequality, debt and deficits, economic development, and the environment. While the first two chapters here are presented largely from a U.S. perspective, the second half of this Part widens the lens to explore current global issues of poverty and inequality, economic growth, human development, and current global environmental challenges including climate change and issues of limits to growth and "degrowth."

In order to focus on "contextual" discussions, we have generally placed more formal instruction in algebraic modeling techniques in optional appendices to the chapters. Also, while this book reviews the basics of supply and demand and includes "new classical" macroeconomics among the theories discussed, it devotes fewer pages to the concept of efficient markets than many texts, certainly less than texts that adopt a "new classical" slant. In taking this approach, we have followed the lead of researchers who convincingly argue that "micro foundations" based on the assumptions of perfect competition are of limited usefulness in explaining macroeconomic phenomena. This approach also makes the course less repetitious for students who take both Introduction to Microeconomics and Introduction to Macroeconomics courses.

WHAT MAKES THIS BOOK DIFFERENT FROM OTHER TEXTS?

This text covers the traditional topics included in most macroeconomics texts but treats them from a broader, more holistic perspective. The following chapter-by-chapter synopsis shows how this book manages both to be "similar enough" to fit into a standard curriculum and "different enough" to respond to commonly expressed needs and dissatisfactions with standard approaches, both by instructors and students.

■ Chapter 0, "Macroeconomics and Well-Being," presents graphically illustrated data on 20 variables, in each case showing where the United States stands among 10–13 other countries. The student supplements section at the related web site www.bu.edu/eci/macro allows users to see the same variables listed in order for all countries in the world where such data are available. This innovative chapter can be used in a variety of ways, including as an introduction to later topics, as a reference for use with other chapters, or as material to draw on in designing research projects.
■ Chapter 1, "Economic Activity in Context," offers a basic roadmap presenting major macroeconomic theory concepts in historical context. The goals of macroeconomics are defined in terms of (1) improvement in living standards, (2) stability and security, and (3) financial, social, and ecological sustainability. Brief descriptions of the four essential economic activities—production, consumption,

distribution, and resource management—are presented along with a discussion on what the economy produces, how it is produced, and who benefits from economic growth.

■ Chapter 2, "Foundations of Economic Analysis," introduces standard concepts of economic modeling, efficiency, scarcity, opportunity cost, and the production-possibilities frontier. In addition to the usual economic "circular flow" diagram, this chapter presents a model of economic activity as embedded in social and physical contexts, and taking place within three "spheres": business, public purpose, and "core" or household/ community spheres. Concepts of externalities, public goods, market power, transaction costs, information, expectations, and concern for human needs and equity are introduced to demonstrate why markets, while effective for many purposes, are not on their own sufficient for organizing economic life in service of well-being. A review of graphing techniques is presented in the Appendix.

■ Chapter 3, "Supply and Demand," contains a brief but clear exposition of traditional supply-and-demand curve analysis, including discussions of the slopes of the curves, factors that shift the curves, equilibrium and market adjustment, and a simple discussion of elasticity. Our contextual approach, however, leads to some subtle shifts in presentation. First, the model is explicitly presented as a thought experiment—a humanly created analytical tool that may help us gain insight—rather than as a set of "laws" about "the way the world works." Second, discussions of price changes that are either too slow (i.e., "sticky") or too volatile (e.g., financial market speculation) lead students to consider how a market adjustment in the real world may not be as smooth and welfare-maximizing as the model is often taken to imply.

■ Chapter 4, "Macroeconomic Measurement: The Current Approach," presents an introduction to national income accounting, emphasizing that the accounts have been created for specific purposes, with conventions that reflect particular assumptions or choices. It notes how production and investment undertaken by households and communities have historically been deemphasized in national accounting.

■ Chapter 5, "Macroeconomic Measurement: Environmental and Social Dimensions," gives a thorough introduction to alternative measures of economic performance, including the Genuine Progress Indicator, the Better Life Index, the Human Development Index, and other current approaches for assessing well-being. It includes discussions of issues in the valuation of environmental and household services and of satellite accounts for environmental and household production.

■ Chapter 6, "The Structure of the U.S. Economy," describes key features of production and employment in the U.S. economy, broken down into its primary, secondary, and tertiary sectors. This discussion presents the context to illustrate several current economic issues, such as the loss of manufacturing jobs, the rising costs of health care, the increased role of the service sector, and the growing financialization of the economy.

■ Chapter 7, "Employment, Unemployment, and Wages," discusses labor topics including the definition of the unemployment rate, the different types of unemployment, and theories of the causes of unemployment. The chapter discusses changes in labor force participation rates, questions about labor market "flexibility," the sources of wage differentials and inequalities, and the impact of technological change on the structure of employment. In addition, there is a special focus on labor market institutions and alternative theories of labor markets.

■ Chapter 8, "Aggregate Demand and Economic Fluctuations," introduces the analysis of business cycles, macroeconomic circular flow, and the market for loanable funds. It develops Keynesian aggregate demand analysis of consumption, investment, and government spending. While presenting both classical and Keynesian approaches, the contextual approach emphasizes the possibility of instability and unemployment, rather than focusing primarily on adjustment to full-employment equilibrium.

■ Chapter 9, "Fiscal Policy," balances formal analysis of fiscal policy with up-to-date real-world data and examples. Analysis of fiscal policy impacts is presented in fairly simple terms, with an algebraic treatment of more complex multiplier effects in appendices. While the basic analysis presented here follows the Keynesian model, the text also discusses classical and supply side perspectives and issues of "crowding out" and "crowding in." The section on budgets and deficits should give students a basic understanding—developed further in Chapter 15—of deficits, debt, and how these affect the economy. The difference between automatic stabilizers and discretionary policy is made clear, and recent fiscal policies are discussed, including a new section on infrastructure and social investment.

■ Chapter 10, "Money, Banking, and Finance," presents the basics of money and the banking system, including inflation, deflation, liquidity, and the different aggregate measures of money. Students are introduced to asset and liabilities tables, different banking institutions, and the process of money creation through the fractional reserve system. The chapter presents a discussion of nonbank financial institutions, financialization, and financial bubbles along with theories of financial instability. The appendix discusses the 2008 financial crisis and regulatory reforms to prevent future crises. (The material on financial instability and crises was formerly in Chapter 15 of the 3rd edition).

■ Chapter 11, "The Federal Reserve and Monetary Policy," focuses on the role of the Federal Reserve and the implementation of monetary policy. Here we discuss the Federal Reserve's structure, functions, and monetary policy tools that it employs to create money. The chapter also spotlights theories of money, prices, and inflation, and discusses monetary policies used to respond to inflation and recession from the 1970s to the 2020s. Appendices present a more detailed view of the bond market and interest rates.

■ Chapter 12, "Aggregate Supply, Aggregate Demand, and Inflation: Putting It All Together," addresses the relationship between output, unemployment, and inflation. The model presented in this chapter has many features that will be familiar to instructors. But unlike *AS/AD* models that put the price level on the vertical axis, implying a static equilibrium at a certain level of prices, this model has the inflation rate on the vertical axis, which makes it more relevant for discussing historical examples as well as current events.[*] Rather than focusing on long-run full-employment equilibrium output, we emphasize how the macroeconomy adjusts dynamically to often-unpredictable economic events. The discussion has been updated to take into account combinations of unemployment and inflation during the 2020–2022 period, and includes a discussion of the differences between cost-push and demand-pull inflation. A variety of different perspectives, including classical, Keynesian, New Classical, and Post-Keynesian, are presented in the Chapter and the Appendix.

■ In Chapter 13, "The Global Economy and Policy," the foreign sector is added to the circular-flow picture, which now includes savings, investment, taxes, government spending, exports, and imports. This chapter discusses trade and provides a detailed treatment of the factors that influence currency exchange rates. Chapter 13 also highlights open-economy macroeconomics, analyzing the increasingly important links between fiscal and monetary policies and the global economy, with new material on supply chain issues, capital flight, and impacts of the pandemic. It concludes with a description of the operation of international financial institutions.

■ Chapter 14, "Inequality: Economic and Social Perspectives," provides an overview of key issues on economic and social inequality, looking beyond income measures to explore inequalities based

---

[*] Regarding the theoretical underpinnings of our model, our downward-sloped AD curve is based on the AD curve developed by David Romer ("Keynesian Macroeconomics Without the LM Curve," Journal of Economic Perspectives 14:2 [2000]: 149–169) and adopted by other introductory textbooks writers, including John B. Taylor (Principles of Macroeconomics, Houghton Mifflin, various editions). Our curved AS is based on the notion of an expectations-augmented Phillips curve, translated into inflation and output space. The idea of a dynamically evolving economy, rather than one always headed toward settling at full employment, is an approach based on Keynes' own (rather than new Keynesian) thought, as explained in the appendix to Chapter 12.

on demographic factors, such as race, ethnicity, and education, as well as labor market discrimination. It presents empirical data on inequality in the United States, global inequality between and within countries, and discusses the impact of the pandemic on increasing existing inequality. The chapter concludes with a detailed examination of macroeconomic policy impacts on inequality, and possible policy solutions. (In the 3rd edition, this chapter was Chapter 15, "Financial Instability and Economic Inequality." In this edition, to allow for an expanded treatment of inequality the material on financial instability has been moved to Chapter 10: "Money, Banking, and Finance").

- Chapter 15, "Deficits and Debt," focuses on the fiscal implications of deficits and debt, including issues of internal and external debt, and sovereign debt. The chapter discusses recent increases in debt and concludes with a discussion of deficit projections and policy responses, including consideration of budgetary and tax policy for managing deficits and debt.
- Chapter 16, "How Economies Grow and Develop," presents basic concepts related to economic growth, such as the linear growth and structural change models, which emphasize the importance of investment in manufactured capital. The chapter also focuses on broader concepts of development and provides examples of how investment in other types of capital—e.g., human or natural capital—can be equally, if not more, important. It also explores in detail the question of whether less developed countries have been "catching up" with the industrialized world ("convergence") or falling behind. Country diversity is a central theme; the chapter emphasizes that the "one size fits all" approach to economic development emphasizing structural reforms—such as those embodied in the Washington Consensus—has produced disappointing results and that different approaches are required to meet sustainable development goals.
- Chapter 17, "Growth and Sustainability in the Twenty-First Century," examines global ecological challenges, including a section on global climate change with updates on per capita emissions, recent policies, and national pledges for carbon emissions reduction. While the chapter covers standard theories such as the environmental Kuznets curve, it raises serious challenges to the belief that economic growth and markets can solve this century's social and environmental problems on their own. The chapter presents ideas for alternative approaches to macroeconomic policy including "green Keynesianism," limits to growth and degrowth, and sustainable employment strategies.

SPECIAL FEATURES

Each chapter in this text contains many features designed to enhance student learning.

- *Key terms* are highlighted in boldface throughout the text, and important ideas and definitions are set off from the main text for easy comprehension and review.
- *Discussion Questions* at the end of each section encourage immediate review of what has been read and relate the material to the students' own experience. The frequent appearance of these questions throughout each chapter helps students review manageable portions of material and thus boosts comprehension. The questions can be used for participatory exercises involving the entire class or for small-group discussion.
- *End-of-Chapter Review Questions* are designed to encourage students to create their own summary of concepts. They also serve as helpful guidelines to the importance of various points.
- *End-of-Chapter Exercises* encourage students to work with and apply the material, thereby gaining increased mastery of concepts, models, and investigative techniques.
- Throughout the chapters, boxes enliven the material with real-world illustrations drawn from a variety of sources regarding applications of economic concepts and recent macroeconomic developments.
- In order to make the chapters as lively and accessible as possible, some formal and technical material (suitable for inclusion in some but not all course designs) is concisely explained in chapter appendices.
- A glossary at the end of the book contains all key terms, their definitions, and the number of the chapter in which each was first used and defined.

SUPPLEMENTS

The supplements package for this book includes an *Instructor's Resource Manual* and *Test Bank* to accompany *Macroeconomics in Context*. To access these electronically, send a request via e-mail to eci@bu.edu with information to verify instructor status.

For each chapter, the *Instructor's Resource Manual* includes an introductory note, detailed lecture notes, and answers to all review questions and end-of-chapter exercises, in addition to complete data sets for the Chapter 0 variables. The "Notes on Discussion Questions" section provides suggested answers to these questions and ideas on how the questions might be used in the classroom.

The Test Bank includes multiple-choice and true/false questions for each chapter. The correct answer for each question is indicated.

PowerPoint slides of figures and tables from the text and a *Student Study Guide* that provides ample opportunity for students to review and practice the key concepts are available for free download at www.bu.edu/eci/macro.

HOW TO USE THIS TEXT

The feedback that we have received from instructors who have used the first three editions of this text has been enthusiastic and gratifying. We have found that this book works in a variety of courses with a variety of approaches, and we would like to share some of these instructors' suggestions on tailoring this book to meet different course needs.

On pages xxxiv–xl, you will find several possible course plans based on different emphases (such as ecological, global, human development, and structural). We hope that this will help in planning the course that will best suit the needs of instructors and students.

NOTE ON DIFFERENCES FROM THE THIRD EDITION

The third edition of this book was published in 2018; much has happened in the world since then—and many real-world events have been reflected in new ways of understanding and teaching about the macroeconomy. In addition to updating data in the text, tables, figures, and boxes, the fourth edition of *Macroeconomics in Context* has been extensively revised and refreshed in response to new macroeconomic developments.

In Part I, Chapter 0 retains the same innovative data, all updated. The graph on life expectancy has been replaced with data on the more comprehensive index on the quality of health care systems across countries. Also, data on internet users has been deleted and a new graph on the gender gap index has been added to this chapter. The three introductory chapters in the third edition have now been cut down to two chapters, presenting a more concise discussion on the introductory topics. Chapter 1 now includes discussion on key economic activities and the five types of capital, which was presented in Chapter 3 in the third edition. The chapter also discusses some impacts of the COVID-19 pandemic and puts increased focus on issues such as inequality, environmental sustainability, and the role of government, initiating a narrative that will continue in various places throughout the book. In Chapter 2, the discussion on economic models has been made more concise. The discussion on market institutions now appears in Chapter 2. Chapter 3 is largely unchanged, presenting the detailed supply and demand analysis which appeared in Chapter 4 in the third edition. Note that starting with Chapter 3, the chapter numbers in the fourth edition are one less than the chapter numbers in the third edition. This provides for a more compact introduction in Chapters 1 and 2, but the order of the following chapters has not been changed.

In Part II, Macroeconomic Basics, Chapter 4 on basic national income analysis is largely unchanged except for updated material on applications including the recovery from the 2020 recession, while Chapter 5 on alternative approaches includes updated research on various well-being indicators, expanded description of new indices related to the Human Development Index, and some discussion on the impacts of COVID-19 on non-market work and gender inequality. Chapters 6 and 7 on the structure of the U.S. economy and the labor market have been thoroughly updated while retaining the same basic structure. Discussion on the impact of the pandemic on various economic sectors and on labor market outcomes has been added to these chapters.

In Part III on macroeconomic theory and policy, Chapter 8 retains the same explanation of the derivation of "aggregate expenditure" in the Keynesian model (we return to the broader term "aggregate demand" when we introduce price changes and inflation in Chapter 12). Boxes in Chapter 8 have been updated to discuss the 2020 recession and subsequent recovery. Chapter 9 likewise updates the discussion of fiscal policy to include the Biden administration's infrastructure and social investment spending.

Chapters 10 and 11, on money and monetary policy, include discussion of cryptocurrencies, pension fund investments, fiduciary rules, and recent changes in the definition of the M1 money supply measure. The discussion on financial instability that appeared in Chapter 15 in the third edition now appears in Chapter 10, and the description of the 2008 financial crisis is now presented as an Appendix to Chapter 10. Chapter 11 includes treatment of negative interest rates, "modern monetary theory", and the return of significant inflation in 2021–2022. Chapter 12, on Aggregate Supply, Aggregate Demand, and Inflation, goes into more detail on recent inflation and policy responses, differentiating between cost-push and demand-pull inflation, and explaining how advocates of contrasting theoretical perspectives interpret the recent inflation experience. Chapter 13 likewise updates the treatment of open-economy macroeconomics, including discussion of transnational corporations and international supply chain problems, varying policy responses to the pandemic, and emerging debt problems in developing nations.

In Part IV on issues and applications, Chapter 14 now focuses exclusively on the issue of economic and social inequality. (The sections of the former Chapter 15 dealing with financial instability now appear in Chapters 10 and 11). Chapter 14 has been thoroughly revised to include recent data on inequality in the U.S. and across countries. A new section on labor market discrimination has been added and the discussion on causes of inequality and policies to respond to inequality has been updated. A topic box focuses on the effect of the COVID-19 crisis in exacerbating pre-existing inequality. Chapter 15 includes updated information and data on deficits and debt, with a focus on recent increases in the U.S. national debt, resulting both from the Trump tax cuts and pandemic-related spending. Chapter 16 includes more material on poverty measures, differing theories of development, the impact of COVID on sustainable development goals and a new box on development aid from China. Chapter 17, Growth and Sustainability in the Twenty-First Century, includes more discussion of recent developments in macro-level environmental issues such as population growth, forest loss, and climate change. It presents updated analysis of "green growth", limits to growth, and degrowth, and economic policies for sustainability including recent green infrastructure investments such as expanding renewable energy, modernizing the electric grid, upgrading water systems, and promoting climate resilience.

Note: In order to better reflect the diversity of users of this text, we now vary our use of pronouns between "he", "she", and "they" (singular).

Acknowledgments

Macroeconomics in Context was written under the auspices of the Economics in Context Initiative (ECI) at Boston University's Global Development Policy Center. All contributors of written materials were paid through grants raised by the ECI.

Contributors to earlier editions, whose work continues to appear in this edition, include Dr. James Devine of Loyola Marymount University, Los Angeles, who contributed to the macro modeling chapters; Ben Beachy, now Director of the Sierra Club's Living Economy Program, who contributed to the section on the 2008 financial crisis, now appearing as the appendix to Chapter 10; and Dr. Nathan Perry of Colorado Mesa University, who contributed to Chapter 15 on deficits and debt.

We thank a number of instructors who were exceptionally generous in giving us detailed comments on previous editions, including Alison Butler, Willamette University; Gary Flomenhoft, University of Vermont; Robin King, Georgetown University; Dennis Leyden, University of North Carolina, Greenville; Valerie Luzadis, SUNY-ESF, Syracuse; Eric Nilsson, California State University San Bernardino; Chiara Piovani, University of Utah; Rebecca Smith, Mississippi State University; Saranna Thornton, Hampden-Sydney College; Marjolein van der Veen, Bellevue Community College; and Thomas White, Assumption College.

Mohish Agrawal of Boston University did essential support work on research and manuscript preparation, including data analysis for Chapter 0 and other data and figures throughout the text. We also thank the staff at Routledge, particularly Michelle Gallagher and Chloe Herbert, for their enthusiasm and meticulous work in getting this book to press.

Sample Course Outlines

The timespan of an academic term imposes severe constraints on what an instructor can teach, which require choices regarding which topics to include and how much time to devote to each. *Macroeconomics in Context* can be used as the basis for a variety of approaches, depending on which topics and approaches are of particular interest.

To help identify the chapter assignments that make the most sense for individual instructors, we have put together some ideas for course outlines below. Arranged in terms of broad selections and more specific emphases, they are designed to help instructors choose among chapters when there is not enough time to cover everything in this textbook.

We understand that in many departments one primary objective of the introductory course is to teach in some detail "how (neoclassical) economists think." For instructors who choose to focus primarily on neoclassical content, the most traditional combination of the selections described below—the Base Chapters, combined with some or all of the Basic Macroeconomics Selection and the Macro-Modeling Emphasis—will provide what you need. This combination of chapters does not come close to exploiting fully the richness of *Macroeconomics in Context,* but the contextual discussions (a hallmark of this text) that are woven into the standard material will broaden the students' understanding of macroeconomic theory and provide tools for critical thinking.

Many instructors seek to combine coverage of traditional neoclassical ideas with other material. Ecological sustainability, for example, is an issue of increasing importance and is deeply linked to the functioning of the macroeconomy. For this focus, the Base Chapters Selection and most of the Basic Macroeconomics Selection could be combined with the "Ecological Emphasis" Selection.

Some instructors and students may have less interest in the formalities of macroeconomic modeling, in which case it might make sense to cover the Base Chapters Selection, some material from the Basic Macroeconomics Selection, and much more material from the topical emphases.

Summary of Possible Course Options

Curriculum Focus	Likely Selections (see descriptions below)
Traditional macroeconomics	Base Chapters Basic Macroeconomics Modeling Emphasis
Strong focus on traditional macroeconomics, with other themes woven in	Base Chapters Basic Macroeconomics Choose from other Emphases
Coverage of basic traditional concepts within course tailored to instructor and student interests	Base Chapters Choose selections from Basic Macroeconomics Choose from other Emphases

BASE CHAPTERS SELECTION

- Chapter 1, "Economic Activity in Context"
- Chapter 2, "Useful Tools and Concepts"
- Chapter 3, "Supply and Demand"

BASIC MACROECONOMICS SELECTION

- Chapter 4, "Macroeconomic Measurement: The Current Approach"
- Chapter 7, "Employment, Unemployment, and Wages"
- Chapter 8, "Aggregate Demand and Economic Fluctuations"
- Chapter 9, "Fiscal Policy"
- Chapters 10 and 11, "Money, Banking and Finance," and "The Federal Reserve and Monetary Policy"
- Chapter 12, "Aggregate Supply, Aggregate Demand, and Inflation: Putting It All Together"
- Chapter 16, "How Economies Grow and Develop"

ECOLOGICAL EMPHASIS

- Chapter 1, Section 2 "Macroeconomic Goals" and Section 3 "The Issues that Define Economics"
- Chapter 5, "Macroeconomic Measurement: Environmental and Social Dimensions"
- Chapter 6, Section 1, "The Three Major Productive Sectors in an Economy," and Section 2, "The Primary Sector in the United States"
- Chapter 17, "Growth and Sustainability in the Twenty-First Century"

GLOBAL EMPHASIS

- Chapter 13, "The Global Economy and Policy"
- Chapter 16, "How Economies Grow and Develop"
- Chapter 17, "Growth and Sustainability in the Twenty-First Century"

HUMAN DEVELOPMENT EMPHASIS

- Chapter 1, Section 2 "Macroeconomic Goals"
- Chapter 5, "Macroeconomic Measurement: Environmental and Social Dimensions"
- Chapter 16, "How Economies Grow and Develop"

STRUCTURAL EMPHASIS

- Chapter 7, "The Structure of the U.S. Economy"
- Chapter 14, "Inequality: Economic and Social Dimensions"
- Chapter 15, "Deficits and Debt"

KEYNESIAN/POST-KEYNESIAN/INSTITUTIONALIST EMPHASIS

- Chapter 2, Section 4, "The Role of Markets"
- Chapter 3, Section 5, "Macroeconomics and the Dynamics of Real-World Markets"
- Chapter 8, "Aggregate Demand and Economic Fluctuations"
- Chapter 9, "Fiscal Policy"
- Chapter 10, Sections 4.3, "Financialization and Financial Bubbles", 4.4 "Financial Instability" and Appendix, "The 2007–2008 Financial Crisis"
- Chapter 12, "Aggregate Supply, Aggregate Demand, and Inflation: Putting It All Together", including Appendix A3, "Post-Keynesian Macroeconomics"

MACRO-MODELING EMPHASIS

- Chapter 8, Appendix, "An Algebraic Approach to the Multiplier"
- Chapter 9, Appendix, "More Algebraic Approaches to the Multiplier"
- Chapter 12, Appendix, "More Schools of Macroeconomics"
- Chapter 13, Section 4, "Macroeconomics in an Open Economy" and Appendix, "An Algebraic Approach to the Multiplier, in a Model with Trade"
- Chapter 16, Section 1, "Economic Growth and Development"

MONEY AND FINANCE EMPHASIS

- Chapters 10 and 11, "Money, Banking and Finance," and "The Federal Reserve and Monetary Policy"
- Chapter 15, "Deficits and Debt"

POVERTY/INEQUALITY/SOCIAL JUSTICE EMPHASIS

- Chapter 5, "Macroeconomic Measurement: Social and Environmental Dimensions"

xxxix

- Chapter 7, Section 3, "Theories of Employment, Unemployment, and Wages"
- Chapter 14, "Inequality: Economic and Social Perspectives"
- Chapter 16, "How Economies Grow and Develop

CONTRASTING SCHOOLS OF THOUGHT EMPHASIS

- Chapter 1, Section 4, "Macroeconomics in Context,"
- Chapter 12, Section 4, "Competing Theories," and Appendix, "More Schools of Macroeconomics"
- Chapter 17, "Growth and Sustainability in the Twenty-First Century," Section 4, "Economic Growth and the Environment" and Section 5, "Policies for Sustainable Development"

The Context for Economic Analysis

Macroeconomics and Well-Being

What comes to your mind when you think of the word "economics"? Perhaps you think about things like money, unemployment, GDP (gross domestic product), inflation, and supply and demand. These things are important in our study of economics, and we will spend much of our time in this book studying these concepts.

But the goals of economics are about much more than these. As we will see in Chapter 1, economics is *the study of how people manage their resources to meet their needs and enhance their well-being.* The term "well-being" can mean different things to different people. Traditional macroeconomic indicators like growth, inflation, money, investment, and unemployment clearly affect our well-being. But so do our health, the quality of our environment, our leisure time, our perceptions of fairness and justice, and many other factors. In this book, we will take an inclusive approach to well-being.

If the goal of economics is to enhance our well-being, then it helps to have an idea about our current level of well-being—where we are doing well, and where some improvement is desired. Since in this book we are studying *macro*economics (as opposed to *micro*economics), we are often concerned with various measures at a national level. This chapter provides you with an overview of how a variety of countries compare across different measures of macroeconomic performance and well-being. In the discussion below, we categorize high-income countries as developed, and middle and low-income countries as developing. The classification of high-income, middle-income, and low-income groups is based on the definition provided by the World Bank.* If you are interested in the performance of specific countries not included here, we provide detailed tables on the book's eResource: www.bu.edu/eci/macro.

---

* For the fiscal year 2022, the World Bank defines low-income countries as those with a GNI per capita of US$1,045 or less in 2020; lower middle-income countries are those with a GNI per capita between US$1,046 and US$4,095; upper middle-income countries are those with a GNI per capita between US$4,096 and US$12,695; and high-income countries as those with a GNI per capita above US$12,695.

The topics covered here preview many of the issues that are covered in more detail in later chapters. You may find some of the information in this chapter surprising. Sometimes the data-based results differ from common perceptions and media representations. But we have tried to be as objective as possible by presenting a wide range of data from reliable sources. Good data are essential for informed debates about how to enhance well-being in our communities, our country, and our planet.

NOTES ON GRAPHS

For each measure included in this chapter, we provide a bar graph showing the data for selected countries. (Tables presenting the available data for all countries can be found on the book's eResource: www.bu.edu/eci/macro). The countries shown here have been chosen to convey the full range of results, with a focus on the United States (the U.S. results are always highlighted). Major countries, such as China, India, and the UK, are also included in most figures. Country rankings are provided, based on the available data, including the highest and lowest values for each variable. While there are over 200 countries in the world, data are not available for all countries for each variable. Thus, the number of countries ranked for each variable differs. For example, in our first chart (GDP per capita) the lowest ranking for a country is 178, indicating that reliable, accessible data on this variable are available for only 178 countries.

The rankings are presented with the "highest" at the top and the "lowest" at the bottom. However, this does not always mean that it is best to be at the top. For example, we present graphs showing the unemployment rate, percentage of people living in absolute poverty, and carbon dioxide emissions per capita. Obviously, it is not a good thing to be ranked first (the highest) for these variables.

For each graph, the names of the countries selected appear on the left. The bar to the right of the country's name shows the value for that country, reading down from the end of the bar to the horizontal axis. For example, we can see in the first graph that GDP per capita is a little under US$15,000 in Brazil, it is about US$60,000 in the United States, and is almost US$64,000 in Norway. (For precise values, refer to the textbook's Web site.) Finally, to the right of each bar is that country's ranking for that variable. So, Norway has the sixth-highest GDP per capita, the United States the eighth-highest, and Brazil the seventy-eighth-highest. Among the 178 countries with reliable GDP per capita data, Burundi has the lowest GDP per capita. In our discussion of each graph, we generally mention some countries that are and some that are not listed on the graph.

The list of graphs that appear in this chapter are:

1. GDP per Capita
2. Growth Rate of GDP per Capita
3. Net National Savings
4. Government Debt
5. Labor Productivity
6. Average Annual Hours Worked
7. Unemployment Rate
8. Inflation
9. Taxes Received by Central Government
10. Trade Balance
11. Income Inequality
12. Gender Gap Index
13. Absolute Poverty
14. Foreign Aid (Donors)
15. Foreign Aid (Recipients)
16. Educational Performance
17. Healthcare Access and Quality
18. Subjective Well-Being
19. Carbon Dioxide Emissions per Capita
20. Local Air Quality

1. GDP PER CAPITA

What it is: Media stories of economic performance frequently refer to gross domestic product (GDP). A country's GDP per capita measures economic production per person per year, which gives us an idea of the average material living standards in the country. While GDP is perhaps the most commonly used macroeconomic metric, it does not necessarily measure well-being. We discuss how GDP is calculated in Chapter 4 and the limitations of, and alternatives to, GDP in Chapter 5.

The results: The United States ranks eighth, with a GDP per capita of around US$60,000. Luxembourg has the world's highest GDP per capita at around US$110,000, with the country's economy driven by its banking, steel, and industrial sectors. Burundi has the lowest GDP per capita, at only US$731 (Figure 0.1).

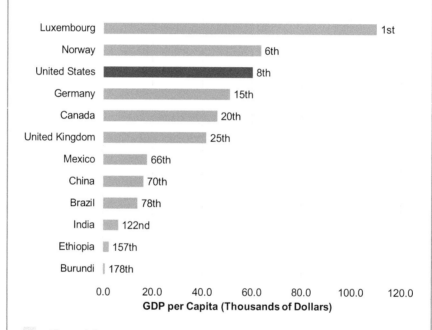

Figure 0.1 GDP per Capita (Thousands of Dollars), 2020

Source: World Bank, World Development Indicators database.

Data are adjusted for purchasing power differences across countries (e.g., a dollar in India buys more than a dollar in the United States).

2. GROWTH RATE OF GDP PER CAPITA

What it is: In macroeconomics, we seek to explain not only why some countries have a higher GDP per capita but also what conditions lead to strong GDP growth rates. In this graph, we compare the growth in GDP per capita, after adjusting for inflation, across countries over the ten-year period 2010–2019, in order to observe growth trends over a long term. For the same reason, we have chosen not to include data from 2020, as this was an exceptional year for most countries due to the COVID-19 pandemic. Of the 179 countries with data on GDP per capita available, 162 experienced negative GDP per capita growth in 2020. We discuss measuring GDP growth rates in Chapter 4 and theories of GDP growth in Chapter 16.

The results: GDP per capita grew rapidly from 2010 to 2019 in some countries, slowly in others, and even declined in several countries. The highest growth in GDP per capita (excluding some tiny countries with exceptional circumstances) occurred in China, primarily from market-oriented reforms and rapid productivity growth, with high growth also in Turkmenistan, Ethiopia, and Bangladesh. The fastest growth among developed countries took place in Ireland. Twenty-five countries experienced a decline in GDP per capita over this time period, including Brazil, Qatar, Greece, Angola, Kuwait, the Central African Republic, and Equatorial Guinea (Figure 0.2).

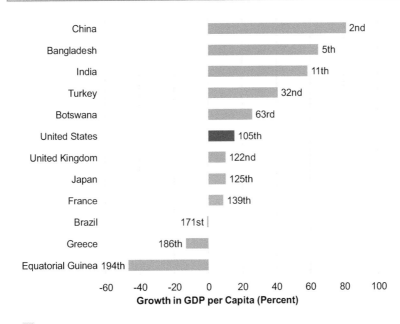

Figure 0.2 Growth in GDP per Capita (Percent), 2010–2019

Source: World Bank, World Development Indicators database.
Data are adjusted for purchasing power differences.

3. NET NATIONAL SAVINGS

What it is: How much a country saves and invests is widely considered an important factor in explaining differences in GDP growth rates. Here we present data on net national savings rates, which equal total national savings minus the depreciation of productive capital such as factories and machinery. A negative net national savings rate implies that a country's productive capacity is declining. We discuss saving, investment, and growth in detail in Chapter 16.

The results: In 2019, Brunei—a country with oil and gas as major sources of national income—had the highest net national savings rate. Other countries with high savings rates include Nepal, Sudan, Qatar, Singapore, and China. Fourteen countries (among those with data) had a negative net savings rate in 2019, including the UK, Ukraine, Kenya, and Greece (Figure 0.3).

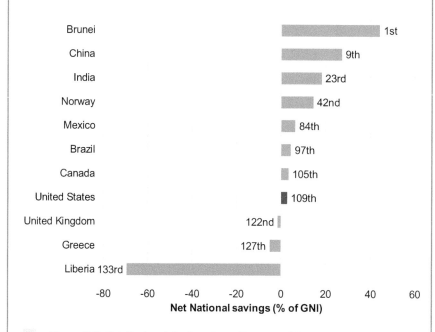

Figure 0.3 Net National Savings Rate (Percent of GNI), 2019

Source: World Bank, World Development Indicators database.

GNI is gross national income, a measure similar to gross domestic product, but including income from residents abroad and excluding income earned by foreigners within the country. GNI is also sometimes referred to as Gross National Product (GNP).

4. GOVERNMENT DEBT

What it is: The level of government debt has been a focus of media stories in recent years. What matters is not so much the size of debt in dollars but government debt relative to a country's GDP. This variable portrays the amount of debt owed by the government of a country, including debts owed to domestic and foreign entities. What level of debt should be considered a problem? This is a topic we discuss in more detail in Chapter 15.

The results: In 2017, Japan had the highest government debt in the world, measured as a percentage of GDP, followed by Greece and Barbados. The United States had the thirty-sixth-highest debt, but many other developed countries had higher debt, including Singapore, Canada, France, and the UK. While some developing countries, such as Mozambique and Sudan have high levels of government debt, others, such as Libya and Afghanistan, have relatively low government debt (Figure 0.4).

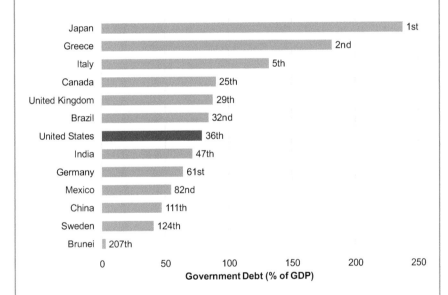

Figure 0.4 *Government Debt (Percent of GDP), 2017*

Source: United States Central Intelligence Agency, *CIA World Factbook.*

5. LABOR PRODUCTIVITY

What it is: One measure of the economic efficiency of a country is labor productivity. This is calculated by dividing a country's GDP by an estimate of the total number of hours worked. Thus, labor productivity tells us how many dollars of GDP are generated for each hour worked. We discuss labor productivity in Chapters 6 and 7.

The results: Data on labor productivity are available for only 39 countries. Ireland has the highest labor productivity in the world. The United States ranks fifth, behind Luxembourg, Norway, and Denmark. Productivity is slightly lower in France and the UK. Less developed countries have lower labor productivity. We see that productivity in Mexico is only about one-third of the U.S. level (Figure 0.5).

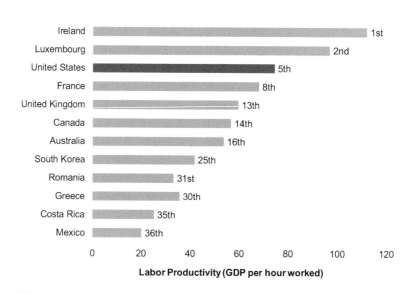

Labor Productivity (GDP per hour worked)

Figure 0.5 *Labor Productivity (GDP per Hour Worked), 2020*

Source: Organisation for Economic Co-operation and Development, OECD online statistical database.

10

6. AVERAGE ANNUAL HOURS WORKED

What it is: This graph shows the average number of hours worked each year per employee. Note that this includes only hours actually worked; vacations, holidays, and sick days are excluded. Thus, the average annual hours worked in a country may be high if work expectations are more stringent and time off is limited. Work hours may also be high if workers choose to work long hours and there are very few part-time workers. We discuss work hours further in Chapter 7.

The results: Data on hours worked are available for only 39 countries. The average annual hours worked per employee are the lowest in Germany. Other countries with relatively low annual work hours are the Netherlands, Norway, the UK, and Denmark. One reason for the relatively low work hours in these countries is federal laws that mandate minimum vacation times and paid holidays. In the United States, where such laws do not exist, average work hours are higher. Work hours tend to be highest among countries with lower levels of GDP per capita. In 2020, Mexico had the highest average annual hours worked, followed by Costa Rica and South Korea (Figure 0.6).

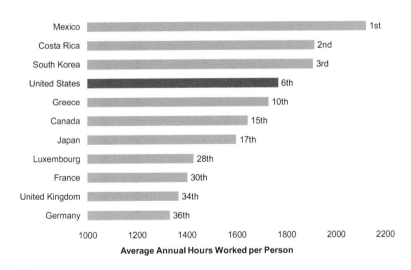

Figure 0.6 *Average Annual Hours Worked per Person, 2020*

Source: Organisation for Economic Co-operation and Development. OECD online statistical database.

7. UNEMPLOYMENT RATE (PERCENT OF TOTAL WORKFORCE)

What it is: The unemployment rate is defined as the percentage of workforce actively seeking a job. This is an important macroeconomic metric—not only does having a job provide a source of income, but it also provides a sense of identity and contributes to overall well-being. Estimating the unemployment rate is somewhat complex, and the method used to measure unemployment rate may differ across countries. In Chapter 7, we discuss issues involved in estimating the unemployment rate including defining what it means to be in the workforce.

The results: Unemployment rates vary tremendously across countries and they also fluctuate a lot over time. In 2020, Cambodia had the lowest official unemployment rate at 0.3 percent and South Africa had the highest unemployment rate at about 29 percent. While many low-income countries, such as Lesotho and Sudan have very high unemployment rates (15 percent or more), other developing countries such as Uganda and Myanmar have rather low unemployment rates, at less than 2 percent. The unemployment rate in the United States, usually in the range of 4–6 percent, rose sharply in 2020 due to the lockdowns imposed by the COVID-19 pandemic, peaking at 14.8 percent in April 2020, and has since declined to about 3.5 percent as of mid-2022 (Figure 0.7).

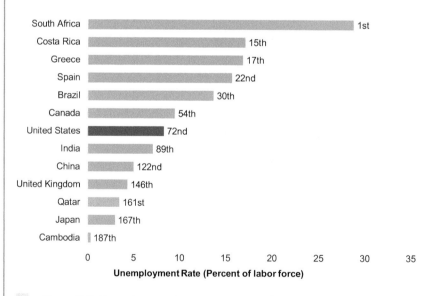

Figure 0.7 Unemployment Rate (Percent of Labor Force), 2020

Source: World Bank, World Development Indicators database.

8. INFLATION

What it is: The rate of inflation summarizes how average prices change in a country in one year. Rapidly rising prices could result in a decline in overall living standards if wages don't rise at a similar pace. In Chapter 4, we discuss how inflation is measured, and we focus on macroeconomic theories of inflation in Chapters 11 and 12.

The results: Over the period 2011–2020, Switzerland had the lowest inflation rate in the world, with prices actually declining slightly during some years and hardly increasing overall. However, this is not necessarily a good thing, as we see later in the book. A low and stable—but not negative—inflation rate is generally considered an important macroeconomic policy goal. In the last few decades, most developed countries had generally been successful at controlling inflation. But the pandemic-related supply chain disruptions and the Russia-Ukraine war have resulted in higher inflation rates more recently. High and fluctuating inflation rates in a country are a sign of macroeconomic instability. With an average inflation rate of over 90 percent between 2011 and 2020, South Sudan had the highest inflation rate over this period. Extremely high inflation rates of over 10,000 percent in Venezuela and over 500 percent in Zimbabwe have been observed in recent years (Figure 0.8).

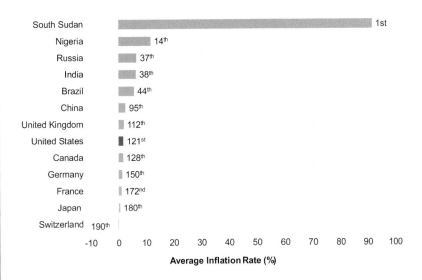

Figure 0.8 Average Annual Inflation Rate, 2011–2020

Source: World Bank, World Development Indicators database.

The average inflation rate is calculated as the average of the inflation rate for each year from 2011 to 2020.

9. TAXES RECEIVED BY CENTRAL GOVERNMENT (PERCENT OF GDP)

What it is: Tax policies are among the most significant ways a government can influence the well-being of the citizens, as we discuss in Chapter 9. Taxes received by the central government, expressed as a percentage of GDP, includes taxes collected at the federal level. Note that some countries also collect a significant amount of taxes at the local level.

The results: Overall tax revenues vary significantly across countries. While Western European countries tend to have relatively high taxes, some other countries with high taxes (more than 25 percent of GDP) include Lesotho, Jamaica, and South Africa. The United States has relatively low tax rates—by far the lowest of any major industrialized country. The countries with the lowest tax revenues (less than 10 percent of GDP) include relatively poor countries in Africa and Asia. The United Arab Emirates, a high-income country in the Middle East, has the lowest tax revenue of less than 1 percent of its GDP (Figure 0.9).

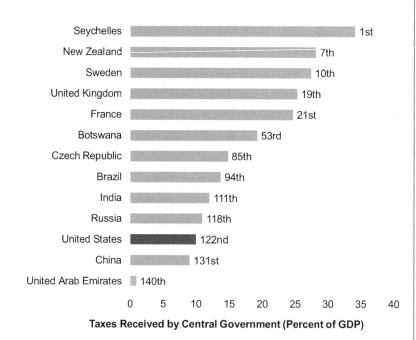

Taxes Received by Central Government (Percent of GDP)

Figure 0.9 *Taxes Received by Central Government (Percent of GDP)*

Source: World Bank, World Development Indicators database.

Data are mostly 2019 estimates.

10. TRADE BALANCE (PERCENT OF GDP)

What it is: Economists refer to a country's trade balance as the dollar value of its exports minus its imports, normally expressed as a percentage of GDP. Thus, a negative trade balance, when a country imports more than it exports, indicates a trade deficit. A positive trade balance indicates a trade surplus. The trade deficit of the United States is often considered a cause for concern in media stories. We discuss trade balances, and other trade issues, in more detail in Chapter 13.

The results: Of the 176 countries with available data, 72 have a positive trade balance (exports exceed imports) and 104 have a negative trade balance. Those countries with the largest trade surpluses tend to be smaller countries (such as Luxembourg and Singapore) or oil-producing countries (such as Qatar and the United Arab Emirates). The U.S. trade deficit is about 3 percent of GDP, with other countries, such as Canada, France, and Turkey, in a similar range. The countries with the largest trade deficits tend to be poorer countries, although some poor countries do have trade surpluses (Figure 0.10).

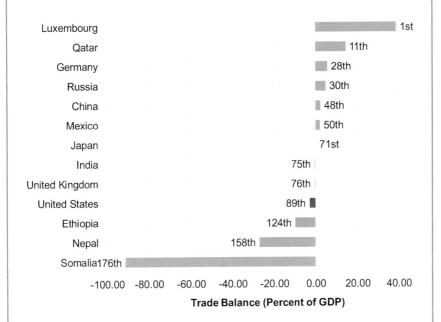

Figure 0.10 *Trade Balance (Percent of GDP)*

Source: World Bank, World Development Indicators database, and authors' calculations.

Data are mostly 2019 estimates.

11. INCOME INEQUALITY (GINI COEFFICIENT)

What it is: A Gini coefficient is a measure of economic inequality in a country. It is most commonly calculated according to the distribution of income (as is done in the figure here), but it can also be calculated according to wealth distribution or other variables. It can range from 0 (perfect equality where everyone in the country has the same exact income) to 1 (perfect inequality where one person receives all the income in a country). We learn more about Gini coefficients and economic inequality in Chapter 14.

The results: Countries in Central and Eastern Europe including Slovenia, Czech Republic, Belarus, and Ukraine and Scandinavian countries such as Denmark, Norway, and Finland tend to be the most equal countries in the world, by income (with the lowest Gini coefficients). Several African countries, including Botswana, Zambia, Namibia, and South Africa are the most unequal countries in the world. In general, countries with high GDP per capita have lower inequality than those with low GDP per capita (compare Figures 0.1 and 0.11). However, this is not always true. The United States, for example, is among the most economically unequal of the developed countries.

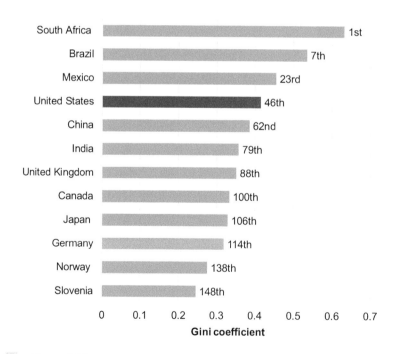

Figure 0.11 Gini Coefficient (Least Equal to Most Equal)

Source: World Bank, World Development Indicators database. Data for the most recent year available, between 2011 and 2019.

12. GENDER GAP INDEX

What it is: The gender gap index tracks the change in gender-based inequality along four main dimensions—economic participation and opportunity, educational attainment, health and survival, and political empowerment. It is measured on a scale of 0–1, with the score representing the percentage of the gender gap that has been closed. Hence, a higher score indicates greater progress in closing the gender gap.

The results: Nordic countries, including Iceland, Finland, and Norway rank the highest on the gender gap index. While, in general, developed countries have made much more progress in closing the gender gap than most developing countries, some developing countries such as Namibia, Rwanda, and Costa Rica rank relatively high on this index. Countries in South Asia and the Middle East, including Kuwait, Saudi Arabia, Syria, Pakistan, and Afghanistan rank the lowest, in the gender gap index. Issues on gender-based inequality will be addressed at several points throughout this textbook (Figure 0.12).

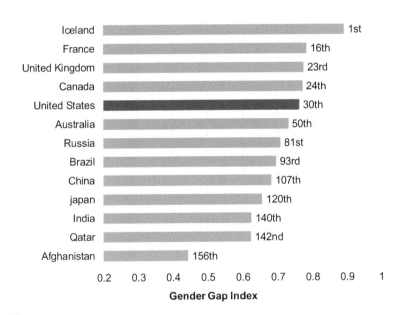

Figure 0.12 Global Gender Gap Index, 2020

Source: Global Gender Gap Report 2021, World Economic Forum.

13. ABSOLUTE POVERTY

What it is: The US$1.90-per-day poverty line has been defined by the United Nations as a measure of absolute poverty. One of the Sustainable Development Goals set by the United Nations is to eradicate absolute poverty worldwide. Extreme poverty had been declining steadily over the last 20 years as the percentage of the global population living under the US$1.90 per day threshold fell from 36 percent in 1990 to about 8 percent in 2019. However, extreme poverty rose for the first time in 2020, with an additional 120 million people falling into poverty, due to the compounded effects of conflicts, climate change, and the COVID-19 pandemic. We discuss poverty and economic development in Chapter 16.

The results: Note that this is one of the two graphs in this chapter that does not include the United States or any other developed countries (few people in developed countries live below the US$1.90-a-day poverty line, though homelessness and food insecurity continue to plague many cities in the U.S.). A majority of people do live below that poverty line in 13 countries, including Madagascar, South Sudan, Malawi, Rwanda, and Mozambique. A small portion of the population lives in absolute poverty in some upper middle-income countries such as Argentina, Costa Rica, Thailand, and Turkey (Figure 0.13).

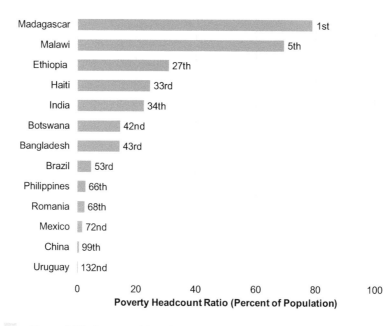

Figure 0.13 *Percent of Population Living Below $1.90/day Poverty Line*

Data are for the most recent year available, between 2011 and 2019.
Source: World Bank, World Development Indicators database.

14. FOREIGN AID (DONORS)

What it is: In 1970, the "economically advanced" countries agreed to a United Nations resolution on foreign aid to developing countries. The resolution set a target for official development assistance (ODA) of 0.7 percent of gross national income (GNI). ODA is defined as government flows to promote economic development and welfare in developing countries. The 0.7 percent target has been reaffirmed at subsequent international meetings. We discuss the role of foreign aid in promoting economic development in Chapter 16.

The results: In 2020 only six countries met the 0.7 percent target: Sweden, Turkey, Norway, Luxembourg, Denmark, and Germany. Turkey began giving aid recently, mostly to Muslim-majority countries in the Middle East and Sub-Saharan Africa. ODA from the United States was 0.17 percent of GNI. Cyprus, Israel, and Taiwan had the lowest ODA percentage, at less than 0.1 percent. Though China is not included in the OECD database on aid, China has emerged as a major donor over the last two decades spending over $350 billion in the period from 2000 to 2014.[1] A common criticism of foreign aid is that it is given to gain political and economic influence (Figure 0.14).

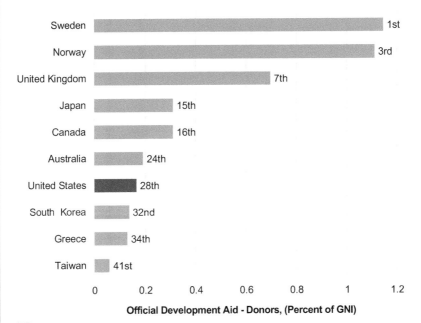

Figure 0.14 Official Development Assistance (Percent of GNI), 2020

Source: Organisation for Economic Co-operation and Development, Official Development Assistance—2020 Update.

15. FOREIGN AID (RECIPIENTS)

What it is: Official Development Aid (ODA) received by a country includes bilateral aid from another country as well as multilateral aid from international organizations. Net ODA as a percentage of GNI (Gross National Income) shows the size of aid received by a country relative to the country's gross national income. It is an indicator of how dependent a country is on foreign aid. Foreign aid may be an important source of revenue for funding development programs and for providing relief from natural disasters or conflicts in developing countries.

The results: This is one of the graphs in this chapter that does not include any developed country, as developed countries do not usually receive aid. Countries in Sub-Saharan Africa including Somalia, the Central African Republic, and Rwanda are highly dependent on foreign aid. A significant amount of foreign aid is directed toward conflict-affected countries such as Afghanistan and Syria. Some middle-income countries such as Brazil and Vietnam also receive small amounts of foreign aid (Figure 0.15).

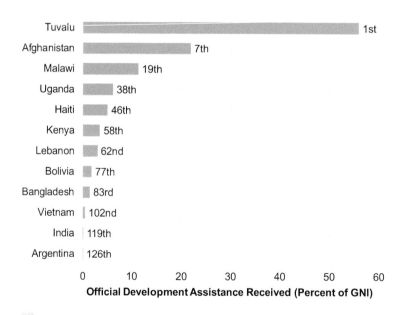

Figure 0.15 Official Development Assistance Received (Percent of GNI), 2019

Source: World Bank, World Development Indicators database.

16. EDUCATIONAL PERFORMANCE

What it is: To compare the educational performance of students in different countries we present data from the Programme for International Student Assessment (PISA), which administers standardized math, science, and reading tests to 15-year-olds in over 60 countries every three years. The graph below provides results from the science test. The country rankings were similar for the math and reading tests, with some variations (e.g., the UK ranked tenth on the science test, eleventh on the reading test, and thirteenth on the math test).

The results: Students in European countries, including Estonia, Finland, Poland, and the UK, tended to achieve the highest test scores. Among Asian countries, students received high scores in Japan and Korea. The United States did relatively well, ranking thirteenth on the science test and ninth on the reading test, but it did poorly on the math test ranking 33rd out of the 43 countries with available data. For less developed countries, scores tended to be lower. Costa Rica, Colombia, Brazil, and Indonesia ranked the lowest in terms of the scores for the science test (Figure 0.16).

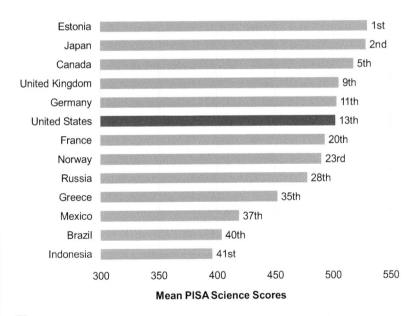

Figure 0.16 *Average PISA Science Test Score (15-year-olds), 2018*

Source: Organisation for Economic Co-operation and Development, Programme for International Student Assessment, PISA 2018 Key Findings.

17. HEALTH ACCESS AND QUALITY

What it is: The Healthcare Access and Quality (HAQ) Index measures health outcomes in a country based on death rates from 32 causes of death that could be avoided by timely and effective medical care. The HAQ index ranges from 0 to 100, with the lowest score representing the worst health outcomes. We discuss health as one component of well-being indices in Chapter 5 and as a topic of economic development in Chapter 16.

The results: The highest ranking countries on the HAQ index include Iceland, Norway, and the Netherlands. Other European countries, such as Finland, Sweden, Italy, and Ireland also rank relatively high in terms of their health outcomes. The United States ranks twenty-ninth—lower than most developed countries, including Australia, Japan, Canada, and the UK. The HAQ index is the lowest, in several African countries, including Sierra Leone, Ethiopia, Somalia, and the Central African Republic (Figure 0.17).

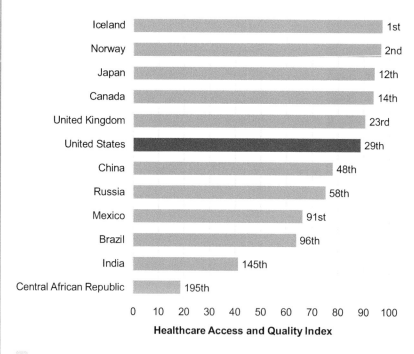

Figure 0.17 *Healthcare Access and Quality Index, 2016*

Source: Institute for Health Metrics and Evaluation, Global Burden of Disease Study 2016.

18. SUBJECTIVE WELL-BEING

What it is: Researchers are increasingly using surveys to measure well-being or happiness directly. The most common approach is to ask people to rate their overall satisfaction with their lives, on a scale from 1 (dissatisfied) to 10 (satisfied). The responses are referred to as "subjective well-being." We discuss subjective well-being in more detail in Chapter 5.

The results: According to the most recent data, which cover 149 countries, Finland has the highest level of average subjective well-being. Other relatively happy countries include Denmark, Switzerland, Iceland, and Netherlands. Happiness levels in the United States are about average for a developed country. Happiness levels are relatively low in countries that have recently experienced conflicts such as Afghanistan and Palestinian territories, and in the poorest countries such as Zimbabwe, Rwanda, Malawi, and Haiti (Figure 0.18).

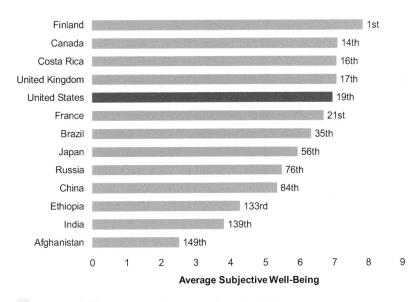

Figure 0.18 *Average Subjective Well-Being Index*

Source: World Happiness Report 2021.

19. CARBON DIOXIDE EMISSIONS PER CAPITA

What it is: Carbon dioxide (CO_2) is the most important gas responsible for global climate change. CO_2 is emitted whenever fossil fuels are burned. Scientific analysis indicates that the accumulation of CO_2 in the atmosphere is raising global temperatures, leading to serious negative impacts on human societies and ecosystems. CO_2 per capita gives us an idea of how much the average person in a country is affecting the environment. We learn more about CO_2 and climate change in Chapter 17.

The results: The countries with the highest CO_2 emissions per capita are several oil-producing countries, including Qatar (the highest, at 32 tons per person), Kuwait, and United Arab Emirates. The United States has the eleventh-highest emissions per capita, around 15 metric tons per person. Emissions per person in European countries such as the UK and France are about one-third of U.S. levels. While China is the world's largest emitter of CO_2 overall, on a per-capita basis its emissions are about half of those in the United States. CO_2 emissions per capita are negligible in the world's poorest countries (Figure 0.19).

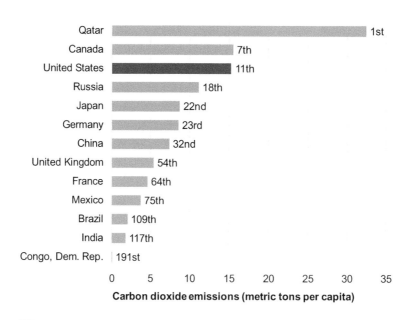

Carbon dioxide emissions (metric tons per capita)

Figure 0.19 Carbon Dioxide Emissions per Capita (Metric Tons per Year), 2018

Source: World Bank, World Development Indicators database.

20. LOCAL AIR QUALITY

What it is: While CO_2 emissions contribute to climate change, breathing air with elevated levels of CO_2 does not cause any adverse health effects. Local air pollutants, on the other hand, can cause numerous health effects, including asthma, lung cancer, and heart problems. One of the most important local air pollutants is particulate matter, which is emitted from power plants, industrial factories, motor vehicles, and other sources. Particulate matter pollution can be reduced through effective environmental regulations and technology. We discuss pollution further in Chapters 5 and 17.

The results: A country with high CO_2 emissions does not necessarily have poor local air quality. The United States is a prime example—CO_2 emissions are high, but local air quality is relatively good due to environmental laws and modern technologies. Other developed countries have as good, or better, local air quality. Developing countries can have good or poor local air quality, depending on their level of development, regulations, and technologies. Oil-producing countries such as Qatar and Saudi Arabia as well as poor countries in South Asia and Africa have a very poor quality of local air. China is almost as well-known for its poor air quality as it is for its high GDP growth rate (Figure 0.20).

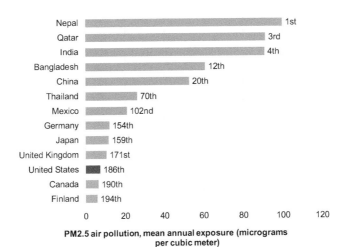

PM2.5 air pollution, mean annual exposure (micrograms per cubic meter)

Figure 0.20 Average National Particulate Matter Concentration (Micrograms per Cubic Meter), 2017

Source: World Bank, World Development Indicators database.
Data are for particulate matter smaller than 2.5 micrometers, referred to as PM2.5. For reference, the European Union pollution standard for average PM2.5 is 25 micrograms/cubic meter ($\mu g/m^3$); California has a stricter standard of 12 $\mu g/m^3$.

NOTE

1 Based on a report from AidData: https://www.aiddata.org/china.

Chapter 1

Economic Activity in Context

What do you expect—and what do you want—from the economic system in which you live? Life, liberty, and the pursuit of happiness? Justice, peace, national security, a pleasant environment, and general welfare? Secure housing, education, and health care? Do you feel that you have the right to a job when you need or want one? And will you feel satisfied with just any job, or do you hope for one that will use your knowledge and talents, will provide you with a decent income, and will earn respect from others?

Your goals and expectations, taken together with those of many other people, contribute to the mood of optimism or pessimism that helps create economic booms or slumps. Other aspects of your economic behavior, such as the skills you have gained or the kind of work you choose to do, contribute to the country's overall productivity. Your activities as a consumer help to shape the country's output patterns. Your role as an active citizen has an impact on economic policy, including in such important areas as environment, health and social security, and general well-being.

One important reason to ask you about your life goals, at the outset, is that goals are an important element of what makes up the economy. When the economy works well people have more opportunities to achieve their goals than when it is working badly. Macroeconomics is about how economies work. As you read through this book, you will have plenty of opportunities to consider this idea, and to think about how an understanding of basic economic principles can be used to judge, or even to make, economic policies. The study of economics can help us to achieve our goals as individuals and create a society in which we are satisfied to live.

1 WHAT IS MACROECONOMICS ABOUT?

Economics is the study of how people manage their resources to meet their needs and enhance their well-being. The term **well-being** refers broadly to a good quality of life. Our well-being is closely connected to meeting our basic needs, such as requirements for food, shelter, and

DOI: 10.4324/9781003251521-3

physical security, but well-being also goes beyond "needs." Virtually everyone desires such things as a decent income, enough leisure time, good family and friends, freedom to express one's opinions, a clean environment, and access to good education and health care. Some people may place a higher emphasis on some of these goals than others. Also, people clearly have different opinions on the best ways to improve our well-being. These opinions are often shaped by social forces, individual personality, and value judgments. We discuss some key components of well-being in Section 2 of this chapter.

---

economics: the study of how people manage their resources to meet their needs and enhance their well-being

well-being: a term used broadly to describe a good quality of life

---

Economics is often defined as the discipline that helps people make optimal choices under scarcity. Economic activities include production, distribution, and consumption. In addition, a major concern of economics is the important activity of resource management. The resources available for economic activity include natural resources such as forests, soils, water, and air, as well as human-made productive resources such as factories, trucks, computers, and roads. Our resources also include our time, knowledge, and skills; financial resources; and the social relationships that improve the quality of our lives. We will look more closely at the activity of resource management in Section 3.1 of this chapter.

The study of economics is generally broken down into two parts: microeconomics and macroeconomics. This book, *Macroeconomics in Context*, is the companion to another textbook called (not surprisingly) *Microeconomics in Context*. Where **microeconomics** emphasizes the economic activities and interactions of individuals and particular organizations (such as businesses, households, community groups, nonprofit organizations, and government agencies), **macroeconomics** looks at how all of these activities join together to create an overall economic environment at the national—and often the global—level.

---

microeconomics: the study of the economic activities and interactions of individuals, households, businesses, and other groups at the subnational level

macroeconomics: the study of how economic activities at all levels create a national (and global) economic environment

---

Economic conditions at the aggregate level create the environment in which individual economic actors make their decisions. These conditions

27

include rates of unemployment and inflation, ecological limits and constraints, degrees of economic inequality, and social/cultural assumptions about trust and responsibility.

For example, when you seek paid work in your chosen field, your success will depend in part on both micro- and macroeconomic factors. On the microeconomic side, you will need to have prepared yourself for the work and found either a business that can use your skills or direct buyers for your services, if you decide to strike out on your own. You will want to find work that gives you a combination of job satisfaction, income, and benefits that you like.

But will employers, in general, be hiring? Some graduating classes are unlucky and flood the job market just as the national economy is "going sour"—that is, entering a **recession**. No matter how well-prepared you are, finding a job can be tough during a period of high **unemployment**, when many people who seek jobs are not successful in finding one. And if you do find a job, how far will your paycheck go toward meeting your standard-of-living desires? If you start working during a period of high **inflation**, when the overall level of prices is increasing, the purchasing power of a fixed paycheck will be quickly eroded.

---

recession: a downturn in economic activity, usually defined as lasting for two consecutive calendar quarters or more

unemployment: a situation in which people seek a paying job, but cannot obtain one

inflation: a rise in the general level of prices

Macroeconomic conditions also affect personal debt. Many students will need to plan on paying back student loans for a number of years. The higher the prevailing real interest rates in the economy, the more costly this borrowing will be. Your own economic well-being will also be tied to global issues such as trade flows and currency exchange rates—especially if you work for a business that is strongly affected by imports or exports. Currency rates will also be important if you send money to family members in another country, or if you do a lot of foreign travel. These macroeconomic issues are considered "short run"—economists refer to them as having to do with macroeconomic "fluctuations." Sometimes unemployment is high, and sometimes it is low, and the same goes for inflation, interest rates, trade deficits, and exchange rates.

Other macroeconomic issues have to do with the long run. Can you expect your standard of living 20 years from now, or the standard of living of your children, to be higher or lower than what you enjoy now? Are you living in a society where people have equal access to opportunities, or are extremes of wealth and poverty becoming more pronounced over time? What is the supply of natural resources used in production processes, and what is the quality of those resources? What other social and environmental factors affect the ability of the economy to prosper, or threaten its success?

Macroeconomics seeks to explain an especially interesting phenomenon: the fact that bad things can often happen on a national or global level even though virtually no individual or microeconomic-level organization *wants* or *intends* them to happen. People generally agree that high unemployment, persistent high inflation, and destruction of the natural environment, for example, are bad things, yet they occur nonetheless.

Microeconomics and macroeconomics are terms that are applied rather loosely, and many issues have both macroeconomic and microeconomic aspects. For example, the imposition of a sales tax will affect microeconomic behavior—people may consume less or shift their patterns of consumption toward untaxed items—but it also affects government revenues, which, as we will see, are an important element of macroeconomic analysis. There is no single "microeconomy"—rather there are many subnational economic systems of varied sizes that are studied in the field of microeconomics. However, the term **macroeconomy** is used to refer to a national economic system.

---

macroeconomy: an economic system whose boundaries are normally understood to be the boundaries of a country

---

People also speak of the **global economy**, meaning the system of economic rules, norms, and interactions by which economic actors and actions in different parts of the world are connected to one another. **Economic actors (or economic agents)** include all individuals, groups, and organizations that engage in or influence economic activity. As the global economy has become an increasingly important part of the experience of more and more people, it has become more essential to include its study in introductory macroeconomics courses. You will find global macroeconomic issues extensively covered in this book.

Another area that has increased in importance for macroeconomics is environmental considerations, including climate change. Thirty years ago, environmental and climate issues would probably not have been considered in a macroeconomics text. Today it is clear that many fundamental considerations, such as agricultural production, economic losses from disasters, rising sea levels, and international migration, are strongly affected by climate change. As the global economy grows, it presses up against natural limits including in such areas as water supplies, natural resources, biodiversity and species loss, ocean degradation, and atmospheric pollution. We will deal with such issues, especially in Chapters 5 and 17, but they also affect other macroeconomic topics such as economic growth and finance.

---

global economy: the system of economic rules, norms, and interactions by which economic actors and actions in different parts of the world are connected to one another

economic actor (economic agent): an individual, group, or organization that is involved in economic activities

---

Discussion Questions

1. You have evidently made a decision to dedicate some of your personal resources of time and money in college to studying economics. Why? What do you hope to learn in this course that will be helpful for you in reaching your goals?
2. Are you familiar with the following terms? While you will study them in detail in this course, see how well you can come up with a definition for them just from your previous knowledge. (It does not matter at this point if you are not familiar with them.)

unemployment	investment
inflation	recession
economic growth	economic boom
development	money
GDP	sustainability

2 MACROECONOMIC GOALS

Social scientists often make a distinction between **positive questions**, which concern issues of fact, or "what is," and **normative questions**, which have to do with goals and values, or "what should be." For example, "How many people live below the poverty line in our country?" is a positive question, which requires facts as an answer. "How much effort should be given to poverty reduction?" is a normative question, requiring us to think about our values and goals.

In our study of economics, we often find that positive and normative questions are inextricably intertwined. For example, consider the definition of poverty. To construct this definition, we need to combine facts about income distribution with a normative assessment of where to draw the poverty line. We also need to consider whether the definition of poverty should be based solely on income, or whether it should include information about people's **assets** or opportunities. Life rarely offers us a neat distinction between "what is" and "what ought to be"; more often, we have to deal with a combination of the two.

> **positive questions:** questions about how things are
> **normative questions:** questions about how things should be
> **assets:** property owned by an individual or company

Note that positive statements often carry normative implications. Consider the statement: "The total share of federal taxes paid by the top 1 percent of households, by income, rose from 13 percent in 1981 to 25 percent in 2017."[1] This is a positive, factual statement, based on reliable data from the U.S. government. But it also implies that taxes on the top 1 percent have increased rather dramatically. But is this implication true? A more complete analysis reveals that the main reason that the share of federal taxes paid by the top 1 percent has risen so much is that this group has also received a much larger share of all income over that period. So we need to be careful about making conclusions based on incomplete or misleading positive statements.

Economics also seeks to answer questions about what will happen in response to specific policies. For example, an economist might ask whether and by how much poverty rates will be reduced if the minimum wage is increased to a certain level. Answering this question requires both positive and normative analysis. Two economists relying upon the same objective data may come to different answers to this question, as they will need to make subjective assumptions about how to analyze and interpret the data. As we will see as we go through the book, on some policy questions economists largely agree on basic principles, while other issues remain strongly debated.

Much of this textbook is concerned with positive issues. Using both empirical evidence and various theories, we describe—using the best available economic research—how an economy functions at the macro level. However, we cannot avoid the normative question of what goals the macroeconomy *should* achieve. Our goals are significantly affected by our beliefs and values. For example, we can rely on positive economic analysis to estimate the extent to which various government policies will reduce poverty rates. But decisions about the appropriate role of the government in reducing poverty necessitate a normative debate.

A useful way to look at different goals is to rank them in a kind of hierarchy. Some are **intermediate goals**—that is, they are important because they are expected to serve as the means to further ends. Goals that are sought for their own sake, rather than because they lead to something else, are called **final goals**. For example, you might strive to achieve high grades as a final goal—it just makes you feel good to excel. Or maybe it is an intermediate goal toward the final goal of getting a good job. Of course, we might also think of the goal of "getting a good job" as itself being intermediate to other final goals, such as obtaining income, or overall satisfaction with life.

31

> **intermediate goal:** a goal that is primarily desirable because its achievement will bring you closer to your final goal(s)
>
> **final goal:** a goal that requires no further justification; it is an end in itself

Economists have often focused on the goals of increasing income and wealth. But these may better be considered as intermediate goals, which help achieve broader final goals of attaining a good standard of living and creating a stable and sustainable economic environment. What should we consider to be the final goals of economic activity? One possible listing of such goals is shown in Box 1.1. Some of the goals involve *making life possible*, some involve *making life worthwhile*, and others involve both of these types of goals. Of course, opinions about goals can differ—our purpose is not to achieve a precise definition of well-being but to emphasize that well-being is a fundamentally multidimensional concept. In the discussion that follows, we will focus on three important components of well-being—good living standards, stability and security, and sustainability.

BOX 1.1 ELEMENTS OF WELL-BEING

The following are some elements that might go into a broad concept of well-being. When you think about a good life for yourself, are there elements that you would wish to add to or subtract from this list?

- **Satisfaction of basic physical needs**, including nutrition and a comfortable living environment.
- **Security** that one's basic needs will continue to be met throughout all stages of life, as well as security against aggression or unjust persecution.
- **Happiness**, expressed through feelings of joy, contentment, and pleasure.
- **The ability to realize one's potential**, including physical, intellectual, moral, social, aesthetic, and spiritual development.
- **A sense of meaning** in one's life; a reason or purpose for one's efforts.
- **Fairness**, including appropriate rewards for one's efforts and fair and equal treatment by others and within social institutions.
- **Freedom** to make personal decisions within the limits of responsible relations with others (and the limits of their decision-making capacity, as in the case of children).
- **Participation** in social processes in which important decisions are made.
- **Good social relations**, including those with friends, family, business associates, and fellow citizens, as well as peaceful relations among countries
- **Ecological balance**, meaning that natural resources are preserved and, where necessary, restored to a healthy and resilient state.

2.1 Good Living Standards

Achieving good living standards refers to people being able to live long, healthy, and enjoyable lives, with access to opportunity to accomplish the things that they believe give their lives meaning. The most basic living standard issues relate to the quality of people's diets and housing, their access to means of transportation and communication, and the quality of education and medical attention that they receive.

Taking a somewhat broader view, we might also include less tangible aspects of life, such as the variety of entertainment that people can enjoy, the amount of leisure time they spend with friends and family, and the ways in which they participate in producing and consuming goods and services. Aspects such as political freedom, social inclusion, and environmental quality that go beyond economic issues also affect our overall living standards. **Living standards growth** is a top concern for macroeconomics. How can living standards be maintained or improved? Increased access to resources such as nutritious food, clean water, good schools, better housing, and better jobs as well as advancements in the various aspects of well-being listed in Box 1.1 could all contribute to this goal.

---

living standards growth: improvements in people's diet, housing, medical care, education, working conditions, and access to transportation, communication, entertainment, and other amenities

---

BOX 1.2 LIVING STANDARDS GROWTH AND THE IMPACT OF THE COVID-19 PANDEMIC

In the last two decades, significant progress has been made in improving people's living standards at the global level. Between 2000 and 2017, the share of the world's population living in extreme poverty (under $1.90/day) declined from 27.8 percent to 9.3 percent. During the same period, the percentage of primary school-age children out of school declined from 15 percent to 8 percent, access to drinking water and safely managed sanitation increased by about 10 percentage points, and fewer women and children died during childbirth.

However, with the COVID-19 pandemic that hit the world in 2020, progress halted or reversed for the first time since 1990. Estimates for 2020 indicate that about 119–124 million people were pushed back into extreme poverty, and the number of people experiencing hunger increased by 70–161 million. The pandemic also resulted in a decline in life expectancy, reduced access to education, increased inequality, and an increase in the incidence of child labor and in gender-based violence. At the same time as the COVID-19 pandemic, the climate crisis has persisted with concentrations of greenhouse gases reaching new highs in 2020 and increased occurrence of severe weather events affecting overall well-being outcomes.

The impacts of the pandemic fell most heavily on the poor and the most vulnerable population. A large share of those pushed into poverty in 2020 was concentrated in countries that already had high poverty rates. An estimated 255 million full-time jobs were lost during the pandemic—most of these were in the informal sector. The shift to remote learning and the disruption in the provision of essential health services during the pandemic also affected the poorest population most adversely. A concerted effort from individual governments as well as local, national, and international organizations to provide social protection measures, universal health coverage, and access to education, and to support a global transition to a low-emission and climate-resilient future are essential to ensure improvements in living standards in the long term.[2]

For a long time, "living standards growth" was considered nearly synonymous with "economic growth." **Economic growth** has been traditionally measured by the growth in the **gross domestic product (GDP)**—a measure of the market value of all final goods and services produced within a country's borders over a specific time period, usually one year.

> **economic growth:** increases in the level of marketed production in a country or region
>
> **gross domestic product (GDP):** the market value of all final goods and services produced within a country's borders over a specific time period, usually one year

Global economic growth has been impressive in recent decades. Figure 1.1 plots the sum of GDP for all countries from 1960 to 2020. By this measure, the value of global production in 2020 was about 7.2 times the value in 1960. Some of this increase in global production is simply a result of population growth: there are more people producing goods and services. An increase in consumption levels can result only if production *per person* (GDP *per capita*) on average rises. When we adjust for the growth in the world's population, we see that production per capita, measured by dividing global production by global population, has also grown over the past several decades, but not by as much. Figure 1.2 shows that global production per capita (adjusted for inflation) increased by about a factor of 2.8 between 1960 and 2020.

If we were to disaggregate from the global figures, we would see that increases in economic production over these years vary significantly across different regions and countries. Between 1960 and 2020, GDP per capita increased more than fivefold in East Asian countries. In Sub-Saharan Africa, however, GDP per capita increased by only about 1.4 times. Such disparities in economic and social achievements across countries, measured through indicators such as GDP per capita, absolute poverty, life expectancy, educational performance, and subjective

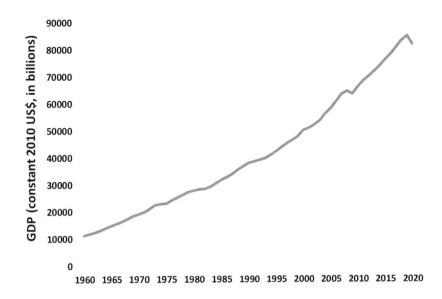

Figure 1.1 *Global Production, 1960–2020*

Source: The World Bank Group, World Development Indicators Online.

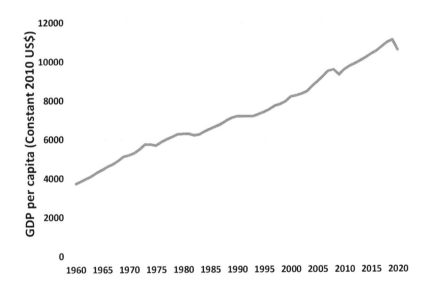

Figure 1.2 *Global Production Per Capita, 1960–2020*

Source: The World Bank Group, World Development Indicators Online.

well-being, are also illustrated in Chapter 0 (see Figures 0.1, 0.12, 0.16, 0.17, and 0.18).

One reason economists have focused strongly on measures of economic growth is that extreme poverty is a major concern in many developing countries. According to the World Bank, about 697 million people in the world were living on less than $1.90 per day in 2017. Of these people over 60 percent lived in Sub-Saharan Africa and about 25 percent lived in South Asia. Poverty can mean that people are crowded together in unsanitary urban slums or isolated in rural huts, have barely enough to eat, receive little or no education, and never see a doctor. The production of more and better housing, better roads, more food, more schooling, and more medical care—*more goods and services*—along with more equitable access to these resources is necessary to raise living standards in such situations. This process of moving from a general situation of poverty and deprivation to one of increased production and plenty is what has traditionally been referred to as **economic development**.

> **economic development:** the process of moving from a situation of poverty and deprivation to a situation of increased production and plenty, through investments and changes in the organization of work

Generally, economic development has been thought of as a process of increasing agricultural productivity, investing in machinery and technology, and making changes in the organization of work (from home-based shops to factories, for example), so that **labor productivity** rises—meaning that people can produce more in each hour that they work.

> **labor productivity:** the level of output that can be produced per worker per hour

While economic growth is necessary to increase well-being in low-income regions, the situation may be different in wealthier regions. In most highly industrialized countries, where the population is generally growing very slowly or even declining and where the majority of families already enjoy decent housing, safe water, plenty of food, readily available heating and refrigeration, a car or two, airline travel, TVs and the like, do we really need *more* in general?

Some people would say that we do, but others believe that we should instead switch our national priorities to making sure that production is designed to increase well-being. In countries that already have a high level of production, *living standards growth* may be achievable even in the absence of *economic growth*, by improving cultural, educational, and environmental conditions, raising the quality of work-life and the quantity of leisure, and by promoting an equitable allocation of economic rewards. We return to these questions—and to the critical issue of the relationships between economic growth and well-being—in later chapters.

2.2 Stability and Security

While closely linked to goals for living standards, the goal of stability and security brings in a dimension that we have not yet discussed. Imagine that you are elderly, and looking back over your life you can say that *on average,* you enjoyed a good standard of living. This might arise from two quite different scenarios. In one scenario, you enjoy a fairly steady, or gently rising, living standard and are always able to plan confidently for your financial future.

In the other scenario, you are quite successful at some points in your life but also periodically have to face the possibility of "losing it all." You do well and buy a nice house, but then you become unemployed and your house is foreclosed on because you fail to make the mortgage payments. Then you start to do well again and believe you are on a path to a pleasant retirement, but steeply rising prices or a falling stock market reduces the value of your savings and pension. Even if, after the fact and "over the long run," you have done OK *on average* in terms of your living standards, the uncertainty and anxiety of living with economic fluctuations in the second scenario would take a toll on your overall well-being, relative to the more stable case.

High rates of unemployment are associated with many indicators of individual and social stress, such as suicide, domestic violence, stress-related illnesses, and crime. Unpredictable fluctuations in employment levels, prices, interest rates, and foreign exchange rates make it difficult—and, in the worst cases, impossible—for individuals and organizations to make productive and economically sensible plans for the future.

One common pattern is for fluctuations in the level of production to occur as a cycle in which recessions (or "contractions" or "slumps") and their attendant problem of high unemployment alternate with booms (also called "expansions" or "recoveries"), which sometimes bring with them the problem of inflation. This is called the **business cycle** or **trade cycle**. Even if these problems are "short run"—people eventually find jobs or inflation slows down—fluctuations cause considerable "ill-being" while they last. So creating a stable, secure economic environment is a separate important macroeconomic goal.

---

business cycle (trade cycle): recurrent fluctuations in the level of national production, with alternating periods of recession and boom

---

If we use GDP as an overall measure of economic activity and consider the example of GDP for the United States since 1850, as shown in Figure 1.3, we can see that while the general trend is upward, the curve is somewhat wavy indicating that there has not been *steady* growth.

37

During some periods GDP fell as the country experienced economic contractions, and during other periods GDP rose very steeply due to rapid economic expansion.

One widely accepted macroeconomic goal is the achievement of sufficient economic stability to enable individuals and families to enjoy economic security and to be able to make reasonable predictions about their future. In the light of new knowledge about our dependence on the natural world, which is undergoing radical alterations due to human economic activity, the goal of security now must also include a much longer time horizon, recognizing a serious responsibility to future generations. This leads us to our third goal: sustainability.

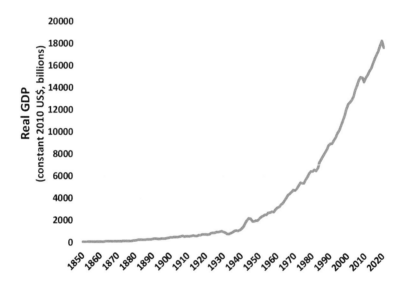

Figure 1.3 *Real GDP in Billions of Dollars (Constant 2010 US$) in the United States, 1850–2020*

Sources: World Development Indicators, World Bank.

2.3 Sustainability

We want good living standards and stability not only for ourselves right now but also for ourselves later in our lives and for our children, grandchildren, and other generations to come. In order to understand the goal of sustainability, we must address the questions:

- Are economic activities *financially* sustainable into the future? Or is a country incurring such a high amount of debt that it may create a heavy burden on its future inhabitants?
- Are economic activities *socially* sustainable into the future? Are disparities between the "haves" and the "have-nots" accelerating or diminishing? Are they based on justifiable causes or on unequal

power relations? Are young people receiving the upbringing and education required to enable them to contribute to a healthy economy and society? Or is the current structure of economic activity setting the stage for future social disruption and political strife?

■ Are economic activities *ecologically* sustainable into the future? Is the natural environment that supports life being treated in a way that will sustain its quality into the future? Or is it becoming depleted or degraded?

For many generations, it seemed that **technological progress** and economic growth were magical keys that unlocked the door to unlimited improvements in the standard of living. For example, real output per person in the United States in 1980 was about ten times what it had been in 1840, and it was 2.7 times greater in 2020 than it was in 1980. "Developed" countries in North America, Western Europe, and elsewhere have experienced long-run rising standards of living through industrialization, improvements in agricultural technology, and the development of service industries.

---

technological progress: the development of new products and new, more efficient, methods of production

---

Can this process continue indefinitely? Some have argued that sustainability problems can be remedied by *more* GDP growth. For example, the issue of financial sustainability includes both concerns about the level of government debt (which accumulates whenever governments spend more than they take in) and external debt (what all people and organizations in a country owe to foreigners). Too much debt is a problem since it means that a large proportion of a country's income in the future may need to be directed toward paying back the debt rather than other, more socially beneficial, uses. Indebtedness, however, is usually considered manageable as long as the growth of GDP is at least keeping pace with the level of debt, so that debt does not increase as a percent of GDP.

To the extent that a country's economic prosperity depends on excessive borrowing, prosperity may be unsustainable. For example, many low-income countries were encouraged to borrow heavily from richer countries for decades, but many of them did not achieve the high rate of economic growth that was supposed to result from the borrowing, and a severe "debt crisis" resulted. Some low-income countries currently spend more funds on debt repayment than on health care for their own population.

39

Some industrialized countries, including the United States, also borrow heavily to fund their activities. Many fear that such borrowing may result in dramatically higher taxes in the future in order to pay interest on the debt. Those called on to pay these higher taxes would be future workers like you. Setting good priorities about how we borrow—and what we borrow for—is important for long-run sustainability. This issue will be discussed in detail in Chapter 15.

Regarding social sustainability, some people believe that economic growth is also the way to relieve social ills and political strife. They reason that the bigger the pie, the bigger everyone's share can be, and that rising personal incomes will naturally lead to a peaceful and productive population. But many scholars have questioned whether economic growth alone will solve the problem of global disparities in living standards. Some analysts suggest that historical factors such as the legacy of colonization, and political factors such as rich countries' protection of their own industries within the system of global trade, mean that it is impossible to expect currently low-income countries to "develop" in the same way as countries that industrialized earlier.

Traditional goals of unlimited material affluence have also been called into question within richer countries, and some social scientists have suggested that consumerist and "more-is-better" values may actually contribute to personal and social discontent and the weakening of social norms of trust and reciprocity. Societies that suffer wide divisions between "haves" and "have-nots" are more likely to suffer a social and political breakdown—perhaps to the point of violence—than societies where people enjoy a greater sense of social cohesion.

Concerning ecological issues, some economists have argued that the negative effects of economic growth on the environment can be remedied by additional economic growth since higher incomes give countries the wherewithal to invest in new exploration for resources and new pollution-controlling technologies. In this perspective, "sustainable growth" simply means making sure that the growth rate of GDP stays high well into the future.

In contrast, by the end of the twentieth century, some economists had started asking whether growth might instead *contribute to* environmental problems. For example, land development as well as intensive agricultural practices and exploitation of forests have caused the extinction of some species and notable decreases in genetic diversity in others. Expansion of economic activity especially in arid and semi-arid areas has caused severe depletion of water supplies. Contemporary "developed" economies are presently heavily dependent on the consumption of fossil fuels, but scientists warn that carbon dioxide emissions from the burning of fossil fuels are rapidly exacerbating global climate change.

Analysts have also estimated that giving everyone in the world an American lifestyle (which is one of the most resource-consuming lifestyles in the world), including a meat-rich diet and multiple cars per family, would require an extra two to four planets to supply resources and absorb waste! Not everyone can have the same consumption pattern as we have in the industrialized world today. There is, indeed, a reason to question whether dwellers in rich countries will be able, in the long term, to maintain current consumption patterns. These issues point toward the need for '**conscious consumption**' where consumption decisions are made responsibly, considering the environmental impacts and reducing waste to achieve a more sustainable lifestyle.

> **conscious consumption:** being aware of the costs of consumption on others and on the planet, and making consumption decisions responsibly to minimize waste and achieve a more sustainable lifestyle

The graphs of economic growth, seen earlier in this chapter, illustrate an impressive human ability to increase production. The growth in global atmospheric carbon dioxide (CO_2, the principal gas associated with climate change) illustrated in Figure 1.4 is equally impressive but more sobering, as it shows the human ability to affect our environment significantly—sometimes in dangerous ways. CO_2 is released in fossil fuel–burning industrial production, transportation, and heating, and the more such production takes place, the more is released. Deforestation also contributes to increases in atmospheric CO_2.

This raises the question of whether it is sufficient to sustain the financial, economic, and ecological systems *as they are now*. Some of the ecological systems that support economic activity may already be severely degraded. In such cases, it is not enough to sustain what exists now—rather, we need to take on a goal of **restorative development**, to

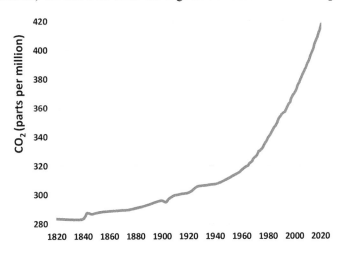

Figure 1.4 *Growth in Atmospheric Carbon Dioxide, 1815–2021*

Sources: Carbon Dioxide Information Analysis Center, and National Oceanic and Atmospheric Administration Earth System Research Laboratory data.

rebuild systems that are no longer supporting well-being in the present and the future.

> **restorative development:** economic progress that restores economic, financial, social, or ecological systems that have been degraded and are no longer adequately supportive of human well-being in the present and the future

Some ecologically oriented economists have suggested that, instead of placing blind faith in technological progress and economic growth, society should adopt a **precautionary principle**. This principle says that we should err on the side of caution, or, as stated by one group of experts, "When an activity raises threats of harm to the environment or human health, precautionary measures should be taken even if some cause and effect relationships are not fully established scientifically."[*] Such attention to environmental sustainability need not preclude also giving attention to the goals of living standards improvement and stability, but it does clearly call into question the idea that economic growth, in itself, is always the only or the best goal.

> **precautionary principle:** the principle that we should err on the side of caution when facing a significant possibility of severe damage to human health or the natural environment

Many economists in the twentieth century did not explicitly address the question of macroeconomic goals, content with the belief that economic growth would naturally contribute to the achievement of any other goals that we might choose. The authors of this book have found it helpful to view the economy as though it exists with a purpose, and that purpose is not simply growth in output (as has been assumed in many other macroeconomic texts) but also improvement in human well-being in the present and the future. This requires learning how to balance ideas on how to achieve economic growth with questions about what kinds of growth actually contribute to well-being and ideas on how present and future well-being can be enhanced by restorative development. This broader approach may be referred to as **contextual economics**—economics viewed in the context of social and environmental realities—and is the approach taken throughout this text.

---

[*] This well-known formulation of the precautionary principle was spelled out in a 1998 meeting of scientists, lawyers, policymakers, and environmentalists at Wingspread, the headquarters of the Johnson Foundation in Racine, Wisconsin.

> **contextual economics:** economic analysis that takes into account the social and environmental realities within which the economic system operates

Discussion Questions

1. Which of the macroeconomic goals discussed above do you think should have the highest priority? Why? Are there other major goals that you think are missing from the preceding discussion?

2. No one would argue that the goal of macroeconomics is to make people *worse* off! Yet the above outline of macroeconomic goals suggests that trying too hard to achieve some narrowly defined goals may lead to such a result. Why do you think that some economists would view economic growth as the major goal, while others view it as potentially in conflict with other goals such as economic, social, or environmental sustainability?

3 THE ISSUES THAT DEFINE ECONOMICS

In discussing goals, we have addressed the question of what economics is *for*—what its purpose is. Now we summarize what economics is *about:* what activities it covers, and which questions it addresses.

3.1 The Four Essential Economic Activities

We think of an activity as "economic" when it involves one or more of four essential tasks that allow us to meet our needs and enhance our well-being. The four essential economic activities are resource management and the production, distribution, and consumption of goods and services.

3.1.1 Resource Management

Resource management means tending to, preserving, or improving the resources that contribute to the well-being of current and future generations. These stocks of resources, that are valued for their potential economic contributions, are referred to as **capital stocks** or "capital assets."

> **resource management:** preserving or improving the resources that contribute to the enhancement of well-being, including natural, manufactured, human, and social resources
> **capital stock:** any resource that is valued for its potential economic contributions

43

We can identify five types of capital that contribute to an economy's productivity. **Natural capital** refers to physical assets provided by nature, such as land that is suitable for agriculture or other human uses, fresh water sources, healthy ocean ecologies, a resilient and diverse stock of wild animals and plants, and stocks of minerals and fossil fuels that are still in the ground. **Manufactured capital** means physical assets that are generated by applying human productive activities to natural capital. These include such things as buildings, machinery, stocks of refined oil, transportation infrastructure, and inventories of produced goods that are waiting to be sold or to be used in further production. **Human capital** refers to individual people's capacity for productive work, particularly the knowledge and skills each can personally bring to his or her work. **Social capital** means the existing institutions and the stock of trust, mutual understanding, shared values, and socially held knowledge that facilitates the social coordination of economic activity.

---

natural capital: physical assets provided by nature

manufactured capital: physical assets that have been produced by humans using natural capital

human capital: people's capacity for engaging in productive activities and their individual knowledge and skills

social capital: the institutions and the stock of trust, mutual understanding, shared values, and socially held knowledge that facilitates the social coordination of economic activity

---

In addition, there is a fifth sort of resource, **financial capital**, which is a fund of purchasing power available to economic actors. While financial capital is not part of any physical production activity, it indirectly contributes to production by making it possible for people to produce goods and services in advance of getting paid for them. It also facilitates the activities of distribution and consumption. An example of financial capital would be a bank checking account, filled with funds that have been either saved up by the economic agent who owns it or loaned to the agent by a bank.

---

financial capital: funds of purchasing power available to purchase goods and services or facilitate economic activity

---

Notice that economists' description of "capital" is different from what you might hear in everyday use. People sometimes take "capital" to mean *only* financial capital, for example, in references to "capital markets," "undercapitalized businesses," "venture capital," and so on.

Economists take a broader view that includes all five types of capital stocks.

Capital stocks may increase or decrease as a consequence of natural forces, as in the case of a forest growing over time; or they may be deliberately managed by humans in order to provide needed inputs for the production of goods and services. When people work to increase the quantity or quality of resources for future benefits, this is what economists mean by **investment**. Advances in technology also expand or improve the stocks of capital, including manufactured, human, natural, and social capital, thereby increasing the productivity of economic activity.

> **investment:** an activity intended to increase the quantity or quality of a resource over time

When capital stock is reduced, we say it has undergone **depreciation**. Natural capital depreciates when rivers become fouled by pollution or more trees are cut down than are naturally regenerated. Manufactured assets commonly lose their usefulness over time, as roads develop potholes, and equipment wears out or breaks. Human capital depreciates if skills are forgotten or not kept up to date; and social capital can depreciate if norms of trust and peaceful interaction become less widely held.

> **depreciation:** a decrease in the quantity or quality of a stock of capital

The activity of "resource management" is about ensuring that all kinds of capital stocks are maintained and rebuilt so as to create an economy with a good asset base for future generations. They include such activities as monitoring the water quality of a lake, repairing machinery, or keeping employees' skills up to date. Going beyond maintenance of the status quo, restoration means bringing back qualities that have been lost; for example, farming in such a way that the quality of the soil is enhanced.

Sometimes resource management "activity" means *not* engaging in an activity. For example, many fishing communities, sometimes under government regulation, have ceased fishing for species that are declining in order to allow fish populations to recover. Similarly, people who make voluntary decisions to minimize their gasoline consumption are helping to maintain petroleum resources and the health of the climate. While this may look like inactivity, including resource management as an economic activity implies that minimizing some kinds of consumption can contribute to well-being.

45

3.1.2 Production

Production is the conversion of resources into usable products, which may be either goods or services. Goods are tangible objects, such as bread and books; services are intangibles, such as TV broadcasting, teaching, and haircuts. Factories producing automobiles, farms growing crops, popular bands performing music, recording companies producing digital music for sale, local governments building roads, and individuals cooking meals at home are all engaged in the economic activity of production.

> **production:** the conversion of resources to goods or services

The economic activity of production converts some resources, which we call **inputs**, into new goods and services, which we refer to as **outputs**. Some goods, such as machines and computers, are produced to assist in the production of other goods and services, and are called **investment goods**. The way in which production occurs depends on available technologies. Production processes can also lead to undesirable outputs, such as pollution and **waste products**. We consider only *useful* outputs to be economic goods and services.

> **inputs:** resources that go into production
> **outputs:** the goods and services that result from production
> **investment goods:** goods such as machines and computers that aid in further production
> **waste products:** outputs that are not used either for consumption or in a further production process

Inputs include materials that become part of the produced good, supplies that are used up in the production process and labor time. For example, a chef explaining the process of preparing one of their specialties, say, ginger chicken, would mention the ingredients (chicken, ginger, oil, etc.) and a method for combining them. These ingredients become part of the produced goods. Other inputs used in the process include the chef's labor time and other supplies, such as natural gas that provides heat, paper towels, etc.

But the recipe, the chef's skills, and the cooking equipment that are used in production neither become part of the produced good nor are "used up," although they are crucial for the production process. These can be best understood as *flows of services* arising out of *capital stocks* (see Box 1.3). The production process draws on services from social capital, in the form of the knowledge embodied in a recipe; services from human capital in the form of the chef's acquired knowledge; and services from manufactured capital in the form of the cooking equipment.

In the case of commercial production, the services of financial capital are also vitally important. This is because the production process *takes time.* If the chef is also an entrepreneur, they need to have financial capital available at the start of the process to be able to buy the ingredients, buy or rent kitchen space, and get to work well *before* they can prepare the meal and sell it. The reliance of commercial production on manufactured and financial capital is very important for macroeconomics, as we will see when we study issues of credit and investment.

BOX 1.3 STOCKS VERSUS FLOWS

When non-economists use the term "stock," they usually mean ownership shares in enterprises that are traded on the "stock market." To an economist, however, the concept of **stock** refers to something as it is measured at a particular point in time. For example, the amount of water in a bathtub can be measured at one particular instant, and that quantity would be considered a stock. The balance in your checking account at the beginning of the month is stock, as is the number of trees in a forest at two o'clock on Saturday afternoon.

In contrast to stocks, **flows** are measured *over* a period of time. For example, the water that goes into a bathtub from a faucet is a flow that occurs over a period of time; its quantity can be measured per minute or per hour. The deposits and withdrawals you make to your checking account can be understood as flows; your bank statement will tell you what the various flows were during a month. As trees grow or are cut down or felled by lightning, these flows add to or subtract from forest resources.

Figure 1.5 is a "bathtub"-style **stock-flow diagram**. It represents the relation of stocks and flows, showing stock at only *one* point in time. Like water flowing through the tap (additions) and the drain (subtractions) of a bathtub, flows raise or lower the level of the water in the tub (stock).

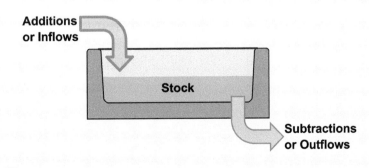

Figure 1.5 *"Bathtub"-Style Stock-Flow Diagram*

> **stock:** the quantity of something at a particular point in time
> **flow:** something whose quantity is measured over a period of time
> **stock-flow diagram:** an illustration of how stocks can be changed, over time, by flows

3.1.3 Distribution

Distribution is the sharing of products and resources among people. In contemporary economies, distribution activities take two main forms: exchange and transfer. In **exchange** relations, two actors trade with each other on mutually agreed-upon terms—one thing is delivered with something else expected in return. For example, when customers buy shoes from a shopping mall shoe store, the store receives monetary payment in exchange for shoes. This monetary payment is used to pay wages to the workers at the store, rent to the owners of the mall, and profits to the owners of the business. How this income is distributed among the various economic actors is one of the key questions of interest to macroeconomists.

> **distribution:** the sharing of products and resources among people
> **exchange:** the trading of one thing for another

The distribution of income among the owners of a business and the workers may become a source of conflict, as each economic actor is inclined to want a greater share of income for themselves. Usually, the owners have more bargaining power than the workers and are likely to get a greater share, as they own the capital goods required for production and control the process of hiring and firing workers. Workers, on the other hand, also have some bargaining power to negotiate for higher wages, as labor input is essential for the production process. Often, workers organize themselves into labor unions to bargain collectively for a fair share of income. In recent decades, union membership in the United States has fallen, and wages have grown much more slowly than profits and rents earned by owners. These relationships between the distribution of income, the declining power of workers, and increasing inequality will be discussed further in Chapter 14.

Distribution also takes place through one-way **transfers**, in which something is given with nothing specific expected in return. Social Security payments are an example of a transfer payment, and transfers can also take place among individuals. Parents are engaged in transfer when they provide their children with goods and services. Gifts and inheritances are also transfers. Local school boards, for example, distribute education services to students in their districts, tuition-free (although public education is, of course, supported by tax revenues). These sorts of nonmonetary transfers are called **in-kind transfers**.

> **transfer:** the giving of something, with nothing specific expected in return
> **in-kind transfers:** transfers of goods or services

Macroeconomists are particularly interested in transfers involving the government. Transfers *from* the government are often made in response to people's **dependency needs**. Our individual basic needs during some portions of our lifetimes— as infants and children or when incapacitated by age or illness—cannot be satisfied through exchange, because at those times we can produce little or nothing that can be sold in a market. During childhood or when incapacitated by illness or old age, we have to rely on our families, communities, and government agencies to transfer to us the care, shelter, food, and education that we need to survive and flourish.

> **dependency needs:** the need to receive care, shelter, or food from others when one is unable to provide these for oneself

Other funds flow *toward* the government. The government collects federal income taxes on the income of individuals and businesses. Most states also collect income taxes, real-estate taxes, and sales taxes on purchases in stores, or online. Policies on transfers and taxes affect the level and distribution of income across different groups. We will discuss the impacts of specific transfer and tax policies in the United States on the distribution of income in more detail in Chapters 9 and 14.

3.1.4 Consumption

Consumption is the process by which goods and services are put to final use by people. In some cases, such as eating a meal or burning gasoline in a car, goods are literally "consumed" in the sense that they are used up and are no longer available for other uses. In other cases, such as enjoying art in a museum, the experience may be "consumed" without excluding others or using up material resources.

In macroeconomics, the activity of consumption is frequently contrasted with the resource-management activity of investment. The two activities are linked by the activity of **saving** or refraining from consumption today in order to gain benefits in the future.

---

consumption: the final use of a good or service
saving: refraining from consumption in the current period

For example, suppose that a subsistence farmer grows a crop of corn. To the extent that the farmer eats some of the corn, the farmer *consumes*—the corn is used up in the process of eating and is not available for future use. To the extent that the farmer sets aside seeds from this year's corn crop for planting next season, the farmer *saves.* This is an example in which saving is directly turned into *investment:* It puts aside a resource that will aid production in the future.

Many real-world economic undertakings involve more than one of the four economic activities. A steelmaking firm, for example, engages in *production* of steel while also *distributing* the revenues from sales among its employees, managers, and stockholders. A family that grows crops for its own use is engaged first in *production* and then *consumption.* Resource management in particular often overlaps with production, consumption, and distribution. For example, the production of paper using recycled materials can be classified as both production and resource management because a good is being produced and natural resource use is reduced.

3.2 The Three Basic Economic Questions

The four economic activities that we have listed give rise, in turn, to the three basic economic questions:

- First, it matters *what* is produced. An economy may experience "economic growth" by increasing its production of military hardware or large public monuments, for example, but these kinds of production raise living standards less than growth in the production of nutritious food, widely available health care, or the quality of basic education.
- Second, it matters *how* it is produced. Production can involve high technology or simple manual labor. Production processes can be efficient or inefficient, and equitable or inequitable. In some poorer countries today, many workers—including young children—work 14-to 16-hour days in unsafe, badly ventilated mines and factories; many suffer severe illnesses and early death. And in both rich and poor countries, production is often carried out in ways that deplete or degrade essential natural resources.
- Third, it matters *for whom* economic growth occurs. How are the increases in production, or in incomes arising from production, dis-

tributed among the population? Do some regions, or some groups of people as defined by income class, race, ethnicity, gender, or other factors, receive more of the gains from growth than others? If the benefits of economic growth go primarily to a privileged group, the bulk of the population may remain very poor.

These questions clearly overlap. For example "what" and "for whom" may be intertwined—choosing whether to produce luxury goods or necessities like food and medicine may be affected by whether the economic system tilts toward production for the rich, or whether production is more equitably distributed. "How" may also have implications for "what"; choosing to produce in an environmentally sound manner may mean that certain goods, such as highly toxic pesticides, should not be produced at all. And "for whom" should include both present and future generations, illustrating the need for resource-saving production.

Discussion Questions

1. Think of a common activity that you enjoy. For example, perhaps you like to get together with friends and listen to music on your smartphone while popping popcorn in the microwave. List the stocks of natural, manufactured, human, and social capital that you draw on while engaging in this activity.
2. Classify each of the following according to which economic activity, or activities, it involves, from this list: production, resource management, distribution, and consumption. If any seem to include aspects of more than one activity, name the activities and explain your reasoning.

   a) Harvesting a crop of corn
   b) Attending college
   c) Building an addition to a factory
   d) Receiving a Social Security payment
   e) Cutting someone's hair

4 MACROECONOMICS IN CONTEXT

Macroeconomics, as a field of study, is not a set of principles that is set in stone. Rather, the field has developed and changed over time as new empirical and theoretical techniques have been invented and as historical events have raised new questions for which people have urgently desired answers. To give you an idea of how the various principles in this book fit into the historical context, we end this chapter with a short overview of major developments in macroeconomics. This historical perspective is important to understand current macroeconomic issues and debates.

4.1 The Classical Period

Centuries ago, most people in the world were involved in agriculture or in home production, such as when a family would work together to turn raw wool into cloth. Merchants were a minority, and industrial production and large-scale trade were unknown. All this changed with the coming of the Industrial Revolution, which began in England in the mid-eighteenth century. In many countries, technological progress led to new methods of production, and more productive economies both increased and diversified their output. Necessities like food and clothing used up a decreasing proportion of the average family income, while a growing fraction of the population was able to acquire more comforts and luxuries. As academic thinkers tried to understand and explain these changes, **classical economics** was born.

> **classical economics:** the school of economics, originating in the eighteenth century, that stressed issues of growth and distribution, based on an image of smoothly functioning markets

During this period, macroeconomic study focused on economic growth and distribution. The most famous classical economist was the Scottish philosopher Adam Smith (1723–1790), whose 1776 book *An Inquiry into the Nature and Causes of the Wealth of Nations* set the terms of discussion for centuries to come. Smith attributed the growing "wealth of nations" to various factors. One was changes in the organization of work, particularly the **division of labor** that assigned workers to **specialized**, narrowly defined tasks. Whereas in family-based production each individual had usually performed a variety of tasks, in industrial production a person would repeat one specific task over and over, presumably becoming more proficient with practice, thereby increasing labor productivity. Another factor was technological progress, such as the invention of new machines powered by burning coal. The third was the accumulation of funds to invest in plants and machinery ("capital accumulation").

> **division of labor:** an approach to production in which a process is broken down into smaller tasks, with each worker assigned only one or a few tasks
> **specialization:** in production, a system of organization in which each worker performs only one type of task

Classical economists, including Smith, David Ricardo, Thomas Malthus, John Stuart Mill, and Karl Marx, were interested in several questions that are still among the most important issues for macroeconomics: How is the total wealth generated by a society divided between those who own the means of production (landlords and **capitalists**) and those who work for them? Is the existing division optimal? What are the forces that determine how society's wealth will be divided?

Smith is known in particular for promulgating the idea that market systems could coordinate the self-interested actions of individuals so that they would ultimately serve the social good. While Smith himself supported a number of government interventions and discussed the moral basis of social and economic behavior in his other works, the school of classical economics has been popularly identified with the idea that individual self-interest is a positive force and that governments should let markets function with little interference—that economies should be **laissez-faire**.[†]

---

capitalists: those who own capital goods used in production, hire wage workers, and sell the products to make profits
laissez-faire economy: an economy with little government regulation

---

The classical economists, with the exception of Malthus and Marx, did not much address the problem of economic fluctuations. Most of them thought that a smoothly functioning market system should be entirely self-regulating, and full employment should generally prevail. This view was summarized in **Say's Law**, named after the French classical economist Jean-Baptiste Say (1767–1832), which was said to prove that "supply creates its own demand." The example Say gave was of a tradesman, for example, a shoemaker who sold $100 worth of shoes. Say argued that the shoemaker would naturally want to spend the $100 on other goods, thereby creating a level of demand that was exactly equal in monetary value to the supply of shoes that he had provided. If this example is extended to the whole economy, it suggests that the quantities demanded and quantities supplied of goods will exactly balance. From this, Say also deduced that the system would always generate the right number of jobs for those needing work. Classical economists also discussed issues related to a country's monetary system, but most tended to assume that monetary issues affected only the price levels, and not the level of production.

Say's Law: the classical belief that "supply creates its own demand"

[†] "Laissez-faire," a French term, means "leave alone" and is pronounced "lez-say fair."

Malthus and Marx were the classical economists most concerned about possible instability in market systems. Malthus spoke of the possibility of a "general glut" where production would exceed consumption, leading to economic crisis and depression. He was also concerned about population outrunning food supply and resources (an issue we take up in Chapter 17). Marx saw economic development as a process of class conflict between capitalists and workers, leading ultimately to the breakdown of capitalism and workers' revolution. But these concerns did not dominate classical economic thinking. The leading classical economists, such as David Ricardo and John Stuart Mill, tended to assume that the market system would prevail and would advance human welfare, with limited government intervention.

4.2 The Great Depression and Keynes

In practice, however, economies do not always work so smoothly. Some periods, like 1904–1906, the 1920s, or the late 1990s in the United States, were boom years in which everyone seemed eager to invest and spend. People with extra funds would buy stocks (ownership shares in companies), invest in real estate, or deposit their funds in banks (to be lent to others) with great confidence. But these booms frequently ended in painful recessions. Suddenly, the tide would turn, and everyone would want to sell—not buy—and stock prices would plummet. A lack of confidence in banks could lead to "bank runs" or "banking panics," such as occurred in 1907 and 1930–1933 in the United States when many people tried to withdraw their deposits all at once. With financial markets in tatters, businesses and individuals would be unable or unwilling to maintain or expand their activities and banks would be unwilling to lend. As people cut back on spending, produced goods went unsold, businesses cut back on production, and large numbers of people became unemployed.

A great many people in the United States and much of the rest of the industrialized world suffered considerable hardship during the Great Depression that followed the 1929 U.S. stock market crash. Production dropped by about 30 percent between 1929 and 1933, and unemployment peaked at 25 percent in the United States. High unemployment persisted throughout the 1930s, exposing the flaws in the classical theory of self-adjusting markets with full employment—a perspective that was unable to explain or correct for this long and persistent period of high unemployment.

The publication of *The General Theory of Employment, Interest, and Money* in 1936 by British economist John Maynard Keynes was a watershed event. In this book, Keynes (pronounced "canes") argued that Say's Law was wrong. It *is* possible, he said, for an economy to have a level of demand for goods that is insufficient to meet the supply from production. In such a case, producers, unable to sell their goods, will cut back on production, laying off workers and thus creating economic slumps. The key to getting out of such a slump, Keynes argued, is to increase **aggregate demand**—the total demand for goods and services in the national economy.

> **aggregate demand:** the total demand for all goods and services in a national economy

Keynes suggested a number of ways to achieve this. People could be provided with incentives (such as tax cuts) to consume more, the government could buy more goods and services, or businesses could be encouraged to spend more. Some economists thought that the best way to encourage business spending was to keep interest rates low so that businesses could borrow easily to invest in their enterprises. While Keynes believed that increasing investment would help the economy recover, he thought that low interest rates alone would be insufficient to tempt discouraged and uncertain businesses to start investing during economic downturns. Keynes believed that the solution to business cycles lay in having the government take more direct control of the level of national investment and aggregate demand. This is one of the main tenets of **Keynesian economics**. The administration of Franklin Roosevelt partially adopted a Keynesian approach in what was known as the New Deal, which expanded government spending and government employment programs. But despite some reduction in unemployment, the Great Depression continued for the remainder of the 1930s. It was the high government spending associated with national mobilization for World War II that finally brought the Great Depression to an end.

> **Keynesian economics:** a school of thought, named after John Maynard Keynes, that argues for an active government involvement in the economy, to keep aggregate demand high and employment rates up, through changes in government spending and taxation

The Keynesian approach strongly influenced macroeconomic policymaking in the United States and many other countries after the Second World War. Between 1946 and the 1960s, the U.S. government made huge investments in the economy through infrastructure development and the implementation of various social welfare and anti-poverty programs. This era in the United States was characterized by strong growth, low unemployment, low inflation, and increases in productivity and wages. The idea became popular that the government might even be able to "fine tune" the economy, counteracting any tendencies to slump or excessive expansion with policy changes, thereby largely eliminating business cycles.

4.3 The Crisis of the 1970s and Retreat from Keynesian Economics

In the early 1970s, this rosy picture was shattered, however, as many industrialized countries began to experience rising unemployment *combined with* increased inflation. Several factors contributed to the economic problems of this era. First, the U.S. economy faced increasing competition from industrialized nations in Europe and Japan, as these nations finally recovered from World War II. This resulted in declining profits for U.S. businesses. The strengthening of labor unions and the consolidation of corporations in the United States in the decades after the war had created an environment where demands for wage increases by workers were accommodated through increases in the price of goods, resulting in an inflationary spiral. Also, high expenditures by the government, including spending on the Vietnam War, and sharp rises in energy prices due to the oil embargo in 1973 contributed to the rising inflation. Overall, growth during the 1970s and early 1980s remained sluggish (under 3 percent).

The government was largely blamed for many of the problems of the 1970s. Too much regulation of businesses, high government spending on social programs, high taxes on corporations and individuals, and the creation of too much money by the government were seen as the key causes of the crisis.

Most notable, among those who took this view, was University of Chicago economist Milton Friedman. Friedman had strongly challenged Keynesian ideas even before the problems of the 1970s surfaced. His most prominent theory, **monetarism**, argued that a government limited to allowing central banks to keep the nation's money supply growth on a steady path was all that was required to prevent economic downturns. Monetarists also claimed that deliberate efforts by the government to push unemployment levels too low would lead to inflation—a prediction that was borne out in the problems of the 1970s. Like the classical economists, monetarists believed that the economy would best be left to adjust on its own. As economic conditions worsened in the late 1970s, this set of beliefs gained momentum.

---

monetarism: a school of economic thought that argues that governments should aim for steadiness in the money supply rather than playing an active role

---

This change in economic ideology led to a decline in the regulation of businesses and finance, cuts in social welfare programs, privatization of public services, and a shift in tax burden from corporations to the middle class. Other notable changes since the 1970s include stagnant real wages, an increase in inequality, and an increase in the size and power of big businesses. We will discuss these issues, and possible policy responses, in later chapters.

Starting in the 1980s there have been periods with long economic expansions: 1983–1990, 1992–2000, 2002–2007, and 2009-2019; but these were interrupted by sharp declines in 1990–1991, 2001, 2007–2009, and 2020. Large asset bubbles, driven by speculation, led to economic crisis and recession in 2001 and 2007–2009. This in turn led some economists to argue that the trend toward reduced government intervention had been overdone, and that a return to more Keynesian approaches was needed to prevent or respond to recessions.

Debates on the value of active government policies have continued, with macroeconomists at the classical end of the spectrum asserting that markets work efficiently and that large-scale government intervention discourages private sector activities and hurts growth. Economists on the Keynesian end of the spectrum, meanwhile, tend to emphasize the way in which unemployment can cause severe human suffering, with recessions possibly continuing for long periods. They therefore argue for a more active role for government. Waiting for markets to adjust on their own, they believe, may mean waiting too long. As Keynes himself put it, "In the long run, we are all dead."

New developments in recent years have revived many of these long-running debates about the appropriate role of government in the economy. But the discussion has also changed to include a new focus on current issues including inequality and environmental damage—so while we need to be aware of the major historical schools of thought, we also need to be open to new approaches to macroeconomic analyses.

4.4 Macroeconomics for the Twenty-First Century

While issues of economic growth and the business cycle dominated macroeconomic thinking for generations, in the twenty-first century, new developments are demanding new ways of looking at the economic world.

The global recession of 2007–2009—which resulted in a huge loss of income and homes—raised concerns over issues of financial instability and inequality, and there has been intense debate on appropriate policy responses. More recently, great suffering, including loss of lives and the increased social and economic insecurity arising from the COVID-19 pandemic, in which the heaviest impact has fallen on the most vulnerable population, has exposed deep inequalities within and between countries, and heightened the need for stronger social safety nets. In a broader perspective, the persistence of substantial global poverty and the continuation of political instability and armed conflicts in

57

some regions of the world have called into question the appropriateness of traditional ideas about economic development.

The changing nature of the labor market, where more people are taking up temporary or part-time jobs and workers are being replaced by machines, could also have important implications on the well-being of workers. Increasing income inequality, unequal distribution of resources, and disparities in power on local, national, and global scales, are rising to the fore as critical issues for human well-being. With economies around the world becoming more integrated and the financial sector's increasing size and influence on the economy, there is a need to develop new models that consider the challenges of the current century. We will discuss these issues in Parts II, III, and IV of this book.

In the twenty-first century, climate change and deterioration of the natural environment have become major concerns as the scale of human activity continues to grow. Most previous economic theories assumed that resources and the capacity of the environment to absorb the by-products of economic growth were essentially unlimited—or at least that continued developments in technology would keep problems of depletion and pollution at bay. This has been increasingly questioned as the incidence of climate-related disasters, such as severe disturbances to agriculture, disruptions in water supply, expansion of tropical diseases, and threats from increasingly severe weather including hurricanes, floods, and droughts, have escalated. Reconciling ecological sustainability and restoration with full employment and growth in living standards is rising in prominence as a macroeconomic issue.

This is an exciting moment for you to be beginning the study of economics when so much is at stake—including the kind of work, recreation, and consumption that you will be able to expect in your life—and when there is both need and opportunity for creative new ideas. If you had embarked on this course 30 years ago, you would likely have read a textbook that implied that "everything we need to know about the macroeconomy is here—just learn it." Given recent developments, it is more appropriate to invite you to contemplate and discuss how the economy works, how it doesn't, and how it should.

Discussion Questions

1. Which major historical events influenced the development of macroeconomics as a field of study? In addition to the problems listed in the text, do you think there are other current problems that macroeconomics should be addressing?
2. The fact that economists do not always agree, and that there are alternative "schools" of macroeconomic thought, can sometimes seem confusing. It may help to think about how economics compares to other subjects that you have studied. What kinds of changes in the fields of physics or biology have occurred in the past hundred

years? Are there major debates, disagreements, and unsettled issues in other fields such as psychology, sociology, or political science?

REVIEW QUESTIONS

1. What is economics?
2. How does macroeconomics differ from microeconomics?
3. What is the difference between positive and normative questions?
4. What is meant by "living standards growth"? Is this the same as "economic growth"?
5. Why are macroeconomic fluctuations a cause for concern?
6. What global developments have caused financial, social, and ecological sustainability or restoration to become increasingly prominent as macroeconomic concerns?
7. What is the "precautionary principle"?
8. What are the four essential economic activities?
9. What five types of capital contribute to productivity? Describe them.
10. Describe the difference between a stock and a flow, giving examples.
11. Describe the economic activity of production.
12. What are the two main forms that the activity of distribution takes? Describe.
13. Describe the relationship between consumption and saving.
14. What do economists mean by "investment"?
15. What is a sustainable socioeconomic system? What is the difference between sustaining and restoring a system?
16. What historical developments and concerns motivated—and what beliefs characterized—the classical economists? The school of Keynesian economics? The work of the monetarists?
17. Name two or more global issues that will likely shape the development of macroeconomics in the twenty-first century.

EXERCISES

1. The more you pay attention to what is going on in the macroeconomy around you, the more meaningful this class will be to you. Find an article in a newspaper or newsmagazine (hard copy or online) that deals with a macroeconomic topic. Make a list of terms, concepts, people, organizations, or historical events mentioned in the article that are also mentioned in this chapter.
2. Classify each of the following as to whether it is an example of a positive question or a normative question (some may have elements of both).
   a) "What is the level of the U.S. national debt?"
   b) "Is the national debt too high?"
   c) "How low should the unemployment rate be?"
   d) "What kinds of production should be counted in measuring gross domestic product?"
   e) "Is it better to have low unemployment or low inflation?"
3. Which of the following are flows? Which are stocks? If a flow, which of the five major kind(s) of capital does it increase or decrease? If a stock, what kind of capital is it?
   a) The fish in a lake
   b) The output of a factory during a year
   c) The income that you receive in a month
   d) The reputation of a business among its customers

    e)   The assets of a bank

    f)   The equipment in a factory

    g)   A process of diplomatic negotiations

    h)   The discussion in an economics class

4. State whether the following statements are true or false. If false, also write a corrected statement.

    a)   Macroeconomics is about the activities of government agencies.

    b)   Economic growth always leads to improvements in living standards.

    c)   The three aspects to consider in thinking about sustainability are financial, monetary, and ecological.

    d)   Low-income countries have had little problem paying back economic development loans.

    e)   Monetarists believe that the government should actively manage the money supply to counter economic fluctuations.

    f)   Specialization and the division of labor are characteristics of industrial production.

    g)   Classical economists believe that the Great Depression was caused by aggregate demand that was too low.

    h)   Keynesian economists believe that an economy that experiences a high rate of unemployment will quickly self-correct.

5. Match each concept in Column A with a definition or example in Column B:

Column A	Column B
a. Keynesian economics	1. Implementation of urban reforestation programs
b. Classical economics	2. Studies how economics applies at the national and global level
c. Restorative development	3. Supply creates its own demand
d. Conscious consumption	4. Expansion in GDP as a result of new production
e. Living standards growth	5. A school that focuses on aggregate demand and encourages government action
f. Business cycle	6. Switching from plastic to reusable bags for shopping
g. Monetarism	7. A factory building
h. Manufactured capital	8. The school of economic thought originally associated with the idea of laissez-faire economics
i. Say's law	9. More of the population gets access to basic health care
j. Microeconomics	10. Studies how economics applies at the level of households, businesses, and other organizations
k. In-kind transfer	11. A school of economic thought that argues that active government monetary policies usually make economic fluctuations worse
l. Social capital	12. The short-run fluctuations of a national economy

m.   Economic growth   13. A gift of food

n.   Macroeconomics   14. A shared language within a community

NOTES

1   Data for 1981 from CBO, 2001 and data for 2013 from CBO, 2016 reports.
2   Data in Box 1.2 is based on the Sustainable Development Goals Report, 2021.

REFERENCES

Congressional Budget Office (CBO). 2001. "Effective Federal Tax Rates, 1979–1997." *Table G1-b. October.*

Congressional Budget Office (CBO). 2016. "The Distribution of Household Income and Federal Taxes, 2013." Figure 1, June.

Johnston, Louis D., and Samuel H. Williamson. 2008. "The Annual Real and Nominal GDP for the United States, 1790–Present." *Measuring Worth,* Economic History Services.

The Sustainable Development Goals Report 2021, United Nations. https://unstats.un.org/sdgs/report/2021/

World Bank. 2017. "Atlas of Sustainable Development Goals 2017: From World Development Indicators." *World Bank Atlas,* Washington, DC.

World Development Indicators Database.

Chapter 2

Foundations of Economic Analysis

You cannot build a secure house without a good understanding of construction materials and building techniques. Likewise, in order to understand how societies might be able to achieve the goals of good living standards, stability, and sustainability we first need to examine some of the "building blocks" of the economy. In this chapter, we develop a foundation for understanding how the economy works, introducing basic concepts and methods of analysis.

1 OUR TOOLS FOR UNDERSTANDING

Explaining economic phenomena involves using two main modes of investigation: empirical and theoretical.

1.1 Empirical Investigation

Empirical investigation involves making observations and recording of specific happenings in the world. These observations can be represented in words, images, or numerical data.

---

empirical investigation: observation and recording of the specific phenomena of concern

---

Economists often rely on numerical observations to understand economic phenomenon. When the observations show how a variable changes over time, we call them **time-series data**. We saw examples of time-series data in Chapter 1, in graphs that showed how GDP and atmospheric carbon dioxide (CO_2) levels have grown over time. In contrast, when observations on a variable are collected for many subjects (such as individuals, firms, countries, or regions) at one point in time, we call them **cross-sectional data**. The graphs in Chapter 0 comparing the data for variables like GDP per capita, unemployment, and labor

DOI: 10.4324/9781003251521-4

productivity in different countries for a certain year, are examples of cross-sectional data. We will see both types of graphs in this book. The appendix to this chapter will help you refresh your skills in working with data and graphs.

---

time-series data: observations of how a numerical variable changes over time

cross-sectional data: observations on a variable for different subjects at one point in time

---

Empirical investigation also includes **historical investigation**, which involves using knowledge of historical events and the evolution of political, economic, and social life to help explain macroeconomic phenomena. The Great Depression of the 1930s, major wars, changing roles of women in the workforce, the invention of computers, and the financial crash of 2007–2008—are all examples of historical events that have had a significant macroeconomic impact.

---

historical investigation: study of past events

1.2 Theoretical Investigation

Theoretical investigation refers to statements made on the basis of abstract thought, making assumptions and logical deductions. In the physical sciences, much theorizing is based on controlled experiments in the laboratory. While it is sometimes possible for economists to carry out controlled experiments at the microeconomic level (as is done in the field of "experimental economics"), this is rarely possible in macroeconomics. Economists seeking to describe the behavior of the economy as a whole therefore create theories based on assumptions about economic agents and institutions, from which, with careful reasoning, they draw out potential implications for economic behavior and macro-level results.

---

theoretical investigation: analysis based on abstract thought

---

In order to build a theory, it is sometimes useful to create **models** that examine specific aspects of the economy by isolating these aspects from their larger historical, social, and environmental contexts. A model is an analytical tool that highlights some aspects of reality while ignoring others. It can take the form of a simplified story, an image, a graph, or a set of equations, and it always involves simplifying assumptions. An important part of many models is the assumption of **ceteris paribus**, a Latin phrase that means "other things equal" or "all else constant." In order to focus on one or two variables, we assume that no other variables change. Of course, in the real world, many things are changing at the same time. Often after a basic model is constructed, we can vary the *ceteris paribus* assumption, to see how changes in other variables will affect the model's conclusions. We look at some examples of economic models in Sections 2 and 3 of this chapter.

---

model: an analytical tool that highlights some aspects of reality while ignoring others

ceteris paribus: a Latin phrase meaning "other things equal" or "all else constant"

Theories and models essentially simplify reality. Is this justifiable? It is if it gives us greater insight into how things actually work. A model plane, for example, cannot carry passengers or freight, but it can give aerodynamic engineers insights into how a real plane works and help them to design better features for real aircraft. In the same way, simplified models can help economists to understand the working of very complex real-world economies. Of course, economists may disagree about which models to use, and as a result, may come to different policy conclusions. In this text, we try to make clear what simplifying assumptions we are using to build models and to indicate when there are different economic theories that may lead to conflicting policy recommendations.

Discussion Questions

1   Consider the following examples of investigation. For each one, indicate which mode of investigation it most closely represents—empirical, theoretical, or historical.

    a)   A biologist tries to determine the number of different species of plants found on a plot of rainforest

    b)   Albert Einstein develops his theory of relativity

    c)   An economist measures how GDP varies across countries

    d)   A sociologist examines the impact of movements for equal pay for women on women's social and economic status

    e)   An economist states that a rise in investment will lead to a fall in unemployment

2   Model building is sometimes compared to map-making. If someone asks you how to get to your house, what will you put on the
map you draw for them? What if the question asked has to do with
the town's political boundaries, the public transit system, or how
your dwelling links up to the local sewer system? Is it possible for
a single, readable map to answer every possible question? Does the
goal you have in mind for the map affect what you put on it?

2 ECONOMIC TRADEOFFS

Tradeoffs are a central concept in economics. Sometimes resources for
economic activity may be available in **abundance**—meaning that there
are more than enough to meet our goals. More commonly, we experience **scarcity**, or limits on available resources, and have to decide on
how to allocate these resources. If we allocate more resources toward
one objective, then less are available to meet other goals. This is particularly important when we recognize that well-being is multidimensional, and that progress in one dimension may come at the expense
of other dimensions. Macroeconomics is centrally concerned with how
decisions on resource use made by individuals, organizations, and the
government influence the overall economic environment.

---

abundance: availability of resources in plentiful supply for meeting various goals
scarcity: limits on resources such that they are not sufficient to meet various different goals at once

---

2.1 Society's Production-Possibilities Frontier

Economists use the model of a production-possibilities frontier (PPF)
to illustrate the concept of tradeoffs. Let's assume that society is deciding between only two possible choices of what to produce over the
coming year, using currently available resources and the existing technology. (This is an example of a simplifying assumption that reduces
the complex reality of many goods to only two in order to illustrate a
principle). The classic example is to take "guns" and "butter" as the two
outputs. In general, the guns-and-butter tradeoff can refer to any society's choice between becoming more militarized ("guns") and becoming more civilian- or consumer-oriented ("butter").

  With limited resources, our simple, imagined society can only produce a given quantity of guns or butter. Also, allocating more resources
toward one output means fewer resources will be available to produce
the other output. For example, if more labor resources go into gun production, fewer workers will be available to make butter. These concepts
can be graphically represented using a **production-possibilities frontier**

65

(PPF), which shows all the combinations of two outputs that can be produced by a society in a given time period.

production-possibilities frontier (PPF): a curve showing the maximum amounts of two outputs that society could produce from given resources, over a certain time period

Figure 2.1 shows a production-possibilities frontier (PPF) for guns and butter. In this graph, the quantity of "butter" produced over a year is measured on the horizontal (or *x*-) axis. The quantity of "guns" is measured on the vertical (or *y*-) axis. We measure butter in tons and guns in hundreds. The points on the PPF curve illustrate various maximum quantities of guns and butter that the society could produce. For example, at point A, the society is directing all its resources into butter production to produce 120 tons of butter. Point B illustrates the production of 100 tons of butter and 500 guns, and point C illustrates that the society can produce 900 guns if it decides to produce no butter. While it may seem odd to think about a society that only produces two goods, the PPF figure is nevertheless helpful for illustrating three important economic concepts.

1. *Scarcity.* Point D in Figure 2.1 represents a production combination (80 tons of butter and 800 guns) that is not attainable, given existing resources and technology. To produce at that point would take more resources, or better technology, than this society currently has. The PPF is specifically defined so that only those points on or inside it (the blue-shaded region) represent outputs that can actually be produced.
2. *Tradeoffs.* Points that lie on the PPF illustrate the fact that scarcity creates a need for tradeoffs. Along the frontier, one can get more of

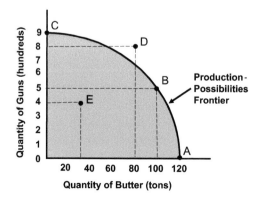

Figure 2.1 *Society's Production-Possibilities Frontier*

one output only by "trading off" some of the other. Figure 2.1 also illustrates the concept of **opportunity cost**, which is defined as the value of the best alternative to the choice that one actually makes. Looking at the PPF, we see that the cost of increasing gun production is less butter. For example, when the economy moves from point A to point B, it gains 500 guns at a cost of a loss of 20 tons of butter.

> **opportunity cost:** the value of the best alternative that is forgone when a choice is made

3. *Efficiency.* Resources are used with **efficiency** when they are used in a way that does not involve any waste. Points that lie *on* the PPF illustrate the maximum combinations that a society can produce from its given resources if these are used efficiently. But what about points *inside* the frontier, such as point E? At point E, the economy is not producing as much as it could. It is producing 30 tons of butter and 400 guns, even though it *could* produce more of one or the other, or both. This could occur for at least three reasons:

- Resources may be left idle, for example, when workers are unemployed, or cows are left unmilked.
- The technology and social organization being applied to the resources may not be optimal. For example, if the gun factory is poorly designed, a lot of the workers' time is wasted carting parts from one area to another. In this case, a better organization of the workflow could increase production, with no increase in resources.
- The allocation of resources between the two outputs (i.e., guns and butter) might not be optimal. For example, locating gun factories on the best pastureland would not be optimal if cows are grazing on poor land that would be fine for gun factories.

> **efficiency:** the use of resources in a way that does not waste any inputs

Note that the PPF has a bowed-out shape. This is due to the fact that some resources are better suited for the production of one good than the other. Suppose our society is initially producing only butter, at point A. It can get the first 500 guns by giving up only 20 tons of butter production (point B). In shifting its resources from butter to guns, we assume the society will start with resources that are best-suited for gun production and least-suited for butter production. For example, we would locate our first gun factories on land that is poorly suited for grazing and hire workers who have better gun-making skills.

But the more we shift resources from butter to gun production, the more we will have to shift resources that are better suited for butter production to producing guns. We have to pull workers off of the most productive pastureland and direct them to the now-crowded gun assembly line. So in order to produce 400 more guns (to go from point B to point C), we will have to give up all remaining 100 tons of butter! We can see that the rate of tradeoff varies at the different points along the PPF.

Of course, we could use the PPF to show the tradeoffs between many other pairs of outputs, such as Coca-Cola and pizza, cars and bicycles, or health care and highways. In some cases, the PPF could have a different shape. For example, if we considered the tradeoff between producing two very similar goods such as bread and muffins, the PPF might be fairly straight since almost exactly the same resources are required for both (think of allocating ten ovens between producing bread or muffins). We could also imagine a multidimensional PPF to evaluate tradeoffs among more than two goods. This classic example of guns and butter, however, does illustrate some real-world concepts. Decisions about guns/butter or militarization/peacetime tradeoffs are important social and political issues (see Box 2.1).

What precise combination of outputs, such as guns and butter, or health care and highways, should society choose to produce? The PPF does *not* answer this question. To determine this, we would have to know more about a society's requirements and priorities. Is food security a high priority? Then the society would lean toward the production of butter. Does the society fear attack by a foreign power? Perhaps then it would choose a point more toward the guns axis.

In a democratic society, there is wide room for disagreement about what the best mix of outputs might be. The PPF shows the range of efficient possibilities, such as points A, B, or C, but does not tell us which one of these combinations of outputs would maximize social well-being.

BOX 2.1 THE OPPORTUNITY COST OF MILITARY EXPENDITURES

What do military build-ups and wars really cost? One way to look at this is to consider what else could have been bought with the money spent on armaments.

In 2020, world military expenditures totaled US$1.9 trillion, or 2.2 percent of world economic output.[1] The United States is by far the biggest spender—with US$778 billion in spending it accounts for 40 percent of the global total. China was second (US$252 billion), followed by India (US$73 billion), Russia (US$62 billion), and the UK (US$59 billion). Many poor countries spend a significant share of their economic output on the military. For example, Pakistan spends over 4 percent of its GDP on the military, Botswana 3.5 percent, and Colombia 3.4 percent (about the same share as the United States).[2]

Military spending comes at the expense of other objectives. In 2015 the United Nations approved a set of 17 Sustainable Development Goals (SDGs) including global goals related to ending poverty, protecting the planet, increasing access to education and health care, lowering inequality, and securing prosperity for all.[3] According to a 2015 analysis,[4] many of these goals could be met for a fraction of world military expenditures. For example, meeting SDG Goal#3—ensuring healthy lives, including reducing maternal and infant mortality and providing universal health coverage—would cost an estimated US$70–90 billion per year, or about 5 percent of annual military expenditures. Providing universal access to safe water and sanitation (SDG Goal #6) would cost about US$40 billion annually. Overall, the entire set of SDGs could be achieved with an annual investment of about US$1.4 trillion, less than the world's military spending.

As U.S. president Dwight D. Eisenhower said in 1953, "Every gun that is made, every warship launched, every rocket fired, signifies in the final sense a theft from those who hunger and are not fed, those who are cold and are not clothed."

2.2 Tradeoffs over Time

A PPF can also be used to think about production allocations across time. If, say, we cut down all our forests or use up all our copper in order to maximize immediate production, that leaves fewer resources available for the future. The economic question of *for whom* directs us to look at the allocation of resources between the present and the future.

Production of goods and services that protect the environment or that encourage the formation of new forms of knowledge and social organization leads to an improved resource base. Technological progress can also *add* to the production possibilities for the future through long-run improvements in productive capacity. The PPF may expand over time, out and to the right, making previously unobtainable points obtainable, as shown in Figure 2.2. With the initial PPF, points A, B, and C are attainable, but points D and E are unattainable. With technological progress and an expanded PPF, points D and E become attainable.

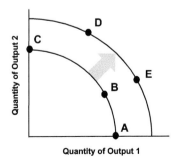

Figure 2.2 *An Expanded Production-Possibilities Frontier*

Some productive activities contribute to increasing outputs without drawing down the stock of capital resources, such as organic farming that maintains the nutrient levels in the soil. But many other productive activities lead to resource depletion. For example, agricultural production processes that deplete soil or pollute watersheds leave us worse off for the future.

Taking a longer-term view, it is clear that focusing only on maximizing current production is not a wise goal. Decisions such as guns vs. butter need to be accompanied by another decision about *now* versus *later*. The choice between current and future production can be presented in terms of a different PPF as shown in Figure 2.3. In this case, the tradeoff is between current production and resource availability for the future. If the society chooses Point A, current production is high but resource availability for the future is low. However, choosing Point B reduces current production and results in significantly greater resource availability in the future.

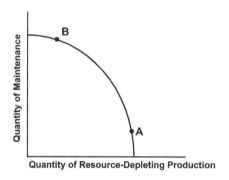

Figure 2.3 *Society's Choice between Current Production and Future Resource Availability*

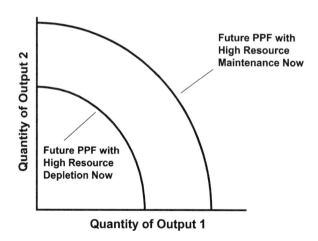

Figure 2.4 *Potential Future Production-Possibilities Frontiers*

70

The consequences of choosing between points A and B are illustrated in Figure 2.4 where once again we portray a two-output PPF with a graph that illustrates how future conditions are affected by the current choice between A and B in Figure 2.3. As Figure 2.4 shows, a decision to maintain more resources for the future, by choosing point B in Figure 2.3, leads to a larger set of production possibilities in future years. A decision to engage in more resource depletion today in Figure 2.3 (Point A) leads to the smaller future PPF shown in Figure 2.4. Decisions about resource management have become more important in recent decades with the threat of large-scale and irreversible consequences due to biodiversity loss, climate change, and other environmental impacts.

Discussion Questions

1. Suppose that a farmer can devote land to production of apples or vegetables. Draw a production possibilities curve for the farm. Do you think the curve would be shaped like the PPF in Figure 2.1? What factors would affect its shape?
2. Consider the following activities. Which ones do you think would expand society's PPF in the future? Which ones would shrink it? (There may be room for disagreement on some.)

   a) Increasing education spending
   b) Expanding timber production
   c) Building a wind power facility
   d) Restoring wetlands
   e) Using larger trawlers to catch more fish.

3 DIFFERENT ECONOMIC MODELS

Like most areas of academic discussion, economics has a long history of varying approaches, assumptions, and beliefs. We have already discussed some of these differences in Chapter 1 and will consider some other approaches in later chapters. Here we present two basic theoretical models for understanding the economy: the neoclassical model, which has dominated much of standard economics, and the contextual economic model, which is the approach taken in this text. These approaches have some overlap, but they differ in their scope and emphasis, and can lead to different understandings of economic theory and policy.

3.1 The Basic Neoclassical Model

The **basic neoclassical model** was developed in the early twentieth century by economists who followed the classical school in assuming smoothly functioning markets but attempted to construct a more

71

specific model to describe them.* (The prefix "neo-" in "neoclassical" means "new.") This model is illustrated by the **circular flow diagram** shown in Figure 2.5. In this model, the world is simplified into two kinds of economic actors: households and firms—represented by two rectangles. The activity of exchange between these two actors is illustrated using arrows. It is assumed that households consume with the goal of maximizing their **utility** (or satisfaction) and firms produce with the goal of maximizing profits.

---

basic neoclassical model: a model that portrays the economy as a collection of profit-maximizing firms and utility-maximizing households interacting in perfectly competitive markets

circular flow diagram: a graphical representation of the traditional view of an economy consisting of households and firms engaging in exchange

utility: the level of usefulness or satisfaction gained from a particular activity

---

In this model, households are considered the ultimate owners of all resources of land, labor, and capital, called "factors of production" by economists. Households rent the services of these productive factors to firms through **factor markets**, (dark blue arrow from households to firms) receiving monetary payments in the form of wages, rents, interests, and profits (light blue arrow from the firms to households). Firms produce goods and services, which they sell to households on **product markets** (dark blue arrow from firms to households) in return for monetary payments (light blue arrow from households to firms). The model further assumes that there are so many firms and households involved in the market for any good or service that a situation of "perfect competition" reigns, in which prices are determined purely by forces of supply and demand.

---

factor markets: markets for the services of land, labor, and capital

product markets: markets for newly produced goods and services

---

In this idealized world, goods and services are produced, distributed, and consumed in such a way that the market value of production is as high as it can be. Full social and economic efficiency is said to arise because:

---

* Neoclassical economists of the early twentieth century included Stanley Jevons, Maria Edgeworth, Leon Walras and Vilfredo Pareto.

- The prices set by the forces of supply and demand in smoothly functioning markets carry signals throughout the economy, coordinating the actions of many individual decision makers in a highly decentralized way
- The profit motive gives perfectly competitive firms an incentive to look for low-cost inputs and convert them into highly valuable outputs
- Consumption decisions made by individuals and households are assumed to maximize the "utility" or satisfaction of consumers
- Maximizing the market value of production is assumed to be a reasonable proxy for maximizing human well-being

While the circular flow diagram is useful in portraying the economic functions of two major actors (households and firms) and the activities of production, exchange, and consumption, it leaves out some key aspects of the economy. For example, while "land" is included as a factor of production, the fact that natural resources can be used up or polluted is not portrayed. Because of this, the circular flow diagram is like a "perpetual motion machine", where the economy can apparently keep on generating products without any inputs of materials or energy. The necessity of resource management activities is not included.

Also, the diagram only takes into account flows of goods or resources that are paid for through the market. This ignores unpaid work and free use of natural resources, among other things. The importance of sociocultural norms and historical factors in influencing economic behavior are also neglected and there is no role for government in this model. While these oversimplifications have some value in allowing us to focus only on the workings of specific markets, it limits our ability to present a broader picture that considers the *environmental* and *social contexts* within which economic activities take place.

Figure 2.5 *The Circular Flow Diagram for the Basic Neoclassical Model*

3.2 The Contextual Model

We present a more inclusive and more realistic model in Figure 2.6. Because all economic production requires the input of natural resources and generates some waste, the economy operates in an *environmental context*. Energy supplies, for example, are fundamental to economic activity, as are water supplies. If we overburden a river with toxic chemicals, the water may not be usable for drinking water supplies. And if we rely heavily on fossil fuel energy, we damage the atmospheric balance that governs climate. Sometimes, economic activity can also generate positive environmental effects, such as restorative care for soils that makes them more fertile, or sustainable forestry that allows forests to continue growing and increase in area.

The economy also operates in a *social context*, including history, politics, culture, ethics, and other human motivations. The social context influences what constitutes acceptable economic activity, and it determines the relative weight that a society attaches to different macroeconomic goals discussed in Chapter 1, such as improved living standards, stability and security, and social equity.

Much economic activity would become impossible without aspects of the social context such as laws, norms, trust, and honesty, which could be considered as essential inputs to the economy. Like the environment, society is also the recipient of both positive and negative outputs from the economy, such as inventions, products, services, as well as perceptions about what is a "good life". Advertising, for example, provides consumers with information, but may also work to shape their

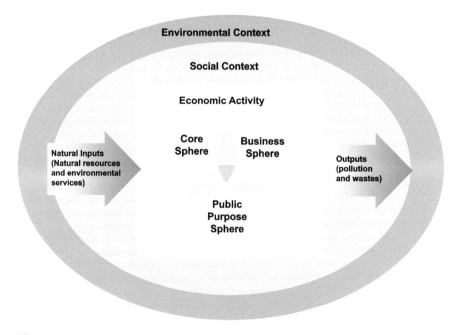

Figure 2.6 *Social and Environmental Contexts of Economic Activity*

preferences in ways that may not be in their best interests. Better communication through the internet and social media, made possible by advancing technology, has increased the availability of information and social contacts—but also of misinformation and social conflict.

In Figure 2.6 we show the social context as existing inside the environmental context because all human activities—not only those of the economic system—are ultimately completely dependent on the environmental context. A useful understanding of economics must take into account the most critical interactions between the economy and its environmental and social contexts, showing how the economy is in various ways enabled and constrained by these contexts, and how these contexts are in turn affected *by* the economy.

Instead of showing economic activity as occurring between just two actors, households and firms, the contextual model presents economic activity as occurring within three spheres: core, public purpose, and business. The core sphere includes households, families, and communities. The public purpose sphere includes government and other local, national, and international organizations, and the business sphere includes firms producing goods and services for sale. Individuals may move among these three spheres—a woman may be a mother in the core sphere, a volunteer for an environmental group in the public purpose sphere, and a business executive in the business sphere. Thus, Figure 2.6 shows the three spheres as overlapping. We discuss economic activities in these three spheres next.

3.2.1 Core Sphere

The **core sphere** includes households, families, and community institutions that undertake economic activities, usually on a small scale and largely without the use of money. We use the term "core," instead of the commonly used term "households," to emphasize the importance of communities, in addition to households, in the "core" activities. Important economic activity occurs *within* the core sphere—it is the primary site for raising children, preparing meals, maintaining homes, organizing leisure time, and caring for individuals who are sick, elderly, or needy but not in institutions such as hospitals or nursing homes.

core sphere: households, families, and communities

Many economic activities are conducted outside of formal markets through the organization of human societies along lines of kinship and community. For example, the conversion of many goods and services (often bought on markets) into forms suitable for final use, such as cooking pasta or planting seeds for a home garden, occurs within the core sphere. Decisions on how to allocate income among consumption, savings, or financial investments are also made within the core sphere. Households decide whether to buy denim pants or DVDs, sports cars or fuel-efficient hybrids, and whether to invest their money in real estate or mutual funds. Often family and friends use savings to make gifts or loans among themselves—for example, to finance food and rent in times of need.

Decisions that affect labor market outcomes, such as allocation of time between labor and leisure, and whether to work in the labor market, to become self-employed, or to engage in household production are also made in the core sphere. The core sphere is also the primary location for developing good social relations as activities of recreation and relaxation are largely organized around core sphere networks of family and community.

One distinguishing characteristic of the core sphere is that economic activities are rewarded by what they produce instead of by monetary rewards. For example, work in a home garden is rewarded with tomatoes, and the reward from good childcare is a happy and healthy child. Activities in the core sphere respond not only to *wants* but also to *needs*—unlike market activities which respond only to what people are willing to pay for. The core sphere is critical for subsistence economies, where societies may produce for themselves most of what they consume, with little outside trading. Although reliance on the core sphere has been reduced in some countries by the increasing use of prepared foods, child-care centers, nursing homes, and the like, it remains of central importance for the flourishing of any economy.

Core sphere activities are sometimes described as non-economic or non-productive because they generally do not produce goods and services for trade through a market. But this can be misleading. Consider the activity of providing care to sick, disabled, or elderly family members who need assistance in their daily activities. According to a 2020 analysis, 53 million people in the United States provided an average of nearly 1,200 hours per year of unpaid "family caregiving" labor.[5] For comparison, a full-time worker in the United States works an average of about 1,800 hours per year.[6] The estimated economic value of this unpaid labor in 2017 was $470 billion, based on an average value of about $13.81 per hour.[7] This exceeds the value of out-of-pocket spending on health care in the United States and is approximately equivalent to the total annual revenue of Walmart, the world's largest company.

While activities in the core sphere promote human well-being, there are limits to what can be accomplished within small-scale, largely informal networks of personal relations. For example, impoverished communities may not have sufficient resources to provide care for children or the sick and elderly. One extreme case is the situation of communities in sub-Saharan Africa trying to care for the large number of children orphaned by HIV/AIDS or by war, without adequate resources to feed and clothe the children, let alone provide for education and physical safety. In such cases, more formal and larger-scale organizations are needed. The public purpose sphere is uniquely capable of meeting these broader well-being needs.

3.2.2 The Public Purpose Sphere

The **public purpose sphere** includes governments and their agencies, as well as nonprofit organizations such as charities and professional associations, and international institutions such as the World Bank and the United Nations. They may be as large as a national government or an international organization or as small as a local soup kitchen. The distinguishing characteristic of these institutions is that they exist for an explicit purpose related to the public good and they do not seek to make profits. Organizations in the public purpose sphere tend to be larger and more formally structured than those in the core sphere and often rely on paid labor, though many are dependent on volunteers.

---

public purpose sphere: governments and other local, national, and international organizations established for a public purpose beyond individual self-interest and not operating with the goal of making a profit

---

We can break down the economic functions of public purpose organizations into two broad categories: *regulation* and *direct provision.*

Regulation involves setting the standards and "rules of the game" by which economic actors "play," so as to create the legal, informational, and social infrastructure for economic activity. Government regulation of financial markets, for example, plays an important role in macroeconomics. Though regulation is mostly carried out by the government, many nonprofit groups also participate in regulating economic activity, particularly in the area of standard setting. For example, standardized exams like the AP, SAT, or GRE are developed and administered by the Educational Testing Service, which is a private nonprofit organization.

---

regulation: setting standards or laws to govern behavior

Direct public provision is often used to supply goods or services that cannot be supplied equitably or efficiently by the core or business spheres. Some of the goods and services provided by the public purpose sphere are what economists call public goods. A **public good** (or service)

is a good whose benefits are freely available to all (**non-excludable**), and whose use by some does not diminish the quantity available to others (**non-rival**).

> **direct public provision:** the supply of goods or services from government or non-profit institutions
>
> **public good:** a good whose benefits are freely available to anyone, and whose use by one person does not diminish its usefulness to others
>
> **non-excludable good:** a good whose benefits are freely available to all
>
> **non-rival good:** a good whose use by one person does not reduce the quantity available to others

For example, when a local fire department provides firefighting services, all the residents benefit. Public roads (at least those that are not congested and have no tolls) are also public goods, as is national defense. Some of the larger public purpose organizations, both government agencies and nonprofit groups, are charged with purposes such as relieving poverty, providing basic health care and education, protecting the natural environment, and stabilizing global financial markets. Some things are provided by the public purpose sphere because, as a society, we believe that everyone should have access to them, regardless of their ability to pay. Public schooling from kindergarten through high school is a primary example.

In some instances, public purpose organizations offer goods and services for sale as businesses do, though this is generally not their primary focus. They usually raise much of their support by soliciting monetary contributions or, in the case of governments, requiring such contributions in the form of taxes or fees. Your college or university, if it is operated by a nonprofit or government entity, would be part of the public purpose sphere. For-profit universities, however, would fall in the business sphere.

The public purpose sphere is a substantial contributor to economic activity. Figure 2.7 presents the share of GDP attributed to government spending in selected countries. In some countries, mainly in Europe around half of the economy is a result of government spending. In the United States, the government comprises 36 percent of the economy. In poorer countries, however, the share of government in the GDP tends to be lower.

In order to estimate the full scale of the public purpose sphere, we also need to consider the contribution of nonprofits. Unfortunately, this data is not available for most countries. Non-profits contributed 5.6 percent to the U.S. GDP in 2016.[8] A 2016 analysis on the scale of the nonprofit sector in 16 countries shows Canada (8.1 percent), Israel (7.1 percent), and Mozambique (6.7 percent) as countries with the largest

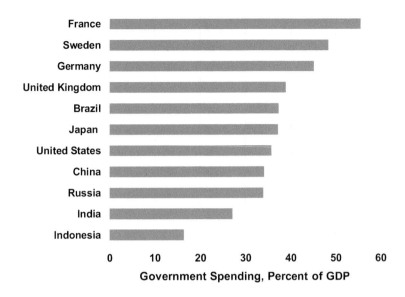

Figure 2.7 *Government Spending, Percentage of GDP, Select Countries, 2019*

Source: International Monetary Fund, World Economic Outlook database, April 2021.

share of GDP attributed to non-profits, and Portugal (2 percent), the Czech Republic (1.6 percent), and Thailand (0.8 percent) as countries with the smallest nonprofit sectors.[9] The United States has traditionally been one of the leading nations in charitable and philanthropic activities.

The main strength of public purpose institutions is that (like core institutions) they can provide goods and services of high intrinsic value, but (unlike core institutions) they are big enough, or sufficiently well-organized, to take on jobs that require broader social coordination. Unlike in the business sphere, the provision of goods and services itself, and not the financial results of these activities, remains the primary intended focus of public purpose organizations.

The public purpose sphere has its weaknesses, of course. Institutions in the public purpose sphere are sometimes accused of being rigid and inefficient because of excessive regulation and a bloated bureaucracy. Organizations can lose sight of the common-good goal of providing "public service" and focus more on increasing their organizational budget. Because public purpose organizations are commonly supported by taxes or donations that often don't have financial incentives to improve the quality of what they provide. Many current debates about reforms in governments and non-profits concern how incentives for efficiency can be improved without eroding these organizations' orientation toward providing goods and services of high intrinsic value.

Finally, because different public purpose institutions may have diverse views on what might improve social well-being, their goals may be in conflict with each other. A continuing issue with government institutions is the question of *whose* interests are represented—the majority, minority groups, or special interests who donate money to campaigns? Yet, because of many important functions of the public purpose sphere, the question isn't whether to have a public purpose sphere but how to make it operate as effectively as possible while serving human well-being as inclusively as possible.

3.2.3 The Business Sphere

The **business sphere** is made up of firms that buy and manage resources in such a way that, after the product is sold, the owners of the firm will earn profits. Whereas the core sphere responds to direct needs, and the public purpose sphere responds to its constituents, business firms are responsive to demands for goods and services, as expressed through markets by people who can afford to buy the products.

---

business sphere: firms that produce goods and services for profitable sale

---

It is sometimes thought that maximizing profits is the *only* goal of businesses. While businesses do need to make profits to stay afloat, firms may also consider social and ethical aspects and make business decisions with regard to the well-being of their workers, communities, or the environment. Additionally, the activities of "the firm" are made up of the activities of many people, including its stockholders, board of directors, managers, and employees. The interests of these individuals may be in conflict. Sometimes, top managers may act, for example, not in the profit-making interest of the owners but according to their *personal* self-interest seeking to maximize their own prestige and incomes.

One strength of businesses is that, because they have a clear goal of profit-making, they are likely to be efficient at achieving this goal. Market forces are commonly thought to drive firms to produce the most economically valuable outputs at the least possible cost. The profit motive also encourages *innovation*—people are motivated to come up with new ideas to generate profits. We all benefit from innovations when they bring us improved products at lower prices. We should note, however, that the public purpose sphere has also often played a critical role in innovation (see Box 2.2).

The relative weakness of the business sphere comes from the fact that business interests may or may not coincide with overall social well-being. Firms *may* act to enhance social well-being—for example, by making decisions that consider the full needs of their customers and their workers, as well as taking into account environmental impacts. But business sphere production has no *built-in* correction for

---

BOX 2.2 THE GOVERNMENT'S ROLE IN INNOVATION

Much economic analysis focuses on entrepreneurship and innovations in the business sector as the key drivers of the economy. The proponents of free market argue that private enterprises—motivated by profit-maximizing goals—are more efficient and more innovative than the public sector. Many of the innovations in the private sector, however, have only been possible due to investments and innovations by the public sector.

Take, for example, the case of iPhone. The success of iPhone has been largely attributed to Apple—a private corporation. However, each of the core technologies of an iPhone, including capacitive sensors, solid-state memory, the click-wheel, GPS, internet, cellular communications, Siri, microchips, and touchscreen, are innovations that came from research supported by the U.S. government and military. Economist Mariana Mazzucato argues that long-term and steady government funding in technological research has been a nearly invariable prerequisite for breakthrough innovations. She points out that the public sector is, in fact, more innovative than the private sector, as the government is more willing to make riskier investments.[10]

In the U.S., the government has also taken a lead in the research and innovations in the health care sector, with almost 75 percent of all revolutionary new drugs coming from funding through the National Institutes of Health. Major pharmaceutical companies do develop innovative drugs, but they also invest heavily in advertising, and in developing 'me-too' drugs to try to undercut their competitors.[11]

---

adverse social and environmental impacts. A more detailed discussion of some of the key limitations of the business sphere can be found in Section 4.3.

3.2.4 The Size of the Three Spheres

Figure 2.8 presents estimates of the monetary value of the annual production of goods and services in the United States by the three spheres

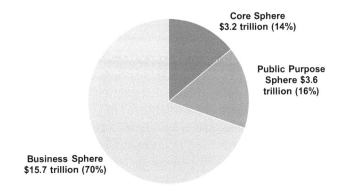

Figure 2.8 *Estimates of the Size of the Three Spheres in the United States, 2020*

Sources: U.S. Bureau of Economic Analysis, National Income and Products Account database; Hess et al., 2020; and authors' calculations.

in 2020. The business sphere contributed 70 percent of production, the core sphere 14 percent, and the public purpose sphere 16 percent. The dollar figures add up to 22.6 trillion, which is more than the GDP in that year ($20.9 trillion) because an estimate of the value of unpaid household labor as equal to 8 percent of GDP has been included.[12] This differs from government estimates of GDP in the U.S., which do not currently include the value of household production.

While the business sphere comprises the majority of economic activity in the United States based on these estimates, that is not the case in all countries. For example, some rough estimates indicate that the largest sphere in France is the public purpose sphere (about 40 percent of the GDP)[13] and statistics published by the UK government indicate that the core sphere is relatively large, with unpaid labor constituting about 60 percent of GDP.[14]

3.2.5 The Informal Sphere

In addition to the three spheres discussed so far, all countries have an **informal sphere**, comprised of market enterprises, normally small in scale, operating outside government oversight and regulation. Although this sphere could be classified as "business" because it involves private production for sale, it is also similar to the "core sphere" in that the activities tend to be small-scale and often depend on family and community connections. Economic activities in the informal sphere may be illegal, as in the case of illicit drugs or prostitution. Other informal sphere activities are legal but do not appear in GDP statistics, such as housecleaning services provided "off the books" and barter transactions.

---

informal sphere: businesses, usually small in scale, operating outside government oversight and regulation. In less industrialized countries, it may constitute the majority of economic activity

---

Accurate data on the size of the informal sphere are difficult to obtain, as such businesses often seek to hide their activities. Nonetheless, estimates of the informal sphere are available for most countries. As shown in Figure 2.9, the informal sector is less than 15 percent of the economy among OECD (Organization for Economic Co-operation and Development) countries, but over 30 percent in less developed countries in Latin America and Sub-Saharan Africa. A 2018 study suggests an even larger informal sphere in less developed countries, showing that the informal sphere accounts for 89 percent of employment in Africa, and 68 percent of employment in Asia and the Pacific.[15] According to the

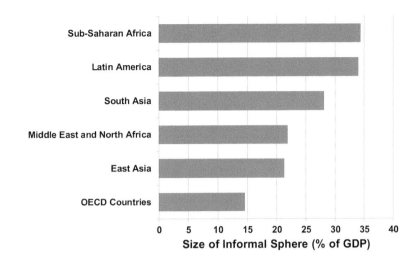

Figure 2.9 *The Average Size of Informal Sphere, Percent of GDP, by World Region*
Source: Medina, Leandro, and Friedrich Schneider. 2019.

International Labour Organization, informal workers are more likely to be in vulnerable forms of employment (i.e., lacking decent working conditions and legal rights, along with inadequate pay) and more likely to be women.[16] A 2021 report from the World Bank found that the COVID-19 pandemic was particularly damaging to informal workers, who generally lack access to social safety nets.[17]

While informal economic activity is more significant in less developed countries, it can be important even in industrialized nations. Informal economy activity that is clearly illegal might do little to enhance well-being, but the informal sphere also provides employment to those who would have difficulty obtaining employment in the other spheres, such as illegal immigrants or women facing discrimination. The challenge is to ensure that these workers are treated fairly and can eventually transition to formal employment.

Discussion Questions

1. Describe some situations in which economic activities could affect their environmental context and some ways in which economic activities could affect their social context. How might these influences that the economy exerts on its contexts result in changing how the contexts, in turn, affect (either support or constrain) economic activity?

2. Education is sometimes provided within the core sphere (at-home preschool activities and home schooling), often provided by the public purpose sphere (public and nonprofit schools), and sometimes provided by for-profit firms (including some "charter schools" or

firms offering specific training programs). Can you think of some possible advantages and disadvantages of each type of provision?

4 THE ROLE OF MARKETS

One of the major areas of interest—and dispute—among economists concerns how markets function. Those who favor the classical approach believe that markets are largely self-regulating and function fairly smoothly to promote economic prosperity. Other economists recognize the effectiveness of markets but believe that problems such as poverty, inequality, environmental degradation, and declining social ethics may be caused or exacerbated by unchecked and unregulated markets. Hence, they advocate for modifications through government policies and other forces of culture and ethics, to serve the overall goals of human well-being. Before delving into these debates, it is essential to understand what economists mean by "markets".

4.1 The Meaning of Markets

The language of economics has at least three different uses of the word "market," ranging from very concrete to very abstract, and the appropriate meaning must be judged from the context in which it appears. We start with the most concrete and move toward the more abstract definitions.

The most commonsense definition of a **market** is that it is a place where people interact physically or virtually to buy and sell things. Historically, markets have been physical locations. Examples include the Grand Bazaar in Istanbul, African village produce stands, and shopping centers or malls. In the electronic age, the market "location" may also be virtual, where buyers and sellers come together on platforms like Amazon and eBay.

---

market (first meaning): a physical place or web location where there is an expectation of finding both buyers and sellers for the same product or service

---

Economists also use the term "market" more generally to refer to *institutions* that bring buyers and sellers together. **Institutions** are ways of structuring the interactions between individuals and groups. Like markets, institutions can also be thought of in concrete or abstract terms. An institution can operate in a physical location, such as a hospital facilitating interactions between doctors and patients, or a university facilitating the interactions between professors and students. But

84

institutions can also be embodied in the customs and laws of a society. For example, marriage is an institution that places some structure on family relationships. Laws, police forces, and cultural and social norms are institutions that structure the acceptable and unacceptable ways that individuals and groups interact.

> **institutions:** ways of structuring interactions between individuals and groups, including both formally constituted establishments and patterns of organization embodied in customs, habits, and laws

Thinking of **markets** as institutions leads to various ways of discussing *particular* markets. For example, we can talk of the "real estate market" for a particular city or country. We can define market for used cars, the market for wind turbines, or the market for luxury goods. Economists often study trends in specific markets, such as heating oil or AT&T bonds, try to forecast what might happen in the future, or advise on the specifics of market structures.

> **market (second meaning):** an institution that brings buyers and sellers into communication with each other, structuring and coordinating their actions

In the most abstract terms, people sometimes talk of **"the market"** as an economic system, for example, describing the United States as having a "market economy" or indicating a preference for "free markets". In this sense, a market economy is one that relies on markets (as social institutions) to conduct economic activities, rather than relying on other institutions.

> **"the market" (third meaning):** an economic system (a "market economy") that relies on market institutions to conduct many economic activities

One alternative to a market economy is a system that relies on central planning to conduct economic activities, as was the case in the Soviet Union. China retains many elements of a central planning system, though the role of markets in China has also been expanded. But even in modern market economies, not all activities are structured by markets. For example, the distribution of resources within the core sphere is mainly based on social and family relationships, and decisions about resource management are often based on scientific evidence or political preference, rather than market forces.

4.2 The Institutional Requirements of Markets

Contemporary large-scale markets do something amazing: They allow many, many separate decision makers, acting on decentralized information, to coordinate their behavior, resulting in highly complex patterns of economic activity. To function smoothly markets rely on a number of basic institutions. We classify these in four broad groups:

1. institutions related to property and decision making
2. social institutions of trust
3. infrastructure for the smooth flow of goods and information
4. money as a medium of exchange.

4.2.1 Institutions Related to Property and Decision Making

For markets to work, people need to know what belongs to whom. Ownership is usually defined through systems of property rights set out in law and enforced by courts and police. **Private property** is the ownership of physical or financial assets by non-government economic actors. **Common property** is ownership of physical or financial assets by the government or particular subsections of society.

---

private property: ownership of assets by non-government economic actors
common property: ownership of assets by government or particular subsections of society

---

Within a market economy, actors must also be allowed to make their own decisions about how to allocate and exchange resources. Prices, in particular, should be set by the interactions of market participants themselves and not controlled by the government. The institutions of private property and individual decision making exist both formally, in codes of law, and informally, in social norms. Countries that have not historically had such norms, such as former communist countries, often take time to develop them or continue with a mix of market and state institutions. Some traditional and indigenous societies reject market-oriented norms in favor of more social cooperation and less market activity. In most Western economies, market-oriented norms dominate, though they may change over time, for example in people's attitudes toward health care and how it should be provided.

4.2.2 Social Institutions of Trust

A second critical institutional requirement for markets is that a degree of trust must exist between buyers and sellers. When a buyer puts down her payment, she must trust that the seller will hand over the merchandise and a seller must be able to trust that the payment offered is valid. Cultural norms and ethical or religious codes can help to establish and maintain an atmosphere of trustworthiness. As businesses and customers engage in one-on-one exchanges, they build trust and make future transactions smoother. Consumers also rely on the reputation of firms based on perceptions about quality and prices associated with brand names or on online reviews to make consumption decisions.

Markets also depend on legal structures, especially in large, complex, mobile societies where buyers and sellers may not know each other, and formal, usually written, agreements (**explicit contracts**) are needed to provide a legally enforceable description of the agreed-upon terms of exchange. In other cases, the terms of exchange may be determined informally, based on verbal terms of cultural and social norms (**implicit contracts**). In effect, social norms and formal legal structures must exist side by side to make complex contracts work, as detailed formal contracts are costly to write and enforce, and it is not practical to police every detail of every contract and cover every possible contingency.

---

explicit contract: a formal, often written, agreement that states the terms of exchange and may be enforceable through a legal system
implicit contract: an informal agreement about the terms of exchange, based on verbal discussions and on common norms, traditions, and expectations

---

In highly marketized economies, many other institutions have evolved to deal with the issue of trust. For example, credit bureaus keep track of consumer credit trustworthiness, Better Business Bureaus keep track of complaints against businesses, and money-back guarantees give consumers a chance to test the quality of a good before they commit to purchasing. Government agencies such as the U.S. Food and Drug Administration and local boards of health are charged with monitoring the quality and purity of many goods that are sold.

4.2.3 Infrastructure for the Smooth Flow of Goods and Information

Another requirement of market is the **physical infrastructure** that enables a smooth flow of goods, services, and information. Physical infrastructure includes such things as roads, ports, railroads, warehouses, utilities, and telecommunications.

> **physical infrastructure:** the equipment, buildings, physical communication lines, roads, and other tangible structures that provide the foundation for economic activity

Infrastructure is also needed to allow the flow of information. Producers and sellers need information on what, and how much, their customers want to buy; in a well-functioning marketized economy this information indicates what, and how much, should be produced and offered for sale. At the same time, consumers need to know what is available, and how much they will have to pay, to get the products that are on the market. It seems unlikely that this ideal condition for perfect markets will ever be reached, but Web-based exchange systems such as Amazon and eBay have brought it much closer to realization.

4.2.4 Money as a Medium of Exchange

The final critical institution required for markets to operate smoothly is a generally accepted form of money. Coins made from gold, silver, and other metals were the most common type of money for many centuries; paper currency developed later. Today, financial instruments such as bank account balances and electronic transfers play an even larger role. While once backed by precious metals in Fort Knox, the value of a U.S. dollar is now based only on the understanding that other people will accept it in exchange. In this sense, money is also a social institution that depends on trust, as well as part of the institutional infrastructure of functioning markets. Money is discussed at greater length in Chapter 10.

4.3 The Advantages and Limitations of Markets

The many advantages of markets as a way to conduct economic activities include the provision of a steady flow of information, in terms of prices and volumes of sales, enabling producers to respond flexibly to consumer desires. Profits provide feedback to sellers about whether resources are being transformed in ways that individuals are willing (and able) to pay for. Markets also give people a considerable amount of freedom in deciding which activities to engage in, and they encourage some beneficial forms of innovation and social cooperation. Markets promote economic efficiency and encourage technological innovation and entrepreneurship.

As we have noted, however, the basic neoclassical model of a completely free private market rarely exists in practice. Actual market-oriented economies always include a mixture of decentralized private decision making and more public-oriented decision making. Social and environmental issues, often neglected in the traditional market model,

88

are central to understanding real-world economies. We will briefly discuss some of these issues here and will expand on them more fully in later chapters.

4.3.1 Public Goods

As discussed above, a public good (or service) is one whose use by one person does not diminish the ability of another person to benefit from it ("non-rival") and whose benefit it would be difficult to keep any individuals from enjoying ("non-excludable"). Examples of public goods include public roads, parks, libraries, schools, clean air and water, other environmental goods and services, police protection, and the national defense system.

Because it is difficult to exclude anyone from benefiting from public goods, they cannot generally be bought and sold on markets. Even if individual actors would be willing to pay for them if necessary, they have little incentive to pay because they cannot be excluded from the benefit. Economists call people who seek to enjoy a benefit without paying for it **free riders**. Because of the problem of free riders, it often makes sense to provide public goods through government agencies, supported by taxes, so that the cost of the public benefit is also borne by the public at large.

---

free riders: people who seek to enjoy the benefit of a good without paying for it

---

4.3.2 Externalities

Some market activities create **externalities**—spillover effects on parties that are not directly participating in the market exchange. These effects can be either beneficial ("positive externalities" or "external benefits") or harmful ("negative externalities" or "external costs"). Externalities are one of the primary reasons why the true *social* value of a good or service can differ from its *market* value.

---

externalities: spillover effects of market activities on parties who are not directly participating in the activity

---

Examples of negative externalities include a situation of a manufacturing firm that dumps pollutants in a river, degrading water quality downstream; or a bar that plays loud music that annoys its neighbors. Examples of activities that have positive externalities include child rearing by parents who, out of love for their children, raise them to become law-abiding citizens, thereby creating benefits for society at large; and getting vaccinated against communicable diseases, which people do to protect themselves, but at the same time protect those around them from the disease's spread. In both these cases, individual actions have social benefits.

Some of the most important externalities relate to the environmental impacts of economic activities. Relying on markets alone to coordinate economic activities may allow activities that damage or deplete the nat ural environment to take place, because the cost of pollution may not be felt by the economic actor that created it. Environmental regulations attempt to counteract this, using fines or other disincentives to bring home to the party that causes the damage some of the pain related to it. It is often difficult, however, to estimate the cost of environmental damage. Moreover, people in future generations, who are likely to bear the environmental costs of current activities, are not direct parties to current decision making.

If economic activities affected only the actors directly involved in decision making, we might be able to think about economic activity primarily in terms of individuals making decisions for their own benefit. But we live in a social and ecological context, in which actions, inter-actions, and consequences are generally both widespread and interrelated. If decisions are left purely to individual self-interest, then from a societal point of view too many negative externalities and too few positive externalities will be created. The streets might be strewn with industrial wastes, while children might be taught to be honest in dealings within their family but not outside it. Market values and human or social values do not always coincide.[†]

4.3.3 Transaction Costs

Transaction costs are the costs of arranging economic activities. The neoclassical model assumes that transaction costs are zero. For example, if a firm wants to hire a worker the only cost involved is the wage paid. In the real world, however, the process of hiring may involve other costs, such as costs related to searching by placing an ad or paying for the services of a recruiting company. The prospective worker may need to pay for the preparation of a résumé and transportation to an interview. One or both sides might hire lawyers to make sure that the contract's terms reflect their interests. Because of the existence of such costs, some economic interactions that might lead to greater efficiency in an idealized, transaction cost–free world, may not happen in the real world.

[†] Some people criticize the economics profession for relegating many important consequences of economic activity to the category of externalities, mistakenly assuming that this means that economists believe that anything "external" to the market is not important. In fact, economists take externalities very seriously, recognizing that their presence indicates a failure of the market to operate as it should.

> **transaction costs:** the costs of arranging economic activities

4.3.4 Market Power

In the basic neoclassical model, all markets are assumed to be "perfectly competitive," such that no one buyer or seller has the power to influence the prices or other market conditions. In the real world, however, we see that many firms have **market power**. For example, when there is only one firm (a monopolist) or a few firms selling a good, they may be able to use their power to charge socially inefficient prices, squelch innovations by competing firms, and create inefficient allocations of resources. Workers may also be able to gain a degree of market power by joining together to negotiate as a labor union. A government, too, can have market power, for example when the Department of Defense is the sole purchaser of military equipment from private firms.

> **market power:** the ability to control, or significantly affect, the terms and conditions of the exchanges in which one participates

Businesses may also gain power by their sheer size—many corporations that function internationally have revenues in the tens of billions of dollars. The decisions of individual large corporations can have substantial effects on the employment levels, living standards, economic growth, and stability of regions and countries. Hence, governments may need to factor in the responses of powerful businesses in making their policy decisions. National leaders may fear, for example, that raising business tax rates or the national minimum wage may cause companies to leave their country, and go elsewhere. Corporations frequently also try to influence government policies directly, through lobbying, campaign contributions, and other methods.

4.3.5 Information and Expectations

In the neoclassical model, in which decentralized decisions lead to efficient outcomes, people are assumed to have complete information needed to make choices. This analysis is **static**—it does not consider the time taken to obtain information or make decisions. In the real, **dynamic**, world, obtaining good information and dealing with future uncertainties may make economic decision making difficult.

> **static analysis:** analysis that does not take into account the passage of time
> **dynamic analysis:** analysis that takes into account the passage of time

A manufacturing business, for example, might be considering whether to borrow funds to build an additional factory. If the company's directors were able to know exactly what the future demand for its products will be along with information about the future interest rates, wages, energy costs, and returns on alternative investments, the decision would be a simple matter of mathematical calculation. But the directors will have to guess at most of these things based on their expectations about the future, which may turn out to be incorrect. If their expectations are optimistic, they will tend to make the new investment and hire new workers. Often optimism is "contagious," and if a lot of *other* business leaders become optimistic, too, then the economy will boom.

If, however, people share an attitude of pessimism, they may all tend to cut back on spending and hiring. Because no one business wants to take the risk of jumping the gun by expanding too soon, it can be very difficult to get a decentralized market economy out of a slump. How people get their information, how they time their actions, and how they form their expectations of the future, then, are all important topics in macroeconomics that are not addressed in the basic neoclassical model. Taking these factors into account suggests why markets sometimes do not work as smoothly as that model suggests or lead to such efficient results.

4.3.6 Human Needs and Equity

Another important issue concerns the distribution of income and the ability to pay for goods and services. In the basic neoclassical model, the only consumer demands for goods and services that can affect the market are those that are backed up by a consumer's ability to pay. This has several implications.

First, there is nothing in the model that ensures that resources are distributed in such a way that people can meet their basic human needs. If a few rich people have a lot of money to spend on diamonds, for example, while a great number of poor people lack the money to pay for basic health care, "free markets" will motivate producers to respond to the demand for diamonds, but not to the need for basic health care. For this reason, governments often adopt more deliberate policies of government provision, subsidies, or income redistribution, to try to ensure that decent living standards become more widespread.

Second, the model does not take into account non-marketed production, such as the care given to children, the sick, and the elderly by family and friends. There is nothing in the basic neoclassical model that ensures that these sorts of production will be supplied in adequate quantities and quality.

Lastly, it is also the case that problems such as unemployment and inflation tend to affect some people more than others, so how a country deals with these problems also has distributional consequences.

92

Clearly, although market systems have strong advantages in some areas, they cannot solve all economic problems. Economists sometimes use the term **market failure** to refer to a situation in which markets lead to inefficient or harmful results. Because of the existence of market failures, macroeconomic systems cannot rely on "free markets" alone if they are to contribute effectively to present and future human well-being.

---

market failure: a situation in which markets yield inefficient or inappropriate outcomes

---

To some extent, *private* non-market institutions may help remedy "market failure." For example, a group of privately owned factories located around a lake may voluntarily decide to restrict their waste emissions, because too much deterioration in water quality hurts them all. Likewise, a widespread custom of private charitable giving may help alleviate poverty. But sometimes the problems are so large or widespread that only government and *public* actions at the national or international levels seem to offer a solution. Exactly how much government action is required, and exactly what governments should do, however, are much-debated questions within contemporary macroeconomics.

Discussion Questions

1. In what sense is the term "market" being used in each of the following sentences?
   "Go to the market and get some bananas."
   "The market is the best invention of humankind."
   "The labor market for new Ph.Ds is bad this year."
   "The advance of the market leads to a decline in social morality."
   Can you think of other examples from your own readings or experience?

2. "Indeed it has been said that democracy is the worst form of government," said British Prime Minister Winston Churchill (1874–1965), "except all those other forms that have been tried from time to time." Some people make the same claim about more marketized forms of economic systems. What do they mean? Would you agree or disagree?

REVIEW QUESTIONS

1. What are the two main modes of economic investigation? Describe each.
2. What is a model? How does the ceteris paribus assumption simplify the creation of a model?

3. How do abundance and scarcity create the possibility of, and the necessity of, economic decision making?
4. Draw a societal production-possibilities frontier, and use it to explain the concepts of tradeoffs (opportunity cost), attainable and unattainable output combinations, and efficiency.
5. What kinds of decisions would make a PPF expand over time? What kinds of decisions would make it shrink over time?
6. What are some of the assumptions of the basic neoclassical model? Why are markets said to be efficient according to this model?
7. What are some of the shortcomings of the neoclassical model? In what ways does the contextual model overcome these shortcomings?
8. What are the three spheres of economic activity?
9. What are some major characteristics and functions of the core sphere?
10. What are some major characteristics and functions of the public purpose sphere?
11. What are some major characteristics, and strengths and weaknesses, of the business sphere?
12. What is the informal sphere? Where is it most significant?
13. What are the three different meanings of the term "markets"?
14. What are the four institutional requirements of markets?
15. What is a public good? Why will private markets generally undersupply public goods?
16. What are negative and positive externalities? Give examples of each.
17. Besides public goods and externalities, describe four real world factors that can cause market outcomes to be less than ideal.

EXERCISES

1. The notion of "scarcity" reflects the idea that resources cannot be stretched to achieve all the goals that people desire. But what makes a particular resource "scarce"? If there seems to be more of it around than is needed, such as desert sand, is it scarce? If it is freely open to the use of many people at once, such as music on the radio waves, is it scarce? What about resources such as social attitudes of trust and respect? Make a list of a few resources that clearly are "scarce" in economists' sense. Make another list of a few resources that are not.
2. How is the concept of efficiency related to the concept of scarcity? Consider, for example, your own use of time. When do you feel time to be more, and when less, scarce? Do you think about how to use your time differently during exam week, compared to when you are on vacation?
3. Suppose that society could produce the following combinations of pizzas and books:

Alternative	Quantity of pizzas	Quantity of books
A	50	0
B	40	10
C	30	18
D	20	24
E	10	28
F	0	30

A. Using graph paper (or a computer program), draw the production-possibilities frontier (PPF) for pizza and books, being as exact and neat as possible. (Put books on the horizontal axis. Assume that the dots define a complete curve.)

94

    B.   Is it possible or efficient for this society to produce 25 pizzas and 25 books?

    C.   Is it possible or efficient for this society to produce 42 pizzas and 1 book?

    D.   If society is currently producing alternative B, then the opportunity cost of moving to alternative A (and getting 10 more pizzas) is _____ books.

    E.   Is the opportunity cost of producing pizzas higher or lower moving from alternative F to E than moving from alternative B to A? Why is this likely to be so?

    F.   Suppose that the technologies used in producing both pizzas and books improve. Draw one possible new production-possibilities frontier in the graph above that represents the results of this change. Indicate the direction of the change that occurs with an arrow.

4.   Match each concept in Column A with a definition or example in Column B:

Column A		Column B	
a.	An important function of the core sphere	1.	Apple growers will seek to maximize their profits
b.	Theoretical investigation	2.	The annual harvest of apples in a country from 1970 to 2000
c.	Time-series data	3.	Producing a combination along a production-possibilities frontier
d.	Opportunity cost of buying an apple	4.	You do not get to have an orange
e.	A positive externality	5.	Does not take into account the passage of time
f.	Scarcity	6.	Can expand a production-possibilities frontier outward over time
g.	Efficient production	7.	Data on the unemployment rate in ten European countries in 2016
h.	A negative externality	8.	There is only one apply producer who is able to make very high profits
i.	Technological progress	9.	An orchard used to grow a full crop of apples cannot also be used to grow a full crop of pears
j.	An important function of the public purpose sphere	10.	The apple tree you plant for your own enjoyment also pleases people passing by
k.	Market power	11.	Raising children
l.	An assumption of the basic neoclassical model	12.	Einstein develops the theory of relativity
m.	Cross-sectional data	13.	Regulation
n.	Static analysis	14.	The production of apple pie creates water pollution that harms downstream communities

APPENDIX: GRAPHING REVIEW

This review covers the two most common ways that economic data are presented in this book. The first way is in a table, such as Table 2.1, which presents time-series data on the annual real growth rate of GDP and the annual average unemployment rate for the U.S. economy over the period 2008–2020. We can determine from the table, for example, that in 2016 the unemployment rate was 4.9 percent and real GDP grew at a rate of 1.7 percent.

While tables can present detailed numerical data, it is not always easy to determine the overall trends over time using a table as unemployment is rising in some years and falling in others. Instead, it is often useful to present data in visual form, using graphs, to "see" what is happening in an economy more clearly. Figure 2.10 presents a time-series graph of the unemployment rate. Graphs have a horizontal axis (also called the "x-axis") and a vertical axis (also called the "y-axis"). It is common practice to present time-series data with the time intervals on the x-axis. Presented this way, we can easily see that unemployment was high and increasing between 2008 and 2010. It declined gradually from a high of 9.6 percent in 2010 to 3.7 percent in 2019. In 2020, it rose significantly to over 8 percent due to the economic impacts of the COVID-19 crisis. You can test yourself by using the data in Table 2.1 to construct a time-series graph for the GDP growth rate.

Table 2.1 *Unemployment Rate and Real GDP Growth Rate, United States, 2008–2020 (in percent)*

	Unemployment rate	Real GDP growth rate
2008	5.8	−0.1
2009	9.3	−2.5
2010	9.6	2.6
2011	8.9	1.6
2012	8.1	2.3
2013	7.4	1.8
2014	6.2	2.5
2015	5.3	3.1
2016	4.9	1.7
2017	4.4	2.3
2018	3.9	3.0
2019	3.7	2.1
2020	8.1	-3.5

Sources: U.S. Bureau of Economic Analysis and U.S. Bureau of Labor Statistics.

We can also use graphs to explore the relationship between two different variables—this provides a way to test specific economic hypotheses. Referring to Table 2.1, we might form the hypothesis that unemployment rates tend to be higher when GDP growth rates are lower. We call this a **negative, or inverse, relationship**—when an increase in one variable is associated with a decrease in another variable (or, vice versa, when a decrease in one variable is associated with an increase in another variable).

---

negative (or inverse) relationship: the relationship between two variables if an increase in one variable is associated with a decrease in the other variable (or vice versa)

Figure 2.11 plots the relationship between unemployment rates and GDP growth rates. Each "data point" on the graph tells us the values of *both* variables for a specific year. In the graph, we have kept the unemployment rate on the *y*-axis and the GDP growth rate on the *x*-axis. So the data point for 2016, for example, indicates that the GDP growth rate was 1.7 percent (across the *x*-axis) and the unemployment rate was 4.9 percent (up along the *y*-axis). You can test yourself by figuring out which data points match which years.

A visual inspection of Figure 2.11 can help us determine whether our hypothesis of an inverse relationship between unemployment and GDP growth rates is correct. We can see that unemployment is low when

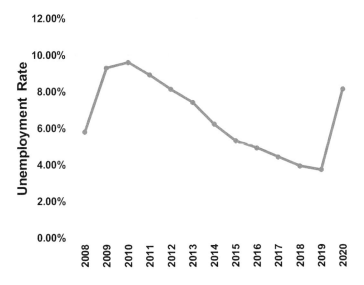

Figure 2.10 *Unemployment Rate, United States, 2008–2020*
Source: U.S. Bureau of Labor Statistics.

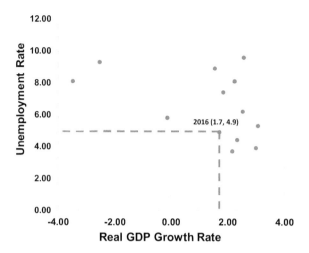

Figure 2.11 *Relationship between Unemployment and GDP Growth Rate, United States, 2008–2020*

Sources: U.S. Bureau of Economic Analysis and U.S. Bureau of Labor Statistics.

GDP growth rates are higher in general, but there are some exceptions. For example, in 2010 when unemployment was at its maximum, GDP growth was about average at 2.6 percent. To determine more accurately whether our hypothesis is supported by the data, we would need to undertake statistical analysis (called "econometrics.")

Figure 2.11 can tell us whether our two variables are related, or "correlated," but we cannot determine whether there is a causal relationship between the two variables. While we suspect that low GDP growth causes high unemployment, we cannot prove it using a graph. The causality could be random, or it could potentially be in the opposite direction—that high unemployment causes low GDP growth.

The opposite of an inverse relationship is a **positive, or direct, relationship**. In this case, an increase in one variable is associated with an increase in another variable—or a decrease in one variable is associated with a decrease in another.

---

positive (or direct) relationship: the relationship between two variables if an increase in one variable is associated with an increase in the other variable

---

A good example of a positive relationship is between the growth rate of GDP and the growth rate of greenhouse gas emissions, such as carbon dioxide and methane. When the economy is growing, manufacturing industries tend to produce more goods, people tend to fly and drive more, and construction activity tends to increase. All these factors tend to increase greenhouse gas emissions. As shown in Figure 2.12, the relationship between GDP growth and the growth of greenhouse gas

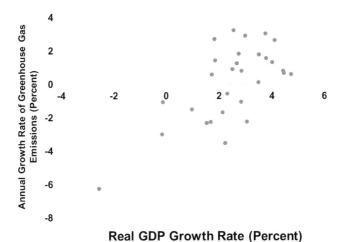

Figure 2.12 *Relationship between GDP Growth Rate and Greenhouse Gas Emissions Growth Rate, United States, 1991–2020*

Source: Greenhouse Gas data from United States Environmental Protection Agency and Real GDP data from Bureau of Economic Analysis, Table 1.1.1.

emissions is positive—when the economy is growing rapidly greenhouse gas emissions also tend to increase. Again, we cannot demonstrate causality just by looking at a graph, but the graph indicates that a positive relationship between the two variables is likely.

NOTES

1   Military spending data from the Stockholm International Peace Research Institute. Web site: www.sipri.org/research/armament-and-disarmament/arms-transfers-and-military-spending/military-expenditure.
2   Data on military spending as a share of GDP from the World Bank's World Development Indicators database. Data from 2015.
3   See www.un.org/sustainabledevelopment/sustainable-development-goals/.
4   Guido, 2015.
5   AARP and NAC, 2020.
6   Annual hours worked statistic from the OECD Labor Force Statistics online database. Value from 2020.
7   Reinhard et al., 2019.
8   NCCS project team, 2020.
9   Casey, 2016.
10   Upbin, 2013.
11   Farley, 2021.
12   Value of unpaid labor of 8 percent of GDP in the United States calculating using unpaid time data from Hess et al., 2020 combined with replacement wage data from the U.S. Bureau of Labor Statistics.
13   Estimate for France based on the value of unpaid labor from Folbre (2015) and the value of non-profits from Casey (2016).
14   Rawlinson, 2018.
15   International Labour Organization, 2018.

16   International Labour Organization, 2015.
17   World Bank Group, 2021.

REFERENCES

American Association of Retired Persons (AARP) and National Alliance for Caregiving (NAC). 2020. *Caregiving in the U.S. Research Report*, May.

Bureau of Economic Analysis. 2009. "Concepts and Methods of the U.S. National Income and Product Account," October.

Casey, John. 2016. "Comparing Nonprofit Sectors around the World." *Journal of Nonprofit Education and Leadership, 6(3)*: 187–223.

Farley, Rebecca. 2020. "Do Pharmaceutical Companies Spend More on Marketing than on Research and Development?" *PharmacyChecker.com*, July 24. https://www.pharmacychecker.com/askpc/pharma-marketing-research-development/#

Folbre, Nancy. 2015. "*Valuing Non-market Work.*" 2015 UNDP Human Development Report Office Think Piece.

Guido Schmidt-Traub. 2015. "Investment Needs to Achieve the Sustainable Development Goals." *Sustainable Development Solutions Network. SDSN Working Paper Version 2*, November 12.

Hess, Cynthia, Tanima Ahmed, and Jeff Hayes. 2020. "Providing Unpaid Household and Care Work in the United States: Uncovering Inequality." *Institute for Women's Policy Research, IWPR #C487*, January.

International Labour Organization. 2015. "Five Facts about Informal Economy in Africa." *ILO News*, June 18. http://www.ilo.org/addisababa/whats-new/WCMS_377286/lang—en/index.htm.

International Labour Organization. 2018. *Women and Men in the Informal Economy: A Statistical Picture* (Third Edition). Geneva.

McKinsey & Company. 2015. "The Power of Parity: How Advancing Women's Equality Can Add $12 Trillion to Global Growth." *McKinsey Global Institute*, September.

Medina, Leandro, and Friedrich Schneider. 2019. "Shedding Light on the Shadow Economy: A Global Database and the Interaction with the Official One." *CESifo Working Paper No. 7981*, December. https://papers.ssrn.com/sol3/papers.cfm?abstract_id=3502028

NCCS Project Team. 2020. "The Nonprofit Sector in Brief 2019." *Urban Institute*, June.

Office for National Statistics (UK). 2016. "Women Shoulder the Responsibility of 'Unpaid Work'," November 10. http://visual.ons.gov.uk/the-value-of-your-unpaid-work/.

Rawlinson, Kevin. 2018. "British People Do More Than £1 Trillion of Household Work Each Year – Unpaid." *The Guardian*, October 2.

Reinhard, Susan C., Lynn Friss Feinberg, Rita Choula, Ari Houser, and Molly Evans. 2019. "Valuing the Invaluable: 2019 Update, Charting a Path Forward." *AARP Public Policy Institute*, November.

Upbin, Bruce. 2013. "Debunking The Narrative of Silicon Valley's Innovation Might." *Forbes*, June 13.

UN Women. 2015. "Progress of the World's Women 2015–2016: Transforming Economies, Realizing Rights." New York: UN Women. https://www.unwomen.org/en/digital-library/publications/2015/4/progress-of-the-worlds-women-2015

U.S. Bureau of Economic Analysis. http:// bea.gov/iTable/index_nipa.cfm.

U.S. Bureau of Labor Statistics. http://bls.gov/cps/cpsaat01.htm.

U.S. Environmental Protection Agency. http://www.epa.gov/climatechange/ghgemissions/usinventoryreport.html.

Vreel, Miranda. 2011. "Cooking, Caring, and Volunteering: Unpaid Work around the World," *OECD Social Employment and Migration Working Papers No. 116*.

World Bank Group. 2021. *The Long Shadow of Informality: Challenges and Policies* (Advance Edition). Franziska Ohnsorge and Shu Yu, editors. Washington, DC.

Chapter 3

Supply and Demand

Understanding how prices are determined in the market and how they change over time is central to the study of economics. During the COVID-19 pandemic, the prices for many goods and services fluctuated significantly. For example, lumber prices in the United States increased by a factor of five from March 2020 to May 2021.[1] As COVID-19 spread across the world in late 2019 and early 2020 global oil prices fell by about 75 percent. But by mid-2021 oil prices were higher than they were before the pandemic, and in 2022 they approached all-time highs.[2] How can economics explain these price variations?

Closely related to *prices* are the *quantities* of things that are bought and sold in the market. The number of new automobiles sold in the United States reached a high of 6.9 million in 2016, then fell steadily to about 4.7 million in 2019 and dropped further to a low of 3.4 million in 2020 due to the economic slowdown caused by the COVID-19 pandemic.[3] Meanwhile, new automobile sales in China increased by a factor of six between 2005 and 2017, but have been decreasing in recent years.[4]

To understand these fluctuations in prices and quantities, it is necessary to understand how markets function. This chapter introduces the famous relationship between supply and demand, which goes a long way toward explaining the workings of the markets.

1 MARKETS AND MACROECONOMICS

As we discussed in Chapter 2, markets are places where individuals, businesses, and other organizations engage in buying and selling. The economic theory of supply and demand is an exceptionally useful example of a "thought experiment" that seeks to describe, in abstract terms, how people make their decisions about buying and selling.

The theory provides a simple, elegant picture of how potential sellers decide how much of a good or service to offer to sell (supply) on a market, and how potential buyers decide how much to purchase (demand). The term **demand** indicates the willingness and ability of purchasers to buy goods and services, while **supply** indicates the willingness of producers to produce, and merchandisers to sell, goods and services. The theory then goes on to show how a well-functioning market coordinates these decisions to determine the price and quantity traded.

---

demand: the willingness and ability of purchasers to buy goods or services
supply: the willingness of producers and merchandisers to provide goods and services

---

In the real world, markets sometimes work much as the theory predicts; at other times, there are other forces that push decisions, and prices, away from the result predicted in the theory. When real-world corresponds closely to the theory, the result is that "the market"—not any particular individual agent or bureaucracy— determines the number of units of a good or service that is actually sold on a market and the price at which the units sell.

1.1 Differing Perspectives on Markets

The direct study of markets is more of a *micro*economic topic than a *macro*economic one. One reason that we particularly need to introduce (or review, for students who have taken microeconomics) the model of supply and demand here is that this model is crucial for understanding many specific markets that are relevant to macroeconomic analysis, and is especially central to the classical approach to macroeconomics. Classically oriented macroeconomists tend to believe that markets generally function smoothly, as portrayed in this model—at least as long as governments do not interfere. They argue that when individuals and businesses make decisions for their private gains, markets will operate efficiently and produce optimal outcomes through adjustments in prices.

Other economists, especially those from the Keynesian school, agree that the model of supply and demand has an important role to play in economics, but emphasize that understanding the workings of the macroeconomy requires that one goes beyond this model, for two reasons. First, real-world markets may deviate in important ways from the one portrayed in the abstract model. People's decisions on production and consumption are affected by social norms and values, expectations about the future, information available (or not available) to buyers and sellers, and other factors. Second, explaining economic phenomena at the national level may require a different set of theoretical tools from those designed for analyzing individual markets for particular goods. The operation of market systems can create problems such as economic instability, unemployment, inflation, inequality of wealth and power, and neglect of negative externalities, which may need to be addressed at the macroeconomic level.

102

We will explore some of these alternative theories in further chapters. Here, we focus on the basic demand and supply model. The first four sections of this chapter lay out this model. In the last section, we return to the question of how this model sometimes may be, and sometimes may not be, helpful in understanding macroeconomics.

1.2 Characteristics of Markets

The sort of market imagined in the classical world has two noteworthy characteristics. It is envisioned as:

- **Perfectly competitive**. In a perfectly competitive market, there are many buyers and sellers of a good, all units of the good are identical, anyone can enter or leave the market at will, and everyone has perfect information about the products being sold and their prices.
- **Self-correcting**. In a market that is self-correcting, imbalances between buyers and sellers do not persist because the market naturally adjusts through price and quantity changes without any outside influence (e.g., government).

> **perfectly competitive market:** a market in which there are many buyers and sellers, all units of the good are identical, and there is free entry and exit and perfect information
>
> **self-correcting market:** a market that automatically adjusts to any imbalances between sellers (supply) and buyers (demand)

In the real world, no market is perfectly competitive in the literal sense (although some are far more competitive than others), and although markets do tend to be self-correcting, in many cases, imbalances persist for some time. Why, then, do we make such assumptions about markets? The real world, as we know, is complex, and models are, by their nature, simplifications of this reality. Just as economists frequently invoke the *ceteris paribus* condition even though we know that it can never be so, the general sense in modeling is that it is acceptable to use assumptions that are not literally true as long as they can tell us something useful about reality.

A good real-world example of a market in which there are many buyers and sellers acting voluntarily is eBay—the online auction site with more than 178 million active users—where over 1.5 billion products—recreational vehicles, high-definition televisions, commemorative coins, T-shirts, condominiums, you name it—are listed for trading.[5] From its beginnings in the United States in 1995, eBay has grown into a global marketing service for individuals and small businesses. Perhaps you have bought or sold something on eBay. If you have, then you have had direct experience with a real-world market very similar, in some ways, to the sort of idealized market that forms the basis for economists' theory of supply and demand.

103

Other kinds of markets are less perfectly competitive. If you want to buy the Microsoft Windows operating system, for example, the sole ultimate supplier is Microsoft. Microsoft's dominance means that prices are controlled by Microsoft—not determined in the market. Also, it is not easy for new firms to enter this market as they face competition from a much larger firm that already has a significant consumer base. Other operating systems such as MAC and Linux hold a much smaller market share. Hence Microsoft has significant market power in the market for computer operating systems and this market is far from perfectly competitive.

The market for airline tickets illustrates the idea of self-correction. When demand for flights rises sharply during the peak season, it creates a temporary shortage that is very quickly eliminated by increased prices. Labor markets often behave differently. When business demand for labor diminishes, wages tend *not* to fall accordingly—instead, some workers are laid off.

Many of the controversies in macroeconomics come down to a question of the degree to which real-world markets—and, in particular, real-world labor markets and financial markets—are similar to, or differ in important ways from, the perfectly competitive and self-correcting markets assumed in basic market theory.

Discussion Questions

1. Have you ever traded on eBay or a similar Internet auction site? If you have, describe to your classmates how it works.
2. Think about a case recently in which you exchanged money for a good or service. Was that market "perfectly competitive"?

2 THE THEORY OF SUPPLY

We start with an example: a simplified market for coffee. Let us assume, to start with, that all cups of coffee sold in the market are identical. We will also assume that the coffee sellers are all well informed and interested primarily in their potential monetary gain.

Each seller has a slightly different idea of what is an acceptable price, based on their costs of production and desire to make a profit. In our simplified market, we will assume that no producer will accept less than $0.70 for a cup of coffee, but at a price of $0.70, sellers would supply 300 cups to the market. At a price of $0.80, 400 cups would be offered. In fact, it turns out that each time the price rises by 10 cents an additional 100 cups of coffee are supplied. This precise relationship is of course unlikely in the real world, but the general principle holds true: at higher prices, more of the product will be offered. Either existing sellers will want to sell more because it is more profitable, or new sellers will enter the market at a more profitable price.

2.1 The Supply Schedule and Curve

The result of this pattern is shown in Table 3.1, which we call a supply schedule. A supply schedule shows us, in the form of a table, the quantity of a good or service that would be offered by the sellers at each possible price.

From the supply schedule, we can graph a **supply curve**, as shown in Figure 3.1, which shows the same information in a different form. If we asked how much coffee would be offered for sale at a price of $1.00, for example, we could look across from $1.00 on the vertical (price) axis over to the supply curve and then drop down to the horizontal (quantity) axis to find that the answer is 600.

Note that the supply curve in Figure 3.1 slopes upward. This seems reasonable, consistent with an expectation that suppliers of a good or service will tend to offer more for sale, the higher the price they receive. Price and quantity have a positive (or direct) relationship along the supply curve.

We see *movement along a supply curve* when we note, for example, that the quantity of coffee that will be offered for sale rises from 600 to 700 as the price rises from $1.00 to $1.10. This is a case of **change in quantity supplied**. It is important to refer to movement *along* a supply curve as a change in the *quantity supplied* in order to avoid confusion with the topic of the next section, which deals with shifts in the supply curve.

---

supply curve: a curve indicating the quantities that sellers are willing to supply at various prices

---

Table 3.1 *A Supply Schedule for Coffee*

Price ($/cup)	Cups of coffee supplied/week
0.70	300
0.80	400
0.90	500
1.00	600
1.10	700
1.20	800
1.30	900
1.40	1,000
1.50	1,100
1.60	1,200

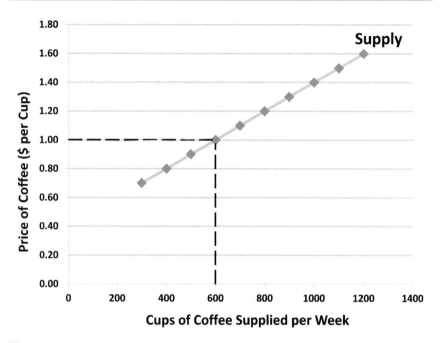

Figure 3.1 *The Supply Curve for Cups of Coffee*

---

change in quantity supplied: movement along a supply curve in response to a price change

---

Check yourself by answering this question with reference to Table 3.1 or Figure 3.1: By how much does the *quantity supplied* change when the price changes from $1.10 to $1.40?

2.2 Changes in Supply

In contrast to *changes in quantity supplied*, we say there has been a **change in supply** when the whole supply curve shifts.

Why might the whole curve shift? As we noted in Chapter 2, models make frequent use of *ceteris paribus* assumptions. The supply curve shown in Figure 3.1 holds, we presume, for a given set of circumstances. But what if circumstances were different?

---

change in supply: a shift of the supply curve in response to some determinant other than the item's price

---

Suppose that an increase in global production of coffee beans leads more coffee sellers to enter the market, with the result that 400 more cups of coffee would be offered at each price. The supply curve would shift to the right from S_1 to S_2 as illustrated in Figure 3.2. Now, at a price of $1.00, for example, 1,000 cups of coffee are offered, instead of 600. We can describe the increase in supply by saying either that "supply has risen" or that "the supply curve has shifted." (It may seem confusing that a supply *in*crease shifts the supply curve *down.* Remember to start the "story" by reading horizontally from the price axis. Then you will notice that the shift goes toward *higher* numbers on the quantity axis.)

We would see a similar result if a new coffee-making technology made its production less costly. With lower costs of production, suppliers become willing to accept, say, $0.40 less per cup. In this case, as well, 1,000 cups would be offered at $1.00, whereas before it took a price of $1.40 to elicit a supply of this size. This would also be termed an "increase in supply" and again the supply curve would shift, as illustrated in Figure 3.2.

If instead, the number of sellers goes *down,* or the cost of production for each cup of coffee *rises,* the supply curve will move to the *left* of the original one, as shown in Figure 3.3. We say that "supply has decreased," or "supply has fallen," or "the supply curve has shifted back." It is also possible to view this as a shift *upward* in the supply curve, reflecting factors such as increased supply costs. For any given quantity of production, such as 600 units, sellers will require a higher price. (This may seem a bit confusing since a *decrease* in supply leads to an *upward* movement of the curve, but remember that this is a move up in *price*).

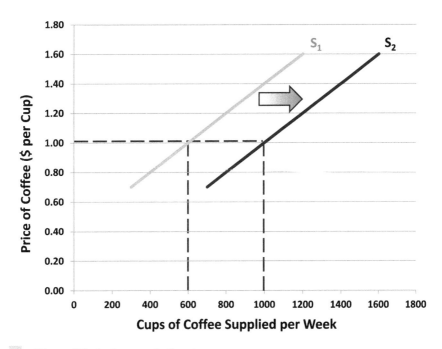

Figure 3.2 *An Increase in Supply*

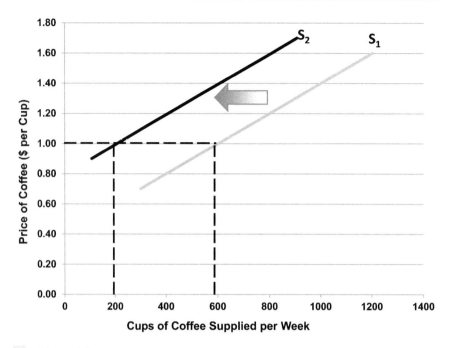

Figure 3.3 *A Decrease in Supply*

Thus, the number of sellers and the costs of production are among the things that can affect the location of the supply curve. Many other factors, such as expectations about the future, prices of related goods and services, and changes in the physical supply of natural resources, also affect the location of the supply curve. These non-price determinants of supply generally depend on what, specifically, is being sold in a market. While we have rather arbitrarily chosen a simple coffee market for our example, the determinants of supply will vary depending on whether the item in question is an asset, a produced good, or a service and on particular characteristics of the item.

For example, in the market for oil, the determinants of supply will include the success of oil exploration and discovery (a big new discovery will increase supply), while in the market for computers, technological innovations that lower chip costs will increase supply. In the market for corn, a bad harvest would reduce supply, but new, more productive varieties of corn would increase it. You can easily think of similar examples for other goods and services.

Discussion Questions

1. Explain in words why the supply curve slopes upward.
2. Verbally explain the difference between a change in *quantity supplied* and a change in *supply.* Considering the supply side of the market for lawn-mowing services, what kind of change (*increase* or *decrease,* in *quantity supplied* or *supply*) would each of the following events cause?

a) A rise in the going price for lawn-mowing services
b) More people decide to offer to mow lawns
c) Gasoline for lawn mowers becomes much more expensive (assume that the person doing the mowing buys the gas)

3 THE THEORY OF DEMAND

Now let us consider the market from the point of view of potential *buyers* of coffee. Potential buyers will also consider price, but of course, they will prefer a lower price. Let's suppose that in this market no potential buyers are willing to pay more than $2.30 for a cup of coffee. But a drop in the price per cup would induce more purchases of coffee. This reasonable assumption about the way potential buyers behave allows us to construct a demand schedule.

3.1 The Demand Schedule and Curve

In Table 3.2, we show the demand schedule that reflects these assumptions. A demand schedule describes, in the form of a table, the quantity of a good or service that buyers are willing to purchase at each possible price.

From the demand schedule, we can graph a **demand curve**, as shown in Figure 3.4. Note that the demand curve in Figure 3.4 slopes downward. It seems reasonable to expect that, generally, the higher the price of a good, the fewer people will want to (or be able to) buy. Price and quantity have a negative (or inverse) relationship along the demand curve.

---

demand curve: a curve indicating the quantities that buyers are ready to purchase at various prices

---

Suppose that the price of coffee rose from $1.40 to $2.00. According to our demand schedule, the number of cups of coffee that will be purchased falls from 600 to 400. The demand curve has not shifted, but movement *along* the demand curve is referred to as a **change in quantity demanded**.

---

change in quantity demanded: movement along a demand curve in response to a price change

---

109

Table 3.2 *A Demand Schedule for Coffee*

Price ($/cup)	Cups of coffee demanded/week
0.20	1,000
0.50	900
0.80	800
1.10	700
1.40	600
1.70	500
2.00	400
2.30	300

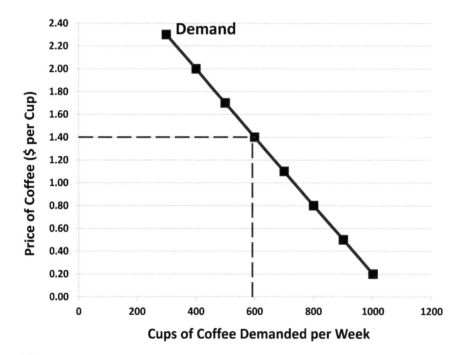

Figure 3.4 *The Demand Curve for Cups of Coffee*

Check yourself by answering this question with reference to Table 3.2 or Figure 3.4: By how much does the *quantity demanded* change when the price changes from $2.00 to $0.80?

3.2 Changes in Demand

As with supply, we distinguish between *a change in quantity demanded* and a **change in demand**. When there is a change in demand, the whole curve shifts.

> **change in demand:** a shift of the demand curve in response to some determinant other than the item's price

Why might the whole curve shift? One reason might be the increasing trendiness of drinking coffee. Whereas a generation ago one seldom saw people walking in the street holding a container of coffee, it may soon be almost as rare to see someone *not* holding one. It means that there are now many more buyers, and the change is reflected as a shift in demand. Specifically, suppose that at every price there are now 300 more cups of coffee demanded in the market. Such a change is illustrated by the shift to the right from D_1 to D_2 in Figure 3.5. We say that "demand has risen" or "the demand curve has shifted." (Because of the curve's negative slope, in this case, this also means shifting "up.")

We would see the same result if, instead of new buyers entering the market, the existing buyers each became willing to pay $0.90 more for a cup of coffee. The situation could arise, for example, if the prices of alternatives, such as tea or hot chocolate, had risen substantially. If this were to happen, the lack of reasonably priced alternatives—what economists call **substitute goods**—would likely increase the maximum price that existing coffee drinkers would be willing to pay for a cup. An

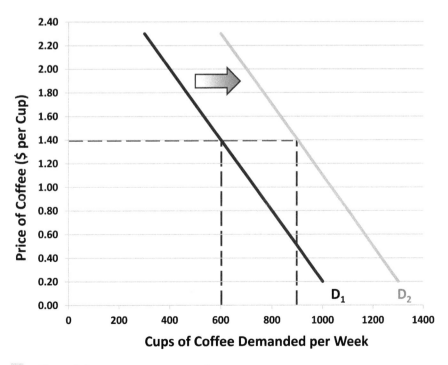

Figure 3.5 *An Increase in Demand*

increase in the price of a substitute good tends to increase the demand for the good in question because people who are unwilling to pay the higher price will shift to the substitute good whose price has not risen. An increase in the price of tea or hot chocolate could thus lead to an "increase in demand" for coffee. The change would also be illustrated in Figure 3.5.

> **substitute good:** a good that can be used in place of another

The coffee market may also be affected by changes in the prices of goods that are **complementary** to coffee. Complementary goods are those that are used along *with* the good in question. A classic example of complementary goods is hot dogs and mustard. For purposes of our example, suppose coffee is frequently consumed with pastries. An increase in the price of pastries would make coffee less attractive since the price of the "package" of coffee plus pastry is now higher. Demand for the good in question tends to decrease with an increase in the price of a complementary good. This is shown in Figure 3.6.

> **complementary good:** a good that is used along with another good

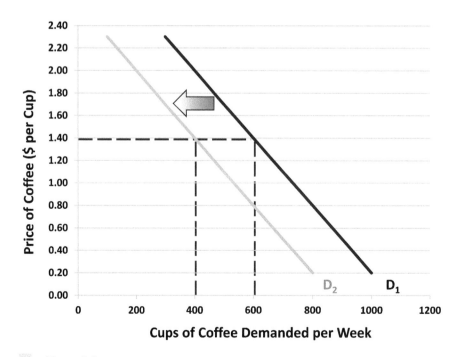

Figure 3.6 *A Decrease in Demand*

Thus, the number of potential buyers, their ability to pay, and the prices of substitutes and complements are among the things that can affect the location of the demand curve. Many other factors, such as changes in preferences, changes in income or wealth levels, or changes in buyers' expectations about future prices, also affect the location of demand curves. The location of the demand curve often depends on the specific market in question.

For example, in the market for steel, overall economic growth will increase the demand for steel, while the development of substitute materials, such as plastic composites for use in automobiles, will decrease it. Hotter weather will increase demand for ice cream but will decrease the demand for sweaters—and so forth. We can easily identify many examples of other demand shifts in everyday life.

Discussion Questions

1. Explain verbally why the demand curve slopes downward.
2. Verbally explain the difference between a change in *quantity demanded* and a change in *demand*. Considering the demand side of the market for lawn-mowing services, what kind of change (*increase* or *decrease*, in *quantity demanded* or *demand*) would each of the following events cause?

   a) A new office park is built, surrounded by several acres of lawn
   b) There is a recession, putting many people out of work; many homeowners have less money, but more time to mow their own lawns
   c) The going price for lawn-mowing services rises
   d) More natural, wild yards become more popular, as people become concerned about the effects of fertilizers and pesticides on the environment

4 THE THEORY OF MARKET ADJUSTMENT

Now that we have considered the sellers and the buyers separately, it is time to bring them together. In our hypothetical market, every cup of coffee will sell at the same price. (Remember, they are identical—why would anyone pay more, or accept less, than the going price?) We are now ready to ask: How many cups of coffee will be sold in the market and at what price?

4.1 Surplus, Shortage, and Equilibrium

Using the original supply and demand curves, reproduced here in Figure 3.7, we can look for the answer by considering possible prices. Suppose that we start with a high price of $1.40. At this price, 1,000 cups of coffee will be offered for sale, but consumers are collectively interested

113

in buying only 600. Economists call a situation in which the quantity supplied is greater than the quantity demanded a **surplus**. It is illustrated in Figure 3.7.

> **surplus:** a situation in which the quantity that sellers wish to sell at the stated price is greater than the quantity that buyers will buy at that price

If a market is in a situation of surplus, what would we expect to happen? Imagine that at the start of the week, coffee sellers are equipped to sell 1,000 cups of coffee. At the end of the week, they find that they have sold only 600 cups, and they have a large leftover inventory of coffee supplies. Coffee sellers realize that they need to attract more customers, so they will respond to the surplus by lowering their prices. Assuming that all sellers respond equally (which is unlikely in the real world, but it simplifies our model at this point), the prevailing price will be somewhat lower the next week. We do not necessarily know how much lower it will be, but there will be downward pressure on prices whenever there is a surplus. Note that if one particular coffee seller lowers price in response to the surplus, pressure will be created on other sellers to lower their prices as well, at the risk of losing customers. Thus, the most likely response to the surplus would be lower prices in general.

Let's say that the next week the prevailing price is lowered from $1.40 to $1.30. Looking at Figure 3.7, we see that there would still be a surplus

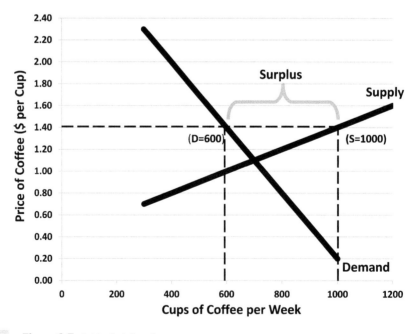

Figure 3.7 *A Market Surplus*

(the quantity supplied exceeds the quantity demanded), but the surplus would be a little smaller. Thus, there would still be downward pressure on prices as long as a surplus existed.

Now let's consider the opposite situation. Assume that the initial price of coffee is relatively low, at $0.80 per cup. As shown in Figure 3.8, at this price sellers are prepared to sell only 400 cups per week while the quantity demanded is 800 cups. A situation in which the quantity demanded exceeds the quantity supplied is referred to as a **shortage**.

> **shortage:** a situation in which the quantity demanded at a particular price exceeds the quantity that sellers are willing to supply

What would we expect to happen in a market with a shortage? Before we even get to the end of the week, the suppliers' inventory will be depleted, and they will end up turning away customers who want to buy coffee. Realizing that there is excess demand for coffee and that there are many buyers who are willing to pay more than $0.80 for coffee, sellers will conclude that they can charge a little more for coffee and still have a sufficient number of customers. Even if all the sellers do not raise prices immediately, the overall tendency will be toward higher prices. So whenever there is a situation of shortage, there will be upward pressure on prices.

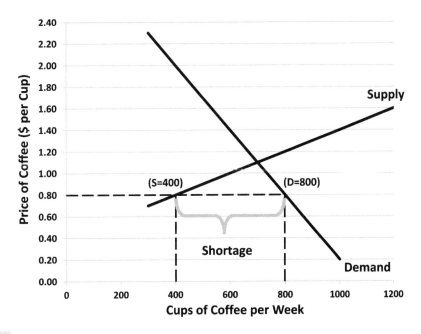

Figure 3.8 *A Market Shortage*

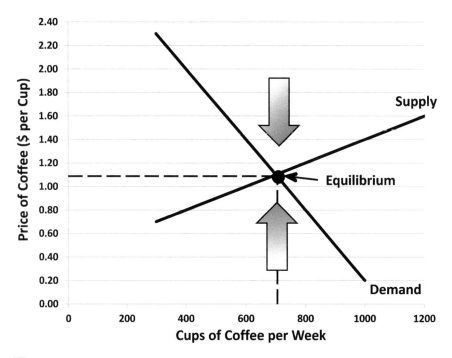

Figure 3.9 *Market Equilibrium*

So if the prevailing price is "too high" (a surplus), there will be downward pressure on prices, and if the price is "too low" (a shortage), there will be upward pressure on prices. Where will prices be "just right"? Starting from either a surplus or shortage, we see in Figure 3.9 that market adjustments will push the price toward $1.10 per cup. At this price, the quantity demanded equals the quantity supplied at 700 cups of coffee per week. (Check Tables 3.1 and 3.2 to confirm this.)

Economists call this a situation in which the "market clears" and a **market equilibrium** is reached. "Equilibrium" describes a situation that has reached a resting point, where there are no forces acting to change it. (Economists borrowed this term from natural science.) In a market situation, equilibrium is reached when the quantity supplied is equal to the quantity demanded. The price will stop falling or rising.

> market equilibrium: a situation in which the quantity supplied equals the quantity demanded, and thus there is no pressure for change in price or quantity bought or sold

The existence of a shortage or surplus is referred to as a situation of **market disequilibrium**. Putting together what we have observed about surpluses and shortages, we can state a **theory of market adjustment**— price changes in a freely working market will tend to make surpluses and shortages disappear.

116

> **market disequilibrium:** a situation of either shortage or surplus
> **theory of market adjustment:** the theory that market forces will tend to make shortages and surpluses disappear

4.2 Shifts in Supply and Demand

With the two curves now combined, we can investigate how market forces will cause equilibrium prices and quantities to change in response to changes in the underlying non-price determinants of supply and demand.

In our coffee market, let us compare the original equilibrium shown in Figure 3.9 to a case in which supply has risen. How would the market result now differ, compared to the original case? In Figure 3.10, the original equilibrium is marked as E_1 with supply curve S_1. When the supply curve shifts to S_2, we see that there is a surplus at the original equilibrium price of $1.10, resulting in a fall in equilibrium price. At point E_2, with a price of $0.80, the market clears, with 800 cups of coffee being sold. As Figure 3.10 illustrates, *an increase in supply will tend to decrease equilibrium price and increase equilibrium quantity.*

Suppose that instead of an increase in supply in this market, we have an increase in demand. In Figure 3.11, we see the effect of that demand increase: At the original equilibrium price of $1.10, a shortage results. The price will be bid up to $1.40, where 1,000 cups of coffee will be

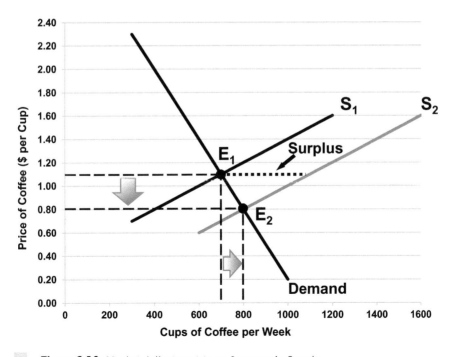

Figure 3.10 *Market Adjustment to an Increase in Supply*

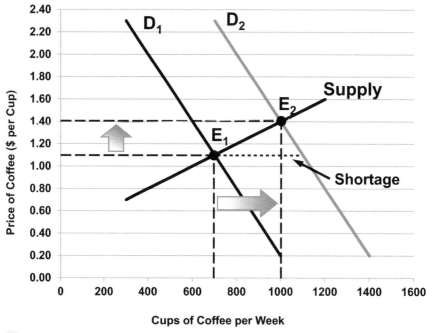

Figure 3.11 *Market Adjustment to an Increase in Demand*

offered. As Figure 3.11 illustrates, an increase in demand will tend to increase equilibrium price and increase equilibrium quantity.

Notice that both supply and demand increases tend to increase the equilibrium quantity transacted. Their price effects, however, go in opposite directions. Increases in supply make the good more plentiful, driving its equilibrium price down. Increases in demand drive up the equilibrium price.

Likewise, decreases in supply and demand both tend to decrease the equilibrium quantity transacted. A decrease in supply will tend to raise the equilibrium price, as the good is harder to get. A decrease in demand will tend to decrease the equilibrium price, as fewer attempts are made to obtain the good. These effects are summarized in Table 3.3.

What if *both* curves shifted at the same time? What if, for example, there were increases in the number of sellers of coffee *and* in the number of buyers? In this case, the new equilibrium would be found at the

Table 3.3 *Effects of Changes in Supply and Demand*

	Effect on equilibrium price	Effect on equilibrium quantity
Increase in supply	fall	rise
Decrease in supply	rise	fall
Increase in demand	rise	rise
Decrease in demand	fall	fall

intersection of two new curves, rather than one new curve and one old one. Comparing the new equilibrium with the original one in the case in which both supply and demand increase, for example, the equilibrium quantity clearly rises, but the effect on the equilibrium price is ambiguous. That is, the equilibrium price may go up, down, or stay the same depending on two factors: how far each of the curves shifts and how steep each of the curves is (the second of these is related to the **price elasticity** of supply or demand, a concept that is discussed in the next section). In other cases, it may be the change in the price that is clear, but the change in equilibrium quantity that is ambiguous—again, depending on the same two factors. You can experiment with various combinations of changes to see how they affect equilibrium. (See Box 3.1 for some examples of changes in the real-world market for coffee).

---

price elasticity: a measure of the sensitivity or responsiveness of quantity supplied or demanded to changes in price

---

BOX 3.1 COFFEE MARKETS IN THE REAL WORLD

Coffee markets are generally characterized by price volatility. After reaching a 14-year high in May 2011, wholesale coffee bean prices declined by about 60 percent by 2013. Coffee prices rose slightly in 2014 but by 2019 they had fallen to almost one-third of their price in 2011.[6] Since 2019 coffee prices have been rising, with steep increases of almost 80 percent in 2021.[7] How can our market model provide insights into changing coffee prices in the real world?

Let us first look at the decline in prices between 2015 and 2019. Our model suggests that falling prices can occur either due to an increase in supply or a decrease in demand, or both. According to data from the United States Department of Agriculture (USDA), global coffee supplies increased over this time period due to production booms in major coffee-producing countries, including Brazil, Colombia, Ethiopia, Indonesia, and Vietnam.[8] At the same time, global consumption of coffee also increased. So these data suggest that the main reason prices fell so much from 2015–2019 was an increase in the supply of coffee. Even though there was some demand increase, which by itself would tend to raise prices, the supply increase was much larger.

What has caused coffee prices to rise since 2019? According to our model, a rise in price can be caused either by a decline in supply or an increase in demand. Data from USDA shows that coffee consumption has increased slightly, which might have contributed to rising prices. But the rise in coffee prices is mainly explained by the drop in global coffee supplies between 2019 and 2021.[9] This decline was mainly driven by a production shortfall in Brazil, the world's leading coffee producer, due to adverse weather conditions including droughts and frosts.[10] There was also a decline in production in some of the other major coffee-producing countries including Colombia, Indonesia, and Vietnam.

While part of this decline was caused by environmental shocks, problems related to the COVID-19 pandemic, such as the disruptions in the supply chain, labor shortages, and rising costs of shipping also contributed to the rise in coffee prices.[11] Volatile prices and supply shocks related to the pandemic create significant uncertainty for coffee growers. According to a 2020 report:

> The pandemic may ... have major implications for poverty and food insecurity for the world's 25 million coffee producers, most of whom are smallholders in low- and middle-income countries that are unprepared to respond to a public health crisis of this proportion.[12]

In the future, the major factor affecting coffee markets is likely to be climate change, as coffee is highly sensitive to temperature variations. By 2050 about half of the world's coffee-producing land may be unproductive due to rising temperatures.[13] Scientists are currently searching for new varieties of coffee that can tolerate hot and dry conditions, while still being palatable to the world's coffee drinkers.

4.3 Elasticity

When there is a change in market price, by *how much* will the equilibrium quantity change? Economists are often interested in the answer to this question. The **price elasticity of demand** measures the degree to which buyers of a good respond to a change in its price. Mathematically, it is defined as the percentage change in quantity demanded divided by the percentage change in price:

$$\text{Price elasticity of demand} = \frac{\text{Percent change in quantity demanded}}{\text{Percent change in price}}$$

price elasticity of demand: a measure of the responsiveness of quantity demanded to changes in price

The larger the quantity response is, relative to the size of the price change, the "more elastic" demand is said to be. If the response is small, demand is said to be relatively "price inelastic." You can think of price elasticity of demand as a measure of the responsiveness of quantity demanded to changes in price.

Figure 3.12 graphs two different demand curves, along with identical supply curve shifts. In Figure 3.12(a), with the relatively flat demand curve, we see that there is a large drop in the quantity demanded associated with a small increase in price. In Figure 3.12(b), by contrast, with a relatively steep demand curve, only a small decrease in quantity

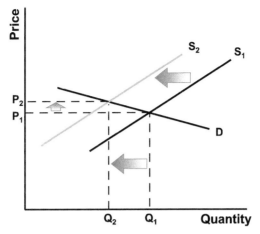

Figure 3.12a *Price Elasticity of Demand (a) Relatively Price-Elastic Demand.*

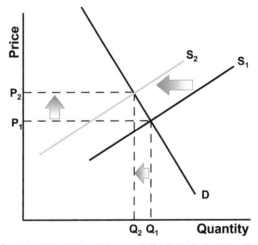

Figure 3.12b *Price Elasticity of Demand (b) Relatively Price-Inelastic Demand*

demanded is associated with a substantial increase in price. The difference derives from the fact that the demand curve shown in (a) is much more price elastic than the demand curve in (b).

Goods for which there are many substitutes, which are merely wanted rather than needed, or which make up a large part of the budget of the buyer tend to have relatively price-elastic demand. Different brands of beverages, for example, will tend to be price-elastic, because they can readily substitute for one another. Demand for automobiles is also price-elastic—because a car is such a large expense that buyers will tend to be sensitive to price. In contrast, goods for which there are few substitutes, that are badly needed, or that make up a small part of the buyer's budget tend to have relatively inelastic demand.

We would expect demand for our earlier example of coffee to be relatively price-inelastic, possibly for all three reasons. Individual brands of coffee, by contrast, would have elastic demand, because they can substitute for one another. Essential medications and gasoline are two other examples of relatively price-inelastic goods.

The **price elasticity of supply** measures the same sort of responsiveness, but this time on the part of sellers. Mathematically, it is defined as the percentage change in quantity supplied divided by the percentage change in price. When suppliers respond to a small increase in price by offering a much larger quantity of goods, we say that supply is relatively elastic. If they hardly react at all, supply is relatively inelastic. Like the price elasticity of demand, the price elasticity of supply is calculated as:

$$\text{Price elasticity of supply} = \frac{\text{Percentage change in quantity supplied}}{\text{Percentage change in price}}$$

---

price elasticity of supply: a measure of the responsiveness of quantity supplied to changes in price

---

Since demand curves slope downward and supply curves upward, the elasticity of demand will generally be a negative number, while the elasticity of supply is positive. A positive change in price will lead to a negative change in quantity demanded, but to a positive change in quantity supplied—this results in the formula for demand elasticity being negative while the formula for supply elasticity is positive. Somewhat confusingly, the negative sign for demand elasticity is often dropped, so that a higher elasticity of demand is reflected by a larger positive number. In technical terms, this amounts to expressing demand elasticity as an absolute value, a common practice in economics.

Discussion Questions

1. Think about the market for high-quality basketballs. In each of the following cases, determine which curve shifts and in which direction. Also, draw a graph and describe, in words, the changes in price and quantity. (Treat each case separately.)

    a) A rise in basketball players' income
    b) An increase in wages paid to the workers who make the balls
    c) A decrease in the price of basketball hoops and other basketball gear
    d) The country's becoming obsessed with soccer

2. Have you ever found yourself shut out of a class that you wanted to take because it was already full? Or has this happened to a friend of yours? Analyze this situation in terms of surplus or shortage. Are classes supplied "in a market"? Do you think that it would be good if they were?

5 MACROECONOMICS AND THE DYNAMICS OF REAL-WORLD MARKETS

Although supply and demand analysis can be a very useful tool for understanding how markets work, few if any markets truly approach perfect competition, and seldom are they as fluid as in the simple models depicted here. Markets may be characterized by market power (as in the example mentioned earlier of Microsoft's dominance in the market for computer operating systems). Goods and services sold in markets may not be as simple as our example of cups of coffee; more commonly there are different brands and types of products, with different characteristics. Indeed, the real-world market for coffee has come more and more to revolve around the quality of the drink, with major firms trying to appeal to consumers with specialty coffees rather than competing mainly on price.

In some markets, buyers and sellers may have imperfect information, or be bound by long-term contracts. The role of assumptions and expectations can also be significant. For example, if advertising leads people to believe that a product is especially good, or if it gains celebrity endorsements, its price may rise simply as a result of its reputation rather than its actual characteristics. Wages, which are a special kind of price paid by firms to workers in exchange for their labor, can be affected by a variety of things aside from simple supply and demand, including market power either of unions or of employers.

There is one additional reason to look closely at the standard market model. This is its assumption that, when the market functions in a smooth, idealized way, taking decisions out of the hands of individuals, the results are purely "objective," with no bias toward any person or group. In fact, this model does have an undeniable bias, toward those with money—and a larger bias toward persons or organizations with more money. This is because "demand" in the context of supply-and-demand interactions means "willingness *and ability* to pay." So pure market results are based on the distribution of purchasing power—money—in the society.

BOX 3.2 MARKET POWER AND PRICE CONTROLS

The prices of most specialty drugs in the United States have been increasing much faster than inflation. In 2020, the annual price of brand-name prescription drugs increased by 2.9 percent—the slowest rise since 2006. But this increase was still twice the country's general inflation rate of 1.3 percent.[14] A 2019 report finds that between 2012 and 2017, the cost of 49 top-selling drugs increased by a median of 76 percent, and 44 percent of these drugs had more than doubled in price.[15]

Such price hikes in the drug market are partly explained by the relatively inelastic demand for drugs and the immense market power that pharmaceutical companies have over controlling market prices. As prices of drugs increase, they become less accessible—especially to the poor. Should prices of such commodities, which may be essential for survival, be dependent on one's ability to pay?

Some economists argue that it is essential for the government to control prices in certain circumstances to protect consumers and producers from rapidly increasing or declining prices. In the case of the market for prescription drugs, the government could set limitations on the rate of price increase or maximum prices for specific drugs to make essential drugs affordable to consumers. Such controls on drug prices have been shown to increase accessibility in other developed countries.[16] While critics of price controls point out that such controls could reduce the ability of the pharmaceutical industry to invest in research and come up with new drugs, it is worth noting that in the United States the federal government puts up most of the risky investments for medical research.

In some other markets, a decline in demand or an increase in supply could result in rapidly falling prices which might hurt producers. For example, in the agricultural sector, technological innovations and an increase in global trade have put downward pressure on the prices of agricultural products, hurting farmers' income levels. Under such circumstances, governments in many industrialized countries have provided farmers with various kinds of agricultural subsidies, or have set price floors, preventing prices from falling below a certain minimum, on some agricultural products.

5.1 When Price Adjustments Are Slow

An issue of particular importance to macroeconomics is the question of the speed at which real-world price adjustments take place. How long will it take our hypothetical coffee traders to reach equilibrium? Minutes? An hour? A day? The theory of supply and demand does not tell us. The graphs represent a static model, meaning that the model does not take into account the passage of time.

Some markets, such as stock markets, tend to clear quickly. But other markets involve significant time delays. For example, consider the market for shirts. When you go into a clothing store, you see a rack of shirts and, on their tags, a given price. The price probably reflects a markup by the retailer over what he or she paid to a distributor to get the shirts. The distributor in turn probably charged a markup over the price charged by the manufacturer. If the shirts were overpriced, they would not sell very well. In the terms we introduced, there would be a surplus. If the market worked as fluidly as just described, the supplier and demander would quickly be able to fine-tune the price and quantity to get it just right, as we saw in our hypothetical coffee market in Figure 3.7. The price would fall, more shirts would be purchased, the surplus of shirts would disappear immediately, and equilibrium would be restored.

In a realistic, complicated case such as this one, however, there is actually a *chain* of markets involved—the manufacturer sells to the distributor, the distributor to the retailer, and the retailer to the final buyer. A quick adjustment of prices is unlikely. More commonly, when retailers mark down the prices on the shirts they have in stock in order to clear them out, the drop in the price will not immediately travel back up the supply chain. Any changes in prices or quantities at the manufacturing level would only develop over time, as the manufacturers saw the level of their inventories either rise (because the shirts are not selling) or fall (because the distributors order more).

Because of the time it takes for all these things to happen, in some cases the most likely first response to a surplus is that manufacturers would cut *production*—perhaps laying off workers—rather than reducing their prices. In such a case, the *quantity* produced adjusts to meet the quantity demanded at a given price, rather than the price adjusting to clear the market. If negative **quantity adjustments** happened throughout the economy, total production could fall, and unemployment could rise.

---

quantity adjustments: a response by suppliers in which they react to unexpectedly low sales of their goods primarily by reducing production levels rather than by reducing the price and to unexpectedly high sales by increasing production rather than raising the price

---

Suppliers may also be reluctant to change the prices that they offer because of **menu costs**—literally, the costs of changing the prices listed on such things as order forms and restaurant menus. Other factors that could slow the process of price adjustment include union contracts, lengthy production processes, and lack of information.

---

menu costs: the costs to a supplier of changing prices listed on order forms, brochures, menus, and the like

---

5.2 When Prices Swing Too Much: Market Instability

Other markets have adjustment processes in which prices may change very rapidly. In electronic stock markets, for example, thousands of trades may take place every minute, as buyers and sellers find each other and quickly negotiate a price. Such a market can probably be thought of as in equilibrium or moving quickly toward one, nearly all the time.

Very rapid adjustments of prices, however, create their own set of problems, especially in relation to the macroeconomic goal of stability. In our hypothetical market for coffee, we assumed that people wanted coffee simply because of the taste or perhaps the energy boost, both reasonable assumptions. But there are markets in which buyers are not really interested in the *item itself* at all—only its price and the direction in which it is likely to go. **Speculation** is the buying and selling of assets with the expectation of profiting from appreciation or depreciation in their values, usually over a relatively short period of time. Speculators buy items such as stocks in companies, commodities futures (e.g., contracts to buy or sell items such as pork bellies or copper at a specific price on a future date), foreign exchange, real estate, or other investment vehicles, purely in the hopes that they will be able to sell them in the future for more than they have paid.

> **speculation:** buying and selling assets with the expectation of profiting from appreciation or depreciation in their value

When many people come to believe that the price of something will rise, a **speculative bubble** can occur, in which people buy the asset because so many other people also believe that its price will continue to rise. In a mass phenomenon often referred to using terms such as "herd mentality" or "bandwagon effect," speculators' mutually reinforcing optimism causes asset values to rise far above any price that could be rationalized in terms of "economic fundamentals."

> **speculative bubble:** the situation that occurs when mutually reinforcing investor optimism raises the value of an asset far above what can be justified by fundamental value

In the case of a stock price, for example, the rational economic basis for valuation should be the returns that an investor can expect from the firm of which the stock represents an ownership share, while in the case of real estate the value should be determined by the stream of likely rents, from the present into the future, or the likely sale value of the property. Someone who buys a home to live in should rationally select one whose costs (mortgage payments plus money used for down payment) are similar to the rent that would be demanded for a comparable property.

During a bubble, however, people pay less attention to (or take a biased view of) such fundamental factors. Instead, demand for an asset is determined largely by purchasers' perception that they will be able to find someone to whom they can sell the asset at a higher price. Eventually, however, people begin to figure out that prices have become unrealistically high. Then the demand drops, the bubble bursts, and prices fall. This happened during the "dotcom" bubble of the late 1990s, as shown

Figure 3.13 *The Nasdaq Composite Stock Index, 1995–2022*

Source: Yahoo! Finance, Monthly data.

in Figure 3.13 when the NASDAQ index of mostly technology stocks rose rapidly and then fell during the period 1999–2002. It took the index 15 years to reach its previous high of over 5,000 points in March 2000. It then increased much further, leading some to wonder whether the new price highs (as of 2021) were justified, or perhaps another bubble in the making.

It is fairly easy, of course, to recognize a bubble after the fact. But during the spectacular rise in stock prices that took place in the late 1990s, many otherwise rational and intelligent people convinced one another—and themselves—that the stock market boom reflected an immense jump in productivity, not a speculative bubble. In spite of the painful lesson of the 2000–2002 crash, soon afterward the buildup began for another boom and bust, this time originating in the U.S. market for **subprime mortgages**. Such mortgages are housing loans given to people whose income or credit history is not good enough to qualify them for regular mortgages.

---

subprime mortgage: a mortgage given to someone with poor credit

---

Many banks aggressively marketed subprime housing loans to prospective homeowners from early 2004 to 2007, sometimes using fraudulent techniques and making profits by collecting fees on each loan made. Some of the world's largest banks moved aggressively into this area, bundling and repackaging the mortgages in such a way that their

127

riskiness was not immediately apparent. This increase in credit increased demand for houses and drove up real estate prices.

Eventually, however, softening of housing prices and rising interest rates caused a steep increase in the number of U.S. homeowners who were defaulting on their loans. Securities based on "bundled" subprime mortgages rapidly lost market value as questions were finally raised about the actual worth of the assets on which they were based. During the subprime crisis, many people lost their homes, and many of the largest commercial banks lost billions of dollars. We will discuss this financial crisis in the appendix to Chapter 10.

Situations of speculative bubbles and volatile (that is, rapidly changing) prices have important implications for macroeconomics, even though there is some disagreement among economists about the importance of market volatility. Those who take a classical point of view tend to downplay such market-related problems, believing that even if market performance sometimes seemed counter to human welfare, it would still be better than what could be achieved by government regulation or intervention. Other economists, in particular those with Keynesian views, or those who are particularly concerned with the economics of less industrialized countries or the fate of the less well-off in any society, believe that some sort of regulation is needed to prevent market volatility. We discuss both the need for and nature of such regulations in later chapters.

5.3 From Microeconomics to Macroeconomics

How far does the model of supply and demand get us in explaining macroeconomic phenomena? That question can be broken down into two parts. First, are markets in the real world similar to the one portrayed in the model? As we have discussed, markets may often not be perfectly competitive, and this can have macroeconomic implications. Second, even to the extent that individual markets do behave as the model predicts, might explaining national-level economic phenomena require different theoretical tools? In other words, does it follow that what works for an individual market, or even for many markets, necessarily works for entire economies?

Later chapters of this book will explore these questions, starting with the ways in which we measure macroeconomic activity, then examining different approaches to analyzing the behavior of the economy as a whole.

Discussion Questions

1. Think of several things that you regularly buy. For which of these goods or services do prices seem to change rapidly? For which do they seem to change slowly? Can you explain why?

2. Has there been any talk of "speculative bubbles" in news reports recently? If so, what markets are being discussed? What explanations are given for why prices may be so high?

REVIEW QUESTIONS

1. Describe two characteristics of the type of market featured in classical analysis.
2. Define and sketch a supply curve.
3. Illustrate on a clearly labeled graph (a) a decrease in quantity supplied and (b) a decrease in supply.
4. Describe two factors that might cause a supply curve to shift.
5. Define and sketch a demand curve.
6. Illustrate on a clearly labeled graph (a) a decrease in quantity demanded and (b) a decrease in demand.
7. Describe two factors that might cause a demand curve to shift.
8. Describe how goods can be "substitutes." Describe how the demand curve for a good may be affected by an increase in the price of a second good that is a substitute for the first.
9. Describe how goods can be "complementary." Describe how the demand curve for a good may be affected by an increase in the price of a second good that is complementary to the first.
10. Draw a graph illustrating surplus, shortage, and equilibrium.
11. Describe, using graphs, how an increase in supply affects equilibrium quantity and price. Repeat for a decrease in supply.
12. Describe, using graphs, how an increase in demand affects equilibrium quantity and price. Repeat for a decrease in demand.
13. Describe what is meant by the price elasticity of demand and the price elasticity of supply.
14. Describe why sellers of a good might adjust the quantity of what they produce, rather than the price.
15. What are some of the problems that can be created by large price swings?

EXERCISES

1   Suppose that the supply and demand schedules for a local electric utility are as follows: The price is in cents per kilowatt hour (kWh), and the quantity is millions of kilowatt hours. The utility does not operate at prices less than 13 cents per kWh.

Price	Quantity supplied	Quantity demanded
17	9	3
16	7	4
15	5	5
14	3	6
13	1	7
12	–	8
11	–	9

129

a) Using graph paper and a ruler or a computer spreadsheet or presentation program, carefully graph and label the supply curve for electricity.
b) On the same graph, draw and label the demand curve for electricity.
c) What is the equilibrium price of electricity? The equilibrium quantity? Label
this point on your graph.
d) At a price of 17 cents per kWh, what is the quantity supplied? What is the quantity demanded? What is the relationship between quantity supplied and quantity
demanded? What term do economists use to describe this situation?
c) At a price of 14 cents per kWh, what is the relationship between quantity supplied and quantity demanded? What term do economists use to describe this
situation?
f) Sometimes cities experience "blackouts," where the demand for the utility is so
high relative to its capacity to produce electricity that the system shuts down,
leaving everyone in the dark. Using the analysis that you have just completed,
describe an *economic* factor that would make blackouts more likely to occur.
2. Continuing from the previous problem, suppose that new innovations in energy efficiency reduce people's need for electricity. The supply side of the market does not
change, but at each price buyers now demand 3 million kWh fewer than before. For
example, at a price of 11 cents per kWh, buyers now demand only 6 kWh instead of
9 kWh.
a) On a new graph, draw supply and demand curves corresponding to prices of 16
cents per kWh or less, after the innovations in efficiency. Also, for reference,
mark the old equilibrium point from the previous exercise, labeling it E1.
b) If the price were to remain at the old equilibrium level determined in part (c) of
question 1 above, what sort of situation would result?
c) What is the new equilibrium price? The new equilibrium quantity? Label this
point on your graph E2.
d) Has there been a change in demand? Has a change in the price (relative to the
original situation) led to a change in the quantity demanded?
e) Has there been a change in supply? Has a change in the price (relative to the
original situation) led to a decrease in the quantity supplied?
3. Using your understanding of the non-price determinants of supply and of demand,
analyze each of the following market cases. Draw a graph showing what happens in
each situation, indicate what happens to equilibrium price and quantity, and explain
why. The first case is done as an example:
Question: Market for gasoline: A hurricane hits the Gulf of Mexico, destroying many
refineries that produce gasoline from crude oil.

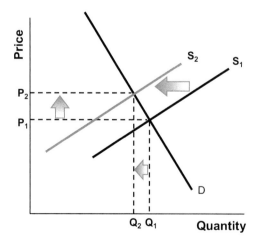

Answer:

S shifts back.

P rises.

Q falls.

The hurricane reduces the number of producers.

    a)   Market for bananas: New health reports indicate that eating bananas leads to important health benefits

    b)   Market for shoes: A new technology for shoe-making means that shoes can be made at a lower cost per pair

    c)   Market for Web design services: Several thousand new graduates of design schools enter the market, ready to supply their services

    d)   Market for expensive meals: A booming economy raises the income of many households

    e)   Market for grapes *from California:* A freeze in Chile, usually a major world provider of fresh fruit, raises the price of Chilean grapes

    f)   Market for salsa dance lessons: The only nightclub in town featuring salsa music triples its entrance fee

    g)   Market for bottled water: A contaminant makes tap water in a community unsafe to drink

    h)   Market for Web design services: Several thousand new graduates of design schools enter the market, ready to supply their services *and,* at the same time, many firms want to create new Web sites

4.   State whether the following statements are true or false. If false, write a corrected statement.

    a)   A fall in the price of a good will cause its supply curve to shift to the left

    b)   Increased costs of supplying a good will cause the supply curve to shift to the left

    c)   A fall in the price of a substitute good will cause the demand for the good in question to fall

    d)   A decrease in supply will have a small effect on the quantity demanded if the demand curve is very elastic

5.   Suppose that a newspaper report indicates that the price of wheat has fallen. Which of the following could be possible explanations? (There may be more than one.) Illustrate *one* case on a supply and demand graph.

    a)   A drought has hit wheat-growing areas

    b)   An increase in the price of rice

    c)   Due to increasing health concerns, tobacco farmers have begun growing other crops

    d)   A new science report suggests that wheat is bad for one's health

6.   For each of the following items, discuss whether you think the demand that the seller faces will be price inelastic or price elastic, and explain why.

    a)   A new song by an extremely popular recording artist

    b)   One share of stock, when there are millions of shares for that company outstanding

    c)   Bottled drinking water at a town in the desert

    d)   Your used textbooks at the end of the term

7.   Calculate the price elasticity of demand for the following cases:

    a)   When price rises by 5 percent, quantity demanded drops by 10 percent.

    b)   When price rises by 10 percent, quantity demanded drops by 2 percent.

    c)   When price falls by 10 percent, quantity demanded rises by 2 percent.

8.   Prices of many financial assets such as stocks and foreign exchange are now readily available on the Internet. Search for a chart like Figure 3.13 for a stock index or foreign currency of your choice and take a printout. During the period covered by the graph that you found, does it seem as if this market is fairly calm, or is it character-

ized by periods of volatility? (Caution: because price swings can be made to look relatively large or small simply by changing the scale of the graph, in answering this question you may want to choose a fairly long time series or compare the behavior of the asset you have chosen with a similar asset.) Is there any evidence of a speculative bubble?

9. Match each concept in Column A with a definition or example in Column B.

Column A	Column B
a. Substitute goods	1. Quantity supplied is equal to quantity demanded
b. Shifts the supply curve	2. A tiny drop in the price of a good leads to a big increase in quantity demanded
c. A "bubble"	3. Shoes and shoelaces
d. Complementary goods	4. A shoe manufacturer responds to a decline in shoe sales by cutting back on production and laying off workers
e. Speculation	5. Tea and coffee
f. Market equilibrium	6. Quantity supplied is greater than quantity demanded
g. Price-inelastic demand	7. Buying an asset largely in the hope of selling it later for a higher price
h. Quantity adjustment	8. Even large changes in price do not influence overall demand
i. Price-elastic demand	9. A change in the number of sellers
j. Surplus	10. When investors' optimism pushes the price of an asset artificially high

NOTES

1   Hernandez, 2021.
2   Oil prices from the U.S. Energy Information Administration, based on European Brent spot prices.
3   New automobile sales data from the BEA, 2021.
4   Richter, 2019.
5   eBay Fast Facts. https://investors.ebayinc.com/fast-facts/default.aspx.
6   https://www.macrotrends.net/2535/coffee-prices-historical-chart-data.
7   Morris, 2021.
8   USDA, 2018.
9   USDA, 2021.
10 Ibid.
11 Teixeira, 2021.
12 International Coffee Organization, 2020.
13 Briggs, 2021.
14 Avery, 2021.
15 Wineinger et al., 2019.
16 Bernstein, 2016.

REFERENCES

Avery, Taylor. 2021. "Prescription Drug Prices Increased Twice the Inflation Rate of US Economy in 2020, AARP report finds." *USA Today*, June 8.

Bernstein, Jared. 2016. "Drug Price Controls Are Vital in a Market That's Not Free." *The New York Times*, June 29.

Briggs, Helen. 2021. "Climate Change: Future-proofing Coffee in a Warming World." *BBC*, April 19.

Bureau of Economic Analysis. 2021. "Auto and Truck Seasonal Adjustment." *National Income and Product Accounts*, Table 7.2.6B.

China Daily. 2021. "Vehicle Sales in China Down 1.9% in 2020." https://www.chinadaily.com.cn/a/202101/13/WS5ffea07ca31024ad0baa25c3.html

Hernandez, Joe. 2021. "Lumber Prices Are Finally Dropping After They Soared During the Pandemic." *NPR*, June 21.

Ho, Patricia Jiayi. 2010. "China Passes U.S. as World's Top Car Market." *The Wall Street Journal*, January 12.

Morris, Jonathan. 2021 "Coffee Bean Prices Have Doubled in the Past Year and May Double AgainWhat's Going on?" *The Conversation*, September 30.

Richter, Wolf. 2019. "China Auto Sales Spiral Down, But This Time It's Different: Government Refuses to Bail Them Out with Big-Fat Incentives." *Wolf Street*, July 11.

Teixeira, Marcelo. 2021. "Shipping Disruptions to Keep Coffee Prices High for Longer, Say Experts." *Reuters*, October 15.

U.S. Department of Agriculture (USDA). 2018. "Coffee: World Markets and Trade." *Foreign Agricultural Service*, June.

U.S. Department of Agriculture (USDA). 2021. "Coffee: World Markets and Trade." *Foreign Agricultural Service*, June.

Wineinger, Nathan, Yunyue Zhang, and Eric J. Topol. 2019. "Trends in Prices of Popular Brand-Name Prescription Drugs in the United States." *Jama Open Network, 2*(5): doi:10.1001/jamanetworkopen.2019.4791

Part II

Macroeconomic Basics

Chapter 4

Macroeconomic Measurement: The Current Approach

In order to understand the workings of the macroeconomy and to make good macroeconomic policy choices, we need to have reliable information on how the economy is performing. The metric that is most often cited to assess overall economic performance is Gross Domestic Product (GDP)—a measure of the total production level of a country over a certain time period. Increases in GDP are generally viewed as a sign of a strengthening economy. On the other hand, the economy is said to be in a downturn if the growth rate of GDP declines or GDP actually decreases.

Of course, other variables, such as unemployment, inflation, and interest rates, are of great interest to economists and policymakers, but they tend to rely most heavily on GDP data to guide their policy recommendations. Rising GDP is often associated with declining unemployment since an expansion in production levels is expected to create jobs. Rapid increases in GDP could, however, cause labor and input shortages and result in increased inflation. Such interactions between GDP and other macroeconomic variables are central to understanding macroeconomic theory and policymaking.

In this chapter, we take a detailed look at GDP and related national economic data. Before we begin, a note of caution is in order. Although GDP growth generally improves average material living standards, GDP growth does not always increase well-being. For example, if GDP grows simply because people are working longer hours, we would need to evaluate this increase in GDP against the loss in leisure time to determine whether well-being has actually increased. GDP growth can also bring with it negative effects, such as increased pollutant emissions and depletion of resources. In Chapter 5, we look at the limitations of, and alternatives to, GDP as a measure of well-being to place our discussion of GDP "in context" with our broader discussion of well-being.

1 AN OVERVIEW OF NATIONAL ACCOUNTING

The first set of U.S. national accounts was created by economist Simon Kuznets in 1937, during the Great Depression when the economy experienced a severe decline. It was obvious that production had fallen, but without a set of national accounts, policymakers had little way of knowing how much the economy had declined, or whether the policies that were implemented in response were actually helping the economy to rebound. In 1937, Kuznets presented the first set of national income accounts to Congress, and they proved important in evaluating efforts to recover from the Depression, and later in measuring the effects of national economic mobilization during World War II. Today every functioning country compiles national accounts using standardized approaches.

National accounting involves more than just measuring GDP. Countries generally maintain a system of **National Income and Product Accounts (NIPA)** that collects data on production, income, spending, prices, and employment. In the United States, the national accounts are maintained by a federal agency, the **Bureau of Economic Analysis (BEA)**.

National Income and Product Accounts (NIPA): a set of statistics compiled by the BEA concerning production, income, spending, prices, and employment

Bureau of Economic Analysis (BEA): the agency in the United States in charge of compiling and publishing the national accounts

---

1.1 Conventions about National Accounting Sectors

Before we focus on how GDP is measured, we need to discuss some of the "conventions" used in the NIPA. **National accounting conventions** are simply practices that are adopted by agencies in order to try to make the accounts as standardized and comparable across different countries and time periods as possible. Some of these conventions concern how data are categorized. For example, there are conventions concerning what is classified as investment versus consumption, or a durable versus a nondurable good. Other conventions address how estimates are made for some components of the NIPA for which readily available data are lacking. Of course, there could be alternatives to the common conventions, but the emphasis tends to be on standardization rather than always choosing the "best" approach.

---

national accounting conventions: practices adopted by government agencies in order to make national accounts as standardized and comparable across different countries and time periods as possible

---

One of the common national accounting conventions concerns how the entire economy is broken down into four national accounting sectors. These sectors, as defined by the BEA, are:

1. *Households and institutions sector:* This includes households and nonprofit institutions that serve households, such as nonprofit hospitals, universities, museums, trade unions, and charities. The BEA also refers to the households and institutions sector as the "personal" sector. (Note how this overlaps with, but is not identical to, the "core sphere" described in Chapter 2.)
2. *Business sector:* The BEA business sector includes for-profit businesses as well as certain business-serving nonprofit organizations, such as trade associations and chambers of commerce. In addition, government agencies that produce goods and services for sale—such as the U.S. Postal Service, municipal gas and electric companies, and airports—are also classified as being in the business sector.
3. *Government sector:* The government sector includes all federal, state, and local government entities, except for the "business-like" government enterprises categorized in the business sector.
4. *Foreign sector:* The entities in the first three sectors include, for the national accounts, only those located within the physical borders of the United States. The foreign sector (or "rest of the world") includes all entities—household, nonprofit, business, or government—located outside the borders of the United States. An individual in another country who buys imported U.S. products, for example, or a company located abroad that sells goods or services to the United States, figures into the U.S. accounts as part of the foreign sector.

1.2 Conventions about Capital Stocks

Although natural, manufactured, human, and social capital are all crucial resources for economic activity, it is primarily *manufactured* capital that is currently included in the accounting of national non-financial assets. This might be because the national accounts were originally devised at a time when the rise of manufacturing made the accumulation of machinery and factory buildings appear to be the main road to prosperity. More recently, some forms of intellectual capital have been added to the asset accounts. (Issues of how to account for other forms of natural, human, and social capital are taken up in Chapter 5.)

The first category of manufactured capital in the national accounts is **fixed assets**. Fixed assets include structures (such as factories and office buildings), equipment, and intellectual property products owned by businesses and governments. Intellectual property products include computer software, which was added as a type of fixed asset in 1999, and knowledge created through research and development. In 2013, expenditures on the creation of intangible assets such as entertainment, literary, and artistic originals, were added as types of fixed assets.

> **fixed assets:** structures, equipment, and intellectual property products owned by businesses and governments

A second—and a much smaller—component of the manufactured capital stock is **inventories**. Inventories are stocks of raw materials, such as crude oil awaiting refining, or manufactured goods, such as the shoe inventory of a retail shoe store, that are held until they can be used or sold. The BEA only counts inventories held by the business sector.

> **inventories:** stocks of raw materials or manufactured goods held until they can be used or sold

In 2003, BEA began including equipment used by households, such as cars and stoves, that are used in household production of goods and services in its accounts of assets. The BEA calls all goods bought by households that are expected to last longer than three years **consumer durable goods**. The BEA estimates of the dollar value of the country's stock of manufactured assets at the end of 2020 are given in Table 4.1.

> **consumer durable goods:** consumer purchases that are expected to last longer than three years. These generally include equipment, such as vehicles and appliances, used by households to produce goods and services for their own use.

Table 4.1 *The Estimated Size of U.S. Manufactured Capital Stock, 2020*

Type of capital	Value in trillions of dollars at the end of the year
Equipment (businesses and government)	8.4
Structures (businesses and government)	29.1
Intellectual Property Products	5.1
Residences	25.1
Inventories	2.9
Consumer durable goods	6.1
The total value of manufactured capital	76.7

Sources: BEA, Fixed Asset Accounts, Table 1.1; NIPA, Table 5.10; and authors' calculations.

1.3 Conventions about Investment

Economists generally use the term "investment" to mean additions to stocks of *non*-financial assets, including human, social, natural, and manufactured capital stocks. This contrasts with the common use of the term "investment" to refer to financial investment, such as the purchase of stocks and bonds. Investment represents a *flow* into the overall capital stock. A machine added to a factory in 2020, for example, is considered part of the national *stock* of non-residential assets every year from the time it is installed until the time it is junked. However, the machine was an *addition* to assets only in 2020, and hence its value would be counted as an *investment* only in that one year.

The total amount of measured flows into the capital stock over a period is referred to as **gross investment**. **Net investment**, by contrast, adjusts this measure for the fact that some portion of the capital stock wears out, becomes obsolete, or is destroyed—that is, **depreciates**—over time.

For example, suppose that an office complex built in 1980 is torn down this year and replaced by a new, larger office complex. Measured gross investment for this year would include the full value of the new office complex. Net investment for this year would be calculated as the value of the new office complex *minus* the value of the depreciated building that was torn down. If the new building is considered to be worth $100 million while the old one was worth $40 million, for example, the economy has a net gain of only $60 million—not the full value of the new building. Net investment gives a better idea of the actual addition to productive capacity.

---

gross investment: all flows into the capital stock over a period of time
net investment: gross investment minus an adjustment for depreciation of the capital stock
depreciation: a decrease in the quantity or quality of a stock of capital

---

Gross investment in fixed assets is always zero or positive. However, if, over a period of time, the capital stock depreciates faster than it is being replaced, the gross investment could be less than depreciation, meaning that net investment would be negative. This can sometimes happen to manufactured capital stocks when a country is hit by major disasters such as wars or floods, or during a period when new investment is very low.

Ideally, productive investments by all sectors would be recognized in the national accounts. But it was not until 1996 that government investment in fixed assets was recognized, and household investment in consumer durables is still, by convention, not considered part of investment in the national accounts.

141

Discussion Questions

1. The BEA definitions of sectors use some conventions that are not obvious. To which sector might the BEA assign each of the following entities? Why?

    a) A local city government-owned golf course that charges fees similar to those at local private courses
    b) A large nonprofit hospital
    c) A U.S.-owned movie company whose offices and studio are in Japan
    d) A nonprofit trade association, such as the Chocolate Manufacturers Association

2. Under the BEA definitions, would spending on education be counted as an investment? Would buying shares in a company be considered an investment? Why?

2 DEFINING GROSS DOMESTIC PRODUCT

As we mentioned earlier, the most-referenced single number that comes out of the national accounts is GDP. According to the BEA, **GDP** measures the total market value of final goods and services newly produced within a country's borders over a period of time (usually one year). This definition contains several key phrases. Let us consider each of them.

---

gross domestic product (GDP) (BEA definition): a measure of the total market value of final goods and services newly produced within a country's borders over a period of time (usually one year)

"Market value": We measure GDP in terms of the market value of goods and services produced in order to have a common unit of measurement—the U.S. dollar—for comparing and adding the contribution of various goods and services that make up the economy. Converting everything into their dollar values makes it possible to aggregate pizzas, cars, healthcare, and educational services into one measure. We can simply refer to the market prices of goods and services for most components of GDP. However, in some cases, we do not have market prices for certain goods and services and thus need to estimate their value using the imputation method (discussed later in the chapter).

"Final goods and services": A **final good** is one that is ready for use. That is, no further productive activity needs to occur before the good can be consumed (if it is a good that is used up as it is put to use) or

put to work producing other goods and services (e.g., if it is a piece of equipment). The reason for limiting measurement to *final* goods and services is to avoid double counting. For example, suppose that over the course of a year, paper is produced by one company and sold to another company that uses it to make books. The books are then sold to their final buyers. Books in this case are the final goods, while the paper used in them is an **intermediate good**. By limiting the accounting to final goods, production is only counted once—the paper is only counted as part of the books.

Sometimes it is not so easy to say what is an intermediate good and what is a final good. As we noted earlier, in 2013 the BEA changed its definitions to include business spending on intellectual property, as well as research and development, as investments (final goods) rather than intermediate goods. Making this change raised the value of GDP by $560 billion—not reflecting any actual increase in production, just a change in the way production is defined.

---

final good: a good that is ready for use, needing no further processing
intermediate good: a good that will undergo further processing

---

"Over a period of time": Since GDP measures a flow, it must be measured over a time period. Macroeconomists usually work with GDP measured on a yearly basis. Estimates of GDP are released more often than once a year—generally on a quarterly basis. However, even when only a part of the year is being covered, GDP and its growth rates are usually expressed in annual terms.

"Newly produced": Only new goods and services are counted. For example, if you buy a book published in 2010 at a used bookshop, the value of the book itself is not included in this year's GDP. Only the retail services provided by the used bookshop are "newly produced," and are part of this year's GDP.

"Within a country's borders": This means that the goods and services are produced within the physical borders of the country. If a U.S. citizen goes abroad to work, for example, what he or she produces while away is *not* part of the U.S. GDP. On the other hand, the work of a Japanese citizen at a Japanese-owned factory *is* part of the U.S. GDP if that factory is located inside the borders of the United States.[*]

---

[*] A closely related measure is gross national product (GNP). The difference between GNP and GDP concerns whether foreign earnings are included. GNP includes the earnings of a country's citizens and corporations regardless of where they are located in the world. GDP includes all earnings within a country's borders, even the earnings of foreign citizens and corporations. GDP is the more common measure used when comparing international statistics.

BOX 4.1 ECONOMIC RECOVERY FROM THE PANDEMIC RECESSION

Following the 2008 financial crisis and recession, the U.S. economy experienced over a decade of relatively stable GDP growth averaging 2.25 percent. This changed abruptly in 2020, when the U.S. economy was hit by a historic contraction, declining by 31.7 percent, in the second quarter. This decline, of course, was caused by business closures and other stringent measures adopted to contain the first wave of the COVID-19 pandemic. This drop in GDP reflected decreases in consumer spending, exports, private inventory investment, and residential and non-residential fixed investment, along with declines in state and local government spending, which was partly offset by an increase in federal spending.[1]

The economy rebounded quickly, growing by 33.4 percent and 4.1 percent respectively, in the last two quarters of 2020. This recovery was primarily driven by increases in consumer spending, reopening of businesses, and resumption of various activities that were restricted earlier in the pandemic.[2] The economic recovery continued in 2021, though growth was much higher in the first two quarters of 2021 (6.3 percent and 6.7 percent) than in the third quarter (2.3 percent).[3] This slowdown is partly explained by the emergence of the delta variant along with the disruptions in the global supply chain, shortage of workers, and a decline in pandemic relief money to households, businesses, and local governments. The economic uncertainties continued into 2022, with projected growth rates ranging from about 3–4 percent, as the appearance of the omicron variant and concerns about rising prices constrained the U.S. economy.[4]

The global economy also experienced a strong recovery from the pandemic in 2021, growing by 5.5 percent—the highest rate in 40 years. Most of this growth was driven by growth in large economies, including the United States, China, and the European Union. The recovery was much slower in less developed countries as they have continued to struggle with the inadequacy of vaccines, resurgences of COVID-19, and lack of government economic support measures.[5]

The figures on the growth rate of GDP are often taken to signal the health of an economy. Hence, a wide range of policymakers and media outlets await the announcement of newly published figures on GDP with great anticipation (see Box 4.1).

3 MEASURING GROSS DOMESTIC PRODUCT

The BEA publishes data on the components of GDP, as well as many other variables related to employment, prices, assets, and other topics in the NIPA. (These are easily accessed at www.bea.gov.) To understand these data, you need to understand how aggregate *production*, *spending*, and *income* are related in an economic system.

Imagine a simple economy with no foreign sector, no depreciation, no inventories, and in which all the profits that companies earn end up in the bank accounts of households after being distributed to stockholders. In this case, three quite different measures of counting GDP would in theory all add up to the same number:

144

$$\text{Value of Production} = \text{Value of Spending} = \text{Value of Income}$$

Using a *production approach*, we could sum up the dollar value of all final goods and services produced in each national accounting sector—by the houshold and institutions sector, the business sector, and the government sector.

Using the *spending approach*, we could look at who *buys* the final goods and services that have been produced. Since we assumed that no goods are carried as inventory in this simple economy, everything produced must be bought. Adding the dollar value of spending on all various kinds of goods and services provides a second way of measuring a country's aggregate production.

Lastly, because in this simple economy everyone who is involved in production also receives monetary payment for their contribution to it, we could, alternatively, take an *income approach.* In this approach, we total the compensation received by everyone involved in production, including workers, investors, creditors, and owners of land or equipment rented for productive use.

In this simple economy if, say, $10 billion worth of goods and services are produced, then the amount spent on goods and services must also be $10 billion and the amount of payment received as income must also be $10 billion. Hence, economists sometimes use the terms "production," "income," and "expenditure" interchangeably when dealing with national accounts. While there is a rough equivalence in theory among the product, spending, and income approaches to calculating GDP, making estimates for an actual economy requires a number of conventions and adjustments. We now consider each approach in more detail.

3.1 The Product Approach

The BEA measures the "value" of final goods and services primarily by their *dollar market value.* For example, if the business sector produces 1 million automobiles this year, which are then sold for $20,000 each, this production contributes $20 billion (1 million * $20,000) to GDP. These sales are considered final since the cars are used by consumers rather than in further production of other goods.

Rather than looking at the final sales, however, it is sometimes useful to think about how much each industry contributes to the value of the final good or service. In the **value-added** approach to GDP accounting, you start with the raw materials—say, iron ore—used in producing a good or service—say, an automobile—and then see how much market value is added at each stage in the production process.

---

value-added: the value of what a producer sells, less the value of the intermediate inputs it uses, except labor. This is equal to the wages paid out by the producer plus its profits

145

Suppose a steel manufacturer buys $500 worth of iron ore from a mining company and spends $200 in additional materials including energy and equipment costs to produce steel automobile frames, which it then sells to Ford Motor Company for $1,800 each. The value added by the steel manufacturer is the difference between the selling price of the automobile frame ($1,800) and the total cost of inputs ($500 + $200 = $700). Hence, the value added at this stage in production is $1,100, which becomes either wages to steel workers or profits to the steel manufacturing company. The BEA maintains an extensive set of tables, called Input-Output Accounts, to keep track of the contributions to GDP by various industries in value-added terms.

Adding up all the value-added contributions at each step in the production process still does not give us the final market price of the good. Many goods are taxed when they are produced and sold. Sometimes governments provide production subsidies, making it possible for producers to sell their goods for less than the actual cost of production. In both of these cases, we need to add production taxes and subtract subsidies to get the market price of the good in question. The fact that GDP should be the same no matter whether it is calculated using the value-added approach or adding up the final sales prices serves as a "check" on the validity of data that the BEA collects from different sources.

While finding the market value of goods and services traded in the market may seem fairly straightforward, in practice it is much harder to estimate the market value of some components of GDP. In such cases, the BEA uses the method of **imputation**, which involves making an educated guess, usually based on the value of similar outputs or on the value of inputs used in production.

---

imputation: a procedure in which values are assigned for a category of products, usually using values of related products or inputs

---

For example, the housing stock of a country produces a flow of services—the services of shelter. For housing units that are rented, the market value of the housing services is the rent paid. But for owner-occupied houses, the BEA has to estimate the value of housing services by using data from the rental housing market to impute what owner-occupiers might be said to be "paying in rent" to themselves.

In cases where no similar marketed product exists, the BEA often looks exclusively at the value of inputs. We know, for example, that governments produce goods and services such as highways, parks, public education, and national defense that are rarely sold on markets. In the GDP accounts, the value of government production is estimated by adding up the cost of inputs, which includes wages paid to workers, payments for intermediate goods and services, and an allowance for depreciation of fixed assets. Likewise, the production of nonprofit institutions is measured in large part by looking at their inputs. For example, payroll expenses are an important part of the value of the services produced by nonprofit agencies.

Imputations are also used when data are difficult or impossible to obtain. The BEA relies on a variety of censuses, surveys, government budgets, and tax records to obtain information. This process of gathering data is laborious and expensive. Market transactions that people try to conceal from the government—such as illegal drug deals or work performed "off the books"—hence are usually not accurately represented in the national statistics, and indeed for a long time were not being represented at all. The BEA updates all its estimates periodically, as it receives better data or improves its statistical techniques.

In one significant case, however, the national accounts do not even attempt to impute a value for production: the production of goods and services within households for their own use. While the value of paid work within the household (i.e., work done by hired housekeepers, babysitters, or private gardeners) is included in the GDP value, activities such as child care, cooking, cleaning, or landscaping of a home done without pay by household members—traditionally, mostly by women— are not counted in GDP. This creates an anomaly in the accounts. The work done may be identical, but it is only *paid and counted* if it is a market transaction. If it takes place within what we have defined as the core economy, it is *unpaid and uncounted*. We will discuss this serious shortcoming of GDP accounts in more detail in Chapter 5.

We can summarize the product approach to measuring GDP using the equation[†]:

$$\text{GDP} = \text{Business Production} + \text{Household and institutions production} + \text{Government production}$$

Note that the foreign sector does not contribute to the production of GDP in the above equation. Can you explain why? (Hint: Look back at the definition of GDP.)

Table 4.2 presents the BEA estimate of GDP in 2020 using the product approach, divided into national accounting sectors and subsectors. Not surprisingly, given the conventions and accounting procedures, the BEA attributes a very large share of productive activity to the business

---

† This sort of equation is called an identity or an accounting identity. It holds simply because of the way in which the various terms have been defined. Once we agree on the definitions of terms, then there remains nothing controversial about an identity. When we begin to deal with macroeconomic modeling in Chapter 8 we introduce another kind of equation, called a behavioral equation. A behavioral equation represents an economist's supposition about how an economic actor behaves—and because it may or may not hold well in practice, it can be more controversial.

Table 4.2 *Gross Domestic Product, Product Approach, 2020*

Sector and subsector	Production by sector (trillions of dollars)	Production by subsector (trillions of dollars)
Households and institutions production	2.75	
Private households		1.53
Nonprofit institutions		1.22
Business production	15.67	
Government production	2.47	
Federal government		0.78
State and local governments		1.69
Total: Gross domestic product	20.89	

Source: BEA, NIPA, Table 1.3.5, September 30, 2021.

Note: Totals may not add up exactly due to rounding.

sector. In 2020, the business sector was estimated to have produced goods and services worth over $15 trillion, or about 75 percent of the total GDP of $20.89 trillion. The household and institutions sector and the government sector were each estimated to have contributed about 12 percent.

3.2 The Spending Approach

The spending approach adds up the value of newly produced goods and services bought by the household and institution, business, government, and foreign sectors. The estimated values for these expenditures for 2020 are listed in Table 4.3.

Purchases of goods and services by households and nonprofit institutions serving households are called "personal consumption expenditures" by the BEA. By convention, they are all considered "final" goods and services, even though many of these are used in household and nonprofit production processes.

Business spending on final goods and services is called "gross private domestic investment" by the BEA. This includes business spending on fixed assets including structures, equipment, and software, as well as the value of changes in inventories within that sector. Note that business spending on wages or on materials such as energy and raw materials are not counted here because these are intermediate goods whose values are already included in the value of the final goods and services produced by businesses.

Table 4.3 *Gross Domestic Product, Spending Approach, 2020*

Sector and type of spending	Spending by sector (trillions of dollars)	Spending by type (trillions of dollars)
Household and institutions spending (*personal consumption expenditures*)	14.05	
Durable goods		1.61
Nondurable goods		3.04
Services		9.39
Business spending (gross private domestic investment)	3.64	
Fixed investment		3.69
Change in private inventories		*0.06*
Government spending (government consumption expenditures and gross investment)	3.86	
Federal		1.50
State and Local		2.36
Net foreign sector spending (net exports of goods and services)	*0.65*	
Exports		2.12
Less: Imports		*2.77*
Total: Gross domestic product	20.89	

Source: BEA, NIPA, Table 1.1.5, September 30, 2021.

Note: Totals may not add up exactly due to rounding. The numbers in italics indicate values that are subtracted to arrive at the final GDP measure.

Next, we come to the expenditures made by the government sector. The BEA calls these "government consumption expenditures and gross investment" and breaks them down by whether they are made at the federal level or at the state and local level. These figures represent only spending for final goods and services, so they exclude the parts of government budgets that go for transfers such as Social Security. We can see in Table 4.3 that most government spending on final goods and services actually takes place at the state and local levels.

The simple economy that we discussed when noting how, in concept, "production = spending = income" was a **closed economy**, with no foreign sector. Although sometimes countries isolate themselves from world trade (North Korea being a prime example), for the most part, global economic relations have become increasingly important as advances in transportation and communication have accelerated.

Because the United States is an **open economy**, we need to take into account interactions with the foreign sector.

---

closed economy: an economy with no foreign sector
open economy: an economy with a foreign sector

Some of the goods and services produced inside the United States are bought by entities in the foreign sector. The value of these exported goods must be added to the value of domestic spending in calculating GDP. In addition, some domestic spending is for goods and services produced abroad. Such spending on imported goods is included in the calculations of spending by different domestic sectors shown in Table 4.3. So the value of imported goods and services must be *subtracted* to arrive at a measure of *domestic* production.

The **net exports** category, defined as the difference in the value of exports and imports, measures the overall impact of international trade on GDP.

$$\text{Net exports} = \text{Exports} - \text{Imports}$$

---

net exports: the value of exports less the value of imports

Net exports are positive if exports are higher than imports, and negative if imports are higher than exports. We can see in Table 4.3 that in 2020 the United States imported goods and services worth $0.65 trillion more than the value of the goods and services exported. (In the table, the fact that the value of imports is subtracted rather than added is denoted by putting the number in italics.) Hence U.S. net exports in 2020 were negative.

Based on the spending by different sectors, we can summarize the spending approach with the identity:

$$
\begin{aligned}
\text{GDP} = \ &\text{Personal consumption} \\
&+ \text{Private investment} \\
&+ \text{Government consumption} \\
&+ \text{Government investment} \\
&+ \text{Net exports}
\end{aligned}
$$

3.3 The Income Approach

The income from production activities earned by all people and organizations located inside the United States can be summed up in a measure called **national income (NI)**. The national income includes income earned by workers in the form of wages and benefits, profits made by businesses, rents and interest payments earned by owners of land and capital, as well as income to the government in the form of taxes on production and imports, minus subsidies that the government provides to individuals and businesses. The national income can be summarized by the identity:

$$
\begin{aligned}
\text{National Income} = {} & \text{Wages and Benefits} \\
& + \text{Profits} \\
& + \text{Rents} \\
& + \text{Interest} \\
& + (\text{Production Taxes} - \text{Subsidies})
\end{aligned}
$$

---

national income (NI): a measure of all domestic incomes earned in production

---

Table 4.4 below presents data on income earned by all people and organizations in 2020. We see that workers received a total of $11.5 trillion in wages and benefits, while $3.89 trillion was earned in profits by businesses, $1.49 trillion was earned in rent and interest by owners of land and capital, and the government received about $1.53 trillion in taxes on goods and services while paying out $0.77 trillion in subsidies. The total national income from adding these components was $17.71 trillion.

If this were a simple economy with no foreign sector and no depreciation, the sum of the incomes from production, which is the national income (NI), would exactly equal GDP. But in our more complex economy, three adjustments are needed to reconcile figures on domestic income and domestic production.

First, we need to note that some domestic incomes reflect *foreign* production. For example, the profits of a U.S. company may include earnings from overseas plants. Conversely, the income from some domestic production may be received by foreign residents. A German-owned factory in the United States may send its profits back to its Berlin headquarters, for example. In order to reconcile the NI measure with the figure for GDP, income from foreign production must be subtracted and foreign income from domestic production must be added to NI.

In 2020, as shown in Table 4.4, receipts from the rest of the world exceeded income paid out to foreign residents by about $222 billion. When net income receipts from the rest of the world are added to GDP, the result is a measure called gross national product (GNP) **or gross national income (GNI)**. For many years, GNP was used as the primary measure of U.S. production. It measures a country's production in terms of the output produced *by its workers and companies,* no matter where in the world they were located. The BEA switched its emphasis from GNP to GDP in 1991to track economic activity *within the borders* of the United States. Most other countries and international economic agencies use both GDP and GNI as standard measures.

> **gross national income (GNI):** the total amount of money earned by a nation's people and its businesses.

Table 4.4 *Gross Domestic Product, Income Approach, 2020*

Types of income and adjustments	*Income and adjustments (trillions of dollars)*
Compensation Received by Workers	11.57
Plus: Rent	0.71
Plus: Net Interest and Miscellaneous Payments	0.78
Plus: Profits	3.89
Plus: Taxes	1.53
Less: Subsidies and other adjustments	*0.78*
Total: National income	17.71
Less: Net income receipts from the rest of the world	*0.22*
Plus: Depreciation *(consumption of fixed capital)*	3.58
Statistical discrepancy	*0.17*
Total: Gross domestic product	20.89

Source: BEA, NIPA, Table 1.12, Table 1.7.5, November 24, 2021, and authors' calculations.

Note: Totals may not add up exactly due to rounding. "Miscellaneous payment" includes current transfer payments from businesses to individuals, governments, and foreign countries for insurance settlements, fines, fees, etc. 'Subsidies and other adjustments' includes government subsidies and the current surplus of government enterprises, which is the difference between the government's earnings and their operating expenses. The numbers in italics indicate values that are subtracted to arrive at the final GDP measure.

Second, we need to account for the fact that not all of GDP creates income since some domestic production simply goes into replacing structures, equipment, and software that have worn out or become obsolete. So we must *add* depreciation (what the BEA calls "consumption of fixed capital") to NI to get a number closer to GDP. This is a bit confusing—but it is in effect the reverse of what we did above when we subtracted depreciation from gross investment to get net investment. (In calculating incomes, depreciation is typically deducted from profits.)

The third adjustment in Table 4.4 is what is called the "statistical discrepancy." It reflects the fact that, no matter how diligently the BEA compiles the accounts, it cannot exactly reconcile the results from the income approach with the results from the product and spending approaches.

We can summarize the relationship between national income and GDP by the identity:

GDP = National income − Net income payments from the foreign sector
      +Depreciation

Discussion Questions

1. The previous section explained why a country's "production" and "income" can be thought of as roughly equal in a conceptual sense. Why, in practice, does the value of domestic production actually differ from the total of domestic incomes?

2. Sometimes GDP is defined as "The total *market* value of all final goods and services newly produced in a country over time." Given the above discussion, how true is this definition, really? Does GDP really count only goods and services exchanged *in markets?* Does it really account for *all* production?

4 GROWTH, PRICE CHANGES, AND REAL GDP

Policymakers are interested in not just the level of GDP but the rate at which it is changing. The rate of change in GDP, often referred to as **GDP growth**, shows how fast the economy is expanding or contracting, and it is directly related to living standards, the creation of jobs, and price levels in the economy. But it is important to distinguish between changes in measured GDP resulting merely from price increases, and those resulting from actual changes in production. To do this, economists use the concepts of nominal and real GDP, based on the calculation of a price index.

GDP growth: rate of change in GDP showing how fast the economy is expanding or contracting

---

4.1 Nominal vs. Real GDP

The measure of GDP discussed in the previous section is **nominal or current-dollar GDP**, or GDP expressed in terms of the prices of goods and services that were current at the time.

---

nominal (current dollar) GDP: the dollar value of all final goods and services produced in a year in that year's prices

---

In 2020 the nominal GDP in the United States was 20,893 billion dollars, more than three times its value of 5,963 billion dollars in 1990. Does this mean that the production level in the United States increased by three times in 30 years? No, since we know that some of the increase in the value of nominal GDP comes from inflation: the increase in the prices at which output is valued. To understand growth in GDP, it is important to be able to separate price changes from actual changes in production.

For example, suppose a very simple economy produces only two goods, apples and oranges, as shown in Table 4.5. Column (2) shows the price of each good in each year, while Column (3) gives the quantity of production, measured in pounds. Nominal GDP is the sum of the dollar values of the goods produced in a year, evaluated at the prices in that same year:

Nominal GDP = Total production valued at current prices

As we can see in Table 4.5, in Year 1 the value of nominal GDP is $200. In Year 2, the value of nominal GDP is $300. So, nominal GDP increased by $100 between Year 1 and Year 2. But only part of the change in nominal GDP is due to an increase in production: The quantity of oranges produced rises from 50 pounds to 75 pounds from Year 1 to Year 2, increasing nominal GDP by $50 (since the price of oranges remained constant at $2.00). The rest of the increase in nominal GDP is due to an increase in the *price* of apples, from $1.00 to $1.50. Note that the quantity of apples produced has not changed.

Hence, in order to measure the change in production level from year to year we need to eliminate the effect of price changes. This is done by constructing **real GDP**—a measure of the actual value of goods and services produced, by removing the effect of changes in prices.

---

real GDP: a measure of gross domestic product that seeks to reflect the actual value of goods and services produced, by removing the effect of changes in prices over time

---

154

Table 4.5 *Calculation of Nominal GDP in an "Apples-and-Oranges" Economy*

(1)	(2)	(3)	(4)
Description	*Price per pound ($)*	*Quantity (pounds)*	*Contribution to nominal GDP [column (2) × column (3)] ($)*
Year 1			
Apples	$1.00	100	$100
Oranges	$2.00	50	$100
			$200
Year 2			
Apples	$1.50	100	$150
Oranges	$2.00	75	$150
			$300

4.2 Calculating Real GDP

A relatively simple way of calculating real GDP is called the "constant-dollar method." This method uses prices from one particular year, called the **base year**, to calculate the value of production in all years. Constant-dollar real GDP is calculated by doing the same sort of multiplying and summing exercise as shown in Table 4.5, but using the base year prices for all years:

Constant-Dollar Real GDP = Total production valued at base year prices

---

base year (in the constant-dollar method of estimating GDP): the year whose prices are chosen for evaluating production in all years

---

Let us consider Year 1 as the base year and apply the constant-dollar method to calculate the real GDP for our simple "apples-and-oranges" example for both Year 1 and Year 2. Calculations of constant-dollar real GDP for each year are shown in Table 4.6. While the quantities in Column (3) are the same as in Table 4.5, the prices in Column (2) are *all from Year 1*, the base year. GDP in Year 2 expressed in "constant (Year 1) dollars" is the sum of quantities in Year 2 multiplied by prices in Year 1. This comes out to be $250. So the change in real GDP between Year 1 and Year 2 is $50, significantly less than the change in nominal GDP of $100 shown in Table 4.5.

Table 4.6 *Calculation of Constant-Dollar Real GDP*

(1)	*(2)*	*(3)*	*(4)*
Description	*Price per pound in base year ($)*	*Quantity (pounds)*	*Contribution to real GDP [column (2) × column (3)] ($)*
Year 1 (Base)			
Apples	**$1.00**	100	$100
Oranges	**$2.00**	50	$100
			$200
Year 2			
Apples	**$1.00**	100	$100
Oranges	**$2.00**	75	$150
			$250

Bold type indicates base year prices

We can also calculate these changes in percentage terms using the standard percentage change formula. For something that takes one value in year 1 (Value$_1$) and another value in year 2 (Value$_2$), this is:

$$\text{percentage change} = \frac{\text{value}_2 - \text{value}_1}{\text{value}_1} \times 100$$

Thus, in percentage terms, real GDP has increased by:

$$[(250 - 200) / 200] \times 100 = [50 / 200] \times 100 = 25\%$$

while nominal GDP increased by:

$$[(300 - 200) / 200] \times 100 = [100 / 200] \times 100 = 50\%$$

The use of a real GDP measure thus allows us to separate out the part of nominal GDP growth that comes from price increases from the part that comes from real production increases.

The convention of using "constant dollars," however, has a number of problems. Its main weakness is that the rate of change in real GDP is dependent on the year chosen as the base. For example, suppose we decide to use Year 2 as the base year in our "apples-and-oranges" economy. Then we would apply Year 2 prices—$1.50 for apples, $2.00 for oranges—to calculate the real GDP for both years. Real GDP now works out at $250 for Year 1 and $300 for Year 2 (you can check this by making a table similar to Table 4.6 but using Year 2 prices). Using the percentage formula, the percentage increase in real GDP between Year 1 and Year 2 is:

$$[(300 - 250) / 250] \times 100 = [50 / 250] \times 100 = 20\%$$

rather than the 25 percent increase that we obtained using Year 1 as the base year.

The constant-dollar method also suffers from various other biases, which become more important the more dissimilar relative prices and spending patterns are between the base year and a current year. Thus it becomes more unreliable over time, as prices and spending patterns change more and more. To provide a more stable way of measuring real economic growth, the BEA calculates real GDP using the "chained-dollar" method. The concept behind this measure is still the same—real GDP should measure output changes free of the influence of price changes. Although there is still one year for which real and nominal GDP are equal, it is now called the "reference year," and real GDP is currently expressed in BEA publications in terms of "chained (2012) dollars." An advantage of the chained-dollar method is that, unlike the constant-dollar method, it yields a unique growth rate. But the chained-dollar method requires a steep jump in computational complexity. A detailed explanation of the chained-dollar method is provided in the Appendix to this chapter.

In Figure 4.1 you can see how measures of real and nominal GDP diverge. Because prices were generally rising over the period 1980–2020, nominal GDP grew faster than real GDP, as shown by the more steeply rising line. But if we are interested in knowing how fast the economy was actually expanding in terms of production, the real GDP line gives

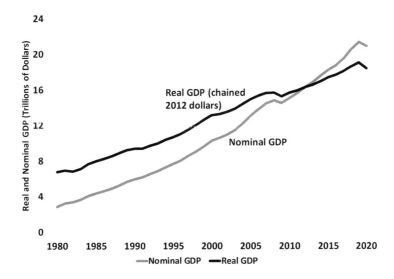

Figure 4.1 *Real versus Nominal GDP, Chained 2012 Dollars, 1980–2020*
Source: BEA NIPA Tables 1.1.5 and 1.1.6, published 09/30/2021.

a more accurate picture. Note that the reference year in Figure 4.1 is 2012; thus real and nominal GDP are the same in that year.

4.3 Price Indexes and Inflation Rates

Price indexes are interesting both for how they relate to the calculation of real GDP and on their own because of their relevance to the issue of measuring (and controlling) inflation. An **index number** measures the change in a given magnitude, in this case, the price level, compared to another period. Generally, the value of the index number in the reference or base year is set at 100, though sometimes other values (such as 1 or 10) are used.

> **index number:** a figure that measures the change in magnitude of a variable, such as a quantity or a price, compared to another period

Economists mainly look at two *price indexes*: the GDP deflator and the Consumer Price Index (CPI). The GDP deflator is derived from the measurement of GDP, and it estimates the average price of all goods and services produced in an economy. The CPI, on the other hand, is a measure of the average price of goods and services purchased by consumers.

4.3.1 GDP Deflator

We have discussed how changes in nominal GDP can come both from changes in production levels and from changes in prices. If prices are rising, nominal GDP increases faster than real GDP, and if prices are falling, real GDP rises faster than nominal GDP. Hence, in order to get from nominal GDP to real GDP, we need to adjust nominal GDP by a measure based on the change in prices. A **GDP deflator** is a price index that is used to make this adjustment. For a specific year, the GDP deflator is the ratio of nominal GDP to the real GDP in that year.

$$\text{GDP deflator} = \frac{\text{Nominal GDP}}{\text{Real GDP}}$$

> **GDP deflator:** price index for measuring the general level of prices and defined as the ratio of nominal GDP to real GDP

Note that the GDP deflator provides a simple way of calculating the real GDP from the nominal GDP. The GDP deflator is an index, and its level is based on the reference year chosen to look at relative prices. The GDP deflator for the reference year when the nominal and real GDPs are equal is 1.

The rate at which GDP deflator changes shows the movement of price levels in the economy, in general. To measure the rate of change in prices, we look at the percentage change in GDP deflator from year to year, using the percentage change formula from the previous section. So the rate of change in price between two years, referred to as the inflation rate when prices rise and deflation rate when prices fall, is given by:

$$\frac{\text{GDP deflator}_{\text{Year 2}} - \text{GDP deflator}_{\text{Year 1}}}{\text{GDP deflator}_{\text{Year 1}}} \times 100$$

For example, between 2019 and 2020, the value of the GDP deflator increased from 1.12 to 1.14. The inflation rate can thus be calculated as:

$$\frac{1.14 - 1.12}{1.12} \times 100\% = 1.78\%$$

4.3.2 Consumer Price Index (CPI)

The price index most often reported in the news is the **consumer price index (CPI)**, calculated by the U.S. Bureau of Labor Statistics (BLS). The CPI measures changes in the prices of goods and services bought by households.

---

consumer price index (CPI): an index measuring changes in the prices of goods and services bought by households

---

Calculating price increases is not quite so straightforward as it might seem at first sight. For example, in Table 4.5 the price of apples increased from $1.00 per pound to $1.50 per pound—an increase of 50 percent. As we noted earlier, the price of oranges did not change between the two years. So how do we calculate the overall price change in our two-good economy? We cannot just average the two price changes because changes in some prices are more significant to consumers than others. Consumers may purchase more of certain products (such as loaves of bread) or may spend a large portion of their incomes on something (such as rent), so prices for these items are more important to them than items on which they typically spend less.

159

Thus, the CPI is calculated using a *weighted average* of the prices of the various goods and services that it tracks. A "weighted average" is an average in which the different numbers being averaged together are "weighted" to indicate their relative importance in the calculation. An example is the calculation of a student's Grade Point Average. Each grade received for a course is "weighted" by the number of credits (or hours) the course is worth. These weighted grade points are added up and then divided by the total number of credits or hours to yield the student's GPA. An "A" received for a two-credit course thus receives less emphasis in the calculation than an "A" received for a four-credit course.

Similarly, in measuring price levels in the economy, we want to give greater emphasis to prices for goods and services that affect consumers the most and less emphasis on the prices of relatively minor goods and services. The way to do this is to weigh each price by the corresponding quantity that is sold at that price.

Once again, however, we face choices about which standards to use. Should we use as weights the quantities bought in Year 1, Year 2, or some combination? Until recently, the BLS used a *constant-weight method* to calculate the CPI. Quantities bought during one period are chosen as the "base." These quantities are said to represent a typical "market basket" of goods bought by households. A constant-weight price index is calculated according to the following formula:

$$\text{Constant Weight Price Index} = \frac{\text{sum of current prices weighted by base quantities}}{\text{sum of base prices weighted by base quantities}} \times 100$$

The price-index problem is analogous to the calculation of "constant-dollar" GDP—only now it is a common set of *quantity weights*, rather than prices, from the base period that is applied to every calculation.

Consider, again, our "apples-and-oranges" economy. Table 4.7 shows how we would calculate the numerator and denominator for the constant-weight price index formula, considering Year 2 the current year and using the Year 1 "market basket" as the base. The sum of current (Year 2) prices weighted by base quantities is $250, while the sum of base prices weighted by base quantities is $200. The CPI for Year 2 is therefore calculated as $(250 \div 200) \times 100 = 125$. The price index for the base year (here, Year 1) always equals 100.

The growth rate of prices—that is, the inflation rate affecting consumers—is measured by the growth rate of this price index:

$$\text{Inflation rate} = \frac{\text{CPI}_2 - \text{CPI}_1}{\text{CPI}_1} \times 100$$

Table 4.7 *Calculation of a Constant-Weight Price Index*

(1)	(2)	(3)	(4)
Description	Price per pound ($)	Quantity in base year	Sum of (prices × base quantities) [column (2) × column (3)] ($)
Year 1 (Base)			
Apples	$1.00	100	$100
Oranges	$2.00	50	$100
Year 2			$200
Apples	$1.50	100	$150
Oranges	$2.00	50	$100
			$250

Bold type indicates base year quantities.

So, in this case, with the price index rising from 100 to 125, the inflation rate is 25 percent.

Unfortunately, when a price index is based on constant weights, it may tend to overstate inflation for periods after the base year. When the price of a good is rising particularly quickly relative to other goods, people tend to look for cheaper substitutes. But a constant-weight index assumes that people are still buying the same quantities of expensive goods. Various innovations have recently been made in the CPI to attempt to get around this problem. Currently, the "market basket" is updated periodically using data from ongoing household expenditure surveys (see Box 4.2). The BLS now also publishes "chained" price indexes. The mathematics of these more advanced calculations will not

---

BOX 4.2 HOW QUANTITY WEIGHTS CAN LOSE VALIDITY OVER TIME

Why do economists and statisticians make a fuss about updating the quantity weights used in calculating the Consumer Price Index? Consider how household expenditure patterns have changed over time.

In 1901, nearly half the budget of a typical urban, working family went toward food, while 15 percent went toward shelter and an equal proportion toward clothing. The family probably spent nothing at all on cars or gasoline—because automobiles were not yet in wide use.

By 1950, the picture had changed considerably. Now only a third of the family's spending was on food, while only 11 percent was on shelter and 12 percent on clothing. On average, families were now spending about 12 percent of their budget on expenses related to private vehicles.[6]

In recent data on consumer expenditures, the share devoted to food has dropped even further—to 11.9 percent (possibly the lowest the world has ever seen). Expenditures on clothing have dropped to less than 3 percent of a household's budget, on average. Meanwhile, families are spending more on shelter (about 35 percent of their budget) and private vehicle expenses (16 percent of their budget), than they were in the mid-twentieth century.[7]

Using expenditure patterns from one of these periods to "weight" the CPI in another would clearly result in biased figures. Using the 1901 expenditure pattern nowadays, for example, would mean that auto and gasoline prices would not figure into the CPI at all. The invention of new goods and services (e.g., electric cars and smartphones) and quality improvements in existing goods (e.g., products for home entertainment and computing) continue to create special challenges for the economists working to measure price changes.

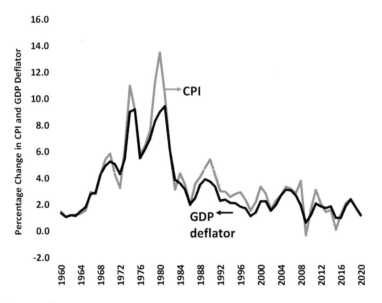

Figure 4.2 *Rate of Change in GDP Deflator vs. CPI, 1960–2020*
Source: BEA NIPA Tables 1.1.4 and BLS Table on CPI-All urban consumers.

be presented here but is similar to the method for calculating chained-dollar real GDP presented in the Appendix to this chapter.

Note that while the CPI is based on the average price of goods and services purchased by consumers, the GDP deflator gives the average price of output produced in a country. The values of the two indices are different since the set of goods produced is not the same as the set of goods consumed. For example, some of the consumption goods may be imported and some goods produced may be exported. Also, some of the goods produced may be bought by firms or the government and may not be counted as consumption. In most cases, however, the two price indices move together, as illustrated by Figure 4.2. The sharp deviation of CPI from the GDP deflator in the 1970s is explained by the rise in the price of oil, much of which was imported and hence not captured by the GDP deflator.

In addition to the GDP deflator and CPI, sometimes other price indices are used. The producer price index (PPI) measures prices that domestic producers receive for their output and it tracks many intermediate goods not included in the CPI market basket. Import and export price indexes track prices of goods traded between domestic residents and the foreign sector. Because they track different goods, these indexes—and inflation rates calculated from them— may vary.

4.4 Calculating GDP Growth Rates

So far, we have concentrated on calculating GDP in only one year. To calculate rates of economic growth, we must look at how GDP changes over time. We can use real GDP to calculate growth rates in order to estimate the change in production level while eliminating the impact of price changes.

The percentage change in real GDP from year to year can be calculated using the standard percentage-change formula. To compute the growth rate of GDP from, say, 2019 to 2020, we calculate:

$$\text{growth rate of GDP} = \frac{\text{real GDP}_{2020} - \text{real GDP}_{2019}}{\text{real GDP}_{2019}} \times 100$$

The real GDP values in the U.S. in 2019 and 2020 were estimated at \$19.03 trillion and \$18.38 trillion, respectively. Hence, the rate of growth of GDP in 2020 is given by:

$$\text{growth rate of GDP} = \frac{18.38 - 19.03}{19.03} \times 100 = -0.034 \times 100 = -3.4\%$$

The BEA commonly reports the GDP growth rates for quarters, expressed in terms of an "annual growth rate"— a measure of how much the economy would grow if it were to continue to expand for the entire year at the speed reported for the three-month period.

We have calculated year-to-year growth rates for GDP and prices. But how do we calculate GDP growth over the past five years or twenty years? The answer to this is rather complicated, but fortunately, you can use BEA's published NIPA tables to answer such questions. A simple (though less precise) way to get a grasp on the relation of annual growth rates to changes over a longer period is by using **the rule of 72**. Taking $72/x$, where x equals the annual growth rate, will give you

---

rule of 72: a shorthand calculation that states that dividing 72 by an annual growth rate yields approximately the number of years it will take for an amount to double

approximately the number of years it will take for an amount to double if it grows at that constant rate (as long as the numbers you are using are not extremely high or low). For example, if real GDP grew at a constant 4 percent rate per year, it would double in about eighteen years (since 72/4 = 18).

Discussion Questions

1. The "constant-dollar" method of estimating real GDP uses prices for one year to calculate measures of GDP for all years. Why is it sometimes important to evaluate GDP in the current year using prices from some other year? Why can't we just always use current prices? Explain.
2. Why are there different ways of measuring inflation? Which indicator would be best for measuring the impact of inflation on people's daily lives?

5 SAVINGS AND INVESTMENT

At a personal level, you produce goods and services, earn income, consume, save, and borrow or lend. One of the reasons that you keep personal accounts might be to try to track your inflows and outflows so that you know whether you are depleting your personal assets or accumulating them. If you can save money out of your current income, you are improving your financial position for the future. However, if you spend down your savings or go into debt to finance a high level of consumption, you may find yourself in trouble later on. Spending down financial savings or taking on debt can be a good choice for your future only if you use the funds to gain another valuable asset. For example, students often go into debt in order to finance their education with the idea that it will pay off later by enabling them to earn a higher income than would have been possible otherwise.

There are analogous issues at the national level. Besides keeping track of economic growth and inflation, systems of national accounting serve another important purpose. They allow us to look at the savings-and-assets situation of a national economy as a whole (at least as far as manufactured assets and financial flows are concerned).

The investment concept used in defining *gross* domestic product (GDP) is *gross* investment. To calculate what the level of production is during a year, above and beyond the production that simply replaces worn-out manufactured capital, we need another concept, **net domestic product (NDP)**. NDP is GDP less depreciation (just as net investment, we saw earlier, is gross investment less depreciation):

$$\text{Net domestic product} = \text{GDP} - \text{Depreciation}$$

164

> **net domestic product (NDP):** a measure of national production in excess of that needed to replace worn-out manufactured capital, calculated by subtracting depreciation from GDP

Similarly, we can differentiate between gross saving and net saving. To really find out the extent to which we have "put something aside for the future," we would subtract depreciation from our gross measure of saving. For example, even if our savings were positive, if they did not finance enough investment to make up for the deterioration of capital stock, we would actually start the next year in a *worse* position. Net saving is thus gross saving minus depreciation.

$$\text{Net saving} = (\text{Gross})\text{Saving} - \text{Depreciation}$$

How much has the United States been "putting aside for the future" lately? According to BEA data, gross savings in the United States were $4.01 trillion in 2020. But since fixed capital depreciation in 2020 was $3.58 trillion, net savings was only about 427 billion. Net savings in the United States were negative between 2008 and 2010, due to a decline in new investments during the recession. Compared to other countries, the United States has had relatively low savings rates for many years. (See Figure 0.3 in Chapter 0 for comparing net national savings across countries).

Discussion Questions

1. Which do you think is a better measure of the true productive capacity of a country, GDP or NDP? What about gross saving versus net saving as a measure of whether a country is well-placed for future production?
2. Do you think it is a problem that the United States has a relatively low savings rate? What might be done to raise this rate, by individuals, corporations, or the government?

REVIEW QUESTIONS

1. For what purpose was national accounting in the United States originally begun?
2. Who compiles the National Income and Product Accounts?
3. What are the four accounting sectors of the economy, according to the BEA? What sorts of entities are included in each sector?
4. What forms of capital assets are tracked by the BEA?
5. Explain the difference between gross investment and net investment.
6. Explain four key phrases that appear in the definition of GDP.
7. What are the three approaches to GDP measurement?
8. Explain why, in a simple economy, the three approaches to GDP measurement would

yield the same figure.

9. Explain why the following two approaches arrive at the same number for the value of a final good: (a) looking at the market price of the good and (b) counting up the value-added at each stage of its production.

10. How are "market values" determined for goods and services that are not exchanged in markets or when data is not available?

11. Describe the components of GDP according to the product approach.

12. Describe the components of GDP according to the spending approach.

13. Describe the components of national income and explain the major differences between GDP and national income.

14. Describe the reasoning behind the "constant-dollar" approach to calculating real GDP.

15. What are some problems with the "constant-dollar" approach to calculating real GDP?

16. Describe the reasoning behind the "constant-weight" method traditionally used in estimating the price indexes.

17. Define GDP deflator and Consumer Price Index. What are some of the key differences between the two price indices?

18. Why is it important to have a concept of Net Domestic Product (NDP)? How does it differ from GDP?

EXERCISES

1. In which line (or lines) of Table 4.2 (the product approach) would the value of each of the following be counted? "Not counted in any category" is also an option.
   a) Production of fresh apples, domestically grown for profitable sale
   b) State health inspection services
   c) Education services provided by a private, nonprofit domestic college
   d) Child-care services provided by a child's parents and relatives
   e) Production by a U.S.-owned company at its factory in Singapore

2. In which line (or lines) of Table 4.4 (the income approach) would the value of each of the following be counted? If it is part of "net income flows from the rest of the world," explain whether it reflects domestic (or foreign) production and whether it reflects domestic (or foreign) income. "Not counted in any category" is also an option.
   a) Wages paid by your local supermarket to its employees
   b) Profits received by a U.S. electronics firm from its factory in Mexico
   c) Business spending to replace worn-out equipment
   d) Wages paid by a U.S. electronics firm to the employees of its factory in Mexico
   e) Profits received by a Japanese automaker from its factory in the United States

3. In which line (or lines) of Table 4.3 (the spending approach) would the value of each of the following be counted? "Not counted in any category" is also an option.
   a) A new refrigerator bought by a family
   b) A book newly produced in Indiana and bought by a store in Mexico
   c) New computers, manufactured in Asia, bought by a U.S. accounting company
   d) Meals produced and served in Virginia to military personnel
   e) New computers, produced in the United States, bought by a U.S. computer retail chain and not yet sold by the end of the year
   f) A three-year-old couch bought by a used furniture store in Arizona
   g) Cleaning services bought by a nonprofit hospital in New York
   h) The services of volunteers in an environmental action campaign

4. Using the relations among accounting categories demonstrated in the tables and identities in the text, use the information on values in the chart below (measured in

Neverlandian pesos) from the country of Neverland in 2020 to find values for the following categories:

Household and institutions spending = 650	Business spending = 50
Household and institutions production = 150	Exports = 225
Net income payments from the rest of the world = 5	Imports = 125
Nonprofit institutions production = 50	Government production = 200
State and local government spending = 30	Statistical discrepancy = 0
Change in private inventories = 2	GDP = 850
Depreciation = 60	

a) Private household production
b) Business production
c) Fixed investment spending (by business)
d) Federal government spending
e) National income

5. Suppose an extremely simple economy produces only two goods, pillows, and rugs. In the first year, 50 pillows are produced and sold at $5 each; 11 rugs are produced and sold at $50 each. In the second year, 56 pillows are produced and sold for $5 each; 12 rugs are produced and sold at $60 each.
   a) What is nominal GDP in each of the two years?
   b) What is real GDP in each year, expressed in terms of constant Year 1 dollars?
   c) What is the growth rate of real GDP (in constant Year 1 dollars)?
   d) What is the growth rate of real GDP (in constant Year 2 dollars)?
   e) Are the growth rates calculated in parts (c) and (d) above same or different? Explain why.
6. Complete the following table.

Year	Nominal GDP (in billions of dollars)	Real GDP (in billions of chained 2009 dollars)	GDP deflator	GDP growth rate (%)
2012	16,155.3	15,354.6		2.2
2013		15,612.2	1.07	
2014	17,427.6			2.6

7. Assume the same simple economy described in question 6.
   a) Calculate a constant-weight price index for the second year, using the first year as the base.
   b) What is the growth rate of prices (inflation rate) from the first to the second year?
8. List the key simplifying assumptions of the traditional macro model concerning:
   a) The forms of capital included in the model
   b) The sectors of the economy
9. Go to the Bureau of Economic Analysis Web site (www.bea.gov). What are the latest figures for real GDP, current dollar GDP, and the growth rate of GDP? What time period do these represent? In what sort of dollars is real GDP expressed?

10. Match each concept in Column A with a definition or example in Column B:

Column A	Column B
a. A negative (subtracted) item in GDP	1. The year in which real and nominal values are equal
b. A constant-weight price index	2. Purchases of computer software
c. An imputed value	3. GDP deflator
d. An entity in the government sector	4. Unpaid household production
e. Reflects the prices of all goods and services counted in GDP	5. A state university
f. Base year	6. Wages
g. Part of business investment (gross private domestic investment)	7. Spending on imported cheese
h. Something not counted in by the BEA in calculating GDP	8. A measure that seeks to remove the effects of price changes
i. Real GDP	9. Uses a fixed "market basket"
j. A component of the "income approach" to GDP accounting	10. What homeowners "pay" themselves in rent

11. Go to the Bureau of Labor Statistics Web site (www.bls.gov) and locate its information on the Consumer Price Index for All Urban Consumers (called the "CPI-U"). What is its current value? What month is this for? How does its value in this month compare to its value for the same month a year ago? (That is, by what percentage has the index risen? Use the "seasonally adjusted" number.)
12. (If Appendix is assigned.) The "chained Year 1 dollar" estimate of real GDP in the apples-and-oranges example (see Appendix) is smaller than the "constant Year 1 dollar" estimate of real GDP. Can you explain why? (Hint: Compare the GDP growth rates derived using the two methods.)

APPENDIX: CHAINED DOLLAR REAL GDP

The key new concept in the "chained-dollar" method is an emphasis on estimating **quantity indexes** for GDP in the current year relative to the year before and relative to the reference year.

> **quantity index:** an index measuring changes in levels of quantities produced

Chained-dollar measures of real GDP and GDP growth are based on the use of index numbers. The ratio of two values of GDP in adjacent years, measured at a common set of prices, can be used as a quantity index to measure production in one year relative to another.

The calculation of chained-dollar real GDP starts with the calculation of a **Fisher quantity index**, which measures production in one year relative to an adjacent year by using an *average* of the ratios that would be found by using the first one year and then the other as the source of prices at which production is valued. The type of average used is a "geometric" average. Instead of adding two numbers and then dividing by two, as you would in calculating the most common type of average (the arithmetic mean), to get a geometric average you *multiply* the two numbers together and then take the *square root*. The formula for this Fisher quantity index is:

Fisher quantity index (for year-to-year comparison)

$$= \sqrt{\left(\frac{\text{Year 2 GDP in Year 1 prices}}{\text{Year 1 GDP in Year 1 prices}} \right) \times \left(\frac{\text{Year 2 GDP in Year 2 prices}}{\text{Year 1 GDP in Year 2 prices}} \right)}$$

> **Fisher quantity index:** an index that measures production in one year relative to an adjacent year by using an average of the ratios that would be found by using first one year and then the other as the source of prices at which production is valued

This index has a value of 1 in the reference year, which we take to be Year 1.

The growth rate of real GDP between the reference year and the next year can then be calculated as:

$$\text{growth rate} = \left(\text{Fisher quantity index} - 1 \right) \times 100$$

For example, we have already made many of the necessary calculations for the "apples-and-oranges" economy in Tables 4.5 and 4.6. Plugging these in, we get

Fisher quantity index (for Year 2 compared to Year 1)

$$= \sqrt{\left(\frac{250}{200} \right) \times \left(\frac{300}{250} \right)} = \sqrt{1.25 \times 1.20} = \sqrt{1.5} = 1.225$$

The growth rate of real GDP for the "apples-and-oranges" economy between these two years is

$$\text{growth rate} = \left(1.225 - 1 \right) \times 100 = 22.5 \text{ percent}$$

Note that this growth rate is *between* the two growth rates (20 percent and 25 percent) we obtained by using the constant-dollar method with various base years. The Fisher quantity index method gives us a unique *average* number for estimated growth.

169

A quantity index for the current year in terms of a reference year that may be several years in the past is created by "chaining together" year-to-year Fisher quantity indexes to make a **chain-type quantity index** comparing real production relative to the reference year. The chain-type quantity index has a value of 100 in the reference year. In any subsequent year, it is set equal to the chain-type quantity index from the previous year multiplied by the Fisher quantity index calculated for the current year.

> **chain-type quantity index:** an index comparing real production in the current year to the reference year, calculated using a series of year-to-year Fisher quantity indexes

Finally, the estimation of real GDP in (chained) dollar terms is made by multiplying the chain-type quantity index for a year times the level of nominal GDP in the reference year and dividing by 100.

For example, suppose that we take our "apples-and-oranges" economy, making Year 1 the reference year. Year 1's chain-type quantity index is thus set equal to 100, and its nominal and real GDP are equal. These are shown in Table 4.8. The chain-type quantity index for Year 2 is the previous year's value (100) times the Fisher quantity index that we just calculated (1.225). We multiply this result, the new index number 122.5 times the nominal GDP in the base year ($200), and divide by 100 to get the real GDP, $245. Whew!

This can be continued for many years into the future—or into the past. (For example, if the Fisher quantity index calculated for Year 3 were to come out to be 1.152, then the chain-type quantity index for Year 3 would be 122.5 × 1.152.) If you want to check to see that this method actually makes some sense, calculate the percentage change in real GDP from Year 1 to Year 2 using the values in the table above. You will find it does, in fact, equal 22.5 percent!

Table 4.8 *Deriving Real GDP in Chained (Year 1) Dollars*

Type of measure	Year 1	Year 2
Nominal GDP	$200	$300
Fisher quantity index (current to previous year)	—	1.225
Chain-type quantity index	100	100 × 1.225 = 122.5
Real GDP (chained Year 1 dollars)	= $200	(122.5 × $200)/100 = $245

The new method has some other drawbacks, as well. The sum of real components of GDP in chained-dollar terms does not generally exactly add up to real GDP. Users of the data are also warned not to make comparisons of chained dollar amounts for years far away from the reference year. The BEA tries to make the data more usable by providing tables in which, for example, year-to-year growth rates in components of GDP are already calculated for the user.

NOTES

1   BEA, 2020.
2   BEA, 2021a.
3   BEA, 2021b.
4   See, for example, estimates from different organizations as discussed in Smart, 2022; Caldwell, 2022; and Kennedy 2021.
5   The World Bank, 2021.
6   Data based on Jacobs and Shipp, 1990.
7   BLS, 2020. Table B.

REFERENCES

Caldwell, Preston. 2022. "2022 Economic Outlook: Recovery Far From Finished." *MorningStar*, January 4.

Jacobs, Eva and Stephanie Shipp. 1990. "How Family Spending Has Changed in the U.S." *Monthly Labor Review*, pp. 20–27, March.

Kennedy, Simon. 2021. "Goldman Cuts U.S. GDP Forecast with Omicron a Drag on Growth." *Bloomberg*, December 4.

Smart, Tim. 2022. "Leading Indicators Suggest Economy Will Keep Growing." *U.S. News*, January 21.

The World Bank. 2021. "The Global Economy: On Track for Strong but Uneven Growth as COVID-19 Still Weighs." June 8.

The World Bank. 2022. "Global Growth to Slow Through 2023, Adding to Risk of 'Hard Landing' in Developing Economies." January 11.

U.S. Bureau of Economic Analysis (BEA). 2017. "Concepts and Methods in the U.S. National Income and Products Account." https://www.bea.gov/sites/default/files/methodologies/nipa-handbook-all-chapters.pdf

U.S. Bureau of Economic Analysis (BEA). 2020. "Gross Domestic Product, 2nd Quarter 2020 (Second Estimate); Corporate Profits, 2nd Quarter 2020 (Preliminary Estimates." August.

U.S. Bureau of Economic Analysis (BEA). 2021a. "Gross Domestic Product (Third Estimate), Corporate Profits, and GDP by Industry, Fourth Quarter and year 2020." March 25.

U.S. Bureau of Economic Analysis (BEA). 2021b. "Gross Domestic Product (Third Estimate), Corporate Profits (Revised Estimate), and GDP by Industry, Third Quarter 2021." December 22.

U.S. Bureau of Labor Statistics (BLS). 2020. "Consumer Expenditures—2020." *Economic News Release*. https://www.bls.gov/news.release/cesan.nr0.htm.

Chapter 5

Macroeconomic Measurement: Environmental and Social Dimensions

In the 80-plus years since the introduction of national income accounting in major industrial countries, GDP has become the official barometer of living standards and business cycles. It appears in newspapers and political debates as an indicator of economic, political, and social progress and it is widely used in formulating national and international policies.

Although GDP numbers are widely used as a proxy for national success, it was never intended to play such a role. Economists dating back to Simon Kuznets, the originator of U.S. national accounting systems, have warned that GDP is a specialized tool for measuring market activity, which should not be confused with national well-being. National well-being is affected by social and environmental factors, such as inequality, political participation, security, quality of healthcare and education, and access to clean air and water, which are no less important than marketed economic activity. In order to measure economic well-being more accurately, national governments need to create new indicators that account for these factors. The metrics used to measure well-being have important implications for designing and assessing economic policies, going beyond a focus only on GDP as an economic goal.

Before we discuss specific options for adjusting, replacing, or supplementing GDP, we need to ask three important questions:

1. *What should we measure?* GDP measures only economic production. Are there some things that GDP excludes that should be included as a component of well-being, such as health outcomes or environmental quality? Should some parts of GDP be excluded because they actually harm well-being?
2. *What should be used as the unit of measurement?* GDP is measured in dollars, but what units should be used to measure other variables affecting well-being, such as education, health, levels of crime, or environmental quality?
3. *Should we seek to combine disparate well-being indicators into a single "bottom-line" number, or should we keep the variables disaggregated*

172

DOI: 10.4324/9781003251521-8

(i.e., split up into component categories)? One tempting approach is to convert all variables to dollars to allow for comparability. But what techniques can we use to measure variables such as environmental quality or social capital in dollars, and should we even try?

This chapter presents some alternatives to national accounting that address these questions and reflect our growing awareness of the importance of social and environmental contexts of economic activity. We begin by listing some of the limitations of GDP as a measure of well-being, and then discuss how the alternative indicators attempt to tackle these limitations.

1 WHY GDP IS NOT A MEASURE OF WELL-BEING

GDP was never intended to measure welfare or well-being. As suggested in Box 5.1, GDP often rises with increases in things that most people would want to have less of, while it often fails to rise with positive contributions to individual and social well-being that are not bought and sold in markets. Even if increases in GDP contribute to increasing well-being, *ceteris paribus*, many other factors, such as inequality levels, environmental quality, and work-life balance, may be equally or more important in determining well-being levels. Thus, if we rely only on GDP to measure well-being, we may obtain policy prescriptions that focus only on the money value of output, with too little attention to questions of what is being produced and how it affects human well-being.

BOX 5.1 THERE'S NO G-D-P IN "A BETTER ECONOMY"

The United States is the largest economy in the world, ranked by total GDP. In terms of GDP per capita, it ranks high but falls below some other countries such as Luxembourg, Norway, Ireland, and Switzerland.[1] But how significant is this measure?

Gross domestic product has become the most watched and most misinterpreted of all economic indicators. It's a measure of economic activity—of money changing hands. Despite the mundane nature of this economic indicator, politicians fiercely compete with each other to see who can promise the fastest GDP growth. Government programs and investments in technology get the green light only when they are predicted to spur GDP growth. Economists, bankers, and businesspeople pop the champagne corks when they hear 'good news' about quarterly GDP numbers.

And while the United States leads in GDP, it also leads in military spending and the number of people in prison. These other first-place finishes seem at odds with America's position atop the GDP standings—that is, until you realize that spending on war, incarceration, and disease, as well as other 'defensive expenditures,' all count toward GDP. The arithmetic of GDP doesn't consider what the money is actually being spent on, and over time, we've been spending more and more money on remedial activities and calling this 'progress'.[2]

> Alternative GDP indicators can be constructed that correct for these negative aspects of production, as well as taking into account positive factors such as a clean environment, household production, or volunteer work that contribute to well-being but are not included in GDP. Such indicators have drawn increasing interest from economists and policymakers in recent years.

Many important issues are not included adequately, if at all in GDP. In addition, some things that are included in GDP can be misleading or represent harmful activities.

- A critical issue is *household production*, which is examined in Section 3 of this chapter. While standard accounting measures include the paid labor from such household activities as childcare and gardening, these services are not counted when they are unpaid.
- Standard measures do not count the benefits of *volunteer work*, even though such work clearly contributes to social well-being. Also, the free services provided by many nonprofit organizations (e.g., a homeless shelter funded by donations) go unaccounted for, even if the workers in the organization are paid.
- Some other significant *services provided for free*, such as free services from Wikipedia, which relies on unpaid volunteer work, are not counted, even though they might increase well-being.
- *Leisure* is another important neglected factor. A rise in output might come about because people spend more time and effort on paid work. The resulting increase in measured output does not take into account the fact that overwork makes people more tired and stressed and takes away from time that they could use for enjoying other activities. But if people spend more time on leisure, increasing their well-being, this will not be reflected in GDP (except insofar as they spend money on leisure-related activities).
- Also inadequately reflected are issues around loss (or gain) of *human and social capital formation*. Social and political factors that may significantly affect well-being include the health and education levels of a country's citizens, as well as political participation, government effectiveness (or lack thereof), and issues of trust, corruption, or other aspects of the economic and social culture. (Expenditures on health and education are counted in GDP, but may not reflect the full picture, since some factors contributing to health and education outcomes come from unpaid activities.)
- Another significant criticism of GDP, when used as a general measure of economic progress, is that interactions between the economy and the natural world are often ignored. GDP generally does not account for environmental degradation and resource depletion, while treating natural resources that do not go through the market (such as the water purification services provided by natural systems such as forests and wetlands) as having no monetary value.

174

■ Some outputs merely compensate for, or defend against, harmful events that result from the economic activity represented in GDP. Referred to as **defensive expenditures**, these show up as positive contributions to GDP, but standard GDP measures do not account for the associated negative impacts. Consider, for example, the 2011 Deepwater Horizon oil spill in the Gulf of Mexico. The billions of dollars spent in clean-up efforts were counted as positive additions to GDP, while environmental and human losses caused by the spill were mostly not accounted for at all. When environmental issues are mostly invisible, there can be an appearance of economic growth even as the ecological basis for future economic health is being seriously undermined.

---

defensive expenditures: money spent to counteract economic activities that have caused harm to human or environmental health

---

■ *Products or production methods that reduce, rather than increase, well-being* may show up as additions to GDP. Unhealthy foods and drugs and dangerous equipment, for example, may lower, not raise, overall well-being. Even if people are willing to pay for such goods and services, such decisions might reflect poor information or bad judgment. In terms of production methods, if people are miserable at their jobs, suffering boring, degrading, or harmful working conditions, their well-being is compromised. The divergence between output and well-being is especially obvious in cases where workers' lives or health are threatened by their working conditions, even while their work results in an increase in GDP.

■ Another gap between GDP and well-being is *financial debt.* GDP counts consumption levels as rising even if the rise is financed by unsustainably large debt burdens, whether the debt is held by consumers or by governments. When debts are high enough to require painful changes in future consumption, not accounting for financial debt is similar to not accounting for unsustainable tolls exacted on the natural environment.

■ Finally, increased economic activity in a given country is counted as an addition to GDP even if it increases inequality. Two countries with the same per-capita GDP may have a significantly different income distribution and, as a result, different levels of well-being. At an individual level, if someone making just $20,000 per year receives a raise of $1,000, this is counted as the same societal gain as it would be if that raise went to someone with an income of $100,000. Obviously, the additional income means much more for the individual well-being of the person with a lower income. Although economists generally accept this concept (called the diminishing marginal utility of income), GDP counts income gains

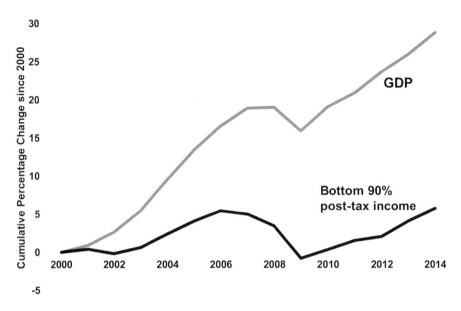

Figure 5.1 *Cumulative Changes in GDP and Average Incomes of the Bottom 90 Percent of Earners, Since 2000*

Sources: Piketty, Saez and Zucman, 2016; Bureau of Economic Analysis; Leonhardt, 2018.

the same regardless of whether the person receiving the increase is rich or poor. The failure of GDP to account for inequality is illustrated in Figure 5.1, showing a significant rise in U.S. GDP over the last two decades, while the average income for a majority of the population has barely risen.

The foregoing examples all indicate the dangers of pursuing policies geared only to raising GDP. A narrow national focus solely on increasing output may result in decreased leisure and less time for parenting, friendships, and community relations; it can increase levels of stress and mental illness, raise economic inequality, or cause environmental degradation. For all these reasons, improvements are needed in the design of measures of national success. The next section describes some leading alternative measures.

Discussion Questions

1. GDP can be characterized as a (rough) measure of the amount of "throughput" taking place in an economy—processes whereby renewable and non-renewable resources (inputs) are turned into new products (outputs). How does "throughput" relate to sustainable well-being? Is more "throughput" always a good thing?

2. In Chapter 1, we discussed how economies are based on natural, manufactured, social, and human capital. Only the value of manufactured capital (structures and equipment)—and recently,

software—is estimated in the current national accounts. Can you think of ways that the stocks of natural, social, and human capital might be measured? What kind of information would be needed?

2 A BROADER VIEW OF NATIONAL INCOME ACCOUNTING

A number of national and international initiatives have been taken to create alternative indicators that account for social and environmental factors in measuring economic progress. One approach to creating alternative indicators focuses on refining measures of national assets and production, supplementing the National Income and Products Account (NIPA) framework with information on resources and environmental impacts. Another approach involves developing separate indicators for the different aspects of well-being and using these additional measures in combination with GDP to get a better assessment of well-being. Other measures rely on creating wholly new indicators based on a composite index including a set of variables measuring different aspects of well-being. Examples of some of these indicators, along with their estimation and application, are presented in this section.

2.1 Satellite Accounts

Satellite accounts supplement standard national income accounts by tracking data on well-being indicators, such as health, education, and other aspects of social and environmental well-being[*]. For example, the UK maintains environmental accounts that track data on forested areas, oil and gas reserves, waste generation, greenhouse gas emissions, and expenditures on environmental protection.

---

satellite accounts: additional or parallel accounting systems that provide measures of social and environmental factors in physical terms, without necessarily including monetary valuation

---

Satellite accounts can be viewed as a "dashboard" approach to national accounting. The dashboard on a car provides indicators of speed, temperature, battery level, and miles driven per gallon of fuel. Though the economy is considerably more complex than a car, a set of indicators that measure various aspects of well-being can be used

---

[*] The United Nations differentiates between "internal" satellite accounts (those that are linked to standard accounts and typically measured in monetary units) and "external" satellite accounts (not necessarily linked and measured in either physical or monetary units). See: http://unstats.un.org/unsd/nationalaccount/AEG/papers/m4SatelliteAccounts.pdf.

177

to measure economic health. Proponents of this approach agree that GDP is a useful measure of national output for historical and international comparisons, but believe that GDP tells us only one of the things that we want to know about the economy. Some of the things that it does not tell us are important, and they deserve to have their own indicators.

The U.S. Bureau of Economic Analysis (BEA) uses dollar-denominated satellite accounts to highlight certain existing components of GDP by presenting data on some special topics.[3] These topics include arts and cultural production, outdoor recreation, travel and tourism, and health care (measuring spending on health care classified by diseases being treated instead of goods and services purchased). More recently satellite accounts to measure the economic contribution of small businesses, the digital economy, the marine economy, and the space economy have been added to the BEA accounts. These satellite accounts eliminate some of the obscurity in the aggregate GDP measure, by estimating the contributions of particular sectors to the national income.

The BEA also tracks the value of unpaid work in the Household Production Satellite Account, based on surveys that ask people how they spend their time (time-use surveys). Unlike the other BEA satellite accounts that are incorporated within broader statistics like GDP, household production measures are not included in BEA's other statistics. The BEA has explored "an accounting framework that covers the interactions of the economy and the environment".[4] Future uses of satellite accounts in the BEA may start counting environmental damages as losses.

In general, the BEA's satellite accounts rely on monetary valuation and are readily comparable to GDP. Other countries use satellite accounts in which the unit of measurement is physical units such as tons of carbon dioxide emitted or numbers of children in poverty.

Even where resources can be easily valued in dollars, data in physical units may be more meaningful. Consider that we can measure the economic value of mineral reserves by multiplying the quantity of reserves in physical units by the market price. But suppose that the market price increases considerably at the same time that reserves are drawn down. Although the economic value of reserves could increase due to the higher prices, the dollar valuation would fail to tell us that our physical reserves have declined.

Moreover, it is often very difficult to convert some variables to monetary units. How can we express changes in crime levels or health status in terms of dollar values? Such questions raise important methodological issues, such as whether the economic value of higher asthma rates includes only medical expenditures and lost productivity, or whether other quality of life factors need to be considered. Some people may also raise ethical objections to attaching dollar values to variables such as traffic deaths or biodiversity.

178

As we delve into additional categories that we might wish to have reported in national accounts, we may find ourselves straying into areas where measurement becomes more difficult. Thus, we can add a fourth question to our list above: Should our "dashboard" include data from surveys that directly ask people about their well-being? We consider this possibility next.

2.2 Measuring Well-Being

Recognizing the limitations of GDP and the need to develop indicators that incorporate social and environmental factors, in 2008 French president Nicolas Sarkozy created the Commission on the Measurement of Economic Performance and Social Progress. The commission, which included many distinguished social scientists, was headed by Nobel laureates Joseph Stiglitz and Amartya Sen, and coordinated by prominent French economist Jean-Paul Fitoussi.

The commission's 2009 report concluded that it is necessary to shift from an emphasis on measuring economic production to measuring well-being. It also distinguished between current well-being and sustainability, recognizing that whether current well-being can be sustained depends upon the levels of capital (natural, physical, human, and social) passed on to future generations. The commission defined well-being based on the following eight dimensions: material living standards, health, education, work and personal activities, political voice, social connections, economic and physical security or insecurity, and the environment.

Objective data can be collected that provide information on many of these dimensions, such as average life expectancy, literacy rates, and air pollution levels. But such data still do not tell us exactly how these factors relate to well-being. If the goal of economics is to promote well-being, you may wonder if we can measure it directly. **Subjective well-being (SWB)** attempts to measure well-being by asking individuals a question such as: "All things considered, how satisfied are you with your life as a whole these days?" Respondents then answer based on a scale from 1 (dissatisfied) to 10 (satisfied).

> **subjective well-being:** a measure of welfare based on survey questions asking people about their own degree of life satisfaction

Although this approach may seem unscientific, a large body of scientific research has emerged in recent decades that suggests that data on SWB provide significant information. For example, higher SWB is generally associated with good health and longevity, stronger social relationships, democracy and freedom, and better work performance and creativity.[5] A wide variety of efforts, such as the World Happiness Report, the Gallup World Poll, and the European Quality of Life Survey,

179

have come up with remarkably consistent measures of "happiness" or "life satisfaction." The Stiglitz-Sen-Fitoussi Commission recommends using SWB data in conjunction with objective data on various well-being dimensions, concluding that:

> Research has shown that it is possible to collect meaningful and reliable data on subjective as well as objective well-being. Quantitative measures of [SWB] hold the promise of delivering not just a good measure of quality of life per se, but also a better understanding of its determinants, reaching beyond people's income and material conditions. Despite the persistence of many unresolved issues, these subjective measures provide important information about quality of life.[6]

We can ask two relevant questions about the relationship between SWB and measures of national welfare such as GDP:

1. Are average SWB levels higher in countries with higher GDP per capita?
2. As GDP per capita increases in a particular country over time, do SWB levels rise?

SWB data have been collected for many developed and developing countries. Figure 5.2 plots average SWB against per-capita GDP, adjusted for differences in purchasing power, for 138 countries. In general, SWB is positively correlated with higher levels of GDP per capita, but note that the benefits of income gains decline at higher income levels, as shown by the curved trendline. However, SWB can be high in both rich and poor countries. For example, middle-income countries like Brazil, Jamaica, and Uzbekistan rank relatively high on the SWB index, with values greater than 6.0.

Figure 5.2 also shows that while SWB varies among richer countries, all developed countries have relatively high SWB. Almost all countries with a per-capita GDP above US$20,000 per year have an average SWB above 5.5, and countries with per-capita GDP below $5,000 have an average SWB of 4.5. Thus, it appears from this graph that for at least some developing countries, increasing GDP could lead to higher SWB levels. But income gains in richer countries are associated with much smaller increases in SWB.

The other way to analyze SWB data is to consider how SWB changes as a country develops economically over time. The longest time series of SWB data comes from the United States, dating back to 1946. While real GDP per capita has increased by about a factor of four since 1946, average SWB levels have essentially remained constant. An analysis of country trends in SWB over the period 1981–2007 found that average SWB rose in 45 of 52 countries, with economic growth associated with greater SWB gains for low-income countries. India is an example of

180

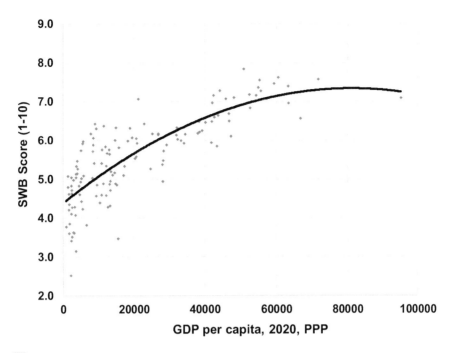

Figure 5.2 *Average Subjective Well-Being 2018-2020 and GDP per Capita 2020, PPP*

Sources: SWB from Helliwell et al., World Happiness Report 2021; GDP per capita data is from World Development Indicators online database.

Note: The trendline is a statistically fitted line showing a "best fit" estimate of the relationship between GDP per capita and SWB. "PPP" is Purchasing Power Parity.

a country that has experienced significant gains in SWB levels as its economy has grown in recent decades.[7]

Based on both approaches to evaluating SWB, the results imply that as people are able to meet their basic needs, such as adequate nutrition and basic health care, their happiness generally increases. Beyond that, further income gains are associated with smaller increases in SWB or no increase at all (as shown by the flattening out of the trendline in Figure 5.2). One explanation for this might be that at higher income levels, people are more likely to judge their happiness relative to others. So even if everyone's income increases by the same percentage, average happiness levels may be unchanged. Another possibility might be that consuming more goods and services is simply not making people any happier, or that the benefits of increased consumption are offset by negative factors such as increased congestion and stress.

As the Stiglitz-Sen-Fitoussi Commission mentions, further work is needed to understand the relationship between SWB and other well-being measures. But the results so far suggest that SWB should be one of the indicators on our "dashboard" of well-being measures.

181

2.3 The Genuine Progress Indicator (GPI)

In 1989, economist Herman Daly and theologian John Cobb Jr. suggested an alternative measure to GDP that they called the Index of Sustainable Economic Welfare (ISEW). This measure was later transformed into the Genuine Progress Indicator (GPI), one of the most ambitious attempts to date to design a replacement for GDP[†]. The GPI is a monetary measure of economic well-being for a given population in a given year that adds many benefits and subtracts many costs that are not included in GDP. It is designed to differentiate

> between economic activity that diminishes both natural and social capital and activity that enhances such capital. . . In particular, if GPI is stable or increasing in a given year the implication is that stocks of natural and social capital on which all goods and services flows depend will be at least as great for the next generation, while if GPI is falling it implies that the economic system is eroding those stocks and limiting the next generation's prospects.[8]

Over time, the GPI measure has been modified to respond to theoretical critiques and to integrate new data sources and valuation methods. The most recent version of GPI (termed GPI 2.0) has three main components: market-based welfare, services from essential capital, and environmental and social costs.[9]

2.3.1 Market-Based Welfare

With the assumption that economic welfare derives at least in part from consumption levels, the personal consumption expenditures (PCE) component of GDP is taken as the starting point of market-based welfare. In the United States, personal consumption accounts for about 70 percent of GDP. In calculating the GPI 2.0, PCE is relabeled as a household budget expenditure (HBE) and components of consumption that have zero or negative contribution to the household's current well-being are subtracted from HBE. This includes defensive and regrettable expenditures, such as medical care, legal services, insurance, food and energy waste, household pollution abatement, and security expenses. Also, to keep the focus on current welfare, expenditures on household investments that may contribute to long-term sustainability, including spending on consumer durables, household maintenance, higher education, savings, retirement, and charitable giving, are subtracted from HBE (though some of these will be accounted for later as "services").

---

† Another predecessor to the GPI and the ISEW was the Measure of Economic Welfare, by William Nordhaus and James Tobin. This 1973 effort was the first serious attempt to create an alternative to GDP.

Next, an adjustment is made for income inequality to reflect the negative impact of inequality on well-being. Finally, benefits from the provision of public goods and services are added to HBE since the exclusion of government spending from PCE underestimates the actual value of household consumption. The resulting value after making these adjustments gives the total market-based welfare.

2.3.2 Services from Essential Capital

Unlike GDP, which focuses on manufactured capital, GPI accounts for welfare benefits from services of human, social, and natural capital. Services from human capital include benefits from higher education, knowledge, and skills. Value of household and volunteer work, leisure time, and benefits from internet services fall under social capital. Services from manufactured (built) capital include benefits from consumer durables, home improvement, and infrastructure. All economically valuable functions of nature such as the provision of food and medicine, pollination of crops, and benefits from lakes, rivers, forests, wetlands, deserts, and other ecosystems constitute the services of natural capital. The gains from services provided by these capital resources are added to the total market-based welfare.

2.3.3 Social and Environmental Costs

Social and environmental costs include aspects of economic activity that have a negative effect on well-being. For instance, homelessness, underemployment, increasing crime rate, more time spent in traffic, and vehicle accidents all have an adverse impact on human well-being and are counted as social costs. Environmental costs include the depletion of natural capital such as the loss of wetlands, groundwater depletion, productivity losses due to soil erosion, as well as the increase in air pollutants, greenhouse gas emissions, and noise and water pollution. Social and environmental costs are subtracted from the total of market-based welfare and services from essential capital to get the final GPI measure.

The adjustments made to household budget expenditure in order to arrive at the GPI for 2014 are shown in Table 5.1.

With the adjustments outlined above, the GPI differs significantly from GDP in magnitude and trends. The largest positive adjustments to GPI come from the benefits of social capital, which include unpaid work and the value of leisure time and internet services. The largest deductions come from the depletion of natural capital.

Over the long term, not only is per-capita GPI much lower than per-capita GDP, but its growth trajectory is different from that of GDP. This can be seen in the case of the United States (Figure 5.3). U.S. GDP per capita and GPI per capita both increased from 1950 to about 1978, but in recent decades GPI has flat-lined while GDP continued to grow,

Table 5.1 *Genuine Progress Indicator ($2012 per Capita), United States 2014*

Indicator	Value
Market-based welfare	
Household budget expenditures (HBE)	$25,529
Defensive and regrettable expenditures	−$3,967
Household investments	−$7,278
Costs of income inequality	−$3,121
Public provision of goods and services	+$7,025
Total market-based welfare	$18,188
Services from essential capital	
Services from human capital	+$5,223
Services from social capital	+$12,857
Services from built capital	+$6,042
Services from protected natural capital	+$1,555
Total services from essential capital	$25,677
Environmental and social costs	
Depletion of natural capital	−$6,496
Costs of pollution	−$3,715
Social costs of economic activity	−$5,195
Total environmental and social costs	$15,406
GPI per capita total	$28,459

Source: Talberth and Weisdorf, 2017.

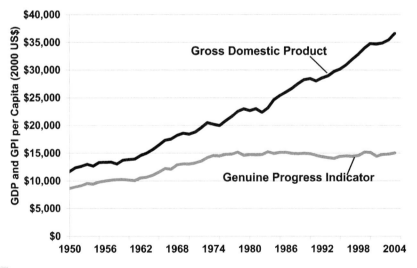

Figure 5.3 *GPI vs. GDP per Capita for the United States, 1950–2004*

Source: Talberth et al., 2007.

indicating that environmental and social costs omitted from GDP have been increasing faster than the value of the omitted benefits.[10] A 2013 study estimating global GPI values, using data from 17 countries covering over 53 percent of the world's population, shows similar trends—both GDP and GPI per capita increased from the 1950s to the mid-1970s, but GPI per capita has remained flat since then while GDP per capita has continued to increase.[11] Relying on the GPI instead of GDP might suggest significantly different policy recommendations, focusing more on reducing environmental damage, increasing reliance on renewable energy, and redressing rising inequality.

GPI estimates have been developed for countries other than the United States, including Australia, China, Germany, India, Japan, Italy, and Brazil. The GPI has also been applied at the subnational level, not only in the United States but also in other countries such as China (Liaoning Province), Italy (Tuscany), Canada (Alberta), and Belgium (Flanders). For example, a 2009 analysis of the Auckland region in New Zealand showed that between 1990 and 2006 the GPI grew at nearly the same rate as the region's GDP. Even in this case, environmental losses grew at a more rapid rate than the GPI—rising 27 percent during this period, while the GPI rose 18 percent. But the positive contributions to the GPI, in particular growth in personal consumption, were enough to more than offset the environmental losses.‡

A 2018 study estimating GPI values for the 50 U.S. states for 2011 ranks Alaska at the top and Wyoming at the bottom, with seven states (Arizona, Arkansas, Louisiana, Mississippi, North Dakota, West Virginia, and Wyoming) estimated to have negative GPI values due to very high environmental and social costs outweighing benefits from consumption and household work.[12]

More extensive analyses on GPI measures have been conducted for the states of Maryland and Vermont and the city of Baltimore. In Maryland, while economic contributions to the GPI rose steadily over the period 1960–2010, the net social contributions increased only slightly, and the environmental costs more than doubled (based on the earlier variation of GPI). In Vermont, 2011 GPI per capita was 40 percent less than the state GDP due to rising income inequality and a strong dependence on fossil fuels.[13] According to a 2017 analysis of the Maryland GPI, "the GPI can help to show net societal benefits of policies such as investing in public transit, increasing the minimum wage and reducing greenhouse gases—giving policymakers and advocates additional ammunition for political battles over such issues," but the actual influence on policy was limited.[14]

---

‡ Note that this study is based on an earlier variation of GPI, but the underlying method of estimation of GPI—taking the total personal consumption expenditure, adding the positive contributions to well-being and subtracting the negative ones—is the same.

2.4 The Better Life Index (BLI)

One of the challenges of using multiple indicators to evaluate well-being, as suggested by the dashboard approach, is that it is sometimes difficult to communicate the results. How do we assess overall well-being if the poverty rate falls by 5 percent, but emissions of greenhouse gases increase by 10 percent? On the other hand, summing up production, poverty, inequality, environmental degradation, and other aspects of well-being in one single index, as is done with the GPI measure, also poses the difficult problem of having to attach monetary values to each dimension to add them up.

The Organization for Economic Cooperation and Development (OECD) has therefore tried a mixed approach[§]. With its **Better Life Index (BLI)**, it combines eleven dimensions, many of which are hard to measure and difficult to value in monetary terms, into one single indicator using different possible weights for each dimension. The 2015 BLI report argues that "a better understanding of people's well-being is central to developing better policies for better lives."[15]

> **Better Life Index (BLI):** an index developed by the OECD to measure national welfare using 11 well-being dimensions

To account for the multidimensional nature of well-being and get a thorough assessment of whether people's lives are improving, the BLI considers the following 11 dimensions:

1. Income, Wealth, and Inequality: The main variables used for this dimension are disposable household income, net financial wealth, and the degree of inequality in income and wealth.[¶]
2. Jobs and Earnings: The main variables comprising this dimension are the unemployment rate, the long-term unemployment rate, and average earnings per employee.
3. Housing: Sufficient housing is important to provide security, privacy, and stability. Rooms per person, dwellings with basic facilities, and housing expenditure are used to measure housing conditions.
4. Health Status: The BLI includes life expectancy and a subjective evaluation of one's overall health status.
5. Work-Life Balance: The proportion of employees who work long (50 or more) hours per week, the time available for leisure and per-

---

§ The OECD is a group of the world's advanced industrialized countries, now including some developing countries, such as Mexico. The BLI was created, in part, as a response to the Stiglitz-Sen-Fitoussi Commission report.

¶ In addition to these main variables, most of the dimensions also consider secondary variables. For example, the dimension of income and wealth also includes data on household consumption and a subjective evaluation of material well-being.

sonal care, and the employment rate for women with school-age children are used as indicators of work-life balance.

6. Education and Skills: This measure is based on the average duration of formal education, percentage of the adult (25–64-year-old) population with a secondary-school degree, and average performance of students in standardized testing.

7. Social Connections: This dimension is measured by the strength of social network, based on the percentage of people who believe they can rely on friends in times of need.

8. Civic Engagement and Governance: This dimension is based on voter turnout data and a composite index that measures citizen input into policymaking.

9. Environmental Quality: The main variable used to measure environmental quality is air pollution levels, specifically levels of particulate matter. Secondary environmental variables include an estimate of the degree to which diseases are caused by environmental factors, people's subjective satisfaction with their local environment, and access to green space.

10. Personal Security: This dimension focuses on threats to one's safety. It is measured using the homicide rate and data on the percentage of people who feel safe walking alone at night.

11. Subjective Well-Being: This dimension measures people's overall satisfaction with their lives, as well as reported negative feelings.

The BLI is designed to produce an overall well-being index. The results for each dimension are standardized across countries, resulting in a score from 0 to 10. But how do we assign a weight to the various components? One approach would be simply to weigh each of the 11 dimensions equally. But it is likely that some dimensions contribute more to well-being than others. The BLI report makes no specific recommendations for weighting the different dimensions, but its Web site allows users to select their own weights for each of the dimensions (see www.oecdbetterlifeindex.org). The OECD collects user input and uses this information to gain a better understanding of the factors that are most important for measuring well-being.

Based on input collected from over 130,000 users about their preferred weight for each dimension, the OECD 2018 report shows a considerable variation in the importance of the eleven well-being dimensions across regions. The highest ranked dimensions are education in South America, life satisfaction in North America, health in Europe, and work-life balance in Asia-Pacific and Australia.[16]

The BLI has been measured for 41 countries, including the 38 OECD member countries,** along with Brazil, South Africa, and Russia. Figure 5.4 shows the total BLI for nine countries. Among these

---

** Costa Rica became the 38th member of OECD in 2021. BLI data is not available for Costa Rica as of early 2022.

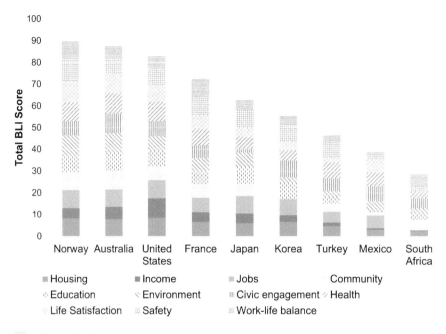

Figure 5.4 *BLI for Selected Countries, 2020*

Source: OECD, 2020.

countries, Norway and Australia rank the highest, scoring highly on life satisfaction, jobs, environment, and health of the population (other Nordic nations along with Switzerland, New Zealand, and Canada have similar scores). Countries with low income and employment levels, poor education, health, and environmental outcomes, including Mexico and South Africa, rank the lowest in BLI. The United States performs well in terms of housing, income, and jobs, but ranks relatively low in terms of work-life balance and inequality in income.

The 2020 BLI report indicates that since 2010 the overall quality of life has improved in all 41 countries. In general, life expectancy has increased, people feel safer and are living in less overcrowded conditions, incomes and jobs have been on the rise, and life satisfaction levels have improved. But these average outcomes do not reflect inequalities across and within countries. For example, housing affordability, relative income poverty, and voter turnout have worsened in some OECD countries, and there has been some decline in social support and time spent with friends and family. Income inequality is still as prevalent as it was in 2010, with those in the top 20 percent of income earners still earning five times more than the people in the bottom 20 percent.

All OECD countries also face new environmental challenges, as nearly two-thirds of people in these countries are exposed to dangerous levels of air pollution. And while there has been a slight reduction in per capita emissions of greenhouse gases, most OECD countries have not done enough to meet climate policy goals.[17]

188

2.5 The Human Development Index (HDI)

In contrast to the BLI, the United Nations' **Human Development Index (HDI)** is calculated based on only three components of well-being: life expectancy at birth, years of formal education, and real Gross National Income (GNI) per capita[††]. Although these are denominated in different units, no attempt is made to translate one into the other. Rather, relative performance is presented in a scaled index (Figure 5.5).

> **Human Development Index (HDI):** a national accounting measure developed by the United Nations, based on three factors: GNI per capita level, education, and life expectancy

Like the BLI, the HDI faces the issue of how to assign relative weights. The standard HDI approach is to give equal weight to each of the three indicators. Although the GNI measure is modified to account for the principle, discussed above, that additional income is worth more to a person with lower income than to a person with higher income, the inclusion of standard measures of income as one-third of the indicator

Human Development Index (Scale 1-100)	
90-100	Norway, Germany, Sweden, Australia, Denmark, Singapore, United Kingdom, Canada, United States, Japan, Korea, France
85-89.9	Italy, Greece, United Arab Emirates, Poland, Lithuania, Portugal, Saudi Arabia, Chile, Croatia
80-84.9	Qatar, Argentina, Russia, Turkey, Costa Rica, Malaysia, Kuwait
75-79.9	Cuba, Mexico, Ukraine, Peru, Thailand, Brazil, China, Ecuador
70-74.9	Lebanon, Botswana, Jamaica, Libya, Philippines, Venezuela, South Africa, Vietnam
65-69.9	Morocco, Guyana, Iraq, El Salvador, Guatemala, Bhutan
60-64.9	India, Bangladesh, Ghana, Nepal, Kenya, Namibia
55-59.9	Cambodia, Zambia, Congo, Syria, Zimbabwe, Pakistan
50-54.9	Uganda, Rwanda, Nigeria, Madagascar, Afghanistan, Haiti, Sudan
45-49.9	Gambia, Ethiopia, Malawi, Yemen, Sierra Leone
40-44.9	Mali, Burundi, South Sudan
35-39.9	Chad, Central African Republic, Niger

Figure 5.5 *Selected Countries as Ranked in the Human Development Index, 2019*

Source: UNDP, Human Development Report, 2019 data.

[††] GNI is another name for GNP or Gross National Product. Recall from Chapter 4 that the key difference between GNI/GNP and GDP is based on whether foreign earnings are included. While GDP includes all earnings within a country's borders, including those earned by foreign citizens and corporations, GNI accounts for the earnings of a country's citizens and corporations, regardless of where they are located.

makes it highly, although not perfectly, correlated with GDP; of the 30 countries with the highest HDI scores in 2019, all were ranked in the top 35 by national income per capita.

At the same time, the results show that in some cases countries with similar income levels measured by GNI per capita vary dramatically in overall human welfare, as measured by the HDI. For example, Jamaica, Guyana, and Namibia have similar levels of GNI per capita, but their HDI scores vary significantly. Jamaica has the highest score in this group, with a relatively high life expectancy of about 75 years, compared to 70 years in Guyana, and 64 years in Namibia. Education levels in Jamaica are also higher than those in Guyana and Namibia. Namibia's low life expectancy and lower average education levels pull down its HDI score.

The relative simplicity of the HDI has made it much easier to apply in countries with less money to spend on data collection; hence, it has been especially valuable for developing countries. The HDI has been an annual feature of every UN *Human Development Report* since 1990, and it is now an official government statistic in a number of countries. One limitation of the HDI is that it does not consider distributional issues, as it is based on average measures of health, education, and income across the population. The HDI has also been criticized for focusing on a narrow set of indicators and failing to account for other important aspects of human well-being, such as social stability and environmental sustainability. Recognizing these concerns, three new indices to monitor poverty, inequality, and gender inequality were launched by the UN in 2010:

1. Multidimensional Poverty Index (MPI): The MPI is based on the same three dimensions as the HDI—living standards, education, and health— but it uses a broader set of indicators to measure each dimension. Living standards is measured using a composite of six variables (cooking fuel, sanitation, drinking water, electricity, housing, and assets); health is measured by nutrition and child mortality; and education is measured by years of schooling and school attendance rate. In 2019, 23 percent of the world's population were identified as being multi-dimensionally poor, compared to a 10 percent global poverty rate based on an income measure using $1.90 a day as the poverty line.[18]

2. Inequality-Adjusted HDI (IHDI): The IHDI measure starts with the same three indicators as the HDI to measure health, education, and living standards. It then makes an adjustment for inequality by discounting the average value of each dimension by the level of inequality. The global HDI value for 2018 dropped by 20 percent after accounting for inequality.

3. Gender Inequality Index (GII): The GII includes measures of reproductive health, women's empowerment, and gender disparities in the labor market to expose the differences in achievements of

men and women. The GII measure shows the highest gender-based inequality in sub-Saharan Africa and Arab states and the lowest gender inequality in Europe and Central Asia. Another indicator for measuring gender inequality, Gender Development Index (GDI), was introduced in 2014. This measure disaggregates the HDI value by gender. In 2018, the average HDI for women was 6 percent lower than that for men.

2.6 Other National Accounting Alternatives

Aside from the measures just described, many other proposals have been made either to supplement GDP, adjust it, or replace it. To give a sense of this landscape, we briefly describe a sample of measures developed for use in specific locales. One alternative measure that has been used more widely, the Happy Planet Index, is discussed in Box 5.2.

- **The Measure of America** presents an HDI modified for application in the United States. For example, although the standard HDI measures access to knowledge using the average number of years that students spend in school, Measure of America uses average achievement scores at various grade levels. The results, calculated down to the level of congressional districts, are available at www.measureofamerica.org.
- **The Canadian Index of Well-Being** was created by collecting information from Canadians about what factors they thought were important for their well-being. The indicator tracks changes in the following eight domains: community vitality, democratic engagement, education, environment, healthy populations, leisure and culture, living standards, and time use.
- Italy has an **Index of Quality of Regional Development**, a composite index of 45 variables pertaining to the environment, economy and labor, rights and citizenship, gender equity, education and culture, health, and democratic participation.
- France has the **Fleurbaey/Gaulier Indicator**, which is similar to the GPI but tries to include more monetary values of non-monetary factors (job security, healthy life expectancy, environmental sustainability), using subjective valuations of these factors to create adjusted "equivalent incomes."
- The **Gross National Happiness (GNH)** concept was proposed in Bhutan in 1972 as a guiding principle for economic development that takes a holistic approach to improving the quality of people's lives. In 2010 it was formally defined along nine different dimensions of welfare (psychological well-being, standard of living, good governance, health, education, community vitality, cultural diversity and resilience, time use, and ecological diversity and resilience), including 33 distinct indicators.[19] The 2015 report from the Centre

for Bhutan Studies, based on a survey of over 7,000 households, indicates that 43 percent of Bhutanese households have sufficiency in at least six domains and are thus considered either "deeply" or "extensively" happy.[20]

■ The government of New Zealand launched the **Well-Being Budget** initiative in 2019 with the goal of reshaping the government's budget toward the well-being needs of the country. A dashboard of indicators on civic engagement and governance, cultural identity, environment, health, housing, income and consumption, jobs and earnings, knowledge and skills, safety and security, social connections, SWB, and time use is used to evaluate the quality of life. Based on this approach, the government allocated billions of dollars to mental health services, child poverty, and measures to tackle family violence, improve conditions of the native population, and build a sustainable, low-emissions, and productive economy.[21]

■ The **Comprehensive Wealth** measure, developed by the International Institute for Sustainable Development (IISD), estimates the total resources that a nation has to continue social and economic activities into the future. This indicator estimates the value of five types of assets—produced capital including roads, ports, machineries, and other manufactured assets; natural capital including resources such as timber, minerals, and gas, and ecosystems such as wetlands and forests; human capital, measuring collective knowledge and skills of the labor force; financial capital covering stocks, bonds, and other kinds of financial assets and investments; and social capital, representing norms that define social behavior, trust on institutions, and inclusivity. The comprehensive wealth measure, initially estimated for Canada for 2018, reveals various concerns including excessive levels of household debt, stagnant human capital, and vulnerability to climate change. More recently the IISD has expanded its effort to measure wealth to countries in Africa, Asia, and the Caribbean.[22]

BOX 5.2 HAPPY PLANET INDEX

The Happy Planet Index, created by the New Economics Foundation of London, asserts that the goal of society is to create long and happy lives for its members. The HPI is made up of three variables:

1. *Average life expectancy:* This measures whether a society's members lead long lives.
2. *Average subjective well-being:* This measures whether a society's members lead happy lives. The data are based on a survey, which asks people how satisfied they are with their lives overall, on a scale of 1–10.
3. *Ecological footprint:* This measures a society's overall ecological impact. It is defined as the amount of land required to provide a society with the resources that it consumes and assimilate the waste that it generates.

In order to obtain the HPI, a country's well-being is multiplied by its life expectancy and divided by its ecological footprint. Some technical adjustments are made to this measure to adjust for inequality in each of the three dimensions and to ensure that no single component dominates the overall score.

In 2019, the HPI was calculated for 152 countries. The countries with the highest HPI scores are those that have rather happy and long-lived citizens, and relatively modest ecological footprints. Examples of countries with high HPI include Costa Rica, Colombia, Ecuador, and Jamaica.

One interesting aspect of the HPI is that a country's HPI ranking tends to be unrelated to its GDP. Most wealthy nations including the United States, Japan, Canada, Australia, and developed countries in Europe all score highly on life expectancy and SWB, but their HPI rank is lower than that of some of the less developed countries in Latin America and Asia-Pacific region because of their larger ecological footprint. Luxembourg, for example, ranks 3rd by GNI per capita and 23rd by the HDI, but ranks 143rd by the HPI. The United States ranks 122nd, just above Tanzania, Namibia, and India, mainly because of its relatively large ecological footprint. The low HPI rank for most sub-Saharan countries, in contrast, is due to the low life expectancy and low SWB despite the relatively low ecological footprint of this region.[23]

The interpretation and policy implications of the HPI are unclear. For example, El Salvador and the Dominican Republic have a higher HPI score than Sweden or Australia.[24] Does this imply that El Salvador and the Dominican Republic are more desirable to live in, or more ecologically sustainable, than Sweden or Australia? Probably not. Another issue is to what extent a country's policies can affect happiness levels, which may be more a result of inherent social and cultural factors rather than policy choices. Despite its limitations, the HPI has received attention as an alternative or supplement to GDP, especially in Europe. So while the HPI is unlikely to become a widespread alternative to GDP, it does provide information that is not currently captured in any other national accounting metric.

One lesson from all these alternatives is that there is not necessarily a positive correlation between economic production in an economy (as measured by GDP) and other measures of well-being. In many instances, GDP is rising while other measures stay flat or fall.

The next two sections focus on the issues surrounding two particular elements that have been seriously underrepresented in GDP. Section 3 discusses issues of accounting for household production. Section 4 takes up environmental accounting, including subsections on the methodological problems of how to assign values to things that are not sold through markets.

Discussion Questions

1. Does the GPI include anything that you think should be left out or fail to account for something that you think should be included? Think hard about what you really think human well-being is about.

2. Give examples of each of the following:

- Efforts to supplement GDP
- Efforts to adjust GDP
- Efforts to replace GDP

Are there some alternatives discussed above that would fit into more than one of these categories? Are there some that are difficult to fit into any of them? Would you suggest any other ways of categorizing efforts that are being made to improve how we measure the success of an economy in achieving well-being for the present and future people?

3 MEASURING HOUSEHOLD PRODUCTION

As discussed above, one key limitation of GDP is that it ignores productive activity that occurs outside the market and without the exchange of money, such as caring for families, raising children, and maintaining homes. Hence, many countries, including the United States, Australia, Canada, India, Japan, Mexico, Thailand, and the UK, have conducted national time-use surveys to aid their understanding of unpaid productive activities. The United Nations Statistical Commission and Eurostat (the statistical office of the European Union) are encouraging countries to develop satellite accounts to take into account both household production and interactions between the economy and the environment.

3.1 Measuring Household Labor

Efforts to measure household labor predate standard GDP accounts. In 1921 a group of economists at the National Bureau of Economic Research calculated that the value of household services would be about 25 to 30 percent of marketed production. Decades later, in 1988, economist Robert Eisner reviewed six major proposed redesigns of the National Income and Product Accounts (NIPA), all of which included substantial estimated values for household production.[25] Despite numerous demonstrations of its practicality dating back over 100 years, household production has never been included in the U.S. GDP accounts.

The COVID-19 pandemic has underscored the importance of recognizing work done within the household, as closures of schools, childcare centers, and other businesses, shifted the burden of providing these services to households. One study, based on data from 16 countries, reveals that on average women spent 5 more hours on childcare per week during the pandemic (increasing from 26 hours/week to 31 hours), while men spent 4 more hours (increasing from 20 hours/week to 24 hours).[26] In the U.S., during the first wave of the pandemic (March-April 2020), some 3.5 million women with school-age children left active work, either to provide care to family members or because of job losses.[27]

This increase in non-market work was not reflected in GDP, which dropped by over 30 percent in the second quarter of 2020 due to business and school closures. This recent example shows why the exclusion of household production in the GDP accounts means that GDP values are significantly understated, as a substantial area of valuable productive activity has been overlooked (see Box 5.3).

BOX 5.3 WHAT ARE STAY-AT-HOME MOMS REALLY WORTH?

What is the fair market value of all the work a typical stay-at-home mom does in a year? To answer this question we can multiply the hours spent on different tasks by the typical wage paid to workers who perform those tasks. For example, if a typical mom spends 14 hours per week cooking, and the average wage for cooks is $10 per hour, then the market value of this work would be $140. Applying this approach to a selected set of household tasks, including child care, cleaning, shopping, yard work, and driving, the annual value of a full-time stay-at-home mom in 2021 is estimated to be $116,022.[28] Other research yields an even larger market value—$178,201 for 2019.[29]

While the share of stay-at-home dads in the United States has increased in recent decades, up to 7 percent in 2016 compared to 4 percent in 1989, they are still a minority, representing 17 percent of all stay-at-home parents in 2016.[30] In recent decades, the number of stay-at-home moms has been declining as more women have entered the workforce. While this brings additional income to households, the income is partially offset by additional expenses, especially in childcare. According to the Economic Policy Institute, the cost of full-time childcare exceeds the typical annual cost of college tuition in 33 of the 50 U.S. states.[31]

Even the most conservative estimates of the total value of household production arrive at numbers equal to about 25–30 percent of standard GDP in the United States, and less conservative estimates put the value as equal to or greater than half of the value of marketed production. An analysis of 27 mostly high-income countries shows that the value of unpaid labor, primarily household production, equates to an average of more than 25 percent of GDP.[32] A recent study by Oxfam estimates the global value of women's unpaid work in 2019 as being close to $10.9 trillion—greater than the combined revenue of the 50 largest companies in the world.[33] The UK Office of National Statistics estimated that the value of unpaid labor in 2018 was equivalent to $1.6 trillion (55 percent of GDP), with the largest components of the value of unpaid work being child care and transportation.[34]

Neglecting household production not only underestimates the level of GDP but might also give a wrong impression about growth trends. One of the major economic shifts during the twentieth century was the movement of a large proportion of women from unpaid employment as full-time homemakers to paid employment outside the home. In 1870, 40 percent of all U.S. workers were women working as full-time homemakers; by 2000, the proportion had dropped to 16 percent. Trends in many European countries were similar, but timing often differed. This increase in work outside the home, as well as the increase in

195

purchases of substitutes for home production, such as paid childcare and prepared foods, was counted as an increase in GDP. The value of *lost* household production, however, was not subtracted. This failure to account for reductions in some home-produced goods and services means that GDP growth during the period was overstated.

For example, a 2019 article in the *Survey of Current Business* found that if "home production" were counted nominal GDP would have been 24 percent higher in 2017 and 37 percent higher in 1965, when fewer women were in the formal labor force. Because the inclusion of "home production" would have added more to GDP in 1965 than in 2017, factoring in non-market activities reduces the average annual growth rate of GDP over this period.[35]

The International Labor Organization estimates that globally about 76 percent of non-market work is carried out by women and that on average women spend three times more time per day on unpaid care work than men.[36] Data on unpaid labor from the UK indicate that men do an average of 16 hours per week of unpaid labor, while women do an average of 26 hours.[37] In the United States, women spend an average of 2.4 hours per day on household production while men spend 1.6 hours.[38] The gender imbalance is even more significant in developing countries, where household production makes up a much higher proportion of total production than in developed countries. Hence, GDP is even more inadequate as an indicator of national production in developing countries.

We see in Figure 5.6 that when we add paid and unpaid labor, women almost always do more total work than men (Mexico is the only exception in the figure). The overall gender imbalance is greatest in India, where women do 21 percent more total work than men, and in South Africa where women do 18 percent more total work than men. If we only consider paid work, we might reach the conclusion that men contribute more to the economy than women. But when we consider both paid and unpaid work, women generally contribute more time on economically productive activities overall.

Why does this matter? One important reason is that the omission of most household production from the national accounts may contribute to a subtle bias in the perceptions of policymakers who base their economic decisions on them. The U.S. Social Security retirement system, for example, makes payments to people based only on their market wages and years of paid work. Some advocates suggest that people should also get credit for time spent raising children—for example, a year of Social Security credit for the time taken off with each child, in recognition of the contribution that such unpaid work makes to social and economic life. Having home production counted in GDP might help make policymakers more aware of its productive contributions.[‡‡]

[‡‡] A prominent advocate of this view is Marilyn Waring, author of *If Women Counted* (San Francisco: Harper and Row, 1988).

196

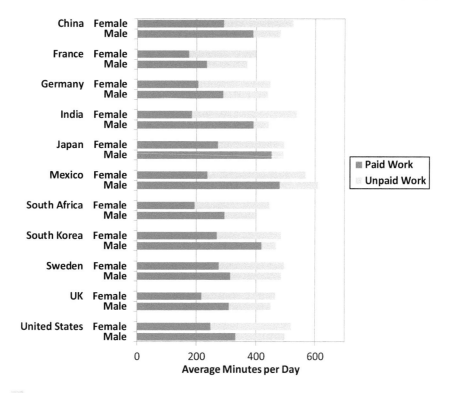

Figure 5.6 *Paid and Unpaid Work by Gender, Selected Countries*

Source: OECD, OECD Stat, Time Spent in Paid and Unpaid Work, by Gender.

3.2 Methods of Valuing Household Production

Standard national accounting procedures require that time spent on household productive be valued using market or quasi-market prices. Economists have developed two main methods of assigning a monetary value to household time use: the replacement-cost method and the opportunity-cost method.

In the **replacement-cost method**, hours spent on household labor are valued at what it would cost to pay someone else to do the same job. In the most popular approach—and the one used to generate the most conservative estimates   economists use the wages paid in a general category such as "domestic worker" or "housekeeper" to impute a wage. A variant of this method, which usually results in higher estimates, is to value each type of task separately: childcare time is valued according to the wage of a professional childcare worker, housecleaning by the wages of professional housecleaners, plumbing repair by the wages of a plumber, and so forth (as discussed in Box 5.3).

> **replacement-cost method** (for estimating the value of household production): valuing hours at the amount it would be necessary to pay someone to do the work

The **opportunity-cost method** starts from a different view, based on microeconomic "marginal" thinking. Presumably, if someone reduces their hours at paid work to engage in household production, they might value time spent in household production (at the margin) at least at the wage rate that they could have earned doing paid work. That is, if you give up $30 that you could have earned working an extra hour to spend an hour with your child, the value of spending that hour with your child is at least $30. This method uses the wage rate that an individual would have earned in the market to value the time spent doing household work. In this case, estimates of the value of non-market production can be higher than using the replacement-cost method, since some hours would be valued at the wage rates earned by doctors, lawyers, and other more highly paid workers.

> **opportunity-cost method (for estimating the value of household production):** valuing hours at the amount that the unpaid worker could have earned at a paid job

Neither approach to imputing a wage rate is perfect. However, it would be hard to argue that perfection has been achieved in any of the other measurements and imputations involved in creating the national accounts, and many argue that imputing any value for household labor time, even using minimal replacement costs, is more accurate than imputing a value of zero.

Similar arguments have been made concerning unpaid volunteer work in communities and non-profit organizations—the time that people spend coaching children's sports teams, visiting nursing homes, serving on church and school committees, and so on. In the United States, 8 percent of men and 13 percent of women reported participating in organizational, civic, and religious activities, a figure that includes organized volunteer activities. If volunteer work and household work were counted in national accounts, the proportion of production attributed to the core sphere of the economy would rise considerably.

Discussion Questions

1. Do you think that national governments should incorporate a monetary estimate of the value of household production in national accounting statistics? How do you think the inclusion of household production would affect the measurement of economic activity in developed versus developing countries?

2. Think back on at least one household activity in which you have engaged in the past couple of days that in principle could be replaced by market or third-person services. How would that activity be valued by the replacement-cost method? By the opportunity-cost method? What sorts of manufactured capital goods were important, along with your labor, in the activity?

4 ACCOUNTING FOR THE ENVIRONMENT

The natural environment underpins all economic activities. Recall Figure 2.6, which indicated that the natural environment provides resources and environmental services as inflows to economic activity and that economic activity also releases waste products into the environment. Environmental economists describe the economic functions of the natural world under three headings:§§

1. *Resource functions:* The natural environment provides natural resources that are inputs into human production processes, including renewable resources, such as fisheries and forests, and nonrenewable resources, such as minerals and crude oil.
2. *Environmental service functions:* The natural environment provides clean air, drinkable water, and a suitable climate that directly supports all forms of life on the planet. Water filtration provided by wetlands and erosion control provided by tree-covered hillsides are other examples of services provided by ecosystems. People receive the services of the natural environment directly when they enjoy pleasant scenery or outdoor recreation.
3. *Sink functions:* The natural environment also serves as a "sink" that absorbs (up to a point) the pollution and waste generated by economic activity. Car exhaust goes into the atmosphere, for example, while used packaging goes into landfill, and fluid industrial waste ends up in rivers and oceans. Some waste breaks down relatively quickly into harmless substances. Others are toxic or accumulate over time, eventually compromising the quality of the environment.

Although for centuries these environmental functions were treated as though they were provided "free" and in unlimited amounts, more recently the problems of depletion of resources, degradation of environmental services, and overuse of environmental sink functions have become increasingly apparent. Consider the example of a country that depends heavily on natural resources. If its forests are cut down, its soil fertility depleted, and its water supplies polluted, surely the country has become poorer. But national income accounting will merely record the market value of the timber, agricultural produce, and industrial output as positive contributions to GDP.

Global declines in soil fertility and depletion of water resources, along with the increased incidence of droughts, extreme weather events,

---

§§ A fourth category of environmental value stems not from use but from mere appreciation of the existence of species and environmental amenities; this is felt by some people even if they do not expect to see, for example, a blue whale or Victoria Falls. The "existence value" of a given species or resource is difficult to quantify, but it is recognized as a legitimate economic value by economists.

199

biodiversity loss, and rising global temperatures are already increasing global food prices and threatening to worsen food insecurity.[39] In the United States, food prices increased by 6.3 percent in December 2021 compared to the previous year, and the price of poultry, meat, fish, and eggs jumped by 12.5 percent. While part of this increase is due to supply disruptions caused by the pandemic, the increase in extreme weather events (especially droughts in the West and Midwest) and the rise in energy costs also contributed to this price increase.[40]

As increased greenhouse gas emissions lead to serious disruptions in climate, more severe storms, and rising sea levels, more and more money must be spent in what we have described as "defensive expenditures." Omitting such important environmental considerations from our measures of success could seriously undermine our goals for sustainability. We therefore need to account for the environmental costs of economic activity.

4.1 Methods of Valuing the Environment

4.1.1 System of Environmental-Economic Accounting

In 1993 the United Nations put forth a comprehensive framework, called the **System of Environmental-Economic Accounting (SEEA)**, to add statistics on environmental accounting to the existing methods of national accounting, using supplementary tables. The SEEA framework, revised most recently in 2014, covers the measurement of the environment and its relationship with the economy using three key approaches:

1. *Measuring the physical flows of materials and energy.* This approach measures the physical flows of natural capital from the environment to the economy as inputs to production, such as extracting metal, drilling for oil, and cutting trees. It also looks at flows from the economy to the environment, such as disposal of solid waste and emission of air and water pollutants. Flows into, or out of, different sectors of the economy are quantified in tables. A table for water pollution, for example, would include quantities of chemical waste, insecticides, fertilizers, and industrial discharges into the water from various sectors of the economy.
2. *Measuring the stocks of environmental assets.* The SEEA lists seven categories of environmental assets: mineral and energy resources, land, soil, timber, water, aquatic resources, and other biological resources. These assets are either measured in physical units such as tons of soil, or acres of wetlands, or in monetary units by multiplying a physical quantity of an environmental asset by its per-unit market price or through some non-market valuation process discussed in Section 4.2 below.
3. *Measuring economic activity related to the environment.* This approach lists monetary transactions related to the environment,

such as the amount of spending on environmental protection and resource management, and environmental taxes and subsidies. The measure also includes the production of environmental goods and services, "environmentally friendly" products and technologies, and pollution-control equipment.

These approaches are not necessarily mutually exclusive—we could theoretically implement all of them simultaneously. While many countries have adopted one or more of these accounts to some extent, no country has fully implemented the SEEA recommendations, and there is currently no universally accepted approach to environmental accounting.

4.1.2 Green GDP

The most basic approach to "green" accounting is to start with traditional measures and make adjustments that reflect environmental concerns. As discussed in Chapter 4, the current national income accounting recognizes that some of each year's economic production is offset by the depreciation of manufactured, or fixed, capital such as buildings and machinery. National accounting methods produce estimates of net domestic product (NDP), which start with GDP and then deduct the annual depreciation value of existing fixed capital. For example, in 2020 the GDP of the United States was $20.9 trillion. But the depreciation of fixed capital that year totaled $3.6 trillion. Thus, the NDP of the United States in 2020 was $17.3 trillion.

Extending this logic, we can see that each year the value of natural capital may also depreciate as a result of resource extraction or environmental degradation. In some cases, the value of natural capital could also increase if environmental quality improves. The net annual change in the value of natural capital in a country can simply be added or subtracted from NDP to obtain what has been called an environmentally adjusted measure of national product, or **Green GDP**. Thus:

$$\text{Green GDP} = \text{GDP} - D_m - D_n$$

where D_m is the depreciation of manufactured capital and D_n is the depreciation of natural capital.

Green GDP: GDP less depreciation of both manufactured and natural capital

---

This measure requires estimating natural capital depreciation in monetary terms, rather than physical units such as biomass volume or habitat area. Estimating the value of all types of natural capital depreciation in monetary terms is a daunting task that would require many assumptions. For this reason, the estimates of Green GDP that have been produced generally focus on only a few categories of natural capital depreciation.

Attempts to estimate Green GDP date back to the 1980s. A pioneering 1989 analysis estimated the value of depreciation in Indonesia for three categories of natural capital: oil, forests, and soil.[41] The analysis found that accounting for natural capital depreciation could reduce GDP by 25 percent or more. A 2001 analysis in Sweden looked at a broader set of natural resource categories, including soil erosion, recreation values, metal ores, and water quality.[42] The results found that accounting for these factors would reduce GDP in Sweden by about 1–2 percent between 1993 and 1997, with some sectors being particularly affected, such as agriculture, forestry, and fisheries. Another study estimated the value of changes in forest resources in India in 2003.[43] Based on timber and firewood market prices, the results indicated that while the overall physical stock of timber decreased, the value of timber resources actually increased due to higher prices. This illustrates the potential distortionary effect of looking at natural capital in monetary, rather than physical, terms.

A significant effort to estimate Green GDP occurred in China in the early 2000s. The initial findings by China's State Environmental Protection Agency (SEPA) in 2006 indicated that environmental costs equaled about 3 percent of China's GDP. The report was widely criticized because it failed to include numerous categories of environmental damage, such as groundwater contamination. Shortly afterward, a separate report concluded that environmental damage was closer to 10 percent of China's GDP. And in a 2007 report jointly produced by the World Bank and SEPA, the costs of air and water pollution alone were estimated at 5.8 percent of China's GDP.[44] Green GDP efforts in China were subsequently canceled in response to opposition from provincial officials who viewed Green GDP as a threat to their efforts to promote high growth. But in 2015 China announced it was restarting its efforts with the implementation of "Green GDP 2.0," with pilot projects in certain regions. Most recently, a 2020 journal article estimated China's Green GDP in 2017 to be 4 percent less than its traditional GDP.[45]

A 2019 analysis, estimating Green GDP for 44 countries, found that Green GDP was lower than standard GDP in all cases, from 1 to 10 percent. Countries with the highest environmental impacts included China (5 percent), Chile (9 percent), Norway (7 percent), and Mexico (4 percent). Some countries, including Japan, Germany, and France had Green GDP adjustments of less than 0.5 percent.[46] This does not mean that environmental damage in these developed countries was insignificant, but rather that it amounted to a smaller percentage of their relatively high GDP values. Such studies have also been criticized for inadequately valuing damages due to carbon emissions and climate change.

4.1.3 Adjusted Net Savings

The World Bank has developed an indicator of **Adjusted Net Saving** that seeks to measure what a society is truly saving for its future, starting with net savings (gross savings minus manufactured capital depreciation) and making adjustments for education, pollution, and the depreciation of natural capital.[47] Expenditures on education are added to national savings to reflect investment in human capital. Adjustment for pollution damages accounts for the negative impacts of carbon dioxide emissions and local air pollution. Accounting for depreciation of natural capital involves deducting the depletion of non-renewable fossil fuels (oil, coal, and natural gas), extraction of non-renewable minerals, and adding the net change in the forest area.

Adjusted Net Saving: a national accounting indicator which aims to measure how much a country is actually saving for its future

---

The World Bank has calculated ANS rates for most countries of the world, with selected results presented in Table 5.2. For many countries, the environmental adjustments are relatively minor, but in some cases, they are a large proportion of net savings. The deduction for energy

Table 5.2 Adjusted Net Saving (ANS) Rates, Selected Countries, Percent of Gross National Income, 2019

Country	Net national saving	Education Spending	Energy depletion	Mineral depletion	Net forest depletion	Pollution + Carbon damage	ANS
Brazil	4.4	6.3	−1.7	−0.3	0.00	−1.3	7.4
China	27.0	1.8	−0.6	−0.2	0.00	−3.5	24.5
Congo, Dem. Rep.	17.1	2.1	−0.5	−2.4	−2.4	−1.9	12.0
Germany	9.7	4.5	−0.0	−0.0	0.0	−0.8	13.3
India	18.1	3.1	−0.4	−0.4	−0.1	−5.1	15.1
Kenya	−7.5	4.9	−0.0	0.0	−0.6	−1.9	−5.0
Mexico	6.4	4.5	−1.6	−0.1	0.0	−1.8	7.4
Nigeria	10.9	0.9	−3.7	−0.0	−0.6	−3.7	3.7
Philippines	19.8	1.8	−0.1	−0.2	−0.1	−2.1	19.1
Russia	15.6	4.4	−7.3	−0.1	0.0	−4.6	8.0
Uganda	15.5	1.7	0.0	0.0	−6.2	−2.2	8.9
United States	2.7	4.4	−0.3	−0.0	0.0	−1.0	5.8

Source: World Bank, World Development Indicators database.

203

depletion is particularly high in Russia and Nigeria. High rates of both mineral and forest depletion are observed in the Democratic Republic of the Congo. The pollution adjustment tends to be a smaller share of national income but is still high in such countries as India, Russia, Nigeria, and China.

About 20 countries have a negative ANS, most of them in Africa and the Middle East. On average, ANS rates are highest in middle-income countries such as China and India, which helps explain why these countries have generally been growing faster in recent years than high-income countries. But note that their high ANS is based on a high basic savings rate; they have significant environmental adjustments in the range of 4–5 percent of GDP. Low-income countries have the lowest average ANS rates, suggesting that low financial saving rates and natural capital degradation are undermining future well-being in these countries.

4.2 Monetary Valuation of Environmental Factors

Estimating monetary values for natural assets requires various assumptions, as these assets are rarely traded in markets unless they are exploited commercially. For example, in recent decades there has been a worldwide decline in populations of amphibians (frogs, toads, and salamanders), along with a large increase in deformities in these animals. Clearly, degradation of the natural environment is occurring. But since the market value of most frog species is zero, there are wide disagreements about how—or even whether—a monetary value can be put on these losses.

As another example, suppose that a hillside is stripped of its forest covering, and the wood is sold as pulp for papermaking. The lack of vegetation now means that runoff from rain increases, and could lead to flooding in downstream towns. In the national accounts as currently constructed, the timber from logging contributes to GDP, but so does the cost of repairing flooding damage (since this is considered an economic activity). Two things are wrong with this accounting approach. First, there is no accounting for the loss of the flood protection benefits of the forest. Second, the costs of repairing the flooding damages count as a positive contribution to GDP, instead of as a net cost that could have been avoided with better resource management.

How could we go about evaluating the environmental services received from the trees on the hillside? Using the **damage-cost approach**, an environmental service can be valued based on the damages done when the service is withdrawn. Suppose that the cost of flooding repairs is $5 million—we can then say that the value of the flood protection services of the hillside forest is $5 million.

---

damage-cost approach: assigning a monetary value to an environmental service that is equal to the actual damage done when the service is withdrawn

---

Another approach to valuing the water retention services of an existing forest would be to consider the costs of replicating these services. Let's suppose that the damage from flooding could be avoided, despite the loss of the forests, by spending $100,000 on sandbagging. Using a **maintenance-cost approach**, we could say that the value of the forest's services is $100,000. As often happens, the results of the two approaches may differ significantly—in this case the value of the forest's services could be estimated at either $5 million or $100,000.

---

maintenance-cost approach: assigning a monetary value to an environmental service that is equal to what it would cost to maintain the same standard of services using an alternative method

---

Economists and environmental scientists face a similar choice in many other areas; for example, whether to measure the value of unpolluted air in terms of effects of pollution on human health (damage) or in terms of the cost of pollution-control devices (maintenance). So far, some national and international agencies have adopted one convention and some the other in their experimental environmental accounts.

If the withdrawal of environmental services makes people suffer or die, then we enter the even more controversial area of trying to assign dollar values to human suffering and human lives. And many environmental effects cross national lines. What is the monetary value of a global "public good" such as a stable climate? On whose account should we tally the loss of deep-sea fisheries located in international waters?

One approach to the problem of valuation is simply to use satellite accounts, as described above, which can be recorded in physical terms, without monetary valuation. So, for example, we might note that the forest cover in a country has declined by 10 percent without attempting to value all the ecological functions of forests. Many governments have already committed in principle to creating such accounts for their own country, and some, such as Norway, maintain extensive satellite accounts for many resource and environmental categories.

Discussion Questions

1. In Burgess County, current irrigation methods are leading to rising salt levels in agricultural fields. As a result, the number of bushels of corn that can be harvested per acre is declining. If you are a county agricultural economist, what two approaches might you consider using to estimate the value of the lost fertility of the soil during the current year? What sorts of economic and technological information would you need to come up with your estimates?
2. Some people have argued that the monetary valuation of environmental costs and benefits is important because "any number

is better than no number"— without valuation, these factors are omitted from GDP accounts. Others say that it is impossible to express environmental factors adequately in dollar terms. What are some valid points on each side of this debate? How do you think this debate should be resolved?

5 CONCLUSION: MEASURING ECONOMIC WELL-BEING

No one—and especially not their creators—would argue that alternative macroeconomic indicators have been perfected. Nor has any single approach emerged as the "best" way to adjust, replace, or supplement GDP. As we have seen, any macroeconomic indicator involves numerous assumptions. One of the strengths of some of the new measures is that they allow users to see how the results change under different assumptions. For example, the BLI allows users to adjust the weights on each of the 11 well-being dimensions according to their personal preferences. Some have suggested that the best approach is to use multiple indicators, along the lines of the "dashboard" analogy mentioned earlier. One thing is clear—reliance on a single traditional GDP measure omits or distorts many crucial variables. Thus, all the alternative approaches discussed in this chapter have some value in providing broader perspectives on the measurement of well-being.

Discussion Questions

1. Of the various alternative indicators presented in this chapter, which one would you advocate as the best approach for measuring economic well-being? What do you think are the strengths and weaknesses of this indicator?
2. Suppose that your national government officially adopted your preferred indicator from the previous question. How do you think this would change specific policy debates in your country? What new policies do you think could be enacted?

REVIEW QUESTIONS

1. What are the two major contexts for economic activity?
2. What are some of the main critiques of GDP as a measure of well-being?
3. What are satellite accounts?
4. What is subjective well-being (SWB), and how is it commonly measured?
5. Based on scientific research, what is the relationship between the average level of SWB in a country and its GDP per capita?
6. Do average levels of SWB increase as a country develops economically?
7. What is the Genuine Progress Indicator (GPI), and how is it measured?
8. What is the relationship between GDP per capita and GPI per capita in the United States over the past several decades?
9. What is the Better Life Index, and what components are used to construct it?

206

10. What is the Human Development Index?
11. In what ways has the HDI measure been modified to better account for poverty and inequality?
12. What are some examples of household production?
13. What is the difference between the replacement-cost method and the opportunity-cost method for valuing household production?
14. What are the three main functions of natural systems?
15. What is Green GDP? How is it calculated?
16. What is adjusted net savings? How is it calculated?
17. What are the potential problems with estimating environmental impacts in monetary terms?
18. What is the damage-cost approach to estimating the value of environmental services?
19. What is the maintenance-cost approach to estimating the value of environmental services?

EXERCISES

1. Describe in a short paragraph why measures of *output* do not always measure *well-being.* Include some specific examples beyond those given in the text.
2. Indicate whether each of the following actions or impacts would increase GDP
   a) An individual purchases bottled water to avoid a contaminated municipal water supply.
   b) An individual obtains her drinking water from a water fountain at her workplace to avoid a contaminated municipal water supply
   c) A homeowner pays a lawn-care company for landscaping services
   d) A neighbor agrees to help a homeowner with landscaping work in exchange for assistance with plumbing work
   e) A paper company employs workers to plant trees
   f) An environmental organization provides volunteers to plant trees
3. In calculating the GPI,
   a) Which factors are subtracted because they represent negative effects on well-being?
   b) Which factors are *not* included in GPI, even though they are included in GDP, because they are defensive expenditures or because of differences in accounting methods?
4. Go to the OECD's Web site for the Better Life Index (www.oecdbetterlifeindex.org). Note that you can adjust the weights applied to each of the 11 well-being dimensions using a sliding scale. Adjust the weights based on your personal opinions. To which factors do you assign the most weight? To which factors do you assign the least weight? Briefly summarize the rationale for your weights. Also, which countries rank the highest according to your weighted BLI?
5. The UNDP *Human Development Report* is available at its Web site (www.undp.org). Consult this report, and pick a country of your choice. Write a paragraph describing this country's performance on the HDI as well as on three other indicators reported in the tables (such as inequality, personal security, hunger, or violence against women and girls).
6. Suppose that you buy a bread-making machine, flour, and other foodstuffs, take them home and bake bread with a group of young children who are in your care (unpaid). How would these activities be accounted for in current GDP accounting? How might they be accounted for in an expanded account that includes household production?
7. Estimate how much time you spend each week doing two unpaid household production tasks (e.g., cleaning, cooking, or repairs). Then, locate data on the typical wages paid to workers who perform these tasks on the Bureau of Labor Statistics Web site

(www.bls.gov/bls/blswage.htm). Based on these data, what is the monetary value of your weekly household production for these tasks?

8. Which of the following describe a resource function of the natural environment? An environmental service function? A sink function?
   a) A landfill
   b) A copper mine
   c) Carbon dioxide (a byproduct of combustion) entering the atmosphere
   d) Wild blueberries growing in a meadow
   e) A suitable temperature for growing corn
   f) A view of the Grand Canyon

9. In 2011, the Deepwater Horizon oil spill in the Gulf of Mexico caused heavy damage to the fishing and tourism industries of Louisiana and other coastal states. In addition, there were long-term ecological impacts on fish and wildlife. Describe how this might be accounted for in the 2011 national accounts of the United States if they were environmentally adjusted:
   a) In terms of depreciation of assets
   b) In terms of flows of produced goods and services. (Describe in detail how two approaches to assigning dollar values might be applied)

10. Consumption of oil, gas, and coal currently fuels the U.S. economy but also has other effects. How might the following be accounted for in the U.S. national accounts, if they were environmentally adjusted?
    a) Depletion of domestic oil, natural gas, and coal reserves
    b) Release of greenhouse gases into the atmosphere
    c) Smoggy air that hides scenery and makes outdoor activity unpleasant

11. Match each concept in Column A with a definition or example in Column B.

Column A	Column B
a. Depreciation of natural capital	1. Valuing time at the wage that someone gives up
b. Satellite accounts	2. Comparison with GDP supports the diminishing marginal utility of income
c. An indicator of well-being including 11 dimensions	3. Costs of cleaning up a toxic waste site
d. An example of non-market production	4. The value of fish killed by toxic waste
e. Opportunity-cost method	5. Government production
f. Subjective well-being	6. The effect on copper reserves of copper mining
g. Maintenance costs	7. Better Life Index
h. Defensive expenditures	8. The service performed by a garbage dump
i. A way of measuring well-being (not production) using dollar amounts	9. Clean-up costs following an oil spill
j. Damage costs	10. Monetary or physical measures that can be related to GDP
k. Sink function	11. Genuine Progress Indicator

NOTES

1   Based on 2020 data from the World Development Indicators, World Bank.
2   Dietz and O'Niell, 2013.
3   Information on BEA Satellite Account is available at: https://www.bea.gov/resourc-es/learning-center/what-to-know-special-topics.
4   BEA, 1994.
5   Diener, et al. 2018; Jorm and Ryan, 2013.
6   Stiglitz, Sen and Fitoussi, 2009, p. 16.
7   Ingelhart et al., 2008.
8   Talberth et al., 2007.
9   Talberth and Weisdorf, 2017, p. 142.
10   Talberth et al., 2007.
11   Kubiszewski et al., 2013.
12   Fox and Erickson, 2018.
13   Ceroni, 2014.
14   Hayden and Wilson, 2018, p. 462.
15   BLI, 2015.
16   OECD, 2018.
17   OECD, 2020.
18   World Development Indicators database, World Bank.
19   Ura et al., 2012.
20   Center for Bhutan Studies, 2015.
21   The Treasury of New Zealand, 2019.
22   IISD, 2014.
23   Well-being Economy Alliance, 2021.
24   Ibid.
25   Eisner, 1988.
26   UN Women, 2020.
27   Heggeness et al., 2021.
28   Shelton, 2021.
29   Salary.com, 2020.
30   Livingston and Parker, 2019.
31   Economic Policy Institute, 2020.
32   Folbre, 2015.
33   Oxfam, 2019.
34   Yeginsu, 2018.
35   Kanal and Kornegay, 2019.
36   ILO, 2018.
37   Office for National Statistics (UK), 2016.
38   BLS, 2021.
39   Flavelle, 2019.
40   Swanson. 2022.
41   Repetto et al., 1989.
42   Skånberg, 2001.
43   Gundimeda et al., 2007.
44   World Bank and SEPA, 2007.
45   Wang et al., 2020.
46   Stjepanović et al., 2019.
47   See World Bank data on environmental accounting.

REFERENCES

Briody, Blaire. 2012. "What Are Stay-at-Home Moms Really Worth?" *Fiscal Times*, May 4.

Centre for Bhutan Studies. 2015. "A Compass towards a Just and Harmonious Society: 2015 GNH Survey Report." Centre for Bhutan Studies and GNH Research.

Ceroni, Marta. 2014. "Beyond GDP: US States have Adopted Genuine Progress Indicators." *Guardian*, September 23.

Diener, Ed, Shigehiro Oishi and Louis Tay. 2018. "Advances in Subjective Well-Being Research." *Nature Human Behavior, 2*: 253–260.

Dietz, Rob and Dan O'Neill. 2013. "There's No G-D-P in 'A Better Economy.'" *Stanford Social Innovation Review*, January 7.

Economic Policy Institute. 2020. "The Cost of Childcare in Massachusetts." https://www.epi.org/child-care-costs-in-the-united-states/#/MA

Eisner, Robert. 1988. "Extended Accounts for National Income and Product." *Journal of Economic Literature, 26*(4): 1611–1684, December.

Flavelle, Christopher. 2019. "Climate Change Threatens the World's Food Supply, United Nations Warns." *The New York Times*, August 8.

Folbre, Nancy. 2015. "Valuing Nonmarket Work." *2015 UNDP Human Development Report Office Think Piece*. UNDP Human Development Report Office: New York, USA. https://hdr.undp.org/system/files/documents//folbrehdr2015finalpdf.pdf

Fox, Mairi-Jane V. and Jon D. Erickson. 2018. "Genuine Economic Progress in the United States: A Fifty State Study and Comparative Assessment." *Ecological Economics, 147*: 29–35.

Goossens, Yanne, Arttu Mäkipää, Philipp Schepelmann, Michael Kuhndt and Martin Herrndorf. 2007. "Alternative Progress Indicators to Gross Domestic Product (GDP) as a Means towards Sustainable Development" New Economics Foundation. London.

Gundimeda, Haripriya, Pavan Sukhdev, Rajiv K. Sinha, and Sanjeev Sanyal. 2007. "Natural Resource Accounting for Indian States—Illustrating the Case of Forest Resources." *Ecological Economics, 61*(4): 635–649.

Hayden, Anders and Jeffrey Wilson. 2018. "Taking the First Steps beyond GDP: Maryland's Experience in Measuring "Genuine Progress." *Sustainability, 10*(2): 2-24.

Heggeness, Misty L., Jason Fields, Yazmin A. Garcia Trejo, and Anthony Schulzetenberg. 2021. "Tracking Job Losses for Mothers of School-Age Children during a Health Crisis." *The U.S. Census Bureau*, March 3.

Helliwell, John F., Richard Layard, Jeffrey Sachs, Jan-Emmanuel De Neve, Lara B. Aknin, and Shun Wang. 2021. "World Happiness Report 2021." *Sustainable Development Solutions Network*, New York.

Ingelhart, Robert, Roberto Foa, Christopher Peterson, and Christian Welze. 2008. "Development, Freedom, and Rising Happiness." *Perspectives on Psychological Science, 3*(4): 264–285.

International Institute for Sustainable Development (IISD). 2014. "Measuring Wealth to Promote Sustainable Development." https://www.iisd.org/projects/measuring-wealth-promote-sustainable-development

International Labor Organization (ILO). 2018. *Care Work and Care Jobs: For the Future of Decent Work*. Geneva.

Jorm, Anthony F. and Siobhan M. Ryan. 2014. "Cross-National and Historical Differences in Subjective Well-Being." *International Journal of Epidemiology, 43*: 330–340.

Kanal, Danit, and Joseph Ted Kornegay. 2019. "Accounting for Household Production in the National Accounts: An Update, 1965–2017." *Survey of Current Business*, U.S. Bureau of Economic Analysis, June.

Kubiszewski, Ida 2019. "The Genuine Progress Indicator: A Measure of Net Economic Welfare." *Encyclopedia of Ecology* (Second edition), *4*: 327–335.

Kubiszewski, Ida, Robert Costanza, Carol Franco, Philip Lawn, John Talberth, Tim Jackson and Camille Aymer. 2013. "Beyond GDP: Measuring and Achieving Global Genuine Progress." *Ecological Economics, 93*: 57–68.

Leonhardt, David. 2018. "We're Measuring the Economy All Wrong." *The New York Times*, September 14.

Livingston, Gretchen and Kim Parker. 2019. "8 Facts about American Dads." *Pew Research Center*, June 12.

Office for National Statistics (UK). 2016. "Women Shoulder the Responsibility of 'Unpaid Work'," November 10.

Organization for Economic Co-operation and Development (OECD). 2018. "What Matters the Most to People? Evidence from the OECD Better Life Index Users' Responses," July 23.

Organization for Economic Co-operation and Development (OECD). 2020. *How's Life? 2020: Measuring Well-Being*. OECD Publishing, Paris.

Oxfam. 2019. "Time to Care," Jan, 19. https://www.oxfamamerica.org/explore/research-publications/time-care/

Piketty, Thomas, Emmanuel Saez, and Gabriel Zucman. 2016. "Distributional National Accounts: Methods and Estimates for the United States." National Bureau of Economic Research Working Paper Series, Working Paper 22945, December 2016.

Repetto, Robert, et al. 1989. *Wasting Assets: Natural Resources in the National Income Accounts*. World Resources Institute. Washington, DC.

Salary.com. 2020. "How Much Is a Mother Really Worth?" https://www.salary.com/articles/mother-salary

Semega, Jessica, Melissa Kollar, Emily A. Shrider, and John Creamer. 2020. "Income and Poverty in the United States: 2019." *The U.S. Census Bureau*, Report Number P60–270, September 15.

Shelton, Jennifer. 2021. "Mother's Day Index 2021: Mom's Salary Hits Triple Digits for the First Time in Index History." *Insure.com*, May 3.

Skånberg, Kristian. 2001. *Constructing a Partially Environmentally Adjusted Net Domestic Product for Sweden 1993 and 1997*. National Institute of Economic Research. Stockholm, Sweden.

Stiglitz, Joseph E., Amartya Sen, and Jean-Paul Fitoussi. 2009. *Report by the Commission on the Measurement of Economic Performance and Social Progress*. https://ec.europa.eu/eurostat/documents/8131721/8131772/Stiglitz-Sen-Fitoussi-Commission-report.pdf

Stjepanović, Saša, Daniel Tomić, and Marinko Škare. 2019. "Green GDP: An Analysis for Developing and Developed Countries." *E+M: Ekonomie a Management, 22*(4): 4–17.

Swanson, Ana. 2022. "Food Prices Approach Record Highs, Threatening the World's Poorest." *The New York Times*, February 3.

Talberth, John, Clifford Cobb, and Noah Slattery. 2007. "The Genuine Progress Indicator 2006: A Tool for Sustainable Development." *Redefining Progress*, February, 2007.

Talberth, John and Michael Weisdorf. 2017. "Genuine Progress Indicator 2.0: Pilot Accounts for the US, Maryland, and City of Baltimore 2012–2014." *Ecological Economics, 142*: 1–11, December.

The Treasury New Zealand (2019) 'The Wellbeing Budget', https://www.treasury.govt.nz/sites/default/files/2019-05/b19-wellbeing-budget.pdfUN Women. 2020. "Whose Time to Care? Unpaid Care and Domestic Work during Covid-19," November.

Ura, Karma, Sabina Alkire, Tshoki Zangmo, and Karma Wangdi. 2012. "*A Short Guide to Gross National Happiness Index*." Centre for Bhutan Studies. Thimpu, Bhutan.

U.S. Bureau of Economic Analysis (BEA). 1994. "Integrated Economic and Environmental Satellite Accounts." *Survey of Current Business*. https://apps.bea.gov/scb/account_articles/national/0494od/maintext.htm

U.S. Bureau of Labor Statistics (BLS). 2021. "American Time Use Survey – May to December 2019 and 2020 Results." *BLS News Release*. July 22, 2021. https://www.bls.gov/news.release/pdf/atus.pdf

Wang, Feng, Ruiqi Wang, and Junyao Wang. 2020. "Measurement of China's Green GDP and its Dynamic Variation Based on Industrial Perspective." Environmental Science and Pollution Research, vol. 27. doi.org/10.1007/s11356-020-10236-x.

Wellbeing Economy Alliance. 2021. "How Happy is the Planet?" October. https://happy-planetindex.org/wp-content/themes/hpi/public/downloads/happy-planet-index-briefing-paper.pdfWorld Bank and State Environmental Protection Agency (World Bank and SEPA), People's Republic of China. 2007. "Cost of Pollution in China." Rural Development, Natural Resources and Environment Management Unit, East Asia and Pacific Region, World Bank, Washington, DC.

World Development Indicators database. *The World Bank.* www.databank.worldbank.org

Yeginsu, Ceylan. 2018. "What's Housework Worth? $1.6 Trillion a S in U.K., Officials Calculate." *The New York Times,* October 4.

Chapter 6

The Structure of the United States Economy

The U.S. economy is both complex and rapidly evolving. Important issues include the changing nature of jobs, a decline in some manufacturing areas and expansion in technology and some services, as well as the growing dominance of financial institutions. This chapter will address some of these issues and will present information on which we can begin to build a picture of the total economy.

To start with, the U.S. economy is the largest in the world, producing almost 25 percent of total global economic output as measured by the GDP of all the world's countries.[1] While it has grown since its beginning, the economy has also changed. A dramatic example of this change is the role of agriculture. Early in U.S. history, most people worked on small farms. But now less than 2 percent of the workforce is directly engaged in agriculture, even though the United States is the third largest agricultural producer in the world, based on agricultural value-added, behind China and India.

What is the rest of the workforce doing? You may, or may not, be surprised to know that more than three-quarters of the workforce is engaged in producing "services" of one kind or another, with about 16 percent working in government, while as of 2020 only about 13.2 percent of workers were employed in manufacturing and construction.[2] This chapter provides some insight into what is going on in this complex macroeconomy.

1 THE THREE MAJOR PRODUCTIVE SECTORS IN AN ECONOMY

1.1 A Quick Review of Categories

Although macroeconomics often considers "the economy" as a whole, the economy is very far from being a homogeneous entity. We have already considered some ways to classify a macroeconomy into smaller units.

- In Chapter 2 we defined the *three economic spheres:* core, business, and public purpose.
- In Chapter 4 we saw that the U.S. national accounts classify the economy into *four accounting sectors* based on *who* produces goods

DOI: 10.4324/9781003251521-9

and services: households and institutions, businesses, government, and the foreign sector.

■ Within each of these groupings, economic actors carry out what, in Chapter 1, we described as the *four essential economic activities*: production, distribution, and consumption of goods and services, and resource management.

In this chapter, we turn to different classification groups, which we refer to as **output sectors**, based on *what* is being produced. While the classification of the macroeconomy into three economic spheres shows where economic activities are occurring and the classification by the four accounting sectors is useful in measuring overall economic activity, classification into the three output sectors—presented in this chapter—provides an insight into structural changes in the economy and in the job market. This is helpful in understanding which sectors are experiencing growth, which are facing decline, and in which direction the economy is headed.

> **output sectors:** divisions of a macroeconomy based on what is being produced

The three productive sectors that constitute any national economy are called primary, secondary, and tertiary. The **primary sector** involves the harvesting and extraction of natural resources and rudimentary processing of these raw materials. Industries in the primary sector include agriculture, commercial fishing, mining, and the timber industry. Generally, the products produced in the primary sector are not sold directly to households for final consumption but to manufacturers as inputs. For example, the wheat grown, harvested, sorted, and dried in the primary sector would be sold to milling and baking companies in the secondary sector, which would then process the wheat into bread.

> **primary sector:** the sector of the economy that involves the harvesting and extraction of natural resources and simple processing of these raw materials into products that are generally sold to manufacturers as inputs

The **secondary sector** involves converting the outputs of the primary sector into products suitable for use or consumption. The secondary sector includes manufacturing industries such as automobile production, the chemical industry, petroleum refining, the pharmaceutical industry, and electronics production. It also includes utilities such as those that generate and distribute electricity as well as the construction of buildings and highways.

> **secondary sector:** the sector of the economy that involves converting the outputs of the primary sector into products suitable for use or consumption. It includes manufacturing, construction, and utilities

Finally, we have the **tertiary sector**, also called the service sector. This sector involves the provision of services rather than tangible goods. This sector comprises a great variety of activities, including education, health care, real estate transactions, insurance, banking, and finance.

There is no simple mapping from the three spheres that make up the economy (as described in earlier chapters) into the three output sectors just described. Firms in the *business sphere* of the economy are distributed among all three sectors. Entities from the *public-purpose* and *core spheres* can also be classified as working in one or more of the sectors. In the core sphere, for example, a household growing food in a garden is contributing to the primary sector. Production of home-cooked meals is a secondary-sector activity. The activities of care and maintenance in the home are best understood as services—thus in the tertiary sector. Much of the work of government and nonprofit organizations (in the public purpose sphere) is accounted for in the tertiary sector, but they may also be active in each of the other two sectors.

> **tertiary sector:** the sector of the economy that involves the provision of services rather than tangible goods

1.2 The Relative Size of the Output Sectors in the United States

Table 6.1 below presents the market value of the production in 2020 of the three output sectors, along with the proportion of the population employed in each sector in that year. This data is provided by the National Income and Product Accounts (NIPA) from the U.S. Bureau of Economic Analysis (BEA). (Note that this official measure does not include such "nonmarket" activities as volunteer work and household production.)

You might be surprised to see that less than a fifth of GDP comes from production that has to do with physical things, and only about 15 percent of workers are involved in that production—when production is measured in terms of the money value of output. In the United States, as in most countries, the extraction of physical things from nature is a relatively small part of the measured economy, accounting for just 1.7 percent of GDP, and employing only 1.3 percent of the workforce. The secondary sector, including utilities, construction, and manufacturing, accounts for about 16.8 percent of the economy and employs about 13.6 percent of the workforce.

215

Table 6.1 *Value-added and Employment by Output Sector in the United States, 2020*

Industry	Value-added (billions of dollars)	Percentage of GDP	Employment (in thousands)	Percentage of Employed
Primary Sector, Total	356.6	1.7	1,930	1.3
Agriculture, forestry, fishing, and hunting	174.5	0.8	1,391	0.9
Mining	182.1	0.9	539	0.4
Secondary Sector, Total	3,509.6	16.8	20,055	13.6
Utilities	341.7	1.6	545	0.4
Construction	895.9	4.3	7,401	5.0
Durable goods Manufacturing	1,268.8	6.1	7,544	5.1
Nondurable goods Manufacturing	1,003.1	4.8	4,565	3.1
Tertiary Sector, Total	14,357.1	68.8	101,158	68.5
Real estate and rental and leasing	2,804.4	13.4	2,237	1.5
Wholesale and retail trade	2,445.5	11.8	20,542	13.9
Transportation and warehousing	572	2.7	5,773	3.9
Information	1167.9	5.6	2,715	1.8
Finance and insurance	1,787.7	8.6	6,506	4.4
Professional, scientific, and technical services	1,627.8	7.8	9,547	6.5
Administration, waste management services, and management of companies and enterprises	1,062.1	5.1	10,948	7.4
Educational services	251.3	1.2	3,493	2.4
Health care and social assistance	1,547.3	7.4	19,829	13.4
Arts, entertainment, and recreation	163.4	0.8	1,766	1.2
Accommodation and food services	508.7	2.4	11,166	7.6
Other services, except government	419.0	2.0	6,600	4.5
Government Sector	2,670.6	12.8	24,457	16.6
Total	20,893.7	100	147,600[a]	100

Source: Bureau of Economic Analysis.

Note: [a]Includes estimates of foreign professional workers and undocumented Mexican migratory workers employed temporarily in the United States.

216

We see that the dominant element in the U.S. economy is now the private (i.e., non-government) tertiary sector, contributing 68.5 percent of total GDP—over two-thirds. Because the majority of government activities (about 13 percent of GDP) also involve providing services, this implies that about four-fifths of the U.S. GDP derives from services. This is also where over four-fifths—85 percent—of U.S. workers are employed.

Does this mean that the other sectors are relatively unimportant? Not at all. The tertiary sector is completely dependent on outputs from the other two sectors. Consider, for example, that a restaurant would not be able to provide food services without meat and vegetable products, furniture made from wood, and building and equipment based on rock, metal ores, or petroleum products (plastics). Some of the money that the restaurant pays for the products derived from agriculture, wood, and metal finds its way back to workers and owners in the primary sector, but the larger portion goes to secondary industries such as construction and fabrication of equipment. Even a partner in an investment firm will need a desk in an office building, with computer and communications media, all ultimately based on outputs from the primary and secondary sectors. In the latter case, the economic value-added in the tertiary sector is a giant step beyond what had been created in the other two sectors. You might wonder whether this is a sensible assessment of "value." Has the investment manager, compared to the restaurateur, contributed much more to the real human well-being of the economy? (We discuss this issue further in Chapters 7 and 14.)

1.3 Historical Trends and Global Comparisons

The relative shares of the three output sectors in GDP have changed over time in the United States. Figure 6.1 shows the share of the U.S. private economy (excluding government) attributed to each of the three output sectors since 1800. The primary sector's share of GDP was about 40 percent in 1800 but has since declined to its current share of about 1.9 percent of GDP. Perhaps the most surprising information given in the graph is that the tertiary sector has always comprised the largest share of economic production in the United States, even in 1800. The tertiary share of GDP held steady at around 50 percent from 1800 until about 1950, then steadily climbed to its current share of about 79 percent. The secondary sector's share of GDP increased from 13 percent in 1800 to about 37 percent in 1950 (taking up the share that was being lost from the primary sector, as the economic value of manufacturing eclipsed that of agriculture) but has decreased since then to about 19 percent in 2020.

The sectoral distribution of economic production in a representative sample of other countries is given in Table 6.2. The classification of output sectors in the table, based on data from the World Bank,

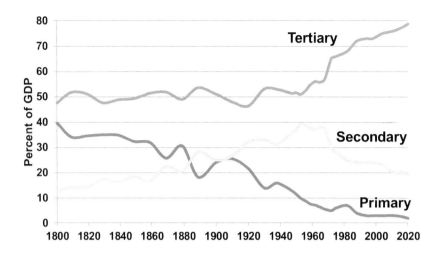

Figure 6.1 *Relative Shares of United States Economic Production, by Output Sector, 1800–2020*

Sources: Historical Statistics of the United States, 1789–1945, U.S. Census Bureau, 1949 (1800– 1938); Historical Statistics of the United States, Bicentennial Edition, Colonial Times to 1970, U.S. Census Bureau, 1975 (1947–1968); various annual editions of the Statistical Abstract of the United States, U.S. Census Bureau (1969–2020).

Note: This graph shows relative, not absolute, magnitudes.

is slightly different from the definitions given above. The World Bank defines agriculture as its own output sector. The World Bank's "industrial" sector includes the secondary sector as defined above but adds fishing, forestry, and mining output. The tertiary sector is unchanged, including all services.

As in the United States, the tertiary sector comprises at least 60 percent of economic production in the UK, Sweden, Japan, and Brazil. Largely because of its oil reserves, Norway is an example of a developed country with a relatively large share of GDP, about 35 percent, coming from the secondary sector. The secondary sector is the dominant share of GDP in several countries, including China, Saudi Arabia (because oil production is classified as "industrial"), Indonesia, and the Republic of the Congo (also heavily dependent on oil production). The agricultural sector is the largest sector only in a handful of lower-income countries, including Ethiopia. Even in most developing countries, the tertiary sector is the dominant output sector.

The sectoral data for different countries indicate that economic development is commonly associated with a declining share of GDP from agriculture. Economic growth in most countries is associated with a significant increase in the relative share of manufacturing, but this is not universally true. Some countries, such as Hong Kong, Bermuda, and Singapore, have achieved income growth primarily by expanding the service sector. (We consider these and other issues of economic development in more detail in Chapter 16.)

Table 6.2 *Division of GDP by Output Sector, Selected Countries, 2019*

Country	Agricultural Sector (%)	Industrial Sector (%)	Tertiary Sector (%)
Ethiopia	34	31	37
Congo, Rep.	8	59	39
Indonesia	13	59	44
India	16	39	49
Saudi Arabia	2	60	50
Bangladesh	13	49	53
China	7	66	54
Russia	3	45	54
Argentina	6	36	54
Norway	2	35	58
Mexico	3	48	60
South Africa	2	38	61
Germany	1	46	63
Brazil	4	27	63
Sweden	1	35	65
Japan	1	50	69
UK	1	26	71
United States	1	30	77

Source: World Bank, World Development Indicators database, 2019.

Note: These data are organized by a ranking, from lowest to highest, of the size of the tertiary sector.

Discussion Questions

1. Think about the businesses and industries in your community. How would you classify those businesses according to each of the three sectors described above? Does your answer to this question concur with the notion that the majority of economic activity takes place in the tertiary sector?
2. Try to estimate what share of your total expenditures is spent on products from the primary, secondary, and tertiary sectors. How do you think your expenditure patterns will change in the future? For example, assuming that your income will rise after you graduate, do you think that your share of expenditures on services will increase or decrease?

2 THE PRIMARY SECTOR IN THE UNITED STATES

The primary sector, as we have noted, is concerned with the harvesting and extraction of natural resources. Countries vary widely in their natural resource endowments, and their particular resource advantages or deficits affect their economic development and future prospects. This is especially true of the United States. When Europeans arrived in North America in the fifteenth through the nineteenth centuries they found extraordinary natural resources: fresh and salt waters teeming with fish, forests full of birds and animals, huge stocks of valuable timber, and great plains suitable for highly productive agriculture. Europeans and later immigrants brought with them, and developed after their arrival, methods of using these resources that have changed the landscape and the human experience of living here to an extraordinary extent. A quick look at the food, water, and energy systems illustrates the evolution of the production and use of primary sector products in the United States.

2.1 The Food System

Throughout its early history, the United States was an agrarian economy. In the late 1700s, approximately 90 percent of the labor force (as well as many family members not counted as in the labor force) were engaged in farming. By 1880, farmers still made up about half the labor force. Now less than 1 percent of the U.S. workforce is employed in agriculture; yet agriculture currently occupies about 897 million acres (over 40 percent) of land area and thus continues to dominate the geographic landscape of the country.

As material inputs and mechanization replaced labor in U.S. agriculture over the course of the twentieth century, the total farm population declined, along with a decrease in the total number of farms, while average farm size increased. According to data from the USDA, of the 2.02 million farms in the United States in 2020, 89.2 percent were small farms earning less than $350,000 a year and accounting for only 20.4 percent of the total production. Mid-sized farms, earning between $350,000 and $999,999 per year, account for another 20.2 percent of production. Meanwhile, large farms with over $1 million in sales account for only 2.9 percent of all farms, but 46 percent of all sales.[3] The largest farms in the country are generally owned as corporate enterprises with annual sales of millions of dollars.

The agricultural products that people consume are generally not obtained directly from farmers but undergo significant processing prior to being sold to consumers. As shown in Figure 6.2, less than 8 percent of each dollar spent on food in the United States is paid to farmers. Food services—restaurants and other places serving food away from home—receive more than one-third (about 38 percent) of what Americans pay for food. The next largest portion (14 percent) is spent on food processing before the point of sale to consumers or food services. In addition, 20.5 percent goes to the retail and wholesale traders who mediate between the producers/processors and consumers. The remainder is spent for packaging, transportation, finance, insurance, legal and accounting services, advertising and energy.

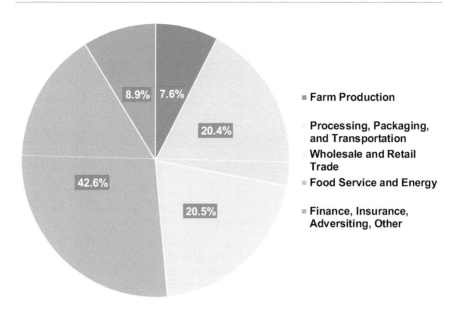

Figure 6.2 *The Allocation of a Dollar Spent on Food in the United States, 2019*

Source: U.S. Department of Agriculture (USDA), Food Dollar Series, 2019.

Note: "Other" includes two industry groups, Agribusiness plus Legal and Accounting.

Agricultural production provides an important application of the notion of productivity—a concept that is important to all economic analysis. What we see in the case of agriculture is a great increase in **labor productivity**, as mechanization and the use of intensive agricultural technologies made it possible to reduce, by a remarkable amount, the number of people needed to provide the farm products needed by the whole economy. Another input, land, has also increased in productivity: for example, in the past 100 years, average corn yields in the United States have risen from around 25 to 175 bushels per acre, and wheat yields have increased from 12 to 53 bushels per acre.[4]

As shown in Figure 6.3, while the total input into agricultural production has remained nearly constant since 1948 and the use of land and labor has declined, the total farm production has increased by over three times. This is largely due to the increase in **total factor productivity** (TFP), which in the agricultural context refers to the ratio between total agricultural output and an aggregate measure of land area, labor, capital equipment, and purchased materials used in production—or:

Total factor productivity (TFP) = (total output of crops and
(in agriculture) livestock)/total inputs

where total inputs = land area, labor, capital equipment and purchased materials used in production.

labor productivity: the level of output that can be produced per worker per hour

total factor productivity (in agriculture) (TFP): the ratio between agricultural output and an aggregate measure of all inputs including land area, labor, capital equipment, and purchased materials used in production

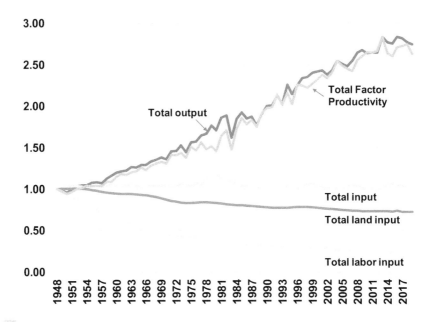

Figure 6.3 *U.S. Total Factor Productivity Growth, 1948–2017*

Source: USDA, Economic Research Services data, Table 1. Indices of farm output, input, and total factor productivity for the United States, 1948–2017.

BOX 6.1 U.S. AGRICULTURAL EXPORTS AND IMPORTS

U.S. agricultural exports have been larger than U.S. agricultural imports since 1960, generating a surplus in U.S. agricultural trade. This surplus helps counter the persistent deficit in non-agricultural U.S. merchandise trade. With the productivity of U.S. agriculture growing faster than domestic food and fiber demand, U.S. farmers and agricultural firms rely heavily on export markets to sustain prices and revenues.

China, Mexico, and Canada are the top three destinations for U.S. agricultural exports. Other important destinations for U.S. agricultural exports include the European Union and Asia. The top 10 destinations for U.S. agricultural export have varied little since 1990, but Europe, which was the largest market in prior decades, has declined in relative importance as China, Canada, Mexico, Asia, and the rest of the Americas have risen.

For the fiscal year 2022, U.S. agricultural imports were forecast to be $172.5 billion, while agricultural exports were projected at $183.5 billion. The U.S. agricultural trade surplus was expected to increase to $11 billion in fiscal 2022.[5]

Global trends in agriculture follow a similar pattern. Between 1960 and 1990 global food output increased sharply, while inputs of fertilizer, hybrid seeds, and farm machinery also greatly increased. But in the 1990s and the first decade of the twenty-first century, the use of these inputs increased only a little from the high level established over the previous 30 years, while three-fourths of the continued increases in total (global as well as the United States) agricultural output were accounted for by an increase in total factor productivity. This growth in TFP is partly explained by dissemination of new technologies to improve local farming systems through investment in research and development, and international spillovers of agricultural knowledge. In particular, human labor as a "factor" became more productive due to increases in human and social capital. This was achieved through institutional and policy reforms, improvements in farmer education and health, increased investment in rural infrastructure, and strong rural education and agricultural services.[6]

Figure 6.4 shows the huge growth in inputs such as fertilizer, machinery, and purchased seeds that occurred following the introduction of the Green Revolution in the early 1960s. Innovations in plant breeding created varieties of corn, wheat, and rice that, under the right conditions, could produce much more food per hectare. The "right conditions" included fertilizer applications as well as amounts of water that

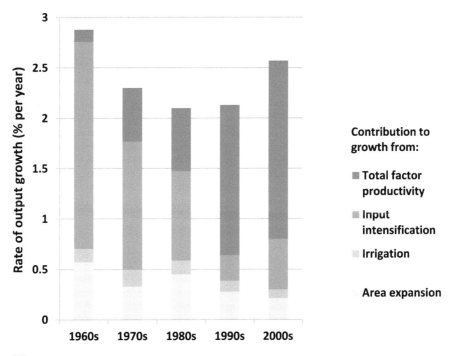

Figure 6.4 *Average Annual Growth Rate in Gross Global Agricultural Output (1960s–2000s)*

Source: Fuglie and Wang, 2012.

often required expanded irrigation. Figure 6.4 shows that from 1990 on, there continued to be an increase in area under cultivation, irrigation, and input intensification, but the big contribution to growth in output came from TFP.

Of course, productivity in agriculture ultimately depends on natural inputs of soil and water, a fact often obscured by the importance of manufactured inputs and technology in current agriculture. Over the past two centuries, both the fertility of the soil and the depth of fertile soil have declined significantly in North America. Globally, according to a 2011 FAO report, 33 percent of the earth's land is moderate to highly degraded, and an additional 5–7 million hectares of agricultural land are lost to soil degradation annually.

"Restorative agriculture"—farming in a way that restores soil—has recently gained attention as a way of rebuilding soils. It also has the potential to avert some significant portion of the dangers of climate change (see Box 6.2). Restorative agriculture usually involves higher labor costs, but these may be offset by the long-term productivity, health, and environmental benefits.

BOX 6.2 SOIL FERTILITY

Soil fertility depends upon a large number of factors, including not only the presence of such chemicals as nitrogen and phosphorous, but also a vast variety of biota (living organisms). One important component of soil fertility is the presence of carbon. This is of vital importance not only for food production but also for reducing the atmospheric carbon that contributes to climate change.

Worldwide, soils hold about 2,300 Gigatons of carbon, about three times as much as the atmosphere, and a sufficient increase in the global carbon content of soils could help to close the "emissions gap" between carbon dioxide reductions pledged at the Paris Agreement of 2015 and those deemed necessary to limit warming to 1.5°C or less by 2100. Today agricultural soils contain 25–75 percent less soil organic carbon than their counterparts in undisturbed or natural ecosystems. Intensive forms of farming using chemical fertilizers, pesticides, herbicides, and fungicides, are a leading cause of degradation of soils worldwide, as are destructive grazing practices in pasturelands.

Several international efforts to build soil carbon have been launched, with similar measures underway in the United States. Proposed policies include reforestation and innovative farming, ranching, and land management approaches that will enhance degraded soil and restore its carbon stock. The French-initiated effort, "4 per 1000: Soils for Food Security and Climate," calls for an annual increase of 0.4 percent in global soil carbon storage which, if achieved, would be equal to nearly one-third of the total carbon emissions from human activities. Professor Ratan Lal, the co-founder of the 4 per 1,000 initiative, estimates that between 1.45 to 3.44 Gigatons of carbon can be sequestered in the terrestrial biosphere (soils and vegetation) per year.

Increasing soil carbon at the root zones of crops would increase agricultural yield and contribute to food security as well as climate stabilization. On average, adding 10 tons of organic carbon per hectare of land is estimated to increase agricultural yield by 400–1,000 kg, depending on the type of crop.[7] This could help

---

reduce hunger and undernourishment among the over 690 million people at the brink of starvation, as estimated by the United Nations.

The cost of sequestering an additional ton of carbon has been estimated at US$70 to US$140 in cropland soils, per year, and US$180 to US$280 in grasslands and forests. These are primarily labor costs, as improved practices tend to be labor intensive.[8] Thus, these costs translate into jobs, and this opportunity to create new jobs in rural areas could reduce the exodus of impoverished rural populations flocking to urban slums worldwide.

Although water is often considered an abundant and almost free good, in fact, it is an essential and increasingly scarce input not only for agriculture but also for all economic activity. Depletion of groundwater supplies in the United States is a serious threat to agriculture as well as to people who live in areas of diminishing water resources. Agriculture is responsible for about four-fifths of U.S. water use, much of it used to irrigate crops in Western states. More than one-third of the irrigation water used in the country comes from groundwater aquifers, which are renewable resources that recharge very slowly and can become depleted when withdrawals exceed the rate of natural recharge.

Currently, the United States is withdrawing groundwater approximately four times faster than it is being replenished, most obviously in Texas, Kansas, and Nebraska, which rely on water from the Ogallala Aquifer, the world's largest known aquifer. The water table for the Ogallala Aquifer is declining as much as 2 feet per year, and water supplies from the aquifer have already been exhausted in some areas. The declining water table in the aquifer has motivated the increased use of efficient irrigation practices, but over time many more areas will lose access to this resource. Most likely, these areas will need to either switch to different crops that require less water or be removed from agricultural production.

Fortunately, water conservation methods have dramatically reduced both the absolute and per-person amount of fresh water used in the United States since their peaks in 1980. Water withdrawal per day in the US declined by over 33 percent between 1980 and 2015.[9] The reasons for this include higher energy costs, resulting in energy conservation (more fresh water is used to produce electricity than for any other purpose except farming), as well as improved water management strategies by large companies, and federal and state laws mandating efficiency in appliances. For example, through technology and redesign the average amount of water in a standard flush toilet—the domestic appliance with the largest water use—fell from 6 gallons to 1.6. And farmers have been increasingly relying on a variety of strategies to reduce water use, including crops that require less water, and drip irrigation, which applies small amounts of water directly to the roots of crops.

225

2.2 The Energy System

Modern production and consumption systems require a lot of energy. Although the United States has less than 5 percent of the world's population, it uses about 20 percent of the world's energy. It is the world's second-largest consumer of energy, behind China, but in per capita terms, U.S. energy consumption is about three times that of China. Indeed, the per-capita energy usage rate in the United States is one of the highest in the world. On average Americans consume twice as much energy as Europeans, 10 times as much as Indians, and about 50 times as much as the average person in sub-Saharan Africa. Only a few countries, such as the high-latitude countries of Canada, Norway, and Iceland have higher per capita energy consumption levels.[10] But these three countries derive most of their electrical sector energy from renewable sources (Norway 98 percent, Iceland 100 percent, Canada 60 percent).

Each stage of economic development has been accompanied by a characteristic energy transition, from one major fuel source to another. Industrialization in the nineteenth century began with a transition from energy sources such as wood, whale oil, and the muscles of animals and people, to coal. By the end of the century other fossil fuels—oil, and natural gas—were replacing even more of the older sources. Through the twentieth century, fossil fuels remained by far the dominant energy source in industrial economies. As of 2020, about 78 percent of the energy consumed in the United States still came from fossil fuels, including petroleum, coal, and natural gas. Petroleum, the single most important energy source, provides about 90 percent of the fuel for transportation. Natural gas and coal are the two main sources of fuel for electricity generation in the U.S., accounting for 38 percent and 22 percent respectively. About 19 percent of the country's electricity supply comes from nuclear power.

In the twenty-first century, the next great transition in energy sources has started—from non-renewable fossil fuels to renewable energy sources. This transition is being motivated by many factors, including concerns about environmental impacts (particularly climate change), limits on fossil fuel supplies, and prices. As of 2020, the United States obtained only about 5 percent of energy from renewable wind, solar, and geothermal sources, and about 12.5 percent from all renewables including biomass and hydro power (see Figure 6.5). But the currently small percentage from renewables is growing at a rapid rate. Over two-thirds of new electricity generating capacity in the United States in 2021 was from renewables, with solar (39 percent) and wind (31 percent) accounting for the largest shares.[11] As swiftly advancing technology brings down the price of renewable energy sources, they have become increasingly competitive with fossil fuels. Globally, the world still obtains over 80 percent of its energy from fossil fuels, but the renewable sector has been growing rapidly. The amount of global energy obtained from solar and wind power has tripled in the last 10 years.

226

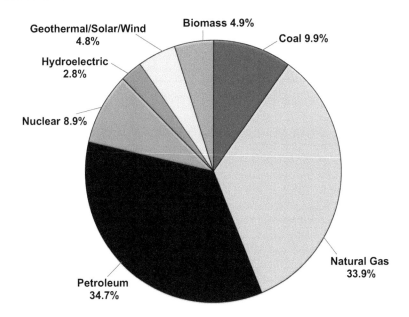

Figure 6.5 *Energy Consumption in the United States, by Energy Source, 2020*

Source: Monthly Energy Review, United States Energy Information Administration, 2020.

Solar energy has grown exponentially in the United States from just 0.34 gigawatts (GW) in 2008 to an estimated 97.2 GW by 2020. At the same time, the cost of solar PV panels has dropped significantly by nearly 70 percent just between 2014 and 2021.[12] Wind energy use has also grown rapidly in the U.S., accounting for about 42 percent of the new energy capacity in 2020. In 16 states, wind energy provided more than 10 percent of total in-state electricity. Most notably Iowa got 57 percent of its electricity from wind, and a few other states, such as Oklahoma and South Dakota, got over 30 percent of their electricity from wind.[13]

A 2013 article in *Energy Policy* outlined how New York State could supply all its energy needs from wind, solar, and water power by 2030, creating 58,000 jobs in the process. The main author of the study commented, "You could power America with renewables, from a technical and economic standpoint. The biggest obstacles are social and political—what you need is the will to do it."[14]

The United States is not only the world's second-largest consumer of energy; it is also the world's second-largest energy producer (again, behind China). Since 2012 there has been a significant increase in US energy output, due primarily to increased production of natural gas and oil. Novel extraction technologies, particularly hydraulic fracturing, commonly known as "fracking," have made it economically viable to tap fossil fuel deposits 2 miles or more below the ground (see Box 6.3 for a discussion of the debate over fracking). Recent weather events such as the 2021 hurricanes in Texas and Louisiana have emphasized the vulnerability of the Gulf States' oil industry, and homes and businesses, to a rising sea level and other effects of climate change. Such events increase the pressure for the U.S. to accelerate the switch to a post-carbon energy era.

BOX 6.3 FRACKING AND THE U.S. ENERGY BOOM

Fracking is the process of pumping fluids under high pressure into fossil fuel deposits, creating numerous fractures that release the fuel from the surrounding rock and allow extraction. Combined with deep-well horizontal drilling techniques, this technology allows the development of previously uneconomic oil and gas reserves across the United States, including in Texas, North Dakota, and Pennsylvania. Increased U.S. production of natural gas has resulted in falling prices—a decline of more than 70 percent between 2007 and 2019. The U.S. energy boom that resulted from fracking has increased employment in previously impoverished areas. Note that natural gas prices rose steeply after 2020 with increased demand from the post-pandemic recovery. The crisis in Ukraine that began in early 2022 put further pressure on rising natural gas prices.

Proponents of fracking in the United States argue that obtaining oil from domestic sources is better than importing it. Burning natural gas emits less carbon dioxide than coal; thus it was expected that substituting natural gas for coal in electricity generation would reduce carbon emissions and other air pollutants. The reality has been somewhat disappointing, however, as it has been found that significant amounts of pollutants are often released in the process of retrieving natural gas.

Opponents of fracking point to the potential for water contamination. While the fuel deposits are normally much deeper underground than drinking water aquifers, drilling through these aquifers means that leaks in the concrete casings could threaten water supplies. A 2016 study found that toxic chemicals such as arsenic, benzene, cadmium, and mercury are a few of the 200 toxins found in fracking fluids and wastewater.[15] A comprehensive 2016 report from the U.S. EPA also found a potential for fracking to contaminate drinking water sources.[16] Fracking activities have been linked to a 900-fold increase in earthquakes in Oklahoma starting in 2008, though the number of quakes has fallen since 2015, with stricter fracking regulations.[17] Another concern is that the increased availability of domestic fossil fuels distracts us from the need to develop renewable substitutes.

In December 2012, the U.S. Environmental Protection Agency (EPA) noted that "responsible development of America's oil and gas resources offers important economic, energy security, and environmental benefits. However, as the use of hydraulic fracturing has increased, so have concerns about its potential human health and environmental impacts, especially for drinking water."[18] Several EPA case studies have found evidence of detrimental impacts of fracking on health and the environment. For example, 9 of the 36 drinking water wells in Northeastern Pennsylvania were found to be contaminated by stray gas from nearby hydraulic activities.[19] Meanwhile, in 2011 France became the first country to ban fracking, and several other countries have prohibited the process. A few states in the United States, including Vermont, Maryland, and New York have also permanently banned fracking.

Although energy *use* permeates every aspect of economic activity in the United States, the *production* of energy currently employs less than a million workers, or about 0.5 percent of the workforce, and directly contributes only a small share to GDP. Yet fluctuations in energy supply and prices can have significant impacts on economy-wide variables such as GDP growth, inflation, and employment. Increases in energy prices lead to downstream increases in the price of many other products and thus contribute to higher inflation rates. In the last half-century, whenever there have been dramatic energy price increases, particularly in the price of oil, the macroeconomy has responded with recessions at both the national and international levels. For this reason, an increase in oil prices in 2022, due to the Russia-Ukraine conflict, increased concerns about recession.[20]

Because so much of the capital stock and infrastructure of modern economic systems are based on fossil fuel energy use, any transition from fossil fuel dependence will involve massive restructuring and new investment. While private markets will play a critical role in this process, appropriate government policies are necessary to foster the transition. Fossil fuel subsidies by governments around the world total about $5 trillion annually, while subsidies for renewable energy are significantly less—about US$167 billion in 2017.[21] Removing distortionary subsidies could significantly speed the transition from fossil fuels to renewable energy sources. Other relevant policies would involve investment in new energy infrastructure, upgrading transmission networks with "smart grid" technologies, and promoting energy efficiency. Energy efficiency may be the most cost-efficient energy "source"—well-designed energy efficiency programs cost, on average, only about half the cost of providing new energy supplies.[22]

Discussion Questions

1. How do you obtain most of your food? Does it come from a supermarket, or do you get some from a farmers' market or grow your own? Are you surprised to learn that less than 8 cents of a dollar spent on food goes to the primary sector, where the food is actually produced?
2. Do you think that the heavy dependence of the United States on fossil fuels for energy is a problem? How likely is it that this might change in the future?

3 THE SECONDARY (INDUSTRIAL) SECTOR IN THE UNITED STATES

The secondary sector includes construction and utilities as well as manufacturing. As was shown in Table 6.1, these industries together comprise 16.8 percent of GDP in the United States and employ 13.6 percent of the workforce, with about 8 percent in manufacturing and the rest in construction and utilities. In this section, we will consider the changes in output and employment in the secondary sector and examine why employment in this sector has declined in the last few decades.

229

3.1 Manufacturing

When asked what makes up an economy, many people think first of manufacturing. The United States remains a major manufacturer, but since about 1950 employment in the secondary sector has declined. The main cause of this decline is essentially the same as the reason for the earlier decline in primary sector employment: the rise in labor productivity—specifically, **manufacturing productivity**, which is commonly measured as an index of the value of the manufactured goods produced per hour of labor. Manufacturing productivity in the United States has been rising for more than a hundred years. During the 1980s, manufacturing productivity increased by an average of 2.6 percent per year. The rate rose to 3.8 percent per year during the 1990s, and to 4.3 percent per year from 2000 to 2007. Between 2008 and 2020, manufacturing productivity fell to an average of about 0.2 percent per year, with productivity being negative on average since 2014.[23]

---

manufacturing productivity: an index of the value of the goods produced per hour of labor in the manufacturing sector

---

The increase in manufacturing productivity means that more manufactured goods can be produced using fewer human labor hours. Although global demand for manufactured goods (and for food and other primary sector products) continues to grow, it has not grown as rapidly as productivity. More goods and services are produced and sold, but fewer people are required to produce them. In addition to a loss of U.S. manufacturing jobs due to increased productivity, jobs are also lost to imports when manufacturing shifts overseas, usually as a result of lower foreign labor costs.

The decline in U.S. manufacturing industries does not indicate declining demand for manufactured goods. The United States imports significantly more manufactured goods than it sells abroad, resulting in a trade deficit in goods of over $1 trillion in 2021. When we combine data on both foreign and domestic goods, the U.S. demand for goods increased by almost 90 percent between 2002 and 2021, even after adjusting for inflation. So while the U.S. economy is becoming more service-oriented, as a share of GDP, this does not mean that people want fewer manufactured goods. In fact, during the COVID-19 pandemic, the demand for goods accelerated, while the services industry suffered (see Box 6.4).

In 2002, American manufacturers met 61 percent of the domestic demand for goods. In 2021 they met only 49 percent. The major sources of imports in goods are (in order of the 2021 value of imports): China, Mexico, Canada, Germany, and Japan. The U.S. trade deficit with all these countries has grown, especially with China. The value of imports of goods from China increased by about 400 percent between 2001 and 2021 alone.[24]

230

BOX 6.4 SERVICES SECTOR HIT HARDEST BY THE PANDEMIC

When the COVID-19 pandemic swept the world in early 2020, people's consumption habits shifted quickly. In the U.S., the fear of infection and uncertainties about the health impacts of the virus along with shuttering of businesses and stay-at-home orders meant people were spending more time at home. Many of their everyday activities such as going to the movies, or to the spa or gym, and eating out at restaurants, declined sharply. At the same time, people switched to cooking more meals at home, while their purchases became more focused on household goods and furniture. How did these lifestyle changes affect the different sectors of the economy?

The service sector suffered the steepest decline during the initial months of the pandemic. As people canceled their vacation plans and cut down on social activities, spending in the services sector declined by 7.3 percent in 2020. The largest drops were seen in recreation (31.8 percent), transportation (23.2 percent), and food and accommodation (21.8 percent) services.

Spending on durable and non-durable goods, on the other hand, continued to increase in 2020. As people spent more time indoors, they turned to online shopping to update their homes and buy more household equipment. In 2020, the purchase of durable goods increased by 6.3 percent, compared to a 4.8 percent increase in 2019, and the largest increases were seen in the purchases of recreational goods and vehicles (18 percent), furnishings, and household equipment (5.7 percent). Spending on groceries also went up by 6.9 percent, while spending on gas as well as clothing and footwear declined by 12.6 percent and 7.7 percent, respectively.[25]

By 2021, however, as vaccines became widely available and people's anxiety about the virus declined, the services sector recovered rapidly, growing by an average of 2.4 percent in the first three-quarters of 2021. The strongest recovery was seen in the food services and accommodations sectors, while spending on transportation and recreation recovered more slowly. In fact, by the end of 2021, demand for services had mostly recovered while there were constraints on the supply side with labor shortages, and supply chain bottlenecks resulting in increased pressures on prices.

Although imports have clearly played a role, the decline in the absolute number of U.S. manufacturing jobs predates the dramatic increase in imports from China. In fact, the decline is not unique to the United States but is a worldwide phenomenon. The absolute number of manufacturing jobs peaked years ago in virtually all industrial countries. The same is true, or is rapidly becoming true, in emerging markets, where rapid productivity growth allows real wages and output to rise, while the number of manufacturing jobs declines and the service sector expands relative to manufacturing. China, the trading partner that has been perceived as the greatest threat to jobs in the United States, has also generally been losing manufacturing jobs. For example, between 2013 and 2017 China lost 12.5 million manufacturing jobs, even though value-added manufacturing in China grew by nearly 20 percent in real terms during this period.[26]

What is the cause of this global phenomenon? It appears that in recent decades an acceleration has taken place in the process that began

231

with the Industrial Revolution in the mid- to the late eighteenth century, in which technological change makes it possible for industries to substitute manufactured capital (i.e., machinery and automation) for human labor.

The general topic of the changing structure of jobs will be taken up again in Chapter 7. For now, we will look at the historical record to see what has been happening in two types of manufacturing that provide good case studies for the sector as a whole.

3.1.1 Textiles

In the 1800s the textile and apparel industry arose as this country's first large-scale manufacturing industry, with the majority of the mills located in the Northeast. The mills, employing mostly women and girls, were the scene of some of the nation's early labor union battles, as the women fought to limit the workday to ten hours. The textile industry expanded rapidly, increasingly using immigrant labor and becoming the largest manufacturing employer in the country by the start of the twentieth century. In 1920 nearly 2 million workers were employed in textiles. Then, faced with foreign competition, particularly from Japan, the industry stopped expanding. Employment in the American textile industry remained at around 2 million workers for the next 50 years or so.

Textiles and clothing are outstanding examples of a category of manufactured items that (1) are labor intensive (i.e., their production requires a large number of labor hours in proportion to the cost of other inputs) and (2) can be produced with large numbers of unskilled laborers. These characteristics create conditions in which countries with large populations of poor people can compete in the international market.

Since the 1970s the textile and apparel industry in the United States has been decimated—employment in the industry has declined about 90 percent, and the decline appears likely to continue into the future. There is no question that, in this industry, imports from China played a large role in job losses in the United States. In 2002 import quota restrictions were removed from 29 categories of apparel. In just two years the United States more than doubled its imports of textiles and apparel from China. Chinese imports can be produced at a lower cost than domestic goods primarily because of lower wages. China currently dominates global textile manufacturing, but this may be changing. In recent years, textile manufacturing has been leaving China for countries with even lower wages, including Bangladesh, Cambodia, and India.

At the same time, technological change plays a significant role in this industry like others. The use of information technology in the production of clothes—including nearly instantaneous "made to order" operations that cannot be reproduced by garment workers—creates more and more situations where even the lowest-wage workers can hardly be competitive in cost considerations.

3.1.2 Automobiles

In contrast to textiles, the automobile industry in the United States had a number of special advantages in the twentieth century. One was the "first-mover advantage" gained by the leadership of Henry Ford and others who innovated and created strong businesses before most foreign competitors. Another was the fact that the United States has a huge domestic market. Not needing to rely on exports is an advantage in an industry in which the transaction cost involved in shipping automobiles over long distances creates a cost disadvantage for foreign producers. In addition, for a long time, the technology of automobile production was such that the greater productivity of more skilled workers enabled them to compete successfully against lower-wage workers who had less education, training, and skill.

The first challenge to the pre-eminence of U.S. auto companies in the enormous domestic market came with the oil crises of the 1970s. This motivated a surge in imports of high-quality, relatively fuel-efficient vehicles from Japan. By 1980 the Japanese automobile industry, virtually non-existent 20 years earlier, had captured over 20 percent of the U.S. market. The impact of this first wave of foreign competition on the domestic motor vehicle industry was severe. Between 1977 and 1982 employment in the industry in the United States declined by 30 percent.

In the 1980s and 1990s, the domestic automobile industry recovered, for several reasons. First, U.S. automobile manufacturers improved the quality of their vehicles, often either emulating Japanese production methods or forming joint ventures with foreign producers. Another factor was the decline in gasoline prices in the 1980s, which shifted demand back toward larger domestic vehicles. Sales of pickup trucks and sport utility vehicles, initially produced almost exclusively by American companies, increased dramatically during this period.

The U.S. auto industry again fell on hard times in the 2000s, first from a significant decline in sales of fuel-inefficient vehicles due to higher gas prices and then from the global financial crisis. Between just 2006 and 2009, annual vehicle production by U.S. automakers fell more than 50 percent. In 2008 and 2009, the federal government rescued General Motors and Chrysler through loans exceeding $60 billion, made through the Troubled Asset Relief Program (TARP). The federal government also took an ownership share of each company. As the economy improved and manufacturers shifted toward more fuel-efficient (and eventually hybrid and electrical) vehicles, the two companies were able to repay their TARP loans. Employment in automotive manufacturing, which peaked at 1.3 million workers in 2000, dropped to 0.66 million workers in 2009 but has since recovered and reached 0.96 million workers in 2021.[27]

3.2 Construction

The construction industry is particularly affected by macroeconomic conditions, as was evident in the aftermath of the global financial crisis.

233

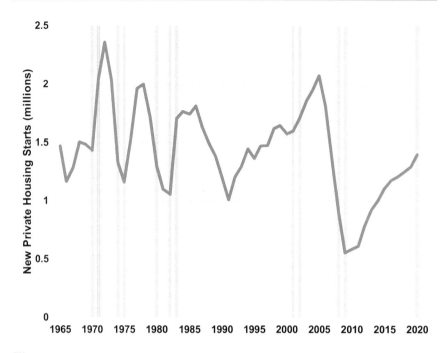

Figure 6.6 *Annual Number of Private Housing Starts in the United States, 1965–2020*

Sources: U.S. Census Bureau, Department of Housing and Urban Development.

Figure 6.6 shows how the number of housing starts decline during recessionary periods but then recovers after a recession is over. (The data follow housing *starts* because only the flow of newly constructed housing, not the level of pre-existing housing, counts in measuring the production of the secondary sector.) Note that housing starts bottomed out in 2009 at the end of the 2008 recession and have slowly begun to recover. But the collapse from the mid-2000s peak was so severe that as recently as 2020 starts were still only about 72 percent of what they were at the peak.

Importantly, construction is about more than housing. Perhaps the best hope for reviving jobs in the secondary sector is a topic that is much discussed in policy circles: the need to maintain, rebuild, and build infrastructure in the United States (see Box 6.5).

BOX 6.5 THE POTENTIAL FOR INFRASTRUCTURE JOBS

The collapse of a major bridge in Minnesota, poisonous water in Flint Michigan, and the failing power grid in Texas all highlight the vulnerable state of the U.S. infrastructure. In the 2021 report from the American Society of Civil Engineers, America's infrastructure received a C-grade, with an estimated 6 billion gallons of treated water lost per day due to water line breaks, and over 43 percent of public roadways in the country reported as being in poor or mediocre conditions.[28]

Increased investment in infrastructure is one of the few issues in the United States that has generally received bipartisan support. Various survey reports find that a majority (about 80 percent) of Americans—regardless of their political affiliation—believe that the country's infrastructure is in critical need of repair and that federal investment in infrastructure would be good for the economy.[29] In November 2021, President Joe Biden signed a $1 trillion infrastructure bill to funnel billions of dollars to state and local governments to upgrade outdated roads, bridges, transit, and water systems, and to modernize the nation's energy system to better manage climate risks. Biden claimed that the bill would make key investments that would create millions of good-paying union jobs.[30]

According to a report by Moody's Analytics, the infrastructure bill has the potential to create about 2.4 million jobs by the end of 2025.[31] Another report from S&P Global estimates that Biden's plan could add $1.4 trillion to the economy and create over 1 million jobs over the next eight years. Most of these jobs would be good middle-class jobs in construction, engineering, and accounting.[32]

For years, the U.S. government's spending on infrastructure has been flagging. As a share of GDP, public expenditures on infrastructure spiked toward the end of the 2008 recession, due both to shrinking GDP and investment funded by the American Recovery and Reinvestment Act of 2009 (the Recovery Act). Since then, however, infrastructure investment has fallen to its lowest levels since peaking in the late 1970s. In 2021, the U.S. only spent 2.4 percent of GDP on infrastructure, compared to 5 percent on average in European countries, and 8 percent in China.[33]

3.3 Rising Productivity in the Secondary Sector

When we consider the value-added from manufacturing, adjusted for inflation, the size of the secondary sector has stayed fairly constant over the past half-century. Its share of GDP has declined, however, because the size of the service sector has grown so much. The most important fact, for many people, is that manufacturing *employment* has declined. As shown in Figure 6.7, from a peak of about 20 million workers in 1979, the number of manufacturing jobs has declined by 37 percent.

What does the shift away from the primary and secondary sectors mean for human well-being? An economist a hundred years ago, if imagining the situation we are now in, might have said that it is exactly what progress is supposed to be about—that people can get more of what they want with less work. However, people can only purchase the output of a market economy if they have income, and for most people income comes primarily through wages, which are attached to jobs. Historically, many of the most stable and well-paid jobs were in the manufacturing sector, and with the decline of manufacturing these have often been replaced with less secure jobs with lower benefits in the service sector, or the "gig" economy. These shifting job patterns in contemporary economies will be discussed further in Chapter 7.

235

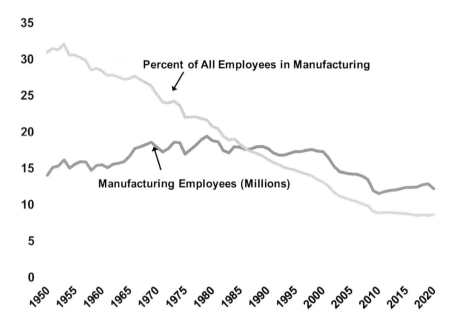

Figure 6.7 *Total U.S. Manufacturing Employment and Manufacturing Employment as a Percentage of Total Employment, 1950–2020*

Source: Various editions of the Statistical Abstract of the United States.

Discussion Questions

1. One of the main impacts of the Great Recession in the United
    States was a significant decline in housing prices in most areas of
    the country. However, at the same time, the number of homes sold
    also declined dramatically. Shouldn't the decline in housing prices
    have resulted in an increase in home sales, as suggested by a basic
    model of supply and demand?
2. Some people cite the return from the suburbs to urban areas and
    the lower percentage of young people getting driver's licenses as
    indications that "the age of the automobile is drawing to a close."
    Do you think that this is true? If automobile use were to fall in
    half over the next 15 years, what impact would this have on the
    economy?

4 THE TERTIARY (SERVICE) SECTOR

Looking back to Table 6.1, you will see that the tertiary sector includes
a wide variety of industries, including education, retail trade, financial
services, insurance, waste management, and entertainment. The tertiary sector also includes direct services without the distribution of any
physical goods, such as consulting, technology, finance, administration,
education, and a category called arts, entertainment, and recreation.
This variety, and the abstract nature of many tertiary-sector activities,

makes it hard to get a grasp on this important portion of the economy. In this section we will address the following questions:

- Why has the tertiary sector grown, relative to the other two sectors?
- What are the major sub-categories of the service sector?
- We will then examine some industries within this sector: retail services, finance, health care, and education.

4.1 The Growth of the Tertiary Sector

Earlier in this chapter, we gave an intuitive explanation for why, even though people are just as dependent as they have always been on the materials extracted from nature, the primary sector has shrunk in economic importance as societies have industrialized. It was not hard to explain how manufacturing came to claim a larger part of every household budget and therefore the total economy in the nineteenth and early twentieth centuries; today, we need to understand why "services" have more recently become so significant.

One reason for the rise in the relative size of the service sector is globalization and trade. Traditionally, most international trade has involved the exchange of physical goods, but trade in services is now expanding rapidly. While it is easy to picture a physical good moving between countries, it might be harder to imagine how *services* can be internationally traded. A service is "exported" if United States producers provide a service used by an individual or organization based abroad. For example, if someone from Argentina stays in a U.S. hotel, this is considered an "export" of U.S.-produced accommodation services. A service is "imported" if agents in the foreign sector provide a service used by individuals or organizations based in the United States. For example, if a U.S. manufacturer ships its goods using freighters registered in Liberia, it is said to "import" transportation services from Liberia.

Between 1995 and 2020, global trade in services increased by a factor of 4.2, while trade in goods increased by a factor of 3.4.[34] By 2020, almost 28 percent of all international trade was in services, an increase from about 9 percent compared to the amount of trade in services in 1970.

Improvements in information technology have made services such as customer call centers, software development, and data processing more easily transferable across national boundaries. The United Nations notes that cost savings of 20–40 percent are commonly reported by companies that offshore their service needs to low-wage countries. Thus, technological opportunities for cost reductions play an important role in the growth of trade in services. Other reasons include changes in technology and in tastes (such as the growing value of leisure activities such as tourism).

237

In 2020, the United States exported more in services ($705.6 million) than it imported ($460.3 million). The principal services exported by the United States are travel, transport, educational, financial, and other business services, while the main service imports are transport, insurance, telecommunications, and professional, management, and legal consulting.

Since the U.S. exports more services than it imports, this does not, on the face of it, appear to predict a loss of service sector jobs (a topic that will be considered in Chapter 7), but it does contribute to our understanding of the growth in the service sector. Additional explanations emerge when we add in technology, especially the rise in computing and other aspects of information technology, as well as the growth of finance as a share of GDP. From 1947 to 2020, the percentage of U.S. value-added from finance and insurance has more than tripled, from 2.3 percent to 8.6 percent.

The growth of finance is related to the growth of wages in this area. A common perception is that jobs in the service sector pay poorly. In fact, overall, service jobs pay only slightly less on average than manufacturing jobs. In January 2022 the average hourly wage in goods-producing industries was $31.88, while the average pay in the service industries was $31.50 per hour.[35] But as is often the case, averages hide as much as they reveal. Many of the "care-work" jobs that are critical to human well-being are low-paid (or, when they take place in the core sphere, not paid at all). These include child-care, early childhood education, and basic physical and mental care for the aged, ill, or disabled. At the same time, there are relatively highly paid service workers, such as doctors and lawyers; and many jobs in finance have wages that far exceed most of those in manufacturing. This raises the *average* service sector wage, but it does not mean that workers in other parts of the service sector are well off.

4.2 Analyzing the Tertiary Sector by Sub-Categories

Even more than the other sectors, the tertiary sector cannot be defined as a homogeneous economic category. Because it is difficult to get a handle on the array of disparate activities that make up this seemingly immaterial, yet enormously important, part of our economy, we offer a way of understanding the sector in aggregated categories. Figure 6.8 shows the size of the tertiary sector relative to the other private (non-government) GDP sectors, based on the value-added approach to national accounting that was used for Table 6.1, and also offers a classification into four different types of activity. (These divisions are the authors' classification, to indicate the different types of economic activity in the sector, and do not represent any official government classification scheme.)

We will identify the largest category of the tertiary activities in GDP as "Ownership Transactions," which includes 31.9 percent of private GDP. About 11 percentage points of this category represent

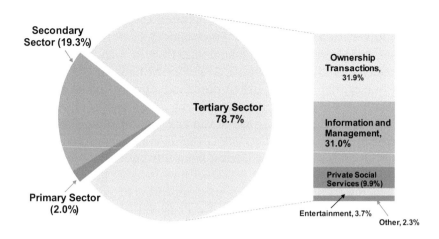

Figure 6.8 *Classification of Private GDP in the United States, 2020*

the imputed value, to each homeowner, of the ongoing value of being able to live in that house. Other real estate activities in this grouping involve the buying and selling of properties. The remainder—about 21 percent of private GDP—is essentially about activities related to buying and selling, including transportation and warehousing, wholesale and retail trade, and real estate rental and leasing (aside from the above-mentioned imputed value of homeownership). We include transportation in "ownership transactions" since the transport of goods is essential in most markets for consumer products, food, etc.

A significant portion of the value-added in this category may be traced to "the middleman"—the person or organization that facilitates the transaction between the final buyer and the original producer, or between the previous owner and the next one (as is often the case with stocks and bonds, real estate, fine arts, and other things that tend to have a sequence of owners). In an advanced economy in which there is a huge amount of choice, for buyers, among objects that can come from anywhere in the world, it is not surprising that a significant portion of GDP should be devoted to making these connections.

The next largest category, "Information and Management" covers diverse marketed services that keep the economy going. These include information, finance and insurance, and professional, scientific, and technical services. This category also includes the activities that the Census Bureau calls administrative and waste management, and management of companies and enterprises.

The size of this category—31 percent of private GDP—is not surprising, given the complexity of modern economies. Our society has come a long way from the relatively simple economies that we described early in this chapter when discussing how the secondary sector grew relative to the primary sector. Firms are more numerous; large (and enormous) firms are more numerous; and there is much organization and management to be done in negotiating the networks of relations

239

inside these firms, among them, and between the producers and consumers (advertising is included in this category). Governments do some of this organization and management, and they, in turn, along with the firms, need many kinds of support. Many individuals and families, too, have resources that they can use to purchase support for the complexities of operating in an industrialized world. The kinds of support that individuals and organizations want and can pay for include insurance and financial services, as well as advice and assistance with the management and operation of technologies, from automobile repair to computer hardware and software.

"Private Social Services" covers those portions of education, health care, and social assistance that are not provided or contracted for by the government. The category "Entertainment" (formally "Arts, Entertainment, and Recreation") is primarily about "what we do for fun"; it covers services sold in relation to arts, entertainment, and recreation, as well as accommodation and food services.

The remainder of this section offers some specific information about the service sector, especially with regard to retail, financial and insurance services, and human services (including health and education).

4.3 Retail Services

Retail services are examples of activites within our category, "ownership transactions." Few manufacturers sell their products directly to consumers. Instead, manufacturers typically sell their output to retailers, perhaps also using wholesalers as intermediaries. Retailers are categorized in the service sector because they normally do not manufacture any of the goods that they sell. Prominent retailers such as Walmart, Home Depot, and Target purchase virtually all their products from suppliers, in the United States and in other countries.

Retail services as a whole are not becoming a larger share of the national economy, but there is a clear trend toward dominance by a small number of very large retailers. We can use data on concentration ratios to illustrate the ascendancy of these firms. A "four-firm concentration ratio" is calculated by dividing the domestic revenues of the four largest firms in an industry by the total domestic revenues in the industry. Figure 6.9 shows the change in the four-firm concentration ratios for several types of retailers between 1992 and 2007.

Large retailers have come to dominate their industries by offering consumers a large number of choices and low prices. In the parlance of microeconomics, the retail industry is oligopolistic, meaning that it is dominated by a small number of companies. However, the economic scale of the largest retailers has become so large that the behavior of individual firms has implications at the macroeconomic level.

In 2021 Amazon became the world's largest retailer, surpassing Walmart which had held the title for years. Propelled in part by the surge in online shopping during the pandemic, people spent more than

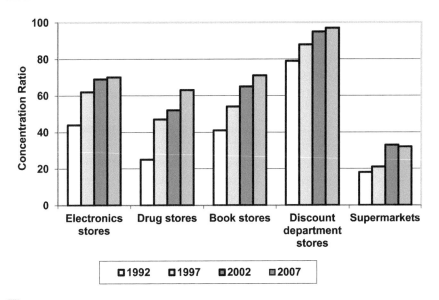

Figure 6.9 *Four-Firm Concentration Ratios in Retail Industries, 1992–2007*

Source: *Economic Census publications, United States Census Bureau.*

$610 billion on Amazon over the 12 months ending in June 2021, compared to the total sales of $566 billion for Walmart during the same period. Walmart is still the largest employer in the U.S., employing 1.6 million workers compared to 1.3 million workers at Amazon.[36]

Some researchers believe that a major reason that productivity increased so much in the United States in the late 1990s was Walmart's pressure on suppliers to increase their efficiency. As another example of Walmart's pervasive reach, the decline of the American textiles industry can be attributed in part to Walmart's foreign sourcing of low-priced apparel. Consider that an estimated 10 percent of Chinese imports to the United States are for Walmart. Economy-wide impacts like these blur traditional distinctions between microeconomics and macroeconomics, and demand new lines of research and analysis.

4.4 Finance and Financialization

Finance falls within our category of "information and management." According to standard economic theory, the principal function of banks and other financial institutions is to *intermediate* the movement of funds throughout the economy. For example, banks absorb savings (when we deposit money in banks), and then they redirect these funds back into the economy in the form of loans that pay higher rates of interest, to cover the banks' costs of operation and give them a profit. These loans may be used by households to buy a car or a house or to pay for college. Businesses borrow from the financial sector to invest in capital goods, like machinery and building, resulting in increases in production and employment.

Intermediating institutions such as banks thus help the real economy to function. The "real economy" refers to the part of the economy that is concerned with actually producing goods and services, as opposed to the financial side of the economy (sometimes called "the paper economy"), whose activities focus on buying and selling on the financial markets.

The financial sector also facilitates investment in **financial assets**, such as stocks (shares in ownership of companies); bonds (certificates indicating that the holder has lent money to a government entity or a business, which will repay the loan over time, with interest); foreign currencies (held when the investor expects either that his own currency will depreciate or that a foreign currency will rise in relative value); certificates of deposit and money market accounts (specially designed savings accounts at banks, which pay higher interest than normal savings accounts, but generally place restrictions on withdrawals or set a minimum deposit level). Households, non-financial businesses, and governments hold about half the country's financial assets directly. The rest are held by **financial institutions**, which include banks, credit unions, pension and retirement funds, mutual funds, securities brokers, and insurance companies. The functions of these institutions are discussed in detail in Chapter 10.

---

financial assets: a variety of holdings in which wealth can be invested with an expectation of future return

financial institution: any institution that collects money and holds it as financial assets

---

Given that the primary role of the financial sector is to facilitate activities in the real economy, there is no inherent reason to expect the financial sector to grow faster than the overall economy. Yet the relative size of the financial sector has increased considerably over time. This process of increasing size and importance of the financial markets in the operation of the economy—with the financial sector accounting for a greater share of GDP and acquiring an increased ability to generate and circulate profits—is known as '**financialization**'.[37] As shown in Figure 6.10, although finance only constituted about 8 percent of the economy and employed 4.4 percent of the workforce, it took over 20 percent of the corporate profits in 2020. What are the reasons for this disproportionate growth of finance?

---

financialization: a process in which the financial sector of the economy is increasingly able to generate and circulate profits that are not closely related to the real economy

---

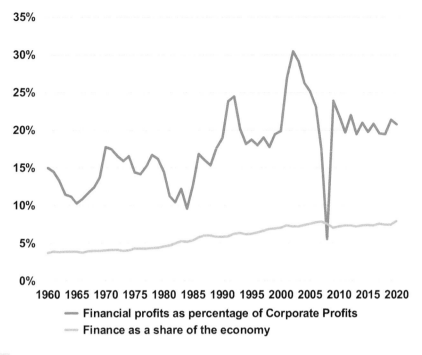

Figure 6.10 *Finance as a Share of the Economy and Financial Profits as a Percentage of Corporate Profits, 1960–2020*

Source: NIPA Tables 6.2A-6.2D, and Piketty, Saez, and Zucman's Distributional National Accounts, Appendix tables II: Distributional series.

One key reason is the deregulation of the financial sector since the 1970s, justified by the "free-market" mantra that financial institutions could be depended on to self-regulate, on the assumption that profit-seeking enterprises would voluntarily avoid risky practices that might cause them to fail. Many of the regulations that were put in place after the Great Depression such as the Glass-Steagall Act (discussed further in Chapter 10), which separated investment banks from commercial banks, interest rate ceilings on savings accounts, and various capital and leverage requirements for banks, were removed in the last three decades of the twentieth century. Deregulation also included loosening restrictions on the movement of capital across borders, repealing prohibitions on interstate banking, allowing banks to measure the riskiness of their own products, permitting financial institutions to offer interest-bearing checking, and increasing the amount of leverage permitted to investment banks.

Deregulation of the financial sector has led to an increase in the size of banks. From 1984 to 2021, the number of banks with more than $10 billion in assets increased from 28 to 160, with thirteen of these banks holding more than $250 billion in assets. The share of banking sector assets held by large banks (more than 10 billion in assets) increased from 28 to more than 85 percent during the same period.[38] The increasing bank size was often justified with the claim that large banks are

243

more efficient and less vulnerable than smaller banks because of their diverse source of income. But there is evidence that the increasing size only encouraged larger banks to take more risks. In the 2008 financial crisis, many big investment banks were seriously impacted by bad mortgage investments, with some failing. And in 2013, megabank JP Morgan Chase agreed to pay $13 billion in a settlement resulting from the bank's questionable mortgage practices.

Deregulation encouraged a proliferation of new kinds of financial institutions and instruments. Finance turned away from its traditional role of lending for consumption and investment, and most of the money in the financial system got directed toward lending against existing assets such as housing, stocks, and bonds—not creating new assets.

From the 1940s to the 1970s, nonfinancial institutions received 15–20 percent of their funding for productive investment from the financial sector; this dropped to 7–10 percent after 1980. Many financial corporations started lending to each other, instead of lending to non-financial corporations (such within-sector lending increased from 10 percent before the 1970s to over 30 percent after 1980).[39]

The operation of the financial sector has also expanded through the rise of the shadow banking system (discussed in Chapter 10), which encouraged putting more money into high-yield financial schemes. Even non-financial institutions have become increasingly involved in investing in financial instruments, rather than funding new investments to expand the production of goods and services. For example, automobile manufacturer General Motors established its financial arm General Motors Acceptance Corporation (GMAC) in 1919. Until the 1980s, the main function of GMAC was to provide credit to their customers to increase car sales. GMAC entered mortgage lending in 1985 and further expanded its services to include insurance, banking, and commercial finance in the 1990s. In 2004, GM reported that 66 percent of its $1.3 billion quarterly profits came from GMAC.[40] Today American companies in every sector earn five times more revenue from financial activities, such as investing, hedging, and offering financial services, than they did before 1980.[41]

Households have also become increasingly dependent on the financial markets, relying more on loans to meet their expenses due to the stagnation of real wages. In 1980, for example, U.S. households held an average debt equal to about 60 percent of disposable income; this figure exceeded 130 percent in 2007, but has since declined to about 101 percent of disposable income as of 2020.[42] In addition, the proliferation of mutual funds and their increased availability in employee accounts has caused a higher percentage of the population than ever before to have a stake in the financial market.

The simplest way of understanding the financialization that has affected the U.S. economy, as well as other advanced economies in recent decades is as a combination of two things: (1) huge increases in debt and debt finance throughout the economy, along with (2) inflation in the price of assets, not necessarily based on growth in the value of real goods and services. This is what occurred in the period 1980–2007 when both asset prices and debt levels throughout the economy ballooned relative to incomes. After crashing in 2008–2009, asset prices once again started a dramatic rise, reflected in a more than fourfold increase in stock values from 2009 to 2021.

Today, the financial sector has expanded far beyond the provision of the financial intermediation services demanded by the economy; what has grown is not only the demand for credit but the overall volume of trading of financial securities, including speculative and risk-taking activities. This expansion of the financial sector has also contributed to the rising inequality in the United States, as will be discussed in Chapter 14.

4.5 Human Services: Health

We now return to the parts of the tertiary sector whose effects are felt in most people's lives, with a consideration of what we categorize as "private sector services." Human services include education, health care, social work, and childcare. These services can be provided by private businesses, non-profit organizations, or governments. We will look in more detail at two of these areas, health care, and education.

Health care is one of the fastest-growing industries in the United States. In 2020, 13.4 percent of the country's workers were employed in the health-care sector. As shown in Figure 6.11, national health-care expenditures grew from about 5 percent of GDP in 1960 to 17.6 percent of GDP in 2019. In 2020, healthcare expenditures increased by almost 10 percent, reaching 19.7 percent of the GDP, primarily due to the 36 percent increase in federal health care expenditures in response to the COVID-19 pandemic. Out-of-pocket costs (the amounts paid by individuals for health care, including payments by those without insurance and co-pays and other expenses by those with insurance) have remained relatively constant at around 2 percent of the GDP over the years, but both private insurance and public costs have risen considerably. In 2020 annual spending on health care in the United States was about $12,530 per person.[43] Health-care costs are expected to increase further and become an even greater share of GDP, as the population ages and medical technology continues to become more sophisticated.

In 2020, the federal government and households accounted for the largest share of national health expenditures—36 percent and 26 percent, respectively—compared to 17 percent of the expenditures by private businesses, 14 percent by state and local governments, and 7 percent from other private revenues. Direct government payments for such programs as Medicare and Medicaid and the Veterans

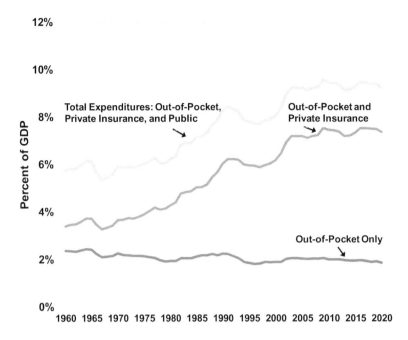

Figure 6.11 *Health Care Expenditures in the United States as a Percentage of GDP, 1960–2019*

Source: Various editions of the Statistical Abstract of the United States.

Administration accounted for 40 percent of overall health spending.[44] Under the Affordable Care Act (ACA) of 2010, the government provides tax credits that cover much of the cost of private insurance for those who are income-eligible (individuals and families making up to 400 percent of the poverty line). Despite attempts by the Trump administration to repeal the ACA, large portions of it remained in place, and this expansion of the government's role in health care continued and expanded under the Biden administration.

Unlike all other developed countries, the United States does not have publicly funded universal health-care coverage. With the passage of the Affordable Care Act, the proportion of Americans lacking health insurance declined significantly, to about 8.6 percent in 2020. While the government's role in providing health insurance has expanded, the actual provision of health care in the U.S. remains primarily a function of the private market.

The dominance of private markets for health care in the United States has not kept health-care spending or costs low. In fact, a higher share of GDP is spent on health care in the United States than in any other developed country. While in the United States health care accounted for about 17 percent of GDP in 2019, in France, Canada, and Sweden health care represents 11 percent, and in Australia and the UK 10 percent.[45] Per person spending on healthcare in the U.S. (about $12,000) is also much larger than in many other developed countries, such as Germany ($6,731), France ($5,564), Canada ($5,370), and Japan ($4,691).[46]

246

Given that these expenditures are so high in the United States, is the quality of health care higher than in other developed countries? Using several common measures of national health, the United States actually ranks lower than most other developed countries. The United States has a relatively low number of physicians per capita and a lower-than-average rate of childhood immunization. Average life spans are shorter than in most other developed countries, and infant mortality rates are slightly above the norm.

As the U.S. population ages, it is likely that health care costs will become an even larger portion of GDP. On the positive side, this offers the potential for expanding job opportunities in the medical sector. But overall cost control and efficiency remain a major concern for the future.

BOX 6.6 THE AFFORDABLE CARE ACT

The passage of the Affordable Care Act (ACA or "Obamacare") in 2010 marked the most significant change to the American health care system in decades. The law was to be phased in over the period 2010–2020, and despite opposition by the Trump administration and Congressional attempts to repeal the ACA, much of the law has remained in effect. The "individual mandate" to buy health insurance that was part of the original law was repealed during the Trump administration, but major continuing provisions include the following:

- The law sets maximum insurance premium rates. For example, an individual making 150 percent of the poverty line cannot pay more than 4 percent of his or her income in premiums.
- The law prohibits insurance companies from denying coverage to individuals with pre-existing conditions.
- As of 2013, the law raised the tax rate on wages by 0.9 percent (from 1.45 percent to 2.35 percent) on individuals making more than $200,000 per year (or couples making more than $250,000). The funds from the tax will be used to subsidize health care coverage for low-income individuals and pay for other costs of the law.
- Firms with more than 50 employees are required to provide health care coverage or pay a fee if the government has to subsidize their employees' health care. Smaller firms that offer health insurance may qualify for subsidies.
- More than 20 million people have gained insurance as a result of the ACA, and the percentage of uninsured Americans has dropped from 16 percent in 2010 to less than 9 percent by 2021. There has also been an improvement in care received, including increased access to personal physicians, preventative care, and care for chronic conditions among low-income adults. The ACA's Medicaid expansions have been especially important in benefiting enrolees—a 2019 report finds that Medicaid expansions have been associated with 19,200 fewer deaths among older low-income adults between 2013 and 2017.[47] Additionally, the gap in uninsured rates between white and Black adults contracted by 51 percent in Medicaid expansion states, compared to 33 percent in non-expansion states.[48]

Recently, the Biden administration has proposed further strengthening the ACA's effectiveness by boosting financial assistance for enrollments, widening the window for sign-ups, and providing states with incentives to expand Medicaid. As of early 2022, enrollment in the plan has reached a record high of 14.2 million Americans.[49]

4.6 Human Services: Education

The situation with respect to education in the United States in many ways mirrors that of health care. The quality of education in the United States can be excellent, which draws many foreigners to come here for higher education. About 20 percent of graduate students in the United States are foreign-born. Spending per student in the United States is significantly higher than the average among members of the Organization for Economic Cooperation and Development (OECD). In 2017, the United States spent $14,100 per student on elementary and secondary education, which was 37 percent higher than the OECD average of $10,300. At the postsecondary level, the U.S. spent $34,500 per student, twice the amount spent by OECD countries on average ($17,100).[50]

The performance of American students below the college level, however, is only mediocre by international standards. In a standardized test given in 2018 to 15-year-old students in over 79 countries with varying levels of economic development, U.S. students ranked thirty-sixth in math, thirteenth in reading, and eighteenth in science. (See Chapter 0 for additional comparisons.)

The costs of education have become a major issue. Between 2010 and 2020, the cost of attending a public four-year institution increased by 32 percent, much more rapidly than overall inflation, which rose 18.6 percent during the same period.[51] While federal college education grants have increased, particularly since 2008, the majority of federal education assistance now comes in the form of loans. Although those who have trouble paying back federal student loans can apply for assistance programs, students who take out loans from private companies tend to face higher interest rates and less flexible conditions. Over the last decade, the federal student debt has increased by 144 percent to $1.7 trillion collectively owed by 45 million Americans. At least part of this increase in student debt is explained by the declining support for higher education at the state level along with easy access to federal loans, which has encouraged schools to continue raising fees without fear of losing students.[52] The average class of 2020 graduate has nearly $30,000 in student loan, up 20 percent from 2010.[53]

Both public and private institutions provide education in the United States. Education services employed about 2.4 percent of the workers in 2020. About 73.5 million students are enrolled in American schools at all grade levels, and about 86 percent are in public schools.[54] Among people 25 and older in the United States in 2020, 90 percent are high school graduates and 37.5 percent have college degrees. Educational attainment differs by race and gender. For example, while 37.5 percent of whites had a college degree in 2020, only 27.8 percent of blacks and 20.8 percent of those of Hispanic origin had completed college. As of 2020, more women are enrolled in college than men, and the proportion of women with a college degree or higher (31 percent) is also higher than that for men (28 percent).[55]

Discussion Questions

1. Economic theory suggests that goods and services provided in competitive markets by private enterprises will result in lower prices. But we have learned that health-care costs in the United States actually are the highest in the world, although Americans do not better have health outcomes than people in countries that provide public health care. How would you explain this result? Do you think that the Affordable Care Act will improve the situation? If not, what alternative solution would you suggest?
2. Amazon has doubled its share of domestic retail from 28.1 percent in 2014 to 56.7 percent in 2021. Are you worried about this increase in market concentration? In what ways might Amazon's rise in market power affect you as a consumer? How does this affect other large retailers like Walmart or Macys? How does this affect smaller businesses?

5 CONCLUDING THOUGHTS

This chapter has provided a bird's-eye view of the U.S. economy. We have looked at primary sector activities that provide the raw materials on which everything else depends, noting that the importance of these activities is belied by the small percentage of GDP devoted to them. We have looked at secondary-sector activities that process physical materials, turning them into goods for sale. And we have looked at the tertiary sector, which accounts for about three-quarters of the economic activity in the United States.

The "marketed" section of the economy, on which we have concentrated here, is not the whole picture. Seemingly inherent in our economic system is a drive to find ever more ways to replace what we do for ourselves with marketed services or products. The replacement of much home cooking with fast food, take-out, and rapid meal delivery is a prime example. Still, the services that people provide as friends, neighbors, family members, and citizens continue to be a large part of the economy, though unmeasured by flows of money and therefore missing from GDP. Recall from Chapter 5 that even the most conservative estimates of the total value of household production are 25–30 percent of measured GDP in the United States. In a more fully accounted economy, covering the core as well as the business and public purpose spheres, the tertiary sector would still loom very large—much of the (non-monetized) economic activity in the core sphere is services—but a greater proportion of its expansion would be in the areas of "private social services" and "entertainment."

As we continue our analysis of the macroeconomy, we will focus primarily on the portion of the economy that is measured by standard GDP. We will be concerned with aggregate figures, concentrating for example on total consumption, total investment, and total government spending. The material covered in this chapter, as well as in the preceding two, may help us to bear in mind the realities that lie behind the abstractions that are necessary to develop macroeconomic theory. Before delving into that theory, we need to review one other important area of the real economy— employment and unemployment—the topic of the next chapter.

REVIEW QUESTIONS

1. List and define the three major sectors of the U.S. economy, as discussed in this chapter.
2. Approximately what percentage of the U.S. GDP is produced in each of the three sectors? How has this allocation changed over time?
3. Summarize how agriculture in the United States has changed over the past century. About how much of each dollar spent on food currently goes to farmers?
4. Does the declining share of the primary sector imply that it is becoming less important?
5. What is the largest source of energy supply in the United States?
6. What is the proportion of U.S. energy supplied by renewables, and what is the trend in this area?
7. Contrast the recent history of the American textile and automobile industries.
8. What are some of the reasons for the decline in U.S. manufacturing jobs?
9. Why does the number of new housing starts in the United States show a cyclical pattern?
10. Is the service sector synonymous with low-paying jobs?
11. What trend was emphasized in the chapter concerning retail services?
12. What is meant by "financialization"? What data suggest the United States has become more financialized in recent years?
13. What are some of the major issues concerning health care in the United States?
14. What accounts for increasing student loan burdens in the U.S?

EXERCISES

1. Match each statement in Column A with a percentage in Column B.

Column A	Column B
a. The government percentage of GDP value-added	1. 16.8 percent
b. The tertiary sector's share of GDP value-added	2. 70 percent
c. The decline in cost of solar PV panels between 2014 and 2021	3. 12.8 percent

d.	Construction starts in 2020 as a percent of their mid-2000s peak	4. 1.3 percent
e.	The percentage decline in U.S. manufacturing jobs since 1979	5. 68.8 percent
f.	The secondary sector's share of GDP	6. 13.4 percent
g.	The percentage of U.S. workers employed in the health-care sector	7. 72 percent
h.	The primary sector's share of GDP	8. 37 percent

2. Search the Internet or other news sources for recent articles discussing the loss of U.S. manufacturing jobs. What factors do you think are most significant in this trend, and what policies might be used to respond to it?

3. Go to the web site for the U.S. Bureau of Economic Analysis https://bea.gov/ and search "Gross Domestic Product by Industry." Look for the "Annual Update." What are recent trends in industry output? What economic sectors were most significant in the changes discussed in the report?

4. Match each statement in Column A with an answer in Column B:

Column A	Column B
a. The largest of the three economic sectors by value-added	1. Cyclical
b. The smallest of the three economic sectors by value-added	2. Ford Motor Company
c. An example of a business in the primary sector	3. Primary
d. An example of a business in the secondary sector	4. Walmart
e. An example of a business in the tertiary sector	5. Declining
f. The current trend regarding the size of the secondary sector	6. Tertiary
g. The current trend regarding the size of the tertiary sector	7. A local farmer's market
h. The typical trend regarding the number of housing starts	8. Increasing

NOTES

1 World Development Indicators database, World Bank.
2 Source: Bureau of Economic Analysis data.
3 Kassel, 2022.
4 Based on data from U.S. Department of Agriculture.
5 Kenner et al., 2022.
6 Fuglie and Wang, 2012.
7 Codur and Harris, 2022.
8 Codur et al., 2017.
9 Nastu, 2019.
10 BP Statistical Review of World Energy 2020.
11 U.S. Energy Information Administration, 2021.
12 U.S. Department of Energy, 2021a.

13 U.S. Department of Energy, 2021b.
14 Jacobsen et al., 2013; quote from Rosenthal, 2013.
15 Elliott et al., 2016.
16 U.S., EPA 2016.
17 Kuchment, 2019.
18 U.S. EPA, 2012.
19 U.S. EPA, 2015.
20 Tan, 2022.
21 Based on data from Taylor, 2020 and Coady et al., 2019.
22 U.S. EPA, 2006.
23 Data from U.S. BLS, Table on Total factor productivity for major industries, 2020.
24 Author's calculation based on data from U.S. Census Bureau.
25 Barua, 2021.
26 Lawrence, 2019.
27 Based on data from U.S. Bureau of Labor Statistics.
28 American Society of Civil Engineers, 2021.
29 Lombardo, 2021a.
30 The White House, 2021.
31 Long, 2021.
32 Lombardo, 2021b.
33 McBride and Siripurapu, 2021.
34 Based on data from World Trade Organization, 2021.
35 Data from BLS on average hourly wages for all employees in goods-producing and services-producing sectors. https://www.bls.gov/web/empsit/ceseeb3a.htm.
36 Weise and Corkery, 2021.
37 Orhangazi, 2007.
38 FDIC, 2021.
39 Real World Macro, 2015.
40 Tomaskovic Dewey and Lin, 2013.
41 Foroohar, 2016.
42 Based on data from OECD.
43 CMS, 2021.
44 CMS, 2021.
45 Based on data from the World Development Indicators.
46 Wager et al., 2022.
47 Miller et al., 2019.
48 Somers, 2021.
49 Mangan, 2022.
50 IES, 2021a.
51 Hanson, 2022.
52 Sheffey, 2021.
53 Kerr and Wood, 2021.
54 IES, 2021b.
55 Based on data from the U.S. Census Bureau.

REFERENCES

American Society of Civil Engineers. 2021. "2021 Report Card for America's Infrastructure." https://infrastructurereportcard.org/.

Barua, Akrur. 2021. "A Spring in Consumers' Steps: Americans Prepare to Get Back to Their Spending Ways." *Deloitte, Ecoomics Spotlight,* June.

British Petroleum (BP). 2020b. *Statistical Review of World Energy 2020.* https://www.bp.com/en/global/corporate/energy-economics/statistical-review-ofworld-energy.html.

Canning, Patrick and Quinton Baker. 2021. Food Dollar Series. *Economic Research Service (ERS)*, U.S. Department of Agriculture (USDA).

Centers for Medicare and Medicaid Services (CMS). 2021. "National Health Expenditures 2020 Highlights." https://www.cms.gov/files/document/highlights.pdf

Coady, David, Ian Parry, Nghia-Piotr Le, and Baoping Shang. 2019. "Global Fossil Fuel Subsidies Remain Large: An Update Based on Country-Level Estimates." *IMF Working Paper WP/12/89*, May 2019.

Codur, Anne-Marie, and Jonathan Harris. 2022. "Climate Challenges After the Glasgow Conference: The Roles of Forests and Soils." *Global Development and Environment Institute*, Climate Policy Brief, No. 15. January.

Codur, Anne-Marie et al. 2017. "Hope Below Our Feet: Soil as a Climate Solution." *Global Development and Environment Institute, Climate Policy Brief No.4*, April.

Elliott, Elise G., Adrienne S. Ettinger, Brian P. Leaderer, Michael B. Bracken, and Nicole C. Deziel. 2016. "A Systematic Evaluation of Chemicals in Hydraulic-Fracturing Fluids and Wastewater for Reproductive and Developmental Toxicity." *Journal of Exposure Science and Environmental Epidemiology, 27*: 90–99.

Federal Deposit Insurance Corporation (FDIC). 2021. "Quarterly Banking Profile." https://www.fdic.gov/analysis/quarterly-banking-profile/qbp/2021dec/qbp.pdf#page=7

Foroohar, Rana. 2016. "American Capitalism's Great Crisis." *Time*, May 12.

Fuglie, Keith and Sun Ling Wang. 2012. "Productivity Growth in Global Agriculture Shifting to Developing Countries." *Choices: The Magazine of Food, Farm, and Resource Issues, 27*(4): 1–7.

Hanson, Melanie. 2022. "Average Cost of College and Tuition." *Education Data Initiative*, January 27.

Institute of Education Sciences (IES). 2021a. "Education Expenditures by Country." *National Center for Education Statistics*. https://nces.ed.gov/programs/coe/indicator/cmd

Institute of Education Sciences (IES). 2021b. "Back-To-School Statistics." *National Center for Education Statistics*. https://nces.ed.gov/fastfacts/display.asp?id=372

Jacobsen, Mark Z. Jacobsonet al., 2013. "Examining the Feasibility of Converting New York State's All-Purpose Energy Infrastructure to One Using Wind, Water, and Sunlight," *Energy Policy, 57*: 585–601.

Kassel, Kathleen. 2022. "Farming and Farm Income." *U.S. Department of Agriculture Economic Research Service*, February 4.

Kenner, Bart, Hui Jiang, Dylan Russell, Wendy Zeng, Steven Zahniser, Maros Ivanic, Fengxia Dong, Megan Husby, and Xuan Pham. 2022. "Outlook for U.S. Agricultural Trade: February 2022" USDA Economic Research Service, USDA, AES-119.

Kerr, Emma, and Sarah Wood. 2021. "See 10 Years of Average Student Loan Debt." *U.S. News*, September 2021.

Kuchment, Anna. 2019. "Even If Injection of Fracking Wastewater Stops, Quakes Won't." *Scientific American*, September 9, 2019.

Lawrence, Robert Z. 2019. "19-11 China, Like the US, Faces Challenges in Achieving Inclusive Growth Through Manufacturing." *Peterson Institute for International Economics*, August.

Lombardo, Jessica. 2021a. "Report: How to Advance US Infrastructure Investment." *For Construction Pros.com*, February 19.

Lombardo, Jessica. 2021b. "Job Creation a Winner Under Infrastructure Plan, But Who Will Do the Work?" *For Construction Pros.com*, August 30.

Long, Heather. 2021. "Biden Infrastructure Bill Will Bring Jobs. He Wants the Safety Net Bill to Reduce Inequities." *The Washington Post*, November 7.

Mangan, Dan. 2022. "Obamacare Enrollment Hits Record High After Biden Makes Post-Trump Tweaks to Health Insurance Program." *CNBC*, January 18.

McBride, James and Anshu Siripurapu. 2021. "The State of U.S. Infrastructure." *Council on Foreign Relations*, November 8.

253

Miller, Sarah, Sean Altekruse, Norman Johnson, and Laura R. Wherry. 2019. "Medicaid and Mortality: New Evidence from Linked Survey and Administrative Data." http://www-personal.umich.edu/~mille/ACAMortality.pdf

Nastu, Jennifer. 2019. "Why Overall Water Use Is Declining in US Despite Population Growth." *Environment + Energy Leader*, January 2.

Orhangazi, Ozgur. 2007. "Financialization and Capital Accumulation in the Non-Financial Corporate Sector: A Theoretical and Empirical Investigation of the U.S. Economy: 1973–2003." Political Economy and Research Institute, Working Paper Series Number 149.

Real World Macro. 2015. "From Boring Banking to Roaring Banking: How the financial sector grew out of control, and how we can change it." *An Interview with Gerald Epstein*, Real World Macro, July/ August 2015, Dollars and Sense.

Rosenthal, Elisabeth. "Life after Oil and Gas." *New York Times*, March 23.

Sheffey, Ayelet. 2021. "4 Reasons Why the $1.7 Trillion Student Debt Crisis is So Bad for 45 Million Americans." *Insider*, November 11.

Somers, Sarah. 2021. "The Affordable Care Act: Reflections on 10 Years." *The Network for Public Health and Law*, May 6.

Tan, Weizhen. 2022. "Analysts Warn of Recession if Oil Prices Continue to Surge Further into 'Unchartered Territory'." *CNBC*, March 9.

Taylor, Michael. 2020. *Energy Subsidies: Evolution in the Global Energy Transformation to 2050*. International Renewable Energy Agency, Abu Dhabi.

The White House. 2021. "President Biden's Bipartisan Infrastructure Law." https://www.whitehouse.gov/bipartisan-infrastructure-law

Tomaskovic-Dewey, Donald and Ken-Hou Lin. 2013. "Financialization and U.S. Income Inequality, 1970–2008." *American Journal of Sociology, 118*(5): 1284–1329.

U.S. Department of Energy. 2021a. "Solar Energy in the United States." *Solar Technologies Office.* https://www.energy.gov/eere/solar/solar-energy-united-states

U.S. Department of Energy. 2021b. "DOE Releases New Reports Highlighting Record Growth, Declining Costs of Wind Power," August 30. https://www.energy.gov/articles/doe-releases-new-reports-highlighting-record-growth-declining-costs-of-wind-power

U.S. Energy Information Administration. 2021. "Renewables Account for Most New U.S. Electricity Generating Capacity in 2021," January 11. https://www.eia.gov/todayinenergy/detail.php?id=46416

U.S. Environmental Protection Agency (EPA). 2006. *National Action Plan for Energy Efficiency.* https://19january2017snapshot.epa.gov/sites/production/files/2015-08/documents/national_action_plan_for_energy_efficiency_report_chapter_6_energy_efficiency_program_best_practices.pdf

U.S. Environmental Protection Agency (EPA). 2015. *Case Studies for EPA's Hydraulic Fracturing Study.* https://www.epa.gov/sites/production/files/2015-06/documents/final_retro_case_study_fact_sheet_6_03_508_km.pdf.

U.S. Environmental Protection Agency (EPA). 2016. *Hydraulic Fracturing for Oil and Gas: Impacts from the Hydraulic Fracturing Water Cycle on Drinking Water Resources in the United States (Final Report).* EPA/600/R-16/236F, Washington, DC.

U.S. Environmental Protection Agency, "Study of the Potential Impacts of Hydraulic Fracturing on Drinking Water Resources: Progress Report," December 2012, and Hydraulic Fracturing Study: Retrospective Case Studies; Edwin Dobb, "America Strikes New Oil," *National Geographic* (March 2013): 28–59.

Wager, Emma and Cynthia Cox. 2022. "How Does Wealth Spending in the U.S. Compare to Other Countries?" *Peterson-KFF Health System Tracker*, January 21.

Weise, Karen and Michael Corkery. 2021. "People Now Spend More at Amazon Than at Walmart." *The New York Times*, August 17.

Chapter 7

Employment, Unemployment, and Wages

Some of the most important issues in the economy relate to questions of employment, unemployment, and wages. For most people, securing a good job with adequate compensation and benefits is central to maintaining their livelihoods and achieving a good standard of living. For this reason, government agencies devote a lot of effort to gathering data relating to current levels of employment, unemployment, and wages. In the first two sections of this chapter, we will look into what exactly these statistics mean. In Section 3 we will discuss various theories about how labor markets work. The final section offers some perspectives on how employment in the future might look, for workers and for society at large.

1 EMPLOYMENT AND UNEMPLOYMENT

We have seen in previous chapters how official data are used to create a macro portrait of the economy—and how these data may emphasize some aspects (especially market activities) and ignore or downplay others. We start this chapter with a similar look at the official data on work issues. These data do not cover all issues related to work (for example unpaid household work is generally omitted), but it is important to know how to read the official data and what they can tell us.

1.1 Measuring Employment and Unemployment

Every month, the U.S. **Bureau of Labor Statistics (BLS)** interviews about 60,000 households, asking whether individual household members have jobs or are looking for work. In addition to conducting this household survey, it collects data every month from nearly 400,000 employers. Based on these two surveys, the BLS publishes monthly data on work issues, including the official unemployment rate.

> **Bureau of Labor Statistics (BLS):** in the United States, the government agency that compiles and publishes employment and unemployment statistics

DOI: 10.4324/9781003251521-10

The BLS statistics only includes the **civilian non-institutional population** which consists of persons 16 years or older living in private households. Hence, children are excluded, as are people who are in compulsory military services, and those who live in prison, nursing homes, mental institutions, and long-term care hospitals. Of the civilian non-institutional population, those who did any work or had jobs as paid employees or business owners, or worked for 15 hours or more at a family business during the reference week are defined as being **employed**. **Unemployed** persons, on the other hand, are those in the civilian non-institutional population, who were not employed during the reference week, but were available to work, and had made specific efforts to find employment sometime in the four-week period ending with the reference week. Let us take a closer look at how the BLS classifies the employed and unemployed population.

---

civilian non-institutional population (BLS definition): persons 16 years or older who do not live in institutions (for example, correctional facilities, nursing homes, or long-term care hospitals) and who are not on active duty in the Armed Forces
employed person (BLS definition): a person who did any work for pay or profit during the week before he or she is surveyed by the BLS or who worked for fifteen hours or more in a family business
unemployed person (BLS definition): a person who is not employed but who is actively seeking a job and is immediately available for work

---

The structure of the BLS household survey is illustrated in Figure 7.1. The survey starts with the three questions in Box A of Figure 7.1. If you can answer "no" to *all* these questions, you are part of the *civilian, non-institutionalized, age sixteen and over population* about which this survey gathers data on employment. If you answer "yes" to any question in Box A, the official employment and unemployment statistics do not include you. Trends in employment statistics over time, then, need to be analyzed in the light of considerations such as changes in age demographics, military policy, and rates of disability and incarceration. (See Box 7.2, for more on incarceration in the United States.)

If you are part of the surveyed population, then you will be asked the questions in Box B of Figure 7.1, starting with: "Last week, did you do any work for pay or profit?" Anyone who answers "yes" will be classified as employed. If you did *any* paid work last week—even if you worked for only an hour or two at a casual job—the interviewer will code you as "employed." If you answer "no," then you will be asked more questions. For example, if you have a paid job but just did not happen to put in any hours last week because you were sick, on vacation, or on a leave, you will be coded as "employed." Also, if you did *unpaid* work in a family-run business, such as a retail store or farm, you will be classified as "employed" as long as you worked for more than fifteen hours a week.

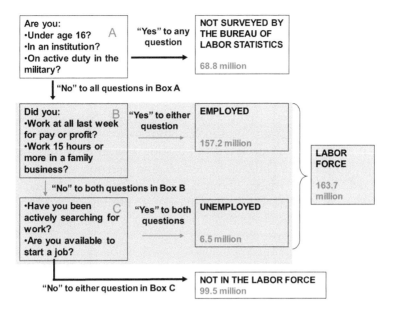

Figure 7.1 *Who Is In the Labor Force?*

Source: BLS News Release, "The Employment Situation—January 2022," February 2022; U.S. Census Bureau Current Population Clock.

Note that the "family business" situation is the only case in which unpaid work currently counts as being employed in the official statistics. If you work fewer than 15 hours in your family business, or are, for example, occupied with caring for your children or other family members or doing community volunteer work, you will *not* be considered "employed." Terms such as "labor," "work," and "employment" in official statistics generally refer only to *paid* work.

If your answers to the household survey do *not* result in your being classified as "employed," you will be asked the questions about job search and availability shown in Box C of Figure 7.1. Activities such as contacting employers and sending out résumés count as an "active" job search. Merely participating in a job-training program or reading employment ads do not. The question about whether you could start a job concerns whether, in fact, you are *available* for work. If, for example, you are a college student searching during spring break for a summer job, but you are not available to start the job until June, you would answer "no" to the availability question. If you can answer "yes" to *both* these questions you are classified as unemployed.

If you are either employed or unemployed, the BLS classifies you as part of the **labor force**. But what if you are neither "employed" nor "unemployed"—if you do not have a job but are not actively seeking one? Then you are classified as "**not in the labor force**." People in this category are often taking care of a home and family, in school, disabled, or retired.

> **labor force (BLS definition):** people who are employed or unemployed
> **"not in the labor force" (BLS definition):** the classification given to people who are neither "employed" nor "unemployed"

Notice, in Figure 7.1, that the vast majority of U.S. residents who are not "employed" either are "not in the labor force" (about 99.5 million) or are not part of the surveyed population (about 68.8 million). The latter group includes children under 16, and persons who are institutionalized. In comparison, about 6.5 million people in January 2022 were counted as "unemployed" while 157.2 million were counted as "employed". (Figures are updated monthly at www.bls.gov.)

1.2 The Unemployment Rate

Every month, having made estimates, based on the survey responses, of the total number of employed and unemployed people in the country, the BLS calculates the official **unemployment rate**. This is defined as the percentage of people in the labor force who do not have paid jobs but are actively looking for and available for paid work. Mathematically, it is calculated as:

$$\text{unemployment rate} = \frac{\text{number of people unemployed}}{\text{number of people in the laborforce}} \times 100$$

> **unemployment rate:** the percentage of the labor force made up of people who do not have paid jobs but are immediately available and actively looking for paid jobs

For example, in January 2022, there were 157.2 million employed people and 6.5 million unemployed people; so a total of 163.7 million people were in the labor force (Figure 7.1). The unemployment rate was thus calculated as 3.97 percent:

$$\text{unemployment rate} = \frac{6.5 \text{ million}}{163.7 \text{ million}} \times 100 = 3.97\%$$

The unemployment rate reported in the media is often "seasonally adjusted." Over the course of a year, some swings in unemployment are fairly predictable. For example, agriculture and construction tend to employ fewer people in the winter months, and each year many students enter the labor force in May and June after graduation. The BLS releases "seasonally adjusted" figures that attempt to reflect only shifts in unemployment that are due to factors *other than* such seasonal patterns.

Table 7.1 *Unemployment Rates for Different Groups, January 2022*

Group	Unemployment rate
All Workers	4.0
Race and ethnicity[a]	
White	3.4
Black/African American	6.9
Hispanic or Latino	4.9
Age	
Teenage (age 16–19)	10.9
Age 65 and older	3.5
Education[b]	
Less than a high school diploma	6.3
Bachelor's degree and higher	2.3
Gender	
Adult male	3.8
Adult female	3.6

Source: BLS News Release, "The Employment Situation—January 2022," February 4, 2022.

[a] *People are allowed to indicate more than one racial group. However, data from people who indicated more than one race are not included in these statistics.*

[b] *Data on unemployment by education is for the age-group 25 years and over.*

The BLS also estimates unemployment rates for various demographic groups, occupations, industries, and geographical areas. Historically, unemployment rates have generally been substantially higher for minority populations than for whites, for teenagers than for older people, and for less educated people than for the more educated. Unemployment rates often have differed somewhat by gender, though not with any consistent pattern. Some representative unemployment rates are given in Table 7.1.

1.3 Discouraged Workers and Underemployment

The fact that some people "not in the labor force" might want jobs but have given up looking for them has long troubled employment analysts. To the extent that people give up looking, the official unemployment rate *underestimates* people's need and desire for paid jobs.

The BLS survey includes questions to determine how many people in the "not in the labor force" population may want employment, even if they are not currently searching for work. Any individual in this population who is available for work, wants to work, and has looked for work in the past 12 months but not in the past 4 weeks, is categorized as "**marginally attached workers**." In January 2022, marginally attached workers numbered 1.5 million.

> marginally attached workers: people who want employment and have looked for work in the past 12 months but not in the past 4 weeks

If these marginally attached workers also say that the reason they are no longer looking is that they believe there are no jobs out there for them, they are called **discouraged workers**. They may have become discouraged because their skills do not match available openings, because they have experienced discrimination, or because they have been turned away time after time. In January 2022 the number of discouraged workers in the United States was estimated at about 408,000. Marginally attached workers who are not discouraged workers typically have not looked for work recently because of school attendance or family responsibilities.

> discouraged workers: people who want employment but have given up looking because they believe that there are no jobs available for them

Let's also take a closer look at the people classified as "employed." In the BLS statistics, people are counted as "employed" if they do any paid work *at all* during the reference week, even if only for an hour or two. Some people prefer part-time work, of course, because of the time it leaves them for other activities, such as schooling or family care. Some are limited to part-time work for health reasons. But others want and need full-time work and are only settling for part-time work until they can find something better. The household survey asks people who work part-time about their reasons for doing so.

In January 2022, 20.2 million people reported working less than 35 hours per week for "non-economic" reasons such as health or family responsibilities. In the same month, an additional 3.7 million people reported working part-time for what the BLS calls "economic reasons"—that is, slack business conditions or because part-time work was all they could find.

What indicator, then, should we look at to see whether the national employment situation is "good" or "bad"? The BLS publishes various measures of labor underutilization that allow you to see the situation from a variety of different perspectives. For example, if the marginally attached workers and people who work part-time involuntarily are added to the number of unemployed, the rate of labor underutilization in January 2022 comes to 7.1 percent, compared to the official unemployment rate of 4.0 percent.

The BLS also counts people as employed even if the kind of work that they did does not match their skills. Suppose that you paint your aunt's living room for cash while you are waiting to hear back on job applications for management or computer positions. The BLS counts you as already employed. People who are working at jobs that underutilize their abilities, as well as those who work fewer hours than they wish to, are said to be **underemployed**.

---

underemployment: working fewer hours than desired or at a job that does not match one's skills

---

If we are concerned about human well-being, underemployment, as well as unemployment, should be of concern. While underemployment due to underutilization of skills is of considerable concern for both efficiency and quality-of-life reasons, BLS official surveys do not currently attempt to measure this sort of underemployment.

1.4 Labor Force Participation

The **labor force participation (LFP) rate** is defined as the proportion of people who either are in paid jobs or are actively seeking paid work out of the total pool of workers who could potentially be working. It is calculated by dividing the number of people officially in the labor force by the number of people age 16 or over who are not institutionalized or in the military:

$$\text{LFP Rate} = \frac{\text{number of people in the labor force}}{\text{number of people age 16+, not institutionalized or in the military}} \times 100$$

---

labor force participation (LFP) rate: the percentage of potential workers either with a job or actively seeking a job or the labor force as a percentage of the civilian non-institutional population

---

In 2021 the LFP rate in the United States was about 62 percent. About 38 percent of the surveyed population are not actively looking for jobs. This is an increase from 2000 when the percentage not participating in the labor force was less than 33 percent.

In the first half of the twentieth century, the labor force participation rates for men and women were very different: In 1948 the LFP rate for men was 87 percent, while for women it was only 33 percent. Since then, men's LFP rate has declined to about 68 percent in 2020 while the rate for women increased dramatically until about 2000 when it began to stabilize at around 60 percent as shown in Figure 7.2. The women's rights movement during the 1960s and 1970s contributed to

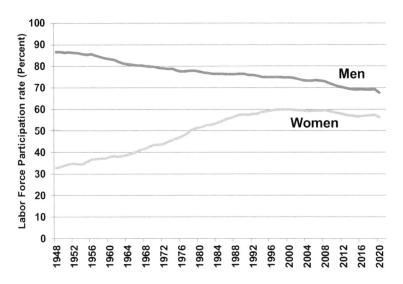

Figure 7.2 *Male and Female Labor Force Participation Rates, 1948–2020*

Source: Bureau of Labor Statistics, Labor Force Participation Rate, retrieved from FRED, Federal Reserve Bank of St. Louis

this expansion in women's labor market activities. Other factors include the expansion of the service sector (discussed in Chapter 6) and reductions in the average number of children per family.

More recently the pandemic has caused a decline in LFP for both men and women. Overall, men's LFP has declined by 1.1 percent, compared to a decline of 1.3 percent for women. Exit from the labor force has been higher for Black and Latina women, as well as for women living with children, and women with lower earnings.[1] Part of this decline can be explained by the loss of jobs in the services sector and the increase in childcare responsibilities during the pandemic.

BOX 7.1 THE DECLINE IN LABOR FORCE PARTICIPATION OF PRIME-AGE MEN

In the past 60 years, the share of men between the ages of 25 and 54 either working or actively seeking work, also known as the prime-age male labor force participation (LFP) rate, has been falling. While over 96 percent of the prime-age men were in the labor force until the 1960s, this number has gradually declined to about 88 percent in 2021.

What explains this decline in men's LFP? Data from the U.S. Current Population Survey suggests that about 47 percent of the prime-age men not in the labor force are going to school, another 26 percent are either disabled or ill, 14 percent are retired, and the remaining 13 percent are either taking care of home or not working due to other reasons. Empirical evidence suggests that the decline in male LFP is concentrated among those with a high school degree or less and that the drop in demand for low-skilled labor, due to the loss of manufacturing jobs, increased technology, and automation explains part of this decline. Other reasons for the decline in LFP cited in the literature include delayed family formation, the rise of substance abuse, and heavy use of video games.[2]

These data raise some obvious questions; for one, how are these individuals getting by? Some males who have dropped out of the workforce might be dependent on income from a working spouse. But less than a quarter of prime-age men who are not in the workforce have a working spouse, and that figure has actually *decreased* during the last 50 years. In case we suppose that these workforce dropouts have other sources of income, data suggests that more than 35 percent of prime-age men not in the labor force lived in poverty in 2014.[3]

Can the trend be explained by generous public assistance? About half of non-working 25- to 54-year-old men are on Medicaid, collect Social Security Disability Insurance, or both, and about two-fifths of them are on food stamps.[4] But it should be noted that disbursements from the Social Security Disability Insurance (SSDI) have increased by only 2 percentage points since 1967, compared to a 7.5 percentage-point decline in prime-age male LFP rates over that period. Analysis conducted in 2016 by the CEA found that increasing SSDI disbursements can explain at most the 0.5 percentage point of the decline in prime-age male LFP over this period. At the same time, other government programs, such as Temporary Assistance for Needy Families (TANF), the Supplemental Nutrition Assistance Program (SNAP), and unemployment benefits have become increasingly hard to access for those out of work, and especially those without children.[5]

Some labor market researchers are also looking at the opioid crisis as an explanation for the decline in LFP of prime-age men with lower education levels. A 2018 paper finds a significant negative relationship between opioid prescription rates and labor market participation.[6] The authors estimate that resolving the opioid crisis would increase labor market participation among prime-aged males by 4 percentage points. It is also possible that the causation runs the other way—loss of good jobs could be leading to higher rates of opioid use.

The fall in LFP for prime-age men has been a hot political topic, as it is presumed to have swung a block of disaffected white male voters toward Donald Trump in the presidential race of 2016. But it should be noted that the decline has been steepest, and the rate remains lowest, for prime-age black men, who also suffer the highest rates of unemployment.

Other issues affecting labor force participation include the aging of the population and higher educational attainment. An increasing share of Americans are retired, and thus voluntarily out of the labor force. As more people attend college and graduate school, for a period of time they voluntarily remove themselves from the labor force. Because of the way LFP is calculated—excluding people who are institutionalized (in prison or jail)—changes in incarceration rates also have a significant effect on the statistics generated on labor force participation (see Box 7.2).

BOX 7.2 INCARCERATION IN THE UNITED STATES

Not only does the United States incarcerate more individuals, in absolute numbers, than any other country in the world but it also has the world's highest incarceration rate. In 2019, the incarceration rate, calculated as the number of prisoners per 100,000 adult population, was 629 for the United States compared to 165 for Australia, 104 for Canada, and 103 for France.[7]

The total cost of public correction in America is estimated to be over $80 billion per year. This figure, however, only includes spending on things like food, staff, and facilities. When spending on judicial and legal systems, policing, health care, private corrections, and costs to families of those incarcerated are added, the total cost is estimated to be over $182 billion.[8] Adding social costs, such as foregone wages and increased health risks of the incarcerated along with adverse health and education effects and increased criminality of children of the incarcerated, could increase the total cost of incarceration to over 1 trillion dollars.[9]

The U.S. prison population has increased dramatically in the past few decades. Between 1980 and 2019, the prison population increased from about 500,000 people to over 2.1 million people.[10] Given that violent and property crimes decreased steeply during this same period, why has the prison population risen so much? Part of the increase is a result of the "war on drugs," which mandated long prison sentences even for minor drug offenses, such as drug possession. However, only 1 in 5 incarcerated people is locked up for drug offenses. A 2020 report from the Prison Policy Initiative finds that most incarcerated people are charged with low-level offenses, including misdemeanors and non-criminal violations, such as probation or parole violations.[11]

Black men are imprisoned at six times the rate of white men. According to Census data from 2014, there are more young black high school dropouts in prison than have jobs. A *Wonkblog* analysis of government statistics noted that about 7.7 percent of prime-age black men are institutionalized, as compared to 1.6 percent of prime-age white men. These facts have a significant impact on reported statistics concerning LFP. The statistics are normally given with reference to the "non-institutionalized" population. Officially, 84 percent of prime-age white men were working in 2014, compared to 71 percent of black men. After including those incarcerated in the population (the denominator), the fraction of white men who have jobs hardly changes, but the black employment-population ratio drops to 66 percent.[12]

When people get out of prison, their chance of getting a job is substantially lower than for a similar individual without a record. One study found that a criminal record reduced the likelihood of a call-back or job offer by nearly 50 percent (28 percent of those without a criminal record get a call-back, vs. 15 percent of those with). Moreover, the negative effect of a criminal conviction is substantially larger for blacks than for whites. The chance of getting a call-back or job offer is reduced by 30 percent for whites, but by 60 percent for blacks.[13] The imprisonment of African Americans affects far more than labor force participation, of course. To mention just one additional aspect of this reality, one in thirteen black adults can't vote because of their criminal records.

Discussion Questions

1. How would the BLS classify you, personally, on the basis of your activities last week? Can you think of an example where someone you think of as *working* would not be considered by the BLS to be officially "employed"? Is it true that people who are *not working* are generally counted as "unemployed"?

2. Would you say that the official unemployment rate provides an accurate estimate of the actual labor market conditions in the economy? What are some of the issues with the way in which this number is calculated? How has the BLS addressed some of these issues?

2 A CLOSER LOOK AT UNEMPLOYMENT

The unemployment rate is one of the most important indicators that economists use to judge the state of a country's economy. As we will see, some degree of unemployment is expected and even considered healthy in an economy. But being unemployed for a long time, against one's wishes, has a significant negative impact on people's well-being, including their mental and physical health.[14] In this section, we will look at a variety of causes for unemployment as well as some historical patterns for the phenomenon.

2.1 Types of Unemployment

Although BLS statisticians are concerned mainly with calculating the number of unemployed, economists try to understand the causes of unemployment. We will discuss four different categories that—while not closely related to BLS categories—can be helpful in thinking about some of the major causes of unemployment.

Frictional (or search) unemployment merely reflects people's transitions between jobs. The fact that some people are unemployed does not necessarily mean that there are no jobs available. In December 2021, for example, the number of job vacancies (10.9 million) was higher than the number of people looking for jobs (6.5 million), implying a shortage of workers, yet unemployment was still at 3.9 percent. An unemployment rate of 0 percent would only be possible if everyone who wants a job always takes one immediately, or at least within the BLS's monthly survey periods. Not only is this unrealistic but it is also in some ways undesirable. Everyone benefits if people take the time to find good job matches—work that puts their skills and talents to good use. Because information about job openings takes time to find, and employers may want to spend time interviewing and testing applicants, making a good job match is not an instantaneous process. Hence, even in a well-functioning economy, it may take time for people and suitable jobs to find each other.

> **frictional unemployment:** unemployment that arises as people are in transition between jobs

For the most part, economists don't worry too much about frictional unemployment because much of it tends to be short term, and some frictional unemployment—about 2 to 3 percent—is seen as inevitable, although innovative web technologies for matching job offers to job seekers may reduce frictional unemployment by reducing search time.

Cyclical unemployment is unemployment due to macroeconomic fluctuations—specifically, unemployment that occurs due to a **recession**. Most economists look to the National Bureau of Economic Research

265

(NBER), a nonprofit and non-governmental economic research organization, to "officially" mark the beginning and end of recessions. The NBER determinations are strongly based on GDP data, though they also consider other indicators, such as the levels of industrial production and wholesale-retail sales. During recessions, when GDP declines for at least two consecutive quarters, unemployment rises as demand for the products of business falls off. During recoveries, this kind of unemployment should decrease.

> **cyclical unemployment:** unemployment caused by a drop in aggregate demand (normally associated with a recession)
> **recession:** a downturn in economic activity, usually defined as lasting for two consecutive calendar quarters or more

Whereas frictional unemployment is almost always present in an economy, cyclical unemployment is variable and is the kind of unemployment that can affect anyone, regardless of his or her education. Hence it is a significant source of insecurity for broad parts of the population. This is why a great deal of macroeconomic theorizing has to do with the causes of cyclical unemployment and the appropriate policy responses. Explanations of why macroeconomic fluctuations occur and what kind of policies might be used to dampen them (and thus reduce cyclical unemployment) are discussed in Part III of this book. In severe recessions, such as the Great Recession of 2007–2008, cyclical unemployment becomes unacceptably high and may remain high even after the economy is no longer formally in recession. This is what has been called a "jobless recovery": Even after GDP starts to recover, job growth can be very slow. In contrast to the experience of the Great Recession, job growth was rapid during the recovery from the 2020 recession (discussed further in Chapter 9).

Many job seekers rely on state unemployment insurance programs to ease their income needs while they spend time searching for work. In many states unemployment compensation benefits are set at half a worker's earnings or a state-set maximum (whichever is less). In normal economic times, people who qualified for unemployment programs usually received up to 26 weeks' worth of benefits. These benefits are often extended during periods of severe economic downturns, in order to allow people more time to find jobs when unemployment rates are high. For example, in the wake of the Great Recession of 2007–2008, unemployment benefits were extended, at one time to as long as 99 weeks. And the Pandemic Unemployment Assistance program, implemented in 2021 in response to the COVID-19 crisis, extended unemployment benefits for up to 79 weeks.[15] However, by February 2022, claims for unemployment benefits had fallen to the lowest point since the 1970s, as the economy had mostly recovered from its lowest point in March and April of 2020.[16]

Structural unemployment arises when there is a widespread mismatch between, on the one hand, the kinds of jobs being offered by employers and, on the other, the skills, experience, education, or geographic location of potential employees. One important cause of structural unemployment is sectoral shifts, such as those described in Chapter 6, where employment has been falling (relative to total population size) in the primary and secondary sectors, with the largest number of new jobs opening up in the tertiary (service) sector. The U.S. economy may have a lot of new openings for financial analysts and nurses' aides in the Southwest, for example. But these will not do you much good if you live in the Northeast and your skills are in engine assembly or Web design. The labor shortage in 2021 was partly caused by the pandemic-related structural changes in the economy (See Box 7.3).

---

structural unemployment: unemployment that arises because people's skills, experience, education, or location do not match what employers need

---

BOX 7.3 LABOR SHORTAGE IN THE U.S.

The COVID-19 pandemic transformed the labor market in the U.S. While the unemployment rate of 4 percent in January 2022 was close to the 3.5 percent unemployment at the end of 2019, there were a record number of job openings and quits, resulting in a shortage of workers and pushing wages higher. What caused this labor shortage?

One factor explaining this shortage is the increase in the number of working-age individuals dropping out of labor market because of job losses or concerns about their health and safety from being exposed to the virus at workplaces. Many who were infected experienced long-term health effects, preventing them from returning to work. Additionally, over 3 million older Americans took early retirement, reducing the size of the labor force.[17] Some working parents, especially women, also left the labor market to provide care to their children and other family members. Hence, the pool of potential workers declined. The number of people employed in 2021 was 3.5 million fewer than the number in 2019, but only about 1.8 million people were actively seeking jobs in 2021.[18]

Another factor contributing to the labor shortage was the increase in the number of people switching jobs. The disruptions caused by the pandemic pushed many people to reconsider their career choices and switch to jobs that allow more flexibility and have better pay and better working conditions.[19] The pandemic-era unemployment benefits may have also provided workers with some cushion against immediate shocks from job losses and allowed them to take time to reconsider their job choices.

Some have blamed the labor shortage on these government benefits, arguing that people became reliant on overly generous unemployment benefits and therefore had little incentive to return to work. But empirical evidence to support this argument is rather weak. States that ended unemployment benefits early did not see a more rapid return of workers to the labor force.[20] Others have argued instead that the labor shortage is caused by the shortage of *good* jobs, i.e., the reason the open positions remain unfilled is that these positions have low wages, poor working conditions, and limited access to basic benefits.[21] A closer look at the problem reveals that labor shortages have been most significant in the accommodations, food, and retail industries—sectors that have low pay and less flexibility for workers. These industries have also had the highest quit rates. Just in September 2021, 4.4 million workers quit their jobs—what has been called "the Great Resignation". More than one-third of these workers were in the accommodations, food, and retail services.[22]

For employers complaining about not being able to fill open positions, the solution seems to be to improve their offers for workers by increasing pay and providing better working conditions. Some firms are already doing this. According to the Bureau of Labor Statistics, average hourly wages have increased by about 4 percent in 2021, with the increases being the steepest in the leisure and hospitality industries (12.3 percent). But addressing the labor shortage requires a much broader change. Most importantly, the wages and working conditions need to be improved for "essential workers" who constitute about half of the workers in low-wage jobs. These workers were on the frontline during the pandemic, risking their health to keep the country functioning, yet they struggle to make ends meet.[23]

Major transitions in the kinds of work that are available—whether caused by new technologies or by sectoral shifts—are inevitably painful, and they have occurred repeatedly over the last few hundred years. Workers have fought back when they saw their jobs disappearing; most famous were the Luddites, a group of English textile workers and weavers in the nineteenth century who destroyed weaving machinery to protest how these machines could be used to replace workers. The term is sometimes applied to anyone opposed to industrialization, automation, computerization, or new technologies in general. It commonly implies opposition to progress—but the grievances of those thrown out of work are real.

Technological unemployment may be considered a special case of structural unemployment. Ever since the beginning of the Industrial Revolution, technology has been recognized as a double-edged sword for workers. On the one hand, it has created circumstances wherein each worker has more natural and manufactured capital to work with, raising workers' productivity and hence (potentially, at least) their earnings. On the other hand, technology can replace workers, leading to a situation in which ever fewer workers are needed to produce a given quantity of output.

technological unemployment: unemployment caused by reduced demand for workers because technology has increased the productivity of those who have jobs

Fears of technological unemployment have been raised repeatedly during the last two and a half centuries. While these fears have been valid in specific areas—for example, tractors introduced in the 1920s were clearly a factor in reducing the need for farm labor, and computers have made many secretarial jobs obsolete—the total quantity of jobs has generally not declined as a proportion of the population. Indeed, in the twentieth century, the number of jobs in the United States increased significantly, as women successfully entered the labor force and increased the LFP rate, as mentioned above.

2.2 Patterns of Unemployment

Figure 7.3 shows the monthly unemployment rate in the United States from January 1975 to January 2022. Unemployment was at a low of 5.6 percent in 1969 and at a high of 10.8 percent in 1982. A steep increase in unemployment was seen during the Great Recession, when the unemployment rate rose dramatically from less than 5 percent in late 2007 to its peak of 10.0 percent in October 2009. By early 2020, the unemployment rate was down to 3.5 percent, but the COVID-19-related business closures in March 2020 shot the unemployment rate to the highest level since the Great Depression, 14.7 percent in April 2020.

Notice in the figure that the U.S. economy experienced six recessions between 1975 and 2021, but the duration of the recessions in the early 1980s and in 2008 was much longer than the other recessions. In fact, the recovery from the 2008 recession was characterized by persistently high unemployment and a dramatic increase in the average duration of

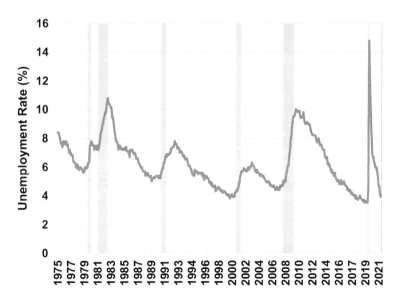

Figure 7.3 *The Monthly Unemployment Rate in the United States, 1975–2021*

Source: U.S. Bureau of Labor Statistics online database.

Notes: Recessionary periods shaded.

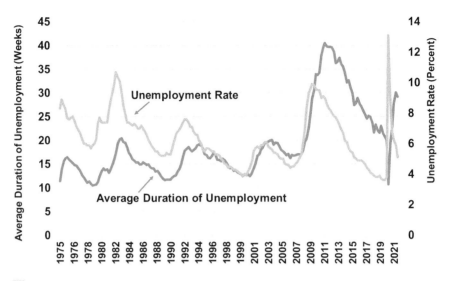

Figure 7.4 *Average Duration of Unemployment and Unemployment Rate, 1975–2021*

Source: U.S. Bureau of Labor Statistics online database.

unemployment. This is shown in Figure 7.4, which plots the average duration of unemployment in addition to the unemployment rate.

The figure shows that when the unemployment rate goes up, the average duration of unemployment also rises. When job opportunities are scarcer, it takes longer for workers who lose their jobs to find new ones. We see in Figure 7.4 that when the unemployment rate exceeded 10 percent in the early 1980s, the average duration of unemployment reached about 20 weeks. As a result of the recession in the early 2000s, the unemployment rate peaked at around 6 percent and the average duration of unemployment again hit 20 weeks. But as the unemployment rate rose during the Great Recession, the average duration shot up dramatically. Even as the unemployment rate began to fall in 2010, the average duration continued to rise, eventually reaching a peak of about 41 weeks in late 2011. The 2020 recession, however, was an exception to this general trend, as the downturn was severe but short—lasting just two months. As pandemic-related restrictions were lifted and businesses reopened in the third quarter of 2020, unemployment fell sharply, and unemployment duration never reached the levels it had in 2011.

As Figure 7.5 shows, unemployment is also unequally distributed by race. The overall unemployment rate reflects a slightly lower rate for whites and a significantly higher rate for black and Hispanic workers. The relationship between these rates has held fairly steady both in times of high and low unemployment. As a result, even in times of close to full employment, the unemployment rate for Black workers remains in the 7–9 percent range.

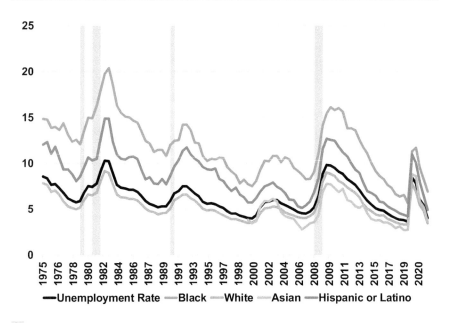

Figure 7.5 *Unemployment Rate by Race, 1975–2021*

Source: U.S. Bureau of Labor Statistics online database.

Discussion Questions

1. Do you know of places in your city or region (or country) that have been hit particularly hard by unemployment and underemployment, recently or in past decades? Do you know why this hardship occurred? Would you characterize this unemployment as frictional, structural, or cyclical? Which kind of unemployment would you say is of deep concern to economists? Why?
2. Some economists believe that "technological unemployment need not lead to structural unemployment". How can this statement be supported? What arguments or data might cast doubt on it?

3 THEORIES OF EMPLOYMENT, UNEMPLOYMENT, AND WAGES

As of 2021, income from wages and salaries accounted for 62.6 percent of national income in the United States.[24] The other sources of income—rents, profits, and interest which make up capital income—are mostly derived from various kinds and degrees of ownership of productive assets, such as buildings, land, or other resources, or stocks, which are ownership "shares" in companies. These sources of income are concentrated in a fairly small segment of the population.

A study from the Tax Policy Center finds that the higher you go up the income ladder, the greater the share of income from capital. For the poorest 20 percent of households, wages and salaries account for about half of all income and government transfers make about a third. For every other income group, except the richest 1 percent, wages and salaries account for over 60 percent of their income. The richest 1 percent gets about 40 percent of their income as wages and salaries and 60 percent from capital income. And for those at the very top (0.1 percent), capital income accounts for about three-quarters of the income, with wages and salaries being only one-quarter.[25] Hence, capital income is mostly concentrated among those at the very top. For most people, wage and salary employment is essential to their livelihoods, comfort, and well-being.

Jobs are easiest to find, and often better paid, under conditions of **full employment**. But often, the economy does not achieve full employment, and rising unemployment can create hardship for many. What explains why labor markets do not always reach full employment? Why don't wages play the role of other types of prices, to bring the market for labor into an equilibrium in which all those who want jobs can find them, and all employers can find appropriate workers? We now explore various theories and perspectives on this issue.

> **full employment:** a situation in which those who wish to work at the prevailing wages are able to find it readily

3.1 The Classical Theory

As we discussed in earlier chapters, a "classical" perspective generally favors the workings of free markets, with little or no government intervention. Applying this approach to the labor market gives us a supply and demand model for labor, as shown in Figure 7.6a. "Quantity," on the horizontal axis, can be understood to mean either quantity of labor *services* or the number of labor hours supplied and demanded. We can think of this quantity as being measured, for example, by the number of full-time equivalent days worked over a given time period. The

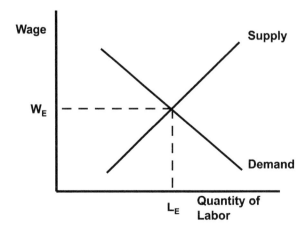

Figure 7.6a *The Classical Labor Market Model*

"price" of labor is the wage, in this case, per day (we assume that this is a "real" wage, i.e., adjusted for inflation.)

Employers demand labor, and as labor becomes more expensive (i.e. wages increase), their demand for labor declines. Hence, the labor demand curve is downward sloping. Workers are the suppliers of labor services. It is assumed that a rise in wages increases their willingness to supply labor; hence, the labor supply curve is upward sloping. This very simple model assumes that every unit of labor services is the same and every worker in this market will receive exactly the same wage. The equilibrium wage in this example is W_E and the equilibrium quantity of labor supplied is L_E.

Because the market pictured in Figure 7.6a is free to adjust, there is no involuntary unemployment. Everyone who wants a job at the going wage gets one. There may be many people who would offer their services in this market if the wage were higher—as the portion of the supply curve to the right of L_E demonstrates. But, given the currently offered wage rate, these people have made a rational choice not to participate in this labor market.

In this model, the only way that involuntary unemployment can exist is if something gets in the way of market forces. The presence of a legal minimum wage is commonly pointed to as one such factor. As illustrated in Figure 7.6b, if employers are required to pay a minimum wage of W^* ("W-star"), which is above the equilibrium wage, this model predicts that they will hire fewer workers. At an artificially high wage W^*, employers want to hire only L_D workers. But at that wage more people (L_S) want jobs. There is a situation of surplus, as we discussed in Chapter 3. In this case, the market is prevented from adjusting to equilibrium by legal restrictions on employers. Now there are people who want a job at the going wage, but cannot find one—that is, they are unemployed.

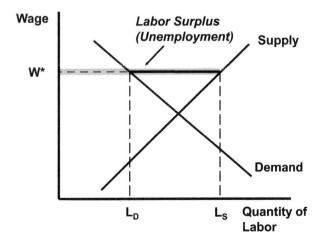

Figure 7.6b *Unemployment in the Classical Labor Market Model*

In the real world, where issues of motivation, labor relations, and power are also important, the classical idea that minimum wages cause substantial unemployment can be called into question. In a well-known study, economists David Card and Alan Krueger found that a moderate increase in the minimum wage in New Jersey did not cause low-wage employment to decline and may have even increased employment.[26] The economic logic behind this result is that the rise in minimum wages could increase people's income and consumption levels, which increases the demand for goods and services in the economy and leads to job creation.* The study came under fire from economists who believed (given the analysis shown in Figure 7.6a) that such a result simply could not be true. But the classical world assumes perfect competition, whereas real-world employers may have enough power in the labor market to be able to pay workers less than they are worth.

Several other studies have since confirmed Card's and Krueger's findings for other regions and other countries, including a number of EU countries. However, the jury is still out on the overall impact of minimum wage increases on employment levels, as some other studies find that higher minimum wages result in fewer jobs, or that raising minimum wages has no impact on employment levels.[27]

The mixed findings might be partly explained by the fact that labor markets are different from the market for goods and services. Factors such as power relations between workers and employers, workers' interests and motivations, as well as social norms may influence labor market outcomes. There may also be an interaction with technology, where employers have a choice on the question of whether to hire more workers or invest in labor-replacing technology. In such circumstances, the wage rate may have a more significant impact on hiring decisions.

In any case, the minimum wage affects only a portion of the workforce—people who are relatively unskilled, including many teenagers—but unemployment tends to affect people at all wage levels. Classical economists suggest other "market interference" reasons for unemployment, as well. The economy might provide less than the optimal number of jobs, they believe, because:

- Regulations on businesses reduce their growth, restricting growth in the demand for labor
- Labor union activities and labor-related regulations (such as safety regulations, mandated benefits, or restrictions on layoffs and dismissals) increase the cost of labor to businesses, causing them to turn toward labor-saving technologies and thus reducing job growth
- Public "safety net" policies, such as disability insurance and unemployment insurance, reduce employment by causing people to become less willing to seek work.

---

* This reasoning is based on the Keynesian theory, which will be introduced in Chapter 8.

Labor-market recommendations derived from a classical point of view tend to focus on getting rid of regulations and social programs that are seen as obstructing proper market behavior. Like other classical proposals, such labor market proposals assume that the economy works best under the principle of laissez-faire. But alternative explanations of the workings of labor markets suggest a different perspective. In considering some of these alternative explanations, we will step away from the assumptions of a single, homogeneous market in which all jobs and all workers are alike and the labor market is characterized by perfect competition. Labor markets are also influenced by many other factors, including history, psychology, power, resources, productivity, and technology.

3.2 Alternative Theories of Labor Markets

Since economics became an academic discipline over 200 years ago, economists have proposed a number of explanations for how wages are set and how overall employment and unemployment levels are determined. As economists have observed the failure of markets to supply jobs to meet the demand, they have sought to explain why wages for each kind of work are not always at the theoretical equilibrium point, where supply would be equal to demand. Some theoretical explanations are based on the real-world fact that supply and demand for labor are not just like markets for any other good: the "good" being supplied and demanded, in this case, is the work done by human beings.

Focusing on why wages don't fall as readily as the price of any other good, economists have come up with a variety of **"sticky wage" theories**. Observations of human behavior include the force of habits and expectations, based on people's memory of recent history. When some types of work are paid more highly than others, people who receive the higher wages are often able to hold out for a long time against other forces (including the forces of supply and demand) that would tend to reverse the relationship. Employers may react to this human reality with a reluctance to reduce wages because they don't want to cause hardship among employees whom they know, or may fear that workers will strongly resist such a move—perhaps with strikes or other labor actions. Often when businesses find that their revenue does not readily support the existing payroll, instead of lowering wages some workers are laid off. In addition to psychological resistance to wage cuts, a minimum wage might also make wages "sticky," or wages may also become set at particular levels by long-term contracts, such as those that some large employers negotiate with labor unions.

"sticky wage" theories: theories about why wages may stay at above-equilibrium levels, even when a labor surplus exists

A more recent attempt to explain why wages may not be at the equilibrium point is the **efficiency wage theory**, which points out that managers must attract, train, and motivate workers if their enterprise is to be productive. Employers may therefore find it to their advantage to pay employees more than would be strictly necessary to get them to work. This theory can be illustrated by looking back at Figure 7.6b, where W* could be read as the efficiency wage.

> **efficiency wage theory:** the theory that an employer can motivate workers to put forth more effort by paying them somewhat more than they could get elsewhere

Efficiency wage theory is a good fit with many observations. When workers are better paid they may be healthier and better nourished and therefore more able to do quality work. (This is especially true when talking about wage rates at the low end of the scale.) Also, workers may be more highly motivated and may have a lower propensity to quit if they know they are getting "a really good deal" from their employer, as opposed to a situation where they are receiving barely enough to motivate them to take the job, or just the same pay as they could get anywhere else. Workers with a lower likelihood of quitting are more valuable to an employer because the employer saves on the costs of training new workers. Workers may also work more efficiently if they believe that they could lose their "really good deal" if they are caught shirking. If a pool of unemployed people results from the higher-than-necessary efficiency wages, those who are employed might have greater incentives to work hard out of fear of losing their good jobs.

Labor markets today have characteristics that can be described using other theories as well. **Dual labor market theory**, developed in the 1970s, is being re-examined for the light it can shed on issues of inequality as well as the quality of jobs. According to this theory, labor markets could be understood as segmented between a primary sector with relatively high wages, long average job tenure, and chances for advancement with the company; and a secondary sector with none of these characteristics.[†] Various issues of class background, education, and employment experience could get some workers stuck in the secondary sector while making it relatively easy for others to enter and stay in a primary sector position.

> **dual labor market theory:** a theory according to which workers tend to get slotted into either a "primary sector" of good jobs, or a "secondary sector" where workers are taken on essentially on an "as needed" basis

---

† Note that the categorization of primary and secondary sectors in the 'dual labor market theory' is different from the classification of the economy in primary, secondary, and tertiary sectors in Chapter 6.

Contemporary versions of this theory emphasize the difference between workers who have a (fairly) secure relationship with the employer, vs. those who are taken on "as needed". Examples of the latter include alternative employment arrangements such as contract work, on-call work, temporary help agencies, and others in the "gig" economy, where employment isn't defined by a steady, full-time job, but by shorter-term freelance or contract projects. In 1995 10.0 percent of employed workers were in such alternative employment arrangements. Recent estimates indicate that between 25 to 35 percent of the workforce in the United States are now involved in the gig economy, though less than half of these workers rely on gig jobs as their primary source of income.[28] A similar shift is occurring in other countries. For example, the number of workers in the gig economy in England and Wales has more than doubled since 2016, and China's gig economy is also rapidly expanding.[29]

Market segmentation is also related to corporate behavior and strategies. Driven by ever-fiercer international competition to reduce costs, many large companies have taken the approach of hiring employees in jobs with primary sector characteristics—good pay, including benefits, etc.—only in the areas defined as their "core competence", while outsourcing the rest (see Box 7.4).

BOX 7.4 THE LOSS OF GOOD JOBS

A 2012 report from the Center for Economic and Policy Research defines "a good job" as "one that pays at least $37,000 per year, has employer-provided health insurance, and an employer-sponsored retirement plan." By this definition, "the share of workers with a "good job" fell from 27.4 percent in 1979 to 24.6 percent in 2010. The writers find that even workers with college degree are less likely to have a good job now than three decades ago. They argue that the decline in good jobs is related to the deterioration in the bargaining power of workers, rather than technological change.[30]

Companies are often able to deny workers many kinds of protections required by U.S. law by classifying them as independent contractors or self-employed workers. Thus, outsourcing and contracting have become popular ways for companies to reduce compensation costs. A 2016 study finds that independent contracting work rose by 30 percent between 2005 and 2015, and most of the increase was among low-wage workers.[31] While independent contractors have certain freedoms in how they operate their business, and some, such as lawyers and real estate agents, have high incomes, a majority of independent contractors suffer from a lack of good pay and benefits.

For example, the hourly wage for Uber drivers after deducting Uber fees and operating expenses is estimated to be about $11.77, but this drops to $9.21 after factoring in the costs of benefits that the drivers must provide for themselves. This is substantially less than the average hourly compensation of $32.06 in the private sector and $14.99 for workers in low-paid service sector jobs.[32] In a 2010 paper, Economists Arindrajit Dube and Ethan Kaplan find that the pay for janitors fell by 4 to 7 percent and for security guards by 8 to 24 percent among American

---

277

companies that outsourced janitorial and security services, hiring services provided by these independent workers as contractors, rather than hiring workers directly.

The rise in outsourcing and contracting has contributed to wage stagnation, rising income inequality, and increasing market power. If these trends are to be reversed to create better jobs that provide good financial security for workers, there will need to be a restructuring of corporate norms along with new legislations at the state and federal levels to strengthen workers' bargaining power.[33]

John Maynard Keynes (pronounced "Kanes"), to whom we referred in Chapter 1, writing during the Great Depression of the 1930s, when unemployment reached over 25 percent, pointed out that aspects of real-world human psychology, history, and institutions make it unlikely and often undesirable for wages to fall quickly in response to a labor surplus. Wages may eventually adjust in the way shown in the classical model, but too slowly to keep the labor market in equilibrium. And even if wages do fall, this will not necessarily result in full employment.

While some Keynesian theorists emphasize sticky wages, Keynes's critique of the classical model actually went much further. In more general terms, the Keynesian perspective challenges the entire classical assertion that unemployment results mainly from wage levels that are too high. The Keynesian perspective sees the labor market as a part of the whole economy and suggests that the problem of insufficient demand for labor may be a consequence of insufficient **aggregate demand**—the total demand for all goods and services in a national economy. Falling wages could make this problem worse, as workers would be less able to buy goods and services. The policy responses that flow from this analysis will be touched on in the next section and elaborated further in Part III of this book.

aggregate demand: the total demand for all goods and services in a national economy

3.3 Policy Responses

We saw in earlier parts of this chapter, that legally or contractually set wages, fear of workers' unrest, and efficiency wages are all possible explanations for "sticky wages," when unemployment is not solved by a lowering of workers' wages, as the standard classical theory would predict. What sort of policies result from such theories? And what kinds of policies can effectively respond to job loss associated with technological change? Or to the forces that are driving a wedge between high and low earners, contributing to growing inequality? Here we will briefly summarize some relevant policies.

Inflation and sticky wages: Some economists argue that a moderate level of economy-wide price inflation tends to relieve some "sticky wage" unemployment. How could this be so? Suppose that you are working for $12 per hour now, and your employer wants to cut your wage to $10 per hour. You would probably resist if asked to accept this wage cut—especially if you see that other people are not suffering such wage cuts. But suppose, instead, that your wage stays at $12 per hour, and, over time, inflation reduces the purchasing power of your wage to $10 per hour (in terms of prices of the base year). Your nominal wage has stayed the same, but your real wage (and thus your real cost to your employer) has fallen. Because this has happened more subtly—and is felt more economy-wide—than a cut in your personal nominal wage, you may not feel as motivated to resist. According to some theories, such a drop in real wages should cause employment to increase. Thus a small amount of inflation might help labor market adjustment without increasing unemployment.

Government job creation: Another policy option is job creation, such as the infrastructure projects mentioned in Chapter 6. The governments of some countries, notably Germany and France, as well as Japan in the 1980s and 1990s, have enacted industrial policies that directly encourage the development and retention of certain key industries through loans, subsidies, and tax credits. During negotiations on international trade (see Chapter 13), one sensitive issue is always the impact that increased trade might have on the employment levels in various industries in each country.

Making unemployment less painful: Governments can also undertake various programs to relieve unemployment-related hardship, most obviously, unemployment benefits. Those benefits could be more effective if they also provided better search assistance as part of the unemployment insurance system, and gave workers more flexibility to use unemployment insurance to integrate into a new job.

Responding to structural unemployment/Education and training: Government policies in the United States that target structural unemployment often focus on helping displaced workers find new employment. For example, the Trade Adjustment Assistance (TAA) Reform Act of 2002 provides benefits for certain workers displaced as a result of increased imports or the shifting of production to other countries. Workers who qualify for the program can receive retraining along with temporary income support payments and assistance with health insurance. The key feature of these programs is that they are targeted at particular workers in particular sectors of the economy. There has been some question, however, as to whether they have actually been successful in getting displaced workers into good new jobs. An evaluation of the TAA program, for example, found that at the end of a four-year observation period TAA participants had almost entirely closed the gap in employment relative to the comparison group of unemployment insurance claimants not eligible for TAA. The total income of the participants, however, was found to be lower than that of the comparison group, implying that the jobs they had landed were not especially good.[34] Another study reveals that trade-displaced workers often end up relying on Social Security and disability benefits.[35]

Business policies at the firm level are also relevant: Firms can help prevent structural unemployment if they make retaining or retraining their employees a priority, even while responding to changes in technology and trade. Community college and training systems could also be strengthened to help place people into jobs where there is strong demand.

More broadly, much of the discussion about structural and technological unemployment—among economists, policy-makers, and the general public—has focused on education as the solution. The problem has been defined as "a mismatch between worker preparation and job requirements," while the solution is described as "education appropriate to the jobs of today and tomorrow." This response seems correct if the "mismatch" is an accurate statement of the problem. An increased focus on computer literacy, starting in the early grades, more math and science, more focused occupational preparation, and expansion of life-long learning programs have been proposed as possible educational policy improvements.

The Keynesian response: raising aggregate demand: An important economic principle is that "the demand for labor is a derived demand"—meaning that it is derived from the demand for the output produced by labor. To Keynes and his followers, fixing the problem of unemployment in a recession or depression is not just a matter of making labor markets work more smoothly. Rather, aggregate demand for goods and services in the economy has to increase in order to stimulate hiring.

In this analysis, falling wages do not improve labor market conditions but would actually make things worse, because workers have less money to buy goods and services, leading to lower levels of business sales and further layoffs. Unlike the classical economists, Keynes believed that government policies in stimulating aggregate demand could be effective in response to an economic downturn.

The impact of Keynes' thinking has been widespread. A major concern of economic theory since the Great Depression has been the relationship between aggregate demand for goods and services, on the one hand, and the demand for, and rewards to, work, on the other. Rather than focusing just on labor markets, in this perspective, the relevant issue is the level of overall economic activity. Part III of this book will provide a discussion of the macroeconomic policies that have been developed in an effort to maintain full employment.

Discussion Questions

1. Which arguments on the relationship between wages and employment levels seem most convincing to you, those of "sticky wage" theorists, "efficiency wages" or economists concerned with aggregate demand? What are some strengths and weaknesses of each argument?
2. A number of policy responses to address job loss associated with technological change have been suggested above. Which of these measures, do you think, would be most effective? Can you suggest some other ways of addressing issues of unemployment?

4 SPECIAL ISSUES FOR THE TWENTY-FIRST CENTURY

4.1 Jobs and Technological Change

How does technological progress affect the overall number of jobs in the economy? There are differing views on this. (See Box 7.5). An optimistic response is that "technological unemployment need not lead to structural unemployment." The standard reasoning along these lines is as follows:

When technology reduces the need for labor in one part of the economy, it also results in more efficient production, increasing the overall wealth of society, because the same resources can produce a greater output, which is likely to be offered for sale at a lower cost. Thus, if a technological innovation results in a reduction of necessary labor inputs in a given sector, then the industry-wide cost of production falls, which lowers the competitive price. As the price goes down along a normal demand curve, the demand is expected to increase. Even if less labor is required per unit of output, increased demand is likely to increase the overall need (or "derived demand") for labor inputs.

BOX 7.5 TECHNOLOGICAL CHANGE AND THE FUTURE OF WORK

Is the current situation of rapid technological change substantially different from previous eras? We are in what some call the second wave of the IT revolution, in which cloud-based platforms that deploy increasingly sophisticated forms of artificial intelligence are used to connect buyers and sellers, manage transactions, coordinate robots, drones, and sensors, and provide other services. While the demand for software engineers is expanding rapidly, taxi and truck drivers are nervously watching the development of ride-sharing programs and self-driving vehicles; and many professions that had seemed immune from technological unemployment—law, banking, retail sales, education, health care, and public services—may now also be in danger.

The COVID-19 pandemic has further accelerated the shift toward automation as companies struggling to keep operating costs low amidst requirements for social distancing increasingly replaced workers with machines. Is there a tipping point ahead, where the total number of jobs will fall behind the number of those seeking work?

While this question has troubled workers for a long time, technological change and employment growth have generally gone hand in hand over the last hundred years. Some economists argue that this trend will continue. For example, the World Economic Forum estimates that by 2025 technology will create at least 12 million more jobs than it destroys.[36]

Automation does not necessarily lead to a disappearance of jobs overall. Rather, new jobs that require a different set of skills could be emerging from the automation of some jobs. Also, changes in other areas, such as the transition to renewable energy, and the rise of the middle class in many emerging markets, could result in the creation of many new jobs.

A 2013 study examining the risks of automation found that some jobs— telemarketers, loan officers, cashiers, tax preparers, taxi drivers, fast-food cooks, and sports referees—are more at risk than others such as therapists, mechanics, dentists, physicians, and health care and social workers. Martin Ford, futurist and author of *Rise of Robots* explains that the jobs that are most at risk are those which "are on some level routine, repetitive and predictable". Jobs involving "genuine creativity" (artists, scientists), building complex social relationships (nurses, counselors), and those that require special skills and ability to deal with rapidly changing situations, such as first responder jobs involving emergencies at different locations, face the lowest risk of automation.[37]

Other researchers have argued that the new wave of automation, with robotics and artificial intelligence (AI), has the potential to cause much wider worker displacement and inequality. A 2019 analysis suggests that the labor-saving shifts from automation are no longer offset by the creation of new jobs, and that the shift to automation has not resulted in a similar increase in productivity.[38] In some cases, such as with the use of self-service kiosks in grocery stores, automation has shifted labor from paid workers to unpaid customers. Additionally, the use of AI to monitor workers can often undermine worker power.[39] Addressing these challenges requires a robust set of policies to ensure that the benefits of automation are widely shared, and workers are helped to adapt to the changing work environment through increased efforts in education and training.

This indeed is what occurred during much of the second half of the twentieth century, when wages kept up with increases in productivity so that on average workers and their families saw their standard of living more than double.

Since about 1980, however, this trend has changed, as shown in Figure 7.7. While productivity has continued to increase, the rate of growth in wages has lagged significantly behind that of productivity growth. This change is a major reason for growing inequality, and it may also give some indications for future trends in employment and unemployment. This is a very important question for future labor market policy. We will consider these issues further in Chapter 14.

4.2 Some Future Possibilities

There is growing recognition of the scale, the significance, and the increase in inequality in the United States today—and, indeed, in much of the world. Also, the possibility of rising unemployment levels due

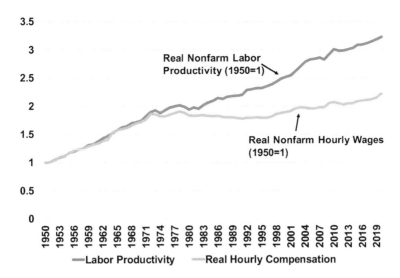

Figure 7.7 *Real Nonfarm Median Wages and Labor Productivity, 1947–2020*

Source: U.S. Bureau of Labor Statistics, Labor Productivity and Costs online database.

to technological change has presented new challenges for the twenty-first century. These changes indicate a rather bleak possibility for the future of work in a hardening "dual labor market" wherein the lucky few have well-paying jobs, while the rest pick up what they can, with little security.

At the same time, there have been other changes in recent decades that suggest more positive possibilities, where it is conceivable that people could enjoy more leisure while maintaining their standard of living. Future transformations in the structure of the labor market, where employment may become more "flexible" for workers, giving workers more control over their time, could reverse some of the trends in inequality and ensure a better future for workers. This final section briefly summarizes some recent changes in the labor market and the ways in which labor and the products of labor might be distributed—and what these changes might mean for human well-being in the future.

4.2.1 Democracy in the Workplace

The dominant model of the firm today is one in which much of the economy consists of large enterprises that are owned by a small percentage of the population who make decisions on whom to hire and how to distribute the income generated from production. In reality, this structure is just one of the many possible ways to organize work.

One alternative which has been growing gradually in the past few decades is a cooperative model, which includes worker cooperatives, employee-owned firms, credit unions, community land trusts, foundation-owned companies, and any form of organization that is owned and controlled by its workers or community. Worker cooperatives are for-profit businesses that are owned and run by workers. Unlike traditional corporations, where profits are distributed among stockholders who often have little connection with or knowledge of the business, profits from cooperatives go to their workers. Workers also control the decision-making process in cooperatives, either through individual votes or by electing a board of members. This allows workers to participate in the decisions related to their working conditions, wages, and job security.

Having a more democratic work space where workers control production and distribution processes could not only encourage workers to be more innovative and dedicated to their work but also help reduce disparities in income levels. Estimates on the pay ratio between highest- and lowest-paid workers in cooperatives range between 2:1 and 5:1 compared to the CEO-to-average-worker pay in corporations being as high as 351:1 in 2020.[40] Also, worker cooperatives are more likely to offer regular work hours, health insurance, and other benefits, than conventional companies.[41] And during economic downturns workers are more likely to decide on working fewer hours rather than laying off people, hence distributing work and income as well as the costs of the economic downturn more evenly.[42]

The cooperative model, of course, is not perfect. Though the democratic process may mitigate inequalities, the structure may be less efficient, and conflicts between workers' interests can present significant challenges. Also, not all employees may want to share the risks of ownership, and it might be difficult for some workers to go against the system of corporate hierarchy.[43] Additionally, having to compete with capitalist firms that focus on cost-cutting and profit-maximization may put severe pressure on worker cooperatives.

Worker cooperatives are still quite marginal in the United States. According to a 2019 Worker Cooperative report, of the approximately 6 million U.S. firms with employees, roughly 465 are worker-owned cooperatives employing about 6,454 workers.[44] Employee ownership in the form of Employee Stock Ownership Plans (ESOPs) is much more common in the U.S., with roughly 6,500 ESOPs benefiting more than 14 million workers.[45] The ESOPs, however, only provide employees with shares of stocks over time; workers may not have control over company operations, as there is no requirement for democratic governance. The cooperative model is better developed in some other countries, mainly in Europe. The world's largest cooperative, the Mondragon Corporation in Spain has about 85,000 employees.

4.2.2 Work Flexibility

In recent years it has become popular to talk about how employment is becoming more "flexible." But the term "flexibility" has two very different meanings, depending on whether it is considered from the point of view of the worker or the employer.

284

One meaning of "flexible" work is that it is more suited to workers' varying needs. Such work arrangements include flexibility in setting hours, job sharing, and the ability to work from home at times. Workers may be able to adjust their starting and quitting times, say to make commuting or dropping off a child at school or day care easier. They may also be able to "compress" a standard workweek by working longer daily hours and taking a weekday off every week. Job sharing typically means that two employees work part-time, essentially sharing a full-time job between them. Working from home, at least occasionally, reduces commuting time and costs, and allows workers to care for children or other relatives at home. Research shows that not only are flexible workers more satisfied with their jobs, but they also tend to be more productive and take sick leave less often.[46]

As a result of the COVID-19 pandemic, many workers worked from home to reduce their exposure to illness. Between 2008 and 2014, the percentage of employers allowing workers to work regularly at home increased from 23 percent to 38 percent.[47] This number rose sharply to over 70 percent during the pandemic. Some of this switch toward remote working is expected to be permanent as workers' demand for flexible work arrangements has increased and many firms have restructured to allow hybrid work arrangements, where workers are allowed to work remotely at least for part of the week.

A 2021 Gallup poll finds that about 45 percent of full-time U.S. workers worked from home at least part-time. Among white-collar workers about 67 percent were able to work remotely, compared to 48 percent of workers in education and 35 percent of workers in health care being able to work remotely. Another Gallup survey finds that 91 percent of the workers working remotely hope to continue doing so at least part-time even after the pandemic, and 3 in 10 are likely to seek another job if they do not have the ability to continue working remotely.[48]

A somewhat different type of employment flexibility from the perspective of workers is "gig" jobs. These are jobs, part-time or full-time, that involve working under short-term contracts doing consulting, freelance, project-based, or other work. A common example is drivers for ride services such as Uber and Lyft who work when they want to and are needed. An increasing number of American workers participate in the gig economy, either by choice or necessity. Gig workers in the U.S. are disproportionately minority and young, with relatively low incomes. While most gig workers describe their work as a side job, more than half say the extra income is "essential" or "important" for meeting their basic needs.[49] The majority of gig workers in the U.S. are satisfied with their work, but gig workers are less likely to have employment benefits such as paid vacations and health care.[50]

There are both winners and losers in the gig economy.[51] Workers with specialized skills and experience can often get good pay while retaining a high level of autonomy and flexibility. Gig jobs are often

285

attractive to retirees, students, stay-at-home parents, and others who want control over working hours and may not need a full-time salary. But many workers are forced into gig jobs because they cannot find "regular" jobs, and end up making low wages with no benefits. (See Box 7.4.)

A desire for flexibility from the employer perspective is driving the gig economy at least as much as the demand for gig jobs by workers. By hiring contract workers, employers avoid providing benefits such as health care and retirement plans. Workers paid as consultants bear the full burden of social insurance taxes, while firms must contribute half of these taxes for regular workers. Firms can also adjust the hours of gig workers, or terminate them, as economic conditions change, much more easily than with traditional employees.

According to conventional economic theory, more "flexible" labor markets— where it is easier for employers to hire and fire workers—are often associated with greater efficiency. Over time, the labor market in the U.S. has become more flexible for employers, characterized by low levels of labor market regulation and employment protections. But it is not clear that this increase in "efficiency" benefits workers. Increased flexibility for employers at the expense of lower employment protection for the workers could be a significant factor in the rise in inequality in the U.S. in recent years.

On a more positive note, workplace flexibility could be designed to allow workers to choose either more work, more income, and more consumption of marketed goods and services or less income but more time to spend engaging in other activities that may satisfy important needs and wants outside of the market. This could be compatible with a less consumption-oriented economy, possibly also reducing pressure on the environment.

4.2.3 More Leisure

Figure 7.7 shows that labor productivity more than doubled between 1980 and 2020. One interpretation of this result is that the United States can now produce twice the quantity of goods and services with the same amount of labor used in 1980. But an alternative possibility is that we could produce the *same quantity* of goods and services produced in 1980, but with *half the amount of labor.*

Consider this statement in light of the notion of labor flexibility. Suppose that workers had the choice between taking productivity gains as either wage increases or labor time decreases. Theoretically, American workers could be living at the same material living standards as in 1980, but working only six months of every year! This example is extreme, but the suggestion that more leisure could be preferable to extra income, at least for some workers, could have significant economic implications. Of course, some workers may always choose more pay over shorter hours, but allowing for more work choice accords with standard economic theory, stated as follows:

> According to economic theory, we should let each worker choose how many hours to work. If workers choose shorter hours, it is because they get greater satisfaction from more free time than they would get from more income. According to the basic principle of market economics, interfering with individuals' choices between more free time and more income reduces total wellbeing, just as interfering with individuals' choices between two products would reduce total well-being by forcing some people to buy the product that gives them less.[52]

If it turns out that many workers are willing to work shorter hours for an equivalent reduction in pay, a choice for more leisure rather than more consumption could have important environmental benefits, in rates of natural resource degradation and extraction.

Various recent studies demonstrate a positive correlation between work-life balance and subjective well-being. For example, a 2018 study asked over 30,000 workers in South Korea how well their work hours fit in with their commitments outside of work.[53] Those with a better work-life balance reported higher subjective well-being. A 2019 study of workers in Pakistan also found that those who were more satisfied with their work-life balance reported higher average subjective well-being.[54] Similarly, a positive correlation between work-life balance and SWB has been observed in the UK,[55] China,[56] and Indonesia.[57]

Unfortunately, in the United States, part-time jobs are generally much less attractive than full-time jobs because hourly wages are often low and few benefits are provided. Some countries have enacted policies to promote higher-quality part-time jobs. One example is the Netherlands where discrimination against part-time workers is illegal and employers must offer the same pay to all workers who are doing the same kind of work, whether they work part-time or full-time, unless the business can prove that hiring part-time workers would impose an economic hardship. Another approach is taken in Denmark, where, in the 1990s "flexicurity" policies were designed to help workers cope with rapid changes in what employers are looking for in their worker force. These policies combine lifelong learning with income support for workers as they transition between skills and jobs.

4.2.4 Other Possibilities

We can imagine a future in which the work that has to be done by humans is reduced by continuing technological progress, while the economy continues to produce enough to satisfy all the people's needs and many of their wants. This scenario could be appealing in terms of flexible work and more leisure, but it could also lead to many being "left out" of the market for good jobs, thus increasing inequality. One policy that could respond to this problem is a **universal basic income (UBI)**. A UBI is a periodic (e.g., monthly) cash payment available to all without means-test or work requirements so that people can at least cover basic expenses such as housing, food, and health care. While some argue that a UBI would reduce incentives to work, experience with experimental UBI programs indicates that this is not the case (see Box 7.6).

---

universal basic income (UBI): a periodic cash payment to all citizens (or all adult citizens) regardless of means-test or work requirements, so that people can at least cover basic expenses such as housing, food, and health care

---

Some economists base a positive view of future employment on demographics; the workforce in the United States (without immigration) is growing at its slowest pace in more than 50 years, as baby boomers who joined the labor force from the 1960s to the 1980s now gradually age out of it. The decline in workforce during the pandemic, discussed earlier in the chapter, could in theory return relative power to employees, in relation to employers. On other hand, a declining workforce could create problems with the availability of labor for key areas such as medical services and elder care, as well as creating strains on the Social Security system.

BOX 7.6 UNIVERSAL BASIC INCOME

With automation replacing many routine and mechanical jobs, some researchers estimate that about half of the current jobs may disappear in the next decade. One policy response that has been suggested is to provide all individuals with a basic minimum income to meet their essential needs. This approach, referred to as the guaranteed or universal basic income (UBI), generally involves providing some form of periodic cash payments unconditionally to all individuals.

Advocates of UBI argue that such a program would provide a basic safety net with some financial security and help relieve work-related stress. The advantages of a UBI system could include lower crime rates, reduced environmental damage from some economic activities, and encouraging innovation by providing individuals with the freedom to explore their interests.

In recent years, several governments and private research groups have conducted experimental trials of basic income policies. The government of Finland, for example, began a two-year experiment in January 2017 making monthly cash payments of €560 (US$590) to 2,000 unemployed individuals and comparing their experience to those receiving unemployment benefits. Results show higher life satisfaction, less mental strain, and a small increase in employment for basic income recipients compared to the control group.[58]

Similar programs have been launched in regions in Canada (Ontario), Germany, the Netherlands, and Spain (Barcelona). Experiments on basic income have also been carried out in developing countries such as India, Namibia, Uganda, and Kenya. Results from a pilot program implemented in the Namibian village of Omitara in 2008 and 2009 showed that the introduction of basic income program increased the rate of those engaged in income-generating activities from 44 percent to 55 percent, mostly by enabling recipients to start their own small businesses.[59] Also, child malnutrition was reduced, school enrollment went up, and crimes declined. Similarly in India basic income led to improved sanitation, nutrition, and school attendance; and in Kenya, cash transfer programs have stimulated the economy.[60]

The most well-known UBI experience in the United States is in the state of Alaska, where each individual gets an annual share of the state's fossil fuel income—$1,600 per person in 2019. A high-profile experiment launched in Stockton, California in 2018 gave 125 randomly selected residents living in low-income neighborhoods $500 per month for two years. The results indicate that the recipients experienced an improvement in their job prospects, financial stability, and overall well-being. Also, the additional income did not dissuade people from working. In recent years, similar UBI programs have popped up in cities across the U.S.[61]

The challenges of instituting a BI system include the following questions:

Would giving people unconditional income disincentivize them from seeking work? Experiments such as those listed above have been neutral, or, more often, encouraging in finding that BI recipients continue to work productively in the economy, appreciating the opportunity to be more flexible in seeking work opportunities.

How would psychological well-being be affected among those who do not participate in the market sphere of the economy? In many parts of the world, during many different eras, women at various socio-economic levels have been responsible for taking care of home and family, without payment from the market. The psychological rewards of such situations have varied widely, but have often been harmful unless the choice to remain at home was truly voluntary. One proposal suggests that UBI income should be directly tied to care work in the home and community; this idea is being looked at for broader contributions to care of the earth (on farms, in relation to forests, wilderness, water, etc.).

Most critically, how would we fund such a program? The World Bank estimates that a comprehensive UBI program set at the national poverty level would cost about 20 percent of GDP in low-income nations and about 5 percent of GDP in upper-middle-income countries.[62] In the United States, giving every American $10,000 a year—an income below the poverty line—would cost at least $3 trillion, which is about eight times the current government spending on social service programs.[63] As has been noted in several places, the U.S. is well behind other developed countries in the level of such spending—but this situation does not seem likely to change soon. Other suggestions are based on the idea that society as a whole owns, and should benefit from "all the creations of nature and society that we inherit jointly and freely, and hold in trust for future generations."[64] This includes, for example, fees from government-created monopolies (such as the broadcast spectrum and utilities), or income from private uses of government land (currently leased out, in general, far below market rates), or income from taxing carbon emissions. Such additional revenues could help to fund a UBI program.

It is also possible that job opportunities could be expanded with benefits both to workers and the environment. New employment opportunities exist for satisfying real needs that are now going unmet—including needs for infrastructure improvement, expanded education, health, and other human services, as well as investment in building a green, post-fossil-fuel economy. Many of these areas are labor-intensive, creating jobs for humans rather than robots.

We will return to some of these issues in Chapter 17, where we deal with growth and sustainability. First, however, we go into detail in Part III regarding macroeconomic theories of stabilization, growth, and employment.

Discussion Questions

1. What evidence have you seen—in your own family or in the media—of increasing "flexibility" in labor markets? Do you think that these changes have been beneficial, harmful, or both?
2. Do you think having more worker cooperatives might help mitigate economic inequality in the United States? What might be some of the challenges in encouraging firms to adopt this model?
3. What do you think of the effectiveness of basic income programs in addressing inequality?

REVIEW QUESTIONS

1. What population is included in the official household survey that measures employment and unemployment?
2. What questions are asked to determine whether someone is "employed"?
3. What makes a person count as "unemployed"?
4. How is the unemployment rate calculated?
5. What are marginally attached workers? Discouraged workers?
6. What is the labor force participation rate and how is it calculated? How has it changed in recent decades for men and women in the United States?
7. What are some of the reasons for the declining labor force participation of men in the U.S. labor force?
8. List and describe the three types of unemployment.
9. What policies may be used to combat frictional and structural unemployment?
10. What is technological unemployment? How might productivity-increasing advances in technology affect employment levels?
11. What is the relationship between the average duration of unemployment and the unemployment rate?
12. Describe how "sticky wages" could lead to unemployment.
13. What are some reasons that wages might be "sticky"?
14. What are "efficiency wages," and why might payment of them lead to unemployment?
15. What is the dual labor market theory? How does this theory contribute to our understanding of issues of inequality and employment?
16. How can high levels of unemployment be explained in the Keynesian model?
17. What are some of the policy measures that might help reduce unemployment levels?
18. What are some of the arguments for and against having more democratic workplaces?
19. What does employment flexibility mean from the perspective of workers? From the perspective of employers?
20. What are some of the advantages of universal basic income programs? What kinds of challenges may be faced in implementing such programs?

EXERCISES

1. The small country of Nederland counts its unemployed using the same methods as the United States. Of the population of 350 people, 70 are under age 16, 190 are employed in paid work, and 80 are adults who are not doing paid work or looking for work because they are doing full-time family care, are retired or disabled, or are in school. The rest are unemployed. (No one is institutionalized, and the country has no military.) Calculate the following:
   a) The number of unemployed
   b) The size of the labor force
   c) The unemployment rate
   d) The labor force participation rate (overall, for both sexes)

2. The population of Tatoonia is very small. Luis works full-time for pay. Robin works one shift a week as counter help at a fast-food restaurant. Sheila is retired. Shawna does not work for pay but is thinking about getting a job and has been looking through employment postings to see what is available. Bob has given up looking for work, after months of not finding anything. Ana, the only child in the country, is 12 years old.
   a) How would a household survey, following U.S. methods, classify each person?
   b) What is the labor force participation rate in Tatoonia?
   c) What is the unemployment rate in Tatoonia?

3. A computer software company advertises for employees, saying "We offer the best-paid jobs in the industry!" But why would any company want to pay more than it absolutely *has to* in order to attract workers? Can this phenomenon help to explain the existence of unemployment? Explain in a paragraph.

4. Locate the most recent news release on employment and unemployment statistics at the Bureau of Labor Statistics Web site (www.bls.gov). In a paragraph, describe how the labor force, overall unemployment rate, and unemployment rates by race and ethnicity, gender, age, and education differ from the numbers (for January 2022) given in the text.

5. Match each concept in Column A with a definition or example in Column B.

	Column A		Column B
a.	"Not in the labor force"	1.	The theory that unemployment is caused by insufficient aggregate demand
b.	Worker cooperatives	2.	Occurs during a recession
c.	Marginally attached workers	3.	An example of an employment flexibility policy
d.	Frictional unemployment	4.	Occurs when the skills, experience, and education of workers do not match job openings
e.	Employed	5.	For-profit businesses owned and run by businesses
f.	Trade Adjustment Assistance Reform Act	6.	Immediately available for and currently looking for paid work
g.	Unemployed	7.	Military personnel
h.	"Sticky wages"	8.	A policy response to structural unemployment
i.	Structural unemployment	9.	Worked 15 hours or more in a family business

	Column A		Column B
j.	Keynesian theory	10.	Occurs as people move between jobs
k.	Cyclical unemployment	11.	Want to work and have looked in the past year but not the past month
l.	Not included in the household survey covering employment	12.	Unemployment may occur because wages are slow to fall
m.	Technological unemployment	13.	Occurs when technology reduces the overall need for workers
n.	Paid parental leave	14.	A retired person

NOTES

1   Lim and Zabek, 2021.
2   Ullrich, 2021.
3   CEA, 2016a.
4   Yarrow, 2020.
5   CEA, 2016a.
6   Aliprantis and Schweitzer, 2018.
7   Based on data from the World Prison Brief, https://www.prisonstudies.org/.
8   Wagner and Rabuy, 2017.
9   McLaughlin et al., 2016.
10 Gramlich, 2021.
11 Sawyer and Wagner, 2020.
12 Guo, 2016.
13 Pager and Western, 2009.
14 Rainer, 2006.
15 Delaney and Scheller, 2015; BEA, 2021.
16 Mutikani, 2022.
17 Faria-e-Castra, 2021.
18 Fowers and Dam, 2021.
19 Hoff and Kaplan. 2021.
20 Leonhardt, 2021.
21 Schweitzer and Khattar, 2021.
22 Ibid.
23 Kinder and Stateler, 2021.
24 BEA data Tables 1.1.5 and 2.1.
25 Stallworth, 2019.
26 Card and Krueger, 1994.
27 See, for example, Neumark and Wascher, 2007; and Cengiz et al., 2019.
28 Gig Economy Data Hub, 2022.
29 Butler, 2021; and Weller, 2021.
30 Schmitt and Jones, 2012.
31 Katz and Krueger, 2016.
32 Mishel, 2018.
33 Bahn, 2019.
34 D'Amico and Schochet, 2012.
35 Autor et al., 2016.
36 World Economic Forum, 2020.

37 Frey and Osborne, 2013.
38 Acemoglu and Restrepo, 2019.
39 Zickuhr, 2021.
40 Estimate on highest-to-lowest paid worker in cooperative is from Austin 2014 and Palmer 2020. Estimate on CEO to average employee in corporations is from Mishel and Kandra, 2021.
41 Gillies, 2016.
42 Rieger, 2016.
43 Gillies, 2016.
44 Palmer, 2020.
45 Based on data from National Center for Employee Ownership: https://www.esop.org/.
46 Gaskell, 2016.
47 Matos and Galinsky, 2014.
48 Saad and Wigert, 2021.
49 Anderson et al., 2021.
50 Molla, 2021.
51 Mulcahy, 2016.
52 Siegel, 2006.
53 Yang et al., 2018.
54 Shams and Kadow, 2019.
55 Fan and Smith, 2017.
56 Wong et al., 2021.
57 Gunawan, 2020.
58 Allas et al., 2020.
59 Claudia and Dirk Haarmann. 2014. Basic Income Grant Coalition. See: http://www.bignam.org/BIG_pilot.html.
60 Samuel, 2020.
61 Lowrey, 2021.
62 World Bank, 2019.
63 Goodman, 2017.
64 Barnes et al., 2003.

REFERENCES

Acemoglu, Daron and Pascual Restrepo. 2019. "Automation and New Tasks: How Technology Displaces and Reinstates Labor." *Journal of Economic Perspectives, 33*(2): 3–30.

Aliprantis, Dionissi, and Mark E. Schweitzer. 2018. "Opioids and the Labor Market." Working Paper 18-07, Federal Reserve Bank of Cleveland. May.

Allas, Tera, Jukka Maksimainem, James Manyika, and Navjot Singh. 2020. "An Experiment to Inform Universal Basic Income." *McKinsey and Company,* September 15.

Anderson, Monica, Colleen McClain, Michelle Faverio, and Risa Gelles-Watnick. 2021. *The State of Gig Work in 2021.* Pew Research Center, December 8.

Autor, David H., David Dorn, and Gordon H. Hanson. 2016. "The China Shock: Learning from Labor-Market Adjustment to Large Changes in Trade." *The Annual Review of Economics, 8*: 205–240.

Austin, Jennifer J. 2014. "Worker Cooperatives for the New York City: A Vision for Addressing Income Inequality." *Federation of Protestant Welfare Agencies,* January.

Bahn, Kate. 2019. "Research Finds the Domestic Outsourcing of Jobs Leads to Declining U.S. Job Quality and Lower Wages." *Washington Center for Equitabel Growth,* August 21.

Barnes, Peter, Jonathan Rowe, and David Bollier. 2003. *The State of the Commons: Report to Owners from the Tomales Bay Institute.* Tomales Bay Institute.

293

Bureau of Economic Analysis (BEA). 2021. "How Will the Expansion of Unemployment Benefits in Response to the COVID-19 Pandemic Be Recorded in the NIPAs?" https://www.bea.gov/help/faq/1415

Butler, Sarah. 2021. "Gig-Working in England and Wales More than Doubles in Five Years." *The Guardian*, November 4.

Card, David, and Alan B. Krueger. 1994. "Minimum Wages and Employment: A Case Study of the Fast-Food Industry in New Jersey and Pennsylvania." *American Economic Review, 84*(4): 774–775.

Cengiz, Doruk, Arindrajit Dube, Attila Lindner, and Ben Zipperer. 2019. "The Effect of Minimum Wage on Low-Wage Jobs." *The Quarterly Journal of Economics, 134*(3): 1405–1454.

Council of Economic Advisers (CEA). 2016a. "Economic Perspectives on Incarceration and the Criminal Justice System." April.

Council of Economic Advisors (CEA). 2016b. "The Long-Term Decline in Prime-Age Male Labor Force Participation." June.

D'Amico, Ronald and Peter Z. Schochet. 2012. "The Evaluation of the Trade Adjustment Assistance Program: A Synthesis of Major Findings." *U.S. Department of Labor Employment and Training Administration*, December.

Delaney, Arthur and Alissa Scheller. 2015. "A Lot Fewer Americans Get Unemployment Benefits Than You Think." *HuffPost*, March 13.

Fan, Jialin and Andrew P. Smith. 2017. "Positive Well-Being and Work-Life Balance among UK Railway Staff." *Open Journal of Social Sciences, 5*(6): 1–6.

Faria-e-Castro, Miguel. 2021. "The COVID Retirement Boom." *The Federal Reserve Bank of St. Louis*, Economic Synopses, Number 25.

Fowers, Alyssa and Andrew Van Dam. 2021. "The Most Unusual Job Market in Modern American History, Explained." *The Washington Post*, December 29.

Frey, Carl Benedikt and Michael A. Osborne. 2013. "The Future of Employment: How Susceptible Are Jobs to Computerisation?" *Oxford Martin School*, September 17.

Gaskell, Adi. 2016. "Why a Flexible Worker Is a Happy and Productive Worker." *Forbes*, January 15.

Gig Economy Data Hub. 2022. "How Many Gig Workers Are There?" *The Aspen Institute Future of Work Initiative.* https://www.gigeconomydata.org/basics/how-many-gig-workers-are-there

Gillies, Benjamin. 2016. "Worker Cooperatives: A Bipartisan Solution to America's Growing Income Inequality." *Kennedy School Review*, June 15.

Goodman, Peter S. 2017. "Capitalism Has a Problem, Is Free Money the Answer?" *The New York Times*, November 15, 2017.

Gramlich, John. 2021. "America's Incarceration Rate Falls to Lowest Level Since 1995." *Pew Research Center*, August 16.

Gunawan, G., Y. Nugraha, M. Sulastiana, and D. Harding. 2020. *"Work-Life Balance and Subjective Well-Being among Employees on Life Science Company in Indonesia"* in *Advances in Business, Management, and Entrepreneurship*. CRC Press, London.

Guo, Jeff. 2016. "America Has Locked Up so Many Black People It Has Warped Our Sense of Reality", *The Washington Post*, February 26.

Hoff, Madoson and Juliana Kaplan. 2021. "13 Reasons that Help Explain the Labor Shortage in the U.S." *Insider*, December 8.

Katz, Lawrence F. and Alan B. Krueger. 2016. "The Rise and Nature of Alternative Work Arrangements in the United States, 1995–2015." https://scholar.harvard.edu/files/lkatz/files/katz_krueger_cws_v3.pdf

Kinder, Molly and Laura Stateler. 2021. "Essential Workers Comprise About Half of All Workers in Low-Paid Occupations. They Deservea $15 Minimum Wage." *The Brookings Institution*, February 5.

Krueger, Alan B. 2017. "Where Have All the Workers Gone? An Inquiry into the Decline of the U.S. Labor Force Participation Rate." *The Brookings Institution*, September 7.

Leonhardt, David. 2021. "Where Are the Workers?" *The New York Times*, November 3.

Lim, Katherine, and Mike Zabek. 2021. "Women's Labor Force Exits during COVID-19: Difference by Motherhood, Race, and Ethnicity." *Finance and Economics Discussion Series 2021–067*. Washington: Board of Governors of the Federal Reserve System.

Lowrey, Annie. 2021. "Stockton's Basic-Income Experiment Pays Off." *The Atlantic*, March 3.

Matos, Kenneth, and Ellen Galinsky. 2014. *2014 National Study of Employers*. Families and Work Institute.

McLaughlin, Michael, et al. 2016. *The Economic Burden of Incarceration in the U.S.* Institute for Advancing Justice Research and Innovation, Washington University in St. Louis, October.

Mishel, Lawrence. 2018. "Uber and the Labor Market." *Economic Policy Insitute*, May 15.

Mishel, Lawrence, and Jori Kandra. 2021. "CEO Pay has Skyrocketed 1,322% since 1978." *Economic Policy Institute Report*, August 10.

Molla, Rani. 2021. "More Americans Are Taking Jobs without Employer Benefits Like Health Care or Paid Vacation." *Vox*, September 3.

Mulcahy, Diane. 2016. "Who Wins in the Gig Economy, and Who Loses." *Harvard Business Review*, October 27.

Mutikani, Lucia. 2022. "U.S. Weekly Jobless Claims Resume Downward Trend: Fourth-Quarter GDP Revised Slightly Up." *Reuters*, February 24.

Neumark, David and William L. Wascher. 2007. "Minimum Wages and Employment." *Foundations and Trends in Microeconomics, 3*(1–2): 1–182.

Ott, Matt. 2022. "Unemployment Benefits Down to Lowest Level since 1970." *NewsNation*, February 24.

Pager, Devah and Bruce Western. 2009. "Investigating Prisoner Reentry: The Impact of Conviction Status on Employment Prospects of Young Men." *Office of Justice Programs*, U.S. Department of Justice. https://www.ojp.gov/pdffiles1/nij/grants/228584.pdf

Palmer, Tim. 2020. "2019 Worker Cooperatives in the United States." *Democracy at Work Institute*, January 29.

Rainer Winkelmann. 2006. "Unemployment, Social Capital, and Subjective Well-Being." *IZA Discussion Paper No. 2346*. Bonn, Germany. September.

Rieger, Shannon. 2016 "Reducing Economic Inequality through Democratic Worker-Ownership." *The Century Foundation*. August 10.

Saad, Lydia and Ben Wigert. 2021. "Remote Work Persisting and Trending Permanent." *Gallup*, October 13. https://news.gallup.com/poll/355907/remote-work-persisting-trending-permanent.aspx

Samuel, Sigal. 2020. "Everywhere Basic Income Has Been Tried, in One Map." Claims for unemployment benefits had fallen to the lowest point since the 1970s, as the economy had mostly recovered from its lowest point in March and April of 2020. *Vox*, October 20.

Sawyer, Wendy, and Peter Wagner. 2020. "Mass Incarceration: The Whole Pie 2020." *Prison policy Initiative*, Press Release, March 24.

Schmitt, John, and Janelle Jones. 2012. "Where Have All the Good Jobs Gone?" *Center for Economic and Policy Research*. Washington, DC, July 2012.

Schweitzer, Justin and Rose Khattar. 2021. "It's a Good Jobs Shortage: The Real Reason So Many Workers Are Quitting." *The Center for American Progress*, December 7.

Shams, Khadija, and Alexander Kadow. 2019. "The Relationship between Subjective Well-being and Work-Life Balance among Labourers in Pakistan." *Journal of Family and Economic Issues, 40*: 681–690.

Siegel, Charles. 2006. *The End of Economic Growth.* Preservation Institute. Berkeley, CA, p. 29.

Stallworth, Philip. 2019. "Let Me Tell You About the Very Rich. They Are Very Different From You and Me." *Tax Policy Center*, Urban Institute and Brookings Institution. https://www.taxpolicycenter.org/taxvox/let-me-tell-you-about-very-rich-they-are-different-you-and-me

Standing, Guy. 2013. "India's Experiments in Basic Income Grants." *Global Dialogue*, 3(5), November.

Ullrich, Laura Dawson. 2021. "Male Labor Force Participation: Patterns and Trends." *Federal Reserve Bank of Richmond*, EconFoucs, First Quarter.

Wagner, Peter and Bernadette Rabuy. 2017. "Following the Money of Mass Incarceration." *Prison Policy Initiative*, January 25.

Weller, Torsten. 2021. "What's Next for China's Gig Economy?" *China-Britain Business Focus*, June 28.

Wong, Ka Po, Fion Choi Hung Lee, Pei-Lee The, and Alan Hoi Shou Chan. 2021. "The Interplay of Socioecological Determinants of Work-Life Balance, Subjective Well-Being and Employee Wellbeing." *International Journal of Environmental Research and Public Health, 18*(9):4525.

World Bank. 2019. *The Changing Nature of Work, World Development Report 2019.* https://www.worldbank.org/en/publication/wdr2019

World Economic Forum. 2020. "The Future of Jobs Report," October. https://www3.weforum.org/docs/WEF_Future_of_Jobs_2020.pdf

Yang, Jae Won, Chunchui Suh, Chae Kwan Lee, and Byung Chul Son. 2018. "The Work-Life Balance and Psychosocial Well-being of South Korean Workers." *Annals of Occupational and Environmental Medicine, 30*: 38.

Yarrow, Andrew L. 2020. "The Male Non-Working Class: A Disquieting Survey." *Milken Institute Review*, July 30.

Zickuhr, Kathryn. 2021. "Exploring the Impact of Automation and New Technologies on the Future of U.S. Workers and Their Families." *Washington Center for Equitable Growth*, December 17.

Part III

Macroeconomic Theory and Policy

Chapter 8

Aggregate Demand and Economic Fluctuations

What makes an economy experience GDP expansion or contraction, high or low employment, and good or bad business conditions? These questions are important both to policymakers and to the general public. For example, in 2020 the United States, as well as the broader global economy, experienced a sharp recession resulting from the COVID-19 emergency, followed by an uneven recovery. This brought a number of macroeconomic issues into focus.

In a sophisticated contemporary economy such as the United States, a decline in demand for goods and services by consumers and businesses generally leads to recessionary conditions and higher unemployment. Recovering demand promotes economic growth, but can also sometimes lead to inflation. These issues have all been present in the recent economic history of the United States and other countries. In Chapter 12 we will discuss some of the events of recent economic history, and in Chapter 15 we will evaluate related issues of deficits and debt. But before getting into these specifics, we need to develop a general theory of how the demand for goods and services varies over time and how this affects economic conditions.

1 THE BUSINESS CYCLE

In Part III of this textbook, we focus in particular on the goal of economic stabilization—that is, keeping unemployment and inflation at acceptable levels over the business cycle. For the moment, we set aside consideration of our two other major goals—the goal of improvement in living standards and the goal of maintaining the ecological, social, and financial sustainability of a national economy—to focus on stabilization.

One crucial key to understanding macroeconomics is how the amount that individuals and businesses want to spend overall influences, and is influenced by, other macroeconomic variables. We referred to total spending in the economy as "aggregate demand" in Chapter 1. One of the key debates in macroeconomic policy is between Keynesians, who believe that aggregate demand needs active guidance if the economy is to be stable, and more classically oriented economists, who believe that aggregate demand can take care of itself.

In Chapter 1 we introduced the notion of the "business cycle," while in Chapter 7 we considered in detail how employment and unemployment vary over the cycle. Now we look in more detail at business cycles, or recurrent fluctuations in the level of national production, with alternating periods of recession and boom.

1.1 What Happens During the Business Cycle

Figure 8.1 shows the pattern of real GDP growth in the United States over the period 1985–2021. In most years, as you can see, GDP grew. But during four periods—1990–1991, 2001, 2007–2009, and 2020—GDP shrank. The level of real GDP actually went *down* from one calendar quarter to the next. As noted in Chapter 7, the National Bureau of Economic Research (NBER) declares a "recession" when economic activity declines for two consecutive quarters, relying on GDP statistics to make this judgment.

In other periods, you can see that GDP grew quite steadily. The positive GDP growth beginning in 2002 shown in Figure 8.1 continued well into 2007, but in 2007–2008 a major financial crisis plunged the economy into a severe recession, lasting from December 2007 to June 2009. After the recession technically ended, it took several years for GDP to recover to its previous level, and as discussed in the last chapter, high unemployment lingered much longer. The recession of 2020 was deeper in the short term but was followed by a more rapid recovery.

While emergencies such as a financial crisis or a pandemic cannot be predicted, and will inevitably have a major effect on the economy,

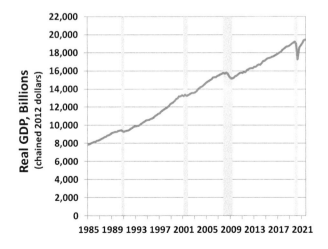

Figure 8.1 *U.S. Real GDP and Recessions, 1985–2021*

Source: BEA quarterly data 1985–2021, and NBER.

the goal of macroeconomic stabilization policy is to smooth out such variations as much as possible.

As we discuss the ins and outs of stabilization policy, you need to keep in mind two "stylized facts." Economists call these "stylized facts" because, while they form a very important base for the way we think about the economy, they are not always literally true. Just as we use simplifying assumptions in microeconomics to draw supply-and-demand curves, we start from a simplified version of reality in constructing our macroeconomic theory.

*Stylized Fact #1: During an economic downturn or contraction, unemployment rises, while in a recovery or expansion, unemployment falls.** This is fairly easy to understand, since, when production in an economy is falling, it would seem natural to assume that producers need fewer workers—because they are producing fewer goods. Similarly, in an expansion, unemployment falls. This relationship is sometimes expressed by an equation called **Okun's law**, which states that a one-percentage-point drop in the unemployment rate is associated with an approximately 3-percentage point boost to real GDP. The equation for Okun's "law" has been estimated many times since then, and in many different variations, and is best regarded as a rule of thumb rather than a "law."

Okun's "law": an empirical inverse relationship between the unemployment rate and real GDP growth

---

We can see some strong evidence of this inverse relationship between output growth and employment by comparing Figure 8.1 with Figure 8.2, which shows the unemployment rate from 1985 to 2021, including the four recessions that occurred during this period, as identified by the NBER. As output turns downward in Figure 8.1, unemployment shoots dramatically upward in Figure 8.2. The inverse relation, however, is not perfect. In all four recessions, the unemployment rate continued to increase even after GDP started to rise again. But with the exception of the periods immediately following a recession, rising GDP is generally associated with increased employment.

Stylized Fact #2: An economic recovery or expansion, if it is very strong, tends to lead to an increase in the inflation rate. During a downturn

---

* In a "jobless recovery," real GDP growth is slow (below average), so it does not create jobs fast enough to keep up with the normal increase in the labor force due to population growth and the decrease in labor demand due to increased productivity (output per worker). So in this case, at least initially, unemployment may not fall as the economy starts to expand.

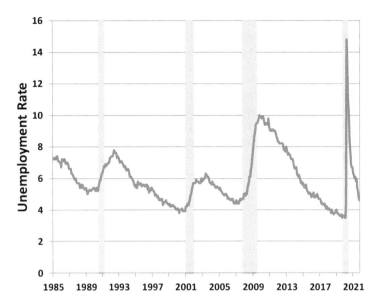

Figure 8.2 *U.S. Unemployment Rate and Recessions, 1985–2017*

Source: BLS monthly data 1985–2021, and NBER.

or contraction, pressure on inflation eases off (and inflation may fall or even become negative). The reasoning behind this result is that, as an economy "heats up," producers increasingly compete with one another over a limited supply of raw materials, labor, and so on. Prices and wages tend to be bid up, and inflation results or intensifies. In a slump, this upward pressure on prices slackens, or even reverses, so inflation may be lower or even, in some cases, negative (deflation). Figure 8.3 shows the inflation rate over the period 1985–2021, including the same three recessions highlighted in Figures 8.1 and 8.2. (Inflation rose further in 2022; we deal with this development in more detail in Chapters 11 and 12).

As you can see, the "stylized fact" that inflation tends to fall during a recession seems to be borne out by the actual data for this period. The three recessions shown in Figure 8.3 were accompanied by distinct downturns in the inflation rate. But wide fluctuations in the inflation rate also occurred during other periods, with both increases and downturns occurring during economic upswings. Business cycle-led variations in the degree of competition for workers and resources are only *one* cause—and, in recent decades, not always the most important cause—of variations in inflation. We look at this issue more closely in Chapters 11 and 12. But for the discussion of business cycles in this and the following two chapters, we assume that booms lead to at least a threat of rising inflation.

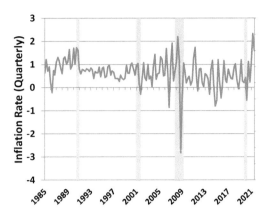

Figure 8.3 *U.S. Inflation Rate and Recessions, 1985–2017*

Source: "Economic Report of the President" 1985–2021; rate is calculated as a three-month moving average of the CPI; NBER.

1.2 A Stylized Business Cycle

When analyzing business cycles, it is often convenient to separate the issue of economic fluctuations from the issue of economic growth. In Figure 8.1 the most striking pattern is the overall growth trend in GDP. For the analysis in Part III of this book, it will be more helpful to mentally remove the upward trend and to think of business cycles in terms of the stylized picture shown in Figure 8.4. (We return to the subjects of growth and development in Part IV.)

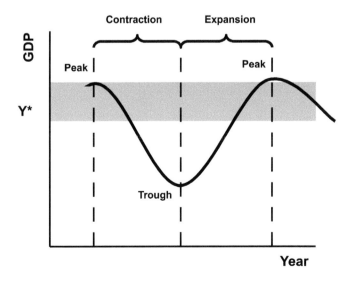

Figure 8.4 *A Stylized Business Cycle*

303

During a contraction, GDP falls until the economy hits the trough or the lowest point. During an expansion, GDP rises from a trough until it reaches a peak. In Figure 8.4, the idea that there is a range of output levels that represent "full employment" is represented by the gray area labeled with the value Y^*. Given the different kinds of unemployment discussed in Chapter 7, there is some controversy about exactly what "full employment" means over the business cycle, so we have used a range rather than a specific level of GDP here to indicate **full-employment output** for modeling purposes. (Sometimes you may also see this referred to as "potential output.")

> **full-employment output** (Y^*): for modeling purposes, a level of output that is assumed to correspond to a case of no excessive or burdensome unemployment, but the likely existence of at least some transitory unemployment

At the full-employment output, the economy is, presumably, not suffering from an unemployment problem. But neither is the unemployment rate actually zero (as measured by the Bureau of Labor Statistics), due to the existence of at least some short-term, transitory, or "frictional," unemployment (as discussed in Chapter 7).

What economists generally do agree on is that there have been episodes when economies have "overheated" and output has gone above this range—giving rise (by Stylized Fact #2) to inflationary pressures. Thus, Figure 8.4 shows employment at the peak levels at the top of, or possibly slightly exceeding, the "full employment" band. And there have also been times when economies have fallen into troughs, with (in accordance with Stylized Fact #1) unacceptable levels of unemployment. In terms of the business cycle model shown in Figure 8.4, the goal of stabilization policy is to keep an economy in the gray area, avoiding the threats of inflation and unemployment.

1.3 The Downturn Side of the Story

It will take this entire chapter and the next four to build up a complete theory of the business cycle! Because this is a large and complex topic, we need to take things one step at a time. We start by looking at the case of economic downturns.

The biggest downturn in U.S. history was, of course, the Great Depression. Production dropped dramatically from 1929 to 1930 and officially measured national unemployment soared, topping out at 25 percent. Some regions were especially hard-hit, with unemployment rates above the national average, and severe underemployment as well.

Not only were times bad—they stayed bad. Unemployment stayed in the double digits all through the 1930s.

Nor was the Great Depression just a U.S. phenomenon. Most of this country's major trading partners were also hard-hit. An important fact about the Great Depression was that during this period prices generally *fell*. You might think that falling prices would be a good thing, but a long period of steadily falling prices, called *deflation*, is actually terrible for businesses, which cannot make a profit, and in turn for workers who get laid off. Between the onset of the Great Depression in 1929 and 1933, prices fell 25 percent, pushing many businesses and farmers into bankruptcy as their sales revenues steadily declined.

Another severe economic downturn hit the United States beginning in 2007. While not as serious as the Great Depression, this "Great Recession" resembled it in that, unlike most recessions of the past, it persisted for more than a few quarters. Even after the economy formally left recession and entered recovery, employment growth was very slow. This severe recession was caused in large part by the financial crisis of 2007 and illustrates the vulnerability of the U.S. economy to excess "financialization," a topic that we discussed in Chapter 6, and to which we will return in Chapter 10.

The recession of 2020 was unusual in that its cause was the deliberate shutdown of many areas of the economy to prevent the spread of COVID-19 (at a time when there were no vaccines for this pandemic disease). This in turn meant that once the shutdowns ended, and especially once vaccines became widely available, the economy rebounded fairly quickly. Notice that in our stylized business cycle in Figure 8.4 there is no scale on the "year" axis. The timing of the cycle is not regular or predictable, so economists in the early years of the Great Depression differed on how to interpret it. Most economists in the 1930s, trained in the classical school, reassured public leaders that this sort of cycle was merely to be expected. They believed that the economy was in the "trough" stage but that it would soon start to expand again. In the long run, they assured officials, the economy would recover by itself, as it had recovered from other downturns in the past.

In response, British economist John Maynard Keynes quipped that "in the long run, we are all dead." He meant that simply waiting for the economy to recover would lead to an unacceptably long period of severe economic damage—which indeed is what happened during the Great Depression. In 1936 Keynes presented a theory on how economies can fall into recessions and stay there for a long time—and some ideas about how public policy might help economies get out of the trough more quickly. We start our detailed study of business cycle theory with models that illustrate classical and Keynesian theories concerning recession and depression.

Discussion Questions

1   What impression do you have of the recession of 2020 and the recovery in 2021? What were the impacts on people whom you know or have heard about? How do you think it compares to earlier experiences with the Great Depression of the 1930s and the Great Recession of 2007–2008?

2   Do you know in what phase of the business cycle we are at present? Is the U.S. economy currently in a recession or an expansion? What does this mean for employment, inflation, and GDP growth?

2 MACROECONOMIC MODELING

For economists, explanations often take the form of theoretical mathematical models. A theoretical model (as we saw in Chapter 2) is a "thought experiment" to help us see the world, which necessarily highlights some aspects of a situation. At the same time, due to simplifying assumptions, it neglects others. A mathematical model expresses the theory in terms of equations, graphs, or schedules. Models contain variables. These are abstract (simplified) representations of important macroeconomic measures—usually related to ones that we can observe empirically, such as GDP or the unemployment rate. Macroeconomists make simplifying assumptions about variables, for example, assuming that all the various interest rates that might coexist in the economy can be summarized as if they were a single one, referred to as "the interest rate." Mathematical models relate these variables together using algebraic formulas, graphs, or tables in such a way as to make clear how these variables affect one another, according to the theorist's understanding.

2.1 Simplifying Assumptions

In Chapter 4, we saw that the economy could be described in terms of four sectors: household, business, government, and foreign. Household expenditures on consumption, business expenditures on investment, government spending, and exchange with the foreign sector expressed as net exports were summed up to obtain total GDP.

This approach simplifies the economy—for example, by assuming that only businesses carry out investment—and the macroeconomic models that we now develop simplify even further†:

■ In constructing our initial macroeconomic models, we assume that the full-employment output level *does not grow.* In designing models,

---

† As noted in Chapter 4, household investment in consumer durables and government investment in fixed assets are not specifically accounted for in national income calculations.

it is often useful to separate different issues into different models. In this chapter and the next, we assume a fixed full employment level in order to focus on the workings of the business cycle. Later, we will introduce the factors that lead to economic growth, and modify our model accordingly.

■ For the initial analysis in this chapter, we assume that the only actors in the economy are *households* and *businesses.* We also assume that all income in the economy goes to households, in return for the labor or capital services that they provide. (In the real world, businesses often hold onto some of their profits as "retained earnings," rather than paying them all out to households, but we ignore that here.) We reintroduce the government in Chapter 9 and discuss the foreign sector in Chapter 13.

■ For the remainder of the present chapter, we concentrate on the difference between the classical and Keynesian theories about the behavior of economies that face a threat of *recession* and rising unemployment due to (potentially) insufficient aggregate demand. Booms and inflationary pressures are discussed in later chapters. While modern macroeconomic models are often not purely "Keynesian" or "classical" anymore[‡] this formulation helps to understand the underlying arguments.

■ These assumptions and simplifications allow us to make some important points while still keeping the stories, with their accompanying math and graphs, reasonably straightforward.

2.2 Output, Income, and Aggregate Expenditure

Recall from Chapter 4 that whether GDP is measured by the product approach, the spending approach, or the income approach, the number will be the same (in theory). For the macroeconomic models that we now develop, we will assume that a single variable, which we will denote as "Y," represents GDP expressed as "output," "product," or "income" interchangeably. This is shown in Figure 8.5. The top arrow in Figure 8.5 illustrates that, in our simplified macroeconomy, production by firms generates labor and capital incomes for households.

But things get more interesting when we examine the flows from income into spending and from spending to supporting a given level of output in the economy. A macroeconomy is in an *equilibrium* situation when output, income, and spending are all in balance—when they are linked in an unbroken chain, each supported by the other at the equilibrium level, as illustrated by the complete circle shown in Figure 8.5.

[‡] Current schools of thought include "New Keynesian," "Post-Keynesian," "Neoclassical," and "New Classical," discussed further in Chapter 12 and its Appendix.

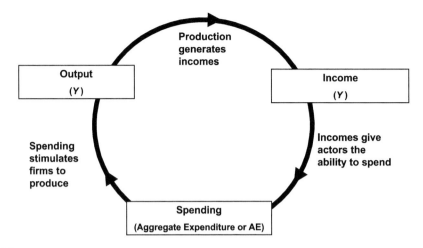

Figure 8.5 *The Output-Income-Spending Flow of an Economy in Equilibrium*

The Keynesian model is based on the idea that total spending or **aggregate expenditure**, which we denote as AE, may (at least temporarily) fall out of balance with the other flows.

---

aggregate expenditure (AE) (in a simple model without government or foreign trade): what households and firms *intend* to spend on consumption and investment

---

Note that for our initial analysis in this chapter and the next, in which we assume a fixed full-employment level and stable prices, we will use the term "aggregate expenditure" to denote total consumer, and business spending, later also adding government and net foreign spending. When we consider the possible impacts of price changes and inflation in our model, in Chapter 12, we will return to the broader term "aggregate demand."

Aggregate expenditure in the economy depends on the spending behavior of the economic actors in the economy. Households make consumption spending decisions, and taking all these decisions together, the household sector generates an aggregate level of consumption, C. We assume that households always consume at the level that they plan to, given their incomes—that what they end up spending is always exactly equal to what they *intended* to spend.

But for firms, the situation can be more complicated. Purchases of final goods by business firms are considered investments, as discussed in Chapter 4. We will denote total investment for a given year as I. But, as we will see, total actual investment is not always the same as what business firms *plan* to invest. We call the amount they *plan* to invest over the course of a year *intended investment, I_I.*

Because the only actors we are looking at right now are households and business firms, we begin our modeling of aggregate expenditure with the equation:

Aggregate expenditure = Consumption + Intended Investment
$$AE = C + I_I$$

AE is the level of spending that results if households and firms are able to follow their plans.

Remembering that if "output," "income," and "spending" are all just different ways of looking at GDP, it must also be true in this simple economy that GDP is equal to consumption plus total (actual) investment:

$$Y = C + I$$

$Y = C + I$ is an **accounting identity**—an equation that must always be true. At the end of any year, when *actual* flows of output, income, and spending are tallied up in the national accounts, the spending by households and businesses (in an economy with no government or foreign sector) are by definition equal to GDP. This equation is true in the same way that, in business accounting, net worth is defined as equal to assets minus liabilities.

---

accounting identity: an equation that is true by definition, regardless of the value of its variables

---

The equation $AE = C + I_p$, in contrast, represents something different. It is what is called a **behavioral equation**, used by economists for modeling purposes—we do not have a national agency that looks into business leaders' minds and measures their *intentions!* We work with both of these equations later in this chapter. The accounting identity involves the *actual* level of investment, while the behavioral equation involves the level of *planned, desired, or intended* investment. While in this simple world households always *actually* spend what they have *intended* to spend (so we do not need a separate symbol for "intended consumption"), Y and AE will only be the same if actual investment (I) is equal to intended investment (I_I). As we will see, this will not always be the case.

---

behavioral equation: in contrast to an accounting identity, a behavioral equation reflects a theory about the behavior of one or more economic agents or sectors. The variables in the equation may or may not be observable

---

309

The link from income (Y) to spending (AE) is the potential weak link in the chain illustrated in Figure 8.5. This is because the people who get the income do not just automatically go out and spend it all. This creates the problem of *leakages*.

2.3 The Problem of Leakages

The household sector, we have assumed, receives all the income in the economy. Households spend some of this income on consumption goods and save the rest, according to the equation:

$$S = Y - C$$

where S is the aggregate level of saving. Saving is considered a "leakage" from the output-income-spending cycle because it represents income that is *not* spent on currently produced goods and services. This is illustrated in Figure 8.6, which shows that some funds are *diverted* from the income-spending part of the cycle into savings.

The other side of the coin, however, is that businesses need funds if they are going to be able to buy investment goods. (Remember, we have assumed that they do not hold onto any of the income they receive, but pass it all along to households as wages, profits, interest, or rents.) In our simple model, we assume that firms must borrow from the savings put away by households in order to be able to finance investment projects.

You can think of households depositing their savings in banks, with firms taking out loans from the banks to buy structures or equipment. In this way, firms can reinject funds to the spending stream in the form of investment. This "injection" of spending through investment is also illustrated in Figure 8.6.

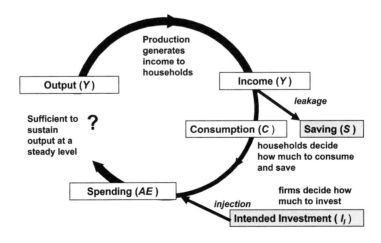

Figure 8.6 *The Output-Income-Spending Flow with Leakages and Injections*

If the amount that households want to save is equal to the amount that firms want to invest, then these two flows will balance each other out:

In equilibrium:

leakages = injections

$$S = I_I$$

If the flows are in balance, then Figure 8.6 is just a more complicated version of the equilibrium situation portrayed in Figure 8.5. The income-spending flow is more complex, but all income still ends up feeding into AE, thus supporting the initial level of output (you can mentally fill in the missing part of the circle, linking savings with investment). This is the kind of equilibrium that might occur in a lake if the inflow of water from rainfall just balances the outflow into a river; the level of the lake remains the same because water is added at the same rate as it flows out.

This can be seen mathematically as well. If we add C to each side of the equilibrium condition above, we get $C + S = C + I_I$. But from the equation that defines saving (S) above, we know that the left side equals Y, while from the definition of aggregate expenditure above we know that the right side equals AE. Therefore, when leakages equal injections:

In equilibrium:

$$Y = AE$$

This equation says that spending is exactly sufficient to buy the output produced—the economy is in a macroeconomic equilibrium. But households and firms are two different sectors—what happens if their plans do not mesh?

Suppose that businesses suddenly lose confidence about the future and cut back on their plans for expansion (that is, they reduce I_I). Or suppose that intended investment is unchanged, but households suddenly decide to consume less and save more, so that the flow into savings is larger than what firms want to use for investment. In either case, leakages will exceed injections. If the savings leakage in Figure 8.6 is larger than the investment injection, the result is that AE will be smaller than income and output:

In the case of insufficient aggregate expenditure:

leakages > injections

$$S > I_I$$

$$Y > AE$$

The question mark in Figure 8.6 indicates that planned spending may or may not be sufficient to support the existing level of output. If the

311

economy is not in macroeconomic equilibrium, something will have to adjust.

Here we reach the dividing point between classical and Keynesian economists. These two theories tell very different stories about how this adjustment comes about. We start with the classical story.

2.4 The Classical Solution to Leakages

In the classical model, we are essentially in a perfectly balanced world, where output is always at its full-employment level. We saw in Chapter 7, looking at business cycles from an employment perspective, that classical economists believed that falling wages in flexible labor markets would bring the economy back to full employment. Classical economists recognize that unemployment is possible, but believe that it will be eliminated fairly rapidly due to flexible labor market responses.

For the moment, we put this labor market story into the background and ask our business cycle question in another way: How does an economy (which we assume to be running at a full-employment level of production) keep leakages into saving *exactly equal to* injections coming from investment spending? Or, to express this another way, how can the economy respond to a sudden shift in saving or intended investment that might cause insufficient (or excessive) aggregate expenditure? The classical argument is again, not surprisingly, that flexible markets will keep the economy at a full-employment level of spending and output.

In this case, the relevant market is what economists call the market for *loanable funds*. In our very simple model, households save out of income from current production. Because they can earn interest on any savings that they deposit in a bank rather than stuff under a mattress, they will prefer the bank. In this market, households are the *suppliers* of loanable funds and firms are the *demanders* of loanable funds. The classical theory about the market for loanable funds is illustrated in Figure 8.7. The vertical axis is the interest rate paid from firms to households, which acts as the "price" of loanable funds.

Classical economists assume that households make their decisions about how much to save by looking at the going rate of interest in this market. The higher the interest rate, the more worthwhile it is to save because their savings earn more. The lower the interest rate, the less appealing it is to save. So the supply of loanable funds (savings) curve in Figure 8.7 slopes upward, like most other supply curves.

To firms, however, the payment of interest is a cost. When interest rates are low, this model assumes that firms will want to borrow more for investment projects because borrowing is inexpensive. High interest rates, in contrast, will discourage firms from borrowing. The demand curve in Figure 8.7 thus slopes downward. Where the curves cross determines the equilibrium "price" of funds—here, the interest rate of 5 percent—and the equilibrium quantity of funds borrowed and lent.

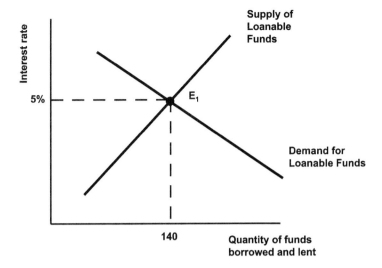

Figure 8.7 *The Classical Model of the Market for Loanable Funds*

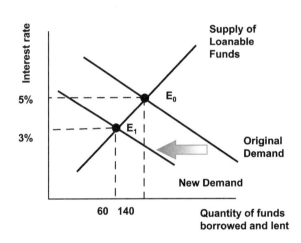

Figure 8.8 *Ajustment to a Reduction in Intended Investment in the Classical Model*

In Figure 8.7, the amount saved by households and lent out is 140—which is also the amount borrowed and invested by firms.[§] (All numbers in our simple models are made up and set to be easy numbers to handle. You could think of the unit for our numbers for Y, AE, C, I, and S as billions of real dollars in a fictional economy.)

In Figure 8.8 we illustrate what happens in the classical model if, after starting from a position at point E_0 (which we assume corresponds

---

[§] In the real world, households and institutions, firms, governments, and the foreign sector all borrow and lend for various reasons, and much of the supply and demand for loanable funds reflects transactions in existing assets that have little to do with current flows of production and income. This model abstracts from these complications to focus on flows of savings and investment.

313

to a full-employment balance of S and I), firms suddenly change their plans, deciding to spend less on investment. The demand for loanable funds curve shifts leftward. If the interest rate remained at 5 percent, we would see a big drop in investment. But because the interest rate falls to 3 percent, part of the drop in investment will be reversed as firms take advantage of the cheaper loans. And because the interest rate is now lower, some households will choose to save less and consume more (indicated by the movement downward along the supply curve).

In the end, saving and (both intended and actual) investment will still be equal, though at a lower level—in Figure 8.8, the level drops to 60. Aggregate expenditure will still be equal to the full-employment level—though now it is made up of somewhat less investment, and somewhat more consumption, than before the shift in investment plans. In short, the fall in intended investment was balanced by an increase in consumer spending (a decrease in saving).

In the classical model, both households' saving activity and firms' investment spending are assumed to be quite sensitive to changes in the interest rate, which serves as the "price of loanable funds." An adjustment in the interest rate, according to this theory, will quickly correct any threat of imbalances between the leakage of savings and the injection of investment. The interest rate is assumed to adjust smoothly in a free-market economy.

With saving and intended investment always in balance, there is no reason to think that the economy would ever diverge from full employment. The economy is thus self-sustaining at full employment due to the smooth working of the market for loanable funds, as shown in Figure 8.9.

We assume (for now) that the level of output that corresponds to full employment is clearly known. As we did in Figure 8.4, we use the symbol Y^* to denote this full-employment level (or range) of output and income. Note that the classical model in Figure 8.9 eliminates the gap between spending and output that we saw in Figure 8.6, closing the loop by achieving a loanable funds market equilibrium.

In the real world, things do not always work out so smoothly (see Box 8.1). This became evident in the Great Depression when the economy clearly did fall into a situation of severe and prolonged unemployment. (High unemployment also occurred during the Great Recession of 2007–2008 and the briefer recession of 2020, though it never reached depression levels). Faced with stubbornly high unemployment levels, people came to be dissatisfied with the classical theory. Could there be something wrong with this story? Could another theory do a better job of explaining the depression—and even better, point toward how the economy might get out of it? The issues that forced attention to these questions in the 1930s returned to prominence in the wake of the Great Recession and the recession of 2020. For this reason, it is especially relevant today to consider the Keynesian theory of macroeconomic adjustment.

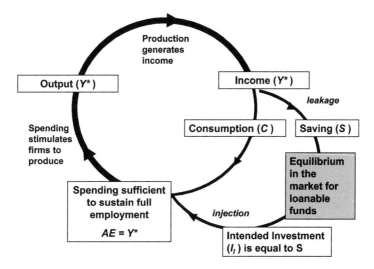

Figure 8.9 *Macroeconomic Equilibrium at Full Employment in the Classical Model*

BOX 8.1 SMALL BUSINESSES STRUGGLE TO GET LOANABLE FUNDS

In the market for loanable funds, banks act as intermediaries between the savings of households and the borrowing of businesses. Banks have to determine the creditworthiness of businesses seeking loans, based on expectations about the overall economy and the profit potential of each business applicant.

One problem with this system is that banks are often reluctant to lend to small businesses. Kenneth Walsleben, who teaches at the Whitman School of Management at Syracuse University noted: "The days of yesteryear when you could go to your corner bank are over. Small, emerging, growing businesses have few traditional sources to turn to."[1]

This has produced essentially two separate markets for loanable funds. Bill Dunkelberg of the National Federation of Independent Business refers to it as a "bifurcated economy." Larger businesses are able to obtain traditional loans from banks at favorable interest rates. Small businesses are frequently forced to seek funds from non-traditional sources, which tend to impose higher interest rates. For example, business "cash advance" loans commonly provided to restaurants and other retailers allow the lender to receive a percentage of each credit card transaction directly. The interest rates on non-traditional loans tend to be at least 15 percent, and rates of 30 percent or more are not uncommon. According to a recent analysis by an associate editor of the *Financial Times*:

lending to Main Street is now a minority of what the largest banks in the country do. In the 1970s most of their financial flows, which of course come directly from our savings, would have been funneled into new business investment. Today, only about 15 percent of the money coming out of large financial institutions goes to that purpose. The rest exists in a closed loop of trading; institutions engage in the buying and selling of stocks, bonds, real estate, and other assets that mainly enriches the 20 percent of the population that owns 80 percent of that asset base. . . Small community banks,

315

which make up only 13 percent of all banking assets, do nearly half of all lending to small businesses.[2]

Since the classical view of the market for loanable funds assumes a single, competitive market, it clearly omits some major features of today's credit markets. At the least, we need to distinguish between credit markets for larger and smaller businesses, and the degree of market control suggests that competitive market theory may not be a good guide to actual behavior in the loanable funds market.

Discussion Questions

1. Who are the actors in the simple macroeconomic model presented here? What is the role of each actor in determining the flow of currently produced goods and services? What is the role of each in the classical market for loanable funds?
2. Explain verbally why, in the classical model, the demand for loanable funds curve slopes downward. Explain verbally why the supply of loanable funds curve slopes upward.

3 THE KEYNESIAN MODEL

Keynes' major contribution was to develop a theory to explain why aggregate demand (or aggregate expenditure) could stay persistently low. He called it *The General Theory* because he believed that the case of full employment (Y^*) represents only a special case, one that may not often be achieved. In this section, we present the basics of his theory using (for the moment) the very simple closed-economy, no-government, no-growth model introduced above.

3.1 Consumption

Many things may affect the level of aggregate consumption in an economy, but one thing that very clearly affects it is the level of current aggregate income. Households are able to spend more on consumption goods and services when the economy is generating a lot of income than they can when it is not (see Box 8.2).

The Keynesian model uses a very simple *consumption function* that expresses aggregate consumption as the sum of two components: an "autonomous" part and a part that depends on the level of aggregate income. In algebraic form, the Keynesian consumption function is expressed as:

$$C = \bar{C} + mpc\ Y$$

where $\bar{C}$ is "autonomous" consumption and *mpc* is called the "marginal propensity to consume" (explained below). We first discuss the

---

BOX 8.2 CONSUMER SPENDING STIMULATES ECONOMIC RE-BOUND

Economists pay careful attention to trends in consumer spending, which represents about 70 percent of aggregate expenditure in the economy. When income rises, consumers tend to spend more. In turn, higher consumer spending tends to stimulate further growth in the economy. According to a *New York Times* article in July 2021:

> Consumers are fueling the economic recovery. Consumer spending rose 2.8 percent in the second quarter, helping to offset declines in other parts of the economy. Spending on services was particularly robust as widespread vaccinations and falling coronavirus cases led Americans to return to restaurants, nail salons and other in-person activities. Spending on goods remained strong, too, partly reflecting the continuing impact of the third round of stimulus checks, which arrived in Americans' bank accounts in the spring.[3]

The *New York Times* article notes that business spending was also strong in early summer 2021, probably reflecting business optimism about expanding consumer demand. The trend continued through fall 2021:

Retail sales jumped 1.7 percent in October, the third monthly increase, as shoppers splurged on electronics and home-improvement projects. . . The continued strength of consumer spending reflects the resilience of the U.S. economy after a year and a half of disruptions, and the success of the government's economic response in insulating many families from the damage.[4] Even after inflation became a significant issue in late 2021 and early 2022, consumer spending continued to be strong, keeping the economic recovery on track.

---

economic significance of these two parts of the function and then put the function to work.

Autonomous consumption is the part of consumption that is not related to income. It can be thought of as a minimum amount that people are obliged to spend for basic needs. It can also be seen as reflecting the amount of consumption spending that people will undertake no matter what their current incomes are, reflecting their long-term plans, their commitments and habits, and their feelings of confidence, or lack of confidence, about the future. Autonomous consumption can change if people's life circumstances or their confidence about the future alters for reasons other than a change in income.

But, of course, much of consumption does reflect current income and its changes. The term "**marginal propensity to consume**" (*mpc*) reflects the number of *additional* dollars of consumption spending that occur for every *additional* dollar of aggregate income. Using the notation Δ (the Greek letter delta) to mean "change in," *mpc* can be expressed as:

$mpc = \Delta C/\Delta Y$

$= \left(\text{the change in } C \text{ resulting from a change in } Y\right) \div \left(\text{the change in } Y\right).$

317

> **marginal propensity to consume:** the number of additional dollars of consumption for every additional dollar of income (typically a fraction between zero and one)

In the following example, we use an *mpc* of 8/10 or 0.8. This means that for every additional $10 in aggregate income, households will spend an additional $8 on consumption. Logically, the *mpc* should be no greater than 1. An *mpc* greater than 1 would mean that people increase their consumption by *more* than the addition to their income. An *mpc* of about 0.8 has been the standard, historically, in Keynesian modeling exercises—though such a value may not correspond well to actual data on consumption in every time period.

Recall that any income not spent by the household sector is saved. Based on the consumption function, a savings function can be derived using the equation for savings and substituting in the equation for consumption:

$$S = Y - C = Y - \left(\bar{C} + mpc\ Y\right) = -\bar{C} + \left(1 - mpc\right)Y$$

> **marginal propensity to save:** the number of additional dollars saved for each additional dollar of income (typically a fraction between zero and one)

The term $(1 - mpc)$ is called the "**marginal propensity to save**":

$$mps = 1 - mpc = \frac{\Delta S}{\Delta Y}$$
$$= \left(\text{the change in } S \text{ resulting from a change in } Y\right) \div \left(\text{the change in } Y\right)$$

For example, if households spend 80 percent of additional income, or $8 out of an additional $10 in income, then they save 20 percent (= 100 percent − 80 percent), or $2 out of $10. If the *mpc* is 0.8, the *mps* is therefore 0.2. The change in savings can be calculated by rearranging the formula above to get $\Delta S = (1 - mpc)\ \Delta Y$ or $2 = (0.2) \times \$10$.

If we assign numerical values to the parameters $\bar{C}$ and *mpc*, we can express the relation between income and consumption stated in the consumption function by a schedule, as in Table 8.1. Various income levels are shown in Column (1). For now, we set autonomous consumption at 20 (as shown in Column [2]). With an *mpc* set equal to 0.8, Column (3) shows how to calculate the second component of the consumption function. Adding together the autonomous and income-related components yields total consumption, shown in Column (4). We also show in Column (5), for later reference, the implied level of saving. For example, the shaded row indicates that when income is 400, $C = 20 + 0.8\ (400) =$

Table 8.1 *The Consumption Schedule (and Saving)*

(1)	(2)	(3)	(4)	(5)
Income (Y)	Autonomous consumption $\overline{C}$	The part of consumption that depends on income, = 0.8 ×Y	Consumption C =20 + 0.8 Y = column (2) + column (3)	Saving S = Y – C = column (1) – column (4)
0	20	0	20	−20
100	20	80	100	0
200	20	160	180	20
300	20	240	260	40
400	20	320	340	60
500	20	400	420	80
600	20	480	500	100
700	20	560	580	120
800	20	640	660	140

20 + 320 = 340. Saving is calculated as 400 − 340 = 60. Consumption and saving both rise steadily as income rises.

We can also see the relationships among consumption, income, and saving in this model in the graph in Figure 8.10. (For a review of graphing techniques, see Box 8.3.) The horizontal axis measures income (Y) while the vertical axis measures consumption (C). The consumption function crosses the vertical axis at the level of autonomous consumption ($\overline{C}$) of 20. The line has a slope equal to the *mpc* of 0.8.

Figure 8.10 also includes a 45° line, which tells us what consumption would be if people consumed all their income instead of saving part of it. So the vertical distance between the 45° "consumption = income" line and the consumption function tells us how much people save. We can see, for example, that at an income of 100, households, in this model, consume all their income. At levels of income higher than 100, households consume less than their total income, and so have positive levels of savings. At levels of income lower than 100, consumption is higher than income, and households have negative savings, or "dissave."¶ At an income of 400, how much do people save? Check for

---

¶ When the household sector "dissaves," it depletes assets (or increases debts) in order to pay for consumption. In this case, consumption exceeds income, and savings are negative. This has happened, at a national level, in only two periods in U.S. history: first, during the Great Depression, when many people suffered extreme hardship, and then again in 2005, when people were feeling wealthy because of large increases in the value of their homes, and so tended to spend more than their incomes. In 2005 the

319

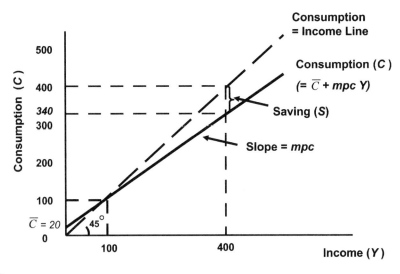

Figure 8.10 *The Keynesian Consumption Function*

BOX 8.3 GRAPHING WITH A SLOPE-INTERCEPT EQUATION

Linear equations are of the form $Y = a + b\,X$. On a graph, the variable Y is measured on the vertical axis and the variable X is measured on the horizontal axis. X and Y are called "variables" and a and b are called "parameters." The parameter a is called "the intercept" and shows where the line representing the linear relationship between X and Y crosses the vertical axis. The parameter b is "the slope," and determines the steepness of the line. It reflects "rise over run": that is, starting from any point on the line and moving to any other point off to the right on the same line, the slope is the ratio of the number of units the line moves *upwards (rises)* to the number of units the line moves *sideways (runs)*.

The consumption function, $C = \overline{C} + mpc\,Y$, is of this same form, only with different variable and parameter names. The consumption function relates the variable C to the variable Y. It has an intercept of $\overline{C}$ and a slope of mpc.

---

yourself that the information given in Table 8.1 and Figure 8.10 for the income levels 0, 100, and 400 are in agreement.

A number of factors can cause the consumption schedule for a macroeconomy to change. Among the significant ones are:

■ *Wealth.* When many people in a country feel wealthier—perhaps because the stock market or housing prices are high—the household sector as a whole may tend to spend more, even if households' actual annual incomes do not change.

---

net household savings figure was –0.5 percent; in 2007, the figure was positive but less than 1 percent. After 2008, with major declines in home values, households started to save more in an effort to reduce debt.

- *Consumer confidence.* When people feel less confident about the future—perhaps due to political turmoil or the fear of a coming recession—they may tend to hunker down and spend less on consumption goods.
- *Attitudes toward spending and saving.* If many people decided to consume less for reasons of health, cultural shifts, or the environment, consumption would also be depressed.
- *Consumption-related government policies.* High levels of saving can be a source of capital for economic growth. Sometimes, a country's leaders will urge people to lower their consumption levels and raise their saving levels, in order to provide funds for investing in the future. (An exercise at the end of this chapter asks you to look at some implications of such a policy.) At other times, leaders may urge people to consume in order to boost the economy. Tax systems may be designed to encourage saving, or to encourage certain types of consumption.
- *The distribution of income.* Poorer people tend to spend more of their income than richer people because just covering necessities can take most or all of their income (or more, forcing them into debt). A redistribution of income from richer people to poorer people will therefore tend to raise consumption relative to saving.

Some of these factors can be thought of as changing $\bar{C}$ in the Keynesian consumption function, causing the consumption schedule to shift up or down, while others may change the *mpc*, causing the schedule to become steeper or flatter.

Note that the classical model assumes that people make their decisions about how much income to consume and how much to save based largely on the interest rate, but the Keynesian model does not mention the interest rate because the effects of interest rates on saving are, in fact, ambiguous. If you saw that a very high interest rate is prevailing in the loanable funds market, you might want to take advantage of it and increase your rate of saving, at least for a while. In this case, you would be acting as classical economists assume: a higher interest rate causes you to save more and consume less.

But what if you are saving primarily to finance your college education or your retirement, so you have a certain target level of accumulated wealth in mind? A higher interest rate also means that you can reach this target *faster* (and so revert to higher consumption sooner) or that you can reach the target in the same amount of time while saving *less*. Common sense suggests that the amount that people save depends mainly on their ability to save, based on their income as well as their needs and plans, rather than primarily on the current interest rate.

In fact, a more significant impact of changes in interest rates on household behavior comes from their effect on what households may *pay* in interest, rather than on what households earn. While the simple classical model assumes that households are only on the saving and lending side of the market, in reality households frequently borrow to spend on capital goods for household production. When interest rates are high, households may postpone buying houses, cars, major appliances, and other consumer durables.

In any case, the simple Keynesian function that we are working with leaves out the interest rate entirely. The most important thing to remember about the Keynesian consumption function is that some income generally "leaks" into saving (and so does not contribute to aggregate expenditure) and that, unlike in the classical model, the interest rate is *not* considered an important factor in determining the size of this leakage.

3.2 Investment

In the real world, firms may take a number of things into account when thinking about how much to invest. The cost of borrowing (the interest rate) is certainly one factor, as are other things, such as the prices of investment goods, their own accumulated assets and debt, and the willingness of investors and banks to lend to them. (Not everyone can qualify for a loan.) The Keynesian approach sees interest rates as one factor helping to determine the level of investment. But Keynes argued that in the case of a severe slowdown of economic activity such as the Great Depression, a low interest rate would not be enough to motivate business firms to invest in building up new capacity.

The most important factor in explaining aggregate investment spending, Keynes thought, is the general level of optimism or pessimism that investors feel about the future, or what he called "animal spirits." If firms' managers believe that they will be able to sell more of the goods or services that they produce in the future, and at a good price, they will want to invest in equipment and structures to maintain and expand

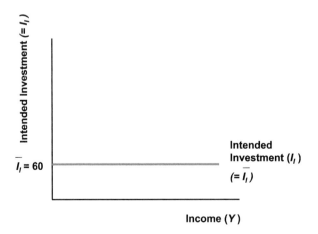

Figure 8.11 *The Keynesian Investment Function*

their capacity. If they do not see such a rosy future ahead, then why would even a very low interest rate persuade them to invest? The borrowed funds will have to be repaid; the major question for the borrower is "are my prospects for success good enough to allow me to repay this loan?" The interest rate will marginally change the amount to be repaid but is not the major determinant of the answer to this question.

The Keynesian view thus sees investment as future directed, rather than related to any current, observable economic variables. For this reason, the "function" for intended investment in the simple Keynesian model just says that investors intend to invest whatever investors intend to invest. All of the intended investment is considered "autonomous" in this model. We can denote this as:

$$I_I = \bar{I}_I$$

where $\bar{I}_I$ is "autonomous intended investment." This is similar in concept to $\bar{C}$ in the consumption function. Just as $\bar{C}$ can go up or down depending on consumer confidence, $\bar{I}_I$ can go up or down depending on investor confidence.

Figure 8.11 graphs investment against income, for the case where $\bar{I}_I = 60$. Because the level of investment does not depend on income, the graph is horizontal. The lack of attention to interest rates is a limitation of the simple Keynesian model. In later chapters, we will go beyond this simple model and consider the effects of interest rates on investment.

3.3 The Aggregate Expenditure Schedule

Earlier we defined AE as the sum of consumption and intended investment. We can now add intended investment to the consumption schedule and curve to get a schedule and graph for aggregate expenditure. In Table 8.2, Columns (1) and (2) just repeat the consumption function from Table 8.1. In Column (3) we have set the level of intended investment at 60, for any level of income, in line with the notion that it is all "autonomous." Column (4) calculates the level of aggregate intended spending in the economy. We can see, for example, that at $Y = 400$, households and businesses together plan to spend 400 on consumption and investment, while at $Y = 500$, they plan to spend 480.

Figure 8.12 shows the relationship between income and aggregate expenditure. The AE line lies exactly 60 units vertically above the C line, at every level of income. Its intercept is the sum of autonomous consumption and intended investment. Its slope is the same as that of the consumption function. We can see that when, for example, $Y = 400$, then $C = 340$ and $AE = 400$.

The AE curve shifts up or down as autonomous consumption or autonomous investment changes. Suppose that intended investment is

Table 8.2 *Deriving Aggregate Expenditure from the Consumption Function and Investment*

(1)	(2)	(3)	(4)
Income (Y)	Consumption (C)	Intended Investment (I_I)	Aggregate Expenditure AE = $C + I_I$ = column (2) + column (3)
0	20	60	80
300	260	60	320
400	340	60	400
500	420	60	480
600	500	60	560
700	580	60	640
800	660	60	720

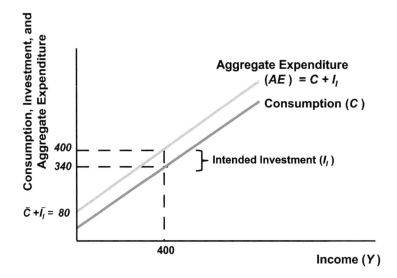

Figure 8.12 *Aggregate Expenditure*

140, instead of 60. Table 8.3 calculates *AE* for selected levels of income like those that we used before, but at this higher level of I_I. Because neither $\bar{C}$ nor the *mpc* has changed, Column (2) is the same as in earlier tables.

This new aggregate expenditure schedule is graphed in Figure 8.13. The intercept is now 160, which is equal to $\bar{C}$ of 20 plus $\bar{I}_I$ of 140, while the slope is still equal to the *mpc*. Notice that now, at an income level of 400, aggregate expenditure is 480 instead of 400. With investment increased by 80, aggregate expenditure at any income level increases by 80 as well.

Table 8.3 *Aggregate Expenditure with Higher Intended Investment*

(1)	(2)	(3)	(4)
Income (Y)	Consumption (C)	Intended Investment (I_I)	Aggregate Expenditure (AE)
0	20	140	160
300	260	140	400
400	340	140	480
500	420	140	560
600	500	140	640
700	580	140	720
800	660	140	800

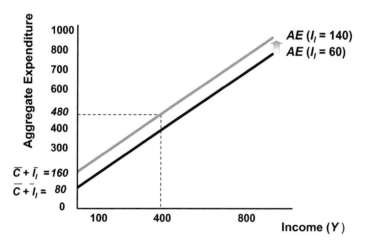

Figure 8.13 *Aggregate Expenditure with Higher Intended Investment*

Figure 8.13 could also be used to illustrate an increase in $\overline{C}$ from 20 to 100 (an increase of 80) while intended investment remains at 60. Any combination of $\overline{C}$ and $\overline{I}_I$, that sums to 160 would yield this graph. In economic terms, any increase in autonomous consumer and investor desired spending increases aggregate expenditure.

3.4 The Possibility of Unintended Investment

The key to the Keynesian model is understanding why and how *unintended* investment can occur and how firms respond when they see it happening. Unintended investment occurs when aggregate expenditure is insufficient because firms will not be able to sell all the goods that they produce.

Recall (from Chapter 4) that a country's manufactured capital stock includes structures, equipment, *and inventories*. Many firms normally

325

plan to keep as inventory a level of supplies that they expect to use soon and products that they have not yet shipped. *Unintended* inventory investment occurs when these inventories build up unexpectedly. A manufacturing firm, for example, experiences *excess inventory accumulation* when it cannot sell its goods as quickly as expected and the goods pile up in warehouses. Conversely, a firm that sells its goods faster than expected experiences *excess inventory depletion*, as the goods "fly off the shelves" and the warehouse empties out.

Actual investment (I, as measured in the national accounts) is the sum of what businesses plan to invest, plus what they inadvertently end up investing if AE and Y do not match up exactly:

I = intended investment (I_I) + excess inventory accumulation or depletion

In Table 8.4, Columns (1) and (2) repeat information from columns (1) and (4) of Table 8.2, showing aggregate expenditure for selected levels of income with an intended investment level of 60. Column (3) calculates levels of *un*intended investment. If, for example, income and output are 600, but aggregate expenditure is only 560, excess inventory accumulation of 40 will occur. Or, if income and output are 300, but firms and households want to buy 320, inventories will be depleted by 20 to meet the demand. Only at an income level of 400 is there a balance between income and spending.

Columns (4) to (6) are included in Table 8.4 to show that the identity $Y = C + I$ holds at all times in this model. Column (5) of Table 8.4 calculates actual investment (I) as the sum of intended and unintended investment. Notice that the figures in Column (6) match those in Column (1)—when we include *unintended,* excess inventory accumulation

Table 8.4 *The Possibility of Excess Inventory Accumulation or Depletion*

(1)	(2)	(3)	(4)	(5)	(6)
Income (Y)	Aggregate Expenditure (AE)	Excess Inventory Accumulation (+) or Depletion (−) = column (1) − column (2)	Intended Investment (I_I)	Investment (I) = column (3) + column (4)	Check that the macroeconomic identity still holds: Y = C + I
300	320	-20	60	40	300
400	400	0	60	60	400
500	480	20	60	80	500
600	560	40	60	100	600
700	640	60	60	120	700
800	720	80	60	140	800

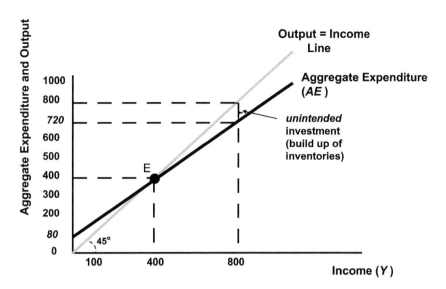

Figure 8.14 *Unintended Investment in the Keynesian Model*

or depletion, the basic macroeconomic identity $Y = C + I$ is true at all levels of income.

Figure 8.14—often called the "Keynesian cross" diagram—illustrates this case for two income levels. The AE curve, as we know, represents the sum of consumption and investment at any income level. The dashed line is a 45° line that (as in our earlier diagram about consumption, income, and saving) illustrates equality between the values on the two axes. With income on the horizontal axis and output on the vertical axis, all points on this 45° line represent situations where output equals income. At an income level of 800, the AE curve indicates that aggregate expenditure is 720. But the "output = income" line indicates that output is 800 and so exceeds spending. There is an unintended inventory build-up of 80, as indicated by the vertical distance between the AE curve and the 45° line, at this income level. (Check to see that this is consistent with Table 8.4.)

At an income level of 400, where the AE line crosses the 45° line, there is full macroeconomic equilibrium, because output, income, and spending are all at the same level. Unintended investment is 0.

At levels of income and output above 400 in Table 8.4 and Figure 8.14, business firms' managers are unhappy because more and more of their goods are gathering dust. For levels of income and output below 400, their inventories are being depleted below intended levels. These are *not* equilibrium levels of income, and the economy will not stay at any of those income levels—things will change.

3.5 Movement to Equilibrium in the Keynesian Model

If firms are unhappy about unsold goods, they will do something to correct the situation. If inventories are building up more than intended, they will cut back on production. Their cutbacks in production will continue until they are no longer seeing inventories build up excessively—that is, until the level of what is actually produced matches what they can sell. Reductions in Y will continue until $Y = AE$. This is a little more complicated than it may at first seem, though, since any reduction in output leads to reduced income, which leads to reduced consumption, so that AE is a moving target. We look at this complication below in Section 3.7, but for now, we continue with the main story.

In Figure 8.14, above, suppose that the economy were initially at an income and output level of 800. From the figure and Table 8.4, we can see that this is not an equilibrium—producers are seeing excess inventory accumulation of 80 because AE is only 720. Producers will cut back on production. The equilibrium point E is obtained only when aggregate output has fallen to 400 and AE has also fallen to 400.

So, what has happened here? If you look back at Table 8.1, you can see that at the income level of 800, there was a "leakage" into saving of 140. But firms, we have assumed, only want to spend 60 on investment. Leakages exceeded injections by 80, aggregate expenditure was insufficient, and inventories of 80 built up. Firms cut back on production. They continued to cut back until inventories were back where they wanted them.

Yet when the economy arrives at an equilibrium, the balance between saving and investing has been restored! Why is this so? Intended investment has not changed—it has been at 60 all along. But now that income has dropped, households have less income to use for consumption and saving, and so saving has dropped from its initial level of 140 to only 60. (See Table 8.1 to check that this is the level of saving at an income level of 400.) It is changes in aggregate income, and the resulting changes in consumption and saving, that have caused leakages and injections to become equal again.

We can also see in the schedules and graphs what would happen if AE were for some reason to be *above* the current level of output. If output were to start out at 300, for example, the desired spending level of 320 (see Table 8.4) would cause produced goods to "fly off the shelves" and deplete inventories. According to this model, this situation would motivate firms to increase production. As production rises, income, consumption, and saving would also all rise. Again, equilibrium would be reached when Y and AE both equal 400, and S and I both equal 60.

3.6 The Problem of Persistent Unemployment

Now that the pieces of the model have been explained, the model can be put together to illustrate how Keynes explained the Great Depression. Assume that 800 represents the full-employment level of output for this economy, as illustrated by the vertical "full-employment range" Y^* in Figure 8.15.

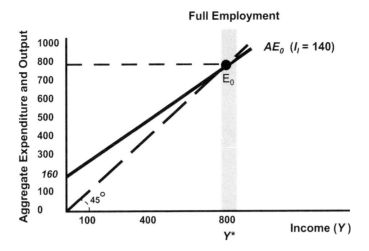

Figure 8.15 *Full Employment Equilibrium with High Intended Investment*

Suppose that intended investment is 140 (represented by the *AE* line in Figure 8.15, which is higher than the *AE* line in Figure 8.14 due to the higher investment level), and the economy is at an initial full-employment equilibrium at E_0. (Refer back to Table 8.3 to confirm that at this level of income $Y = AE$.) A high level of intended investment keeps the economy at full employment.

But suppose intended investment falls? This was the situation at the start of the Great Depression when the 1929 stock market crash and other events caused business and investor confidence to plummet. Producers became very uncertain about whether they would be able to sell what they produced, so they cut back radically on their investment spending.

A similar mechanism can be argued to have worked at the onset of the Great Recession in 2008–2009. The banking crisis in the U.S. and its global repercussions caused such a high degree of uncertainty and disruption that businesses all over the world cut back their investment plans radically. And in 2020, deliberate policies of "lockdowns" pummeled both consumer spending and business investment.

Such a cutback in investment plans is modeled in Figure 8.16 as a drop in aggregate expenditure caused by a drop in intended investment from 140 to 60. (Note that 60 is the number used in Table 8.2 so that AE_1 in Figure 8.16 is identical to the *AE* curve in Figure 8.12.) With the drop in *AE*, the income level of 800 is no longer an equilibrium. Consistent with the adjustments toward an equilibrium that we just discussed, output, income, and spending contract until a new equilibrium (E_1) is reached at a level of 400.

An income and output level of 400, however, is far below the level of production required to provide full employment for workers. Massive unemployment results. And in the Keynesian model, there is no automatic mechanism (as there was in the classical model) to rescue

329

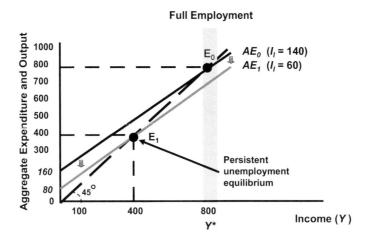

Figure 8.16 *A Keynesian Unemployment Equilibrium*

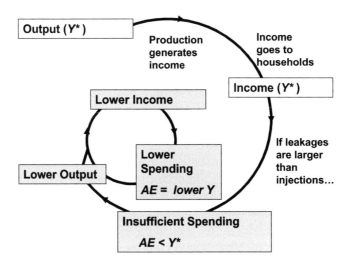

Figure 8.17 *Movement to an Unemployment Equilibrium*

the economy from this situation. The economy experiences a permanent contraction, settling at a new, persistent, self-reinforcing, low-income and high-unemployment equilibrium. The downward economic spiral resulting from inadequate aggregate expenditure is shown in Figure 8.17.

To say that a macroeconomy is "in equilibrium" just means that output, income, and spending are in balance. The basic idea about an equilibrium is that there tend to be forces (such as, in this model, firms' desire to avoid unintended inventories) that are likely to push an economy toward equilibrium and tend to keep it there after it is achieved. But the achievement of an equilibrium is not the same thing as full employment—the equilibrium level at which output, income, and spending balance may or may not be at full employment.

330

In Keynes's view, there was nothing that would "naturally" or "automatically" happen to pull an economy out of such a low-employment equilibrium. A full-employment equilibrium such as E_0 in Figure 8.15 is possible, but it is merely one of a large number of possible equilibria (seen in the model as different points along the 45° line). Equally possible is a persistent unemployment equilibrium such as E_1 in Figure 8.16. Because Keynes, unlike classical economists, did not equate equilibrium with full employment, he believed that there is often a need for government action to stimulate aggregate expenditure. Such policies are the topics of Chapters 9 and 11.

3.7 The Multiplier

In the example above, intended investment dropped from 140 to 60 because of a fall in investor confidence—a decline of 80 units. But output dropped from 800 to 400—a decline of *400* units. Why is the decline in output so much bigger than the decline in investment spending that caused it?

The intuition behind this result is that, while the drop in investment spending leads to a drop in aggregate expenditure, which leads directly to a contraction in output, there are also additional feedback effects through consumption. Because consumption depends on income, and income depends on AE, which in turn depends on consumption, additional effects "echo" back and forth. For example, reducing production in a factory does not merely involve laying off assembly-line workers. The laid-off factory workers now have less income to spend at stores. This means that the stores will also need to lay off some of their employees, who then also have less income. And so on. This process is illustrated in Figure 8.17 as a general downward spiral and is shown in more specific detail in Figure 8.18.

In Figure 8.18, the drop in intended investment of 80 (step 1) leads to an immediate drop in AE of 80 (step 2). Firms see inventories piling up and cut back production by 80. But this decreases the income going to households because firms are now paying less in wages, interest, dividends, and rents (step 3). Consumers react (in step 4) to a change in income according to the relationship $\Delta C = mpc\ \Delta Y$. With 80 less in income, they reduce their spending by $0.8 \times 80 = 64$. (They also reduce savings by 16, according to the formula $\Delta S = (1 - mpc)\ \Delta Y$ or $0.2 \times 64 = 16$, but it is the reduction in consumption that leads to further decreases in income.)

Steps 5 and 6 show how decreases in consumption decrease aggregate expenditure, output, and income, and thus depress consumption even further (step 7). Note that in each round, the decrease in Y gets a little smaller (steps 8, 9, and 10 and onward). Fortunately, a convenient result from mathematics means that we do not need to continue this calculation forever.

331

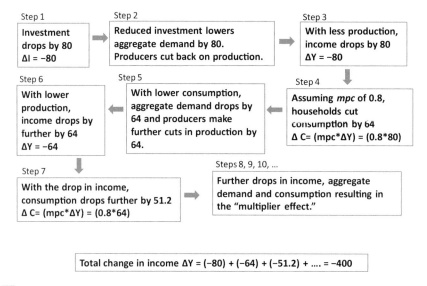

Figure 8.18 *The Multiplier at Work*

A result from the mathematics of infinite series implies that, in the end, the total change in *Y* is related in the following way to the original change in I_I:

$$\Delta Y = \frac{1}{1 - mpc} \Delta \bar{I}_I$$

which means, in this case,

$$\Delta Y = \frac{1}{1 - 0.8}(-80) = \frac{1}{0.2}(-80) = 5(-80) = -400$$

The expression $1/(1—mpc)$ is called "the income/spending multiplier"—or, for short, the multiplier—and is abbreviated *mult:*

$$mult = \frac{1}{1 - mpc}$$

In this case, with *mpc* = 0.8, the multiplier is 5. The initial decrease in intended investment causes, in the end, a decrease in income that is five times its size. We can express this mathematically as $\Delta Y = mult \ \Delta \bar{I}$. In this example the change in equilibrium *Y* is 400, which is five times the original decline of 80 in intended investment.

The value of the multiplier would be the same if it had been a decrease in consumer confidence, acting through a change in $\bar{C}$, that started this cascade in incomes, instead of a decrease in investor confidence. Mathematically, this means $\Delta Y = mult \ \Delta \bar{C}$ as well.

In Chapter 9, we will consider factors other than investor and consumer confidence that can change aggregate expenditure, including government policies.

Discussion Questions

1. If you received a raise of $100 per month, how would you increase your spending per month? How much would you change your saving? What is your *mpc*? What is your *mps*?
2. Describe verbally how, in the Keynesian model, an economy can end up in an equilibrium of persistent unemployment.

4 CONCLUDING THOUGHTS

In classical economic theory, an economy should never go into a slump—or at least it should not stay in one very long. Any deficiency in aggregate expenditure would be quickly counteracted by smooth adjustments in labor markets and in the market for loanable funds. Keynes, by contrast, theorized that deficiencies in aggregate expenditure, due to drops in investor (or consumer) confidence, could explain the deep, long-term slumps that many countries experienced during the Great Depression (as well as some of the other economic depressions that various economies have experienced throughout history). Modern Keynesians argue that this theory also explains more recent recessions including the recessions of 2007–2008 and 2020.

Any excess of "leakages" over "injections" into the aggregate expenditure stream would, in the Keynesian view, lead to progressive rounds of declines in consumption and income, until savings are so low that a new, lower-output-level equilibrium is established. Keynesians generally believe that in this situation some kind of government action is required to get the economy out of its slump and to achieve a higher equilibrium level. In Chapter 9, we explore how the U.S. economy did, in fact, get out of the Great Depression, as well as some of the policies that were instituted in response to the Great Recession and the recession of 2020.

This Keynesian approach turns some classical economics principles upside down. Classical economists, of course, thought that government should interfere in the economy as little as possible, while Keynes suggested that in many circumstances a government role was essential. Another classical belief, that "supply creates its own demand" (known as Say's law, as mentioned in Chapter 1) is reversed in the Keynesian model. According to Say's law and the classical view of the loanable funds market, greater savings should automatically lead to greater investment, which in general would be good for the economy. In the Keynesian model, this is not true. Suppose that consumers become thriftier—that is to say, they decide to save more at every level of income. This pushes the consumption schedule downward and, other things equal, leads to a *decline* in equilibrium income and, at this lower equilibrium income, *lower* total savings. This has been called the **paradox of thrift**,

333

meaning that a seemingly commendable attempt to put more money away for the future actually leads to *lower* economic output and lower savings. This could help to explain why recession or depression might persist: feeling pessimistic about the future, people try to save more for a "rainy day," and the resulting decline in spending keeps the economy below its full-employment level.

---

paradox of thrift: the phenomenon that an increase in intended savings can lead, through a decline in equilibrium income, to lower total savings

---

It is also worth taking a moment to consider the implications of this model as it relates to contemporary controversies over consumerism and the environment. In the Keynesian model, it does, indeed, appear that keeping consumption and spending at high levels is necessary to keep the economy humming. The idea that cutting back on consumption spending would be "bad for the economy" is based on the Keynesian notion that reductions in aggregate spending lead to recessions or depressions, and that these could potentially be deep and persistent. Would our cutting back on the kinds of consumption that are environmentally damaging—especially consumption of fossil fuels—lead to recession and job losses? Or could we perhaps substitute other kinds of economic activity and job creation, such as extensive investment in renewable energy sources and energy efficiency? We revisit this issue in later chapters to see whether it really is the case that what is good for the environment (and for future generations) has to be "bad for the economy", and in Chapter 17 we introduce the idea of "green Keynesianism", attempting to reconcile economic and environmental goals.

Discussion Questions

1. Which theory—classical or Keynesian—seems more realistic in describing today's economy? Or do you think that some combination of the two, or some other approach, is required?
2. Have you ever read articles or editorials that claim that high consumption is essential for a healthy economy? Does the Keynesian model seem to confirm or challenge this idea? What are some arguments for the opposite point of view?

REVIEW QUESTIONS

1. During a business-cycle recession, which of the following typically rises: the level of output, the unemployment rate, the level of investment, or the inflation rate?
2. During the 1930s, how did economists' opinions about the Great Depression differ?

3. In the model laid out in this chapter, who receives income? Who spends? Who saves?
4. What is the definition of aggregate expenditure? How does it differ from measured GDP?
5. What conditions comprise equilibrium in a macroeconomy?
6. Saving is described as a "leakage" from the circular flow. How is it a leakage?
7. How can an increase in saving (if not balanced by an increase in intended investment) cause a shrinkage of the output-income-spending flow?
8. Describe the classical market for loanable funds. Who are the actors, and what do they each do?
9. Describe how the problem of leakages is solved in the classical model.
10. How did Keynes model consumption behavior? Draw and label a graph.
11. List five factors, aside from the level of income, that can affect the level of consumption in a macroeconomy.
12. Why isn't the interest rate included in the Keynesian consumption function?
13. What did Keynes think was the most important factor in determining investment behavior?
14. What determines aggregate expenditure in the Keynesian model? Draw and label a graph.
15. Do firms always end up investing the amount that they intend? Why or why not?
16. Describe how the adjustment to equilibrium occurs in the Keynesian model.
17. Does a macroeconomy's being "in equilibrium" always mean it is in a good state? Why or why not?
18. What is "the income/spending multiplier"? Explain why a drop in autonomous intended investment, or in autonomous consumption, leads to a much larger drop in equilibrium income.

EXERCISES

1. Carefully draw and label a supply-and-demand diagram for the classical loanable funds market. Assuming that the market starts and ends in equilibrium, indicate what happens if there is a sudden drop in households' desire to consume.
    a) Which curve shifts and in what direction?
    b) What happens to the equilibrium amount of loanable funds borrowed and lent? (You do not need to put numbers on the graph — just indicate the direction of the change.)
    c) What happens to the equilibrium interest rate?
    d) What happens to the equilibrium amount of investment?
2. Suppose that you see a toy store increasing its inventories in early December, right before the holiday season. Is this a case of excess inventory accumulation? Why or why not?
3. Suppose that the relation between consumption and income is $C = 90 + 0.75\ Y$.
    a) For each additional dollar that households receive, how much do they save? How much do they spend?
    b) What is the level of consumption when income is equal to 0? 360? 500? 600? (You may want to make a table similar to Table 8.1 in the text.)
    c) What is the level of saving when income is equal to 0? 360? 500? 600?
    d) As income rises from 500 to 600, how much does consumption rise? What formula would you use to derive the mpc from your answer to this question, if you did not know the mpc already?
    e) Graph this consumption function, along with a 45° "consumption = income" line. Label the slope and intercept, and show how the level of savings when income is equal to 600 can be found on this graph.

335

4. Draw a Keynesian cross graph and assume that the macroeconomy starts and ends in equilibrium. Label the initial aggregate expenditure line AE_0. Then show what happens in the diagram when a rise in consumer wealth raises $\bar{C}$ (autonomous consumption) in your diagram. (This event might happen if the stock market or the housing market enjoys large price increases. You do not need to put numbers on the graph — just indicate the direction of the change.)

   a) How does the AE line shift? Label the new line AE_1.

   b) What is the *initial* effect of this change on inventories? How will firms change production in response to this change in inventories?

   c) What happens to the equilibrium level of production, income, and spending? Does each rise, fall, or stay the same?

5. What happens in the Keynesian model if households decide to be "thriftier" — that is, spend less and save more? Do the following multistep exercise to find out.

   a) Suppose that the economy starts out in a situation we already developed in the text: $\bar{C} = 20 + 0.8Y$ and $I_1 = 60$ (see Table 8.2). Carefully graph the resulting AE curve, labeling the levels of aggregate expenditure that result when income is equal to 0, 300, 400, and 500. Label the curve AE_0, add the 45° line, and label the equilibrium point E_0.

   b) What is the equilibrium level of income in this initial case? What is the equilibrium level of saving?

   c) Now suppose that people decide they want to save more of their income and spend less of it. In fact, their new level of autonomous consumption is 0, so the new consumption function is just $C = 0.8\ Y$. Calculate the levels of consumption and aggregate expenditure that would result from incomes of 0, 300, 400, and 500. (You might want to set up a table similar to Table 8.2, but using this new equation for consumption. The level of intended investment is still 60.)

   d) If income stayed at the equilibrium level determined in step (b) of this question, would people now be saving more? How much more? Show your work.

   e) Add the AE curve that arises from your calculations in step (c) on the graph that you drew earlier. Label this curve AE1 and the new equilibrium point E1.

   f) What is the new equilibrium level of income? What is the new equilibrium level of saving? Compare your answers to your answers in step (b).

   g) Explain why this phenomenon arising from the Keynesian model is called "the paradox of thrift." Can you explain why this "paradox" arises?

6. Suppose that the behavior of households and firms in an economy is determined by the following equations:

$$C = 90 + 0.75Y \qquad \bar{I}_I = 35$$

   a) Show in a table what the levels of C and AE would be at income levels of 0, 500, and 600.

   b) If, for some reason, income equaled 600, would there be unintended inventory investment? If so, would inventories be excessive or depleted, and by how much?

   c) If, for some reason, income equaled 500, would there be unintended inventory investment? If so, would inventories be excessive or depleted, and by how much?

   d) What is the equilibrium level of income and output?

   e) What is the income/spending multiplier equal to, in this model?

   f) If the intended investment were to rise by 25, by how much would equilibrium income increase? Use the income/spending multiplier.

7. (Appendix) Suppose that the behavior of households and firms in an economy is determined by the following equations:

$$C = 50 + 0.9Y \qquad \bar{I}_I = 50$$

Answer the following questions, using algebraic manipulations *only*.
a)   What is the equation for the *AE* curve?
b)   What is the level of equilibrium income?
c)   If intended investment increases by 10 units to 60 units, by how much will equilibrium income rise?
8.   Match each concept in Column A with a definition or example in Column B.

Column A		Column B	
a.	*mult* $\bar{I}_I$	1.	Peak
b.	An injection	2.	An inverse relationship between unemployment and rapid GDP growth
c.	An assumption evident in the equation $AE = C + I_I$	3.	Households save more when income rises
d.	Okun's "law"	4.	$I - I_I$
e.	Classical assumption about saving	5.	The proportion of an additional dollar that households spend on consumption
f.	Unintended investment	6.	$\bar{C} + \bar{I}_I$
g.	The turning point from a business cycle expansion to contraction	7.	The amount that equilibrium GDP rises when autonomous investment rises
h.	*mpc*	8.	Households save more when the interest rate rises
i.	The intercept of the *AE* curve	9.	No government sector
j.	A Keynesian assumption about saving	10.	Intended investment

APPENDIX: AN ALGEBRAIC APPROACH TO THE MULTIPLIER

The formula for the multiplier in the simplest Keynesian model can also be derived using tools of basic algebra, starting with rearranging the equation for *AE:*

$$AE = C + \bar{I}_I$$

We can substitute the Keynesian equation for consumption, $C = \bar{C} + mpc\ Y$, and use the fact that in this model all investment is autonomous, to get

$$AE = \left(\bar{C} + mpc\ Y\right) + \bar{I}_I = \left(\bar{C} + \bar{I}_I\right) + mpc\ Y$$

The last rearrangement shows that the *AE* curve has an intercept equal to the sum of the autonomous terms and a slope equal to the *mpc*. Changes in either of the variables in parentheses, by changing the intercept, shift the curve upward or downward in a parallel manner.

337

By substituting this into the equation for the equilibrium condition, $Y = AE$, we can derive an expression for equilibrium income in terms of all the other variables in the model:

$$Y = \left(\bar{C} + \bar{I}_I\right) + mpc\, Y$$

$$Y - mpc\, Y = \bar{C} + \bar{I}_I$$

$$(1 - mpc)Y = \bar{C} + I_I$$

$$Y = \frac{1}{(1 - mpc)}\left(\bar{C} + \bar{I}_I\right)$$

If autonomous consumption or intended investment increases, these each increase equilibrium income by $mult = 1/(1 - mpc)$ times the change in autonomous consumption or investment.

To see this explicitly, consider the changes that would come about in Y if there is a change in I_I from I_{I0} to a new level, $\bar{I}_{I1}$, while autonomous consumption (and the mpc) stays the same. We can solve for the change in Y by subtracting the old equation from the new one:

$$Y_1 = \frac{1}{1 - mpc}\left(\bar{C} + \bar{I}_{I1}\right)$$

$$-\left[Y_0 = \frac{1}{1 - mpc}\left(\bar{C} + \bar{I}_{I0}\right)\right]$$

$$Y_1 - Y_0 = \frac{1}{1 - mpc}\left(\bar{C} - \bar{C} + \bar{I}_{I1} - \bar{I}_{I0}\right)$$

But $\bar{C}$ (and the mpc) is unchanged, so the first subtraction in parentheses comes out to be 0. We are left with:

$$Y_1 - Y_0 = \frac{1}{1 - mpc}\left(\bar{I}_{I1} - \bar{I}_{I0}\right)$$

or

$$\Delta Y = mult \Delta \bar{I}_I$$

where $mult = 1/(1 - mpc)$. A similar analysis of ΔC (holding intended investment constant) would show that the multiplier for that change is also $1/(1 - mpc)$.

NOTES

1   Mount, 2012.
2   Chohan, 20017; Faroohar, 2017.

3   Casselman, 2021.
4   Casselman et al., 2021.

REFERENCES

Casselman, Ben. 2021. "Consumer Spending Was a Big Factor in G.D.P. Expansion," *New York Times*, July 21.

Casselman, Ben, Sapna Maheshwari, and Coral Murphy Marcos. 2021. "Uneasy about the Economy, Consumers Are Spending Anyway," *New York Times*, November 16.

Chohan, Usman. 2017. "How Much Does Wall Street Give Back?" *Big Think Technology and Innovation*, March 3.

Faroohar, Rana. 2017. "How Big Banks Became Our Masters." *New York Times*, September 27.

Mount, Ian. 2012. "When Banks Won't Lend, There Are Alternatives, Though Often Expensive." *New York Times*, August 1.

Chapter 9

Fiscal Policy

Economic theory has real-world implications, as we can see by looking at some recent economic history. The U.S. and global economies experienced major economic recessions in 2007–2009 and again in 2020. In both cases, governments employed policy tools based on macroeconomic theory to respond.

The financial crisis starting in 2007 resulted in the default of the major U.S. investment bank Lehman Brothers in 2008 and brought other large financial institutions to the brink of collapse. This caused the world economy to go into shock. Banks stopped lending, companies stopped investing and world trade collapsed. In the first months immediately after the default, exports in major economies plummeted, much as they had in the Great Depression of the 1930s. In a rare coordinated policy move, governments of many industrialized and developing countries passed large economic stimulus packages. They cut taxes, increased spending on infrastructure, increased transfers for the unemployed, and created incentives for increased consumption.

In the United States, an immediate response put in place by the Obama administration in 2009 was a policy of economic stimulus through expanded government spending and tax cuts. The "stimulus package" involved more than $800 billion in new government spending and reduced taxes. This was followed by further tax cuts over the next two years, including a temporary two-percentage-point payroll tax holiday in 2011 and 2012. Even after the economy started to recover, growth was slow and job creation weak, with unemployment remaining over 7 percent through 2013. This led to a wide-ranging, and continuing, discussion about the best way for the government to respond to the recession and its aftermath. A major package of individual and business tax cuts passed in the United States in December 2017 gave further stimulus to the economy, although it drew criticism for favoring upper-income earners and large corporations.

The recession of 2020 had a different cause—the COVID-19 pandemic. In response to the rapid onset of the pandemic in early 2020, economic shutdowns and limitations on travel and other activities led to a sharp reduction in production and employment, both in the

DOI: 10.4324/9781003251521-13

United States and worldwide. The impact of the recession was unusually severe; according to the World Bank, it was the deepest since World War II, and more than twice as deep as the 2007–2009 recession.[1] In the United States the economy declined by a record 31.4 percent in the second quarter of 2020, a more rapid drop than even during the Great Depression. Unemployment reached nearly 15 percent in April 2020. The recovery from the recession, however, was also unusually rapid, with the economy regaining its pre-recession GDP levels by mid-2021.

The recovery was not just a market phenomenon. It was a result of strong and repeated government actions. The first major policy response, the Coronavirus Aid, Relief, and Economic Security (CARES) Act was adopted in March 2020, shortly after the start of the recession. Adopted on a bipartisan basis, the CARES act and accompanying legislation included spending increases and tax cuts equal to about $2 trillion (about 10 percent of total GDP). It included $1,200 stimulus checks for individuals and $2,400 checks for families as well as significantly expanded unemployment benefits.

Despite significant GDP recovery in the second half of 2020, unemployment remained fairly high, at about 6 percent, in early 2021. For this reason, the incoming Biden administration sponsored the $1.9 trillion American Rescue Plan Act, signed into law in March 2021. This included further direct assistance to households and individuals, an extension of unemployment insurance benefits, and expanded child tax credits, as well as funding for small businesses, education, and health including vaccination programs to address the pandemic.

In addition, the Biden administration proposed the Infrastructure Investment and Jobs Act ($1.2 trillion), which was adopted in November 2021. Unlike the earlier CARES act, this spending bill was spread over a ten-year period, so while it was intended to have some immediate effect, the goal was to promote long-term economic health and improve the nation's infrastructure, such as broadband, water, and energy systems, as well as its social and environmental conditions including childcare, housing, and climate policy.

The common-sense idea behind government policies aimed at economic stimulus is that more spending, either by government or by individuals and families who receive tax cuts or increased benefits, will create demand for goods and thereby expand employment and output. In terms of the macroeconomic theory sketched out in Chapter 8, these policies are intended to increase aggregate expenditure, generating positive multiplier effects.

In theory, any spending could have a positive multiplier effect. But forms of spending, or tax cuts and benefit increases, that promote equity and that strengthen the fundamentals of the economy such as education, transportation, and water systems, have a stronger economic justification. In addition, as we saw in Chapter 8, classical and Keynesian perspectives differ in their analysis of the impacts of government spending and tax cuts. This difference is often reflected in patterns of political support or opposition. For example, while the CARES Act and the Infrastructure Investment and Jobs Act were passed on a bipartisan basis, the American Rescue Plan was adopted by a Democratic majority and signed into law by a Democratic President over Republican opposition.

Our goal in this chapter is to develop a basic theory of government spending and taxes and their effects on the economy, using the principles of aggregate demand/aggregate expenditure and the multiplier developed in Chapter 8. The approach that we outline is primarily based on the Keynesian model developed in Chapter 8, but we will also consider more conservative, or classical, theoretical perspectives.

1 THE ROLE OF GOVERNMENT SPENDING AND TAXES

Economists often disagree about which tax and spending policies are best in different economic situations. These debates are over **fiscal policy**—what government spends, how it gets the money that it spends, and the effects of these activities on GDP levels. To understand these issues, we need to extend the simple macroeconomic model of Chapter 8 to include the role of government.

---

fiscal policy: government spending and tax policy

If the role of the government is added, the equation for aggregate expenditure used in previous chapters becomes:

$$AE = C + I_I + G$$

Government spending on goods and services, including spending by federal, state, and local governments (G) is added to consumption and investment to obtain aggregate expenditure (AE). Taxes do not appear directly in this equation, but, as we will see, they have an impact through their effect on consumer spending.

We examine the effects of these changes in our model one at a time, starting with the impact of a change in government spending.

---

government spending (**G**): the component of GDP that represents spending on goods and services by federal, state, and local governments

---

1.1 A Change in Government Spending

Government spending has a direct impact on the level of GDP. Government purchases of goods and services increase aggregate expenditure, boosting equilibrium output. In Chapter 8, we showed how a decline in intended investment (I_I) lowered the AE line, leading to equilibrium at a lower level of income. This suggests that government spending might be used as an antidote to low investment spending.

Suppose that we start with the macroeconomic equilibrium presented in Table 8.4 and Figure 8.16 in Chapter 8. Remember that this was an unemployment equilibrium. If we start at an unemployment equilibrium, additional aggregate expenditure will be needed to return to full employment. Our first model assumed no government role; hence initial government spending equals 0. Thus, a simple policy would be to increase government spending on goods and services from 0 to 80. As you can see in Table 9.1 and Figure 9.1, the addition of 80 units of government spending causes the equilibrium to shift up by 400, to the full employment Y^* of 800. Why does this happen?

Let's look at a simple example—a new building construction program. Government money is spent on goods such as concrete and steel as well as paying workers. This directly creates new aggregate expenditure. In addition, there are multiplier effects—construction workers will use their incomes to buy all kinds of consumer goods and services. The multiplier effects add to the original economic stimulus resulting from government spending.

The effect is exactly the same as the multiplier for intended investment that we discussed in Chapter 8. The initial change in government spending (ΔG) becomes income to individuals (ΔY), which leads to a round of consumer spending (ΔC) equal to ($mpc^*\Delta Y$), which in turn becomes income to other individuals, leading to another round of consumer spending, and so forth. The whole process can be summarized

Table 9.1 *An Increase in Government Spending*

(1) Income (Y)	(2) Consumption (C)	(3) Intended Investment (I_I)	(4) Original Aggregate Expenditure ($AE_0 = C + I_I$)	(5) Government Spending (G)	(6) New Aggregate Expenditure ($AE_1 = C + I_I + G$)
300	260	60	320	80	400
400	340	60	400	80	480
500	420	60	480	80	560
600	500	60	560	80	640
700	580	60	640	80	720
800	660	60	720	80	800

343

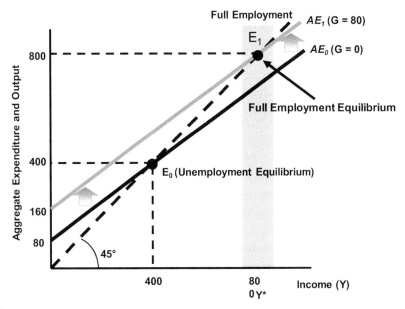

Figure 9.1 *Increased Government Spending*

using the same formula as in Chapter 8, but now applied to government spending rather than intended investment:

$$\Delta Y = \frac{1}{1 - mpc} \Delta G$$

or:

$$\Delta Y = mult \Delta G$$

Using the same *mpc* and multiplier as before (*mpc* = 0.8, resulting in *mult* = 5) allows us to predict the impact of government spending on economic equilibrium. The multiplier applies to government spending in exactly the same way that it does to changes in intended investment. Therefore, an increase in government spending of 80 leads to an equilibrium shift of 80 × 5 = 400. Looking at it the other way, if we start with the goal of an increase of 400 in *Y*, we can divide 400 by 5 to find the needed quantity of ΔG: 400/5 = 80.

Note that at the original *AE* level, there is an equilibrium at 400, where *AE* = *Y*, and there is significant unemployment. After the addition of 80 in government spending (*G*), the new equilibrium is at the full-employment level of 800, where AE_1 = *Y*. (You can check other levels in the table to make sure that it is the only level at which AE_1 = *Y*.)

Figure 9.1 shows the same thing graphically. The aggregate expenditure schedule moves up by 80 at each level of income, so that the horizontal intercept of the *AE* line moves up from 80 to 160. The slope of the *AE* line remains the same, since there has been no change in the *mpc*. The change in equilibrium income is equal to the change in government spending times the multiplier.

Using the multiplier, we can easily calculate the effect of further changes in government spending. For example, suppose that government spending were reduced from 80 to 60. This negative change of 20 in *G* would lead to a change of $(5 \times -20 = -100)$ in equilibrium *Y*. Income would fall from 800 to 700.

So we can see that an increase in government spending will raise the level of economic equilibrium, while a decrease in government spending will lower it. The multiplier effect, which is the same size in both directions, gives the policy extra "bang for the buck"—in this case, a change in government spending leads to five times as great a change in national income.

While we have used a multiplier of 5 to illustrate our hypothetical example, in real life the multiplier is rarely this large (as we will see later in the chapter and also in the algebraic presentation in Appendix A2), but there will usually be some multiplier effects from a change in government spending. The exact size of this multiplier is subject to much debate among economists but is generally estimated to be 2.0 or less for the U.S. economy.

1.2 Taxes and Transfer Payments

To complete the picture of fiscal policy, we need to include the role of taxes and transfer payments. If voters and government officials do not want to raise government spending on goods and services, they have another option. To promote expansion of GDP, the government could cut taxes or increase **transfer payments**. Transfer payments are government grants, subsidies, or gifts to individuals or firms. Examples of transfer payments include unemployment insurance and Social Security payments, and subsidies to, for example, energy or agricultural corporations.

---

transfer payments: payments by government to individuals or firms, including Social Security payments, unemployment compensation, interest payments, and subsidies

---

A fiscal tool frequently chosen by policymakers is tax reductions. (Tax reductions, of course, tend to be politically popular in addition to providing economic stimulus.) Increases in transfer payments would have the same general positive effect on aggregate expenditure. The opposite policies—increasing taxes or decreasing transfer payments—would have a negative effect on economic equilibrium, similar to a reduction in government spending.

Changes in taxes and transfer payments, however, do not have exactly the same effect as changes in government spending on goods and services. The mechanism by which tax and transfer changes affect output differs from the process discussed above for government spending. While government purchases *directly* affect aggregate expenditure and GDP, the effect of taxes and transfer payments is *indirect*, based on their effect on consumption or investment. There are many kinds of taxes and transfers, including corporate taxes, tariffs, and inheritance taxes, but we focus here on the effects of changes in personal income taxes and transfers to individuals.

For example, let's say consumers receive a tax cut of 50. If they spent it all, that would add 50 to aggregate expenditure. But according to the "marginal propensity to consume" (*mpc*) and "marginal propensity to save" principles, consumers are likely to use a portion of the tax cut to increase saving or reduce debt. With the *mpc* of 0.8 that we used for our basic model in Chapter 8, the *mps* will be 0.2 and the portion saved will be 0.2 × 50 = 10, leaving 40 for increased consumption. Thus, the effect on aggregate expenditure would be only 40, not 50 (since saving is not part of aggregate expenditure).

The same logic would hold if consumers received an extra transfer income amount of 50. They would spend only 40, and save 10. The reverse would be true for a tax increase or a cut in transfer payments. With a tax increase or benefit cut of 50, individuals and families would have less to spend and would reduce their consumption by 40.

Economists define **disposable income** (Y_d) as the income available to consumers after paying taxes and receiving transfers.

---

disposable income: income remaining for consumption or saving after subtracting taxes and adding transfer payments

---

Disposable income can be expressed algebraically as:

$$Y_d = Y - T + TR$$

where T is the total of taxes paid in the economy and TR is the total of transfer payments from governments to individuals.

Changes in taxes or transfer payments directly affect disposable income but only indirectly affect consumption and aggregate expenditure. Hence their impact on economic equilibrium is less than that of government spending, which affects aggregate expenditure directly.

For this reason, the multiplier effects of changes in taxes and transfer payments are smaller than the multiplier impacts of government spending. If taxes are "lump sum"—that is, set at a fixed level that does not change with income, then we can write $T = \bar{T}$. The **tax multiplier** for a lump sum tax works in two stages. In the first stage, consumption is reduced by $mpc\ \Delta\bar{T}$, which can be expressed as:

$$\Delta C = -(mpc)\Delta\bar{T}$$

In the second stage, this reduction in consumption has a regular multiplier effect on equilibrium income. The combined effect can be expressed as:

$$\Delta Y = (mult)\Delta C = -(mult)(mpc)\Delta\bar{T}$$

The tax multiplier is equal to $\Delta Y/\Delta\bar{T} = -(mult)(mpc)$. Mathematically, *(mult) (mpc)* always works out to exactly 1.0 less than the regular multiplier. (You can use the multiplier formula from Chapter 8 to work out why this is true.) The tax multiplier is negative because an *increase* in taxes leads to a *reduction* in consumption, and a *reduction* in taxes leads to an *increase* in consumption. Using the figures from our previous example, where $mpc = 0.8$ and $mult = 5$, the tax multiplier would be $-(0.8)\ (5) = -4$. (For a more detailed algebraic account of the tax multiplier for a lump sum tax, see Appendix A1.)

---

tax multiplier: the impact of a change in a lump sum tax on economic equilibrium, expressed mathematically as $\Delta Y/\Delta\bar{T}$

Just as a tax increase has a contractionary effect, a tax cut will have an expansionary effect. Historically, tax cuts played an important role in U.S. economic policy in the 1960s and 1980s, as well as in 2001, 2003, 2009, and 2017. In all cases, the effect on GDP was expansionary, although there is debate about the exact mechanism through which this occurred—not all economists accept the simple tax multiplier process that we have discussed. (The case of the tax cuts of 2017 is discussed in Box 9.3.)

Transfer payments, which as we noted are a kind of "negative tax," affect the level of output through a similar logic. An increase in transfer payments, like a tax cut, will give people more money to spend. But the expansionary effect occurs only when they actually do spend—so, according to the *mpc* logic, the impact of an increase in transfer payments is reduced by whatever portion of the extra income people decide to save. The multiplier impact of a change in transfer payments is therefore the same as that of a change in taxes, except in the opposite direction. A cut in transfer payments, like an increase in taxes, will be contractionary, tending to lower economic equilibrium.

347

In the real economy, income taxes are generally either **proportional** (taking an equal share of income at all income levels) or **progressive** (increasing with income levels). In our model, the effect of a proportional tax would be to *flatten* the aggregate expenditure curve, since it has a larger effect at higher income levels. (See Appendix A2 for a more detailed treatment of the impact of a proportional tax—we omit analysis of progressive taxes, which is a bit more complex.) This in turn will affect the multiplier, reducing it somewhat.[*]

---

proportional income tax: a tax in which the same share of income is collected from households, irrespective of income level

progressive income tax: a tax in which a larger share of income is collected from those with higher incomes

---

How can we explain the effect of a proportional tax on the multiplier? Taxes that rise with income will tend to lower the proportion consumed out of each dollar increase in income. For example, with a 15 percent tax, each extra dollar of income will be reduced to 85 cents of disposable income. Applying our original *mpc* of 0.80 to the remaining 85 cents, we get $0.8 \times 0.85 = 0.68$, indicating that 68 cents will be devoted to consumption (and 17 cents to saving). The result is similar to having a lower *mpc*, which also means a lower multiplier. This will dampen the effect of income changes on aggregate expenditure and economic equilibrium.

You might wonder what would be the effect of an increase in government spending that is exactly balanced by an increase in taxes. Since we have shown that the multiplier effect of taxes goes in the opposite direction from that of government spending, it might appear that the effects would cancel each other out. But this is not the case. Because the tax multiplier is smaller than the government spending multiplier, there is a net positive effect on aggregate expenditure and equilibrium. The difference between the two multipliers equals 1, so the net multiplier effect will also equal 1. In the example we have used, the government policy multiplier is 5, and the tax multiplier is 4, so the **balanced budget multiplier** $= +5 - 4 = 1$. Thus, the impact on economic equilibrium is exactly equal to the original change in government spending (and taxes). So in

---

[*] Not counting "loopholes" that sometimes allow the very wealthy to characterize some of their income in ways that allow them to pay lower effective tax rates (i.e. taxes as a percentage of total income) than do other groups.

the case of an increase in government spending that is "paid for" by an equal increase in taxes we can say that $\Delta Y = \Delta G = \Delta T$.[†]

> **balanced budget multiplier:** the impact on equilibrium output of simultaneous increases of equal size in government spending and taxes

For example, an increase of $50 billion in government spending, balanced by an equal increase of $50 billion in taxes, would be expected to lead to a net increase in equilibrium output of $50 billion. One way of thinking about this is to consider that the original government spending boosts GDP, but the negative multiplier effects generated by the tax increase cancel out the positive multiplier effects of the government spending. This results in a weaker net effect than government spending of $50 billion alone, which would lead to $\Delta Y = (mult)\Delta G = 5\Delta G$, or $250 billion in this example.

1.3 The Circular Flow with Government Spending and Taxes

We can modify the simple circular flow model introduced in Chapter 8 (Figures 8.5 and 8.6) to add government spending and taxes. A circular flow including government spending and taxes is shown in Figure 9.2. As noted above, transfer payments are considered negative taxes, so we do not include a separate arrow for transfers. Instead, we show **net taxes**—taxes minus transfer payments—as a leakage from the circular flow and government spending as a reinjection into the circular flow.

> **net taxes:** taxes minus transfer payments

This model thus has two leakages—savings and net taxes; and two injections—intended investment and government spending. As discussed in the previous chapter, savings and investment flow through the financial system, and may or may not balance. Similarly, taxes and government spending may or may not balance, depending on whether the government has a deficit, a surplus, or a balanced budget.

This model represents a useful, simplified way of thinking about the complex macroeconomic system. If the overall leakages and injections

---

† Technically, simultaneous changes in government spending and taxes of equal size do not imply that the overall budget is balanced. What is required for this is that total spending and total taxes be equal.

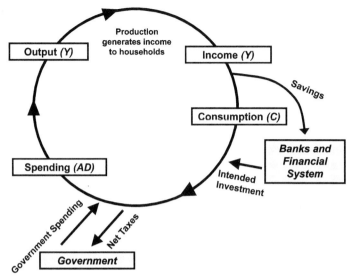

Figure 9.2 *A Macroeconomic Model with Government Spending and Taxes*

balance, the system should be at a full employment equilibrium. From a Keynesian perspective, the object of government policy is to achieve such a balance, by varying government spending and net taxes to offset any imbalances in savings and investment. Classically oriented economists are more skeptical about the ability of government to achieve this and more concerned that government action will unbalance, rather than balance, the circular flow. We discuss some of these policy implications in more detail in later chapters.

In Chapter 13 we will introduce one more modification of the circular flow diagram to take into account the foreign sector, showing the effect of imports and exports. But first, we examine some of the implications of government policies aimed at balancing out the circular flow.

1.4 Expansionary and Contractionary Fiscal Policy

The three fiscal policy tools discussed above—changes in government spending, changes in tax levels, and changes in transfer payments—affect income and employment levels, as well as inflation rates (discussed further below and in Chapter 12). They also, of course, affect the government's budgetary position. The budget could be balanced, in surplus, or in deficit, depending on the combination of spending and tax policy that is employed.

Increasing government spending is an example of what economists refer to as **expansionary fiscal policy**. Other expansionary fiscal policies are increasing transfer payments or lowering taxes. Whether through a direct impact on aggregate expenditure or through giving consumers more money to spend, these policies should increase aggregate expenditure and equilibrium output.

> **expansionary fiscal policy:** the use of government spending, transfer payments, or tax cuts to stimulate a higher level of economic activity

If that were the whole story, macroeconomic policymaking would be simple—just use sufficient government spending or tax cuts to maintain the economy at full employment. But there are complications. One problem is that in order to spend more, the government has to raise taxes, borrow, or "print money" ("Printing money", or increasing the money supply, requires the cooperation of the central bank; this will be discussed in detail in Chapter 11.) Raising taxes tends to counteract the expansionary effects of increased spending. Borrowing money creates deficits and raises long-term government debt that, as we will see, may or may not be a problem. Issues of how government finances its expenditures are discussed later in this chapter and in subsequent chapters on monetary policy and deficits.

Another problem is that too much government spending may lead to inflation. The goal of expansionary fiscal policy is to expand the economic activity to its full-employment level. But what if fiscal policy overshoots this level? It is easy to see how this might occur. For politicians, increasing government spending on popular programs is easy, but raising taxes to pay for them is hard. This can lead to budget deficits, and it can also cause excessive aggregate expenditure in the economy. Excessive demand could also, in theory, arise from high consumer or business spending, but usually government spending, alone or in combination with high consumer and business expenditures, is partly to blame when the economy "overheats." The result is likely to be inflation.

According to our basic analysis, the cure for inflation should be fairly straightforward. If the problem is too much aggregate expenditure, the solution is to reduce aggregate expenditure. We could do this by reversing the process discussed in the previous section and lowering government spending on goods and services. A similar effect can be obtained by reducing transfer payments or by increasing taxes. With lower transfer payments or higher taxes, businesses and consumers will have less spending power. Lower spending by government, businesses, and consumers will result in a lower equilibrium output level, and there will no longer be excess demand pressures to create inflation.

We have thus identified another important economic policy tool—**contractionary fiscal policy**. This is a weapon that can be used against inflation, though it would generally be unwise to use it at times of high unemployment. (The problem of what to do if unemployment and inflation occur at the same time—something that is not shown in our simple model—is discussed in Chapter 12.) Of course, too large a spending reduction could overshoot in a downward direction, leading to excessive unemployment and possibly a recession.

> **contractionary fiscal policy:** reductions in government spending or transfer payments or increases in taxes, leading to a lower level of economic activity

Although the effects of contractionary fiscal policy can be painful, it would be wrong to assume that expansionary fiscal policy is always beneficial and contractionary policy always harmful. Contractionary policy can be useful when previous policies have "overshot" the goal or when the economy is suffering from excessive inflation. We discuss this issue of policy choice extensively in this and the following chapters.

Discussion Questions

1 What recent changes in government spending or tax policy have been in the news? How would you expect these to affect GDP and employment levels?
2 In general, tax increases are politically unpopular. Can you think of specific tax increases that you might favor? Under what circumstances, if any, might a tax increase be beneficial to the economy?

2 THE FEDERAL BUDGET

The federal government's budget includes spending on goods and services, transfer payments, and taxes. (This is also true of state and local government budgets, but our focus for purposes of fiscal policy analysis is mainly the federal budget.) Thus, we can divide total government expenditures, or **government outlays**, into two categories. Total government outlays include not only government spending on goods and services (G) but also government transfer payments:

$$\text{Government Outlays} = G + TR$$

> **government outlays:** total government expenditures, including spending on goods and services and transfer payments

Recalling the earlier discussion, only government spending directly affects aggregate expenditure. Transfer payments do so indirectly through their effect on consumption. As we see below, however, both types of outlay affect the federal budget, since both represent funds that the government must pay out.

On the revenue side, government income comes from taxes (T). When revenues are not sufficient to cover outlays, the government borrows to cover the difference. The actual financing of a deficit is accomplished through the sale of **government bonds** by the U.S. Treasury. Government bonds are interest-bearing securities that can be bought by firms, individuals, or foreign governments. In effect, a government bond is a promise to pay back, with interest, the amount borrowed at a specific time in the future.

> **government bond:** an interest-bearing security constituting a promise to pay at a specified future time

Federal sources of revenue and outlays are shown in Figure 9.3 for the fiscal year (FY) 2021.‡ The major sources of federal revenue are personal income and Social Security taxes. In FY 2021, the federal government also borrowed an amount equal to 40.6 percent of the total budget (an unusually high amount due to stimulus spending following the 2020 recession). Government borrowing varies from year to year, but deficits are more common than surpluses. The major categories of government spending are Social Security, defense spending, and social programs.

Social Security and Medicare taxes are a special case, in that they are collected for a specific purpose—the provision of Social Security and Medicare benefits. Funds raised through such taxes are exclusively for retirement purposes and cannot be used to finance any other government programs, for example, national defense or social programs (except, as we will see, when the federal government borrows from such accounts). For this reason, they are considered to be "**off budget**."

All other tax and spending categories shown are free of such restrictions and are classified as "**on budget**." Each of the on-budget spending items is subject to congressional approval, or **appropriation**, each year.

> **off-budget expenditures:** government-funded programs that are exempted from the normal budgeting process because the taxes that fund them cannot be used for budgetary items that are subject to congressional appropriations
> **on-budget expenditures:** all federal expenditures that rely on general tax revenue subject to congressional approval each year
> **appropriation** (of federal funds): Congressional approval of funds for a particular purpose

---

‡ The Federal Fiscal Year runs from October 1 of the prior year through September 30 of the year being described. For example, FY 2021 ran from October 1, 2020 through September 30, 2021

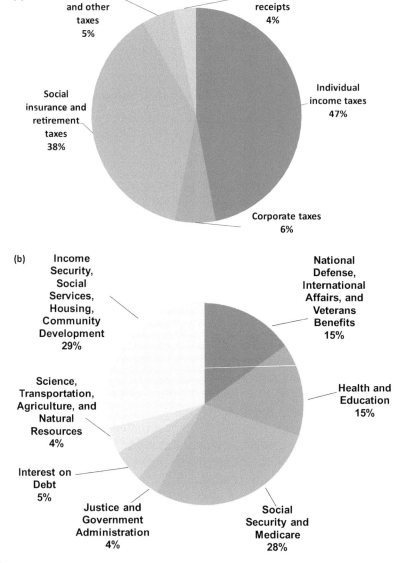

Figure 9.3 *United States Government Source of Funds and Outlays, Fiscal Year 2021*

Interest payments on the existing government debt are another special case. They are "on budget," yet they are not subject to approval by Congress. To fulfill the promise made by the government when issuing bonds, interest on the debt must always be paid. Such payments amounted to 5 percent of federal spending in FY 2021.

Clearly, government borrowing and interest payments on the debt have economic impacts. What is the nature of these impacts? To answer this question, we need to look more carefully at the nature of government deficits.

2.1 Deficits and Surpluses

First, we need to define what we mean by the **government budget surplus or deficit**. This can be calculated by subtracting total government outlays from total government tax revenues. A positive result indicates a surplus; a negative one, a deficit.

---

budget surplus: an excess of total government tax revenues over total government outlays

$$\text{Budget Surplus } (+) \text{ or Deficit } (-) = T - \text{Government Outlays}$$
$$= T - (G + TR)$$

Showing the government's budget deficit as a percentage of nominal GDP is a simple way to correct for the effects of both inflation and the ability of the economy to handle the deficit. The larger the economy—as measured by GDP—the easier it is to manage a given deficit, since both the fiscal and budgetary impacts of the deficit will be relatively smaller compared to the size of the economy. A bigger economy means that people will have higher incomes and a larger flow of savings is likely to be available to purchase more government bonds, making it easier for the government to borrow.

---

budget deficit: an excess of total government outlays over total government tax revenues

---

State and local governments are generally required to separate their current spending and capital budgets. Current spending must be paid for out of current taxes, but money can be borrowed for investment ("capital") projects such as new schools, bridges, and transit systems. The federal budget, however, makes no such distinction between current and capital spending. In fact, the federal government has considerably more flexibility than state and local governments in the conduct of budget operations. A decisive factor in the difference is that the federal government is uniquely empowered to conduct **deficit spending** and, with the cooperation of the central bank, may finance spending through expansion of the money supply (as we will see in Chapter 11), while the states and municipalities have no such power. We return to this point in later chapters.

---

deficit spending: government spending in excess of tax revenues collected

---

355

Economists use the term **countercyclical policy** to describe a federal government policy of increasing spending and cutting taxes in lean times and doing the reverse when the economy strengthens. State and local governments, in contrast, tend to follow a more **procyclical policy**, in which both recessions and booms are reinforced rather than counterbalanced. This is not the intended result but simply a result of the fact that tax revenues usually fall when times are bad, leading to cuts in expenditure, and that tax revenues increase in good times, making it possible to spend more. Also, voters are more inclined to support local spending on schools, for example, when times are good. So in certain respects, countercyclical federal fiscal policy works against not only business-cycle fluctuations but also the unintentional reinforcement of such fluctuations by state and local governments (see Box 9.1).

---

countercyclical policy: fiscal policy in which taxes are lowered and expenditure is raised when the economy is weak, and the opposite is done when the economy is strong
procyclical policy: fiscal policy in which taxes are lowered and expenditure is raised when the economy is strong, and the opposite is done when the economy is weak

---

Over the years, the U.S. Federal budget position has varied from deficit to surplus and back again. After record deficits during World War II, the budget was briefly in surplus, then ran mostly small deficits until about 1980. Deficits increased in the 1980s, then moved back to a surplus in 2001, again only for a brief period (Figure 9.4). In 2002 the government budget moved back into deficit. After moderating for a few years, deficits increased sharply following the Great Recession of 2007–2009. Deficits then fell again, but started to rise following the 2017 tax cuts, and reached very high levels in 2020 and 2021 during and following the COVID-19 recession.

There is much continuing controversy, among economists and the general public, about the significance of budgetary policy and deficits, and many different ideas about the best way to handle issues of government spending, taxes, and transfer payments. We focus on these issues in greater depth in Chapter 15.

BOX 9.1 THE EFFECT OF STATE AND LOCAL GOVERNMENT SPENDING ON GDP

While much of the debate about government spending in the United States focuses on the federal level, changes in government spending at state and local levels can also have a significant impact on the macroeconomy. The U.S. Bureau of Economic Analysis (BEA) has developed economic models that attempt to isolate the impact of state and local government spending on GDP.

The BEA estimated, for example, that in 2009 state and local government spending provided a boost to the national economy—increasing the GDP growth rate by 0.28 percentage points. Some of this spending was money that state and local governments received from the 2009 American Recovery and Reinvestment Act (the Obama stimulus).

But when state and local governments cut spending, their impact on GDP levels can turn negative. This was the case in 2010 and 2011, as federal stimulus money dried up and states mostly looked to balance their budgets by cutting spending. The BEA estimated that state and local budget cutbacks reduced GDP growth by 0.23 percentage points in 2010 and 0.43 percentage points in 2011. The impact of state and local government spending on GDP in 2012 was also negative.[2] By 2017, when the recovery was well under way and state and local government finances had improved, the BEA reported that "the slight acceleration in real GDP in the third quarter reflected an acceleration in private inventory investment and an upturn in state and local government spending."[3] And in 2021 the BEA noted that "The third quarter increase in real GDP reflected increases in inventory investment, consumer spending, state and local government spending, and business investment."[4]

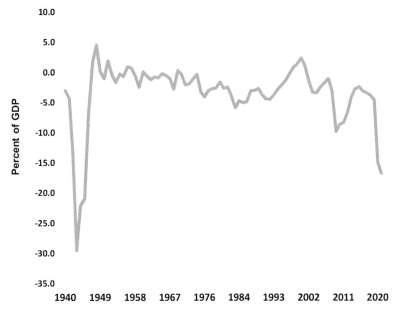

Figure 9.4 Federal Surplus or Deficit as a Percent of GDP, 1949–2020

Source: Economic Report of the President, 2021, Table B-46.

2.2 Automatic Stabilizers

Deficits and surpluses are not just a result of active fiscal policy. A significant portion of the variations in government spending and tax revenues occurs "automatically," due to mechanisms built into the economic system to help stabilize it.

In World War II, U.S. government spending rose to unprecedented levels, close to 50 percent of GDP. After the war, spending fell back, but not to pre-war levels. Since the 1950s, government spending has been a major part of the U.S. economy. As we have seen, this was partly a result of the Keynesian idea that government spending was needed to prevent recessions. In recent decades, the use of expansionary fiscal policy has been controversial, partly as a result of issues such as deficits and inflation. During this period, however, total government outlays (including transfers and spending on goods and services) have not declined, either in money terms or as a percentage of GDP.

As Figure 9.5 shows, government receipts and outlays tend to fluctuate over time. For example, beginning in 2007, when the economy stagnated as a consequence of the financial crisis, government receipts declined as a percentage of GDP, while outlays increased. Part of this change was due to government "stimulus" spending, but part of it was a consequence of declining economic activity, leading to lower tax receipts and higher expenditure on "safety net" items such as unemployment compensation. Economists refer to these changes in tax receipts and transfer payments as the **automatic stabilization** effect of government spending and taxes. The effect is "automatic" because the structure of the government budget moderates fluctuations in aggregate expenditure even without any active decision making or legislation by the government.

---

automatic stabilizers: tax and spending institutions that tend to increase government revenues and lower government spending during economic expansions but lower revenues and raise government spending during economic recessions

---

Even if no specific budgetary action is taken, the government's budget will thus vary over the business cycle. Suppose that the economy is entering a recession. As aggregate expenditure falls, the government deficit generally rises. Tax revenues decline as people have less income on which to pay taxes due to the slowing economy. In addition, as more people receive unemployment insurance, transfer payments related to unemployment and other programs such as food stamps increase. This cushions the fall in personal disposable income—and thus the fall in consumer spending.

If the federal government does not actively move to balance its budget, these automatic changes in spending and taxes tend to moderate the recession. In effect, the recession creates an automatic response of expansionary fiscal impacts—increased spending and lower tax revenues. It will also, of course, tend to increase the government deficit (or reduce any surplus).

Similarly, if aggregate expenditure is rising during an economic expansion, tax revenues increase. At the same time, fewer people receive unemployment or other transfer payments. This means that personal disposable income does not rise as quickly as national income. This, in

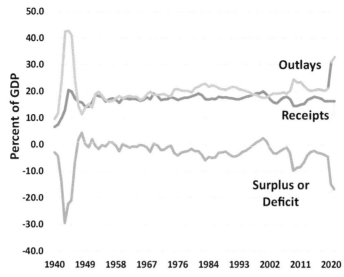

Figure 9.5 *Federal Outlays, Receipts, and Surplus/Deficit, as a Percent of GDP, 1980–2020*

Source: Economic Report of the President, 2021, Table B-46.

turn, puts a damper on increases in consumer spending—and limits the inflationary overheating that can arise from increased aggregate expenditure.

Automatic stabilizers are, therefore, an important part of cyclical budget changes. Economists often say that the portion of the deficit (surplus) that is the result of automatic stabilizers is the **cyclical deficit (or surplus)**. It is, in effect, the part of the budget balance that is sensitive to fluctuations in the macroeconomy.

---

cyclical deficit (surplus): the portion of the deficit (or surplus) that is caused by fluctuations in the business cycle

---

This phenomenon helps explain why, for example, the U.S. government was able to enjoy budgetary surpluses in the late 1990s. It is true that the policies of the Clinton administration, which included raising some tax rates to try to balance the budget, contributed. But as business revenues and personal incomes soared, the resulting increase in tax revenues allowed the government's coffers to fill. The same phenomenon in reverse contributed to the deficit increases of 2009 and 2020.

In addition to the automatic stabilizers, the federal budget has another aspect that levels the fluctuations of output. This is the relative steadiness of government spending. Unlike investment, consumer spending, net exports, and to some extent state and local government spending, most areas of federal spending do not change drastically

359

from year to year. This adds an element of stability to the economy's aggregate expenditure.

2.3 Discretionary Policy

Sometimes, the automatic stabilization effect of government spending and taxes cannot smooth economic ups and downs as much as is needed. Relatively severe problems of recession or inflation often give rise to proposals to use an active, or **discretionary fiscal policy** to remedy the situation. This issue is controversial among economists. Some economists, as we will see, tend to be critical of activist fiscal policy, believing that it is likely to do more harm than good. Other economists argue that activist fiscal policy is essential, especially to respond to severe economic problems such as a deep recession.

Regardless of economists' advice, the fact is that governments are making fiscal policy all the time, whether in a planned or unplanned manner. Every year, the government revises its budget, including levels of spending and taxation. These spending and tax levels have effects on the economy, and it is important to try to understand them.

---

discretionary fiscal policy: changes in government spending and taxation resulting from deliberate policy decisions

---

Historically, the first major experience with the use of expansionary fiscal policy was during World War II. Before the war, President Franklin D. Roosevelt's New Deal had initiated some government spending programs intended to put the unemployed to work during the Great Depression. But these programs were dwarfed by the magnitude of war spending in the 1940s. As a result, unemployment, which had been as high as 25 percent in 1933 and 19 percent in 1938, fell to about 2 percent in 1943. Similarly, in Europe the mass unemployment of the Great Depression was replaced with expanded military and civilian employment as war spending escalated on both sides. The fall in unemployment was a beneficial side effect of the onset of World War II and the war-induced spending.[§]

After the conclusion of World War II, government spending never returned to pre-war levels, and the beneficial effects of the expanded government role—steady economic growth with relatively low unemployment levels—seemed to justify this. In the 1960s, economists

---

§ Employment figures for that era covered a labor force in which a much lower proportion of women were seeking jobs than is the case today. During World War II, an unusually large number of women were employed, filling jobs left vacant by men who were serving in the armed forces.

360

became even more optimistic about the benefits of fiscal policy. At that time, it was suggested that it would be possible for the government to "fine-tune" the economic system using fiscal policy, to ratchet aggregate expenditure up or down in response to changes in the business climate in order to maintain full employment.

"Fine-tuning" was largely discredited in the 1970s and 1980s, as the economy struggled with inflationary problems that were partly a result of sharp increases in oil prices, but were also seen as having been worsened by excessive government spending (we look at this in more detail in Chapter 12). In addition, many economists argued that problems of **time lags** made fiscal policy unwieldy and often counterproductive.

---

time lags: the time that elapses between the formulation of an economic policy and its actual effects on the economy

---

To understand the problems with fine-tuning and time lags, we can use a common-sense example. Imagine that when you wake up it is too cold in your apartment, so you turn up the temperature on the thermostat. It might take so much time for the apartment to warm up that you do not get the benefits before you leave for work. You might become impatient, raising the temperature again. As a result, the apartment gets too hot during the day, so when you get home you have to turn the thermostat down again. Thus, delayed responses make your management of the apartment's temperature less effective. The best strategy is to set the thermostat at a single temperature (or, with a programmable thermostat, a specific daily pattern) and then resist fiddling with it.

Similarly, time lags can make active fiscal policy less effective as a way to stabilize the economy. There are two types of lags: *inside* and *outside* lags. Inside lags refer to delays that occur within the government, while outside lags refer to the delayed effects of government policies. There are four major types of inside lags:

1. *A data lag:* It may take some time for the government to collect information about economic problems such as unemployment.
2. *A recognition lag:* Government decision-makers may not see an event as a problem right away.
3. *A legislative lag:* Discretionary fiscal policy must be instituted in the form of legal changes in the government's budget. The government's economists may want to increase spending or decrease tax rates, but they have to convince both the President and Congress to act to solve the problem.
4. *A transmission lag:* These legal changes take time to show up in actual tax forms and government budgets. One solution is that

changes can be made retroactive to speed up their implementation—for instance, a tax cut legislated now may apply to income received during the previous year. However, this is not always done.

In addition, even if all these lags have been overcome, it takes time for the new policies actually to affect the economy (the "outside lag"). Suppose, for example, that the government responds to an increase in unemployment with increased government spending or a tax cut. By the time these policies are in place and create an economic stimulus, the economy may have recovered on its own. In that case, the additional aggregate expenditure will not be needed and is likely to create inflationary pressures.

Despite these issues with discretionary fiscal policy, governments have continued to use it, with mixed results. Government fiscal stimulus, with or without a formal economic justification, was applied during the periods 1964–1968, 1975–1977, 1980–1987, 2001–2003, and 2009–2012, as well as in 2020–2022 in response to the COVID-19 recession. Most major stimulus packages included a significant amount of tax cuts, a policy especially popular in the U.S. Such tax cuts as part of stimulus packages were implemented under Presidents Kennedy, Reagan, George W. Bush, as well as by the Obama administration as part of a stimulus policy in response to recession (see Box 9.2). The Trump administration passed a major package of tax cuts in 2017 (see Box 9.3). Perhaps because these 2017 tax cuts were seen by many economists as excessive, the stimulus packages of 2020 and 2021 did not include further tax cuts but concentrated on providing stimulus spending.

BOX 9.2 THE OBAMA STIMULUS PROGRAM

In February 2009, in response to a severe recession that had pushed the unemployment rate over 8 percent, the Obama administration proposed a $787 billion stimulus package, including $288 billion in tax cuts, $224 billion in extended unemployment benefits, education, and health care, and $275 billion for job creation through federal contracts, grants, and loans. The stimulus, formally known as the American Recovery and Reinvestment Act (ARRA), was enacted by Congress, providing for increased spending and tax reductions over a period of ten years. For the first three fiscal years, $720 billion, or 91.5 percent, was budgeted to maximize the impact in fighting the recession. Later estimates by the Congressional Budget Office (CBO) indicate that the total impact of the stimulus package over the period 2009–2019 would be about $830 billion.

From the point of view of economic analysis, the stimulus amounted to a major expansionary fiscal policy, including all three fiscal policy tools: changes in government spending including spending on infrastructure investment, changes in tax levels, and changes in transfer payments. According to the economic theories discussed in this chapter, the effects of such a program should be to expand economic activity, boost GDP, and lower unemployment (although classical economists are skeptical, especially about the effectiveness of government spending).

Was the stimulus successful? The answer was not immediately obvious, because the recession was severe, with unemployment rates peaking in late 2009 at 10 percent, and the subsequent recovery was slow, giving many people the impression that the stimulus failed. But there is now sufficient evidence to indicate that in fact it was very effective.

According to the CBO, the ARRA "added as many as 3.3 million jobs to the economy in the second quarter of 2010, and may have prevented the nation from lapsing back into recession." An analysis by economists Alan Blinder and Mark Zandi in 2010 found that the stimulus "probably averted what could have been called Great Depression 2.0... [W]ithout the government's response, GDP in 2010 would be about 11.5 percent lower [and] payroll employment would be less by some 8½ million jobs."[5] Blinder and Zandi's analysis takes into account negative multiplier effects. The decline in economic activity in 2009 was so steep that, without an increase in aggregate expenditure, a negative spiral of lower demand, lower incomes, and even lower demand would have taken place, as it did in the Great Depression in the 1930s.

The CBO report indicates that "the effects of ARRA on output peaked in the first half of 2010 and have since diminished." Even so, the stimulus continued to exert a positive impact on GDP in 2012: "ARRA raised real GDP in 2012 by between 0.1 percent and 0.8 percent, and increased the number of people employed in 2012 by between 0.2 million and 1.1 million." The CBO also estimated output multipliers for stimulus spending between 0.5 and 2.5, for middle-income tax cuts between 0.3 and 1.5, and for transfer payments between 0.4 and 2.1.

In a survey conducted by the University of Chicago Booth School of Business in 2012, 80 percent of economists agreed that the stimulus had reduced the unemployment rate. On long-term effects, economists were more divided: 46 percent believed that "the benefits of the stimulus will end up exceeding its cost," while 27 percent were not certain, and 12 percent thought that long-term costs would outweigh benefits.

Worldwide, using fiscal policy to stabilize the economy made a global revival during the Great Recession of 2007–2009. During this time, many major economies passed large stimulus packages, and these packages are credited by many with having prevented further deterioration of the world economy. The same logic applied to the 2020 recession; soaring unemployment and looming economic collapse convinced governments that immediate action was necessary.

At such times of extreme crisis, the expansionary impact of government policy is obvious. But in more normal times, it is sometimes difficult to evaluate the extent to which fiscal policy is expansionary or not. In economically good times, governments are often faced with an increase in tax revenue (resulting from a general rise in incomes), and one common government response is to use this money for increased spending or tax cuts. In this case, an increase in spending does not appear to cause any increase in the deficit, because it is covered by increased revenues. Nonetheless, the underlying fiscal position of the government has changed, and a new downturn in economic activity would result in a larger deficit. In order to see how the fiscal position has really changed, economists have come up with the concept of a **structural deficit (or surplus)**.

> **structural deficit (surplus):** the portion of the deficit (or surplus) that results from tax and spending policy dictated by the President and Congress at their discretion

We can (loosely) think of the structural deficit as the deficit that would occur at a given level of spending and taxation if the economy were at full employment. Structural deficits thus represent the portion of the overall deficit that is determined by the President and Congress (or by the corresponding authorities in other countries), even though a significant portion of discretionary expenditures often result from decisions made years earlier. Only changes in the structural budget balance truly reflect the direction of fiscal policy—that is, whether it is more stimulative or more contractionary—since other changes are related to the automatic stabilizers.

Changes in tax policy—tax cuts, for example—are also classified as discretionary (in contrast to changes in tax revenues resulting from business-cycle fluctuations). Proponents of tax cuts sometimes appeal to **supply-side economics** (first popularized during the Reagan administration of 1981–1989) to support their policies. The supply-side argument for tax cuts is essentially that lower tax rates encourage more work, saving, and investment, thereby creating a more dynamic economy. According to the most enthusiastic advocates of supply-side economics, economic output will grow so rapidly in response to a cut in tax rates that total tax revenues will actually increase, not decrease (more on this in Chapter 15). This is different from the logic of increased aggregate expenditure that we have discussed, which implies that tax cuts will create an economic stimulus, but are also likely to raise the government deficit.

> **supply-side economics:** an economic theory that emphasizes policies to stimulate production, such as lower taxes. The theory predicts that such incentives stimulate greater economic effort, saving, and investment, thereby increasing overall economic output and tax revenues

The economic record seems to show that tax cuts do indeed create an economic stimulus—but debate continues among economists as to whether this effect is demand-led (as implied by our fiscal policy model) or based on supply-side effects, or possibly a combination of both. And in general, the "supply-side" argument that tax cuts will pay for themselves with increased revenues has not proved true—tax cuts have usually led to lower revenues and higher deficits. This was true of the Reagan tax cuts in the 1980s, the Bush tax cuts in the 2000s, and the Trump tax cuts in 2017. According to projections by the Congressional Budget Office and Joint Committee on Taxation, the 2017 tax cuts will lead to an increase in deficits of between $1 and $1.5 trillion over a ten-year period (see Box 9.3).

BOX 9.3 THE TRUMP TAX CUTS

In December 2017, a major package of tax cuts known as the Tax Cuts and Jobs Act (TCJA) was passed by Congress and signed into law by President Trump. Major elements of the TCJA included:

■ Reductions in personal income tax rates and changes in exemptions and deductions, delivering major gains to wealthy households with smaller reductions for the middle class and lower-income earners.
■ A reduction in the corporate tax rate from 35 percent to 21 percent.
■ Repealing the Affordable Care Act's mandate for individuals to purchase health insurance.

While most economists agreed that the tax cuts would exert a stimulative effect on the economy, opinions differed on the mechanisms involved, as well as the overall impact of the Act. Advocates of the tax cuts envisioned a positive supply-side effect, with the corporate tax cuts especially anticipated to increase investment and economic growth. But these presumed positive effects on growth proved difficult to measure, especially given the impact of the 2020 recession. And supply-side projections that tax cuts would increase government revenues proved wrong, with federal tax receipts declining as a percent of GDP and deficits increasing in the years following the tax cuts.

Since the individual tax cuts mainly benefited upper-income earners, the multiplier effects would be likely to be limited. For the same reason, the tax cuts would tend to increase overall inequality. According to a 2020 report, the Trump tax cuts benefited the richest 1 percent of taxpayers by about $50,000 each, while the bottom 80 percent averaged just $645. The Congressional Budget Office projected that after-tax income shares of the top fifth of taxpayers would increase by 1.2 percent between 2016 and 2021, while those of the bottom and middle fifths would decrease by 0.2 percent and 0.3 percent respectively. In addition, the individual tax cuts were slated to expire in 2027, resulting in net tax increases for many taxpayers after that date, while the corporate tax cuts were permanent. The repeal of the ACA individual mandate was also expected to add millions to the number of uninsured Americans and increase health premiums in the individual market.

The tax cuts also came under fire from economists who argued that the TCJA "weakens revenues at a time when the nation needs to raise more revenue". These critics predicted that larger deficits resulting from the tax cuts would make it more difficult to invest in such priorities as infrastructure, education, and health, while increasing pressure for cutbacks in social programs such as Social Security, Medicare, and Medicaid.

---

1. Are budget deficits necessarily bad? Which factors affecting budget deficits are controlled by the President and Congress, and which are related to changes in economic activity?
2. Why doesn't the government run surpluses every year instead of deficits, or at least balance the budget? Wouldn't doing so be better for the economy?

3 POLICY ISSUES

3.1 Crowding Out and Crowding In

A common concern of fiscal policy critics is that federal government spending gets in the way of consumption and private investment. We have already seen that while government expenditures boost aggregate expenditure, the tax revenues required to finance such expenditures have the opposite effect. But the expenditure effect is stronger, dollar for dollar, than the tax effect, which is why the effects do not exactly cancel each other out and why the balanced budget multiplier equals 1 instead of 0.

That would be the end of the story if raising taxes were the only means of financing government expenditures. Yet we know that the government frequently runs deficits and, when it does so, it must borrow money. It borrows from the capital markets. Using the theory of loanable funds introduced in Chapter 8, government borrowing in theory could absorb some of the available supply of funds, leaving less money available for private investment. The reduced availability of loanable funds can have the effect of raising interest rates, which, by making borrowing more expensive, makes investment less likely, *ceteris paribus*. Economists therefore say that borrowing to help cover budget deficits may have the effect of "**crowding out**" private investment. Using this argument, economists who favor the classical approach often claim that replacing dynamic private investment with less efficient government spending is undesirable, as well as ineffective in stimulating the economy.

---

crowding out: a reduction in the availability of private capital resulting from federal government borrowing to finance budget deficits

---

Figure 9.6 uses the classical model of the loanable funds market, introduced in Chapter 8 (Figure 8.7) to illustrate how government demand for loanable funds could crowd out private borrowing. The supply curve (*S*) represents savings or, more concretely, the supply of loanable funds.

For a given supply of loanable funds, the interest rate will be pushed up from i_1 to i_2 when the government borrows money to pay for a budget deficit, represented by a shift in the demand curve from D_1 to D_2. The result is that private investment is now more expensive and saving becomes more attractive.

The difference between Q_2 and Q_3 represents the amount of funds borrowed by the government. Because this additional demand raises the interest rate, private investment becomes less attractive, and some is "crowded out." Q_3 now represents the quantity of loanable funds available for private investment. The amount of "crowding out" is shown on the graph as the difference between Q_1 and Q_3. The implication of this analysis is that government deficit spending is counterproductive to the aim of promoting private investment.

Keynesian economists generally disagree with this conclusion. Keynes himself acknowledged the potential for crowding out. He did not, however, believe that deficit spending would crowd out private spending to a significant degree if, as during the Great Depression, there was considerable slack in the economy. In other words, if owners of capital are reluctant to invest anyway, there is no reason for government borrowing to drive up interest rates. Remember that in the Keynesian view, recessionary conditions are characterized by an excess of savings over investment. If there is a large excess of savings, there is no reason to worry that government borrowing will absorb too much of the available loanable funds.

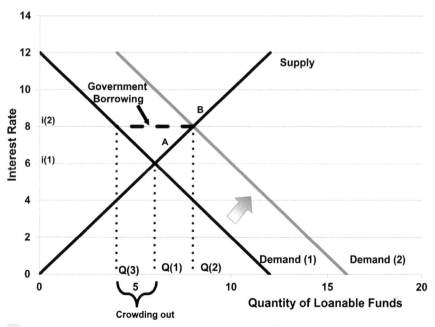

Figure 9.6 *Crowding Out in the Loanable Funds Market*

Keynes also minimized the importance of crowding out for other reasons. First, recall from Chapter 8 that, according to Keynes, investment decisions are not dependent only on the rate of interest. He believed that investment decisions also are a function of expectations of future profit, what he called "animal spirits." In good economic times, investors purchase more capital goods because their growing profits reinforce an optimistic outlook about the future. And they are likely to do so despite the historical tendency for interest rates to *rise* in good economic times. The opposite might well be true in a recession. Despite low interest rates, business spending will be lower due to growing pessimism.

For these reasons, government borrowing to finance deficits may not raise interest rates during a recession, and even if it does, this might not have any significant effect on investment, since investors will not want to invest anyway—at least until the economy starts to recover. Once the recovery is under way, the prospect of growing demand will encourage "animal spirits" and increased investment.

Modern Keynesian economists also point out that the theory of loanable funds is outdated in modern financial systems. As will be discussed in Chapters 10 and 11, the banking sector can create the money demanded by other sectors. There is therefore no fixed amount of loanable funds; instead, the amount of loanable funds will depend on firms' willingness to invest and the banking sector's creation of funds to finance this investment. As long as government spending does not lead to overheating the economy by pushing aggregate expenditure beyond the economy's capacity limits, there will be no crowding out.

In fact, from a Keynesian point of view, the opposite of crowding out might occur. This is because there is significant scope for complementarity between public and private investment. According to this argument, certain government expenditures on, say, transportation, energy, or communications networks enhance the potential profits of private investment by providing critical infrastructure. Rather than being a substitute for private investment, government spending supports the productivity of private investment and is therefore likely to encourage more of it. When such government spending generates more private investment, it is called **crowding in**.

---

crowding in: the process in which government spending leads to more favorable expectations for the economy, thereby inducing greater private investment

---

This argument was used to justify the stimulus programs of 2009–2012 and 2021, which promoted infrastructure spending to get a sluggish economy moving again. Box 9.2 discussed how this process worked in the Obama stimulus of 2009–2012, and in the next section, we take a closer look at how it may apply to the Biden administration's programs for infrastructure and social investment.

3.2 Infrastructure and Social Investment

While the main focus of our fiscal policy analysis thus far has been on achieving the "right" level of aggregate expenditure to promote full employment without inflation, there are other significant issues involved in the formulation of fiscal policy. In particular, government spending can achieve other goals in addition to full employment. Spending can also serve to strengthen important foundations of economic activity, including education, health care, transportation, communication, and the power grid, as well as fundamental environmental functions including water systems, climate, atmosphere, and oceans. This principle was the basis for the Biden administration's Infrastructure Investment and Jobs program of 2021. The $1.2 trillion infrastructure package included:

- $110 billion for roads, bridges, and major infrastructure projects (https://edition.cnn.com/2021/03/30/politics/infrastructure-us-investment-cost-engineers/index.html)
- $39 billion to modernize public transit and $66 billion for passenger and freight rail
- $65 billion to improve the nation's broadband infrastructure (https://edition.cnn.com/2021/06/09/politics/infrastructure-broadband-digital-divide/index.html)
- $17 billion in port infrastructure and $25 billion in airports
- $7.5 billion for zero- and low-emission buses and ferries
- $7.5 billion for a nationwide network of plug-in electric vehicle chargers
- $65 billion to upgrade the electric grid
- $55 billion to upgrade water infrastructure
- $50 billion to protect essential infrastructure from drought, floods and cyberattacks

Unlike the previous $1.9 trillion American Rescue Plan, which disbursed funds immediately, the infrastructure funding will be spread over a ten-year period. Some funding was made available within six months of the bill's passage in November 2021, but other portions would take years to come into full effect. "Infrastructure spending has a bigger effect on jobs when we're in an economic recession," according to Jon Huntley, senior economist for the Penn Wharton Budget Model. "The benefits of infrastructure spending take a while, but are very, very long lasting," he added.

The infrastructure bill would provide a modest economic stimulus spread over a long time period, but clearly its main principle is the value of the investments that it makes in transportation, energy, water systems, and climate protection. Proponents argue that these projects will improve well-being, environmental sustainability, and workforce quality over the long term. This could be viewed as a case of "crowding in", where the initial government investment will encourage and facilitate extensive private investment in areas such as renewable energy, electric vehicles, and communications systems. Senators of both parties favoring the bill claimed that it was "fully paid for" by user fees and the use of other unspent government funds, but the Congressional Budget Office projected that it would lead to a small increase in the deficit over the period 2022–2031. Independent analysts concluded that while the bill might slightly raise deficits initially, in the longer term its positive effects on output would lead to deficit reduction.

The Infrastructure Investment and Jobs Act was followed by the Inflation Reduction Act of 2022, with a similar rationale of social and environmental investment. This bill authorized $369 billion in spending on investments related to renewable energy and climate change. But it also included $737 billion in new revenues through increased corporate taxes, a tax on stock buybacks, and more effective tax enforcement, especially targeting high income earners who evade taxes. Thus it would have an overall effect of reducing the Federal deficit. According to the nonpartisan Committee for a Responsible Federal Budget, deficit reduction would be $1.9 trillion over a 20-year period, and "deficit reduction, along with other elements of the bill, is likely to reduce inflationary pressures and thus reduce the risk of a possible recession." The bill also has provisions to lower prescription drug prices and extend Affordable Care Act subsidies. Despite the bill's title, however, the Congressional Budget Office and the University of Pennsylvania Wharton Budget Model find that it would have little long-term effect in reducing inflation.

3.3 Different Multiplier Effects

Another issue of considerable policy controversy is which items in the budget deserve priority. A principal goal of government spending—especially discretionary spending—is to stimulate the economy. The multiplier effect outlined in Chapter 8 implies that every additional dollar of government spending increases aggregate expenditure by more than one dollar. But we have also seen that much of the effect can be offset by taxes. In addition, it is unrealistic to assume that the multiplier effect is the same regardless of the type of government expenditure.

As seen earlier, the larger the *mpc,* the greater the multiplier. Until now, we have assumed that the *mpc* is uniform—that is, that it represents the marginal propensity to consume of all individuals and groups in society. But there may be significant variations in the *mpc* depending on which income groups are involved.

The typical wealthy individual is capable of saving a significant percentage of income, a much greater percentage than that of lower-income people. Of course, what is saved is not consumed; the average lower-income person spends a higher percentage of each additional dollar received than would a rich person. In other words, a lower-income person's *mpc* tends to be higher. Because a higher *mpc* translates to a larger multiplier, Keynes argued that the multiplier is largest when government spending is directed toward those who have the highest *mpc*. Spending or tax cuts that benefit middle- and lower-income people are thus likely to have larger multiplier effects than spending or tax policies that primarily benefit the rich.

Considering both crowding out/crowding in effects and different *mpc* effects, we can conclude that multipliers:

- Are not stable over time, but might be larger in a recession, when crowding out is less of a problem.
- Are larger if the spending benefits lower-income households.
- Are larger if the government spends money on investment for infrastructure, as in this case, crowding in of private investment might result.

Table 9.2 Different Multiplier Effects

Tax Cuts	Multiplier
Nonrefundable lump-sum tax rebate	1.02
Refundable lump-sum tax rebate	1.26
Temporary Tax Cuts	
Payroll tax holiday	1.29
Across the board tax cut	1.03
Accelerated depreciation	0.27
Permanent Tax Cuts	
Extend alternative minimum tax patch	0.48
Make income tax cuts permanent	0.29
Make dividend and capital gains tax cuts permanent	0.37
Cut corporate tax rate	0.30
Spending Increases	
Extend unemployment insurance benefits	1.64
Temporarily increase food stamps	1.73
Issue general aid to state governments	1.36
Increase infrastructure spending	1.59

Source: M. Zandi, "The Economic Impact of the American Recovery and Reinvestment Act," Moody's Economy.com, 2009

Table 9.2 presents estimates for the multiplier effects of different fiscal policy initiatives. (The multipliers listed here are smaller than those seen in earlier examples because of offsetting effects and leakages such as those discussed in Appendix A2.) Note that unemployment benefits, food stamps, aid to state governments (which help prevent layoffs), and infrastructure spending all have relatively large multiplier effects. All of these were featured in the response to the 2007 2009 recession, as well as in recent stimulus policies in 2020 and 2021. The smallest multiplier effects tend to be associated with tax cuts, especially those for wealthy individuals or corporations, such as those included in the 2017 tax cut package. Tax cuts in this case get less "bang for the buck" due to the generally smaller *mpc* exhibited by the beneficiaries of such policies.

3.4 Applying Fiscal Policy

We have now identified a number of different fiscal policy approaches that can be used by the government to respond to various economic conditions. We have also noted some of the differences in opinion among economists as to the effectiveness and appropriate use of fiscal policy. In future chapters, we examine the application of fiscal policies to specific problems, considering the impacts on both unemployment and inflation.

Before doing this, we need to add another very important aspect of the economy to our analysis: money, credit, and monetary policy. Monetary policy is a very important factor affecting, among other things, interest rates and inflation. We need to understand how money is created, how the money and interest rates are influenced by the central bank, and how this relates to other macroeconomic factors. This is the topic of Chapters 10 and 11.

After we have added an analysis of money and monetary policy, we will return to a consideration of the issues of unemployment and inflation, and appropriate policies to respond to them, in Chapter 12. We will then introduce the international economy in Chapter 13. In Chapter 14 we discuss the macroeconomics of economic inequality, and in Chapter 15 we focus on issues of debt and deficits.

Discussion Questions

1   Under what conditions would government spending tend to displace private investment spending? Under what conditions might it contribute to increasing private investment spending?

2   Looking at Table 9.2 on different multiplier effects, which kinds of government fiscal policy do you think are most effective? Which are least effective? What might be some implications for evaluation of the Obama stimulus program (Box 9.2), the Trump tax cuts (Box 9.3), or the Biden administration American Rescue Plan, Infrastructure Investment and Jobs Act, and Inflation Reduction Act?

REVIEW QUESTIONS

1. What is the impact of a change in government spending on aggregate expenditure and economic equilibrium?
2. What is the impact of a lump-sum change in taxes on aggregate expenditure and economic equilibrium? How does it differ from a change in government spending?
3. Give some examples of expansionary and contractionary fiscal policy.
4. How is the federal budget surplus or deficit defined? How has the federal budget position varied in recent years?
5. What is meant by an automatic stabilizer? Give some examples of economic institutions that function as automatic stabilizers.
6. What are some of the advantages and disadvantages of discretionary fiscal policy? Give some examples of the use of discretionary fiscal policy.
7. What is a cyclical deficit? What is a structural deficit? How are they different?
8. What is crowding out? How specifically does crowding out happen? Explain. What is crowding in?
9. What are some recent examples of the use of fiscal policy to respond to longer-term issues of infrastructure and social investment?

EXERCISES

1. Using the data in Table 9.1, determine the economic equilibrium for a government spending level of 60.
2. Using Table 9.1 and the formulas and numbers given in the text for the multiplier and tax multiplier, calculate the effect on equilibrium GDP of a government spending level of 100 combined with a tax level of 100. What does this imply about the impact of a balanced government budget on GDP, compared to government spending alone?
3. Go to the *Economic Report of the President* at https://www.whitehouse.gov/cea/economic-report-of-the-president/Consult the most recent *Report*'s table on "Gross Domestic Product." For the last year with final rather than preliminary figures, find the values of gross domestic product personal consumption expenditures, and gross private domestic investment. Now find the value for fixed investment. If we assume that all inventory changes are unintended, fixed investment is the same thing as what we call intended investment. You will note that the column on the right titled "Change in Private Inventories" is equal to the difference between total and fixed investment (just as we have noted that total investment equals intended investment plus the change in inventories). Calculate personal consumption expenditures (C) and intended investment (I_1) as percentages of gross domestic product (Y). Calculate a simple measure of aggregate expenditure ($C + I_1$) without government spending.
4. Which of the following are examples of automatic stabilizers, and which are examples of discretionary policy? Could some be both? Explain.
   a) Tax revenues rise during an economic expansion
   b) Personal tax rates are reduced
   c) Government spending on highways is increased
   d) Farm support payments increase
   e) Unemployment payments rise during a recession
5. Match each concept in Column A with a definition or example in Column B.

Column A	Column B
a. Tax multiplier	Reduction in income tax rates
b. Disposable income	Unemployment compensation

373

c. Expansionary fiscal policy	$Y - T + TR$
d. Contractionary fiscal policy	$G + TR$
e. Government outlays	Reduction in government spending
f. Automatic stabilizer	Intended investment
g. Injection into the circular flow	$-(mult)\,(mpc)$

APPENDIX: MORE ALGEBRAIC APPROACHES TO THE MULTIPLIER

A1 AN ALGEBRAIC APPROACH TO THE MULTIPLIER, WITH A LUMP-SUM TAX

A lump-sum tax is a tax that is simply levied on an economy as a flat amount. This amount does not change with the level of income. Suppose that a lump-sum tax is levied in an economy with a government (but no foreign sector). Consumption in this economy is

$$C = \bar{C} + mpc\, Y_d$$

(the consumption function from Chapter 8, but using after-tax or disposable income in the formula). Since disposable income is

$$Y_d = Y - \bar{T} + TR$$

we can write the consumption function as:

$$C = \bar{C} + mpc(Y - \bar{T} + TR)$$

Thus, aggregate expenditure in this economy can be expressed as:

$$AE = C + I_I + G = \bar{C} + mpc\left(Y - \bar{T} + TR\right) + I_I + G$$
$$= (\bar{C} - mpc\,\bar{T} + mpc\,TR + I_I + G) + mpc\,Y$$

The last rearrangement shows that the AE curve has an intercept equal to the term in parentheses and a slope equal to the marginal propensity to consume. Changes in any of the variables in parentheses, by changing the intercept, shift the curve upward or downward in a parallel manner.

By substituting this into the equation for the equilibrium condition, $Y = AE$, we can derive an expression for equilibrium income in terms of all the other variables in the model:

$$Y = (\bar{C} - mpc\,\bar{T} + mpc\,TR + I_I + G) + mpc\,Y$$

$$Y - mpc\,Y = \bar{C} - mpc\,\bar{T} + mpc\,TR + I_I + G$$

$$(1-mpc)Y = \bar{C} - mpc\,\bar{T} + mpc\,TR + I_I$$
$$+G\,(\bar{C} - mpc\ \bar{T} + mpc\,TR + I_I + G)$$

If autonomous consumption, intended investment, or government spending change, these each increase equilibrium income by *mult* = $1/(1 - mpc)$ times the amount of the original change. If the level of lump-sum taxes or transfers changes, these change Y by either negative or positive *(mult)(mpc)* times the amount of the original change.

To see this explicitly, consider the changes that would come about in Y if there were a change in the level of the lump sum tax from T_0 to a new level, T_1, if everything else stays the same. We can solve for the change in Y by subtracting the old equation from the new one:

$$Y = \frac{1}{1 - mpc}(\bar{C} - mpc\,\bar{T} + mpc\,TR + I_I + G)$$

$$\left[Y_0 = \frac{1}{1 - mpc}\bar{C} - mpc\,\bar{T}_0 + mpc\,TR + I_I + G) \right]$$

$$Y - Y_0 =$$
$$\frac{1}{1 - mpc}\left(\bar{C} - \bar{C} + I_I - I_I + G - G - mpc\,\bar{T}_1 + mpc\,\bar{T}_0 + mpc\,TR - mpc\,TR\right)$$

But $\bar{C}$, I_1, G, TR (and the *mpc*) are all unchanged, so most of the subtractions in parentheses come out to be 0. We are left with (taking the negative sign out in front):

$$Y - Y_0 = \frac{1}{1 - mpc}mpc\left(\bar{T}_1 - \bar{T}_0\right)$$

or

$$\Delta Y = -(mult)(mpc)\Delta\bar{T}$$

As explained in the text, the multiplier for a change in taxes is smaller than the multiplier for a change in government spending, because taxation affects aggregate expenditure only to the extent that people *spend* their tax cut or pay their increased taxes by reducing *consumption.* Because people may also *save* part of their tax cut or pay part of their increased taxes out of their *savings,* not all the changes in taxes will carry over to changes in aggregate expenditure. The tax multiplier has a negative sign, since a *decrease* in taxes *increases* consumption, aggregate expenditure, and income, while a tax increase decreases them.

A2 AN ALGEBRAIC APPROACH TO THE MULTIPLIER, WITH A PROPORTIONAL TAX

With a proportional tax, total tax revenues are not set at a fixed level of revenues, as was the case with a lump sum tax but, rather, are a fixed *proportion* of total income. That is, $T = tY$ where t is the tax rate. The equation for AE becomes

$$
\begin{aligned}
AE &= \bar{C} + mpc\left(Y - tY + TR\right) + I_I + G \\
&= \left(\bar{C} + mpc\ TR + I_I + G\right) + mpc\left(Y - tY\right) \\
&= \left(\bar{C} + mpc\ TR + I_I + G\right) + mpc\left(1 - t\right)Y
\end{aligned}
$$

With the addition of proportional taxes, the AE curve now has a new slope:

$mpc(1 - t)$. Because t is a fraction greater than 0 but less than 1, this slope is generally flatter than the slope we have worked with before. A *cut* in the tax rate rotates the curve *up*ward, as shown in Figure 9.7.

Substituting in the equilibrium condition, $Y = AE$, and solving yields:

$$
Y = \left(\bar{C} + mpc\ TR + I_I + G\right) + mpc\left(1 - t\right)Y
$$

$$
Y - mpc\left(1 = t\right)Y = \bar{C} + mpc\ TR + I_I + G
$$

$$
\left(1 - mpc\left(1 - t\right)\right)Y = \bar{C} + mpc\ TR + I_I + G
$$

$$
Y = \left[\frac{1}{1 - mpc\left(1 - t\right)}\right]\left(\bar{C} + mpcTR + I_I + G\right)
$$

The term in brackets is a new multiplier, for the case of a proportional tax. It is smaller than the basic (no proportional taxation) multiplier, reflecting the fact that now any change in spending has smaller feedback effects through consumption. (Some of the change in income "leaks" into taxes.) For example, if $mpc = 0.8$ and $t = 0.2$, then the new multiplier is $1/(1 - 0.64)$, or approximately 2.8, compared to the simple model multiplier $1/(1 - 0.8)$, which is 5. Changes in autonomous consumption or investment (or government spending or transfers) now have less of an effect on equilibrium income—the "automatic stabilizer" effect mentioned in the text.

Is there a multiplier for the tax rate, t? That is, could we derive from the model a formula for how much equilibrium income should change with a change in the rate (rather than level) of taxes? For example, if the tax rate were to decrease from 0.2 to 0.15, could we calculate the size of the change from Y_0 to Y_1 illustrated in Figure 9.7? Yes, but deriving a general formula for a multiplier relating the change in Y to the change

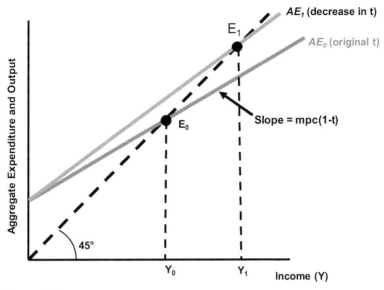

Figure 9.7 *A Reduction in the Proportional Tax Rate*

in the tax rate requires the use of calculus, which we will not pursue here. (If you are familiar with calculus, you can use the last formula above to calculate the change in Y resulting from a change in *t*.)

NOTES

1   Kose and Sugawara, 2020.
2   Francis, 2012
3   BEA, 2017.
4   BEA, 2021.
5   Blinder and Zandi, 2010.

REFERENCES

Bernstein, Jared. 2020. "The Trump Tax Cuts in Action: Socialism for the Rich." *Washington Post,* January 2.

Blinder, Alan S. and Mark Zandi. 2010. "How the Great Recession Was Brought to an End." https://www.economy.com/mark-zandi/documents/End-of-Great-Recession.pdf

Clemente, Frank. 2020. "Eight Ways the Trump-GOP Tax Cuts Have Made the Rich Richer While Failing Working Families." https://inequality.org/research/trump-tax-cuts-inequality/

Committee for a Responsible Federal Budget. 2022. "What's in the Inflation Reduction Act?" July 18. https://www.crfb.org/blogs/whats-inflation-reduction-act

Congressional Budget Office (CBO). February 2012. *Estimated Impact of the American Recovery and Reinvestment Act on Employment and Output from October 2012 through December 2012.* Washington, D.C.: Congressional Budget Office.

Congressional Budget Office (CBO). 2021. Summary of Cost Estimate for H.R. 5376, the Build Back Better Act." https://www.cbo.gov/publication/57627

Francis, Norton. 2012. "State and Local Budget Cuts Hurt the Recovery." *Christian Science Monitor*, VOX, July 30.

Kose, M. Ayhan, and Naotaka Sugawara. 2020. "Understanding the Depth of the 2020 Global Recession in 5 Charts." *World Bank Blogs,* June 15.

Lobosco, Katie. 2021. "Here's How Long It May Take Biden's Infrastructure Package to Jolt the Economy." *CNN*, November 9.

Marr, Chuck, Brendan Duke, and Chye-Ching Huang. 2018. "New Tax Law is Fundamentally Flawed and Will Require Restructuring." *Center on Budget and Policy Priorities,* August 14.

Montgomery, Lori. 2012. "Congressional Budget Office Defends Stimulus." *Washington Post*, June 6.

Moss, Wes, Robert C. Kelly, and Ariana Chavez. 2021. "How Has the Tax Cuts and Jobs Act Affected the US Economy?" *The Balance*, February 2022.

Penn Wharton. 2022. "Inflation Reduction Act: Estimates of Budgetary and Macroeconomic Effects." *University of Pennsylvania*, August 2. https://budgetmodel.wharton.upenn.edu/issues/2022/8/12/senate-passed-inflation-reduction-act

Robertson, Lori. 2021. "Senators Claim Infrastructure Bill Is 'Paid For'; Experts Disagree." *FactCheck.org.*, August 5.

U.S. Bureau of Economic Analysis (BEA). 2017. "Gross Domestic Product: Third Quarter 2017."

U.S. Bureau of Economic Analysis (BEA). 2021. "Gross Domestic Product, Third Quarter 2021."

Chapter 10

Money, Banking, and Finance

Everyone would like to have more money, right? Well, maybe not. In 2004 it was very easy to be a millionaire in Turkey—many times over. A million Turkish lira were worth about US$0.75. A 20 million lira bill was worth about US$15. People routinely just put their thumb over the last six digits when looking at a value expressed in liras. *Guinness World Records* named the Turkish lira the world's least valuable currency. But you could have lots of it! This chapter will explore what gives money its value—and how it can lose it.

1 WHY MONEY?

So far, this book has said very little about money. This is in line with early views on money, according to which money was seen as a mere facilitator in the process of employing scarce resources—including labor—in the production of goods and services that contribute to economic well-being. But in modern economies, money is more than a mere facilitator. Money, and the banking system by which money is made available to the public, are crucial to the effective functioning of the economy. This is especially the case as the financial sector gains in relative importance. The Great Recession of 2007–2009 made clear that if there are problems in the banking system and the financial markets, deep and long-lasting recession can result. And the more recent pandemic recession brought a renewed focus on the role of monetary and financial systems in recession and recovery.

If companies would like to invest, but cannot obtain the money necessary to do so, they often have to cancel their investment plans. The same applies to families who want to build or buy a home. Without money, such plans cannot be realized. And if business and residential investment decline, the economy is likely to go into recession. Hence, money and finance as well as interest rates, which represent a price for borrowing money, are clearly important macroeconomic issues.

How does the existence or availability of money impact economic behavior and the economy at large? Before we get into the details about the functions of money in a sophisticated contemporary economy, let's

DOI: 10.4324/9781003251521-14

picture a few simpler—and dramatically different—scenarios, drawn from real-world situations and events, that inform how economists have come to think about money and the macroeconomy.

1.1 Money and Aggregate Expenditure

Before discussing a specific definition of money, let's look at some ways that money works in the economy. In a modern economy, "money" does not just refer to cash, but also to bank accounts and various electronic forms of payment.

Let's start with the case of an economy in which inflation is low to moderate. Suppose, further, that this economy has a banking system that is sophisticated and in reasonably good shape. You are a businessperson who has a great idea about how to expand your business. Or, in your role as a household member, you are interested in buying a home for your family. But you do not have the cash. You go to a bank and ask for a loan. The bank will evaluate your creditworthiness, see whether lending you the requested amount is sensible within its business strategy and regulatory requirements, and then either deny you the loan or offer it to you on particular terms. If you and the bank come to an agreement, you obtain the loan and go out and spend the money. If you are denied the loan, or if you think the terms are too unfavorable, you will probably forgo expansion of your business or purchase of the house.

Government policy, implemented by the country's central bank, can influence the volume and terms of loans made by banks, and as a result, can also influence the level of money and spending in the economy. We have already seen in Chapters 8 and 9 how the level of spending (or aggregate expenditure) in an economy is related to levels of employment and output. Policy that affects the behavior of banks (referred to as **monetary policy**), can therefore also be a significant factor in achieving the goals of macroeconomic stabilization and low unemployment.

---

monetary policy: the use of policy tools controlled by a nation's central bank, to influence interest rates, available credit, and the money supply.

But not all economies enjoy low inflation rates and stable banking systems. Our next two cases illustrate alternative scenarios in which serious monetary problems affect the economy.

1.2 "Running the Printing Press"

Consider a country with a very simple government and banking system. The country's government is housed in a single building and pays its employees and its bills in cash. In the basement of the building is a printing press that prints paper money. The government finds it very difficult to collect enough taxes to pay its operating expenses, so it just runs the printing press every time an employee needs to be paid or a bill comes due.

How would such behavior affect the economy? If the national economy were very large and growing in relation to the volume of government expenditures, the fresh bills might just be absorbed into circulation without much impact. But if the economy were stagnant and government expenditures were significant relative to national output, the result would be inflation caused by "too much money chasing too few goods." And if more and more money were put into circulation, prices would rise at an increasingly rapid rate.

If this went on for long, a situation known as hyperinflation, often defined as any annual inflation rate higher than 100 percent, could result (see Box 10.1). Germany after World War I, Hungary after World War II, Bolivia in the mid-1980s, Argentina during various periods, Ukraine in the early 1990s, Zimbabwe in 2008–2009, and Venezuela in 2016–2018, all experienced notable hyperinflations.

In Germany in the 1920s, for example, the economy was in tatters after the war and the government found it impossible to collect sufficient tax revenue to support its operations, to say nothing of paying the reparations dictated by the Treaty of Versailles. So Germany effectively resorted to running the printing presses. Inflation reached a high of 41

BOX 10.1 EXPERIENCES OF HYPERINFLATION

During the period of German hyperinflation in the 1920s, a story was told of someone taking stacks of Deutsche marks (the German currency at the time) to town in a wheelbarrow in order to make a modest purchase, and—after leaving it for a moment—returning to find the wheelbarrow stolen but the bills left stacked on the ground. Other stories told of people in a bar ordering their beers two at a time because the time it took for the price of beer to rise was less than it would take for the beer to get warm.

After the fall of the Soviet Union, in the 1990s, Russia suffered from severe inflation. Many people who had saved money in cash found that it had become nearly valueless. A Russian colleague told one of the authors of this text how his mother had thought, at the beginning of the 1990s, that she had enough money saved to take care of her in old age. She watched the value of her stash of bills go down and down until finally, in desperation, rather than watch it disappear, she took it to the store and bought a bag of sugar.

And hyperinflation is not a thing of the past. Venezuela has been trying to emerge from a recent episode, with its 686 percent inflation in 2021, an improvement over 2020, when domestic prices increased by almost 3,000 percent.[1] Meanwhile, in Turkey, the inflation rate rose from 20 percent in November 2021 to over 50 percent by early 2022, while its central bank stubbornly continued to cut its main interest rate amid soaring prices, which could be like throwing fuel on the fire. By mid-2022, the lira had lost about two thirds of its value relative to 2020, raising memories of the Turkish hyperinflation of the early 2000's.[2]

percent—per *day!* In 1920, a German postage stamp cost 4 marks; in 1923 the same stamp cost *50 billion* marks.

In such a situation, it becomes very difficult to keep a modern economy going. People tend to resort to **barter**—exchanging goods, services, or assets directly for other goods, services, or assets—to try to avoid having to deal with a rapidly deteriorating currency. It becomes impossible to think about making a deposit at a bank or to work out reasonable terms for a loan, and so normal patterns of saving and lending are disrupted. If they can, people may try to acquire—or at least keep their accounts in—a "hard," stable currency issued by a foreign country. Hyperinflation is obviously a very damaging economic situation; production tends to decline, and unemployment is increased by the chaos that it causes.

---

barter: exchange of goods, services, or assets directly for other goods, services, or assets, without the use of money

---

Hyperinflation usually ends when the nearly valueless currency is abandoned, and people exchange very large denominations of the old currency for small denominations of a new currency. If the new currency is accompanied by a credible government promise to stop "running the printing press," the episode of hyperinflation draws to a close. This is what happened after the hyperinflation of the early 2000s in Turkey; the old lira was abandoned in favor of a new currency that removed six zeros. In 2017, the new Turkish lira had a value of about US$0.26, but by 2022 this had fallen to US $0.06 as hyperinflation again threatened.

Even if price increases do not reach hyperinflation levels, rapid inflation tends to be disruptive to an economy. It can, over time, wipe out the value of people's savings, and it hurts people who are on fixed incomes (such as non-indexed pensions). It redistributes wealth from creditors to debtors, since people now repay debts in money that is worth less than the money that they originally borrowed. Inflation also creates "menu costs"—literally, the cost of time and effort made to update printed menus and other sorts of price lists. Rising or variable inflation rates create a great deal of uncertainty, which can make it very difficult for households and businesses to make sensible plans regarding savings, retirement, investment, and so on. For these reasons, the stabilization of a country's price level is among the important goals of macroeconomic policy.

1.3 Deflation and Financial Crises

Now consider an economy in the opposite situation, in which insufficient money is entering the system. In this case, people are not spending—either because they simply want to hold on to their money, or because banks do not want to lend them the money that they need. Such a case, if sustained, can result in a general *fall* in prices—also known as **deflation**. At first glance, deflation might appear to be a good thing. Wouldn't people benefit from lower prices? While deflation does indeed make people's savings *more* valuable and *helps* people who are on fixed incomes, it is highly disruptive to the broader economy.

With deflation, wealth is redistributed from debtors to creditors. You borrow "cheap" money, but later have to pay it back with money that is "expensive." This can force consumers and businesses into bankruptcy. Deflation also creates menu costs as well as uncertainty. When people come to expect deflation, it may also cause them to cut back on spending. Why buy a big item such as a car or computer now, if you believe you will be able to buy the same item for less next year?

---

deflation: when the aggregate price level falls

Deflation is often touched off by a financial crisis in which many people lose access to loans, and possibly even access to their own deposits at banks. If you cannot withdraw money from your account at a bank, and you cannot get a loan, then you cannot pay for things. If many people are in this situation, the economy grinds to a halt—or at least slows down considerably. Because less money is spent, prices fall. Once prices start to fall, business failures follow. With debts fixed in nominal currency terms (e.g., in dollars or euros), falling prices mean an increasing debt burden. Business failures in turn lead to loan defaults and more banking failures, not to mention substantial layoffs.

The Great Depression was accompanied in the United States by just such a collapse in the banking system. The "bank runs" or "banking panics" of 1930–1933, in which people rushed to try to withdraw their deposits all at once, caused many banks to fail. Because deposit insurance did not yet exist, people's accounts at those banks were wiped out. The price level dropped 25 percent in just a few years. Falling prices bankrupted businesses and farmers, thus making conditions even worse.

But deflation is also not merely "ancient history." Japan has experienced protracted deflation that was touched off by a financial crisis in late 1989 after a speculative bubble in real estate and stocks came to a sudden end. Japanese banks had, it turned out, racked up huge amounts of bad loans—loans on which they would never be able to collect. Some banks were ordered to shut down, while others teetered. People became justifiably leery of spending, with the future so uncertain. Because banks had to write down their capital on account of losses on their loan portfolios, they were unable to lend as much. And because spending was falling, the Japanese economy slid into a long-term recession. As

383

BOX 10.2 THE DEFLATION TRAP IN JAPAN

Inflation was in the news in 2022 in the United States and a number of other countries, as a result of supply chain disruptions during the "reopening" following widespread coronavirus lockdowns and restrictions. But Japan continued to face the opposite problem. Consumers pay less over time for many goods and have been doing so for decades. While in the United States average prices surged in 2021–2022, prices in Japan dipped 0.1 percent over the same period.

As Japan continues to learn, low inflation—and worse, deflation—can become an enduring hazard. That experience may carry a warning for the United States and other economies.

"Most economists, me included, are pretty confident that the Fed knows how to bring inflation down, [but] it's much less clear, partly because of Japan's experience, that we're very good at bringing inflation up," said Joshua Hausman, an associate professor of public policy and economics at the University of Michigan.

Consumers may often look favorably upon falling prices. But economists know that persistent deflation is a major problem. A small amount of inflation increases profits and wages, and reduces debt burdens, which are generally positive for the economy. Deflation, in contrast, postpones consumer spending, hurts business profits, and fosters a sometimes-self-fulfilling economic pessimism.

Prior to about 2008, economists tended to view Japan's experience not as a warning to the world, but as an anomaly produced by bad policy choices and cultural quirks. But this view began to change with the financial crisis of 2008 when inflation rates around the world plummeted and many central banks reduced interest rates and adopted "easy money" policies. Interest rates have since mostly remained at historical lows. While inflation finally reared its head as of early 2022, concern remained that the United States and other countries could eventually follow Japan into long-term stagnation.[3]

---

can be seen from Box 10.2, the problem has hardly, if at all, improved in the ensuing three decades.

Many experts feared a similar deflation in the United States both after the 2007–2008 financial crisis, and again following the global pandemic recession. But in both cases, measures aimed at providing cheaper credit pumped more money into the system, with the result that a severe collapse in economic activity was averted. The feared deflation did not materialize. Unemployment rates fell, slowly after the Great Recession, and rapidly following the pandemic recession. The official unemployment rate, which peaked at over 14 percent early in the pandemic, had dropped below 4 percent by December 2021. Europe came close to deflation in the aftermath of the Great Recession but managed to avoid it through changing central banking policies to inject more money into the system.

Deflation can be very damaging when looked at from the perspective of the real potential productivity of an economy. Businesses might have great ideas for expansion, and people might want to work, earn money, and make purchases, but all are held back by a falling price level. With the prospect of debt becoming harder to service over time, companies are far less inclined to borrow. Hence, investment is postponed or even canceled, with rising unemployment a direct consequence. For these reasons, avoiding deflation is a major concern for most governments.

The stability of the monetary system is, thus, a fundamentally important policy goal—to prevent both rapid inflation *and* deflation. Success in achieving price stability is closely related to the goal of raising living standards.

Discussion Questions

1. Which of the three conditions just described—low inflation, high inflation, or deflation best characterizes the U.S. economy right now? Do you know of any country currently in one of the other conditions?
2. Unemployment and inflation are usually considered the "bads" that can come with business cycles. Compare the costs to society of unemployment to the costs to society of inflation.

2 WHAT IS MONEY?

You have no doubt that the bills and coins you have in your wallet are "money." And you would probably also say that you have "money" in your bank account, that you can spend using a debit card or other electronic payment system. Economists would agree with you about that. But the cash in your pocket or the balance in your bank account only represent specific *forms* of money. Economists use the term "money" in a much broader sense. Money, to an economist, is formally defined as something that plays three specific roles in an economy, which we will define in the next section. It is not always entirely clear that money is an entity or thing in the way a saleable commodity might be. In fact, the line between money and debt can sometimes be a bit blurry and, as we will see, the two can sometimes even be thought of interchangeably.

2.1 The Roles of Money

Money is a special kind of financial asset (a form of financial capital) that has three important functions.

First, it is a *medium of exchange*. When you sell something, you accept money in return. When you buy something, you hand over money to obtain the good or service that you want. Without a functional medium of exchange, an economy would have to operate as a barter system, as mentioned in the earlier example of German hyperinflation. You would have to trade tangible objects or services directly in order to get other goods or services in exchange. This could be quite inconvenient— there would have to be what is called a "double coincidence of wants." For example, if you want pizza and can offer Web design services, you would need to hunt around for pizza-makers in need of Web design.

385

Such merchants may or may not exist, but even if they did, you would certainly have to spend some considerable time finding them. With money, on the other hand, you can sell your services to anyone who wants them and use the money you receive to buy pizza from anyone who supplies it.

Second, money is also a *store of value*. That means that, even if you hold onto it for a while, it will still be good for transactions when you are ready to use it. This is obviously a necessary property since the pizza-makers are unlikely to accept your money in exchange unless they know that, a month from now, their landlord will also accept the same money when they pay their rent. In serving as a store of value, money serves as a way of holding wealth—like any other form of financial or real capital that is held because it is worth something. The thing that makes money distinct from other assets is its **liquidity**, that is, the ease with which it can be used in exchange. Money is highly liquid—you can take it to the store and use it immediately. If you own a car, shares in a business, or a valuable piece of jewelry, these are also ways of storing your wealth, but they are not liquid. In most cases, you must convert the value stored in them to money before you can buy something else.

---

liquidity: the ease of use of an asset as a medium of exchange

---

The third role of money is that it is a *unit of account*. The price of a pizza can be expressed in monetary units that, presumably, reflect the pizza's "value." So, in this example money is a unit of account for the pizzeria calculating its revenue and profit and for the household calculating the expenditure portion of its monthly budget. Yet even things that are not actually being bought and sold are often assigned money values. When a firm estimates the value of unsold inventories in its warehouses in order to calculate its profits or losses, for example, or a town assesses the dollar value of a house even though there are no plans for it to be sold, they are using money as a unit of account.

Some ways in which we commonly use the term "money" differ from how economists use it. For example, we might say that someone "makes a lot of money" because they have a high annual *income*. Income, how-ever, is a *flow* variable, measured over a period of time (as described in Chapter 1). Money is a *stock* variable—a particular kind of asset. A person who makes a lot of income over a year may or may not acquire a large stock of money. If the income is quickly spent on goods and ser-vices, the person may have a high *income* (over the year) but accumulate little *money* (measured at a point in time).

We may also say that someone "has a lot of money" if they have accumulated a lot of *wealth*. But this is also not technically correct. A wealthy person may hold assets in the form of corporate shares, real estate, or Renaissance paintings, rather than as spendable, liquid money. Some middle-class families are sometimes described as "house rich, but cash poor" exactly for this reason. If they hold a high proportion of their assets as home equity, they may end up with very little in the way of funds that they can actually spend—that is, *money.*

Liquidity issues aside, holding money (a particular financial asset) is not the same as holding a tangible asset with useful physical properties. Money is thus not the same thing as wealth or income (although the concepts can overlap). This is an important distinction to keep in mind to better understand the material that follows.

2.2 Types of Money

Historical accounts about the origins of money differ. While economists often tell a story in which money was introduced to eliminate the need for barter, the truth appears to be a bit more complicated. First, as noted earlier, barter exists to this day, and not only in extreme situations like those of hyperinflation. In vibrant, local communities, for example, friends or neighbors might exchange dog-walking services for tutoring or guitar lessons. Second, it is far from clear that barter was *ever* the principal means of exchanging goods. Indeed, money may have been in existence for even longer than markets themselves, in the form of debits and credits. The use of **credit money** may even predate the use of gold or other metals as money and has over the course of history seen periods where it was the dominant form of money (see Box 10.3).

---

credit money: money that is transferable to another through credit and debit book-keeping entries

---

Over significant periods in history, at least in some major geographical areas, gold and other forms of metal served as important forms of money. Gold is an example of **commodity money**, which is money made up of something that is used in the exchange of goods and services, giving it what economists call **exchange value**, but also contains an **intrinsic** value (value based on its own properties). While coins made of gold or silver are probably the most familiar example, decorative beads, shells, fishhooks, and cattle have also served the purpose in some cultures. In prisons and prisoner of war camps, even cigarettes sometimes developed into a medium of exchange. "Prices" for chocolate or other goods and services were quoted in terms of the numbers of cigarettes required in exchange. Cigarettes thus had exchange value in this system even to non-smokers, for whom they had no intrinsic value.

BOX 10.3 MONEY AS A FORM OF DEBT

In his book, *Debt: The First 5,000 Years,* anthropologist David Graeber makes the claim that the human system of credit is the original means of "quantifying" (by specifying a debt amount) what is fundamentally *qualitative*: one's obligation to someone else. According to Graeber, debt is "an agreement between equals to no longer be equal." In other words, as commerce and markets grew to play a more important role in human interactions, the qualitative norm of reciprocity came to be replaced by the "ruthlessness" of hard numbers.

The gradual change is consistent with the parallel development of economic systems where those who were in debt and unable to pay ended up at the mercy of their creditors. Debt, as well as the asymmetric power relations that it produced, has thus a hand in the development of class-based systems like slavery, feudalism, the caste system, as well as modern capitalism. By this account, debt relations from millennia past have shaped much of human history.

Graeber is critical of the "pure exchange" narrative claiming that money was introduced to benefit all people, by eliminating the need to barter. He believes it to be a convenient myth to conceal its role in the construction of a highly unequal global economic order. Indeed, historians and anthropologists have documented the important role that debt has played in class structures and power. The close relationship between debt and money established over centuries continues in today's complex economic systems.[4]

---

commodity money: a good used as money that is also valuable in itself
exchange value: value that corresponds to the value of goods or services for which the item can be exchanged
intrinsic value: value related to the tangible or physical properties of the object

---

To be used as money, a commodity must be *generally acceptable, standardized, durable, portable, scarce,* and, preferably, easily *divisible.* Standardization is important so that disputes do not arise about the quality and value of the money. Coins stamped by the government are a popular kind of money because the stamp is a sign that they are of equal weight and purity of mineral content. Gold and silver have historically been popular because coins made from them are durable. The scarcity of gold and silver was also an important factor. Coins made of, say, wood, in an area with many forests, would rapidly lose value as everyone could just make their own. Divisibility is also important. Heavy gold ingots might be used to buy expensive real estate but are not very useful for buying pasta for dinner. Smaller coins, and coins made of less valuable minerals, were historically minted to provide a medium of exchange for smaller purchases.

Gold and silver coins, while fairly portable, can still be inconvenient to carry around in large quantities. Individual banks, state governments, and national governments have at various times issued paper monies that represent claims on actual commodities, usually gold or silver. In a sense, this is a variation on the system of credit money, in which the debt issuer is the government itself. It would not be incorrect to think of the paper money as an "I.O.U."* issued by the government to the holder of the note. For many years, starting in the late 1880s, government-issued silver certificates were the main form of domestic paper money in the United States. International transactions were, for many years, based on gold reserves, in what came to be known as the **gold standard**. When people carried such a piece of paper, they could think of it as a certificate showing that they owned a bit of an ingot in Fort Knox.

---

gold standard: a monetary system in which the monetary unit is based on some fixed quantity of gold

---

Systems in which the value of paper notes is tied to commodities with intrinsic value such as gold and silver were, during their time, considered necessary for people to have faith in the exchange value of the notes and, by extension, for the economy to function smoothly. One problem with this system, however, was that fixing money to scarce gold or silver seriously limited the ability of the banking system to create money, something that at least some researchers blame for the economic turmoil of the past, such as the Great Depression. Why constraints on money creation might be a problem will become clearer in the next two chapters.

In the 1960s, due to an increase in the price of silver, the government eliminated silver certificates and replaced them with what you probably have in your pocket today. What is commonly called a "dollar bill" is, if you look at it, officially called a Federal Reserve note. It states that it is "legal tender for all debts, public and private," but it is not backed by silver or gold. The U.S. government also removed silver coins from circulation, replacing them with look-alike coins made from cheaper nickel-clad copper. Finally, in 1971, President Richard Nixon took the U.S. economy off the international gold standard, ushering in a new monetary era that dates to the present.

Did you ever stop and think about what is the basis for the value of the coins and dollar bills we use today? The basis for the value is—precisely and no more than—the expectation that the dollar bill will be acceptable in exchange. The currency and coins we use now are what are called **fiat money**. "Fiat" in Latin means "let it be done," and a legal authority does something "by fiat" when it just declares something to be so. *A dollar bill is money because the government declares it to be money.* In other words, its intrinsic value is no more than the value of the piece of paper of which it is made; but fiat money possesses exchange value,

---

* An IOU (short for "I owe you") is an acknowledgement of a debt by the borrower.

which is the value of the goods or services that such money can pay for in the market.

> **fiat money:** a medium of exchange that is used as money because a government says it has value, and that is accepted by the people using it

Fiat money is what some people call a "social construction"—something that works in society because of how people think and act toward it, not because of something it intrinsically "is." Fiat money works well as long as people are generally in agreement that it has value. As will become clear, it *is* a form of credit money in the sense that the branch of government that issues it is "indebted" to the individual holding it. But it is also very different from credit money in the traditional sense. In the past, credit money represented a direct claim that one had on someone else's assets. Nowadays, in contrast, it is far more impersonal; your "claim" is based on other people's willingness to accept fiat money as payment for something.

As many economies continue to modernize, even carrying around paper money is inconvenient for many purposes. A growing number of establishments today do not even accept cash. Nowadays, most of us carry debit cards, which instantly transfer money from one of our accounts to a merchant. There has also been a proliferation of "payment apps" like PayPal, Venmo, Zelle, Apple Pay, and Cash App. These convenient means of payment can be linked either to a bank account or an existing credit card.

Checks are today used with far less frequency than in the past. We are instead likely to make many of our transactions by other means, such as electronic funds transfers from our banks. Commercial banks can, in turn, create electronic "money" when granting you a loan (we will discuss how this is done in more detail in the next section). Once again, we are dealing with credit money—the only difference here being that a modern bank is now the "creditor." So, paper money and bank credit can both be considered as "money."

Are there other types of money? Many people think of Bitcoin or the numerous other cryptocurrencies as alternative forms of money. But for two important reasons, none of them officially count as money. First, "currencies" like Bitcoin are inadequate as a medium of exchange. While it is true that some merchants and firms accept them as payment, these establishments are still far too few to make cryptocurrencies reliable for market exchange. Their frequent association with the criminal underworld also causes most people to opt for the safety of fiat money. Second and more important, cryptocurrencies are very unreliable as a store of value. Bitcoin, for example, lost close to 50 percent of its value from November 2021 to January 2022. While it is true that since its inception its value has multiplied many times, this fact makes it more of a speculative asset (about which more later) than a stable representation of value.

A full understanding of what types of transactions can be said to involve "money" requires understanding how various assets differ in their liquidity—that is, the ease with which they can be used for exchange.

2.3 Measures of Money

Because different assets have different degrees of liquidity, it is difficult to draw distinct lines between which assets are actually money (economists sometimes use the term "pure money" to distinguish it from other categories), which are "near-money," and which are "not money." As a result, economists have devised various ways of defining and measuring the volume of money that is circulating in a given economy.

Despite their diminished popularity, coins and bills are obviously money. Coins in the United States are manufactured by the U.S. Mint in Philadelphia, Denver, San Francisco, and West Point, NY, while bills are created by the Bureau of Engraving and Printing in Washington, DC, and Fort Worth, Texas. When economists measure a country's "money supply," only currency—that is, coins and bills—that is *in circulation* is included. In other words, currency sitting in a vault at the Mint or at a bank is not officially "money." In December 2021, currency in circulation in the United States totaled about $2.13 trillion.

But the "money" residing in most bank accounts is also extremely liquid. Although checks are less frequently used than in the past, people can still pay for many things using paper checks. Because of this, economists have long considered checking accounts to be on par with currency as "pure money." Checking accounts are considered pure money regardless of whether they are used to write paper checks or for electronic fund transfers. Economists define the most basic measure of the amount of money in an economy at a given point in time, known as **M1**, as including not only the currency in circulation but also the value of checkable deposits.

M1: a measure of the money supply that includes currency, checkable deposits, and other liquid accounts like savings, shares, and money market accounts

---

In 2020 there were two important changes made in what constitutes M1. First, travelers' checks, previously a small portion of the total, have fallen into such disuse due to changes in technology that they effectively register as zero. Second, and more importantly, other forms of money non previously classified as M1—such as savings accounts, share accounts at credit unions, and money market accounts—count as part of M1 since May 2020. The reason for their inclusion is their increased liquidity. Until recently a withdrawal from, say, a savings account usually required a trip to an ATM or a visit to a bank counter. But with the recent proliferation of debit cards, it would make no sense to continue classifying such accounts separately. In December 2021, checkable deposits totaled about $4.88 trillion, and "other" liquid accounts amounted to about $13.66 trillion, so M1 (cash plus checks plus savings and other liquid accounts) totaled $20.67 trillion.

A broader measure of money called **M2** includes everything in M1, plus small certificates of deposit (CDs)—where "small" is defined as $100,000 or less—and retail money market funds (those owned by individuals and businesses). While more liquid than most other assets, these cannot be instantly converted to cash, so they fall into the "near-money" category. While the traditional system of classification used by monetary economists was slow to adapt to changes in banking technology, it finally has been updated. Consequently, while the difference between M1 and M2 was formerly three- or fourfold, with the movement of savings and other balances to M1 the difference between them is now very small. M2 totaled $21.77 trillion as of December 2021. When economists talk about "the money supply" they usually mean either M1 or M2.

M2: a measure of the money supply that includes all of M1 plus small certificates of deposit and retail money market funds

---

If we include large certificates of deposit and money market funds owned or managed by large financial institutions, we arrive at a more expansive measure of money called M3. Specialists even use other yet broader categories of money for purposes of classification. The principal reason for the different classifications is to allow for different points on the liquidity continuum that distinguish money from other kinds of assets (see Figure 10.1). While it is clear that currency is money and that real estate is not, the line separating money from non-money assets is not clearly defined.

Are credit cards money? What about payment apps? Debit cards? From the user's point of view, using a credit card often seems to be like using a debit card or cash from one's pocket. In economists' terms, however, one does *not* use "money" when paying with a credit card. When paying on credit, you are, technically speaking, taking out a temporary loan from the credit card company. Most economists would not count this loan as money, since it occurs outside the banking system. Only one day a month, when you send a check or electronic transfer to your

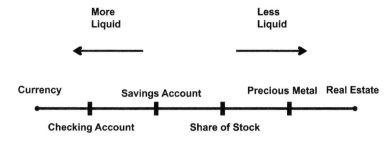

Figure 10.1 *The Liquidity Continuum*

credit card company from your checking account to pay your monthly bill (or at least the minimum payment), do you make a "money" transaction.[†] Apps like Paypal or Venmo are merely vehicles through which accounts can be settled through funds transfers – they are therefore not money but rather a way of transferring money. Likewise, debit cards are not themselves a form of money, but rather a mechanism to transfer liquid money from one account to another.

Discussion Questions

1. Why do dollar bills have value? Are they backed by any commodity such as gold or silver? Are there conditions under which they might lose their value?
2. What do you commonly use to make payments? Cash? Credit cards? Online payments? In which of these cases are you using "money"?

3 THE BANKING SYSTEM

It is easy to understand how the U.S. Mint and the Bureau of Engraving and Printing create currency, and how they could create more or less of it. But how does currency make its way into people's wallets? How are bank deposits such as checking accounts created? How can the volume of currency and deposits be influenced over time, as a matter of macroeconomic policy? To understand the answers to these questions, we need to know more about how a contemporary banking system works.

The central bank of the United States, known as the Federal Reserve (or "Fed," for short) determines how much currency should be produced and puts it into circulation. In addition, the actions of the Fed, together with the actions of commercial banks, create the economy's volume of checkable deposits. For much of Europe, now that many

---

† Here is where matters can become confusing. Even the credit card transaction *could* count as money from a credit money perspective since the new debt to your credit card company could be considered to be a transfer of "money." But this transfer occurs outside the banking system (whereas the use of a check or electronic transfer to pay the bill is within the banking system).

countries have agreed to use the euro as a common currency, the equivalent institution to the Fed is the European Central Bank (ECB). Most countries have combined systems of commercial and central banking. The workings of this combined system are discussed in this chapter, where we focus on commercial banks, and in greater detail in Chapter 11, where we examine the role of the central bank.

3.1 Commercial Banks‡

In the discussion of the market for loanable funds in Chapter 8, we assumed that some agents lend, and others borrow, but we paid no attention to how borrowers and lenders would find each other. An individual might go to a relative or friend for a loan. But when the borrower is operating in a more impersonal way—perhaps because the borrower is a business, not an individual, or does not have personal contacts with individuals who can make the needed loan—an intermediary is needed to put together would-be lenders with would-be borrowers.

A commercial bank is a type of institution called a **financial intermediary**. Individuals and organizations deposit funds with financial intermediaries for safekeeping, to provide the convenience of making bank transfers, paying with debit cards, writing checks, or earning interest. The financial intermediaries use the funds deposited with them to make loans to individuals and organizations that seek to borrow funds. Commercial banks as a special type of financial intermediary can also "create" money by extending loans to customers, based on deposits at the bank.

---

financial intermediary: an institution such as a bank, savings and loan association, or life insurance company that accepts funds from savers and makes loans to borrowers

---

A commercial bank is a for-profit business, meaning that it seeks to make earnings on its activities. It does this by charging interest on the loans it makes, and perhaps other fees on loans or deposits. One of its functions is to screen the parties seeking loans, in order to determine their creditworthiness. Lending is a risky business—not all loans made will be paid back in full. Demanding physical assets as collateral can alleviate some of the risks.

For example, mortgages and home-equity loans are collateralized by the value of a house; if the owner defaults on the loan, the bank may

---

‡ What we call a commercial bank is sometimes called a 'private bank.' Some previous editions of this text used this terminology. To avoid confusion, in this text edition we limit the use of the term "private bank" to a specific kind of bank that caters to wealthy customers, discussed in Section 3.2 of this chapter.

take possession of the house. Consumer loans are made on the basis of available income and job security of the applicant. Many educational loans are backed up by government guarantees. Other loans are made on the basis of an evaluation of, say, the strength of a business plan and a business's record in paying back past loans. Banks may charge different interest rates depending on the riskiness of a loan or deny a loan request outright.

To understand what happens in a banking system, we start with a commercial bank's simplified balance sheet, shown in Table 10.1. A balance sheet is a standard double-entry accounting representation of a commercial bank's assets and liabilities. It must "balance" in the sense that assets and liabilities must add up to the same amount. The right-hand side of a balance sheet, as shown in Table 10.1, lists an organization's liabilities. An **economic liability** is anything that one economic actor owes to another. The funds that you deposit in a bank are listed among the bank's liabilities because it has an obligation to repay these funds to you.

---

economic liability: anything that one economic actor owes to another

---

Except in the case of banking panics, depositors are not likely all to show up at the same time, demanding their funds in cash. Although the bank must keep some funds on hand to meet depositors' withdrawal needs, normally it can use most of the deposits that it holds to obtain earnings.

Assets of an organization are listed on the left-hand side of a balance sheet, as shown in Table 10.1. **Bank reserves**, shown as an asset, include vault cash that the bank keeps on hand to meet likely short-term calls, such as depositors' withdrawals. Reserves also include deposits that the commercial bank has made in an account at the Federal Reserve (discussed in Chapter 11). The bank owns these Federal Reserve deposits in the same way that bank customers "own" the deposits on their liability side. Banks are required to maintain a certain portion of their assets with the Federal Reserve. While such deposits had traditionally not earned interest, a provision of the Emergency Economic Stabilization

Table 10.1 *A Simplified Balance Sheet of a Commercial Bank*

Assets		Liabilities	
Loans	$70 million	Deposits	$100 million
Government bonds	$20 million		
Reserves	$10 million		

Act of 2008 (introduced in the wake of the financial crisis) stipulated that the Fed would thenceforth pay interest to banks for their reserve assets.

> **bank reserves:** funds not lent out or invested by a commercial bank but kept as vault cash or on deposit at the Federal Reserve

One relatively safe way for the bank to earn some interest on funds not held as reserves is to hold government bonds. Recall from Chapter 9 that the U.S. Treasury borrows from the public when it needs to finance a government deficit or refinance part of the debt. It does this by issuing government bonds, which give the buyer the right to specific payments in the future. Depending on the duration of the loan, these securities may be called "bills" (sometimes called Treasury bills, or "T-bills for short), "bonds," or "notes." We will use the term "government bonds" to represent any type of federal government security.

Very active markets exist for trading federal bonds, and a particular bond may change hands many times before it is paid off. Banks tend to keep some of their assets—about one-quarter, on average—in government bonds, because they are among the safest of investments and they earn interest. They are also relatively liquid. If it looks as if depositors will want more cashback than a bank has in its vault, the commercial bank can quickly sell some of its government bonds on the open bond market.

The major asset of a commercial bank—and the main way that it makes its earnings—is its portfolio of loans other than government bonds: funds that are owed to the bank by businesses, households, non-profits, or non-federal levels of government. Unlike T-bills, which can be liquidated quickly, if necessary, some of these may be business loans, home mortgages, or consumer loans that will not be repaid for years.

Since such assets are generally far less liquid than vault cash or T-bills, in difficult times it could be problematic if banks own too many of them. The health of a commercial banking system depends on having depositors who are confident about the safety of the funds that they have entrusted to the banking system and are not trying to withdraw their funds more rapidly than such loans are repaid. If confidence in the banks diminished, and many customers wanted to withdraw their money, some banks might find themselves with insufficient liquidity (i.e., with too many of their assets in long-term loans) to service all requests, further undermining confidence in the system.

3.2 Bank Types

The banks with which most people are familiar are known as commercial banks, which perform the functions that we have already described:

Table 10.2 *Bank Types*

	Chief Functions
Commercial or Retail	Safekeeping of money, checking accounts, loans to individuals and businesses
Savings & Loan	Similar to retail bank but specializing in loans, particularly mortgages
Credit union	Same as a retail bank, but cooperatively owned by customers
Private	Caters almost exclusively to high-net-worth individuals; functions extend beyond traditional banking into variety of financial services
Investment	No traditional banking functions; involved in underwriting and issuing securities, assistance with company mergers and acquisitions, market making, and general advice to corporations
Central	Overseeing the monetary and interest rate stability of the national economy by directly influencing the money supply

keeping money in secure deposits, providing check writing services and clearing checks, and extending loans. Commercial banks are also sometimes known as retail banks (Table 10.2). Savings and loan banks are like commercial banks but specialize in the provision of home loans to their customers. Credit unions are also similar to commercial banks, except that instead of being privately owned they are collectively owned by their customers.

Private banks are exclusive, catering to high-net-worth individuals and companies. Their functions range widely from traditional banking to many forms of investment, some of which are moderate to high risk. Investment banks mostly deal with companies instead of individuals and do not offer any traditional banking services. In other words, their principal function is to make asset values grow. Usually, this will entail preparing a diverse portfolio of investments—e.g., in growth stocks, corporate bonds, commodities, etc.—that balances moderate to high investment risk with the goal of a considerably higher annual return, on average, than most retail customers obtain.

Central banks are entirely different institutions. They exist to regulate the banking system and ensure monetary and interest rate stability in the economy. Chapter 11 deals specifically with the U.S. central bank, the Federal Reserve.

The functions of banks are subject to government regulation. The Banking Act of 1933, introduced in the depths of the Great Depression, put in place a number of changes in banking law designed to ensure greater security and stability and, most notably, to prevent panics or runs on banks. An important component was the Glass-Steagall Act, which required that traditional banking functions be strictly separated from the financial and investment activities of private banks and investment banks. While the most common way in which a bank was able to make money was simply to charge higher interest rates to lenders than the rate given to depositors, private banks and investment banks could engage in riskier types of investments and often enjoy much higher returns on their money. The purpose of the Glass-Steagall Act was to protect bank customers from excessively risky investment activities by their banks that might jeopardize the value of their savings accounts.

In 1999, with the passage of the Gramm-Leach-Bliley Act, major provisions of Glass-Steagall were overturned, eliminating the separation between traditional and investment banking. Yet even in the years preceding this Act, many were saying that the Glass-Steagall Act survived in name only. In the late 1980s, many savings and loan banks (S&Ls) went bankrupt because they had invested too many of their assets in precisely the dubious and risky real estate ventures that Glass-Steagall was designed to prevent. Savings and loans had been suffering for many years because higher interest rates in the late 1970s made many customers averse to taking out loans, and the growth of money market accounts gave depositors an attractive alternative to the S&Ls. In response, the government relaxed regulations on their activity, allowing them to invest in "higher return" areas but without adequately overseeing where the money was going.

The S&L crisis would be the first notable instance since the Great Depression of the federal government bailing out the banking system after it suffered substantial losses. But it would not be the last. Looser regulation contributed to subsequent crises requiring some form of government intervention or assistance, such as the Asian financial crisis of 1997, the Long-Term Capital Management failure of 1998, the dotcom crisis of 2001–2002, and – most notably – the financial crisis of 2007–2008. These, in turn, led to changes aimed at tightening some of the rules and minimizing the excessively risky activities of banks.

Another important element of the 1933 Banking Act was the creation of the Federal Deposit Insurance Corporation (FDIC), initially on a temporary basis but made permanent in 1935. The FDIC is empowered to insure the savings deposits of retail customers up to a specified amount and is funded by insurance premiums paid by banks to the FDIC. At the time of its creation, the FDIC insured only up to $2,500 of each savings account, but this limit has increased considerably over the years. Today, as a consequence of the Dodd-Frank Act passed in the wake of the 2007–2008 financial crisis, the limit stands at $250,000.

3.3 How Banks Create Money

As we saw earlier, the U.S. Mint and the Bureau of Engraving and Printing are responsible for producing the country's supply of currency. But there is another way in which money is created, and commercial banks play a critical role in the process.

If you have ever taken out a loan from a bank, you know that the money that you borrow is seldom, if ever, delivered to you as a bundle of cash. Rather, the bank credits your bank account—if you have one—for the amount of the loan, or it creates a new transactions account in your name. Consequently, and recalling our earlier discussion of monetary measures, when banks make loans they *increase the money supply* because transaction accounts make up part of M1, M2, and the broader money supply.

You might think that depositing money in the bank would similarly increase the money supply because doing so also leads to an increase in deposits at the bank. But merely making a deposit does not, in fact, increase the money supply. While making a cash deposit does increase total bank deposits, it also takes the same amount of currency out of circulation (i.e., into the bank's vault). In this instance, the composition of the money supply is altered—less currency, more transactions deposits—but its total remains unchanged. And, of course, depositing a check drawn on another bank simply shifts deposits from one bank to another.

Yet a cash deposit does enable a bank to increase the money supply because the bank can now make new loans—hence, create new money—based on the deposit. To see how this works, it is important to keep in mind that banks are not required to hold in their vaults or on reserve all the money that they receive in deposits. Far from it. As noted earlier, banks can use most of their assets to obtain earnings.

The banking system is a **fractional reserve system** in which only a small percentage of the total value of deposits, usually around 10 percent, must be kept on reserve. The portion of bank reserves that are kept to satisfy the minimum requirement is known as **required reserves**. If banks must hold 10 percent of every new deposit on reserve, it means that banks can lend out the other 90 percent. So, when you make a deposit at your local bank, 90 percent of its value is classified as **excess reserves**, which a bank is free to lend to other customers.

---

fractional reserve system: a banking system in which banks are required to keep only a fraction of the total value of their deposits on reserve
required reserves: the portion of bank reserves that banks must keep on reserve
excess reserves: the portion of bank reserves that banks are permitted to lend to their customer

---

Even though your deposit does not *directly* increase the money supply, it does help increase it to the extent that banks are willing to lend out their excess reserves. (We discuss this process in more detail in the next chapter). Banks are usually eager to lend out excess reserves because this is how they can make money on them. But sometimes, in periods of financial crisis, banks prefer to hold onto excess reserves.

If the whole process strikes you as a bit peculiar, well, it is. And it gets stranger. As we saw, money can be thought of as analogous to debt. So, when money is created by the banking system, the economy as a whole is essentially taking on more debt. What are the implications of this? Some may argue that the effect is positive, enabling more economic activity. Others may feel that the process may lead to excessive debt, creating risks to the economy including inflation or debt dcfault. Chapter 11 will consider the Federal Reserve's role in controlling the banking system's process of money creation, and Chapter 15 will go into further detail on the different types of debt as well as the consequences of its continued growth.

Discussion Questions

1. How do banks lend their customers money that they do not physically possess? Are they *really* creating money in the process?
2. Does it bother you that banks hold only a small fraction of the value of their deposits on reserve? Why or why not?

4 THE FINANCIAL SYSTEM

In the past, the average person with a little extra money had few options for what to do with it other than putting it in the bank. Today, however, people have numerous financial investment alternatives available. Many people, including those classified as "small investors," find themselves with funds that they do not need at the moment and would like to use to accumulate a nest egg. But how can they choose among the many different options, including mutual funds, individual stocks, bonds, or other assets?

This book does *not* attempt to offer specific advice on this question. From the point of view of an individual or business, finance mostly concerns strategic decision-making aimed at growing one's assets (tangible or financial). But viewed more broadly, finance is an essential and growing factor in the macroeconomy. Thus, it is important for us to consider all the implications of the financial system, especially given the lasting impacts of the financial crisis of 2007−2008 (discussed in detail in the Appendix to this chapter). In this section, we look at the relationship between individual investment decisions and the role of finance in the economy as a whole.

4.1 Functions of Finance

The primary and most long-standing function of the financial system is the provision of money to support investment in real capital. Such "real" investment is the same as the "intended investment" described in Chapter 8, an important reinjection into the circular flow that comes from the financial system. The banking system is involved in this key function, but here we are interested in the broader financial system, of which banks form only a part.

In recent years, finance for other purposes has grown in importance. **Portfolio investment**, once available only to rich individuals, is much more widespread today. This refers mostly to investing funds in securities such as stocks or bonds. To an economist, portfolio investment is merely another form of saving, a means of postponing consumption while hoping to earn a greater return than in a traditional bank. It is not a true investment in the sense of the national accounts covered in Chapter 4, because when one buys a stock or a bond, ownership of an existing security is simply transferred from one person to another. There is, in other words, no addition to the economy's stock of capital.

> **portfolio investment:** the purchase of financial assets such as stocks and bonds

A century ago, only the wealthy used this kind of financial planning. Indeed, only a minority of the population earned enough to save significantly. Even as this changed, most people saved money in traditional banks instead of securities. Only more recently, over the past three or four decades, have stocks and bonds been "democratized" in the sense that a sizable percentage of the population now owns such assets. The change is largely due to the introduction of collective (also called "pooled" or "commingled") investment vehicles, such as mutual funds, and their association with defined contribution pension plans which provide retirement income usually in the form of annuities (i.e. regular monthly payments).[§]

Finance now provides not only a variety of ways to invest but also more choices for long-term saving. It also supports speculation, that is, buying securities in the hopes of short-term gain. Individuals who speculate are not truly saving—they hope to exploit changes in prices to achieve short-term financial gain. The financial system offers them a vast, and growing, array of possible securities, each with its own market. The opportunities for speculation are therefore substantial. Speculators, unlike "true" investors, entrepreneurs, or businesspeople, do not directly contribute to economic well-being. As we will see, however, at a large enough scale, speculative activity has the potential to influence the economy through its impact on income, wealth, and spending.

---

§ Defined contribution plans are retirement plans where a specified amount is contributed each month. The eventual income from these plans depends on investment returns. In contrast, a defined benefit plan offers a specific amount of retirement income. Defined benefits plans are becoming much less common in the private sector, though many government workers still have them.

As long as speculators are risking their own funds, the potentially adverse economic impact of their activity is limited. Most problems emerge when they borrow funds for the purpose. Speculators may borrow money in order to exploit what they see as market opportunities based on short-term price movements. This can create problems when speculators use excessive **leverage**—investments based on borrowed funds. Borrowing excessively to finance risky speculative ventures carries the potential to destabilize the entire financial system and, with it, the economy. Another possible problem, not unrelated, occurs when lenders extend large lines of credit to borrowers who would not ordinarily satisfy minimum loan criteria. Both of these were recurrent problems during the 2007–2008 financial crisis. Unfortunately, the crisis put the federal government "on the hook" since it had no choice but to provide financial assistance to failing companies in order to keep the economy from collapsing (see Appendix to this chapter).

> **leverage:** the use of debt to increase the potential rate of return of one's investment (at greater risk)

Finally, public finance relates to how governments finance their activities. We say relatively little about this in the present chapter. Chapter 9 has already covered government finance with particular attention to taxes and spending, and Chapter 15 elaborates on the subject of government deficits and debt.

4.2 Non-bank Financial Institutions

There was a time when banks were responsible for most, if not all, economic matters relating to money. Today, many other types of financial intermediaries exist. Indeed, over the past few decades, banks have been declining in importance relative to these **non-bank financial institutions**. Most savings today go through such institutions, which invest in stocks, bonds, and other assets.

> **non-bank financial institution:** a financial institution that performs a number of services similar to those offered by banks but that is not a licensed bank and is not subject to banking regulations

For instance, many people have their money in what are known as **collective investment vehicles** (CIVs), which basically offer people alternatives to saving money in a bank. Many types of CIVs fall into the category of **pooled funds**, which accept investments from many different investors and reduce the cost of making decisions about investing by managing them all together.

---

collective investment vehicle or pooled fund: an investment vehicle that pools investments from many different sources, making investment decisions for them all as a group

---

The best-known example of a CIV is a mutual fund.¶ Many individuals place their savings in such funds, which offer customers a variety of "baskets" or "pools" of investments. They purchase "shares" of a given fund, instead of individual stock shares or bonds. Some funds are invested in high-growth stocks with moderate to high risk, for example, while others are mostly in government bonds. The number of possibilities is large, as many thousands of pooled funds exist, invested not only in different classes of stocks and bonds but also in commodities and other assets (as well as combinations of two or more of these forms of asset).

Pooled funds have lower fees than funds managed by a broker because they do not have a paid manager looking after each individual investor's money (the manager in this case is paid to look after the pool of funds on behalf of multiple investors). At the same time, many believe that they offer better returns than bank savings accounts. The returns may, however, vary greatly, depending on the general state of the economy, and on whether the managers have made good bets about the future— what industries are in decline or on the rise, and which companies are likely to make profits.

Hedge funds are a special category of CIV that often engage in highly speculative investments, including "short" investments, which are essentially bets that the value of a given stock, or of the market as a whole, will fall. Hedge funds promise greater earnings potential than most other funds, along with higher risk. Because they carry greater risk, hedge funds are only permitted to do business with particular (high net worth) individuals and institutions. Hedge funds are not necessarily commingled; though it is unusual, a hedge fund can be created by a single very large investor.

---

hedge fund: a type of pooled fund that often engages in highly speculative investments and to which access is generally restricted to wealthy clients

---

¶ The term "mutual fund" is most appropriately applied to CIVs that are regulated under the Investment Company Act of 1940 and are open to the general public. This act was updated by the Dodd-Frank Act of 2010.

403

Pension funds are another type of CIV that accumulate savings from workers, sometimes including a matching contribution from employers, usually over a long period, to be disbursed as benefits in retirement. Access to the funds before retirement is highly restricted, with significant penalties for early withdrawals. To encourage workers to participate (thereby voluntarily deferring a percentage of their pay that they could otherwise use for current consumption), such funds are granted generous tax breaks, both by reducing taxable income by the amount of the employee's contribution, and by deferring taxes on earnings. Most retirement fund dollars are invested in some form of pooled fund. The availability of and extent of choice among funds offered to workers depend on the terms of the specific company or government pension plan.

---

pension fund: a fund with the exclusive purpose of paying retirement benefits to employees

---

Some of the largest investors in the world are pension funds that pool the retirement and health savings accounts of workers in the public sector. For example, the California Public Employees Retirement System (CalPERS) had about $500 billion in investments as of December 2021. CalPERS' income comes from returns on its investments and from the healthcare and pension plans of more than a million workers and their employers, which include government agencies at the state or local level, as well as public schools. CalPERS provides health-care benefits to about 1.8 million beneficiaries and their families, and retirement benefits to over 600,000 individuals.

Given their large investments, such U.S. pension funds can often influence corporate behavior (even far beyond U.S. borders), and some have been pivotal in removing CEOs who have performed poorly. Some have also taken seriously issues of socially responsible investment, including environmental issues such as climate change, and are gradually adjusting their asset mix by divesting from securities such as fossil fuels that are likely to be disadvantaged as markets adjust both to climate risks and to opportunities for businesses that invest in mitigating or adjusting to a changing climate. Yet others, including CalPERS, have recently taken on more leverage, and hence risk, in hopes of combating low average returns in recent years (see Box 10.4). Since pensions, more than other funds, are expected to provide security for retirement, this move is highly controversial.

Another example of a non-bank financial institution is an **insurance company**. You might not think of insurance companies as similar to banks, but over time they have come to resemble them in some ways. The principal difference is that instead of making a deposit with an insurance company, you pay it a premium (monthly, quarterly, or annually)

> **insurance company:** a company that pays to cover all or part of the cost of specific risks against which individuals and companies chose to insure themselves

---

BOX 10.4 CALPERS RESHUFFLES ALLOCATIONS IN BID TO COMBAT LOW RETURNS

The California Public Employees' Retirement System (CalPERS), the public pension plan that serves California workers is going to begin making riskier investments. The board of the largest pension plan in the country voted to make changes in its portfolio allocation in response to the lower average returns expected in the near future.

The aim of public pension systems is to offer employees investment portfolio choices that maximize returns while also protecting the existing assets. It will be especially difficult to strike a balance in the coming years since lower average returns are expected economy-wide. The pension expects to take on more risk merely to keep its expected rate of return constant.

"The portfolio we've selected incorporates a diverse mix of assets to help us achieve our investment return target," CalPERS said in a statement. "By adding five percent leverage over time, we'll better diversify the fund to protect against the impact of a serious drawdown during economic downturns."

What the company means by "leverage" is using some of the pension assets as collateral to borrow funds to invest in other securities. It is an increasingly common practice by financial investors and speculators. But CalPERS had never previously added leverage to its portfolio, and it is a potentially problematic step for an institution entrusted with the preservation of half a trillion dollars in retirement assets for about 2 million California employees.

In the fiscal year ending June 2021, CalPERS returned 21.3 percent. But in the year ending 2020, it only returned 4.7 percent. Its "assumed" annual rate of return is 6.8 percent, but this can be controversial. "Paying more to satisfy pension obligations can mean crowding out what can feel like more immediate budget needs such as education, road repair, and other municipal services."[5]

---

that is meant to protect you against a particular risk. The company, however, must have sufficient funds available to pay to beneficiaries that have the bad fortune (fire, flood, theft, accident, ill health, etc.) against which they had been insured. It must therefore earn a return sufficient to cover the cost of these pay-outs. In this way, an insurance company resembles a bank: It holds a pool of money that it lends to governments and companies and sometimes invests in stocks or other riskier investments.

The difference is that insurance companies can usually, through the use of sophisticated statistical models, much better predict (especially for life insurance) when pay-outs will come due. For example, in anticipation of higher mortality rates in Europe in the coming years (owing to the rapidly aging population in many European countries) most

European insurance companies have taken steps to ensure adequate reserve for future pay-outs. Especially in the United States, however, some insurance companies have engaged in very risky business. The huge insurance company American International Group (AIG), for example, put billions of dollars into risky investments and had to seek a government bailout during the financial crisis of 2007–2008.

Brokerage services also fall into the category of non-bank financial institutions. **Securities brokers**, for example, keep an inventory of different financial assets—mostly stocks and bonds—that result from playing the role of middleman in transactions between buyers and sellers. They earn a commission, a percentage of the transaction, for the service of linking the buyer and the seller. Their service provides another option for customers who might otherwise put all their savings in a bank account.

---

securities broker: an agent responsible for finding a buyer for sellers of different securities, thereby offering enhanced liquidity to the seller

---

From the customer's point of view, funds invested with a broker are very liquid—in other words, a broker can easily convert a stock or bond into cash for a client. But since the broker is earning his or her own fees based on what products the client buys, questions have recently been raised about whom the broker is most likely to be serving: the buyer or the seller? The sellers are apt to be large organizations with close, sometimes financially rewarding, relationships with the broker. In some instances, brokers have encouraged the purchase of stocks or other assets that they knew were unlikely to offer the advertised return, simply because they themselves stood to gain from the transaction. This has led the Department of Labor to adopt a "fiduciary rule" that requires brokers to act in the interests of their clients. The rule is still controversial, with some arguing that it has too many loopholes, and others that it goes too far in restricting activities by brokers. But the movement in the direction of stricter fiduciary rules seems already to have benefited investors by causing financial service companies to cut back on risky and high-cost retirement annuities.[6]

Mortgage brokers perform a similar function, except that their role is specific to real estate purchases. Most homebuyers lack sufficient funds to buy a property outright, so they must borrow a portion of the sale price. The mortgage broker earns a fee for helping the homebuyer and a lender find each other. Traditionally, banks held home mortgages for their duration, satisfied with the interest income that they provided. Today, banks will often "flip" the mortgage—that is, sell it to another financial interest. This has sometimes led to significant financial risk, as noted in the Appendix to this chapter.

> **mortgage broker:** an agent who assists in identifying a lender for prospective homeowners looking to borrow money for their purchase

The non-bank financial institutions described above blur the line between banks and non-banks. And since they are, for the most part, not subject to the regulations that restrict banking activity, such institutions are often referred to as **shadow banks**. Their proliferation relative to the much slower growth of traditional banks has raised the concern of many analysts since it effectively means that a greater share of "banking activity" is conducted by institutions that are not highly regulated. Possible policy responses to this new set of risks and regulatory challenges are discussed in the Appendix.

> **shadow banking:** credit intermediation that involves entities and activities outside the regular banking system, such as collective investment vehicles or hedge funds

4.3 Financialization and Financial Bubbles

By almost any measure, the U.S economy is more dependent than ever on finance. Total financial assets were less than four times GDP in 1970; as of 2020, they are nearly ten times GDP. When we consider financial transactions—the buying and selling of financial assets—we find that they are about 65 times GDP, primarily a result of rapid growth in high-frequency trading, which permits speculators to buy and then quickly sell large quantities of assets.[7] This is the trend that we referred to in Chapter 6 as "financialization."

The fact that the economy depends so much on finance does not pose a problem in and of itself. It may, however, contribute to widening economic inequalities, and contribute to significant economic damage if financial investment behavior becomes excessively risky. When economies grow on the basis of mass investment in assets with questionable foundations that nevertheless experience rapid price increases, the growth is unstable and destined to be of short duration. Such irrational speculative price rises are called bubbles, as discussed in Chapter 3.

Possibly the most famous historical example of a speculative bubble is the Dutch tulip frenzy (called tulipomania) in the early 1600s. Different tulip types had different values, and since no one knew which type would bloom from a given tulip bulb, mass speculation ensued. Initially, only the wealthy Dutch were buying them, but eventually, the rest of the population caught the fever. Because everyone was buying tulips, their price rose rapidly, until the peak in March 1637 when some select bulbs sold for several times the yearly income of a skilled craftsman.

407

Shortly thereafter, however, confidence in their value vanished, and almost overnight the tulip market crashed, ruining many speculators.

Almost three centuries later, the U.S. stock market experienced a speculative bubble in the run-up to the 1929 stock market crash. Many at the time believed that the rapid increase in stock prices during the 1920s was entirely justified by a growing economy. But what was really driving the bubble was the same factor underlying the Dutch tulip craze—the "herd" instinct that causes people to follow what everyone else is doing and to believe what everyone else believes. In the 1920s it seemed as if everyone was buying stocks. This drove up share prices, in turn making stocks seem much more attractive. The period was also characterized by heavy borrowing, with many people going into debt to buy stocks. When the stock market finally crashed in October 1929, the Great Depression followed, rapidly spreading from the United States to the rest of the world.

In recent years, many other bubbles have developed, such as in East and Southeast Asia in 1997, in Russia in 1998, in Argentina in 1999, and in Iceland in 2008, as well as the 1999–2000 "dotcom" stock market bubble and the housing bubbles in the United States, Britain, Ireland, Spain, and other European countries six to eight years later. All were rooted in the widespread but misguided belief in the value of assets driven or reinforced by speculative borrowing. Some fear that little has been learned from the experience and that new asset bubbles may have been inflated in recent years.

Widespread confusion about bubbles can be traced to a fundamental misunderstanding about how the economy relates to the financial markets. On the one hand, financial bubbles are not based on economic reality—that is, they are characterized by rapid price increases that are independent of prevailing economic conditions. People who see rapidly rising prices assume that they must reflect real economic value, but this is an illusion. On the other hand, the *collapse* of a financial bubble usually has very real—and very negative—economic consequences, as bankrupt investors set off a domino effect that can bring down major financial institutions. Ordinary people holding assets caught up in the bubble can rapidly lose wealth, causing them to spend less, setting off a recessionary chain reaction throughout the economy.

4.4 Theories of Financial Instability

Why, despite having so much experience with bubbles, do we fail to learn from past mistakes? One of the mistakes commonly made is extrapolating values over time. If, for example, home prices in a particular area rise rapidly, say at 30 percent per year, large numbers of buyers may enter the market, mistakenly believing that such a growth rate must be sustained and that they therefore "can't lose" on their investment.

408

Another common mistake, as we have noted, is the tendency to follow the herd. Even someone who doubts that prices could continue to increase might find it difficult to resist buying an asset when everyone s/he knows has already done so (and has already made money!). The same phenomenon is at play among money managers. Those who take a conservative or contrarian position during a bubble risk performing worse than nearly everyone else, as long as the bubble continues to expand – which may be a period of several years, or even more than a decade. Keynes was famously quoted as saying that "markets can remain irrational longer than you can remain solvent." This accounts for the tendency of fund managers to "follow the herd" in the investment advice given to clients.

Such behavior contradicts the conventional theory of financial markets, which is based on the "efficient market hypothesis." This theory maintains that financial asset prices always reflect *all* the information available about its true value. As new information becomes available, market participants simply revalue the asset. The theory therefore portrays the economy as consisting of rational individuals who live in a world of perfectly competitive markets and possess complete information about the price of assets. Yet we have just seen that it is often unrealistic to assume that people act rationally, especially when potentially profitable investments are concerned. Another problem with the efficient market hypothesis is that it ignores how uncertainty, herd psychology, and the expectations of market participants influence the value of assets Theories of efficient markets thus lack an explanation for the creation of such bubbles, and of their eventual collapse.

An alternative to efficient market theory is the 'financial instability hypothesis' proposed by Hyman P. Minsky. Minsky's key argument is that unregulated markets will always, given sufficient time, produce instability and crisis. When an economy is just recovering from a crisis, investors will be cautious since they still have a memory of having been "clobbered" in the recent crash. Yet as the economy emerges from its slump investors become more confident and again start taking more risks.

Minsky identified three phases through which the financial system cycles: hedge, speculative, and Ponzi financing. Hedge finance (used here in a quite different sense from "hedge funds" discussed earlier) is the safest form of financing, where the borrowers have enough cash flow to cover both interest and principal payments on their debt. Speculative finance is riskier, in that borrowers are only able to cover interest payments—not principal—with near-term income flows, but future financial flows are expected to cover the principal. Ponzi is the riskiest profile, where near-term income flows are insufficient to cover even the interest payments; hence interest on current debts will have to be rolled

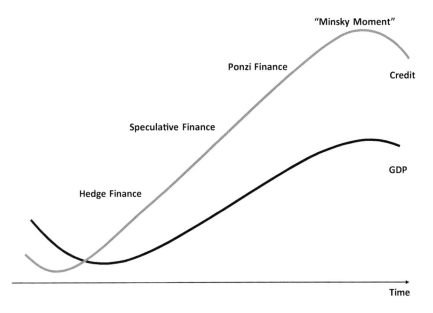

Figure 10.2 *Minsky's Financial Instability Hypothesis*

over such that new loans are taken to pay off the older ones.** During an economic expansion, financial firms tend to move from safer hedge financing to speculative and then to Ponzi financing (Figure 10.2). As a result, their financial strength—which is determined by the way they finance their debt—weakens. This makes the economy overall more credit-dependent and fragile.

Minsky argued that stability is in effect *de*stabilizing, since it is when market conditions are stable that changes in policymaking behavior and business opportunities move toward more risk-taking and deregulation. For example, financial markets were regulated in the wake of the Great Depression, when banks were reeling from huge losses, investors were more cautious about taking risks, and the general market sentiment was focused on preventing future crises. By the 1980s, much of the pain of the Great Depression was forgotten, allowing a movement toward relaxing regulations to gain momentum.

Minsky's theory is derived from Keynes' notion of 'fundamental uncertainty', which argues that, since it is impossible to know the future, our actions are guided by our expectations, and these expectations are based on conventions that have been socially and historically created. Unlike the classical view of the economy, where things are in equilibrium until affected by some external event, expectations about the future, confidence levels, and risk-taking behavior are all endogenous to the economic system in the Keynesian world ("endogenous," as used by economists, means originating within the system, as opposed to arising from an

---

**The term "Ponzi finance" is based on a fraudulent investment scheme promoted by Charles Ponzi in the 1920s, where current investors were paid out of funds raised from new investors; when the flow of new funds ran out, the scheme collapsed.

external force). This theory helps explain numerous crises of the past few decades, including the stock market crash in 1987, the savings and loans crisis in 1989, the dotcom bubble of 2001, and the Great Recession of 2008. In fact, the 2008 crisis (discussed in more detail in the Appendix to this chapter) was referred to as a 'Minsky moment."

Although Minsky's theory is very helpful in understanding the roots of financial instability and the need for adequate regulation (discussed further in the Appendix), it only locates the roots of instability in the financial sector, seeing it as an unavoidable cyclical phenomenon. But it does not explain the *structural* aspect of increased financialization. The latter is both a cause and consequence of greater inequality. Rising inequality since the 1970s is of increasing concern to economists today, as it lies at the center of many current economic problems (discussed in detail in Chapter 14).

Money and finance can therefore play both positive and negative roles in the economy. Government policy is an important factor in shaping money and finance and their impacts. In Chapter 11, we explore how monetary policy, as carried out by central banks such as the U.S. Federal Reserve, can affect the economy as a whole, and in Chapter 12 we bring together fiscal and monetary analyses to develop a theory of macroeconomic activity, recession, inflation, and government policy.

Discussion Questions

1. What is the difference between the real, monetary, and financial economies? In what way are they related to each other? Should growth in one imply growth in the others?
2. Think about the ways in which uncertainty and expectations about the future may affect your current economic decisions and give two examples of such decisions. What role does expectation about the future play in Minsky's theory of financial instability?

REVIEW QUESTIONS

1. Describe three scenarios that could describe economies in very different situations, with regard to their banking systems and price (in)stability.
2. Describe the three roles played by money.
3. Describe at least three different types of money.
4. Describe at least two measures of money.
5. Draw up and explain the components of a balance sheet for a commercial bank.
6. What characteristics are needed to make commodity money effective?
7. What is meant by leverage? What are its advantages, and its dangers?
8. What are "pooled funds"? Describe two different kinds of pooled funds. What is the primary advantage of the pooling process?
9. What is a financial bubble? Give some examples and explain some of the causes of financial bubbles.
10. What is Minsky's financial instability hypothesis? What does it suggest about the need for regulation in financial markets?

411

EXERCISES

1. Search for the "World Economic Outlook Database" on the internet and locate the most recent version. Use this database to select inflation data (units of percentage change) for Germany, Japan, and the United States for the period 1995–2021. Construct a table of annual inflation rates for these countries. Now construct a graph using annual inflation rates on the vertical axis and the year on the horizontal axis. Plot the annual inflation rates from your table in three separate lines on the same graph. How would you compare the experiences of these three countries based on your graph?

2. Use FRED (https://fred.stlouisfed.org/categories), which stands for Federal Reserve Economic Database, "Money, Banking, and Finance," to locate monetary data for M1 money and M2 money (monthly data of each stock, seasonally adjusted). How do the two series relate in size? How do the changes in the two series compare to one another? Does your understanding of the definitions of M1 and M2 help you make sense of what you observe?

3. Determine whether each of the following belongs on the asset side or the liability side of the balance sheet identified in parentheses. (a) $20,000 loan for a new automobile (balance sheet for an individual) (b) Ten-year government bonds (balance sheet for a bank) (c) $1,000 checking account (balance sheet for a bank) (d) $500 in Federal Reserve notes—also known as cash! (balance sheet for an individual) (e) $10,000 student loan (balance sheet for a bank)

4. Assume a required reserve of 0.10 to complete the following:

	Assets		Liabilities
Reserves	$800,000	Deposits	$2,000,000
Loans	$1,000,000		
Bonds	$400,000		
Total	$2,000,000	Total	$2,000,000

   a) Calculate the required reserves for this bank.
   b) Calculate the initial excess reserves for this bank. What can the bank do with these excess reserves?

5. Assume a required reserve of 0.20 to complete the following:

	Assets		Liabilities
Reserves	$3,000,000	Deposits	$11,500,000
Loans	$6,000,000		
Bonds	$2,500,000		
Total	$11,500,000	Total	$11,500,000

   a) Calculate the required reserves for this bank.
   b) Calculate the initial excess reserves for this bank.

6. State whether the following statements are true or false. If false, also write a corrected statement.
   a) Inflation erodes the value of savings.
   b) Inflation creates "menu costs."

c) Inflation reduces uncertainty.
d) Inflation hurts people on fixed incomes.
e) Inflation redistributes wealth from debtors to creditors.

7. Match each concept in Column A with a definition or example in Column B.

Column A		Column B	
a.	Excess reserves	1.	The ease of use of an asset as a medium of exchange
b.	Barter	2.	A measure of the money supply that includes currency, checkable deposits, and other liquid accounts like savings, share accounts, and money market accounts
c.	Deflation	3.	An institution such as a bank, savings and loan association, or life insurance company that accepts funds from savers and makes loans to borrowers
d.	Required reserves	4.	A good used as money that is also valuable in itself
e.	Liquidity	5.	When the aggregate price level falls
f.	Commodity money	6.	A medium of exchange that is accepted as money accepted because the government says it has value
g.	Fiat money	7.	A measure of the money supply that includes all of M1 plus small certificates of deposit and retail money market funds
h.	M1money	8.	Exchange of goods, services, or assets directly for other goods, services, or assets, without the use of money
i.	M2 money	9.	The portion of bank reserves that banks *must* keep on reserve
j.	Financial intermediary	10.	The portion of bank reserves that banks are permitted to lend to their customers

APPENDIX: THE 2007–2008 FINANCIAL CRISIS

The 2007–2008 financial crisis brought the United States and world financial systems almost to the brink of collapse. In their wake, the "Great Recession" caused massive unemployment that lasted for years before returning to more normal levels. The lessons of this period therefore have lasting importance for financial systems and policy.

The immediate cause of the crisis was a bubble in home prices. Low interest rates and steadily rising home prices fed a speculative frenzy where millions of would-be homeowners, as well as speculators, rushed to buy, believing that prices would only continue to go up. Between the mid-1990s and the mid-2000s, the average annual value of mortgage loans borrowed by U.S. households rose from $200 billion to over $1 trillion.

Many of the mortgages granted during this period were classified as "**subprime**," as borrowers taking these loans typically had low income, high debt, and poor credit history. Historically, subprime borrowers

413

were charged higher interest rates to compensate for the increased lending risk. But during the housing bubble, they were allowed to borrow at low rates, often tied to risky conditions.

---

subprime mortgage: a mortgage given to someone with poor credit

---

Why were lenders willing to provide such high volumes of high-risk mortgages? First, financial institutions had a lot of funds to lend, and they made a tremendous amount of income from fees for originating and trading loans. Also, financial innovation in the form of **securitization**, which involved pooling various kinds of loans (mortgages, auto loans, credit card debts, and commercial bank loans), slicing and sorting them according to their presumed risk levels, and repackaging them into new financial instruments, motivated the lenders to create more loans. After making an initial loan, the lender could quickly sell it off to another financial intermediary (such as an investment bank). These financial intermediaries would then repackage the loans and sell them off to other investors (hedge funds, pension funds, or foreign investors). This ability to sell off the loans to other financial investors freed up capital for the lenders to make new loans, but this also meant that the lenders had little incentive to ensure the credibility of borrowers to make their payments down the road. The creation of such perverse incentives is what economists refer to as the "**moral hazard**" problem. In this case, the loan originators had no financial incentive to protect against the risk of default by the borrower.

---

securitization: the process of pooling various kinds of loans, slicing and sorting them according to their risk levels, and repackaging them into financial instruments

moral hazard: the creation of perverse incentives that encourage excessive risk-taking because of protections against losses from that risk

---

Why weren't the investors buying these financial assets worried about the creditworthiness of the borrowers? Unfortunately, most investors were not aware of the risks because securitization made these assets very complex. Investment in these securities was mainly driven by their attractive rates of return. In addition, the credit rating agencies (Standard and Poor's, Moody's, and Fitch Group) on whom investors relied to evaluate the risks associated with these securities mostly rated them as being very safe. This was partly because these assets were too complex to understand. But there was also a moral hazard problem: the credit rating agencies were paid by the investment banks trying to sell the securities, so they had an incentive to understate the risks of default.

The investment banks, which were most likely aware of the high-risk nature of these financial securities, also continued to create and trade them. This high risk-taking behavior of the banks is partly explained by their being "too big to fail", meaning if these banks reached the verge of failure, the government would have to save them as their failure could hurt the entire economy. Knowing that the government would come to their rescue, large banks had little incentive to manage risks well. This is what happened in 2008: as large financial companies like Lehman Brothers and Merrill Lynch faced huge losses, other big companies that provided credit to these banks faced the risk of failure. As a result, federal regulators "bailed out" other large institutions that came close to failure, despite public resistance to helping the banks whose recklessness had led to the crisis.

The impacts of the crisis were felt widely throughout the economy. Large mortgage companies, such as Countrywide and Washington Mutual, and securities firms and investment banks such as Lehman Brothers and Bear Stearns either went bankrupt, were bought by larger banks, or bailed out by the government. With the failure of large financial firms, lenders became much less willing to give out new loans leading to a "credit crunch" in which families and businesses were unable to obtain loans or refinance mortgages. This led to further intensification of the crisis. Approximately 11 million homebuyers faced foreclosure from 2008 to mid-2012, accounting for about a quarter of the mortgages in the United States. Additionally, an immense amount of financial wealth disappeared as U.S. families lost $10.9 trillion in financial investments related to stocks and bonds (amounting to an average loss of nearly $100,000 per household) from mid-2007 to early 2009.

The impacts of the crisis quickly spread from the financial sector to the real sector. From 2007 to 2009, the U.S. economy lost nearly 9 million jobs. The official unemployment rate hit 10 percent in October 2009 and stayed above 7 percent through late 2013. Total unemployment and underemployment numbers, including marginally attached workers and those working part-time involuntarily, were much higher reaching over 17 percent in late 2009, staying above 13 percent until the end of 2013, and only declining gradually to about 8 percent by 2017.

Income and wealth inequality, already severe before the crisis, only intensified after it. From 2007 to 2010, the median household lost nearly 40 percent of their wealth, while the average household net worth of the poorest 25 percent fell to zero. The wealth of middle-income families had increased by 68 percent (from $95,879 to $161,050) between 1983 and 2007, but most of this gain had disappeared by 2013 as their wealth levels fell to $98,000. At the same time, upper-income families saw their wealth more than double from 1983 to 2007 (from $323,402 to $729,930), and although they also faced losses during the recession, by 2013 their wealth had risen to $650,074.

415

To address the economic decline after the crisis, the government instituted a massive fiscal stimulus, the American Recovery and Reinvestment Act (ARRA) (discussed in Chapter 9). Independent analysts estimate that ARRA created between 1.5 million and 7.9 million new jobs from 2009 to 2012.

The recovery efforts of the government also included a $700 billion Treasury bailout—known as the Troubled Asset Relief Program (TARP)—to make emergency loans to firms that were in critical condition. Major recipients of this bailout included the insurance giant AIG, along with large financial corporations such as Citibank, JP Morgan Chase, Bank of America, and Goldman Sachs. Even non-financial firms, such as General Motors and Chrysler, received billions of dollars in TARP loans as they had invested heavily in financial assets. Though TARP loans were paid back to the government by 2014, there was widespread criticism of a policy that bailed out the banks that created the crisis, rather than helping the middle and low-income homeowners who lost so much wealth as a result.

A major policy response to the crisis, the 2010 Dodd-Frank Wall Street Reform and Consumer Protection Act (Dodd-Frank), was adopted to help avert future crises. The goals of the Dodd-Frank reform include protecting consumers by ensuring they get clear and accurate information needed to shop for credit, preventing predatory lending, discouraging risky practices, controlling executive pay, protecting investors by requiring rating agencies to disclose the methods used to rate each security, discouraging the formation of large banks by adding restrictions on the activities of firms that are too large, and strengthening oversight and regulations over financial fraud and conflict of interests.

POLICIES TO PROMOTE FINANCIAL STABILITY

Regulating the Financial System

The Dodd-Frank legislation was a step toward promoting financial stability, but many economists feel that more is needed. Other policies that might help insure against future crises include:

- Giving the central bank greater oversight of the financial health of borrowing institutions, including requirements for large financial institutions to hold sufficient capital reserves to cover the risks associated with the financial instruments they create.
- Greater oversight and regulation of non-bank institutions in the shadow banking system.
- Reinstituting a version of the Glass-Steagall Act, separating banking and investment functions, promoting the role of smaller and regional banks, and possibly breaking up financial institutions in the "too big to fail" category.

■ locking the revolving door between finance and politics by instituting requirements that individuals must wait a significant number of years between the time they leave a government position in which they can affect legislation on industry sectors and when they can begin work in those sectors

Channeling Financial Resources to More Socially Useful Investments

One of the criticisms of the current financial system is that it directs too much effort and money toward short-term financial profitmaking while providing insufficient support for productive investment. Policies to reverse this bias might include:

■ Promoting regional and community financial institutions, credit unions, and other smaller financial institutions whose main orientation is toward supporting local businesses and homebuyers.
■ Instituting a small tax on financial transactions. Both Keynes and the Nobel laureate economist James Tobin supported such a tax as a way of discouraging short-term speculation. What has come to be known as a "Tobin tax" could be at a very low rate, but would still raise substantial revenues due to the very large volume of financial transactions. Speculators would end up paying much more than long-term investors because they buy and sell securities much more frequently.
■ Restricting companies from buying back their stock, and rewarding them through the tax system for investing in their employees; linking executive pay to productive performance of the company instead of share prices; adding worker representatives on corporate boards so their interests are represented when decisions are made.[8]
■ Encouraging cooperative-based organizations, as discussed in Chapter 7, could also help create a stronger and more equitable economic system. Cooperatives have a motive to invest in the long-term viability of the company and improve the well-being of workers. Worker-owned companies, community development corporations, and credit unions tend to be locally oriented and resilient to economic fluctuations at the national level.

NOTES

1   Armas, 2022.
2   Pitel, 2021 and data from https://tradingeconomics.com/ "Turkey inflation rate", March 2022
3   Dooley, 2021.
4   Graeber, 2011.
5   Riquier, 2021.

6   Sommer, 2020.
7   According to figures from the Tax Foundation, approximately $90 trillion in stocks and $216 trillion in bonds were traded on U.S. exchanges in 2018. While the size of the market in derivatives (indirect forms of investment such as options to buy or sell stocks) is harder to determine, the Tax Policy Center (TPC) estimated that $1.1 quadrillion of derivatives was traded in 2015. This gives a total of $1.3 trillion in financial trading, about 65 times U.S. GDP.
8   Lazonick, 2012.

REFERENCES

Armas, Mayela. 2022. "Venezuela's Inflation Hit 686.4 Percent in 2021." *Reuters*, January 8.

Dooley, Ben. 2021. "Inflation? Not in Japan. And That Could Hold a Warning for the U.S." *New York Times*, July 15.

Graeber, David. 2011. *Debt: The First 5,000 Years*, Melville House, Brooklyn.

Lazonick, William. 2012. "How American Corporations Transformed from Producers to Predators." *HuffPost*, April 3.

Pitel, Laura. 2021. "Is Turkey on the Brink of Hyperinflation?" *The Financial Times*, November 28.

Riquier, Andrea. 2021. "America's Biggest Pension Fund CalPERS Votes to Reshuffle Allocations, Add Leverage, in Bid to Combat Low Returns." *Marketwatch.Com.*, November 18.

Sommer, Jeff. "Even the Threat of a Tougher Rule on Financial Advice has Helped Investors," *New York Times*, September 11.

Chapter 11

The Federal Reserve and Monetary Policy

One of the most frequent items in U.S. financial news reports concerns interest rates and the Federal Reserve Bank (or, in other countries, the central bank of the country in question). Are interest rates rising or falling? What is the Fed expected to do next and when? The answers to these questions affect many financial markets and the broader economy. We have seen that the central bank controls the amount of currency and holds a certain percentage of commercial bank reserves. But in addition, the Fed pursues active policies that affect the level of interest rates throughout the economy, including rates that people pay for mortgages and consumer loans. In this chapter, we explore how the Fed does this, and what its primary policy objectives are in terms of how these policies affect the economy.

In the wake of the financial crisis of 2007–2008, much attention was focused on the appropriate monetary policy responses, particularly actions by the Federal Reserve (the Fed) in the United States and the European Central Bank (ECB). The Fed, for example, took extraordinary measures to keep interest rates very low, as well as initiating other measures to promote economic recovery. The slow return to growth that followed the 2007–2009 recession ended in early 2020 with a sudden rapid decline in economic activity precipitated by the global Covid-19 pandemic. In response to the Covid-19 recession, the Fed once again acted to keep interest rates at rock bottom and used other methods (which we will discuss in more detail) to stimulate the economy. By the end of 2021 a new issue— significant price inflation— appeared for the first time in four decades, prompting further Fed policy changes that led to rising interest rates starting in spring 2022.

As this recent history shows, managing monetary policy involves significant challenges and controversies. To get a perspective on these issues, we examine the history, structure, and policymaking of the Federal Reserve System. While the Fed differs from other central banks there are also broad similarities, so the material covered here will give us a basis for understanding the operation of central banks in general.

1 THE FEDERAL RESERVE SYSTEM

In 1907, the U.S. economy experienced a bank panic, in which depositors lost trust in banks, tried to withdraw their deposits all at once, and as a result caused many banks to fail. In response, Congress enacted legislation creating the Federal Reserve System in 1913.

The Fed is a rather odd organization in that it is not exactly part of the government, nor entirely separate from it. Policy decisions made by the Fed are ostensibly independent of other branches of government, although it is impossible to guarantee that there never is any influence exerted on it by the President or other political leaders. The Fed is also technically "private," in that it has commercial banks as private shareholders that even earn dividends on their Fed shares. It is, however, quite different from other private companies or commercial banks in that it does not exist to make profits. Historically, its primary objective had been to maintain stable prices. But in 1977 the goal of ensuring adequate national employment was added to its official mandate.[1] Much controversy remains, however, over the extent of the Fed's role in job creation.

The Fed is overseen by a board of governors whose seven members are nominated by the President and approved by the Senate, and who serve non-renewable 14-year terms. One member of the board is chosen by the President to serve as chair for a four-year term, renewable within the 14-year period if renominated by the President. The long terms of service are intended to help insulate the Fed from short-term political pressures.

The Fed performs a number of important functions. As noted in Chapter 10, it serves as a "banker's bank" by holding deposits made by commercial banks. Another of the Fed's day-to-day functions involves using these deposits to clear checks that draw funds from one bank and deposit them in another. For example, if you give a check to a friend, who then deposits it in her bank, the check goes to a Fed clearinghouse. Your bank's account at the Fed is debited by the amount of the check, while your friend's bank's account at the Fed is credited with the funds. This function is much less important than it once was, however, since, as noted in Chapter 10, the use of electronic fund transfers and direct deposits as an alternative to checks is increasingly widespread.

If a bank is in need of cash to hold in its vault, it can buy currency from the Fed, using the funds in its Fed account as payment. As we have seen, the Fed can order banks to keep a certain percentage of their deposits as required reserves, in the form of either vault cash or in such deposits at the Fed. In recent years, banks were generally required to keep an amount equal to about 10 percent of their checkable deposits as reserves, but this requirement, known as the 'reserve ratio', was lowered to zero in March 2020 to encourage more lending.

If it wishes, a bank may keep reserves in excess of the required amount. The incentive to do so is greater than it once was. In the past, the Fed did not pay interest on bank reserves that it held, so holding reserves in excess of the amount required might have made banks forgo profitable earnings opportunities. This changed in 2010, when the Dodd-Frank Act introduced in response to the 2008 financial crisis called for the Fed to pay interest to banks for the reserves that it holds.

Another of the Fed's important tasks is to stabilize the rate of exchange between domestic and foreign currencies. It does this by buying or selling dollars in exchange for foreign currencies, a process that is detailed in Chapter 13. In addition, the Fed, along with other organizations such as the Federal Deposit Insurance Corporation (FDIC), regulates banks, attempting to ensure that they operate as much as possible without error or fraud, and do not take excessive risks with their investments. Because the FDIC guarantees the value of many accounts, and the Fed is willing to make emergency loans to banks that find themselves short of liquidity, the sorts of crises in depositor confidence that led to bank runs in the past are now far less likely. (Recall from Chapter 10 that "liquidity" refers to the availability of cash.)

The Federal Reserve System consists of a board of governors based in Washington, DC, and twelve regional Federal Reserve Banks based in Atlanta, Boston, Chicago, Cleveland, Dallas, Kansas City (MO), Minneapolis, New York, Philadelphia, Richmond (VA), St. Louis, and San Francisco. The regional Fed banks also have their own branches in many other cities, such as Baltimore, Los Angeles, Miami, and Pittsburgh.

The structure of the European Central Bank (ECB) is somewhat similar to that of the Fed in the United States, the main difference being that it operates across countries. While the ECB has headquarters in Frankfurt, Germany, each of the nineteen member countries also retains its own national central bank.[*]

The Fed keeps close track of the economy and tries to sense whether some adjustment in the money supply or in interest rates might be necessary to support aggregate expenditure or to counteract undesirable changes in the inflation rate. The Fed has the ability to choose "targets" for the rate of growth of the money supply, inflation, or the level of interest rates, which, as we will see, are highly related. Whereas for much of its history the Fed's principal concern was the money supply, in recent years its focus has shifted to interest rates. We examine the macroeconomic consequences of Fed actions later in this chapter, but for right now we concentrate on the mechanics of *how* the Fed influences the money supply and interest rates.

---

[*] The European Central Bank operates in the 19 Member States of the European Union (as of early 2022) that have adopted the euro as their currency. The remaining EU countries either have chosen not to join the euro or do not presently meet the criteria for joining. Some are, however, expected to adopt the Euro in the future. A few other small countries like Andorra and Vatican City, while not part of the EU, nevertheless have agreements with the ECB to circulate the euro.

1. What is the Federal Reserve System? What event or events caused it to be created? Where are its banks found?
2. Is the Federal Reserve truly an independent bank or is it part of the government? What are its principal functions?

2 MONETARY POLICY

2.1 How the Fed Creates Money and Credit

As we saw in Chapter 10, increasing the amount of reserves that banks hold indirectly increases the money supply by permitting banks to lend more money. The additional loans add to the overall supply of money in the economy. Each of the means that the Fed has at its disposal targets the level of bank reserves.

Historically, the most commonly used tool is **open market operations**. In open market operations, the Federal Reserve Bank of New York can affect the level of bank reserves by buying or selling U.S. Treasury bonds. Such operations are directed by the **Federal Open Market Committee (FOMC)**, which is composed of the Board of Governors of the Fed and 5 of the 12 regional Fed bank presidents.[†] Let's see what happens when the FOMC undertakes a purchase of government bonds on the open market.

---

open market operations: sales or purchases of U.S. Treasury bonds by the Fed
Federal Open Market Committee (FOMC): the committee that oversees open market operations. It is composed of the Fed Board of Governors and 5 of the 12 regional Fed presidents

---

A simplified balance sheet for the Fed is shown in Table 11.1. Because currency is issued by the Fed, it is the Fed's major liability. You will recall from Chapter 10 that "liability" refers to anything that someone owes to anyone else. Currency is technically a liability to the Fed because it is legally redeemable for equivalent value. Formerly, in the days of the gold standard and silver certificates, one could, at least in theory, redeem the U.S dollar for gold or silver. Today, the best that one could do is get new currency for old currency. One would be correct, then, to question whether the currency issued by the Fed is a *true* liability. As we noted in the previous chapter, it is really public faith in

---

[†] The President of the Federal Reserve of New York is a permanent member of the FOMC. Presidents from the other 11 regional Fed banks rotate in and out of the other four positions.

422

the value of money that matters, rather than a formal promise to pay by the Fed. Regardless, the Fed backs up the value of its currency by holding assets in the form of government bonds issued by the U.S. Treasury.

The Fed's other major liability is the reserves held by commercial banks. These *are* true liabilities to the banks. Bank reserves consist only partly of their own vault cash, with the majority being their deposits at the Fed. Just as deposits made by individuals at banks are the liabilities of the banks, deposits made by banks at the Fed are liabilities of the Fed.

Until 2008, the Fed's assets consisted primarily of U.S. Treasury bonds. Since then, in response both to the financial crisis and the more recent global pandemic recession, the Fed has acquired about $3 trillion in other somewhat riskier assets, mostly mortgage-backed securities. Its total assets of about $8 trillion amount to about 35 percent of GDP, far more than its earlier peak during the Great Depression.

For now, however, let's keep our story simple and focus on Treasury bonds (as shown in Table 11.1). When the Fed makes an open market purchase of bonds, its holdings of bonds increase. It generally makes such purchases from a commercial bank, so it pays for the purchase by crediting the bank's account with the Fed by the amount of the purchase. By doing this, the Fed can create new money merely by adjusting an entry in a computer database at the New York office. It simply declares that the bank's reserves are now higher by the amount of the bond purchase. Just as the Fed can authorize the production of new currency by the Bureau of Engraving and Printing, it is also empowered to create new bank reserves, which in turn expand the money supply by permitting banks to make more loans. New loans issued by banks will end up as deposits elsewhere in the banking system—i.e., new money. Ultimately, the Fed is the only economic actor with the power to create new money. Although banks in effect create money by making new loans, the Fed controls their power to do so through its policy impacts on bank reserves.

When the Fed makes an open market purchase, it increases something called the **monetary base** (sometimes referred to as "**high-powered money**"). This is defined as the sum of total currency in circulation plus bank reserves—in other words, total Fed liabilities. We noted in Chapter 10 that dollar bills in circulation are "fiat" money, whose value depends on a government declaration that they are money. While technically not

Table 11.1 *A Simplified Balance Sheet of the Federal Reserve*

Assets		Liabilities	
U.S. Treasury bonds	$1,200 billion	Currency in circulation	$1,100 billion
		Bank reserves	$100 billion

"money" according to the definition of M1 and M2, bank reserves are a portion of the monetary base and share with currency the attribute that their value is defined purely by fiat.

---

monetary base (or high-powered money): the sum of total currency plus bank reserves

---

Suppose that the Fed buys $10 million worth of government bonds from ABC Bank. The changes in the Fed's balance sheet and the balance sheet of ABC Bank are shown in Table 11.2. The Fed increases both its holdings of assets and liabilities by $10 million—the bonds being the asset, and the bank reserves the liability. ABC Bank changes only the mix of assets it holds, now holding less in bonds and more in reserves. Note that both the Fed and ABC Bank balance sheets are still balanced. If total assets equaled total liabilities before the change, they will still be equal after the open market purchase.

So far in our story, reserves have risen by $10 million, but the supply of money in circulation (as measured by M1 or other measures) *has not changed.* But if ABC Bank sees opportunities to make loans at a higher rate of interest than that paid by the Fed, it may very well not let its new $10 million in reserves just sit at the Fed. Even if it was only just meeting its reserve requirement before the bond purchase, all of this new $10 million would be *excess* reserves. ABC Bank may therefore use this $10 million to make $10 million in new loans. This movement of $10 million from reserves to new loans is shown in Table 11.3(a).

Suppose that ABC Bank makes a $10 million loan to Jane's Construction, and then, after obtaining the loan in the form of a check, Jane's Construction deposits the entire amount of the funds at XYZ Bank. (We assume a different bank, since in general recipients of loans do not have to deposit them in the originating bank. It also allows us to keep track of changes in balance sheets more easily.)

Table 11.2 *An Open Market Purchase of Government Bonds by the Fed*

(a) Change in the Fed Balance Sheet			
Assets		Liabilities	
Government bonds:	+$10 million	Bank reserves	+$10 million
(b) Change in ABC Bank's Balance Sheet			
Assets		Liabilities	
Government bonds	−$10 million		
Reserves	+$10 million		

Table 11.3 *A Loan by ABC Bank Becomes a Deposit in XYZ Bank*

(a) Next Change in the ABC Bank's Balance Sheet			
Assets		Liabilities	
Loans:	+$10 million		
Reserves:	−$10 million		
(b) Change in XYZ Bank's Balance Sheet			
Assets		Liabilities	
Reserves:	+$10 million	Deposits:	+$10 million

The changes in the balance sheets of XYZ Bank are shown in Table 11.3(b). Because the way that the Fed clears checks is by increasing or decreasing the deposits that it holds for banks, the initial impact on XYZ Bank of the deposit of the check by Jane's Construction is a $10 million increase in both its checkable deposits and its reserves at the Fed.

Note, first, that the money supply *has* now increased. Checkable deposits are part of M1 and M2, and there are now $10 million more in total deposits in the economy than there were before. Through an open market purchase of bonds paid for by a simple computerized book-keeping entry, the Fed has brought new money into being.

Second, note that XYZ Bank now has excess reserves. Assuming that required reserves are 10 percent of deposits, it can lend out as much as $9 million of the $10 million in new funds that it has received while keeping only 10 percent ($1 million) as reserves.[‡] The new loans will, in turn, become new deposits in the banking system (they could return to ABC or XYZ bank, but more likely will end up in other banks). Then the money supply will have increased by the initial 10 million, plus the second-round $9 million—already an increase totaling $19 million, which is quite a bit larger than the initial $10 million increase.

Now, of course, the banks that receive the $9 million in deposits resulting from XYZ Bank's loans will find that they have excess reserves and will also be able to make new loans, and the process will continue. Where will it all end? If each bank that receives new funds lends out as much as it can (given the 10 percent reserve requirement), the total amount of new money will eventually be $100 million.[§] The logic is similar to the government spending multiplier in fiscal policy. Just as

---

[‡] Note that ABC Bank was able to lend out the entire $10 million that it received from the Fed. It did not have to keep 10 percent as reserve because there was no corresponding increase in deposits at ABC—they obtained the $10 million by selling bonds.

[§] This can be calculated by using the formula for an infinite series where x is less than one: $(1 + x + x^2 + x^3 + \ldots + x^n) = 1/(1 - x)$, just as we did in calculating the income/spending multiplier in Chapter 8. In this case x = 0.9. This "*x*" corresponds to "mpc" in the fiscal multiplier formula, but here, rather than the portion of income spent,

re-spending by consumers multiplies the original amount of government spending, so the creation of new loans by banks multiplies the original creation of new reserves.

The story is actually somewhat more complicated than this because banks often hold excess reserves, and people who take out loans similarly often want to hold some of the funds in cash or in types of deposits that are not part of M1 or M2. So not all high-powered money creation will translate directly into new deposits and loans, and monetary expansion will not be quite as dramatic as in the example above.

Economists define the **money multiplier** as the ratio of the money supply to the monetary base:

> **money multiplier:** the ratio of the money supply to the monetary base, indicating by how much the money supply will change for a given change in high-powered money

$$\text{money multiplier} = \frac{\text{money supply}}{\text{monetary base}}$$

Using M1 as the measure of money, empirical studies have shown the money multiplier in the United States is currently very close to 2. That is, if the Fed acts to increase reserves and currency by $10 million, the total increase in the money supply would be expected to be around double that:

$$\Delta\text{money} = \text{money multiplier} \times \Delta\text{money base}$$

$$\$20 \text{ million} = 2 \times 10 \text{ million}$$

Thus, with a simple bookkeeping entry, the Fed open market purchase of government bonds increases the money supply by about twice the value of the initial bond purchase. While our theoretical example implied a money multiplier of 10, the actual effect in the real world is significantly less. (Also in theory, when the reserve ratio was lowered to zero in March 2020, the money multiplier could become infinite, but the tendency of banks to hold excess reserves and for depositors to hold excess cash means that the multiplier did not increase dramatically even with a reserve ratio of zero.)

Note that, looking at the same story in a slightly different way, the action of the Fed can also be seen as increasing the amount of *credit* extended to private actors in the economy. In making an open market purchase of government bonds, the Fed in essence takes over a

---

it reflects the portion of new deposits that are loaned out—90 percent if the reserve ratio is 10 percent.

portion of the public debt that was previously held by private institutions. (Recall from Chapter 9 that government bonds are issued by the Treasury to finance federal budget deficits.) The new bank reserves created by the purchase of government bonds allow banks to extend more credit— that is, new loans—to private actors in the economy.

Traditionally, macroeconomists have tended to look at the asset side of the banks' balance sheets and perceive the story outlined above as a matter of increasing deposits and hence increasing the money supply. More recently, however, many macroeconomists focus more on the liabilities side of the banks' balance sheets and see the process as a story of an expansion of credit. According to this interpretation, the Fed's activist role is more limited. If the economy is booming and "wants" more money, banks and financial institutions will lend and invest to the maximum of their capacity. If the economy is slack, banks may hold excess reserves and there will be less expansion of money and credit.

While, in some sense, the two views are just "two sides of the same coin," looking at the money side of monetary policy tends to draw more attention to people's need for liquidity, while looking at the credit side draws more attention to issues of how financial capital is created and distributed within the economy. This, in other words, recalls the Chapter 10 distinction between money and finance. It is no coincidence that we have these two interpretations since, as we have already explained, money is itself a form of debt. With the growing influence and importance of finance, the distinction is increasingly relevant.

2.2 Other Monetary Policy Tools

As we have seen, if the Fed wants to increase the volume of money and private credit circulating in an economy, it can use open market operations. Open market purchases of government bonds increase reserves. Banks will generally then increase their loans, which increases deposits and hence the money supply.

While this is, in fact, what the Fed usually does when it wants to expand the money supply, it also has other tools at its disposal, and its "toolkit" has enlarged in recent years. Since the financial crisis of 2007–2008, the Fed has expanded its operations by acquiring large amounts of assets other than Treasury bonds, including mortgage-backed assets and other riskier forms of debt purchased directly from investment banks, as opposed to its standard bond purchases from commercial banks. As mentioned earlier, this change in course caused the assets and liabilities on the Fed's balance sheet to balloon from about $800 billion before the financial crisis to about $8 *trillion* as of 2022.

Following the financial crisis, the Fed also began funding so-called special purpose vehicles (SPVs) through initiatives such as the Commercial Paper Funding Facility (CPFF) and the Money Market Investor Funding Facility (MMIFF). These were basically other means of providing short-term liquidity to investment banks and other private investors. More recently, the Fed has responded to the fallout from the pandemic by funding initiatives such as the Primary Market Corporate Credit Facility (PMCCF), aimed at providing banks and companies access to credit, often to help them remain solvent.

The problem with such measures is that investment banks and other non-bank financial institutions that benefit from them exist outside the Fed's usual area of bank regulation. Much of the controversy surrounding the Fed's actions following the financial crisis and the global pandemic, therefore, concerns the possibility that such institutions may have received a disproportionate benefit, often at the expense of individuals and smaller banks and companies, with little or no restrictions on their activities. In the future, the Fed is likely to face a choice between expanding its regulation to cover non-bank financial institutions, or else reverting to dealing exclusively with commercial banks.

Another monetary policy tool available to the Fed is known as the **discount rate**. This is the interest rate at which commercial banks can borrow funds from the Fed at what is called the Fed's "discount window". In theory, a reduction in the discount rate should increase the money supply, because it would lower the cost to a bank of borrowing from the Fed. A bank could then be somewhat more aggressive about making loans. In extraordinary circumstances such as the financial crisis or the pandemic, the Fed has encouraged expanded use of the discount window to promote greater liquidity.

---

discount rate: the interest rate at which banks can borrow reserves at the Fed discount window

---

Finally, another tool that the Fed has at its disposal is the required reserve ratio. Historically, if it wanted to increase the money supply, the Fed could lower the reserve requirement ratio, which would have the effect of expanding the money supply by allowing banks to make more loans on a smaller base of reserves. If, on the other hand, the Fed wanted to restrict increases in the money supply, it could increase the ratio of reserves required, thereby restraining bank lending. The Fed has generally altered the required reserve ratio only rarely, so it is generally considered the least important of the Fed's policy tools. But in response to the pandemic, the Fed took the unprecedented step of reducing all reserve requirements to 0 percent.

Thus far we have almost exclusively discussed monetary expansion, but the Fed can of course cause the money supply (and credit) to contract as well. If instead of making an open market purchase of government bonds, it makes an open market *sale*, everything we have thus far described just happens in reverse. When the Fed sells bonds, the buyer (usually a commercial bank) must pay the Fed. Overall, commercial banks will then hold *more* in government bonds and *less* in reserves. Of course, banks are never *forced* to buy bonds. But if the Fed increases the supply of bonds sufficiently, bond prices will fall to levels that strongly encourage banks to buy (see Appendix A1 for a detailed analysis of the bond market). If banks hold less in reserves, then they must tighten up on loans. If they tighten up on loans, then there will be fewer deposits. The money multiplier also works in reverse, so that the original bond sale has a magnified effect in reducing the total money supply.

The Fed can therefore increase the money supply (or expand credit) by making an open market purchase of bonds (or more recently, as noted, other assets), lowering the required reserve ratio, or lowering the discount rate. It can decrease the money supply (or contract credit) by making an open market sale of bonds, raising the required reserve ratio, or raising the discount rate.¶ Of these policy tools, however, open market operations continue to be the most frequently used and most significant in affecting the money supply.

In a growing economy, a central bank would rarely want to shrink the money supply in absolute terms. A growing economy, as measured by GDP, means ever more transactions need to be facilitated by readily available liquid assets and generally growing demand by private economic actors for loans. "Loose" monetary policy, in the case of a real-world growing economy, then, usually means making the money supply grow *faster* than the economy has been growing. "Tight" policy does not mean actually making the money supply fall; rather it just means making the money supply grow *more slowly* than the growth rate of the economy. Using the credit approach to interpreting monetary policy, we could say that the Fed has the choice of allowing credit to grow either faster or slower with respect to the real economy.

In this section, we have discussed the technical question of *how* the Fed or another economy's central bank can change the volume of money and credit in an economy. Now we can move on to the more interesting questions of *why* it may—or may not—want to do so. We introduce these issues by examining two different situations.

- ■ The first case is where inflation can be assumed to be fairly stable, and the main concerns of policymakers relate to output and employment. This case is addressed in the next two sections.
- ■ The second case is where policymakers are primarily worried about inflation. This is addressed in Section 5.

¶ Selling riskier assets, as described earlier, would be more problematic as there would be a much smaller pool of buyers. Indeed, many have criticized the Fed's actions in purchasing these assets in the first place, believing that it represented a "handout" to some of the biggest investment banks and insurance companies since the price paid may have been far in excess of market value, leaving the Fed "holding the bag" of devalued securities.

These important base cases are useful for analyzing real-world policy situations. The last section of the chapter looks at the more complicated issues of balancing goals related to employment, output, and inflation, and delves into controversies about monetary policies.

Discussion Questions

1. Describe in words how a Fed open market operation can increase the volume of money in the economy.
2. What are some ways in which the Fed has expanded its monetary policy tools to respond to recent challenges? Are there possible risks or problems associated with using these new approaches?

3 THE THEORY OF MONEY, INTEREST RATES, AND AGGREGATE EXPENDITURE

Our discussion up to this point has focused on the volume of money and credit in the economy. In an economy that is experiencing fairly low inflation and has a healthy banking system, most of the concern with the money supply is really a concern about interest rates, the availability of credit, and their consequences for aggregate expenditure. In contemporary discussions of the Fed's monetary policy, the focus is almost always on interest rates. Indeed, some macroeconomists question whether the concept of the money supply is even relevant, given the many variables that we have noted in the way banks and the financial system can choose to expand or contract credit; they would prefer to focus exclusively on interest rates. How does the Fed affect interest rates, and how do changing interest rates affect the economy?

3.1 The Federal Funds Rate and Other Interest Rates

When changes in monetary policy are announced by leaders of the Fed or discussed in the financial pages of the newspaper, attention usually focuses on what is called the **federal funds rate**. This is the going rate of interest on interbank loans determined in a private market. If a bank finds that it has more reserves than it needs to meet its reserve requirements, it offers funds on the "federal funds" market, usually just overnight. If another bank is short on reserves, it borrows in that market and pays back the next day. (Thus, we can think of bank reserves and "federal funds" as being more or less synonymous.)

---

federal funds rate: the interest rate determined in the private market for overnight loans of reserves among banks

---

Although a quick reading of reports in the media often makes it sound as though the Fed directly controls the federal funds rate (for example, headlines may read "Fed Announces Increase in Federal Funds Rate of 0.25 Percent"), this is not, in fact, the case. The Fed announces desired *target* or *benchmark* levels for the federal funds rate and then acts on bank reserves (i.e., by buying or selling assets like bonds) to try to achieve that target. Because the Fed is usually quite effective at this, the difference between the (official) target federal funds rate and the (market-determined) actual federal funds rate is generally quite small.

A simplified model of the federal funds market is portrayed in Figure 11.1(a). The quantity of funds is on the horizontal axis, and the federal funds rate—the price of borrowing in this market—is on the vertical axis. (Note that this is just a specific variant of the sort of "market for

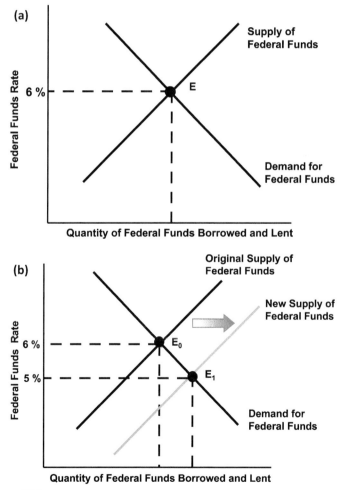

Figure 11.1a *The Market for Federal Funds*

Figure 11.1b *An Open Market Purchase Lowers the Federal Funds Rate*

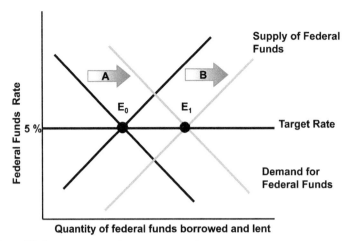

Figure 11.2 *Maintaining the Federal Funds Target Rate*

loanable funds" discussed in Chapter 8.) The actors on both sides of this market are banks.

The supply curve for federal funds slopes upward because higher returns in this market mean that banks with excess reserves will be more likely to lend them here, rather than finding other ways to lend them out. The demand curve for federal funds slopes downward, because the lower the interest rate, the more willing banks are to borrow. Figure 11.1(a) portrays a situation in which the federal funds rate at which the market clears is 6 percent. (Interest rates are generally stated in annualized terms—what borrowers would pay if they held the loan for a year—no matter how long the loan is actually held.)

The Fed undertakes open market operations with the goal of pushing the going rate for loans in that market to the level of its choosing. Recall that when the Fed makes an open market purchase, it increases the quantity of reserves that banks hold. All else being equal, this increases the quantity of reserves available for private lending in the federal funds market. In Figure 11.1(b), this is shown as the supply curve for federal funds shifting to the right. In this example the federal funds rate falls to 5 percent.

Since 1995, the Fed has explicitly announced its target for the federal funds rate and then taken the necessary steps to keep the actual rate as close as possible to the target rate. Figure 11.2 shows how the Fed reacts to a shift in the demand for federal funds. A rise in demand for federal funds is shown by shift A. If the Fed took no action in response to this shift, the increase in demand would cause the interest rate to rise. The Fed counteracts this upward pressure by putting more reserves into the system via open market purchases, shifting the supply curve outward (shift B). Conversely, the Fed would meet a decrease in the demand for federal funds with open market sales. The Fed is thus able to maintain this important interest rate at, or very close to, its targeted level.

Since the passage of the Dodd-Frank Act in 2010 in response to the financial crisis, the Fed pays commercial banks interest on their reserves, something not done previously. This makes the Fed's ability to "target" the fed funds rate even stronger. The rate at which banks receive interest on their reserves represents a "lower bound" on the fed funds rate since no bank will be willing to lend to other banks at a lower rate than this, while the discount rate (the rate at which banks can borrow from the Fed) represents an "upper bound," since no bank would pay more than this to borrow from another bank. As a result, the Fed practically has absolute control of the fed funds rate. If necessary, it can reduce the band within which the rate fluctuates by simply reducing the difference between the discount rate and the fed funds rate.

In today's modern, sophisticated economy financial markets tend to be closely interlinked, so a drop in an important rate like the federal funds rate tends to carry over into other markets. One of the things you might have noticed if you have ever taken out a consumer loan or obtained a mortgage is that the interest rate your bank charges you is much higher than the federal funds rate. There are several reasons for this.

First, most loans granted by banks are relatively long-term loans. Banks usually borrow from the Fed for a few days, while consumer or corporate loans usually run at least over several months, if not years, and mortgages usually for up to 30 years. Banks therefore must charge a higher rate than they themselves pay, as compensation for giving up liquidity for long periods.

Second, the higher interest rate partly compensates commercial banks for the occasional instance when the borrower does not pay back the loan. Indeed, in this sense, the cost of the "bad debts" of some customers is ultimately borne by other customers. Finally, the commercial bank needs to make a profit in order to cover costs for credit administration, staff, and services. These factors also explain why the interest rate on bank loans exceeds the rate paid to depositors on their savings accounts.

Commercial banks charge their most creditworthy commercial customers what is known as the **prime rate**, which moves virtually in lockstep with the federal funds rate. While historically the difference between the two has varied, since the 1990s it has remained at 3 percentage points, so that the prime rate precisely tracks the fed funds rate over time (Figure 11.3).

Rates on loans and mortgages are generally tied to the prime rate, while the interest rate paid on deposits will generally be significantly lower than the prime rate (so that the bank can make a profit). Regardless of the differences in prevailing interest rates (economists call these differences "interest rate spreads"), all rates, including consumer interest rates, tend to rise or fall in accordance with changes in the fed funds rate.

433

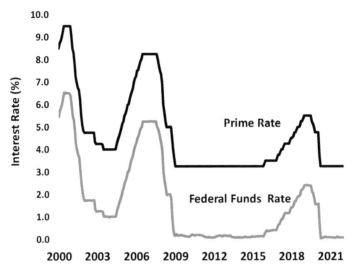

Figure 11.3 *The Federal Fund and Prime Rates, 1955–2021*
Source: Federal Reserve Board, Monthly data.

---

prime rate: the interest rate that banks charge their most creditworthy commercial borrowers

---

As a general rule, an expansionary monetary policy lowers interest rates throughout the economy.** Since lower interest rates make loans cheaper, such a policy usually leads to faster credit growth throughout the economy. Conversely, contractionary monetary policy tends to shrink the volume of credit and raise interest rates throughout the economy. Higher interest rates make loans more expensive, so contractionary policy usually leads to slower credit growth or even credit contraction throughout the economy. Therefore, whichever policy direction it chooses, central bank monetary policy profoundly affects businesses and individuals throughout the economy.

3.2 Interest Rates and Investment

Economists are particularly interested in interest rates because of their effect on investment. To the extent that individuals or businesses make investments using borrowed funds, higher interest rates make investing more expensive and hence less attractive. Even if investment were to be financed directly out of savings, in theory, it would be diminished by a higher rate. With higher interest rates, saving money or investing in

---

**Things get more complicated when we consider the duration of loans and the difference between short- and long-term interest rates. We address this issue in the Appendix.

bonds might be more attractive than buying a new piece of machinery or building a house.

Residential investment in particular has historically been especially sensitive to variations in interest rates. Traditionally, investment in homes has been financed by 15- or 30-year mortgages. A small change in the interest rate can add up, over time, to a very big difference in the total cost of buying a house.

The case for interest rate effects on intended business investment in structures, equipment, and inventories (sometimes referred to as "non-residential investment") is a bit more mixed. We saw in Chapter 8 that Keynes did not think that changes in the interest rate would be sufficient to get the economy out of the Great Depression. Investor pessimism during that period was very deep. Trying to encourage businesses to invest by lowering interest rates at a time when they see no prospect of selling more of their goods has been referred to as attempting to "push on a string."

The idea that business fixed investment primarily responds to changes in sales much more than to changes in interest rates has been called the **accelerator principle**. If businesses see their sales rising, they may need to expand their capacity—that is, invest in new equipment and structures—in order to keep up with demand for their product. Since the best macroeconomic indicator of expanded sales is a rising GDP, this principle says that the best predictor of investment growth is GDP growth. Conversely, a small decline—or even just slowing down—of demand may lead to a disproportionate drying up of intended investment, as firms come to fear being caught with excess capacity. To the extent the accelerator principle prevails, changes in the interest rate may have only a relatively minor effect on levels of business investment.

---

accelerator principle: the idea that high GDP growth leads to increasing investment, and low or negative GDP growth leads to declining investment

---

Given a particular level of optimism or pessimism, however, firms can be expected to pay at least some attention to interest rates in deciding how much to invest. Higher interest rates tend to limit the amount of investment by firms that may need to borrow money to invest. Using the string analogy, it is easier to pull on a string than to push it—tighter monetary policy is likely to restrain overall investment.

Combining this logical assumption with the empirically observed sensitivity of residential investment to interest rates, our simple model of macroeconomic stabilization says that *all else being equal*, lower interest rates will lead to higher intended investment spending (and vice versa for higher interest rates). The quantity of intended investment is inversely related to the interest rate, r, as shown in Figure 11.4.

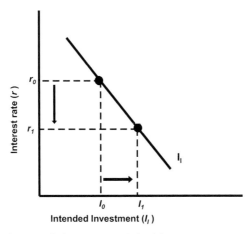

Figure 11.4 *The Intended Investment Schedule*

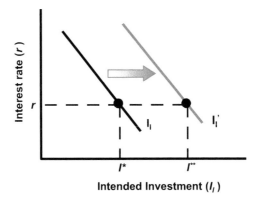

Figure 11.5 *An Increase in Investor Confidence*

Changes in investor confidence, related to actual spending (via the accelerator principle) or to expected levels of spending, can be portrayed as shifting this intended investment curve. An increase in investor confidence, for example, shifts the curve to the right (from $\mathbf{I_1}$ to $\mathbf{I_1}'$) as shown in Figure 11.5. At any given interest rate, firms now want to invest more ($\mathbf{I^{**}}$ rather than $\mathbf{I^{*}}$). A decrease in investor confidence shifts the curve to the left.

3.3 Monetary Policy and Aggregate Expenditure

Our basic model of aggregate expenditure, developed in Chapters 8 and 9, can now be expanded to include the effect of monetary policy. In an economy with relatively low inflation and a stable banking system, expansionary monetary policy tends to lower interest rates (Figures 11.1(b) and 11.3) and, consequently, raise intended investment (Figure 11.4).

Because intended investment spending, I_1 is part of aggregate expenditure:

$$AE = C + I_I + G + NX$$

this increase in investment should shift the *AE* schedule upward and raise the equilibrium levels of aggregate expenditure, income, and output, as shown in Figure 11.6. The chain of causation can be summarized as:

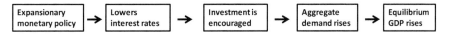

If the economy were headed toward a recession, then monetary policy that is relatively loose, increasing the money supply in order to help maintain output, could have a desirable stabilizing effect. Sometimes such an **expansionary monetary policy** is called an **accommodative monetary policy**, especially when the Fed is reacting to a specific economic event that might otherwise tend to send the economy into recession.

---

expansionary monetary policy: the use of monetary policy tools to increase the money supply, lower interest rates, and stimulate a higher level of economic activity

accommodative monetary policy: loose or expansionary monetary policy intended to counteract recessionary tendencies in the economy

---

Contractionary monetary policy, however, would be prescribed if the economy seems to be heading toward inflation. In that case, the Fed seeks to slow growth and "cool down" the economy. In the aggregate expenditure model, a decrease in the rate of growth of the money supply will raise interest rates, lower intended investment, shift the *AE* schedule downward, and lower the equilibrium levels of aggregate expenditure, income, and output.[††]

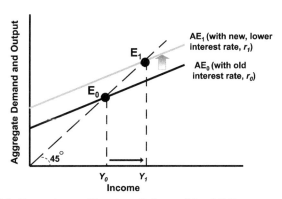

Figure 11.6 *Expansionary Monetary Policy and the AE Curve*

[††]In Chapter 13, we look at how monetary policy can also change *AE* by affecting international capital flows, the relative values of national currencies, and net exports.

> **contractionary monetary policy:** the use of monetary policy tools to limit the money supply, raise interest rates, and encourage a leveling off or reduction in economic activity and inflationary tendencies

Discussion Questions

1. What sorts of interest rates are relevant to your own economic activities? Do you think that Fed policies affect their levels?
2. Is it always true that an increase in the money supply, or a decrease in interest rates, leads to an increase in investment and aggregate expenditure? Why or why not?

4 MONETARY POLICIES IN PRACTICE

4.1 Responding to Inflation

How important are money and monetary policy to the national economy? It is a question lacking an easy answer. While we often observe patterns in economics, sometimes even consistent ones, we lack evidence that pumping more money into the economy *necessarily* makes people spend or businesses invest. Because of the uncertainty, a variety of competing monetary theories have been developed, some of which we will compare and contrast later. First, we explore some lessons from experience, some of which suggest that monetary policy may be more effective when contractionary than when expansionary (see Box 11.1).

The 1970s were characterized by very rapid inflation in the United States. Average prices, as reflected in the consumer price index (CPI), increased by more than 12 percent in 1974 alone, and again by 13 percent and 12 percent in 1979 and 1980. In response, starting in 1979, Fed chair Paul Volcker undertook to limit further increases by increasing interest rates substantially. During his tenure, the Fed raised the fed funds rate target well into the double digits, where it peaked at over 19 percent in early 1981 and did not return to single digits until late 1984.

The monetary "tightening" was successful in slowing inflation substantially; by 1982 inflation was below 4 percent. The unresolved, and still somewhat contentious, issue is whether or not the economic recession that Volcker's policy caused in the early 1980s was too high a price to pay for price stability. This is an issue that we continue to confront:

BOX 11.1 MONETARY POLICY IN PRACTICE

History appears to support the idea that, while monetary policy may be effective as a restraint to the economy, it is limited in its ability to stimulate it.

The United States experienced an estimated one-third decrease in its money supply from 1929 to 1933. This coincided with the greatest economic decline that the U.S. economy has experienced in over a century. Whether or not the decline in money was actually the main *cause* of the Great Depression remains a topic of controversy. But there is significant evidence that restrictive monetary policy contributed to the severity and duration of the Depression.

The period from 1979 to 1982 offers another instance in which recession appears to have been caused by tight money. In this period, the Fed's goal was to counteract inflation, which had reached double digits by the late 1970s. But the resulting application of a highly contractionary monetary policy, while effective against inflation, also caused a severe recession.

U.S. monetary policy has, in contrast, been aggressively expansionary in recent decades. But its effectiveness in stimulating the real economy is uncertain. Several years of low interest rates in the early 2000s provoked unsustainable levels of mortgage refinancing and other forms of consumption that were the seeds of the 2007–2008 financial crisis. Following the financial crisis, the Fed used even more expansionary measures, with mixed results. While very low interest rates may have helped avert an even worse recession, and provided some support for recovery, that recovery turned out to be painfully slow. The Fed was effectively "pushing on a string," and this failed to provide the necessary impetus for a more rapid economic comeback.

At the same time, protracted low-interest rate policy introduced other distortions to the economy, hurting ordinary savers who got almost no return on their investment, while benefiting primarily affluent investors in stocks, whose prices rose very rapidly as a result of the availability of "cheap money" for investment. Inequality has intensified as a result, and the Fed's aggressive response to the near collapse precipitated by the pandemic may have "added fuel to the fire".

how much unemployment should we tolerate in the interest of keeping prices stable?

4.2 Responding to Recession

With generally low interest rates during the 1990s, the United States economy experienced a steady expansion. After having peaked at almost 11 percent in the early 1980s, the U.S. unemployment rate was just 3.8 percent in April 2000. These good times, however, did not last. The "dotcom" stock market bubble burst in 2000, with the NASDAQ index eventually losing more than 75 percent of its value before hitting its bottom in September 2002. Orders for goods slowed down, and inventories consequently built up. Concerned about a weakening economy, the Fed in January 2001 lowered the fed funds rate again. As shown in Figure 11.3, until late 2003 the Fed continued pushing interest rates down, and the fed funds rate bottomed out at 1 percent in early 2004.

One might think that such an aggressive move in lowering rates would spur investment. Yet business investment actually ticked *down*

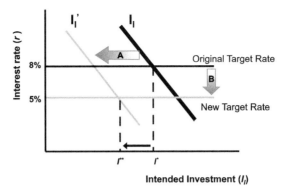

Figure 11.7 *Expansionary Monetary Policy in an Environment of Pessimism*

and did not recover until late 2003. Businesses had too much capacity and inventory and were pessimistic about sales. Moreover, the global security situation, with the terrorist attack in September of 2001 being followed by the wars in Afghanistan and Iraq, caused uncertainty among the business community and tended to reduce investment.

In terms of the model, Figure 11.7 shows this pessimism shifting the intended investment schedule to the left, from I_1 to I_1'. The lower interest rates due to Fed action may have kept investors from cutting back even more, but the lower rates were not enough to prevent the downturn in intended investment, shown on the graph as a shift from I^* to I^{**}.

Residential investment, however, rose steadily during this same period. This boosted the overall economy, and it was partly in response to this economic improvement that the Fed moved to increase rates anew starting in 2004. For the next three years, the Fed steadily increased the federal funds rate in hopes of keeping the economy from "overheating" (as shown in Figure 11.3). But the real estate market nonetheless moved into a speculative frenzy that led to the crash of 2007–2008. Consequently, in late 2007 the Fed had little choice but to again switch to an expansionary stance.

But this time it would move more aggressively than in the past and for much longer. The Fed allowed the federal funds rate to sink to historic lows, and far more quickly than during the previous rate reduction. The rate fell from 5.26 percent in mid-2007 to scarcely above zero (0.16 percent) by the end of 2008 (as shown in Figure 11.3). The economy nevertheless fell into recession, and because the ensuing economic recovery was so slow, then-Fed Chair Ben Bernanke had no choice but to keep rates at rock-bottom levels. The fed funds rate bottomed out at 0.07 percent in early 2014, before starting a gradual rise.

Even a near-zero federal funds rate was insufficient to promote the lending required to kick start the economy. Some analysts suggested that the Fed might even lower rates *below* zero, but the Fed has rejected this approach (see Box 11.2). The Fed instead resorted to an unprecedented approach known as **quantitative easing (QE)**. In addition to its regular open market program of government bond purchases, under QE the Fed also bought other diverse financial assets from banks and non-bank institutions alike. Included among these are what are known as mortgage-backed securities, which are basically "pools" of a variety of private mortgages. The main objective of such purchases is to flood the economy with more money, in hopes of provoking the necessary spending to create an economic stimulus.

---

quantitative easing (QE): the purchase of financial assets including long-term bonds by the Fed, creating more monetary reserves and expanding the money supply

---

BOX 11.2 NEGATIVE INTEREST RATES?

The Federal Reserve took unprecedented measures to help the United States survive the consequences of the COVID-19 pandemic. Until recently, for example, it had never utilized its authority to purchase municipal bonds or exchange traded funds. But there has been heated debate over an even more controversial monetary policy tool: Negative interest rates.

If the Fed were to set a negative target for its fed funds rate, it means interest rates could fall below 0 percent. In theory, negative rates would help the economy by encouraging consumers to borrow and spend. They would make it less appealing to keep cash in the bank since people would be charged a fee instead of earning interest on their savings, and negative interest rates would also incentivize borrowing since they would push loan rates to rock-bottom lows. The European Central Bank (ECB) and the Bank of Japan (BoJ) have both employed negative rates in efforts to stave off deflation. In real terms—that is, adjusting for inflation (see Appendix)—neither has since been able to move rates back into positive territory.

But the Federal Reserve insists that negative interest rates are not on the table. Federal Reserve Chairman Jerome Powell has repeatedly said that they are not something to be considered: "I continue to think...that negative interest rates are probably not an appropriate or useful policy for us here in the United States," said Chairman Powell in a 60 Minutes interview.

It might be for the best. The effects of negative rates on the domestic economy would be highly unpredictable. Seeking to avoid bank fees, people might, for example, keep little money in the bank and possibly seek to prepay their phone and utility bills months ahead out of their savings. And minuscule mortgage rates – Nordea Bank, based in Finland, recently offered 20-year mortgages at 0 percent interest— would likely incentivize the purchase of second or even third homes. Credit card interest rates would, to be sure, remain positive. But who would even want to use the cards when banks might pay consumers to borrow money? In fact, who would even want to lend?[2]

While the Federal Reserve has said that it is not seriously looking at negative rates, it might be worth considering how they could potentially affect you in the future, especially since the moderate to rapid inflation observed up to early 2022 could effectively (that is, in real terms) make rates negative even if they are positive in nominal terms.

By 2014, three rounds of quantitative easing, referred to as QE1, QE2, and QE3 had taken place. Although it took time, the economy did start to recover, and it appears that low interest rates and quantitative easing played an important role. Yet critics warned that such a massive program of monetary expansion could have undesired effects, such as fueling further financial bubbles or causing inflation to rise.

The fourth round of quantitative easing (dubbed QE4) was launched in March 2020 in response to the global pandemic, along with a sharp reduction in the fed funds rate, which was pushed nearly to zero (as shown in Figure 11.3). While it arguably helped stave off an economic collapse, this very expansionary monetary policy is also widely believed to have played an important part in the inflation that appeared starting in the second half of 2021. Average goods prices rose more rapidly in early 2022 than they had in 40 years, bringing inflation to the fore as a major policy concern. This led to the Fed once again reversing course and tighten policy by ending quantitative easing and raising interest rates starting in 2022.

Discussion Questions

1. What economic conditions would cause the Fed to shift from an expansionary policy to a policy of raising interest rates? What risks might be involved with a policy that is too expansionary, or not expansionary enough?
2. Are negative interest rates possible? Are there real-life examples of negative interest rates? Why have they generally been rejected by the U.S. Federal Reserve Bank?

5 THEORIES OF MONEY, PRICES, AND INFLATION

As mentioned above, there are different theories regarding the analysis of money and monetary policy. The relationship between money and the "real" economy has long been a source of controversy. We will review some of the main ways in which economists have conceptualized this relationship and the corresponding implications for government policy.

5.1 The Quantity Equation

One way of thinking about the relationship between the real economy, money, and prices is based on what economists call the **quantity equation**:

$$M \times V = P \times Y$$

---

quantity equation: $M \times V = P \times Y$ where M is the money supply, V is the velocity of money, P is the price level, and Y is real output

---

In this equation, Y is, as usual, real output or GDP. P indicates the price level as measured by a price index, for example the GDP deflator discussed in Chapter 4. The multiplication of these two variables means that the right-hand side of the equation represents nominal output (if necessary, review Chapter 4 for an explanation of the difference between nominal and real output).

On the left-hand side, M measures the level of money balances, such as the M1 measure discussed above. V, the only really new variable here, represents the velocity of money. The **velocity of money** is the number of times that a dollar changes hands in a year, in order to support the level of output and exchange represented by nominal GDP. In other words, since the money in circulation is insufficient to "purchase" everything involved in GDP, velocity represents how often, on average, each dollar changes hands in order for there to be sufficient funds to purchase all the goods and services produced in the economy. (Remember that we are talking both about cash and bank deposits—so "changing hands" could be literal, as when you pay for a pizza with cash, or virtual, as when a bank clears a check on one account, making the funds available to another account holder.)

---

velocity of money: the number of times that a dollar would have to change hands during a year to support nominal GDP, calculated as $V = (P \times Y)/M$

Since nominal GDP and M1 are observable, velocity can be calculated as the ratio of the two,

$$V = \frac{P \times Y}{M}$$

For the quantity equation to become the basis for a *theory*, rather than merely represent definitions of variables, an assumption needs to be made about velocity. Supporters of different economic theories all have subscribed to the irrefutable arithmetic of the quantity equation. Where they have differed is over assumptions regarding the behavior of one or more of the variables.

Two closely related theories that we discuss below—classical and monetarist—assume that velocity is constant—changing very little, if at all, with changing conditions in the economy. If this is true, then the level of the money supply and the level of nominal GDP will be tightly related. We denote this assumption that velocity is constant by putting a bar over V. The **quantity theory of money**, then, is characterized by the relation

$$M \times \bar{V} = P \times Y$$

443

where $\bar{V}$ is read "V-bar." More Keynesian-oriented theories, however, while they may make use of the quantity equation, do not assume that velocity is constant. Their analyses are not based on the quantity theory.

> **quantity theory of money:** the theory that money supply is directly related to nominal GDP, according to the equation $M \times \bar{V} = P \times Y$

5.2 Competing Theories

Classical monetary theory is based on the quantity theory of money, plus the assumption that output is always at or close to its full-employment level.[‡‡] That is,

$$M \times V = P \times Y *$$

where Y^*, as usual, denotes full-employment output. In this case—in contrast to the aggregate expenditure model described in Section 4—changes in the money supply have *no* effect on the level of output. The inability of changes in the money supply to affect real output is called **monetary neutrality**. The only variable on the left-hand side that is not constant is the money supply, while the only variable on the right-hand side that is not constant is the price level. Thus, all that a change in the money supply can do is change prices. Rather than an increase in the money supply increasing output, in this model an increase in the money supply has no effect other than to cause inflation.

Classical economists, then, tend to see no need for discretionary monetary policy. On the contrary, they consider it counterproductive. In the case of an economy that is not growing, the classical theory would

> **monetary neutrality:** the idea that changes in the money supply may affect only prices while leaving output unchanged

prescribe a stable money supply level to avoid unnecessary changes in prices. In a growing economy, the classical theory says that the money supply should grow at the same rate as real GDP in order to keep prices stable. If we assume that the rate of real GDP growth is fairly constant, then the money supply should just grow at a fixed rate, say 3 percent per year. A central bank that enforces this is said to be following a **money supply rule**.

[‡‡] We simplify here, but to be precise, the classical view is that the economy will always tend toward full employment equilibrium in the long run, as discussed in Chapter 8.

> **money supply rule:** committing to letting the money supply grow at a fixed rate per year

Another famous theory based on the quantity equation is **monetarism**, propounded by Milton Friedman and Anna Jacobson Schwartz in their book *A Monetary History of the United States, 1867–1960*, published in 1963. While Keynes had argued that insufficient investment and aggregate expenditure caused the Great Depression, Friedman and Schwartz argued that it was caused by a severe contraction in the money supply.

> **monetarism:** a school of economic thought that argues that governments should aim for steadiness in the money supply rather than playing an active role

Friedman had earlier propounded the quantity theory of money and has become known for his saying that "inflation is always and everywhere a monetary phenomenon." Like classical economists, he thought that bad monetary policy could, at least temporarily, have detrimental effects on the real economy. But unlike the pure classical theorists, he thought that it could work both ways: monetary policy could be deflationary as well as inflationary. During the early years of the Great Depression, he and Schwartz pointed out, both the money supply and the level of nominal GDP fell sharply. This empirical observation can be seen as consistent with the quantity theory of money, assuming a constant velocity of money:

$$M \times \bar{V} = P \times Y$$
$$\downarrow \qquad\quad \downarrow \quad \downarrow$$

Friedman and Schwartz argued that the contraction in the money supply caused reductions in both the price level and real GDP. It is an assertion that remains controversial, and there remains widespread disagreement over whether prices or output are more sensitive to a money supply reduction. Because of his belief in the potential for bad monetary policy to cause harm, Friedman was one of the most vocal proponents of the idea that central banks should simply follow a fixed rule of having the money supply grow at a steady rate. In this regard, he and most classical theorists would have been in agreement.

The quantity equation can also be used to shed light on the problem of very high inflation, described in Chapter 10. Here we move away from the classical assumption of a constant velocity of money. Suppose that the level of output in an economy is stagnant or growing only very

445

slowly. But at the same time suppose that the central bank is causing the money supply to grow very quickly by printing money, for example, to help the government finance a large budget deficit. If people come to expect high inflation, money may become a "hot potato"—people want to hold it for as short a time as possible because it loses value so quickly. They will try to turn money into non-inflating assets—real estate, hard currency, jewelry, or barterable goods as quickly as they can. This means that the velocity of money also increases. A situation of hyperinflation in a stagnant economy can be illustrated as:

$$M \times V = P \times \bar{Y}$$
$$\uparrow \quad \uparrow \quad \uparrow$$

where the bar over Y indicates that output is stuck at a level below full employment. With output stagnant, and both money supply and velocity increasing, inflation must result.

While we imagined a printing press in the government's basement in our earlier story about hyperinflation in Chapter 10, a sophisticated economy can also essentially "run the printing presses" if the agency that issues government debt and the central bank work together. For example, suppose that the U.S. Treasury issues new debt, and the Fed immediately buys the same amount of new debt and injects new money into the economy. The effect is the same as if the Fed had just printed new currency, except that the increase in bank reserves is in the form of a computer entry instead of freshly printed paper. This is a phenomenon referred to as **monetizing the deficit**. In practice, the Fed never *automatically* buys new U.S. Treasury debt although it may, as an accommodating move, monetize some of the government deficit in order to help the economy out of a recession. But since the Fed is, as noted earlier, "independent" of the U.S. government, it is not obliged to do so.[§§]

---

monetizing the deficit: when a central bank buys government debt as it is issued (equivalent to "running the printing presses")

Even in less extreme cases, a "loose money" policy can lead to inflation. For example, suppose that the economy is functioning relatively normally, but output has reached its full-employment level (Y^*). If monetary policy continues to be expansionary, inflation is likely to result. Chapter 12 considers this possibility in greater detail.

[§§] The situation in the United States stands in contrast to the Eurozone, where the ECB is prohibited from buying new government debt. Even if it considered it worthwhile to buy government bonds (e.g., under a new quantitative easing program) it can only buy outstanding bonds—i.e., already-existing as opposed to new government debt.

While the quantity equation can be helpful in thinking about monetary phenomena such as inflation, we get different results if we assume that velocity is variable. For example, an increase in M could be offset by a decrease in V. Even though the central bank pursues a policy of monetary expansion, people and banks might be pessimistic enough that they hold onto excess reserves of money, in effect neutralizing the desired expansionary policy. This is why Keynesian-leaning economists often prefer expansionary fiscal policy measures to stimulate the economy in situations of high unemployment. Similarly, contractionary fiscal policies would be favored by Keynesian economists to control inflation by lowering the AE curve.

Some economists go further in rejecting monetarism. According to the school known as **modern monetary theory** (MMT), it makes little sense even to use the concept of the money supply (M in the quantity equation) as an important factor determining prices or events in the real economy. Rather, the direction of causation runs the other way: the real economy, based on private consumption, investment, government spending, and taxes determines the growth of the money supply. The role of the Fed, in this view, is merely to maintain a target rate of interest by buying or selling bonds. It is possible to measure the money supply, but M is not an independent variable that affects P and Q, as in the monetarist approach. While there is general agreement that setting a target rate of interest rather than focusing on the money supply is how modern central banks operate, the broader assertions of the MMT school remain controversial (see Box 11.3).

---

modern monetary theory: the belief that fiscal expenditure and taxes determine output and price levels, while money is supplied or withheld merely in response to fiscal policy

---

BOX 11.3 "MODERN MONETARY THEORY" AND GOVERNMENT SPENDING

The controversial Modern Monetary Theory (MMT) doctrine holds that governments have the capacity to spend as much as they want and back up this spending with money creation. In this view, debt is not a problem so long as the government retains the power to create money.

In 2020, the $1.9 trillion American Rescue Plan, coming on top of earlier pandemic-related spending, was seen as a victory for MMT since it did not include "payfors"—tax increases or cutbacks in other budget areas to compensate for the increased spending. "We got five or six trillion dollars of spending and tax cuts without anyone worrying about payfors, so that was a good thing," according to L. Randall Wray, an economics professor at Bard College in New York and MMT advocate. "In January [2020], MMT was a crazy idea, and then in March, it was, OK, we're going to adopt MMT."

The U.S. infrastructure act signed into law in November 2021, on the other hand, marked a defeat for advocates of MMT, due to the bipartisan requirement that all the $550 billion of new spending be matched by offsetting revenue (pay-fors).

Critics of MMT argue that monetary excess will lead to inflation. The re-emergence of significant inflation in late 2021 and 2022 strengthened their position, and undercut the early success of MMT. For a while, it seemed that governments had adopted the MMT point of view that high spending was acceptable if needed to promote the economy, and debt was nothing to worry about. But the onset of inflation gave more traditional views of monetary precaution a new lease on life.

In 2022 the Federal Reserve, worried about the upsurge in inflation, moved toward more contractionary monetary policy. But MMT advocates believe that monetary policy does not work. If an expanding economy starts to "overheat," MMT would recommend using tax policy rather than monetary policy, increasing taxes to cool things off. This, however, is a much harder sell than promoting spending, given a strong aversion on both sides of the aisle in Congress to increasing taxes.[3]

5.3 Money Supply, Money Demand, and the Liquidity Trap

Another approach to monetary policy is to look at the money supply in the context of a "market" for money in which there is also a demand side. Since nearly everyone wants more money, what exactly does it mean that money is "demanded?" Here it is important to recall the distinction made in Chapter 10 between money in the sense of a purely liquid asset such as currency, and other less liquid "non-money" assets like stocks or real estate. For our purposes, money demand will represent the extent to which we prefer to hold our household assets in liquid form.

Why not hold *all* our assets as money? Typically, one earns little or no interest from keeping money in cash or checking accounts. So, in a sense, the expected return (interest, dividend, or profit) on one's relatively illiquid assets represents the *opportunity cost* of holding money, since that return is sacrificed whenever one holds liquid money instead of assets. Yet it should be clear that there are also costs to holding no liquid money.

There are essentially three reasons that people choose to hold some of their assets as money. The first of these is known as the **transactions demand** for money, which is based on our need to finance our day-to-day existence. We need liquidity, for example, to make purchases at the grocery store or to pay our monthly bills. The second type of money demand is called **precautionary demand**, which is explained by our general need to always hold "a little extra" in case, for instance, we needed home repairs, or we had to drop everything and travel to help a relative. Finally, some people like to keep some extra money liquid—often in a "cash account" with their broker—to be able to take advantage of any new and often unpredictable investment opportunities. Such a demand for money is known as **speculative demand**.

---

transactions demand: the demand for money to pay for the goods and services that satisfy our day-to-day needs
precautionary demand: the demand for money to pay for contingencies
speculative demand: the demand for money to exploit new expectations of changes in asset prices

---

Together, these three types of demand constitute the overall demand for money in a market. As with any other commodity, the "cheaper" it is, the greater will be the quantity demanded. In this case, since we do not "buy" money in the store, its cheapness amounts to what we give up by holding it (i.e., what the opportunity cost of holding money will be).

So, if we use the prevailing interest rate to represent the return on non-liquid assets,[¶¶] we can show how the money demanded in an economy varies according to its relative cheapness. As with any other theorized demand curve, the one for money is downward sloping. Like other demand curves, the money demand curve may *shift* as a result of a change in transactions, precautionary, or speculative demand for money. (This corresponds to what we have discussed above as a change in the velocity of money.)

The supply curve for money shows the relationship between the quantity of money supplied and the market interest rate. But since the Fed, through open market operations, determines the quantity of bank reserves—and, through the money multiplier, the money supply—this analysis assumes that the Fed more or less "dictates" the money supply independent of prevailing interest rates. The result is a money supply curve that is vertical instead of the more familiar upward sloping curve. Together with money demand, it determines the equilibrium interest rate r^* (Figure 11.8).[***]

In this approach, it is not the case that the interest rate influences or determines the money supply. Rather, it is the money supply—or to be precise, the point of equilibrium between it and money demand—that determines the interest rate. And as shown in Figure 11.9, when the Fed increases the money supply, the interest rate goes down. It should make

---

[¶¶] This is, of course, an enormous simplification, since in the real world there exist an almost endless variety of assets that vary in terms of liquidity, risk, and other factors. Moreover, many pay dividends or distribute profits instead of paying an interest rate. The main point about money demand is in no way invalidated, however, by the simplification.

[***] As noted earlier, theorists of the "modern monetary theory" school disagree with this, rejecting the idea that the money supply is strictly under control of the Fed, focusing instead on interest rate targeting.

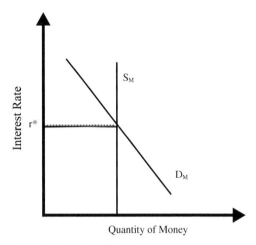

Figure 11.8 *Demand and Supply for Money*

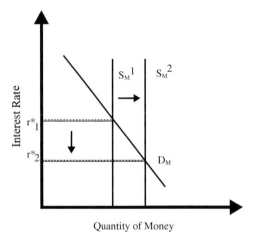

Figure 11.9 *An Increase in the Supply of Money*

sense since, *ceteris paribus*, the more money is available, the "cheaper" it is. The opposite would happen if the Fed decreased the money supply. Using similar logic, you can determine for yourself the consequences of a shift in money *demand*.

5.3.1 The Liquidity Trap and Credit Rationing

Are there limits to the Fed's ability to control the money supply and interest rates? In the 1930s, Keynes introduced the term **liquidity trap** for a situation in which it is impossible for a central bank to drive interest rates down any lower through continued monetary stimulus. This concept may be a good description of the recent periods when the U.S. fed funds rate hovered near zero.

> **liquidity trap:** a situation in which interest rates are so low that the central bank finds it impossible to reduce them further

The way a liquidity trap works is that as the Fed creates money, banks, individuals, and business firms simply hold onto the money, rather than using it in ways that increase aggregate expenditure. Recall that for expansionary monetary policy to work in the predicted way, banks have to respond to increases in their reserves by making new loans. But what if banks do not find many of their customers creditworthy or their usual customers are not very interested in taking out new loans? Or what if banks are weak as a consequence of past losses, and hence are reluctant to expand their balance sheet? In such situations, low interest rates may not translate into new credit and new investment. Instead, the banks may hold the money as excess reserves to protect themselves against problems with bad loans or other financial demands.

Instead of using extra funds to make more loans, banks may tend to engage in **credit rationing** in order to ensure their own profitability. This means that they will lend to the customers whom they deem most creditworthy, using restrictive standards to decide who merits getting a loan. If this happens, some firms and individuals will get the funds that they need, while others—and particularly smaller firms and lower-income individuals—may be frozen out. In this case, monetary policy may have significant distributional effects: in the simplest terms, making the rich richer, and the poor poorer.

> **credit rationing:** when banks deny loans to some potential borrowers, in the interest of maintaining their own profitability

An analytical presentation of a liquidity trap is shown in Figure 11.10. In this figure, the shape of both the money supply and demand curves is modified from the simple version shown in Figures 11.8 and 11.9. The money supply curve slopes slightly upward, reflecting the tendency of banks to hold more excess reserves when interest rates are low, and investments are less profitable. The money demand curve becomes almost flat at lower interest rates, reflecting the unwillingness or inability of businesses and households to make new investments, deciding to hold money instead. Thus, however much new money the Fed pumps into the system—shown in Figure 11.10 by the shift from money supply (1) to (2), (3), and (4)—people simply hold onto the extra money, meaning that interest rates do not fall.

451

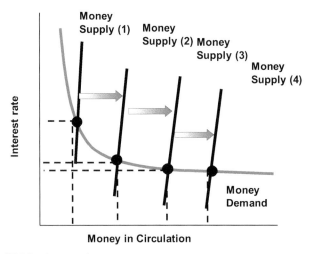

Figure 11.10 *The Liquidity Trap*

The possibility of a liquidity trap, or of reluctance among bankers and investors to lend and borrow, means that the Fed faces limits to its ability to stimulate a sluggish economy (recall Box 11.1). It does not necessarily mean that the Fed's efforts are completely fruitless. For example, the Fed's purchases of existing mortgages from banks in the aftermath of the financial crisis freed the banks to create new mortgages, improving the situation in the housing market. But the creation of so much new money following both the 2007–2009 and 2020 recessions also raised concerns that much of the money might go to the wrong places, creating inflation in asset prices. Indeed, prices of assets, particularly publicly traded equities, rose substantially during the recent period of very low interest rates.

Clearly, then, while the Fed has great powers to affect economic fundamentals, it also faces limits on its policy effectiveness, depending on conditions in the real economy.

Discussion Questions

1. What is the difference between the quantity *theory* of money and the quantity *equation?*
2. Has inflation been reported to be a problem in any recent news reports? Check recent inflation data at https://www.usinflationcalculator.com. How do you think this is related to recent Fed monetary policy?

6 COMPLICATIONS AND POLICY CONTROVERSIES

In the real world, central banks generally have to be concerned about output and inflation, as well as banking regulation and stability, all at the same time. When the goals include *both* stabilization of prices and maintaining output at or near full employment, it complicates the analysis considerably. What does this mean for policy?

6.1 The Fed's Dilemma

As we saw in Section 3, the Fed tries to help get the economy out of a recession through expansionary monetary policy—policies that increase the money supply, lower interest rates, stimulate investment, and increase aggregate expenditure. But if the Fed implements expansionary monetary policy too vigorously or at the wrong time (such as when the economy is already nearing full employment), then it can cause inflation to accelerate (as we saw in Section 4). If inflation is "heating up," then the Fed should use contractionary monetary policy—i.e., reining in the money supply, raising interest rates, and discouraging investment in the interest of stabilizing, if not reducing, aggregate expenditure and "cooling off" the economy.

This may seem very straightforward, but policymaking can have many complications. For one thing, there is the controversial question of what exactly the "full-employment" level of employment is at any given time.

Suppose, for example, that the Fed starts to get nervous about inflation too early in an economic upswing. Perhaps the unemployment rate could have fallen to 4 percent, with little increase in inflation, if the recovery had been allowed to continue, but the Fed switches into inflation-fighting mode at an unemployment rate of 6 percent. By halting the recovery too early, the Fed may end up being blamed for causing unnecessary suffering. But if conditions in the economy are such that letting unemployment fall to 4 percent would cause a "heating up" of inflation, then if the Fed lets the recovery continue, it will instead end up being blamed for inflation.

There is also considerable controversy over what rates of inflation can be considered acceptable. Some economists find only inflation rates from 0 percent to 2 percent acceptable; others do not see an urgent need for monetary control unless inflation is around 4 percent or higher (though all agree that inflation in double digits, as experienced in the 1970s, is very bad for the economy). There is a continuing debate among economists and policymakers over the proper weight to give to employment goals versus price stabilization goals (see Box 11.4).

Another practical problem is that monetary authorities have to pay attention to issues of timing. In Chapter 9 we discussed the "inside lags" of decision making and implementation as well as the "outside lag" of an enacted policy having an effect on aggregate expenditure. In the case of fiscal policy, the "inside lags" tend to be rather long, as Congress and the President try to agree on a budget, but the "outside lag" is relatively short. For monetary policy, the case tends to be reversed. The Federal Open Market Committee is scheduled to meet eight times a year and

453

BOX 11.4 INFLATION RETURNS

From 2009 to 2016, the Fed kept interest rates at very low levels, as shown in Figure 11.3, to promote economic expansion during the very slow recovery from the 2007–2009 recession. After just a few years of slightly higher rates from 2016 to 2019, the 2020 recession once again caused the Fed to push rates to rock bottom—with the fed funds rate close to zero. Although some economists had warned that these low rates could lead to inflation, no significant inflation actually appeared during the earlier period of low rates. But in late 2021 this changed. By early 2022, inflation had reached levels not seen for 40 years, around 8 percent per year. It seemed clear that a monetary policy change was required.

In March 2022 Jerome H. Powell, the Federal Reserve chair,

> signaled that the Fed could make big interest rate increases and push rates to relatively high levels in its quest to cool off demand and temper inflation. . . 'There is an obvious need to move expeditiously to return the stance of monetary policy to a more neutral level, and then to move to more restrictive levels if that is what is required to restore price stability' Mr. Powell said during remarks to a conference of business economists.[4]

Some argued that the Fed had waited too long. According to economist and former Treasury Secretary Larry Summers, writing in early 2022, "the Fed has not internalized the magnitude of its errors over the past year, is operating with an inappropriate and dangerous framework, and needs to take far stronger action to support price stability than appears likely,"[5] Others feared the opposite: that the Fed would move too strongly and push the economy into recession. "High interest rates suppress inflation fairly effectively, but they do so by choking off the demand side of the economy, making it more expensive for both consumers and businesses to borrow. So in trying to steer clear of inflation, the Fed could inadvertently plunge the U.S. economy into recession."[6]

Nobody likes inflation. This is true despite the fact that there are actually some gainers from inflation. Debtors find that the dollar amount of their debt is lower in real terms. In the case of mortgages, the majority of which are fixed-rate 30-year loans, monthly payments remain the same while property values increase. The same inflation benefit applies to anyone paying off federal student loans, which also have a fixed interest rate. As incomes increase, debtors are essentially getting a discount on what they must repay.

People on fixed incomes, though, suffer from inflation as the real value of their incomes declines. In addition, the uncertainty surrounding rapid price increases brings negative psychological effects across the board. One in four people surveyed in December 2021 said inflation has worsened their living standards, and half said they expect inflation to wipe out whatever wage gains they were given over the past year.[7]

There was, however, a major benefit from the combination of low interest rates and increased government spending in 2020—a very rapid jobs recovery from the steep recession caused the response to the COVID-19 recession. Unemployment, which reached 14 percent in 2020, fell to below 4 percent by the end of 2021. Many people who might otherwise have remained unemployed had jobs by 2021—even if they, like everyone else, complained about inflation.

Another factor in the inflation of 2021/2022 was that a large part of it arose from supply chain disruptions due to COVID and the war in Ukraine, in particular high gas and food prices. Since these price increases were not a result of Fed policy, but of factors well beyond the Fed's control, it might be wrong to place all the responsibility for inflation on easy monetary policy, or to see the solution as mainly drastic monetary tightening.

may schedule extra meetings. A monetary policy decision only requires discussion and agreement among the FOMC's twelve members, unlike the much more extensive discussions required to get a tax or spending change through Congress. Hence decisions about monetary policy can generally be made more quickly than decisions about fiscal policy.

But monetary policy only has an effect on aggregate expenditure as people change their plans—including their very long-term plans—about investment and spending. So, the "outside lag" is generally thought to be longer. There is a danger that the effects of a policy intended to counteract a recession may continue too long into recovery, promoting unwanted inflation, or that the effects of policies intended to counteract inflation might continue after the economy has slipped into recession, exacerbating the business cycle instead of flattening it out.

In addition, under some circumstances, it is possible for an economy to suffer *both* recession and inflation at the same time. Because one problem requires expansionary policies while the other calls for contractionary ones, the dilemma facing the Fed is especially acute in this case. We will discuss this issue in detail in Chapter 12.

6.2 Rules versus Activism

Given all these caveats about monetary policy, you might think that the Fed would do better just to follow a money supply growth rule, as suggested by the quantity theory of money. Indeed, a number of classically oriented macroeconomists make just this argument.

But the quantity theory has its problems. For one thing, the velocity of money is not as constant as the theory assumes. Because financial markets have many linkages, people's desire to hold some of their assets as money, as opposed to another asset, can cause wide swings in velocity. In good economic times, people may want to make more purchases and investments, raising the velocity of money. Likewise, when the stock market falls and the economy moves into recession, it is common for many people to seek the relative security of money and near-money assets, driving velocity down. The more unpredictable velocity is, the harder it is to make policy based on the assumption of a stable relationship between money supply and nominal GDP.

As a result, many macroeconomists argue for a relatively flexible and activist monetary policy stance. Rather than having the Fed locked onto a particular rule— as the monetarists would have it—they suggest that the Fed keep an eye on inflation and unemployment but also remain

455

flexible, so that it can respond to new developments, including financial market changes, price shocks, and threats of recession.

In Chapter 12, we bring together monetary policy, fiscal policy, and the twin goals of output and price stabilization. We also take into account some of the effects that world events, and policy responses to them, have had on the U.S. economy over the past several decades.

Discussion Questions

1. What are some arguments in favor of having the Fed follow a money supply rule? What are some arguments against it?
2. How does the issue of time lags affect fiscal and monetary policy?

REVIEW QUESTIONS

1. Draw up and explain the components of the balance sheet of the Federal Reserve.
2. Show what happens to the Fed's balance sheet and the balance sheet of a bank, when the bank sells bonds to the Fed.
3. Describe how a Fed open market purchase leads to a sequence of loans and deposits and thus a multiplier effect.
4. Describe two tools the Fed can use to affect the money supply, other than open market operations.
5. Describe how a Fed open market purchase changes the federal funds rate.
6. How is investment related to the interest rate? What other factors affect investment? Use a graphical analysis to show these relationships.
7. Show the effects of an expansionary monetary policy in a Keynesian cross diagram.
8. Describe how Fed policy has been used to respond to recent problems of recession and inflation. What were the significant changes in Fed policy in 2009, and in 2022?
9. What is the quantity equation? What is the quantity theory of money?
10. What is monetarism?
11. Discuss how monetary expansion can lead to high inflation, using the quantity equation.
12. What are some of the problems with using a monetary rule?

EXERCISES

1. Suppose that the Fed makes an open market purchase of $200,000 in bonds from QRS Bank.
   a) Show how this affects the Fed balance sheet.
   b) Show how this affects the balance sheet of QRS Bank.
   c) Assume that QRS Bank lends out as much as it can, based on this changed situation. What does its balance sheet look like after it makes the loans?
   d) Assume that all the proceeds from those loans are deposited in TUV Bank. What is the effect on TUV Bank's balance sheet?
   e) Assume that the required reserve ratio is 10 percent. What new opportunity does TUV Bank now face? What is it likely to do?
2. Suppose that the Fed makes an open market *sale* of $15 million in bonds to HIJ Bank.

a)   What is the effect on the Fed's balance sheet?

b)   What is the initial effect on HIJ Bank's balance sheet?

c)   Show in a graph the effect on the market for federal funds. (No numbers are necessary, for this or later sections of this exercise.)

d)   Assuming that the level of business confidence remains unchanged, show on a graph how this open market sale will change the level of intended investment.

e)   What is the effect on aggregate expenditure and output? Show on a carefully labeled graph.

f)   What is the effect on equilibrium consumption and saving? (You may need to refer back to Chapter 9 to answer this.)

3.   Suppose that investor confidence falls, and the Fed is aware of this fact. Using the model presented in this chapter, show (a)–(c) below graphically:

a)   How a fall in investor confidence affects the schedule for intended investment.

b)   What the Fed could do, influencing the federal funds market, to try to counteract this fall in investor confidence.

c)   The effect on AE and output if the Fed is able to *perfectly* counteract the fall in business confidence.

d)   Is the Fed likely to be as accurate as assumed in part (c)? Why, or why not?

4.   Suppose that the level of nominal GDP ($P \times Y$ in the quantity equation) for Estilvania is $30 billion and the level of the money supply is $10 billion.

a)   What is the velocity of money in Estilvania?

b)   Suppose that the money supply increases to $15 billion and nominal GDP rises to $45 billion. What has happened to velocity?

c)   Suppose that the money supply increases to $15 billion and nominal GDP rises to $40 billion. What has happened to velocity?

d)   Suppose that the money supply decreases to $8 billion and, as a result, both the price level and real GDP fall, leading to a decrease in nominal GDP to $26 billion. What has happened to velocity?

5.   Match each concept in Column A with the best definition or example in Column B.

Column A	Column B
a. Expansionary monetary policy	1. The idea that changes in the money supply affect only prices, not output
b. Fiat money	2. Residential investment
c. Accelerator principle	3. Standardization
d. Monetary neutrality	4. A dollar bill
e. Velocity	5. The ease with which an asset can be used in trade
f. Liquidity	6. Federal Reserve open market sale of bonds
g. Commodity money	7. A silver coin
h. A good property for money to have	8. A silver certificate
i. A piece of paper representing a claim on something of value	9. Vault cash and bank deposits at the Federal Reserve
j. Bank reserves	10. Currency in circulation and checkable deposits, and other liquid accounts
k. M1	11. The number of times that a unit of money changes hands in a year

l. Very sensitive to interest rates   12. Relates investment to GDP growth

m. Contractionary monetary policy   13. The Federal Reserve lowers the discount rate

6. The chair of the Federal Reserve gives testimony semi-annually before Congress about the state of monetary policy. Search for the most recent such testimony by the Fed chair at www.federalreserve.gov/newsevents.htm. What does the Fed chair identify as the most significant issues facing the economy? How is the Fed proposing to deal with them?

7. (Appendix A1) Suppose that you have a bond with a face value of $200 and a coupon amount of $10 that matures one year from now.
   a) If the going interest rate is 3 percent, how much can you sell it for today?
   b) If the going interest rate is 8 percent, how much can you sell it for today?
   c) What does this illustrate about bond prices and interest rates?

8. (Appendix A2) Suppose that the nominal prime interest rate for a one-year loan is currently 6 percent.
   a) If inflation is 1 percent per year, what is the current real interest rate?
   b) Suppose that many people believe that the inflation rate is going to rise in the future— probably up to 2–3 percent or more within a few years. You want to borrow a sum of money for ten years and are faced with deciding between
   i. a series of short-term, one-year loans. The interest rate on this year's loan would be 6 percent, while future nominal interest rates are unknown.
   ii. A ten-year fixed-rate loan on which you would pay a constant 6.25 percent per year. If you agree with most people and expect inflation to rise, which borrowing strategy do you expect might give you the better deal? Why? Explain your reasoning.

APPENDICES

A1 BOND PRICES AND INTEREST RATES

The process by which monetary policy influences interest rates can be explained by examining the market for federal funds, as was seen in the body of this chapter. Alternatively, it can also be explained by looking at the market for government bonds.

A **bond** represents debt, but, as a particular kind of financial instrument, bonds have some special characteristics. When the government (or a business) borrows by selling a bond it makes promises. It promises to pay the bondholder a fixed amount of money each year for a period of time and then, at the end of this time, to repay the principal of the loan. The fixed amount paid per year is called the *coupon amount*. The date that the principal will be repaid is called the *maturity date*. The amount of principal that will be repaid is called the *face value* of the bond.

> bond: a financial instrument that pays a fixed amount each year (the coupon amount) as well as repaying the amount of principal (the face value) on a particular date (the maturity date)

So far, it seems simple enough—a $100 bond at 5 percent, for example, specifies that its issuer will pay you $5 a year for ten years and then pay you $100 at the end of ten years. What makes bond markets more complicated, though, is that bonds are often sold and resold, changing hands many times before they mature. During the period to maturity, many factors affecting the value of the bond may change, and so the *bond price*—the price at which bondholders are willing to buy and sell existing bonds—may change.

For example, suppose that you bought the bond just described at its face value of $100. The *bond yield to maturity*, or the annual rate of return if you hold a bond until it matures, would obviously be 5 percent ($5 annually is 5 percent of the $100 bond price). Suppose that after a couple of years you want to sell your bond (perhaps you need the cash), but meanwhile, the rate of return on alternative (and equally safe) investments has risen to 10 percent. People will not be interested in buying your bond at a price of $100, because they would get only a 5 percent return on it, whereas they could get a 10 percent return by investing their $100 elsewhere. To sell your bond you will need to drop the price that you demand until your bond looks as attractive as other investments—that is, until the $5 per year represents a 10 percent yield to maturity.

Conversely, if the return on alternative investments has fallen, say to 2 percent, the $5 per year on your bond looks pretty good, and you will be able to sell it for *more than* $100. Bond prices and bond yields are thus inversely related.

If the bond has one year left to maturity, for example, its value one year from now is $105. We can use the formula [Value next year]/(1 + interest rate) = [Value now] to find out what you could get by selling the bond today. If the interest rate on alternative investments is 10 percent, then $105/(1 + .10) ≈ $95.45. The lower the bond price, the higher the bond yield, and vice versa. Conversely, if the return on alternative investments has fallen, say to 2 percent, the $5 per year on your bond looks pretty good, and you will be able to sell it for more than $100. If the interest rate is 2 percent, then $105/(1 + 0.02) ≈ $102.94.

The U.S. Treasury issues a variety of different kinds of bonds. Treasury bills have a zero-coupon amount and mature in one year or less. Because the holder receives no coupons, they are sold at a discount from their face value. Other Treasury bonds pay a coupon amount every six months and have maturities that range from 2 to 30 years. In the real economy, then, there are many different "government bond" prices—and interest rates. It is only for the sake of simplicity of modeling that we assume only one type of bond and one interest rate.

Although many people and organizations buy and sell government bonds on what is called the "secondary market" (the "primary market" being the Treasury's initial offering of the bonds), the Fed is a major player. Its actions in the market for government bonds are large enough to have effects on the whole market. Expansionary policies tend to raise bond prices and lower bond yields and interest rates; contractionary policies do the opposite.

A simplified (secondary) bond market is shown in Figure 11.11(a). The price of bonds (and the corresponding nominal interest rate) is on the vertical axis and the quantity on the horizontal axis. The supply curve, in this case, is determined by the willingness of people to sell bonds—that is, to exchange their government debt for cash. The demand curve is determined by people's willingness to buy bonds. This gives an equilibrium interest rate, shown in this example as 5 percent.

The effect of a Fed open market purchase of bonds is illustrated in Figure 11.11(b). A sizable Fed *purchase* shifts the demand curve for government bonds to the right. As a result, the price of bonds rises. Because bond prices and interest rates are inversely related, the rise in the price of bonds means that the going interest rate on them falls.

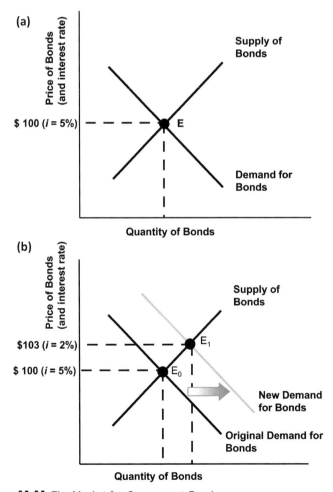

Figure 11.11 *The Market for Government Bonds*

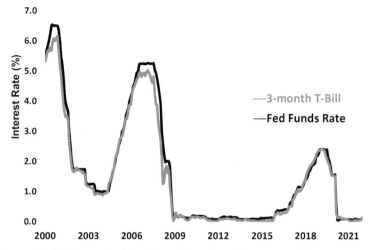

Figure 11.12 *The Federal Funds and Three-Month Treasury Bill Rates, 2000–2021*

Source: Federal Reserve, monthly data.

In this example, the price rises to $103, and the interest rate falls to 2 percent.[†††]

Although this explanation focuses on the market for government bonds, it closely parallels the earlier discussion of the Fed and the market for federal funds. The interest rate for three-month Treasury bills and the federal funds rate are graphed together in Figure 11.12, and we can see that they track each other closely. The bottom line of this story is the same as that given by the model of federal funds used in this chapter: A Fed open market purchase drives down interest rates.

A2 SHORT-RUN VERSUS LONG-RUN AND REAL VERSUS NOMINAL INTEREST RATES

In the model of interest rates and aggregate expenditure discussed in Section 3 of the text, we assumed that the Fed, through open market operations, could change the interest rate that influences investment spending. In Figure 11.8 we used the symbol r to denote a generalized interest rate. In real life, however, many different interest rates have to be taken into account.

Here we present some basic facts about short-run vs. long-run and real vs. nominal interest rates. We also note the difference between the Fed's focus on the short-term, nominal interest rate and the interest rate that is often most important to investors: that is, the long-term, real interest rate.

[†††] This assumes a bond with a maturity date of one year. The exact relationship depends on the time to maturity of the bond. The longer this time, the greater the impact of an interest rate change on the bond price.

In Section 4.1 we discussed the federal funds rate as the principal interest rate targeted by the Fed. This is a short-term, nominal interest rate. It is short term, because while this rate is quoted in annualized terms (that is, what borrowers would pay if they kept the loan for a year), the loans are actually made on one day and paid back the next. The federal funds rate—like any interest rate that you normally see quoted—is a *nominal* interest rate, not adjusted for inflation.

But if you are considering undertaking a substantial business investment project or buying a house, the interest rate that you should be taking into account, if you are a rational decision maker, is the *real* interest rate over the life of the business loan or mortgage. The **real interest rate** is:

$$r = i - \pi$$

where r is the real interest rate, i is the nominal interest rate, and π is the rate of inflation.

---

real interest rate: nominal interest rate minus inflation, $r = i - \pi$

For example, suppose that you borrow $100 for one year at a nominal rate of 6 percent. You will pay back $106 at the end of the year. If the inflation rate is 0, then the purchasing power of the amount that you pay back at the end of the year is actually $6 more than the amount you borrowed. However, if inflation is 4 percent during the year, the $106 that you pay back is in "cheaper" dollars (dollars that can buy less) than the dollars that you borrowed. The *real interest rate* on your borrowing will be only 2 percent. The higher the inflation rate, the better the deal is for a borrower at any given nominal rate (and the worse it is for the lender).

If inflation is fairly low and steady—as we assumed in the aggregate expenditure model—then this difference between real and nominal interest rates is not of crucial importance. If inflation is steady at, say, 2 percent, then both lenders and borrowers mentally subtract 2 percent to calculate the real rate that corresponds to any nominal rate. If the Fed lowers the prime rate from 8 percent to 5 percent, for example, then it correspondingly lowers the real rate from 6 percent to 3 percent.

But inflation is not always so predictable. When inflation is high or variable, it is very important to realize that investors' decisions are in reality influenced by the **expected real interest rate**, r_e:

$$r_e = i - \pi_e$$

where i is the nominal rate the borrower agrees to pay and π_e is the *expected* inflation rate.

---

expected real interest rate: the nominal interest rate minus expected inflation, $r_e = i - \pi_e$

The actual real interest rate (r) can be known only with hindsight. That is, only *after* information on inflation has come for last month or last year, can you calculate what the real interest rate *was* in that period. But you never know with certainty what the real interest rate is right now or what it will be next year. The more changeable inflation is, the harder it is to form reliable expectations about real interest rates.

Since investors are usually interested in long-term, real interest rates, while the Fed controls primarily short-term, nominal interest rates, the impacts of various Fed policies on the economy may not be as straight-forward as our basic models imply. In making decisions that affect economic activity, investors will consider both the short-term interest rates strongly affected by Fed policy, and long-term rates taking into account expected inflation.

NOTES

1   See Federal Reserve Bank of Chicago, "The Federal Reserve's Dual Mandate," https://www.chicagofed.org/research/dual-mandate/dual-mandate.
2   Smith, 2020.
3   Macintosh, 2021; Smialek 2022a.
4   Smialek, 2022b.
5   Summers, 2022.
6   Coy, 2022.
7   Morrow, 2021.

REFERENCES

Coy, Peter. 2022. "Will the Fed Cause a Recession?" *New York Times*, March 16.

Mackintosh, James, "Modern Monetary Theory Isn't the Future. It's Here Now." *The Wall Street Journal*, November 21, 2021.

Morrow, Allison. 2021. "Why Inflation Can Be Good for Everyday Americans and Bad for Rich People." *CNN Business*, December 1.

Smialek, Jeanna. 2022a. "Is This What Winning Looks Like?" *The New York Times* February 6.

Smialek, Jenna. 2022b. "Powell says Fed Could Raise Rates More Quickly to Tame Inflation." *New York Times*, March 21.

Smith, Kelly Ann Smith. 2020. "Negative Interest Rates Explained: How Could They Affect You?" *Forbes*, May 18.

Summers, Lawrence H. 2022. "The Fed Is Charting a Course to Stagflation and Recession." *Washington Post*, March 15.

Chapter 12

Aggregate Supply, Aggregate Demand, and Inflation Putting It All Together

If you read the financial pages in any newspaper (or sometimes the front pages if economic issues are pressing), you will see discussion about government budgets and deficits, interest rate changes, and how these affect unemployment and inflation. You may also see news about changes in the availability of certain crucial resources—particularly energy resources—and about how the impact of such changes in resource supplies spread throughout the country's economy. How does economic theory help to make sense of it all?

In Chapter 8, we started to build a model of business cycles, focusing at first on the downturn side of the cycle and the problem of unemployment. In Chapters 9, 10, and 11 we explained economic theories concerning fiscal and monetary policy. So far, our models have focused on the "demand side," illustrated by shifts in the aggregate expenditure (*AE*) curve. In this chapter, we complete the demand-side story, using the broader term "aggregate demand", so that it includes explicit attention to the potential problem of inflation. Then we move on to the issue of the productive capacity of the economy, or "supply side" issues. Finally, we will arrive at a model that we can use to "put it all together." We then use this model to analyze several real-world economic cases including recent trends in unemployment and inflation.

1 AGGREGATE DEMAND AND INFLATION

The *AE* curve in the Keynesian model used in the previous three chapters was graphed with income on the horizontal axis and output on the vertical axis. We mentioned that if output is above its full-employment level, there may be a threat of rising inflation, but nothing in the figures incorporated this idea. The graphs that we used all measured income, output, and aggregate expenditures without considering changes in price levels. It is time now to remedy that omission by introducing an explicit measure showing changes in prices.

 DOI: 10.4324/9781003251521-16

1.1 The Aggregate Demand (AD) Curve

Recall from Chapter 8 that aggregate demand is the total level of spending in the economy. Since the level of spending is influenced by the changes in price levels, we use the **aggregate demand (*AD*) curve** to represent the relationship between the equilibrium level of output and inflation. To show this graphically, we put output (*Y*) on the horizontal axis and inflation on the vertical axis (denoted by the symbol π).[*] This is shown in Figure 12.1. The *AD* curve shown here differs from the *AE* curve used in the preceding chapters since it takes into account changes in inflation and the reaction of the central bank to different levels of inflation, but the points on the *AD* curve all correspond to macroeconomic equilibrium points where the Keynesian *AE* curve crosses the 45° line. We are building on that previous equilibrium analysis by introducing an extra dimension—inflation—shown on the vertical axis.

---

aggregate demand (*AD*) curve: graph showing the relationship between the rate of inflation and the total quantity of goods and services demanded by households, businesses, government, and the international sector

---

This view of aggregate demand assumes that higher inflation rates will tend to reduce total demand, for several reasons:

- When inflation rises, it reduces the value of money assets. Even if this does not reach the level of hyperinflation discussed in Chapter 10, it hurts savers and people who have money balances. This

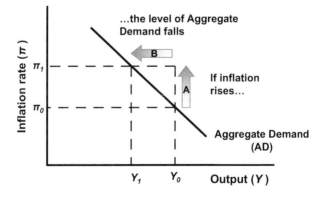

Figure 12.1 *The Aggregate Demand Curve*

---

[*] Some versions of the AD curve use "price level" rather than inflation on the vertical axis. The authors of this text believe that using inflation better represents the reality of an economic system in which prices are rarely constant.

real wealth effect tends to reduce their consumption, lowering total demand.

> **real wealth effect:** the tendency of consumers to increase or decrease their consumption based on their perceived level of wealth

- Inflation also lowers the **real money supply**, defined as M/P, where M is the nominal money supply and P is the general price level. This has an effect similar to contractionary monetary policy, raising interest rates and discouraging investment.

> **real money supply:** the nominal money supply divided by the general price level (as measured by a price index), expressed as M/P

- Inflation hurts net exports by making domestically produced goods more expensive for foreigners and imports more attractive for domestic consumers. This decreases aggregate demand by decreasing net exports.[†]
- The Federal Reserve generally responds to higher inflation by raising interest rates, as discussed in Chapter 11. This also tends to lower investment and total demand.

There is some disagreement among economists about which of these effects are most significant, but there is little doubt about the overall result: higher inflation will tend to result in lower aggregate demand levels.

1.2 Shifts of the *AD* Curve: Spending and Taxation

The downward slope of the *AD* curve shown in Figure 12.1 is based on the indirect impacts of inflation on aggregate demand, as discussed above. What determines the position of the curve? The logic is essentially the same as discussed in our Keynesian *AE* analysis in Chapter 8. The position of the *AD* curve depends on specific levels of government spending, taxation, autonomous consumption, autonomous investment, and autonomous net exports.[‡] Changes in these variables will therefore cause the *AD* curve to shift.

[†] As defined in Chapter 4, and discussed further in Chapter 13, net exports are exports minus imports, and represent a net addition to aggregate demand and GDP levels.

[‡] The specific role of net exports will be discussed further in Chapter 13.

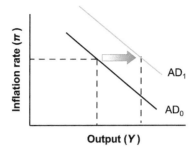

Figure 12.2 *The Effect of Expansionary Fiscal Policy or Increased Confidence on the AD curve*

For example, if the government were to undertake an expansionary fiscal policy, this would shift the *AD* curve to the right, as illustrated in Figure 12.2. At any level of inflation, there would now be aggregate demand sufficient to support a higher level of output.

An increase in autonomous consumption or investment would have a similar effect, as would an autonomous increase in net exports. Recall that autonomous consumption is the part of household spending that does not depend on income, and autonomous investment is the part of business spending that does not depend on the interest rate. These are often used to represent consumer and business "confidence". Thus, an increase in consumer or investor confidence could also cause the rightward shift seen in Figure 12.2. Conversely, of course, contractionary fiscal policy, reductions in consumer or investment confidence, or reduction in autonomous net exports would shift the *AD* curve to the left.

1.3 Shifts of the *AD* Curve: Monetary Policy

As we have noted, the Federal Reserve usually responds to higher inflation by increasing interest rates, and this is reflected in the slope of the *AD* curve. This kind of policy response, which aims to keep inflation near a target level, is a rather passive sort of monetary policy. Including it in the *AD* curve is based on the assumption that this kind of Fed response will be more or less automatic. A more active form of Fed intervention occurs when the Fed's leaders decide to change policy more fundamentally—either by changing their inflation target or by shifting their focus to fighting unemployment. Such a change can shift the *AD* curve.

For example, in a severe recession the Fed might decide that the economy requires additional stimulus. If the Fed instituted significant expansionary monetary policies, driving interest rates down (as it did, for example, in 2007 and again in 2020 to respond to recessions), this would, in theory, have the effect of boosting investment and shifting the *AD* curve to the right. Alternatively, if the Fed decided that its policies on inflation have been too lax, it could tighten monetary policy (this happened, for example, in 1982 and also in 2022 in response to

467

inflation). This would have the effect of shifting the *AD* curve to the left.

To summarize:

■ The *AD* curve indicates levels of equilibrium GDP at different possible rates of inflation.
■ The *AD* curve can be shifted by changes in levels of autonomous consumer spending, autonomous investment, fiscal policy, net exports, or by major changes in monetary policy.

Discussion Questions

1. The negative slope of the *AD* curve means that higher levels of output will lead to lower levels of inflation." Is this statement correct or not? Discuss.
2. Does the Fed always want the inflation rate to be as low as possible? Why or why not?

2 CAPACITY AND THE AGGREGATE SUPPLY CURVE

As we have noted in earlier chapters, increases in aggregate expenditure can push output up toward the full-employment level. In our current analysis, an increase in aggregate expenditure is shown by a rightward shift in the *AD* curve. But what happens when output reaches—or maybe even exceeds—the full-employment level? In a graph such as Figure 12.2, for example, there is nothing in the model that seems to prevent expansionary policies from just shifting the *AD* curve, and output, up and up and up.

Obviously, this cannot be true in the real world. At any given time, there are only certain quantities of labor, capital, energy, and other material resources available for use. The U.S. labor force, for example, comprises just over 160 million people. The United States simply cannot, then, produce an output level that would require the work of 200 million people. This is a *hard capacity constraint*: What happens as an economy approaches maximum capacity can be modeled using the **aggregate supply (*AS*) curve**. The *AS* curve shows combinations of output and inflation that can, in fact, occur within an economy, given the reality of capacity constraints.

---

aggregate supply (*AS*) curve: graph representing the relationship between the rate of inflation and the total goods and services producers are willing to supply, given the reality of capacity constraints

---

2.1 The Aggregate Supply (*AS*) Curve

Figure 12.3 shows how AS is related to the rate of inflation. It will be easiest to explain the shape of the curve starting from the right, at high output levels. Moving from right to left, we can identify five important, distinct regions of the diagram.

First (starting on the right in Figure 12.3), the vertical **maximum capacity output** line indicates the hard limit on a macroeconomy's output. Even if every last resource in the economy were put into use, with everybody working flat out to produce the most they could, the economy could not produce to the right of the maximum capacity line.

---

maximum capacity output: the level of output an economy would produce if every resource in the economy were fully utilized

---

Just below the maximum capacity level of output, the *AS* curve has a very steep, positive slope. This indicates that, as an economy closely approaches its maximum capacity, it is likely to experience a substantial increase in inflation. If many employers are all trying to hire many workers and buy a lot of machinery, energy, and materials all at once, workers' wages and resource prices will tend to be bid upward. But then, to cover their labor and other costs, producers will need to raise the prices that they charge for their own goods. Then, in turn, if workers find that the purchasing power of their wages is being eroded by rising inflation, they will demand higher wages, which leads to higher prices, and so on. The result is a phenomenon called a **wage-price spiral**, in which higher wages and higher prices lead to a steep rise in self-reinforcing inflation.

---

wage-price spiral: when upward pressure on wages creates upward pressure on prices and, as a result, further upward pressure on wages

---

In the real world, such steep increases in inflation are usually the result of dramatic pressures on producers, such as often occur during a national mobilization for war. During World War II, for example, the U.S. government pushed the economy very close to its maximum capacity—placing big orders for munitions and other supplies for the front, mobilizing the necessary resources by encouraging women to enter the paid labor force, promoting the recycling of materials on an unprecedented scale, encouraging the planting of backyard gardens to increase food production, and in general pushing people's productive efforts far beyond their usual peacetime levels. As a result, unemployment plummeted. The government, knowing that such pressures could lead to sharply rising inflation (as shown in the wage-price spiral region of Figure 12.3), kept inflation from getting out of hand by instituting **wage and price controls**—direct regulations telling firms what they could and could not do in the way of price or wage increases.

---

wage and price controls: government regulations setting limits on wages and prices or on the rates at which they are permitted to increase

---

The shaded area to the left of the wage-price spiral region in Figure 12.3 indicates as it did in the national income equilibrium graphs in Chapters 8 and 9, a range of full-employment levels of output. While it is controversial to say exactly where that level may be, it can be thought of as an output level high enough that unemployment is not considered a national problem. And because it must be low enough to allow for at least a small measurable level of transitory unemployment, the *full-employment* level of output is slightly lower than the *maximum capacity* level of output.

Within the full-employment range, Figure 12.3 shows a moderately rising *AS* curve. This is because, even well before an economy approaches the absolute maximum capacity given *all* its resources, producers may tend to run into "bottlenecks" in the supply of *some* resources. Agricultural workers may be plentiful, for example, but professional and technical workers may be in short supply. Or fuel oil may be plentiful, but there may be a shortage of natural gas. Shortages in the markets for particular kinds of labor and other inputs may lead to an acceleration of inflation in some sectors of the economy. Because the measured inflation rate represents an average for the economy as a whole, some aggregate increase in inflation may be observed. If many significant economic sectors experience shortages, as occurred in 2021-2022 during the recovery from the pandemic recession of 2020, the increase in inflation may be significant and cause a rethinking of fiscal and monetary policy.

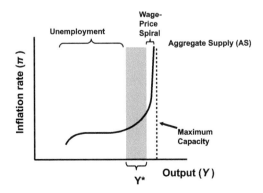

Figure 13.3 *The Aggregate Supply Curve*

Some increase in inflation is what economists expect to happen when the economy nears a business cycle "peak." Note, however, that the *AS* curve has been drawn as flatter toward the left of the *Y** range, indicating that combinations of full employment and stable inflation may also be possible.

Moving further to the left, the *AS* curve shows a region in which the economy is below full employment, perhaps going into recession or recovering from a recession. The flat *AS* line shown in Figure 12.3 for this region indicates that, under these conditions, there is assumed to be no tendency for inflation to rise. Because a significant amount of labor and other resources are unemployed, there is no pressure for higher wages or prices. It is also likely that because wages and prices tend to be slow in adjusting downward, inflation will not fall either—at least not right away.

When the economy is hit not by a regular recession, but by a really deep recession, such as the one experienced in most industrialized countries in 2007–2009 and again in 2020, the level of output is so far below the full employment level that inflation starts to drop, and may even become negative (deflation). In this situation, demand is so weak that a large number of companies may fail. Struggling to stay in business, firms are forced to cut prices in order to maintain at least some sales. Also, in such a situation, workers and their unions might agree to wage cuts which lowers firms' costs and allows them to further reduce their prices. As output declines further (going from right to left on the graph), the *AS* curve in Figure 12.3 slopes downwards as a further fall in aggregate demand accelerates the process of **disinflation** (a decline in the rate of inflation) or even deflation (an absolute decrease in price levels).

---

disinflation: a decline in the rate of inflation

2.2 Shifts of the *AS* Curve: Inflationary Expectations

When people have experienced inflation, they come to expect it. They then tend to build the level of inflation that they expect into the various contracts into which they enter. If a business expects 4 percent inflation over the coming year, for example, it will add 4 percent to the selling price that it quotes for a product to be delivered a year into the future, just to stay even. If workers also expect 4 percent inflation, they will try to get at least a 4 percent cost of living allowance, just to stay even. A bondholder who expects 4 percent inflation and wants a 2 percent real rate of return will be satisfied only with a 6 percent nominal rate of return.[§]

---

§ As noted in Chapter 11, Appendix A2, the real rate of return equals the nominal rate minus inflation, $r = i - \pi$.

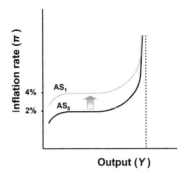

Figure 12.4 *The Effect of an Increase in Inflationary Expectations on the Aggregate Supply Curve*

In this way, an expected rate of inflation can start to become institutionally "built in" to an economy. As a first approximation, it is reasonable to assume that people expect something like the level of inflation that they have recently experienced (an assumption that economists call "adaptive expectations"). Thus, inflation can be, to some degree, self-fulfilling.

Since different contracts come up for renegotiation at different times of the year, the process of building in inflationary expectations will take place only over time. Because of the time that it takes for prices and wages to adjust, we need to make a distinction between short-run and medium-run aggregate supply responses.

The *AS* curve in Figure 12.3 was drawn for a particular level of expected inflation in the *short run*. Before people have caught on to the fact that the inflation rate might be changing, their expectations of inflation will continue to reflect their recent experience. In this model, an economy in recession, or on the horizontal part of the *AS* curve, will tend in the short run to roll along at pretty much the same inflation rate as it has experienced in the past. Tight labor and resource markets caused by a boom could tend to increase inflation, but this will initially come as a surprise to people and will not immediately translate into a change in expectations. For the purposes of this model, you might think of the short run as a period of some weeks or months.

Over a longer period of time—the *medium run*—however, a rise in inflation due to tight markets tends to increase people's expectations of inflation.[¶] If they expected 2 percent inflation but over a period of time they experience 4 percent inflation, the next time that firms set prices or workers renegotiate contracts they may build in a 4 percent rate. Figure 12.4 shows how the *AS* curve shifts upward as people's expectation of inflation rises. Note that the maximum capacity of the economy has not changed—nothing has happened that would affect the physical

¶ As distinguished from the *long run*, discussed in the Appendix.

capacity of the economy to produce. All that has happened is that now, at any output level, people's expectation of inflation is higher.

Similarly, if people experience very loose markets for their labor or products (i.e. low demand), or lower inflation due to a lack of aggregate demand and recessionary conditions, over the medium run the expected inflation rate may start to come down. Employers may find that they can still get workers if they offer lower wages. Unions might agree to lower wage increases as their members might be afraid of unemployment, but only need a small wage increase to guarantee stable purchasing power. Producers may raise their prices less this year than last year or cut prices because they are having trouble selling in a slow market.

When people start to observe wage and price inflation tapering off in some sectors of the economy, they may change their expectations about inflation. As people react to the sluggish aggregate demand that occurs during a recession, they will tend, over time, to lessen their expectations about wage and price increases. The graph for this would be similar to Figure 12.4 but would show the *AS* curve shifting downward instead of upward.

2.3 Shifts of the *AS* Curve: Supply Shocks

The *AS* curve also shifts when the capacity of the economy changes. A **supply shock** is something that changes the ability of an economy to produce goods and services. Supply shocks can be beneficial, as when there is a bumper crop in agriculture or a new invention allows more goods or services to be made using a smaller quantity of resources. Increases in labor productivity also allow an economy to produce more goods and services.

---

supply shock: a change in the productive capacity of an economy

---

In such cases, the real capacity of the economy expands, as shown in Figure 12.5. The line indicating maximum capacity also shifts to the right, showing that the economy can produce more than before. We model the beneficial supply shock as moving the *AS* curve both to the right and downward. It moves to the right because capacity has increased. It moves downward because beneficial supply shocks are often accompanied by decreases in prices. As computer technology has improved, for example, the price of any given amount of computing power has dropped rapidly. Since computers play a significant role in the economy, this tends to reduce inflation.

Supply shocks can also be adverse. Natural occurrences, such as hurricanes or droughts, and human-caused situations, such as wars, that

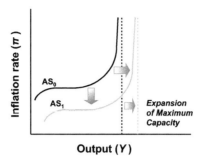

Figure 12.5 *A Beneficial Supply Shock: Expansion of Output Capacity*

destroy capital goods and lives are examples of adverse supply shocks. Restrictions on key supply chains during and after the pandemic recession of 2020 could also be classified as adverse supply shocks. With regard to energy resources, adverse supply shocks can arise from physical changes such as the exhaustion of an oil or gas reserve. They can also arise for economic reasons such as a successful limitation of energy supply by a cartel or major supplier (the OPEC oil cartel was a major factor in promoting inflation during the 1970s, and limitations on Russian natural gas supply have become a concern for many European economies.) Adverse supply shocks reduce the economy's capacity to produce and, by concentrating demand on the limited supplies of resources that remain, tend to lead to higher inflation. Adverse supply shocks would be illustrated in a graph such as Figure 12.5, but with the direction of all the movements reversed.

Discussion Questions

1. Describe in words how the *AS* curve differs from the *AD* curve. What does each represent? What explains their slopes?
2. Do you get "cost of living" raises at your job or know people who do? Why does this practice have important macroeconomic consequences?

3 PUTTING THE *AS/AD* MODEL TO WORK

Economists use the *AS/AD* model to illustrate three points about the macroeconomy:

1. Fiscal and monetary policies affect output and inflation:
   - *Expansionary fiscal and monetary policies* tend to push the economy toward a higher level of output. If the economy is approaching its maximum capacity, it will also cause inflation to rise.
   - *Contractionary fiscal and monetary policies* tend to push the economy toward a lower level of output. Inflation may not fall

quickly, but a persistently lower level of economic activity will tend to lower inflation over the long term.

2. *Supply shocks* may also have significant effects:
   - Adverse supply shocks lower output and raise inflation.
   - Beneficial supply shocks raise output and lower inflation.

3. *Investor and consumer confidence and expectations* also have important effects on output and inflation.

Bearing these principles in mind, we will see how this model helps to explain some major macroeconomic events.

3.1 An Economy in Recession

In Figure 12.6, we bring together the *AS* and *AD* curves for the first time. The (short run) equilibrium of the economy is shown as point E_0, at the intersection of the two curves. Depending on how we place the curves in the figure, we could illustrate an economy that is in a recession, at full employment, or in a wage-price spiral. (We temporarily omit the maximum capacity line, but we reintroduce it when we discuss inflation.)

In this specific case, the fact that E_0 is well to the left of the full-employment range of output indicates that the economy is in a recession. Private spending, as determined in part by investor and consumer confidence, along with government and foreign sector spending, is not enough to keep the economy at full employment. The fact that the curves intersect on the flat part of the *AS* curve indicates that inflation (in the short run) is stable. So in this situation, unemployment is the major problem. What can be done?

Figure 12.6 models the real-world situation of the U.S. economy in the 2007–2009 and 2020 recessions. Unemployment rose to 10 percent in 2009, and briefly to 14 percent in 2020, but inflation was very low in both periods. In this situation, the Federal government implemented major fiscal stimulus programs. The goal of the stimulus programs was to promote employment both through direct impact and through

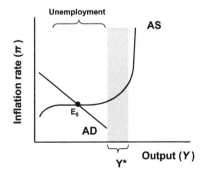

Figure 12.6 Aggregate Demand and Supply Equilibrium in Recession

475

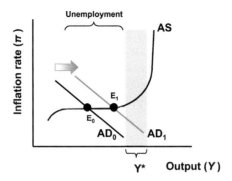

Figure 12.7 *Expansionary Fiscal Policy in Response to a Recession*

multiplier effects expanding private spending and employment. This effect is shown in Figure 12.7 as a rightward shift of the *AD* curve.

As noted in Chapter 9 (Box 9.2), the 2009 stimulus plan was responsible for adding millions of jobs to the economy. While economists are not in agreement about how large the multiplier effects of the program were, many argue that without the program, the economy would have continued to plunge deeper into recession.[1] The effects, however, were not large enough to bring the economy back to full employment. The unemployment rate remained above 7 percent until 2013, and only gradually declined to 5 percent in late 2015. This is reflected in Figure 12.7 as an *AD* shift that moves output toward, but not into, the full-employment zone.

How about the effect of this expansionary program on inflation? As the *AS/AD* model would lead us to expect, inflation did not rise in response to the 2009 stimulus because the economy did not move beyond the flat portion of the *AS* curve. Some economists and political commentators warned at the time that such a high level of government spending and deficits would cause serious inflation—but inflation remained low through 2017, eight years after the initiation of the stimulus program.

Would more macroeconomic stimulus in 2009 have made sense, given that unemployment was still high and inflation relatively low? Some economists argued that it would, but proposals for further fiscal stimulus were not acted on by Congress, largely out of fear that deficits were already too high (for more on this debate, see Chapter 15). So the Federal Reserve stepped in with the expanded monetary stimulus known as "quantitative easing" (as discussed in Chapter 11). The hope was that a combination of this monetary expansion plus recovering confidence on the part of consumers and businesses could lead to a more complete recovery.

When the official unemployment rate hit 4.1 percent in late 2017, many economists believed that the U.S. economy had reached or was close to reaching the goal of full employment. This is illustrated in

476

Figure 12.8, where we see that a larger *AD* shift brings the economy back into the full-employment zone. At this point, the model predicts that there could be at least a slight increase in inflation. Detection of such rising inflation would signal the Fed to cut back on its monetary expansion. In 2017–2018, amid some signs of increasing inflation, the Fed started to reverse its quantitative easing program and cautiously started increasing interest rates (see Box 12.1).

BOX 12.1 UNEMPLOYMENT AND INFLATION: A TALE OF TWO RECOVERIES

By 2018, the U.S. economy had entered its ninth year of expansion following the crisis of 2008–2009. As of early 2018, the unemployment rate was at 4.1 percent—the lowest since 2000—and hourly wages had increased by about 2.6 percent since the previous year.[2] The strengthening conditions in the labor market raised concerns about the possibility of inflation, as the rising demand for workers could drive up salaries and prices. Amid fears of inflation, the Federal Reserve planned to raise interest rates at least three times in 2018.

As of mid-2018, however, inflation rates remained below 2 percent. An Economic Policy Institute report argued that until wages are rising by at least 3.5–4 percent, there would be no threat that inflation would exceed the Fed's 2 percent inflation target.[3] Some economists suggest that a moderate amount of inflation actually provides a good environment for economic activity:

> Economic research suggests that inflation is best in moderation. Price increases lead to wage increases, which make it easier to repay existing debts, like mortgages, and more attractive to incur new debts, like borrowing to start a company. Inflation also functions as a kind of economic WD-40, easing shifts in the allocation of resources. Perhaps most importantly, moderate inflation keeps the economy at a safe distance from deflation, or general price declines, which can freeze activity as would-be buyers wait for lower prices.[4]

The trick for policymakers is to achieve just the right amount of inflation, without either allowing inflationary expectations to get out of hand or pushing the economy back into recession.

The experience of 2021/2022 was different. After a rapid recovery from the recession of 2020, inflation gained a definite foothold in the economy. At the end of 2021, prices had risen 5.8 percent over the year according to the Personal Consumption Expenditures index used by the Federal Reserve to gauge inflation. "Core prices", which exclude volatile food and energy categories, rose 4.9 percent, the biggest increase since 1983.[5] At the same time, job growth was very strong, averaging over half a million jobs per month throughout 2021. So a clear policy success—rapid employment recovery—was accompanied by a problem of significant inflation.[6] By mid-2022, year-over-year inflation has risen to over 8 percent. Economists differed in their interpretation of this combination. Former U.S. Treasury Secretary Lawrence Summers commented in early 2022, "We've got an overheated economy, and the Fed is going to have the very real challenge of cooling that economy off, and doing it in a controlled way." Summers warned that there was "a surfeit of purchasing power and demand relative to the capacity of the economy to

---

produce, and unless we bring those things into balance, we're going to have not just higher inflation but possibly even accelerating inflation."[7]

Economist Paul Krugman, who admitted that he had not seen the inflation coming, nonetheless believed that it was significantly different from the inflation of the 1970s, which had required very drastic Fed action to control. He argued that "overall demand in the United States actually doesn't look all that high" and that inflation had arisen primarily from "supply-chain issues." This could be a time-limited phenomenon since "expected inflation has not (yet?) become entrenched the way it had by the end of the 1970s."[8] But, according to Krugman, engineering a "soft landing" would still be tricky: "The Fed will adjust its policies based on incoming economic data, but monetary policy acts with a substantial lag, so it can be many months before we know whether interest rates are too low, too high or just right."[9]

The achievement of full employment with relatively low inflation could be judged a success (indicated by point E_1 in Figure 12.8). The process of recovery from the 2007–2009 recession was very slow, however, with about 1.39 million workers being long-term unemployed (over 27 weeks), and the unemployment rate including marginally attached workers and those working part-time for economic reasons remaining above 8 percent in February 2018. The uncertainty about whether full employment had really been reached is reflected by our "gray zone" or shaded area denoting a range for what can be considered full employment.

The recovery from the 2020 recession can be contrasted with the earlier experience of recovery from the 2007–2009 recession (see Box 12.1). In both cases, as the economy approached full employment there was concern about the possibility of rising inflation. But in the first case, inflation never became a serious problem, whereas in 2021–2022 it did.

As with the earlier recession, considerable Federal stimulus was applied through expansionary fiscal policy, including the $2.2 trillion CARES Act of 2020 and the $1.9 trillion American Rescue Plan of 2021. The combined size of these programs was several times that of

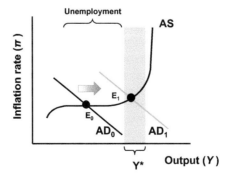

Figure 12.8 *A Greater Expansion of Aggregate Demand*

the 2009 stimulus. At the same time, the Fed implemented expansionary monetary policy, both keeping interest rates very low and expanding "quantitative easing". The result of this combination of expansionary fiscal and monetary policies was a rapid recovery in late 2020 and 2021. But by the end of 2021, inflation had become a definite problem. This was the first time since the 1980s that the U.S. economy had suffered from significant inflation. To analyze this in terms of our *AS/AD* model, it will be useful to recall some lessons from the experience of inflation in the 1960s, 1970s, and 1980s.

3.2 An Overheated Economy

Problems with inflation were a major issue in the United States starting in the late 1960s. High government spending, in particular spending on the Vietnam war, meant that fiscal policy was excessively expansionary. Monetary policy during this period tended to accommodate fiscal expansion. Although unemployment was very low as a result, by the late 1960s the economy started to "overheat," causing inflation to rise.

This period of history is modeled in Figure 12.9. The *AD* curve moves further to the right due to the increases in government spending. It shifts from AD_0, which at E_0 corresponds to a full-employment equilibrium, to AD_1, which crosses the *AS* curve in the wage-price spiral range. The economy became overheated, moving beyond full employment to E_1.

The tradeoff between unemployment and inflation in the 1960s established a pattern that became known as the Phillips curve, after the economist who first identified an empirical relationship between unemployment and inflation. Working on data from 1861 to 1957, A.W. Phillips found that for the U.K. periods of high inflation coincided with periods of low unemployment and vice versa. If one looks at data for

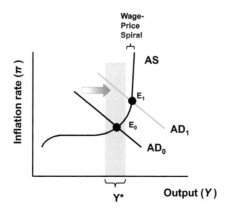

Figure 12.9 *Excessively High Aggregate Demand Causes Inflation*

479

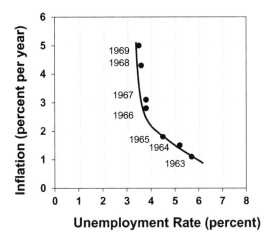

Figure 12.10 *The Phillips Curve in the 1960s*

the United States in the 1960s, this relationship also seems to be evident. The 1960s Phillips curve for the United States is shown in Figure 12.10.

As you can see, the shape of the upward-sloping portion of the *AS* curve is essentially a mirror image of the Phillips curve. This is no coincidence. The models that economists developed during the 1960s grew out of observing such a pattern of unemployment and inflation rates and trying to explain why it occurred. Although, as we will see, subsequent events challenged the simple view of the Phillips curve, the concept of an unemployment/inflation tradeoff is still relevant, as is evident in more recent concerns about rising inflation as the economy approaches full employment (Box 12.1).

3.3 Responding to Inflation

Economic history shows that the Phillips curve is not always a reliable guide to policy. The developments of the 1970s came as a shock to Phillips-curve–minded economists and policymakers. During the 1970s unemployment and inflation, *both* rose, and both stayed fairly high. Oil price increases by the OPEC cartel added considerably to already significant inflationary pressures. This combination of economic stagnation (recession) and high inflation came to be known as **stagflation**. In 1979, the price of oil was *ten* times higher than it had been in 1973. The overall inflation rate in the United States was more than 9 percent in 1979—and exceeded 10 percent (measured at an annual rate) during some months.

stagflation: a combination of rising inflation and economic stagnation

The high rates of inflation experienced in the late 1970s were very damaging to the economy. Once people experienced high inflation over a period of time, expectations of further inflation rose. At the same time, the economic problems associated with stagflation forced cutbacks in consumption, investment, and government spending, lowering aggregate demand. Figure 12.11 shows the combination of these effects, moving the economy from E_0 to E_1. The situation at equilibrium E_1 shows stagflation—a combination of unemployment and high inflation. Even though the economy is no longer in the wage-price spiral range, inflation persists because inflation expectations have risen.

As we noted in Chapter 10, high rates of inflation can wipe out the value of people's savings and make it very difficult for households and businesses to plan, save, and invest. Because unemployment was also high, as shown in Figure 12.11, it was difficult to see how consumers and businesses could ever recover confidence while inflation seemed out of control.

Even though the economy was already in a recession, and the unemployment rate was above 7 percent, the Federal Reserve, under the chairmanship of Paul Volcker, took deliberate and drastic action to

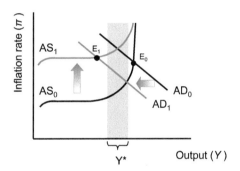

Figure 12.11 *"Stagflation"—A Combination of Unemployment and Inflation*

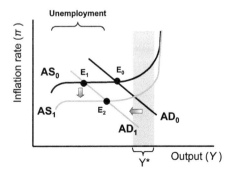

Figure 12.12 *The Effect of Expansionary Fiscal Policy or Increased Confidence on the AD curve*

481

bring the long-term inflation rate down, by implementing very contractionary monetary policies. The effects of these "tight money" policies during the early 1980s can be seen in Figure 12.12.

As discussed earlier, contractionary monetary policy shifts the AD curve to the left. The AS/AD model predicts that the immediate effect of this policy will be to send the economy even deeper into a recession, with output falling even farther below its full-employment level, as shown by equilibrium point E_1. A recession tends to lower inflation, since in recession firms find it more difficult to raise prices, and workers are not able to get wage increases. But there is a further effect, on inflationary expectations. Once people see that inflation is declining, they tend to reduce their expectations of future inflation.

The effect of this decrease in inflationary expectations is shown as a downward shift in the AS curve to AS_1, showing a reduction in inflation. Such a recession with falling inflation is, in fact, what happened in the early 1980s. By 1983, the inflation rate had fallen to 4 percent, but at a significant human and economic cost. Unemployment between 1982 and 1983 rose to nearly 10 percent. But in the years that followed, the economy recovered and employment increased, as shown by equilibrium point E_2.

The experience of the 1980s showed that after inflationary expectations become established, they can be reduced only by policies that cause major economic pain. This has led future policymakers to be very wary of encouraging any new inflationary wage-price spiral.

When inflation once again made an appearance in 2021, after having been relatively low for almost 30 years, the memory of 1970s stagflation spurred policymakers into action (see Box 12.1). It seemed that, in the rapid recovery of 2020/2021, the economy might have "overshot" into the wage-price spiral range. This created an urgency to act *before* high inflationary expectations and "stagflation" set in.

The goal of policymakers in early 2022 is shown in Figure 12.13. Judging that the economy was at an equilibrium similar to E_0, the goal was seen as shifting it to E_1, which would be in an acceptable employment range, while reducing the danger of an inflationary spiral. This called for a more contractionary policy on the part of the Fed. Accordingly, the Fed stopped its policy of bond purchases ("quantitative easing"), moving instead to bond sales ("quantitative tightening') and started to increase interest rates during the second half of 2022. The risk in this type of policy is overshooting in the other direction, pushing the economy into recession. As of mid-2022, it appeared that the Fed might be successful in engineering a "soft landing," reducing inflationary pressures while not forcing the economy into another severe recession.

A complicating factor in 2021/2022 was that the inflation that began in 2021 had an unusual character. Economists differentiate between two major types of inflation: **demand-pull inflation** and **cost-push inflation**.

482

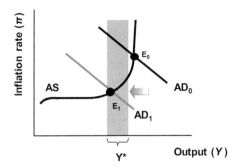

Figure 12.13 *The Aggregate Supply Curve*

Our discussion so far has focused on demand-pull inflation—the result of the AD curve moving too far to the right, exceeding supply capacity and thus forcing up wages and prices. Cost-push inflation, by contrast, results from supply-side restrictions and bottlenecks, and may occur even if overall demand is not high.

This was the case, for example with the oil price increases of the 1970s. It was also evident in the recovery from the 2020 pandemic recession. The impact of COVID-19 led to many supply-chain and transportation problems, as a shortage of workers in key areas made it difficult to meet consumer demands. The fact that many services, which required in-person contact, were impacted by COVID-19 also led consumers to shift their budgets in favor of goods purchases. The combination of greater demand and limited supply for many goods, for example in the automobile market, led to significant price increases.

---

demand-pull inflation: inflation primarily caused by excessive aggregate demand
cost-push inflation: inflation primarily caused by supply restrictions and bottlenecks

---

The appropriate policies for responding to the two types of inflation might differ. In the case of widespread supply-chain problems, it would be best to try to alleviate these problems directly rather than reducing aggregate demand. An overall reduction in demand could hurt the economy and employment without doing anything to remedy the supply problems.

So which type of inflation was the major problem in 20021/2022? There were probably elements of both. There is no question that the pandemic led to widespread supply problems. At the same time, as mentioned earlier, the CARES Act and American Rescue Plan between them had injected about $4 trillion of additional demand into the economy. Even in an approximately $20 trillion economy, that is a large

483

amount of additional aggregate demand! This may well have been an appropriate response to high unemployment, but it did contribute to inflationary pressures.

This logic was what drove the Fed in 2022 to implement a contractionary monetary policy, to cool down excessive demand. But the situation was not as bad as the out-of-control inflation of the late 1970s, which led to much more drastic Fed policies to break the back of inflation even at the cost of plunging the economy into a deep recession. The hope was that inflation could be moderated this time without such drastic impacts on the economy.

In addition to monetary policy, the perception of rising inflation had an impact on fiscal policy. As discussed in Chapter 9, the Biden administration had passed the $1.9 trillion Infrastructure Investment and Jobs Act in 2021. This spending was spread over a ten-year period, so it would have little immediate impact on inflation. Nonetheless, the next major Biden initiative, the Build Back Better Act, also planned to cover a ten-year period and accompanied by revenue-raising provisions, ran into significant problems in Congress due to the perception that more spending at a time of inflation was unwise. Eventually a stripped-down version of Build Back Better, called the Inflation Reduction Act of 2022, was passed, including provisions for new revenue exceeding the amount of new spending. In other words, unlike the earlier initiatives, this Act represented a moderately contractionary fiscal policy.

3.4 Technology and Globalization

We can use our *AS/AD* analysis to focus on one more historical period: the expansion of the 1990s. As with our analysis of the earlier 1960s–1980s period, past economic history may have some lessons for the present. From 1992 to 1998, unemployment rates and inflation rates steadily fell. In 1998, unemployment was 4.4 percent, the lowest it had been since 1971. Inflation was 1.6 percent, lower than it had been in more than ten years. This was clearly the best macroeconomic performance in decades. Unemployment continued to fall for another two years, reaching 3.9 percent in 2000.

What caused this sustained recovery? Significant advances in innovation—in particular enormous leaps in information technology, including the advent of widespread use of the Internet and information systems for business supplies, deliveries, and product design—provided a major impetus for this period of superior macroeconomic performance. This can be modeled as a period of beneficial supply shocks, as shown in Figure 12.14.

Many economists also point to increasing global competitiveness as a factor in the rising productivity of this period. Competition from foreign firms, they argue, made U.S. firms work harder to become efficient. Meanwhile, competition from foreign workers and anti-union

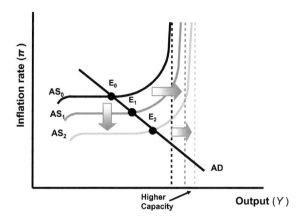

Figure 12.14 *The Effects of Technological Innovation and Increased Efficiency*

government policies weakened the power of domestic unions. This helped keep wage and price inflation low, although it also had negative consequences for the U.S. distribution of income, as described in Chapters 1 and 14.

The strong performance of the macroeconomy in the 1990s inspired economic optimism. A number of commentators wondered whether we were entering a "new economy" in which business cycles would become a thing of the past. Events after 2000 proved otherwise. In 2001–2002 the stock market crashed, as the "dot-com" speculative bubble burst. About a year later, the economy slid into recession. Expansionary fiscal and monetary policies, including tax rate cuts and low interest rates, helped to promote recovery from that recession. But in 2007, another even more significant speculative bubble in housing collapsed, leading rapidly to the most severe recession since the 1930s—often referred to as the Great Recession because of its length and severity. And in 2020 the onset of the COVID-19 pandemic plunged the economy into another recession. Clearly, recessions and the effort to recover from them are not a thing of the past.

This brings us back to the broader issue of application of *AS/AD* analysis. It seems that we have not entered a new, business-cycle–free, "recession-proof" economic optimum. Instead, we have relived some of the recessionary and inflationary problems of previous decades. Although the real productivity gains made during the 1990s did not go away, and many of the effects of that supply capacity expansion persist to this day, the kinds of economic fluctuation and policy response that we have modeled with *AS/AD* analysis clearly remain of prime importance to macroeconomics. Significant declines in aggregate demand require expansionary policy measures to prevent a worsening recession. As the economy moves out of recession and approaches full employment, concerns typically shift to possible excessive aggregate demand and the need for policies to moderate inflation—but if possible without tipping the economy back into recession.

Discussion Questions

1. Under what circumstances can aggregate demand be increased without leading to problems with inflation? Under what circumstances is an increase in aggregate demand likely to cause inflation?
2. Stagflation—a combination of unemployment and inflation—seems to be the worst of both worlds. What policies can be used to respond to stagflation? Why is it important to differentiate between demand-pull and cost-push inflation in formulating policies?

4 COMPETING THEORIES

The *AS/AD* model has given us insight into some of the major macroeconomic fluctuations of the past several decades. But there remains much room for controversy. Was the expansionary fiscal policy enacted in response to the 2007–2008 recession too little or too much? Was it a good idea for the Federal Reserve to lower interest rates to near zero in 2008–2015 and again in 2020 to try to promote recovery? Was a strong contractionary policy required in 2022 to respond to inflation? Economists often differ in their views on these issues, and their theoretical backgrounds tend to inform their answers to these and other more contemporary questions.

Here we review the ways in which classical and Keynesian economics address these questions. Additional theories—some of which take positions between these two poles, and some of which are more radical—are reviewed in the Appendix to this chapter.

4.1 Classical Macroeconomics

As discussed in previous chapters, economists with ties to the classical school tend to believe in the self-adjusting properties of a free-market system. In the classical view, labor markets clear at an equilibrium wage (Chapter 7). Classical markets for loanable funds cause savings and investment to be equal at an equilibrium interest rate (Chapter 8). In theory, then, a smoothly functioning economy should never be at anything other than full employment.

In terms of the *AS/AD* model, the classical theory implies an *AS* curve that is quite different from the one that we have been working with, as shown in Figure 12.15. In such an economy, output would always be at or close to its full-employment level (now shown as a distinct value, rather than a range). The *AD* level would determine the inflation rate, but nothing else.

The rationale for this vertical *AS* curve is as follows. At the full-employment level, people are making their optimizing choices about how much to work, consume, and so on. If for some reason the economy were to produce at less than the full-employment level, the unemployed

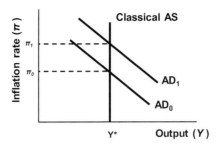

Figure 12.15 *The Classical View of AS/AD*

workers would bid down wages and full employment would be restored. If the economy were to produce at more than its full-employment level, wages would be bid up, and employment would drop back to its full-employment level. Similar adjustments would take place in product markets and financial markets. Such processes are assumed to work quickly and smoothly so that the economy will return to full employment fairly quickly.

What, according to the classical model, is the effect of aggregate demand management policies? As we can see in Figure 12.15, expansionary fiscal or monetary policy can have no effect on the output level. Classical economists believe that increased government spending just "crowds out" private spending (as discussed in Chapter 9), in particular spending on investment. Because the economy is already at its full-employment level of Y^*, more spending by government just means less spending by consumers and businesses.

The extreme version of this view, as expressed in Figure 12.15, is probably not held by many economists. Even most classically oriented economists acknowledge that there can be short-term variations in employment and temporary effects of fiscal and monetary policies. But they argue that in the longer run, the economy will achieve its natural equilibrium (Y^* in Figure 12.15), and government stimulatory policies such as a shift from AD_0 to AD_1 in Figure 12.15, will only lead to inflation, as shown by the move from π_0 to π_1 (The concept of a vertical long-run AS curve is discussed in more detail in the Appendix to this chapter.)

As we saw in our discussion of classical monetary theory in Chapter 11, the classical prescription is that the central bank should just choose a certain growth rate of the money supply or level of the interest rate to support and stick to it, without concerning itself about unemployment and output. Classical theory tends to support politically conservative policies that emphasize small government and strict rules on monetary policy. Classical economists would tend to say that the fiscal expansionary policies put into place in 2009 and 2020/2021 were unnecessary for the purposes of macroeconomic stabilization, but that the anti-inflationary monetary contraction of the early 1980s was a good idea.

4.2 Keynesian Macroeconomics

The original Keynesian belief was that market economies are inherently unstable. The Keynesian notion of the influence of "animal spirits" on investment refers to the tendency of private decision-makers to become overly optimistic and create booms in investing and production. And the higher the boom, the deeper the crash. Firms that have overextended and overproduced during an upswing need time to regroup, sell off inventory, and so on before they will be ready to go on the upswing again. Households that have overextended and overspent during a boom also need to regroup and perhaps pay down debt, before they will be willing to restart an optimistic spending bandwagon.

This view of perpetual business cycles is a fundamentally different worldview from those that presume an automatic "settling down" of the economy at a full-employment equilibrium. Keynes did *not* believe that macroeconomic phenomena could be explained by assuming rational, optimizing behavior by individuals, and then extrapolating from models of individual markets to the macroeconomy. Modern Keynesians argue that this inherent tendency toward market instability requires active government intervention and that the alternative—simply waiting for the market to correct itself—risks major economic damage and long-term depression.

It is important to note that Keynesians do not only favor expansionary fiscal and monetary policies. They believe that such policies are needed in case of recession, but under different circumstances, such as the inflationary periods that we have discussed, contractionary policies may be called for. Keynesians thus find the kind of analysis that we have presented in this chapter very useful for determining what type of policy is needed in different circumstances.

The traditional model of Keynesian business cycles must be modified to deal with new events such as supply shocks (discussed above) and sustainability issues (discussed in Chapter 17). These require models that are flexible enough to address new issues as they arise. Such models are best built on the understanding that economies are subject to a variety of forces, many of which can swamp the market equilibrium logic that would be expected to lead to a classical situation of full-employment equilibrium.

In the modern era, the debate between economists who favor classical approaches and those who argue for Keynesian analysis has continued. The Great Recession of 2007–2009 and the COVID recession of 2020 provided new fodder for these arguments about economic analysis and policy (see Box 12.2).

BOX 12.2 CLASSICAL AND KEYNESIAN VIEWS OF RECESSION AND RECOVERY

The recessions of 2007–2009 and 2020 provided a new arena for the long-running debate between classical and Keynesian views in economics and their impacts on macroeconomic policies.

Two major responses to the recessions in the United States—the fiscal stimulus programs of 2009, 2020, and 2021 and Federal Reserve policies of ultralow interest rates and "quantitative easing"— are right out of the Keynesian playbook of expansionary fiscal and monetary policy.

On the other hand, contractionary fiscal policies of "austerity" (drastic spending cutbacks) implemented in many European countries following the 2007–2009 crisis reflected the classical perspective that excessive government spending is a problem, not a solution, and that budget deficits need to be eliminated. But by 2016 the European Central bank had adopted a different approach, moving to a more expansionary monetary policy. And in response to the 2020 recession Europe followed the lead of the United States in putting expansionary policies into place.

Keynesians argued that the stimulative fiscal and monetary policies implemented in the United States in 2009 prevented a much worse recession, saving or creating millions of jobs and putting the country on a (slow) road to recovery.[10] They believed that the results, in terms of employment creation, were limited mainly because the stimulus was not large enough, and that the stimulus approach was wrongly abandoned after the 2010 Republican congressional victories. Meanwhile, Keynesians pointed to the deepening recession in Europe after 2009 as proof that the "classical medicine" of budget austerity was counterproductive.

Classical economists, by contrast, saw government efforts at economic stimulation in 2009 as a failure, one that would saddle the country with an increased burden of debt. According to conservative economist Allan Meltzer (2011):

> U.S. fiscal and monetary policies are mainly directed at getting a near-term result. The estimated cost of new jobs in President Obama's jobs bill is at least $200,000 per job. . . once the subsidies end, the jobs disappear—but the bonds that financed them remain and must be serviced. Perhaps that's why estimates of the additional spending generated by Keynesian stimulus— the "multiplier effect" have failed to live up to expectations.[11]

Until 2016, the U.S. economy was performing much better than most European economies, which were still well below their production levels of 2007, with unemployment rates in some countries remaining at Great Depression levels of over 25 percent. Predictions by classical economists of the beneficial effects of budget austerity in Europe, and of accelerating inflation in the United States, did not come true.

After 2016, European economies experienced robust growth and declining unemployment. GDP in the EU region rose by 2.6 percent in 2017—the fastest since 2007—and the unemployment rate dropped below 8 percent for the first time since 2008.[12] This progress in European economies was mainly attributed to the expansionary policies of the European Central Bank, including low lending rates and large-scale purchases of securities, which has increased liquidity and boosted growth.[13] This seemed to support the Keynesian argument that activist and expansionary government policy is essential to get out of a severe recession.

489

The experience of 2020–2022 provided some fodder for both perspectives. On the one hand, Keynesians could argue that once again expansionary government fiscal and monetary policy saved the day, bringing economies back from the deep Covid-induced recession in a relatively short time period. According to Keynesian economist Paul Krugman,

> Economic policy in 2021 was actually pretty good...holding back the recovery would have been a serious mistake if — and it's a big if — the inflation spike of 2021 doesn't turn into a wage-price spiral, and we can eventually get inflation back down without having to go through a serious recession.[14]

Krugman pointed to record job growth in 2021 as evidence that the stimulus policies were on target. Federal Reserve Chair Jerome Powell seemed to agree: "The country's early aid was 'a lot,' and it's 'too soon' to say whether the early pandemic aid is at fault for the recent [inflationary] headwinds, Powell said in a press conference in January 2022. Still, the actions were taken while the economy faced a 'shocking' drop in activity, and the recovery since has been superlative."[15]

On the other hand, classically oriented economists could claim that they were right this time about the dangers of inflation. At a minimum, they could find some support for the argument that the stimulus policies of 2020 and 2021 were too large. According to conservative economist Douglas Holtz-Eakin, commenting on the policies of President Biden's first year, "The president's fiscal policy was a disaster. The American Rescue Plan—the $1.9 trillion stimulus passed in March 2021—was a major policy error. It was unnecessary, too large, incredibly poorly designed. It fueled the inflation that is bedevilling the middle class."[16] Yet without any stimulus policies at all, it seems very likely that the recession of 2020 would have been much more protracted.

The real world is the testing ground for economic theories. As events unfold, the economic argument will continue, and new policies and new data will be grist to the mill of continued economic debate.

Discussion Questions

1. What is the effect of expansionary fiscal and monetary policies in the classical model?
2. Which do you think gives a better description of economic realities: classical or Keynesian macroeconomic theory? Explain.

REVIEW QUESTIONS

1. What does the *AD* curve represent, and why does it slope downward?
2. What shifts the AD curve?
3. What does the *AS* curve represent, and why does it have the shape that it has?
4. What shifts the *AS* curve?
5. Describe, using the *AS/AD* model, a combination of events that might cause an economy to suffer from "stagflation."
6. Describe, using the *AS/AD* model, the impact of an adverse supply shock.
7. Describe, using the *AS/AD* model, how Federal Reserve policy might bring down inflation over time.

8. Describe, using the *AS/AD* model, the effects of a series of positive supply shocks.
9. What does the *AS* curve look like in the classical model, and why?
10. What underlying dynamic did Keynes believe is behind the business cycle? Illustrate with an *AS/AD* graph.
11. What is the difference between demand-pull and cost-push inflation? How might policy responses to the two types differ?
12. How do classical and Keynesian economist differ in their analyses of recent policies related to recession, recovery, and inflation?

EXERCISES

1. For each of the following, indicate which curve in the *AS/AD* model shifts (initially), and in which direction(s):
   a) A beneficial supply shock
   b) An increase in government spending
   c) A monetary contraction designed to lower the long-run inflation rate
   d) An increase in taxes
   e) An adverse supply shock
   f) A fall in people's expectations of inflation
   g) A decrease in consumer confidence
2. Suppose the inflation rate in an economy is observed to be falling. Sketching an *AS/AD* model for each case, determine which of the following phenomena could be the cause. (There may be more than one.)
   a) The federal government gives households a substantial tax cut
   b) Agricultural harvests are particularly good this year
   c) Businesses are confident about the future and are buying more equipment
   d) The Fed is trying to move the economy toward a lower long-run inflation rate
3. Suppose that an economy is currently experiencing full employment, and inflation is only slightly higher than had been expected.
   a) Draw and carefully label an *AS/AD* diagram that illustrates this case. Label the point representing the state of this economy $E_{(a)}$.
   b) Suppose that investors' confidence is actually only in the middle of an upswing. As investor confidence continues to rise, what happens to inflation and output? Add a new curve to your graph to illustrate this, as well as explaining in words. Label the point illustrating the new situation of the economy $E_{(b)}$.
   c) What sort of tax policy might a government enact to try to counteract an excessive upswing in investor confidence? Assuming this policy is effective, illustrate on your graph the effect of this policy, labeling the result $E_{(c)}$.
4. Suppose that an economy is in a deep recession.
   a) Draw and carefully label an *AS/AD* diagram that illustrates this case. Label the point representing the state of this economy E_0.
   b) If no policy action is taken, what will happen to the economy over time? Show on your graph, labeling some new possible equilibrium points E_1, E_2, and E_3. (Think about which curve shifts over time, and why, when the economy stagnates. Assume that no changes occur in investor or consumer confidence or in the economy's maximum capacity output level.)
   c) Suppose that the changes you outlined in (b) occurred very rapidly and dramatically. Is government policy necessary to get the economy out of the recession?
   d) Write a few sentences relating the above analysis to the dispute between classical and Keynesian macroeconomists.
5. Check recent inflation rates at https://www.rateinflation.com/inflation-rate/usa-historical-inflation-rate/ What do you think explains the recent pattern of inflation?

491

How does this relate to *AS/AD* analysis, and to the debate among different schools of thought, as discussed in Box 12.2?

6. Empirical data on the macroeconomy can be found in the *Economic Report of the President.* Go to https://www.govinfo.gov/ and search for statistical tables for the "civilian unemployment rate" and "price indexes for gross domestic product." Jot down data on the *seasonally adjusted* unemployment rate and the *percent change in the GDP implicit price deflator* for recent periods. Plot a few points on a graph to show how the economy has performed recently. (Sometimes data is presented for months or calendar quarters, rather than for years. For the purposes of this exercise, you may simply average the numbers within a year to get a number for the year.)

7. Match each concept in Column A with a definition or example in Column B.

Column A		Column B	
a.	Aggregate supply	1.	A rightward shift in the *AD* curve
b.	Real wealth effect	2.	A suggested relationship between inflation and unemployment
c.	Increase in autonomous consumption	3.	People's feelings about prices, based on experience or observation
d.	Maximum capacity output	4.	The economy's total production in relation to inflation
e.	Beneficial supply shock	5.	A sudden shortage of a key resource
f.	Reduction in autonomous investment	6.	A self-reinforcing tendency of wages and prices to rise
g.	Aggregate demand	7.	Increased (or decreased) spending as a result of feeling wealthier (or poorer)
h.	Inflationary expectations	8.	Government regulations to prevent wages and prices rising
i.	Phillips curve	9.	The economy's total production if all resources are fully utilized
j.	Wage-price spiral	10.	A burst of technological progress
k.	Wage and price controls	11.	Total spending on goods and services in an economy
l.	Vertical *AS* curve	12.	A leftward shift in the *AD* curve
m.	Adverse supply shock	13.	Represents the classical model of an economy at full employment

APPENDIX: MORE SCHOOLS OF MACROECONOMICS

A1 NEW CLASSICAL ECONOMICS

In the simple classical model presented above, the economy is nearly always at or close to full employment. Faced with the empirical evidence of widely fluctuating output and unemployment rates, some modern-day economists—often called "new classical" economists—have come up with a number of theories that seek to explain how classical theory can be consistent with the observed fluctuations.

At one extreme, some economists have sought to redefine full employment to mean pretty much whatever level of employment currently exists. Assuming that people make optimizing choices and markets work smoothly, one might observe employment levels rising and falling if, for example, technological capacities or people's preferences for work versus leisure shift over time. For example, during and after the COVID-19 recession, large numbers of people left the labor force in what was called the "Great Resignation".

Some new classical economists, who have worked on what is called **real business cycle theory**, have suggested that "intertemporal substitution of leisure" (i.e., essentially, people voluntarily taking more time off during recessions) could be at the root of the lower employment levels observed during some historical periods. Availability of unemployment compensation, in this view, could also make people more likely to choose not to work.

---

real business cycle theory: the theory that changes in employment levels are caused by a change in technological capacities or people's preferences concerning work

---

Economists of the **rational expectations** school (which originated during the 1970s and 1980s) proposed a theory according to which monetary policy only affects the inflation rate and not output. The basic idea is that people have perfect foresight (i.e., they are perfectly rational), so their decisions already factor in the effects of predictable Fed policy, rendering it ineffective. This model can be explained by using the *AS/AD* model with a classical-type vertical *AS* (as shown in Figure 12.15). This vertical *AS* is interpreted to be the real supply curve for the economy, with an output level unaffected by government policies. Possibly a very unexpected move by the Fed might have a temporary effect on output, but as soon as people understand what policies the Fed is carrying out, the policies will become ineffective due to changes in expectations.

---

rational expectations theory: the theory that people's expectations about Federal Reserve policy cause predictable monetary policies to be ineffective in changing output levels

---

Other new classical economists accept that unemployment is real and very painful to those whom it affects. But they see aggregate demand policies as useless for addressing it. Rather, they claim that unemployment

493

is caused by imperfections in labor markets (the "classical unemployment" described in Chapter 7). To reduce unemployment, new classical economists prescribe getting rid of government regulations (such as rigorous safety standards or minimum wages), restricting union activity, or cutting back on government social welfare policies that make it more attractive (according to the new classical economists) to stay out of work. Market pressures, they believe, will be enough on their own to support full employment—if given free rein.

A2 THE NEOCLASSICAL SYNTHESIS AND NEW KEYNESIAN MACROECONOMICS

Somewhere in the middle ground is what has been called the "classical-Keynesian synthesis" or **neoclassical synthesis**. (It is a bit confusing that the terms "neo-classical" and "new classical" sound so similar, but they represent two different approaches). In this way of looking at the world, Keynesian theory, which allows for output to vary from its full-employment level, is considered a reasonably good description of how things work in the short and medium run. However, this view holds that, for the reasons set out in the classical model, the economy will tend to return to full employment in the long run.

> **neoclassical synthesis:** A combination of classical and Keynesian perspectives

You may have noticed that in the exposition of the AS/AD model above, we talked about the short run and the medium run, but did not mention the long run. This is because in more decidedly Keynesian thought (to be discussed below), the economy is really a succession of short and medium runs. Shocks to the economy are so frequent and so pronounced, and price and wage adjustments (especially downward ones) so slow, that the economy never has a chance to "settle down" at a long-run equilibrium.

In the neoclassical synthesis, however, it is assumed that the economy, if left to its own devices for long enough, would settle back at full employment, due to the (eventual) success of classical wage and price adjustments. Models built on this basis would use an analysis much like that presented in the AS/AD model used in the body of this chapter but add a vertical AS curve such as that shown in Figure 12.15, labeling it "long-run aggregate supply."

To the extent that neoclassical economists and some Keynesians agree on this model, then, debates come down to a question of how long it takes to get to the long run. More classically oriented economists tend to emphasize that excessive unemployment is merely temporary and believe that (at least if the government stays out of the way) the long run comes fairly soon. Some Keynesian economists, often called **New Keynesians**, have accepted the challenge from classical economists to present all their analysis in terms of the workings of markets, individual optimizing behavior, and possible "imperfections" in markets. They have built up theories (such as efficiency wage theory, discussed in Chapter 7) to explain why wages do not just fall during a recession to create a full employment equilibrium. They tend to work within the neoclassical synthesis, but claim that due to institutional factors the long run may be a long, long way away. (As Keynes himself wryly said, "In the long run, we are all dead.") New Keynesians, therefore, believe that activist government fiscal and monetary policy is often justified.

> **New Keynesian macroeconomics:** a school of thought that bases its analysis on micro-level market behavior, but which justifies activist macroeconomic policies by assuming that markets have "imperfections" that can create or prolong recessions

A3 POST-KEYNESIAN MACROECONOMICS

Post-Keynesian economists base their analyses on some of the more radical implications of the original Keynesian theory. (Once again, the similarity between the terms "New Keynesian" and "post-Keynesian" can be confusing, but there is a significant difference in the theoretical perspectives, as we will discuss). Post-Keynesians believe that modern economies are basically unstable and do not accept the idea of a long-run equilibrium at full employment. They stress the view that history matters in determining where the economy is today (a perspective known as **path dependence**). They also believe that the future, although it will depend to some extent on the actions we take now, is fundamentally unpredictable, due to the often surprising nature of economic evolution and world events.

> **post-Keynesian macroeconomics:** a school of thought that stresses the importance of history and uncertainty in determining macroeconomic outcomes
> **path dependence:** the idea that the state of a system such as the economy is strongly dependent on its past history

For example, one post-Keynesian argument is that high unemployment, like high inflation, may also be "toothpaste" that is very difficult to get back into the tube. When people are unemployed for a long time, they

495

tend to lose work skills, lose work habits, and get demoralized. If this is true, then government action to counter unemployment is even more needed, since high unemployment now may tend to lead to high unemployment in the future, even if the demand situation recovers. (Economists sometimes use the term "hysteresis" to refer to an event such as unemployment that persists into the future, even after the factors that cause that event have changed.)

In addition, long periods of high unemployment mean a permanent loss of output and investment—making the economy weaker in the long term. For these reasons, it is essential for the government to act to maintain full, or close-to-full, employment. Post-Keynesian economists would say that the fiscal expansionary policies put into place in 2009 and 2020 were a good idea because they do not believe that an economy left to its own devices will naturally return to full employment, even "in the long run."

Environmental problems, in the post-Keynesian view, add to the unpredictability of the future. Many environmental problems, like climate change and species loss, have long-term implications that are rarely if ever taken into account in market decision making. This strengthens the argument that activist government policy is necessary to ensure a stable macroeconomic future—essentially the opposite of the classical view that the economy is best left to itself for the long run.

NOTES

1. Blinder and Zandi, 2010; CBO, 2013; Montgomery, 2012.
2. Irwin, 2018.
3. Economic Policy Institute, 2018.
4. Appelbaum, 2013.
5. Rugaber, 2022.
6. Mitchell, 2022.
7. Summers, 2022.
8. Krugman, 2021.
9. Krugman, 2022.
10. Blinder and Zandi, 2010; Krugman, 2011.
11. Meltzer, 2011.
12. Based on data from Eurostat, European Commission.
13. El-Erian, 2017.
14. Krugman, 2022b.
15. Winck, 2022.
16. Holtz-Eakin, 2022.

REFERENCES

Appelbaum, Binyamin. 2013. "Yes, We Have No Inflation." *New York Times*, June 27.
Blinder, Alan S. and Mark Zandi. 2010. "How the Great Recession Was Brought to an End." www.economy.com/mark-zandi/documents/End-of-Great-Recession.pdf.

Congressional Budget Office (CBO). 2013. "Estimated Impact of the American Recovery and Reinvestment Act on Employment and Output from October 2012 through December 2012." https://www.cbo.gov/sites/default/files/113th-congress-2013-2014/reports/02-25-2013-ARRA_One-Column.pdfEconomic Policy Institute. 2018. "Nominal Wage Tracker." March 9. https://www.epi.org/nominal-wage-tracker/.

El-Erian, Mohamed A. 2017. "How to Build on Europe's Economic Recovery." *Bloomberg View*, November 20.

Holtz-Eakin, Douglas. 2022. "Bidenomics: Grading Year 1." *American Action Forum*, January 21. https://www.americanactionforum.org/daily-dish/bidenomics-grading-year-1/

Irwin, Neil. 2018. "The Economy Is Looking Awfully Strong,." *New York Times*, March 9.

Krugman, Paul. 2011. "Keynes Was Right." *New York Times*, December 29.

Krugman, Paul. 2021. "History Says Don't Panic about Inflation." *New York Times*, November 11.

Krugman, Paul. 2022. "Can the Fed Let Us Down Easy?" *New York Times*, February 1.

Meltzer, Allan H. 2011. "Four Reasons Keynesians Keep Getting It Wrong." *Wall Street Journal*, October 28.

Mitchell, Josh. 2022. "U.S. Economy Grows as Fourth-Quarter GDP Shows Strongest Year in Decades." *Wall Street Journal*, January 27.

Montgomery, Lori. 2012. "Congressional Budget Office Defends Stimulus." *The Washington Post*, June 6.

Rugaber, Christopher. 2022. "A Key Inflation Gauge Rose 5.8% in 2021, the Most in 39 years." *Associated Press*, January 28.

Wall Street Week. 2022. "Larry Summers: We're Moving towards Higher Entrenched Inflation." *Bloomberg*, January 14, 2022. https://www.bloomberg.com/news/videos/2022-01-14/we-re-moving-toward-higher-entrenched-inflation-summers-video

Winck, Ben. 2022. "US Pandemic Aid Was 'a Lot' – But It Fueled a World-beating Recovery and Inflation Is Being Managed, Fed's Powell Says." *Insider*, January 27.

Chapter 13

The Global Economy and Policy

Do you know how many Philippine pesos, South African rand, or Peruvian nuevos soles you can get for a U.S. dollar? No? If you traveled to one of these countries, you might be surprised to find out that the average person on the street in any city can often easily quote you the going exchange rate between their currency and the U.S. dollar. People in smaller economies have always been very vulnerable to international economic conditions and hence make it a habit to stay current on the rate.

In contrast, because the United States has a large economy and its currency has historically dominated the world financial system, people living in the United States often tend to be relatively unaware of global economic conditions. But this has been changing, as recent events have made increasingly clear the degree to which national economies are interdependent. Global financial imbalances exposed first by the 2007–2008 financial crisis, and more recently by the global COVID-19 pandemic, led to world economic downturns that weakened the relative standing of the U.S. economy. Thus far, the dollar remains the preeminent international currency, but there is continuing discussion about possible alternatives.

International money flows, as we will see, are partly determined by international trade flows. The U.S.–China trade imbalance continues to be a concern, with many arguing that the large U.S. trade deficit means that the United States owes too much money to China and that this will cause economic problems in the future. The great size of the U.S. economy makes it more capable of handling its indebtedness— both domestic and international—than many smaller countries. But many developing countries around the world face immense economic and financial challenges, with international debts far greater than their GDPs. Other political events, such as Britain's exit from the European Union and inflation in Turkey and Argentina, have also led to fluctuation in national currency values. How can we evaluate these and similar issues from an international economic perspective?

DOI: 10.4324/9781003251521-17

1 MACROECONOMICS IN A GLOBAL CONTEXT

In earlier chapters, our macro model has generally limited its scope to three main economic sectors: households, businesses, and the government. We have seen how each of these—through consumption, investment, and government spending—contributes to aggregate expenditure. It is now time to open things up a bit and introduce the foreign sector. Doing so can provide insight into how national economies are linked, and also into the opportunities and problems that such linkages can create.

1.1 Global Connections

An economy with no international linkages is called a *closed economy*, while one that participates in the global economy is called an *open economy*. The economic linkages among countries can take many forms, including:

- international *trade flows*, when goods and services that have been created in one country are sold in another, or when multiple countries are involved in different stages of production as part of a **global supply chain**.
- international *income flows*, when capital incomes (profit, rent, and interest), labor incomes, or transfer payments go from one country to another
- international *transactions in assets*, when people trade in financial assets such as foreign bonds or currencies, or make investments in real foreign assets such as businesses or real estate
- international *flows of people*, as people migrate from one country to another, either temporarily or permanently
- international flows of *technological knowledge, cultural products*, and other intangibles, which can profoundly influence patterns of production and consumption, as well as tastes and lifestyles
- international sharing of, and impact on, *common environmental resources,* such as deep-sea fisheries and global climate patterns
- the *institutional environment* created by international monetary institutions, international trade agreements, international military and aid arrangements, and banks, corporations, and other private entities that operate at an international scale.

---

global supply chain: A network of countries directed at transforming resource inputs into finished products for delivery to the consumer

---

499

Any one of these forms of interaction may be crucially important for understanding the macroeconomic experience of specific countries at specific times. Mexico and Turkey, for example, receive significant flows of income from remittances sent home by citizens working abroad. Trade in "intellectual property," such as technology patents and music copyrights, continues to be an issue of hot dispute. And as made clear by the COVID-19 pandemic, diseases that threaten human health or pests that damage agriculture can travel along with people and goods—with grave consequences.

Thoroughly describing the international economic system is too large a project for even a whole textbook, never mind one or two chapters. This chapter will therefore focus on the critical foundational material required to understand the global economy. It looks at two distinct but interrelated phenomena: *trade*, or specifically how trade in goods and services affects aggregate expenditure; and *finance*, or the flows of money across borders for commercial as well as investment purposes. Additionally, we look at how trade and finance influence the exchange rate of a country's currency. As we will see, these international issues can all affect living standards and macroeconomic stabilization. Later chapters look in more detail at issues of growth and sustainability.

1.2 Major Policy Tools

We say that a country's economy is "open" if it exports and imports large amounts relative to its GDP and "closed" if it exports and imports relatively small amounts. Governments can try to control the degree of openness or "closedness" of their economy through a variety of policy tools. Yet why would a country even *want* its economy to be "closed?" Is trade with other countries not unambiguously favorable? Those who favor globalization believe so; those more inclined to "protectionism" are more skeptical.

The traditional view, which dates back two centuries to Adam Smith and David Ricardo, is that trade is indeed an unmistakable benefit. One of the chief supporting ideas is that through trade, a country can expand the market for its products and therefore increase the benefit of *specializing in* products in which it has a productive advantage. Specialization, moreover, is seen as promoting productive efficiency and thus helping to increase economic output. Finally, through trade a country can translate its improved productivity to greater consumption of a variety of relatively low-priced products available from other countries—hence achieving higher living standards.

While there is a strong economic argument to support such claims, trade skeptics focus on the potential problems. First, trade can sometimes leave a country exceedingly vulnerable to market changes and instability. If, for example, the price of a critical raw material or food item unexpectedly rose and a country specializing in other products no longer produced that item domestically, the country might suffer severe adverse consequences if unable to pay the higher price.

Second, it matters in what products a country specializes. If a country focuses on aircraft and other high-tech products, for example, there is not necessarily a problem as long as it finds sufficient external market demand for these items. On the other hand, if a country specializes in producing bananas and coffee, there are two potential problems. First, such items often yield relatively meager earnings and employment potential, even if trade with other countries is extensive. Second and more problematic, planning an economy around the production of such primary products commits a large portion of the country's valuable resources to the production of such goods, seriously hampering a country's potential to become richer and more diversified.

Trade can also lead some countries, especially those that are poor, to maintain low standards for worker or environmental protection. Lower standards make for "cheaper" production, hence more competitive prices. While richer countries on the whole have lower tolerance for labor and environmental abuses, countries with impoverished populations will sometimes regard lax or even non-existent regulation in these areas as the "price" of trade competitiveness.

Finally, even if trade produces generalized benefits for all participating countries, it does not mean that everyone within a country benefits. In particular, workers in import-competing industries may face lower wages or job loss as a result of cheaper imports. Perhaps the most common example given for restricting trade (often labeled **protectionism**) is that doing so protects domestic workers' jobs—even if at the cost of limiting domestic consumer choice.

---

protectionism: the practice of limiting the extent of trade with other countries through direct policy intervention

---

Because of such controversies, as well as others, few if any countries adopt completely "open" policies. Various restrictions on trade have remained common even as global trade has expanded. What are some of the ways in which a country can restrict trade?

One means of doing so is a **trade quota**, which does not eliminate trade but sets limits on the quantity of a good that can be imported or exported. By restricting supply, a quota generally raises the price that can be charged for the good within the country. This helps domestic producers of the good by shielding them from lower-price competition. It hurts foreign producers because it limits what they can sell in the domestic market. Some foreign producers may, however, get some benefit in the form of additional revenues from the artificially higher price.

> **trade quota:** a restriction on the quantity of a good that can be imported or exported

A second sort of policy—which has been used often throughout history and which is still the most widely used tool of trade policy—is a **tariff** (or "duty"). Tariffs are taxes charged on imports or exports. Tariffs, like quotas, can reduce trade because they make internationally traded goods more costly to buy or sell. Often misunderstood, tariffs are taxes paid to the government of the importing country *by the importing company or entity*, not by the exporting country. Even if a country wanted to tax its trading partners, it would have no manner of compelling them to pay. Taxing the country's own importing entity nevertheless discourages trade with the other country since the product price goes up. Consumers are therefore the ones who ultimately "pay" for the tariff in the form of a higher retail price.

> **tariffs:** taxes on imports or exports

Like quotas, import tariffs benefit domestic producers while raising prices to consumers. Unlike quotas, however, tariffs provide monetary benefit to the government that imposes them. Also, they do not give foreign producers an opportunity to increase prices—in fact, foreign producers may be forced to lower prices in order to remain competitive with domestic producers that do not pay the tariff.

There are also various **non-tariff barriers to trade** that can be imposed. These include the use of specific licensing requirements, standards, or regulations on imported goods, which permit trade but may limit its extent. These may take the form of "disguised" trade barriers that are not always easy to distinguish from reasonable standards or regulations. Perhaps as a consequence, we have seen quite a variety of such non-tariff trade barriers. One well-known case was a German law requiring all the beer that the country imports to be made of a few select ingredients (namely water, barley, and hops). Beer "purity" might have been a plausible pretext, but in 1987 the European Court of Justice found the centuries-old law to be in violation of commercial agreements among European Union member countries, and Germany was required to admit imports of beer that was not "pure." Eventually, Germany even permitted domestic production of "impure" beer, as long as it was not labeled "beer."

> **non-tariff barriers to trade:** use of licensing or other requirements to limit the volume of trade

502

The last important major category of trade-related policies—**trade-related subsidies**—may be used to either expand or contract trade. These are increasingly prevalent as less "visible" alternatives to tariffs or quotas. Export subsidies, paid to domestic producers when they market their products abroad, are motivated by a desire to *increase* the flow of exports. Countries can also use subsidies to promote a policy of **import substitution**, by giving domestic producers extra payments to encourage the production of certain goods for domestic markets, with a goal of *reducing* the quantity of imports.

---

trade-related subsidies: payments given by governments to producers to encourage more production, either for export or as a substitute for imports
import substitution: the policy of subsidizing domestic producers to make products that can be used in place of imported goods

---

Government policies can also influence international capital transactions (financial flows). Central banks often participate in foreign exchange markets with policy goals in mind, buying or selling foreign currencies, as discussed in detail later in this chapter. Countries also sometimes institute **capital controls**, which are restrictions or taxes on transactions in financial assets such as currency, stocks, or bonds, or on foreign ownership of domestic assets such as businesses or land. Restrictions on how much currency a person can take out of a country, for example, are one type of capital control. More sweeping capital controls can restrict investment flows into or out of a country, sometimes based on the concern that rapid large investment flows could destabilize the domestic economy.

---

capital controls: the regulation or taxation of international transactions involving assets

---

Countries may also regulate the form that foreign business investments can take. Some have required that all business ventures within their borders be at least partially owned by domestic investors. Some have required that all traded manufactured goods include at least a given percentage of parts produced by domestic companies. Countries that have adopted such **domestic content requirements** include China, Indonesia, Mexico, and the Philippines; the 2020 U.S.-Mexico-Canada Agreement (USMCA) also contains a regional content requirement. Sometimes such controls are related to a development strategy, while in other cases they simply reflect a desire to avoid foreign domination of domestic markets.

---

domestic content requirement: laws requiring traded goods to contain a certain percentage of goods produced by domestic companies

---

Some trade policies are enacted to try to attract foreign investment by, for example, giving foreign companies tax breaks and other incentives. A popular form of this is the **foreign trade zone**, a designated area of the country within which many tax, tariff, and perhaps regulatory policies that usually apply to manufacturing are suspended. By attracting foreign investment, countries may hope to increase employment or gain access to important technologies.

A well-known example is the *maquiladora* policy in Mexico under which manufacturing plants can import components and produce goods for export free of tariffs. U.S. companies on the other side of the border also benefit from Mexican exports made with much cheaper labor. Maquiladoras and similar foreign trade zones are controversial; critics highlight their frequent labor rights violations, exceedingly low wages, and environmental pollution. Mexican maquiladoras today face far more competition than 30 years ago. Other countries with an abundance of low skilled labor, like China, India, and Pakistan, are now a much bigger factor in the global economy than they once were.

---

foreign trade zone: a designated area of a country within which foreign-owned manufacturers can operate free of many taxes, tariffs, and regulations

---

Migration controls are another important aspect of international policy. Countries generally impose restrictions on people who visit or move to their territory, and a few also impose tight regulations on people when leaving the country. Although beliefs about national culture and population size are often the most obvious concerns behind the shaping of these controls, economic interests also play an important role. For example, policies may be affected by concerns about the skill composition of the domestic labor force, the issue of a "brain drain" of skilled workers, or concern about immigrants competing for jobs with domestic workers.

But migration controls may create their own problems. For example, Brexit brought about the end of unrestricted labor flows from the European Union to Britain. While hailed by some supporters, this has led to severe labor shortages in a number of British industries. More generally, some labor economists argue that aging populations in many industrialized countries will eventually require an influx of young workers from other countries, merely to support the growing ranks of pensioners economically. Finally, intensifying climate change almost ensures that international migration will increase over time regardless, as populations abandon homes made inhospitable by rising sea levels, dangerously high temperatures, and other climate-related disasters.

---

migration controls: restrictions on the flow of people into and out of a country

---

Countries do not necessarily choose sets of policies that consistently lead toward openness or consistently toward "closedness." Often there is a mix—policies are chosen for a wide variety of reasons and can even be at cross purposes. Nor do countries choose their policies in a vacuum. Not only must policymakers take into account the preferences of their country's population, but they must also consider reactions to their policies by foreign governments. Increasingly, they also need to pay attention to whether their policies are in compliance with international agreements.

1.3 Patterns of Trade and Finance

Economists would say that national economies are, on the whole, more "open" than in the past, even if global trade has trended slightly downward in the past few years. One way of measuring a county's economic "openness" is to calculate the sum of its imports and exports of goods and services as a percentage of GDP. Growth in trade according to this measure is shown for 1970–2020 in Figure 13.1. Although trade is a lower proportion of GDP in the United States than in many other countries, a similar pattern of significantly increasing trade over the period 1970–2010 is also evident for the United States, with a slight downturn in the 2010–2020 decade.

Why has trade grown over time? The first and probably most important reason is that many governments have, over time, lowered their tariffs and other barriers to trade. Since the end of World War II, there has been a push for freer trade at the global level. The General Agreement on Tariffs and Trade (GATT), established in 1947, and the **World Trade Organization** (WTO), succeeding it in 1994, have overseen many rounds of tariff reduction. The WTO, with 164 member countries representing over 98 percent of global trade and GDP, also serves as the world's arbiter on trade disputes. It has thus far consistently ruled against countries engaging in trade restrictions and aims for a world in which countries cannot discriminate against one another through unfavorable trade

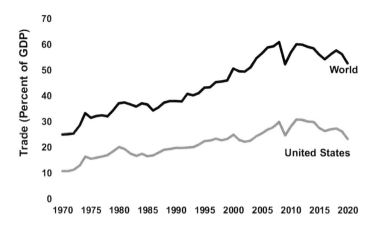

Figure 13.1 *Trade Expressed as a Percentage of Production, World and United States, 1970–2020*

Source: World Development Indicators, World Bank, 2021.

Note: Since this measure includes both imports and exports, it does not mean that over 50 percent of all produced goods and services in the world are traded—it counts the same goods both as exports from one country and imports to another.

policies. Despite general agreement on these broad principles, the WTO has often run into difficulties and disagreements among member nations, especially on issues such as agricultural trade. This may have contributed to the recent stall in expansion of global trade evident in Figure 13.1.

Further complicating matters is the existence throughout the world of so-called "trade blocs"—groups of countries integrating their economies for commercial advantage. Members of a trade bloc grant preferential market access to other participants, usually within the same geographical area. Such economic integration effectively creates a hierarchy of trade preference in which bloc members are favored—with, for example, elimination of tariffs or quotas—even if the goods traded are produced less efficiently or competitively than they could be outside the bloc. It could therefore be said that trade blocs, while promoting free trade within a specific region, countervail the main objectives of the WTO.

World Trade Organization: An international organization that conducts negotiations aimed at lowering trade barriers, and mediates trade disputes between countries

---

The United States-Mexico-Canada Agreement (USMCA)* is an example of one type of trade bloc that is known as a **free trade area**.

---

* USMCA came into force in 2020, succeeding the earlier North American Free Trade Agreement (NAFTA). USMCA is sometimes referred to as "NAFTA 2.0

The participating countries agree, among other things, not to impose tariffs on imports from each other. Members can pursue independent trade policies with countries outside the free trade bloc (for example, Canada has a separate trade agreement with the European Union).

A **customs union** is a free trade area that goes one step further: It also defines common tariffs toward the rest of the world. The Southern African Customs Union (SACU), consisting of Botswana, Eswatini (sometimes referred to as 'Swaziland'), Lesotho, Namibia, and South Africa, is one example. Yet more integrated is a **common market**, which is like a customs union that additionally provides for free movement of labor and capital, as well as goods and services, among its member countries. The European Economic Area (EEA), which encompasses the European countries, Norway, Iceland, and Liechtenstein, is an example of a common market.

An **economic union** is a common market that, in addition, adopts a common set of economic policies. As an example, the Maastricht Treaty (1992) stipulated "convergence criteria" (fiscal policy requirements) for countries belonging to the European Union. Other examples of such unions are MERCOSUR (Argentina, Brazil, Paraguay, and Uruguay) and the Central American Integration System (SICA).

Finally, a **monetary union** refers to an economic union that additionally shares a single currency. The Eurozone (the region that shares the Euro currency) is the by far most well-known example of a monetary union. Some, but not all, members of the European Union participate in the Eurozone. (Denmark and Sweden are examples of European Union members that do not participate in the Eurozone.) The Eastern Caribbean Currency Union is the only other example of note, and it is a subset of the Caribbean Single Market and Economy (CSME), another economic union.

---

free trade area: A group of countries that have abolished tariffs and quotas for goods produced in the area and traded between these countries

customs union: A group of countries that have abolished tariffs and quotas among themselves, and have introduced a common external tariff

common market: A group of countries forming a customs union and additionally permitting free movement of labor and capital between participating countries

economic union: A group of countries forming a common market and additionally adopting a common set of economic policies

economic and monetary union: An economic union in which participating countries share a single currency

---

A second reason for the increase in trade flows is improvements in transportation technology. The costs and time lags involved in shipping products by air, for example, are far less now than in 1950. Fruit from

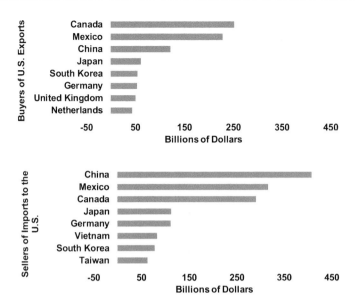

Figure 13.2 *Top Purchasers of Goods from the United States and Suppliers of Goods to the United States, 2021*

Source: U.S. Census Bureau, Foreign Trade Statistics, Top Trading Partners, 2021.

Chile and flowers from Colombia or Costa Rica are now flown into the United States every day—and are still fresh when they arrive. Container ships have hugely reduced the costs of long-distance transport.

The third reason for increased trade is advancements in telecommunications. The infrastructure for phone, fax, and electronic communication has improved dramatically. Better telecommunications make it possible for many kinds of services, such as customer support and many technical functions, to be directly imported from, for example, call centers in India.

Figure 13.2 shows the volume of exports that the United States sells to the top eight buyers of its goods and the volume of its imports that come from the top eight countries that sell to it. Historically, the closest neighbors of the United States—Canada and Mexico—have been very important trading partners. Germany, the UK, and Japan, not surprisingly, have also been leading trade partners.

Over the last several decades, China has become a major source of U.S. imports. Until about 1980, U.S. trade with China was negligible. Since then, U.S. importation of Chinese products—especially electronics (including computers and televisions) as well as clothing, toys, and furniture—has boomed. Although China buys some U.S. goods, including agricultural products and aircraft, the value of U.S. imports from China far exceeds the value of U.S. exports to China, creating a trade deficit with China of over $300 billion in 2020.

1.4 Transnational Corporations and Global Supply Chains

Trade relations have also grown increasingly complex over time. We have thus far been assuming that countries produce all products from start to finish and then sell them to their trading partners. But as the world's markets become progressively more interlinked, private companies known as **transnational corporations** (TNCs) often find it advantageous to schedule different stages of production in different countries through global supply chains. So, for example, goods as diverse as automobiles and clothing are often produced in more than one country. The presence of TNCs in multiple countries means that much of the "international trade" that goes on actually occurs *within one company*.

---

transnational corporation: a company that produces goods or services in more than one country

---

By organizing production and sale through global supply chains, TNCs gain efficiency advantages that increase profits. They are able to arrange each production stage in a country where, for example, labor or vital resource inputs are cheapest. Doing so helps save them considerable amounts of money. Technological advances in transportation and communications have facilitated this progress. Additionally, sophisticated algorithms have in recent years enabled companies to, for example, better anticipate consumer demand. This means that it is often no longer necessary to spend large sums of money storing inventory, as products are increasingly timed to ship as they are needed. Such developments have, over the years, helped increase the interconnectedness of markets. The efficiency gains of such modern trade networks have greatly helped increase TNC profits. But they have also come under criticism, for example for allowing TNCs to choose to operate where safety or environmental standards are most lax.

Global supply chains can also be vulnerable to unexpected events. Today's computer algorithms, increasingly driven by artificial intelligence or 'AI,' have immense computing potential. But when it comes to predicting sudden "shocks" to the system, they often fall short. This was vividly illustrated during the pandemic years of 2020–2022, as disruptions in some sectors spilled over into others, creating a "domino effect" with substantial adverse impacts on global commerce, prices, and employment. Despite optimism that the worst is over, fear remains that global supply chain problems will persist indefinitely (see Box 13.1).

BOX 13.1 GLOBAL SUPPLY CHAIN CRISIS COULD LAST ANOTHER TWO YEARS

Industry experts warn that the pandemic-induced supply chain crisis that began in 2020/2021 could last for up to two years. Many markets are affected. In Britain, for example, it is alcohol; in Canada, maple syrup; in Australia, it is a crucial additive for diesel trucks; and in New Zealand, it is brown sugar.

Maersk, one of the big three shipping companies, said the worst delays were on the US west coast, creating a "ripple effect" around the world. Among consequences are too many containers in some ports in the US and Europe, but not enough in ports throughout Asia.

Inflation touched decades-long highs in western economies not only because of higher shipping costs but also due to greater demand from consumers stuck at home for months and unable to spend any money on treats such as holidays and nights out.

Tiffany Compres, a partner at international law firm FisherBroyles based in Florida, said: "It will take time to get better, for companies to adjust, and for the legal framework to adapt. To add to the challenge, this is very much a political issue, and nations will need to cooperate to really get us to a new sustainable way of operating the supply chain. It seems to be a tall order in our polarized era."

And Dennis Unkovic, a US corporate lawyer, trade expert, and author of Transforming the Global Supply Chain says that for anyone "expecting the post-pandemic world to return to 'normal,' forget it. Whatever was considered normal before the pandemic is not coming back."[1]

Regardless of how the supply chain problem is resolved, there also exists a longer-term political challenge. Concern is growing that TNCs may eventually become so large that they will wield absolute power over the countries that host them. An American or European company might, for example, pressure the government of Brazil to loosen earlier restrictions on deforestation on grounds that more land is needed for cattle ranches or soybean farms. Major agribusiness corporations already wield considerable power over agricultural policy in many African countries. Such cases could mean that private companies would have sovereign rights over the governing of independent countries. As TNCs become more dominant in the global economy, this is not an idle concern.

Discussion Questions

1. How do international linkages affect your own life? Can you give examples of the sorts of linkages listed in Section 1.1 that have had direct effects on you or your family?

2. Production of apparel has been widely globalized in recent years. Before going to class, check the labels on a number of items of clothing that you own. Which countries are represented?

2 THE TRADE BALANCE: COMPLETING THE PICTURE

How does trade affect the economy? In a number of important ways. Consumers who go to any U.S. shopping mall, for example, cannot help but notice that a large proportion of the products available for sale are imported. Many U.S. jobs are in industries that depend on export markets. We often hear concerns expressed about the **trade deficit**. In 2021, the U.S. trade deficit equaled nearly 4 percent of GDP.[2] This means that people in the United States were spending much more on foreign goods and services (importing) than the United States was selling to foreign buyers (exporting). In other words, U.S. net exports (exports minus imports) were negative. In many other countries, the situation is reversed. China, for example, is a large net exporter, meaning that it carries an annual **trade surplus**. Were it not for the United States, however, China would be a much smaller net exporter. Of its $366 billion in net exports in 2020, about $286 billion consisted of its bilateral surplus with the United States.[3]

---

trade deficit: an excess of imports over exports, causing net exports to be negative

trade surplus: an excess of exports over imports, causing net exports to be positive

---

2.1 The Circular Flow Revisited

Our trade balance is also related to the circular flow discussed in earlier chapters. In this section, we look at the impact of our exports and imports on aggregate expenditure and GDP. We can introduce trade into our macroeconomic model by adding net exports (NX) into the equation for aggregate expenditure:

$$AE = C + I_I + G + NX$$

As discussed in Chapter 4, net exports (NX) equals exports minus imports ($X - IM$). Exports, like intended investment (I_I) and government spending (G), represent a positive contribution to aggregate expenditure. More exports mean more demand for domestically produced goods and services. Imports, however, are negative in the equation. That means they represent a *leakage* from U.S. aggregate expenditure—a portion of income that is not spent on U.S. goods and services.

Negative net exports (when $X < IM$) therefore represent a net subtraction from demand for the output of U.S. businesses and a net leakage from the circular flow. In Chapters 8 and 9, we identified savings and net taxes as leakages from the circular flow; now we need to add imports as a third source of leakage. We can also add exports to intended investment and government spending as a third source of *injection* into the circular flow. A decrease in exports (or an increase in imports) reduces the circular flow of domestic income, spending, and output. An increase in net exports, on the other hand, encourages a rise in GDP and employment. For example, an increase in U.S. purchases of foreign cars and a decrease in purchases of domestic cars would lower aggregate expenditure in the United States (and raise it in other car-exporting countries). But an increase in foreign sales by the U.S. computer software industry would raise U.S. aggregate expenditure and employment.

Adding exports and imports completes our basic macroeconomic model. We started with a very simple economy, with just consumers and businesses, then added government spending, taxes, and the international sector. We now have a more complex model, with three leakages (saving, taxes, and imports) and three injections (intended investment, government spending, and exports). Imports are considered leakages because, like saving and taxes, they draw funds away from the domestic income-spending flow. Exports, like intended investment and government spending, add funds to the flow. We can modify our original circular flow diagram to show all these flows (Figure 13.3).

Macroeconomic equilibrium thus involves balancing the three types of leakage with the three types of injection. A change in one or more of the leakages or injections alters the equilibrium level of output. This equilibrium, however, is a moving target. The equilibrium to which the economy *tends* depends on the interaction of all leakages and injections, which are constantly changing. For instance, an increase in foreign car imports lowers the equilibrium level that would balance the economy. But this change might be offset by, for example, an increase in intended investment or government spending.

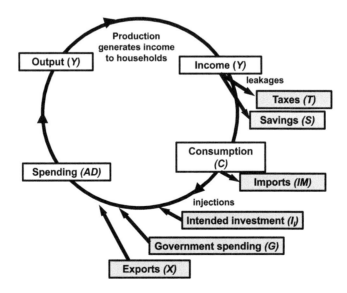

Figure 13.3 *Leakages and Injections in a Complete Macroeconomic Model*

The model that we have constructed allows us to understand how all these factors are related to levels of income and employment. We put it to use shortly to explain how saving and investment are linked to the global economy. But first, we look at the multiplier effects of exports and imports.

2.2 Effects on the Multiplier

The multiplier effect for an increase in exports is essentially the same as that for an increase in I_t or G. Using the same model as in Chapter 9 (with a multiplier of 5), an increase in exports of 40, for example, leads to an increase of 200 in economic equilibrium.

$$\Delta Y = mult \; \Delta X$$

We can use exactly the same logic for a lump-sum increase in imports— the effect on equilibrium income just goes in the opposite direction. An increase in imports of 40 would lower the equilibrium level of income by 200, and a decrease in imports of 40 would raise the equilibrium by 200.

The multiplier logic becomes a little more complicated, however, when we consider how import levels are determined. In general, when people receive more income in an open economy, they spend some of it on domestically produced goods and some on imports. The proportion spent on imports, as we noted above, is a "leakage" that does not add to domestic demand. If we want to account for this fully, we need to modify our multiplier logic.

The effect is similar to that of a proportional income tax (see Chapter 9, Appendix 2): it tends to flatten the aggregate expenditure curve, for the same reason. When people receive additional income, a portion of it "leaks" away into imports, just as taxation causes a "leakage" of a portion of extra income. This portion does not stimulate the domestic economy, so multiplier effects are smaller and the economic response a bit less dynamic. Multipliers in the neighborhood of four or five are seldom observed in the real world because *mpc* is affected not only by our marginal propensity to save but also by the rate of taxation and our marginal propensity to import. For a full treatment of this effect, see the Appendix to this chapter.

In an open economy, a portion of any aggregate expenditure increase goes to stimulate *someone else's economy* via imports. Thus, U.S. consumers who buy imported goods from Canada are creating jobs and income in Canada, not the United States. Does this mean that imports are bad for the United States? Not necessarily. Two other factors are important to consider.

The first is that U.S. consumers and U.S. industry benefit from cheaper imported goods and services, raw materials, and other industrial inputs. The second is that at least some of the money spent on imports is likely to return to the United States either as demand for

U.S. exports—which, as we have seen, stimulates an increase in GDP and employment—or as foreign investment in the United States, which is generally beneficial to the U.S. economy overall. More generally, the U.S. economy and the overall quality of life in the United States improve when other countries have healthier economies and diminish when other countries are suffering economic setbacks. A prosperous world is a happier world for all. Thus, in the largest sense, if China or Canada benefits from exporting to the United States, to some extent this benefits everyone. Problems can arise, however, when trade deficits (negative net exports) are too large for too long. We explore this issue in more detail later in the chapter.

2.3 Balance between Savings, Investment, and Net Borrowing

We can use our macro model to demonstrate that saving and investment are related not only to net exports but also to foreign lending and borrowing. Understanding this link is critical to making sense of much that happens in the global economy.

We start with the usual equation breaking down GDP into consumption, investment, and government spending. In addition, we follow the convention—seen earlier in Chapter 4—of breaking government spending down into "government consumption" and "government investment," which results in the following equation:

> *GDP = Personal consumption + private investment + government consumption + government investment + net exports*

or

$$GDP = C + I_I + G_C + G_I + NX$$

Rearranging, we obtain

$$GDP - C - G_C = I_I + G_I + NX$$

Because saving is what is left over from income after spending on consumption (the left-hand side of the equation above), if we combine private and government savings[†] into a single term S_{total} and private and government investment into a single term I_{total}, we get:

$$S_{total} = I_{total} + NX$$

or:

Total saving = Total investment + net exports

[†] Government savings would occur if government had a surplus of net tax revenues over government consumption; if government consumption exceeded net tax revenues, government savings would be negative.

514

Thinking about these quantities in terms of valuable goods and services, this important identity says, intuitively, that goods and services that are produced in our domestic economy in excess of what we currently use for consumption can become investment goods—additions to our stock of manufactured assets (including replacement of depreciated assets)—or can be sold to foreign countries (in excess of the value of what we import from them).

Another way of understanding this is in terms of macroeconomic equilibrium. If, say, total domestic saving exceeded investment, a net leakage from the circular flow would occur. In order to obtain an equilibrium, this leakage would need to be offset by a trade surplus (an excess of exports over imports, creating a net injection). If total investment exceeded saving, the opposite would result—that is, there would be a trade deficit. In this case, the net leakage from an excess of imports over exports would balance the net injection caused by investment exceeding savings.

Yet another way to look at the relation between saving, investment, and trade is to think of how the various sectors *finance* their purchases of goods and services. In a contemporary economy, goods are rarely traded for goods; rather, money is used as a means of exchange. So, corresponding to any flow of goods and services transacted in exchanges, there is an equivalent flow of monetary funds.

Consider, for a moment, a closed economy. In this case, the last equation would reduce to:

$$S_{total} = I_{total}$$

This says that, in a closed economy, the total amount that is not spent on consumption goods is available for spending on investment goods. How does financial saving get turned into tangible investments?

In the national accounts, it is primarily businesses and the government that are counted as investing (although households may also "invest", for example in second homes). They finance their investment expenditures either from their own savings or by borrowing someone else's savings (by getting a loan from their commercial bank). Savings, in the form of income not spent on consumption, can be made available for investment by the other sectors—as when the funds in a household's bank deposit are lent to a business or when a household or business buys a government bond. The "saving = investment" identity tells us that at an aggregate national level in a closed economy, only what the country as a whole saves out of current income can be available to finance investment for the future.

When we consider an open economy, things get more complicated. Now the country as a whole can also borrow from, or lend to, the foreign sector, and the relevant identity, as noted above, is:

$$S_{total} = I_{total} + NX$$

515

If net exports are positive, we sell more goods abroad than we buy. How would people abroad pay for all our goods, if the value of what we sell to them exceeds the value of what they sell to us? They are not earning enough from their sales to pay us! The main way for them to finance their purchases of our goods is by borrowing from us. They would need to borrow the amount by which our exports to them exceed our imports from them. So, the identity can be (approximately) rewritten as:

$$S_{\text{total}} = I_{\text{total}} + \text{net foreign lending}$$

That is, if we have extra savings, above and beyond what is being used for domestic investment, we can lend it to foreigners so that they could buy our goods. The equation above is only approximate because foreigners can also get more goods and services from us than they sell to us by receiving our goods as gifts, paying for them out of transfer income, or selling us their assets, such as land or businesses, in return. We discuss these possibilities in greater detail in the next section.

In recent years the United States has tended to have net exports that are negative. That is, we tend to buy more from foreign countries than we sell. This means that *we* need to borrow from *them*. In this case, we can rewrite the savings/investment identity as:

$$S_{\text{total}} = I_{\text{total}} - \text{net foreign borrowing}$$

(This means exactly the same thing as the previous equation but is easier to use to represent a situation with a trade deficit.) When we are in a situation of borrowing from abroad, then the amount we are really "putting away for the future"—that is, saving—is less than what we would assume if we looked only at what we are investing. Although we may be investing domestically, if we are using "net foreign borrowing" to obtain investment funds, we are also creating future indebtedness to other countries by borrowing from them.

Should we worry that our country has to borrow from foreigners? As in the case of your personal finances, it makes a difference what the purpose of the borrowing is. If the borrowing financed the purchase of productive new private or government investment goods, then it might be a way of actually improving the country's outlook for the future. As mentioned in Chapter 1, for many decades international authorities encouraged low-income countries to borrow heavily for development projects, using exactly this reasoning.

But if the funds borrowed went largely into investments that did not pay off financially, or if the borrowing only financed a high level of consumption, there would be a reason to worry. A country that borrows a lot may be in trouble when it comes time to pay back its loans. In recent years, some countries have found themselves unable to pay even the *interest* on the foreign debts that they have built up over the years—much less repay the principal. In the case of the United States, the country's creditworthiness has not been seriously questioned, and to date paying interest and principal on foreign debt (known as "servicing" the debt) has never posed problems. However, as discussed further in Chapter 15, a high level of international indebtedness has potential costs over the long term.

Discussion Questions

1. What will be the likely effect of increased imports on U.S. GDP? Do imported goods undercut employment in the United States? What other developments in the economy might counteract this effect?
2. Savings, imports, and taxes are all considered "leakages" from the aggregate expenditure. Are they bad for the economy? Or is there an important function for each? How are their levels related to equilibrium GDP, income, and employment?

3 INTERNATIONAL FINANCE

In addition to trade in goods, countries are also linked through exchange of currencies, flows of income, and purchases and sales of real and financial assets across national borders. As we consider how international finance is related to trade and to domestic macroeconomic policies, the realization that "everything is linked to everything else" can become overwhelming. Most topics that we have discussed earlier in this book—such as supply and demand, interest rates, inflation, aggregate expenditure, and the Fed—will here come back into play. In order to ease into the topic, we begin with a few basic concepts and models. The first is currency exchange rates, followed by purchasing power parity adjustments.

3.1 Exchange Rates

The **exchange rate** refers to the rate at which one country's currency can trade for another's. Consider, for example, the exchange rate between U.S. dollars (US$) and euros (€). As of early 2022, US$1 was worth about €0.889. Equivalently, we could say that one euro was worth US$1.125. The two rates are inverses of one another. When we cite "the exchange rate" for the dollar in terms of a foreign currency, what we mean is the number of units of the foreign currency that you can get in exchange for a dollar.

---

exchange rate: the number of units of one currency that can be exchanged for one unit of another currency

---

What makes exchange rates go up and down? Currencies are traded against each other all over the world, as people offer to buy and sell. The supply-and-demand model explained in Chapter 3 can be applied to foreign exchange markets, once we realize that an exchange rate is really just another kind of price—a price for a national currency.

Figure 13.4 shows an idealized foreign exchange market in which U.S. dollars are traded for euros. The quantity of dollars traded is shown on the horizontal axis, and the "price" of a dollar is given on the vertical axis, in terms of the number of euros it takes to buy a dollar.

In a well-behaved foreign exchange market, domestic residents largely determine the supply curve of dollars, by deciding how many dollars they are willing to offer in order to buy foreign-produced goods and services and foreign assets. Because foreign-produced goods, services, and foreign assets must be paid for in the currency of the country from which they will be purchased, dollars must be traded in the foreign exchange market. Professional currency traders and banks usually do the actual trading. The more euros that U.S. residents can get for their dollars, the cheaper the European items are to them, and the more they will want to buy from Europe rather than from domestic producers. Thus, the higher the exchange rate, the more dollars they will offer on the market. The supply curve slopes upward.

It is residents of other countries who largely determine the demand curve for dollars. They may want to buy goods and services from the United States or invest in U.S. bonds or businesses. To make these purchases, they must acquire dollars. The more euros, or other currencies, they have to *pay* to get a dollar, the more likely they are to go somewhere other than the United States for what they want and the lower will be the quantity of dollars that they demand. But if the U.S. dollar is relatively cheap in terms of euros, they will want to demand more

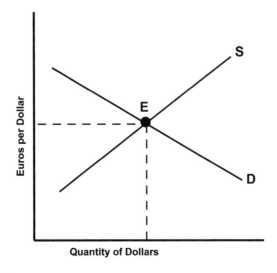

Figure 13.4 *A Foreign Exchange Market for Dollars*

dollars. So, the demand curve slopes downward. Market equilibrium is established at point E.‡

When the exchange rate falls, we say that the currency has **depreciated**. Suppose, for example, that a European technology firm comes out with a new device for listening to music that everyone wants to buy. In their desire to obtain euros to buy the goods, people in the United States will offer more dollars on the foreign exchange market, shifting the supply curve to the right. Excess supply will, as in any other market, cause the price to fall, as shown in Figure 13.5. Commentators may say that the dollar is now "weaker" against the euro. (Conversely, of course, the euro is now "stronger" against the dollar.)

> **currency depreciation:** when a currency becomes less valuable, for example, due to a decrease in demand for a country's exports or an increase in its demand for imports

But an increase in demand for U.S. products or assets would lead to an **appreciation** of the dollar. For example, if European investors became eager to buy U.S. real estate, the demand curve for dollars would shift outward and the dollar would appreciate—that is, gain in value— against the euro. A currency may appreciate or depreciate relative to a specific currency, or it may appreciate or depreciate generally— that is, in relation to all or most other currencies.

> **currency appreciation:** when a currency becomes more valuable, for example, when increased demand for a country's exports causes an increase in demand for its currency

Which factors are most responsible for the depreciation or appreciation of a country's currency? The first potentially important factor is relative prices. If prices in general rose more rapidly in the United States than in, say, Japan (meaning that inflation is lower in Japan), the Japanese would be less interested in purchasing U.S. goods, *ceteris paribus*, and we would be more interested in purchasing theirs. What this means in terms of the foreign exchange market is that the United States would supply more dollars (in order to obtain yen to make purchases from Japan), and the Japanese would demand fewer dollars to purchase our higher-priced goods.

---

‡ For simplicity, this example ignores other sources of supply and demand for currencies, such as foreign lending and currency speculation.

519

A rightward shift in supply coupled with a leftward shift in demand unambiguously lowers the yen "price" of the dollar, meaning that the dollar would depreciate relative to the yen (and the yen would appreciate relative to the dollar). Note that, in this example, the dollar would not depreciate with respect to all other currencies—it would merely depreciate relative to the yen.

A second factor influencing exchange rates may be a country's GDP growth rate relative to that of its trading partners. If, for example, the United States experienced rapid growth in employment and output, it means that imports would also, *ceteris paribus*, increase relatively rapidly, since people would spend part of their increased disposable income on imports. This would lead the United States to demand more foreign currencies (to purchase imports) relative to the foreign demand for our dollars. Our greater demand for foreign currencies (and greater supply of dollars to purchase them) would cause the dollar to depreciate.

One might conclude from this discussion that countries that consistently import more than they export should have a persistently weak currency. The United States has, in fact, imported significantly more than it has exported for many years. Yet the dollar not only has not collapsed but remains one of the most stable currencies. How is this possible?

One reason might have to do with interest rates, which are a third key factor in determining exchange rates. If the interest rate on, say, the six-month U.S. Treasury bill were higher than the rate on comparable investments in other countries, the United States might attract flows of money from foreign investors seeking to exploit the interest rate differential. Because Treasury bills are denominated in dollars, the foreign money would be seeking to buy dollars, raising dollar demand. The

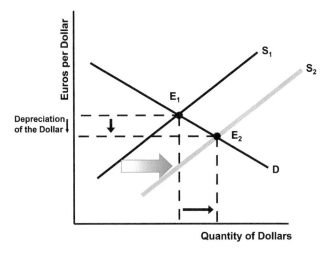

Figure 13.5 *A Supply Shift in a Foreign Exchange Market*

result would be an appreciation in the value of the dollar. As a general rule, then, higher relative interest rates tend to raise demand for the domestic currency and hence lead to a currency appreciation.

Yet it would be misleading to attribute dollar stability solely, or possibly even at all, to higher interest rates. Rates in the United States have been at historically low levels for the past decade and a half. Yet a strong foreign appetite for U.S. assets such as government bonds persists, and it probably explains much of the steady and reliable demand for dollars. Generally speaking, it is a country's relative investment attractiveness that influences its currency exchange rate; the prevailing interest rate is merely one variable in what makes the country attractive to investors. Because U.S. government bonds, as well as other investments in the United States such as real estate, are widely regarded as safe and desirable, there is a steady flow of foreign demand for dollars to purchase these assets—independent of the inter-country interest rate differential.

In addition to currency needs for trade and investment, many traders buy and sell currency for speculative reasons. As discussed in Chapter 3, sometimes people buy something not because they need it (e.g., in this case, for facilitating trade in real items), but because they are betting that its price will go up or down in the future. Speculative buying and selling of currencies often play a large role in foreign exchange markets.

Unfortunately, because the ability of a country to participate in global trade critically depends on its exchange rate, such "bets" have the potential to produce real economic effects that are not always beneficial. As the role of speculation grows in importance relative to other factors that influence exchange rates, the ability of financial decisions to affect entire economies—especially small, relatively vulnerable economies—only increases. As discussed in Chapters 6 and 10, the relationship between speculation and finance, on the one hand, and the "real" economy, on the other, can affect the stability of the domestic economy, and this is also true internationally.

Many confuse domestic currency depreciation with inflation since the latter is often (correctly) understood to be a decline in the "value" of the currency. But "value" can have more than one meaning. Price inflation refers to when a currency weakens in terms of domestic purchasing power (i.e., higher average prices mean that the currency is worth relatively less) while depreciation is the weakening of the currency in relation to other currencies (a reduction of its exchange rate). The two concepts are related, but not always equivalent.

What really matters for trade is the **real exchange rate** between currencies. Economists use the real exchange rate to express the combined effect of exchange rates and domestic inflation. For example, if a country experiences 10 percent inflation while its currency exchange rate is

> **real exchange rate:** the exchange rate between two currencies, adjusted for infla-
> tion in each country

unchanged, the real exchange rate, which measures what foreign buyers can get for their money, is said to fall by 10 percent.[§]

Most foreign exchange transactions are made in "strong" currencies or currencies that other countries would generally not hesitate to accept as payment for goods and services or for some investments. The U.S. dollar tops the list, but the euro and the yen also qualify. Beyond this, the Swiss franc, famed for its remarkable stability, and possibly the British pound sterling, could be considered members of this exclusive club. Many speculate that it is only a matter of time before the Chinese currency makes this short list, but not everyone agrees. Regardless, the dollar, the euro, and the yen stand out as the top three. These currencies are the ones often referred to as **foreign exchange** due to their general acceptability for foreign transactions.

> **foreign exchange:** the class of currencies that is broadly acceptable by foreigners
> in commercial or investment transactions. Generally limited to three currencies —
> the dollar, the euro, and the yen

Weak economies seldom if ever accept one another's currencies, and usually not even *their own* currency, as international payment for goods, services, or assets. As will become clear, it benefits them to be paid in strong currencies. Thus, the overwhelming majority of global currency trades are in dollars, euros, or yen.

3.2 Purchasing Power Parity

Purchasing power parity (PPP) refers to the notion that, under certain idealized conditions, the exchange rate between the currencies of two countries should be such that the purchasing power of currencies is equalized. If, for example, one US dollar can fetch 115 Japanese yen in the market, a coffee maker selling for $100 in the United States should cost exactly 11,500 yen in Japan. If this were not so, the purchasing power of the two currencies would not be equal, and the purchasing power theory would not hold.

[§] The example presumes no inflation in the foreign country or countries. If, say, the other country experienced a five percent inflation, then the real exchange rate in the first country would fall by the inflation rate *differential* between the two countries, or 5 percent.

> **purchasing power parity (PPP):** the theory that exchange rates should reflect differences in purchasing power among countries

If currencies could be traded freely against one another, if goods were freely traded and identical across countries, and if transportation costs were trivial, then there would be a strong logic to the theory of PPP. Take, as another example, a winter jacket that costs US$200 in New York. If you lived in the United States and changed US$200 into euros, the theory of PPP says that the number of euros you would receive in exchange for your dollars in this idealized world should be exactly enough for you to buy the identical winter jacket in Paris. If the exchange rate were 0.80 euros per dollar and the jacket cost €160 (= US$200 × 0.80 euros per dollar) in Paris, PPP would hold. If economies were in fact as smoothly integrated as we are assuming in this idealized world, *any* item (whether a winter jacket or an hour of labor services) should cost the same, no matter where you are.

If this were *not* true, there would be pressures leading toward change. Suppose that the jacket costs US$200 in New York and €160 in Paris, but the exchange rate is higher, at €1: US$1. Why, in this case, would anyone buy a jacket in New York, if by changing their money into euros they could order it from Paris and save US$40? For jackets to be sold in both locations—in this idealized world—the price in New York would have to be bid down, the price in Paris would have to be bid up, or the exchange rate would have to fall.

But the real world is far from ideal. National economies are not nearly as integrated as the **PPP** theory assumes. Transportation costs are often significant; there are many varieties of goods; markets for goods and services do not work as quickly, smoothly, and rationally as is often assumed; and exchange rates are often "managed" by governments and central banks (see Section 4.4).

Any of these factors can mean that converting monetary amounts from one country to another using the prevailing exchange rates may be misleading. Travelers often notice that a particular category of goods, such as books or clothing, are more expensive in one country than in another; this could reflect real-world factors such as transportation costs, as well as tariffs or other market imperfections.

Sometimes we see comparisons of international income levels expressed "in PPP terms." Rather than simply using current exchange rates to convert all the various income levels into a common currency, **PPP adjustments** try to take into account the fact that the cost of living varies among countries. For example, converting Mexican average per capita income figures from pesos to dollars would probably understate the living standard of the average Mexican. Even though the conversion would be "correct"—in the sense that there exists a peso–dollar exchange rate that can easily be used for such an adjustment—many

523

domestic goods and services in Mexico (e.g., haircuts or fresh produce) are generally much less expensive than in the United States. So, the dollar equivalent of what the average Mexican earns each year goes much further in Mexico. Prices tend to vary much more for goods and services that cannot be traded; haircut prices, for example, vary much more across borders than camera or jewelry prices.

> **purchasing power parity (PPP) adjustments:** adjustments to international income statistics to take into account the differences in the cost of living across countries

The "Big Mac Index" published every year by *The Economist* is a somewhat light-hearted attempt to determine how much exchange rates and the price of goods vary from PPP predictions, by comparing the prices (converted into dollars using market exchange rates) of a McDonald's hamburger across various countries. A more sophisticated analysis uses a larger "basket" of goods to make such comparisons and estimate appropriate PPP adjustments.

3.3 The Balance of Payments

The flows of foreign exchange payments into and out of a country are summed up in its **balance of payments (BOP) account**. Table 13.1 shows the BOP account for the United States in 2020. The top part of the table tallies the **current account**, which tracks flows arising from trade in goods and services, earnings, and transfers. The **trade account** refers exclusively to the portion of the current account related to exports and imports.

> **balance of payments (BOP) account:** the national account that tracks inflows and outflows arising from international trade, earnings, transfers, and transactions in assets
> **current account (in the BOP account):** the national account that tracks inflows and outflows arising from international trade, earnings, and transfers
> **trade account (part of the current account):** the portion of the current account that tracks inflows and outflows arising exclusively from international trade in goods and services

Various kinds of transactions lead to payments flowing into this country (hence a demand for dollars in the foreign exchange market). When we export goods, we receive payments in return. So, the first entry under current account inflows is the US$1.4 trillion that the United States earned from exports of goods. Exports of services (such as travel, financial, or intellectual property) also bring in inflows, as do incomes earned

Table 13.1 *U.S. Balance of Payments Account, 2020 (billions of dollars)*

Current account

Trade Account	
Inflows:	
Payments for exports of goods	1,429
Payments for exports of services	705
Total exports	2,134
Outflows:	
Payments for imports of goods	−2,351
Payments for imports of services	−460
Total imports	−2,811
Trade Balance	<u>−677</u>
Other Flows	
Income receipts	958
Income payments	−769
Transfer receipts	166
Transfer payments	−294
Total	<u>61</u>
Balance on current account (= inflows − outflows)	−616

Capital account

Inflows:	1,457
Borrowing from abroad, and portfolio investment or FDI	
Outflows: Lending, portfolio investment, or FDI abroad	−806
Derivatives and other misc. flows, net	6
Balance on capital account (= inflows − outflows)	657

Official reserve account	−9
Statistical discrepancy	−32
Balance of payments	0

Source: U.S. Bureau of Economic Analysis, U.S. International Transactions Accounts Data, Table 1, with rearrangements and simplifications by authors.

abroad (as profits or interest) by U.S. residents. All told, inflows into the United States from exports, incomes, and transfers totaled almost US$3.3 trillion in 2020.

Other transactions lead to payments going abroad (and to a supply of dollars to the foreign exchange market). When we import goods and services, we need to make payments to foreign residents. Foreign residents can take home incomes earned in the United States. The BOP account also includes a line for transfers abroad. The account consists of monies paid out in government foreign aid programs as well as remittances—money sent home to families from the host country by foreign workers. All told, outflows of payments from the United States totaled just under US$3.9 trillion in 2020.

The balance on the current account is measured as inflows minus outflows. Because outflows exceeded inflows on the current account in 2020, the United States had a current account deficit of US$616 billion. The trade deficit, including just imports and exports, was slightly larger at US$677 billion. This is because other flows in the current account (incomes and transfers) added up to a net positive of US$61 billion. As you can see in Figure 13.6, the United States has had trade deficits fairly steadily since about 1980, with the gap between imports and exports widening to about 6 percent of GDP in some years, but more recently narrowing to about 3 percent.

How can a country steadily import more than it exports? If you, personally, wanted to buy something that costs more than you have the income to pay for, you might take out a loan or perhaps sell something that you own, such as your bicycle or your car. Likewise, countries can finance a trade deficit by borrowing or by selling assets. These are the sorts of transactions listed in the **capital account**.

> **capital account (in the BOP account):** the account that tracks flows arising from international transactions in assets

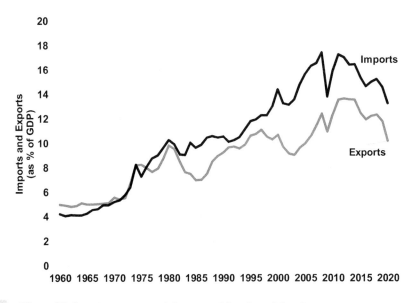

Figure 13.6 *U.S. Imports and Exports of Goods and Services, 1960–2020*

Source: BEA NIPA Tables 4.1 and 1.1.5, 2021

To the extent the United States *lends* abroad (e.g., when the government extends loans to other countries, foreigners borrow from U.S. banks, or people in the United States buy foreign bonds), capital *outflows* are generated. This terminology may be confusing. Think about capital flows as going *in the direction of* the country that ends up with "the cash" or the power to purchase goods, and *away from* the country that provides the cash or purchasing power. In the case of a loan, the borrower received "the cash," while the creditor receives a bond or other security representing a promise to repay; thus, a loan is an *outflow* from the lender and an *inflow* from the perspective of the borrower.

Similarly, in the case of a U.S. firm engaged in **portfolio investment**—investment in the stocks or bonds of a foreign country or company—or **foreign direct investment (FDI)**—the buying of all or part of a business in another country—it is the people abroad who would end up with "the cash," while the U.S. company would receive the asset. This is also counted as an outflow from the United States. From Table 13.1, we can see that the United States had US$806 billion in capital outflows during 2020.

---

portfolio investment: investment in stocks or bonds of a foreign country or company

foreign direct investment (FDI): investment in a business in a foreign country

---

Capital outflows can have widely differing meanings and impacts, depending on where they occur. When a country with a large current account surplus such as China invests the proceeds from its exports abroad, say by buying U.S. Treasury bonds, it increases China's claims against the United States but does not necessarily have negative impact on either country. Holding U.S. bonds may provide China with a secure investment, while the inflow of capital may promote economic activity in the U.S.

Weak, unstable economies are much more vulnerable to large capital flows and frequently suffer from what is known as **capital flight**, which occurs when investors fear investment losses and rush to move their assets to "safer" countries like the United States, the member countries of the European Union, and Japan. Capital flight may represent international investors rushing to take their money out of a weak country—as happened with South Korea, Indonesia, and the Philippines during the East Asian financial crisis of 1997—or wealthy elites seeking to take money out of their own countries. In many such cases, capital flight has the potential to destabilize economies by making foreign exchange scarce, and governments will often go to great lengths to try to stop it (see Box 13.2).

527

BOX 13.2 AFRICA LOSES $89 BILLION A YEAR TO CAPITAL FLIGHT

African countries lose almost $90 billion each year, equivalent to 3.7 percent of the continent's economic output, in illicit capital flight, according to a recent UN Economic Development in Africa Report.[4] A report by the UN Conference on Trade and Development (UNCTAD) states that stopping capital flight would have the potential to generate enough capital by 2030 to finance almost 50 percent of the $2.4 trillion needed by African countries for climate change adaptation and mitigation policies.

"Illicit Financial flows (IFFs) rob Africa and its people of their prospects, undermining transparency and accountability and eroding trust in African institutions," UNCTAD Secretary-General Mukhisa Kituyi said in a statement accompanying the report. The report calls for increased transparency and cooperation between global governments and within the continent to tackle tax evasion and tax avoidance. It also urges the African Tax Administration Forum to become a platform for regional cooperation among African countries. UNCTAD also reports that African countries with the most IFFs spend 25 percent less than countries with low IFFs on health care, and 58 percent less on education.

"The fact remains that the funds involved [in illicit financial flows] often come from jurisdictions with scarce resources for development financing, depleted foreign reserves, a drastic reduction in collectable revenue, tax underpayment or evasion, and poor investment in-flows," said Nigerian President Muhammadu Buhari. As a result of the pandemic, a handful of African states face debt distress, and countries like Chad and Zambia have warned that they will have to default on commercial payments.

"Curbing IFF presents a key policy measure for governments, particularly in Africa, to generate the necessary financial resources to mitigate the impact of COVID-19-induced economic crisis," Alvin Mosioma, executive director of Tax Justice Network Africa, told EURACTIV.

---

capital flight: rapid movement of capital assets out of a country

---

As we have noted, a country receives capital *inflows* when it borrows from foreigners or when foreigners purchase assets there. In the case of the United States, many people abroad buy U.S. government bonds because they are considered a very secure investment. For similar reasons, many also put funds into bank accounts here. These are both capital *inflows*—the sellers of the U.S. securities and the U.S. banks receive "the cash." Likewise, if a foreign multinational bought an interest in a U.S. publishing company, it would be a capital *inflow.* Another large source of inflows is foreign investment in U.S. real estate. In addition, a growing though still relatively minor source of net inflows were financial derivatives and similar instruments used primarily for speculation. In total, the United States received close to US$1.5 trillion in capital inflows in 2020.

528

As with the current account, the balance on the capital account is measured as inflows minus outflows. Thus, the United States had a US$657 billion capital account surplus in 2020. It was the willingness of foreigners to buy U.S. securities (and other assets) that financed the deficit in the current account (as you can see from Table 13.1 the positive balance on the capital account largely cancels out the negative balance on the current account).

Does this mean that the United States is putting itself in a vulnerable position by relying on borrowing to "spend beyond its means" on imports? Notice that *present-day capital inflows* create the obligation to pay *future income outflows*: The interest due in the future on U.S. government bonds sold abroad this year, and future profits made by firms located in the United States that were bought by foreign parties this year, will become part of "income payments" in the outflows section of the current account, in years to come.

Depending on how confident we are that the U.S. economy will be able to handle these payments, we may not need to be concerned about a current account deficit – and indeed some countries have run moderate current account deficits for decades with no ill effects, generating positive economic benefits from foreign investment. But if a current account deficit is very large or lasts for a prolonged period, it could lead to future problems, as has been the case for many developing countries that borrowed too heavily on international markets.

Finally, we have what is known as the **official reserve account**. It represents the foreign exchange market operations of the country's central bank (in the United States, the Federal Reserve). Why the central bank? Here it is probably more helpful to consider the position of a developing country—say, Indonesia. Like any other country, it needs to import some goods and services. How can it pay for the imports? Its currency, the rupiah, will not do. Most exporters will insist on being paid in foreign exchange—that is, dollars, euros, or yen. This presents a problem for Indonesia because it cannot produce its own dollars. It can, however, obtain them.

---

official reserve account: the account reflecting the foreign exchange market operations of a country's central bank

---

For example, when Indonesia exports coffee, it can insist on being paid not in rupiah but in foreign exchange such as dollars. In this way, it has a strong currency available to pay for its imports. It works the same way with the capital account. Indonesia has creditors to whom it owes interest every year (reflected in the income section of the current account) that require payment in foreign exchange. Indonesia obtains this foreign

529

exchange not only by exporting coffee and other products but also by attracting foreign capital, which it also insists should come in the form of dollars, euros, or yen.

Bank Indonesia, the country's central bank, holds reserves of foreign currency so that it can make up for a BOP deficit if necessary. Of course, it cannot do so indefinitely. If the central bank runs short of foreign exchange reserves, the country will have to cut back on imports. But in the short term, the central bank can supply foreign exchange to cover a BOP deficit or acquire foreign exchange if there is a BOP surplus. If the central bank supplies foreign exchange, it is recorded as a positive item in the official reserve accounts; if it acquires foreign exchange, it is recorded as a negative item.

In some versions of the BOP, the official reserve account is lumped with the capital account.¶ When this is done, the total inflows and outflows from the current and capital accounts always "balance." When treated separately, the official reserve account, as we have seen, offsets the discrepancy between current and capital accounts. The United States reduced its official reserve account by about US$9 billion in 2020, which means that the Fed's holdings of these assets *increased* by this amount. If this is confusing, think of it as the negative sign signifying that the Fed removed US$9 billion in reserve assets (mostly foreign exchange) from the U.S. economy.

One additional caveat is the statistical discrepancy. It represents an inability of the BEA to make the accounts balance precisely, given problems in the quality of the data, and some small items in the accounts that we do not get into here. Allowing for this discrepancy, the balances in the current account, the capital account, and the official reserve account *must* add up to zero (the "balance of payments"). The difference between the current and capital accounts *must* be "balanced" by a flow of foreign exchange to or from the central bank. Any gap can be fully attributed to measurement error, which is what the statistical discrepancy reflects.

Discussion Questions

1. Is it better for the United States to have a strong or weak dollar? What are the advantages and disadvantages of each?
2. Is a nation's BOP analogous to a company or household income statement? Is it necessarily a bad thing for a country's trade balance to be in deficit?

¶ In recent years, for example, the International Monetary Fund has adopted the practice of calling the capital account the "financial account," with the latter calculated to include the official reserve account. We prefer to present the traditional approach to the BOP, finding it more transparent about whether a country is truly in surplus or in deficit.

4 MACROECONOMICS IN AN OPEN ECONOMY

In earlier chapters, our discussion of how fiscal and monetary policy can be used to influence aggregate expenditure was limited to a "closed" economy. We are now ready to consider a more complete picture of the effects of such policies in an "open" economy. The bottom line of what is laid out in Sections 4.1 and 4.2 is simple to state: The intended effects of monetary policy are strengthened, or amplified, by interactions with the foreign sector; while trade with foreign partners may either strengthen or weaken fiscal policy actions. The reasons why this is so, however, are rather complex. The value of working through them is that it is a way of showing in action some of the principles of macroeconomic supply and demand that have been laid out thus far. We will then apply our open economy model to the emergency circumstances underlying the global pandemic, and then consider how these, along with exchange rate policy, can bring about serious sovereign debt problems.

4.1 Fiscal Policy

Recall from our earlier concept of a macroeconomic equilibrium that, for equilibrium to be present, injections must equal leakages. We know from Chapter 9 that a budget deficit is a net injection because it occurs when government spending (injection) is greater than tax revenue (leakage). If we assume that private savings and investment are in balance, a government budget deficit requires a net leakage from the foreign sector for macroeconomic equilibrium to be achieved—that is, imports must exceed exports (again, disregarding for now the transfers and net income).

In other words, a government's budget balance is correlated with the country's trade balance—a government deficit, not financed from domestic savings, implies a trade deficit. In common-sense terms, if the government does not obtain the funds it needs from domestic savings, it must borrow from abroad. But what is the economic mechanism by which they are related? A country's budget balance can influence its trade balance through at least two separate channels, each related to the exchange rate of its currency.

First, we have seen that deficit spending has the potential, in economies at or near full employment, to lead to higher interest rates—either through the classical argument of crowding out or through the central bank reacting to growing inflationary pressure with rate hikes. In an open economy, higher interest rates are likely to attract more foreign investment in the form of bond purchases. If foreigners demand more U.S. bonds as a result of the higher interest rates that they offer, the demand for dollars increases (because U.S. bonds are all denominated in U.S. dollars). The resulting increase in demand for dollars, *ceteris paribus*, leads to an appreciation of the dollar compared to other currencies.

We have also seen that a stronger currency makes a country's goods relatively more expensive in the global markets. In other words, if the

U.S. dollar appreciated, we would expect the United States to be able to export less than before. At the same time, imports would increase because a stronger dollar makes other countries' goods (denominated in their currencies) appear cheaper. Through this sequence, an increase in the budget deficit might increase the size of the trade deficit.

Notice, however, that while both deficits grow, the economic effect of the rising trade deficit is to offset the expansionary effect of the budget deficit. Imports (leakage from the circular flow) increase while exports (injection) decrease. Because we do not know the magnitude of each of these changes, we are *not* saying that the open economy effect cancels out the original effect of the fiscal stimulus. What we can say is that it probably dampens it somewhat.

The other channel is a more direct consequence of the fiscal expansion. Deficit spending boosts aggregate expenditure, increasing spending and generating greater employment and more income. Yet, as the economy grows, *all* spending grows, including spending on imports. The greater demand for imports increases the global supply of dollars, as U.S. citizens demand more foreign currency to purchase imports. This causes the dollar to depreciate, reversing the process because a weaker dollar results in more exports and fewer imports.

Depreciation of the dollar will tend to narrow the trade deficit, resulting in a net injection to the circular flow and *reinforcing* the initial fiscal stimulus. Since the two effects we have described go in opposite directions, we cannot say anything specific about the magnitude of the changes, nor can we say overall whether the "open economy" on balance reinforces or countervails the domestic fiscal policy. But we can say that the effect of deficit spending is complicated by consideration of foreign sector effects.

4.2 Monetary Policy

In Chapter 11 we discussed monetary policy in a closed economy. In an open economy, monetary policy is more effective in changing aggregate expenditure, because, unlike fiscal policy, its global effects unambiguously reinforce the domestic policy.

Suppose that the Fed believes the U.S. economy needs a boost and acts to promote lower interest rates in an attempt to increase aggregate expenditure. As we saw in Chapter 11, the decrease in interest rates should encourage investment spending. But in an open economy, the fall in interest rates should also increase net exports, another component of aggregate expenditure.

This is because a reduction in U.S. interest rates is likely to reduce inflows of foreign financial capital. If interest rates in the United States fall, people abroad will be less inclined to buy U.S. government bonds or put their money in U.S. bank accounts. As they send their financial capital elsewhere, the demand for U.S. dollars will decrease. This can be portrayed as a leftward shift of the demand curve in the foreign exchange market. As discussed above (refer to Figure 13.4) a decrease in the demand for dollars would cause the dollar to depreciate.

A depreciation in the dollar means that a dollar now buys fewer units of foreign exchange, which, you will recall, discourages spending on imports. Meanwhile, the fact that a dollar can be purchased for fewer units of foreign exchange means that U.S. exports become "cheap" for foreign buyers. Exports should increase. As we have discussed, an increase in net exports (caused in this case by both a rise in exports and a fall in imports) raises aggregate expenditure. This reinforces the original stimulus effect of the expansionary monetary policy.

The openness of the economy can be thought of as adding an extra loop to the chain of causation discussed in Chapter 11, as illustrated below:

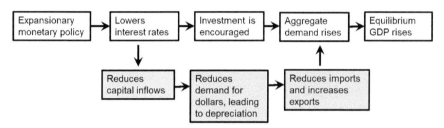

Yet this is not the end of the story. Just as in the earlier case of deficit spending, an increase in aggregate expenditure tends to produce an increase in imports. As we have seen, this leads to dollar depreciation, as U.S. citizens trade dollars for other currencies so that they can purchase imported products.

The effect is to further reinforce the initial domestic stimulus since a weaker dollar tends to narrow the trade deficit and thus increase aggregate expenditure, *ceteris paribus*. So, in contrast to the fiscal policy case, where "opening up" the economy produces ambiguous effects in relation to a domestic fiscal stimulus, for monetary policy the international trade consequences clearly reinforce the domestic policy. A monetary stimulus, in other words, is amplified in an open economy. We should note that a monetary contraction would also be magnified; the same causal mechanisms would be in effect, only in reverse.

4.3 A Special Case: Economic Stimulus in the Pandemic Era

The pandemic experience illustrates a variety of country experiences with macroeconomic policy and its impacts. The initial economic fallout from COVID-19 threatened to plunge the world into a full-blown depression. It is arguably thanks to widespread fiscal and monetary stimulus throughout the world that such an outcome was avoided. Yet not all countries benefited equally from economic stimulus.

Widespread illness and death, along with an imposed economic slowdown in hopes of stemming the pandemic's spread, effectively put a brake on most economies. Most countries pursued fiscal and monetary stimulus in response to the negative economic effects of the pandemic,

533

but with varying degrees of success. In particular, as we might expect from the discussion of fiscal policy in the previous section, countries that attempted very large spending increases did not necessarily see comparable benefits. Some of the benefits of increased spending could "leak" away in the international market, leaving the country with large increases in debt. Public health policy was also a major factor in economic health outcomes: invariably, countries that imposed stricter lockdowns and were slower in inoculating their populations suffered more adverse economic consequences (see Box 13.3).

It matters a great deal whether the country pursuing fiscal or monetary policy is a rich country like the United States or a developing country like the Philippines. Quite simply, markets respond very differently when a country that cannot "afford" a sizable stimulus—often requiring a sizable debt to finance—attempts to undertake one regardless. Developing countries are hurt more even by moderate inflation because it means either higher interest rates, currency depreciation, or both. Either one has the effect of nullifying the impact of the initial stimulus. Countries with stable currencies need not fear such consequences, at least not to the same extent.

The logic underlying fiscal and monetary policy links to the global economy is of less concern to a large economy such as the United States. The U.S. also enjoys the benefits of possessing the dollar, the world's premier international currency. What this means, for example,

---

BOX 13.3 THE PANDEMIC STIMULUS BACKFIRED IN SOME EMERGING MARKETS

According to an analysis in the *Financial Times*, some of the developing countries that stimulated most aggressively got little payoff in terms of faster recovery.[5]

More rapid inflation, higher interest rates, and currency depreciation at least partly canceled out the effects of stimulus in a number of countries. Hungary, Brazil, the Philippines, and Greece, all of which spent at least 16 percent of GDP on stimulus, saw limited results. But the higher deficits and debt that they ran up "will leave them with less ammunition to fight the next battle," according to Ruchir Sharma, global strategist for Morgan Stanley.

Moreover, developing nations often lack the financial resources and the global credibility to increase spending substantially without unbalancing the economy. Those that overspend tend to get punished by global markets.

Comparing countries on an index that includes factors like inflation, currency value, interest rates, and budget deficit highlights the difference between the big spenders and countries that were more conservative. Hungary, Brazil, and the Philippines were among the worst scorers, while light spenders like Taiwan, South Korea, and Mexico scored the best.

According to Sharma, nations that spend in haste are often forced to repent at leisure. Those that attempted to "go big" during the pandemic mostly got less added growth than they imagined and considerably more trouble, in the form of higher deficits and debt. It figures to be a major challenge in the future, as many believe that another international debt crisis looms.

is that the United States government can borrow large sums without worrying unduly about having to offer higher interest rates. Why? U.S. government debt and the currency in which it is dominated continues, arguably at least, to offer global investors the safest existing investment. Consequently, foreigners generally continue to lend to the United States, even at a low interest rate. Unlike other currencies, the dollar is not as likely to depreciate as a result of continued low rates, because investors will be expected to invest in the U.S. economy regardless.

In short, while there exist important links between a country's domestic economic policies and the global economy, we must keep in mind that the picture is invariably complicated by such factors as pandemics and other global shocks, the relative strength of the economy or its currency, or international politics. These intersecting considerations limit the extent to which we can predict the likely global consequences of domestic economic policies.

4.4 Managed Versus Flexible Foreign Exchange

Thus far, we have assumed that exchange rates are determined by market forces, as modeled in Figures 13.4 and 13.5. In a **flexible** or **floating exchange rate system**, countries allow their exchange rates to be determined by the forces of supply and demand. But in practice this may not always be the case: countries may often attempt to control or manage their exchange rates.

> **flexible (floating) exchange rate system**: a system in which exchange rates are determined by the market forces of supply and demand

Flexible exchange rates can create significant uncertainties in an economy. A manufacturer may negotiate the future delivery of an imported component, for example, only to find that exchange rate changes make it much more expensive than expected to complete the deal. Foreign exchange markets can also be susceptible to wild swings from speculation. A mere rumor of political upheaval in a country, for example, can sometimes create a rush of capital outflows as people try to move their financial assets into foreign banks, causing a precipitous drop in the exchange rate. Or an inability to obtain short-term foreign loans may send an economy into crisis—and its exchange rate swinging—even if over a longer period the economy would be considered financially sound. It can be hard to maintain normal economic activities when exchange rates fluctuate wildly.[**]

[**]It is for this reason that importers and exporters frequently resort to futures markets in order to "lock in" a given exchange rate between two currencies hence avoid any risk from such fluctuation. But such markets can also be, and often are, used for financial speculation. Perhaps as a result, futures markets are generally more a focus of finance than of economics.

535

Many countries have tried to control the value of their currencies to create a more predictable environment for foreign trade. The strictest kind of control is a **fixed exchange rate system**. In this case, a group of countries commits to keeping their currencies trading at fixed ratios over time. Starting in 1944, many countries, including the United States, had fixed exchange rates under what is known as the **Bretton Woods system** (named after the international monetary conference in Bretton Woods, New Hampshire that created a post-war financial order including the Intentional Monetary Fund and the World Bank).

---

fixed exchange rate system: a system in which currencies are traded at fixed ratios
Bretton Woods system: a system of fixed exchange rates established after World War II, lasting until 1972

The exchange rates in such a system, however, do not usually remain perfectly fixed. For one thing, to fix an exchange rate precisely, the central bank would need to have perfect (and *continuously* perfect) information about all trades—something that is not feasible in real-world conditions. What the countries that participated in the Bretton Woods conference did—and countries today that fix their currency generally do—is set a "band" or range around a "target rate" and allow the "fixed" rate to fluctuate within this band. In the case of the countries that were part of the Bretton Woods system, the band was very narrow—on the order of plus or minus 1 percent.

Over the long term, the target rate can change, at the government's discretion. When a government lowers the level at which it fixes its exchange rate, what is called a **devaluation** occurs, and when it raises it, a **revaluation** takes place. But the system can be undermined if there are too many changes, and when key currencies such as the dollar come under too much selling pressure a fixed exchange rate system can break up. This is what happened to the Bretton Woods system in 1972. The U.S. dollar had been the linchpin of the system and had been convertible to gold. When the United States suffered large currency outflows, the U.S. eliminated gold convertibility and allowed the currency to float, which was quickly followed by other major countries floating their currencies also.

---

devaluation: lowering an exchange rate within a fixed exchange rate system
revaluation: raising an exchange rate within a fixed exchange rate system

---

After the Bretton Woods system ended, many countries moved to a "floating" system, while others tried to exert some management over their currencies. Such management is performed by trying to maintain certain target exchange rates, by "pegging" the currency to a particular foreign currency, or by letting it "float" but only within certain bounds (something like the Bretton Woods system, only with a much wider band).

How does a country keep its exchange rate fixed, or at least within bounds? A government has at its disposal two main tools. The first is imposing capital controls. For example, a country that wants to limit foreign exchange trading may require that importers apply for licenses to deal in foreign exchange or impose quotas on how much they can obtain. By only allowing highly regulated transactions, it can control the prices at which exchange transactions are made.

The second is **foreign exchange market intervention**. As we saw earlier in our discussion of official reserve accounts, central banks have the power to intervene in foreign exchange markets. They may do this under a floating exchange rate regime, with the object of raising or lowering the rate or building up or lowering their holdings of foreign exchange. When a country is committed to a fixed exchange rate, it is the responsibility of the central bank to respond to upward or downward pressures on the rate with appropriate intervention in order to keep the rate at the prescribed level.

---

foreign exchange market intervention: an action by central banks to buy or sell foreign exchange reserves in order to keep exchange rates at desired levels

---

To see how the intervention works, consider Figure 13.7. Suppose that the government would like to keep the exchange rate of its domestic currency at the level e^*, but market pressures are represented by the curves S_{market} and D_{market}. At the exchange rate e^*, there is an excess supply (surplus) of domestic currency, and so there is pressure on the exchange rate to fall. The central bank must artificially create more demand for the domestic currency, as shown by the demand curve $D_{with\ intervention}$. It does this by going into the market and exchanging foreign currency for domestic currency—essentially "soaking up" the surplus domestic currency.

The problem is that the central bank can do this only as long as it has sufficient reserves of foreign exchange on hand. If it ran out of foreign exchange, it would be unable to support the currency and be forced to devalue. Devaluation is, in fact, fairly common among countries with a deficit in their current account and insufficient surplus in the capital account to cover these deficits. In particularly severe cases, countries can experience a **balance of payments crisis**, in which a lack of foreign exchange means that the country cannot purchase needed imports or make payments on its debt.

537

> **balance of payments crisis:** when a country gets precariously close to running out of foreign exchange and is therefore unable to purchase imports or service its existing debt

Is devaluation a bad thing? The answer to this question is complex. Devaluation is generally thought to be good for exporters because it makes the country's goods cheaper abroad. But it also means that people in the country will find that imports are now more expensive. And sometimes devaluation is taken as a sign of instability or poor policy in a country, which can lead to rapid outflows of capital, forcing further devaluation.

Imagine, for example, an investor who is considering investing US$100 million in Bolivian government bonds. If it seemed likely that the country's currency—the sucre—would at some point be devalued, the best strategy would be to avoid investing in Bolivia. If the exchange rate today were 5,000 sucres to the dollar, the investor could purchase 500 billion sucres worth of bonds with US$100 million. But if the currency were in fact later devalued—to the point where 10,000 sucres would be needed to purchase a dollar—the investment would subsequently only be worth US$50 million if the investor decided to sell the bonds and convert them back to dollars. Because of the potential problems resulting from currency devaluation, many economists have grown cautious about recommending devaluation as a cure for international imbalances.

Not surprisingly, countries will always prefer to *plan* a devaluation rather than be pressured into one by circumstances. Countries that are either export competitive or attractive to foreign investors are able to amass large amounts of foreign reserves and supply much domestic currency on the market. Doing so enables such countries to keep their

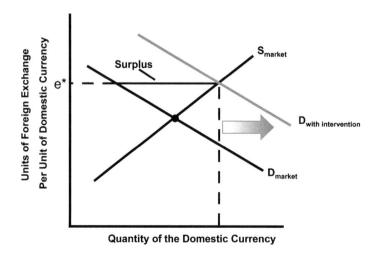

Figure 13.7 *Foreign Exchange Intervention*

exchange rates lower than market forces would dictate. China is generally known to have used this tactic in the past, keeping the value of its currency, the renminbi, artificially low to stimulate exports (the value of renminbi is often cited in terms of its most common unit, the yuan) and, in the process, becoming a large holder of U.S. dollars as well as other currencies. But China has also intervened in the opposite direction, to revalue the renminbi, particularly between 2014 and 2017 when it sold over $1 trillion from its reserves to support the currency.

One complication with fixed exchange rates is that they make it impossible for a country to conduct independent monetary policy. The reason is that intervention by its central bank in money markets to buy and sell its currency for foreign exchange reasons necessarily affects the country's domestic money supply, and consequently (as we saw in Chapter 11) its interest rates. If the domestic interest rate is influenced to a significant degree by the country's exchange rate policy (specifically its desire to fix its rate), this severely limits the effectiveness of domestic monetary policy. If, on the other hand, the central bank intervenes for monetary policy reasons (e.g., to control inflation), the resulting change in the money supply would affect the relative international value of the currency, so it would be impossible to keep the exchange rate fixed. A country, therefore, can set its exchange rate *or* its interest rate, but not both. If it keeps its exchange rate fixed relative to another currency, the interest rates in the two countries will tend to move together.

4.5 Developing Country Problems: Balance of Payments and Debt Crises

Most developing countries opt for some variation of a "managed" exchange rate regime. For them, monetary policy is often necessarily a secondary concern. Their need for scarce foreign exchange is paramount. On the one hand, this makes sense, since it is important that the value of an exporting country's currency not rise too much. Allowing it to do so would make exports more expensive, hence less competitive, in global markets.

Yet it is a delicate balancing act. Too weak a currency severely hampers a country's ability to import. Perversely, developing countries with limited import potential will sometimes even go without necessities since the luxury-consuming middle class has preferential access to scarce foreign exchange. An exceedingly weak currency is also a big liability when it comes to servicing a country's external debt. Creditors always insist on being paid in foreign exchange; the weaker a developing country's currency, therefore, the more of its scarce stock of foreign exchange must go to paying interest on the debt.

The problem is that poor countries often fall short in their BOP. The current account and capital account need not fully offset; as we have seen, the central bank balances things through the operation of the official reserve account. Unfortunately, a country that is a relatively weak exporter (meaning fewer foreign exchange inflows) still depends on imports and must service its debt (both outflows). Consequently, the central bank "makes up the difference" by putting some of its scarce foreign exchange reserves into circulation. Doing so repeatedly is what provokes BOP crises requiring emergency lending.

The worst such case on record is probably the debt crisis of the 1980s, during which several Latin American countries fell into the BOP crises and required emergency bailouts. There have been numerous similar instances in more recent years, such as in Mexico (1994) and East Asia (1997), Russia (1998), Turkey (1999), Argentina (2001), Ecuador (2008), Greece (2012 and 2015), and Venezuela (2017)—to name only the most prominent.

Many fear that a new debt crisis is brewing, possibly more consequential than any earlier one. Dozens of countries have recently applied for emergency assistance (see Box 13.4). The main cause is the unanticipated need for pandemic support. Wealthy nations can afford to "do without" for an extended period, have more fiscal clout, and also have more resources to stem the spread of diseases—in some cases not requiring their populations to undergo strict lockdown. Developing

---

BOX 13.4 POOR COUNTRIES FACING A NEW DEBT CRISIS

The world's poor countries have had their finances destroyed by the global pandemic. Tanzania has called on "our rich brothers" to cancel its debt, and Argentina recently defaulted for the ninth time in its history.

"This is really unlike anything we have seen," said Mitu Gulati, a law professor at Duke University. "The last time we had this many countries likely to go under at the same time was in the 1980s." In Latin America, that period was known as La Década Perdida—The Lost Decade.

While poor countries have historically been able to borrow from the World Bank and International Monetary Fund (IMF), in recent years their debt has become popular with private investment firms. Unfortunately for debtor nations, such entities have their own interests and their own rules.

Argentina's multiyear dispute with a group of hedge funds including Elliott Management is a wake-up call. Elliott and other investors bought Argentine bonds shortly before the country defaulted in 2001 and held out for full repayment—at one point even seizing an Argentine naval vessel—rather than settle through a debt restructuring. It worked. Elliott eventually received nearly 400 percent of its original investment.

As investors around the world seek refuge in the dollar, currencies in many developing countries have plummeted in value. That means it takes more of their own currency to buy the dollars they need to pay their debts, while they have also spent heavily on the logistical response to the COVID-19 pandemic. "The abruptness of this shock is much larger than the 2008 global financial crisis," said Ramin Toloui, assistant Treasury secretary for international finance under Obama.

The IMF has already expanded two emergency loan programs, and more than 100 countries have applied. The programs will help in the short term, Mr. Toloui said, but much more financial assistance will be required. The IMF itself has estimated the borrower countries' total current need, from all sources, at $2.5 trillion.[6]

country economies have been hit especially hard because of economic paralysis and insufficient government funds. The global markets have also not favored them.

As we have seen, persistent BOP deficits tend to provoke vicious cycles of continued debt dependence, except in the rare case when a country is able to export its way out of trouble. The recent economic crisis caused by the pandemic has only intensified an already chronic problem, as many countries find themselves in dire need of external assistance. While the pandemic might only be temporary, its financial consequences on developing countries could persist for decades. Together with the mounting challenges that developing countries face related to climate change, many are likely to experience an unprecedented imbalance in their foreign exchange payments. That might require widespread and massive debt forgiveness to avoid economic collapse.

Discussion Questions

1. Having an "open" economy complicates a country's conduct of fiscal and monetary policy, since international effects must be considered, and these may either reinforce or counteract the original policy. Does this mean that it might be better to have a "closed" economy? What are some of the advantages and disadvantages of "openness"?
2. Why did countries fix their exchange rates in the past? Why did many stop doing so? What are some potential problems involved in letting a country's exchange rate "float"?

5 INTERNATIONAL FINANCIAL INSTITUTIONS

The Bretton Woods system of fixed exchange rates was only one aspect of the international financial structure established in the 1940s. Also formed during this period were the International Bank for Reconstruction and Development (IBRD), which later expanded into the **World Bank**, with the goal of promoting economic development through loans and programs aimed at poorer countries, and the **International Monetary Fund (IMF)**, established to oversee international financial arrangements. Although fixed exchange rates among the major currencies have been abandoned, the World Bank and the IMF continue—with

---

World Bank: an international agency charged with promoting economic development, through loans and other programs

International Monetary Fund (IMF): an international agency charged with overseeing international finance, including exchange rates, international payments, and balance of payments management

---

541

considerable controversy—to play significant roles in international affairs.

When it was created, the IMF was charged with overseeing exchange rates, international payments, and BOP management and with giving advice to countries about their financial affairs. The IMF has a complicated governance structure based on voting shares allocated to member countries, but in fact, its policymaking has historically been dominated by the United States and certain countries in Europe. The appointed members of its executive board represent the United States, the UK, Germany, France, and Japan. In 2010 the IMF restructured its voting system to give China, South Korea, Turkey, and Mexico slightly larger shares. Both the World Bank and IMF have their headquarters in Washington, DC.

When a country is in financial trouble—for example, when it is unable to pay the interest that it owes on its foreign debts or is experiencing wild swings in its exchange rate—the IMF (in conjunction with the World Bank, if the country is poor) often advises the government on how to remedy the problem. The IMF has tended to encourage low- and middle-income countries with debt problems to remove their barriers to trade and capital flows, arguing that such liberalization promotes economic growth. The countries are also advised to minimize the size of their government and its expenditures, as a way to reduce the need for borrowing. They are told to keep their inflation rates down and are often advised about their exchange rate policies as well.

The policy prescriptions of trade liberalization, privatization, deregulation, and small government became known during the 1980s and 1990s as the **Washington Consensus** (described in more detail in Chapter 16). The policies have also become the source of much controversy, as many economists have come to believe that rigid, "one-size-fits-all" application of such policies often works against, rather than for, human welfare and international stability. In particular, as prominent Malaysian economist Jomo Kwame Sundaram has argued, forcing smaller countries to open their borders to capital flows leaves them vulnerable to crises caused by capital flight. This occurred in the Asian financial crisis of 1997 when an "East Asian miracle" of economic growth was rapidly replaced by economic collapse in Indonesia, Malaysia, the Philippines, and elsewhere.[7] High current debt levels, as we have noted, make renewed crises of this kind very likely.

Washington Consensus: specific economic policy prescriptions used by the IMF and World Bank with a goal of helping developing countries to avoid crises and maintain stability. They include openness to trade and investment (liberalization), privatization, budget austerity, and deregulation

---

Many observers are currently calling for reforms in the international financial system and perhaps for new international institutions. Dissatisfaction over the IMF prescriptions for liberalization has caused some changes within the organization itself. But some argue that these changes are not sufficient and that more radical changes are necessary. Suggestions include greater regulation of international banking, substantial reforms and increased transparency in multinational corporate governance, restrictions on short-term capital flows, a tax on speculative transactions in foreign exchange, and the establishment of an international bankruptcy court.

Discussion Questions

1. To check your understanding of international linkages, consider the following hypothetical scenario. Suppose that people overseas become less interested in buying U.S. government bonds (perhaps because they start to think of them as less secure). What would be the effect on:
   a) The BOP financial account?
   b) The supply or demand for U.S. dollars?
   c) The value of the U.S. dollar?
   d) The BOP current account?
2. Have international trade or financial imbalances, or actions of the IMF, been in the news lately? What are the current controversies?

REVIEW QUESTIONS

1. What are the major ways in which economies connected internationally?
2. List three policies related to international trade.
3. List two policies related to international capital transactions.
4. Briefly describe the recent history of United States and world trade and list the major U.S. trading partners.
5. What are some international organizations and agreements dealing with trade relations?
6. List some major reasons why countries often limit trade.
7. What are some of the impacts of the increasing power of transnational corporations?
8. What is the theory of "purchasing power parity"?
9. Who creates the supply of a currency on the foreign exchange market? Who creates the demand?
10. Draw a carefully labeled graph illustrating a depreciation of the dollar against the euro.
11. What are the two principal accounts in the balance of payments, and what do they reflect?
12. How and why is an imbalance (surplus or deficit) in the current account related to an imbalance in the capital account?
13. Does having an open economy make monetary policy stronger or weaker? Why?
14. What is the effect of an open economy on fiscal policy?
15. Distinguish between floating and fixed exchange rate systems.
16. How and why might a central bank "intervene" in a foreign exchange market?
17. Why do developing countries often struggle with capital outflows and debt crises? What does this suggest about inequity in the international financial system?
18. What is the "Washington Consensus"? What are some of the criticisms of its effects on developing countries?
19. What reforms have been suggested for the international financial system?

543

EXERCISES

1. Singapore is a natural-resource-poor country that has built its economy on the basis of massive imports of commodities and raw materials and similarly massive exports of refined and manufactured goods and services. In Singapore, exports were 176 percent of GDP in 2020! But how can a country export *more* than its GDP? (Hint: Remember that imports are subtracted to obtain the measure of *net exports* that is part of GDP.)

2. Classify each of the following as a *trade flow, income flow,* or *asset transaction*:
   a) A U.S. software company sells its products to European consumers
   b) A Saudi investor buys real estate in Europe
   c) A U.S. retailer imports Chinese-made appliances
   d) A worker in the UK sends some of her wages back to her family in India
   e) A Mexican manufacturer pays interest on a loan from a Canadian bank

3. Suppose that, due to rising interest rates in the United States, the Japanese increase their purchases of U.S. securities.
   a) Illustrate in a carefully labeled supply-and-demand diagram how this would affect the foreign exchange market and the exchange rate expressed in terms of yen per dollar.
   b) Is this an appreciation or depreciation of the dollar?
   c) Would we say that *the yen* is now "stronger"? Or "weaker"?
   d) If the rise in interest rates was due to a deliberate Fed policy, does this international connection make such policy more, or less, effective? Explain in a few sentences.

4. Determine, for each of the following, whether it would appear in the *current account* or *capital account* section of the U.S. BOP accounts and whether it would represent an *inflow* or an *outflow*.
   a) Payments are received for U.S.-made airplanes sold to Thailand
   b) A resident of Nigeria buys a U.S. government savings bond
   c) A U.S. company invests in a branch in Australia
   d) A Japanese company takes home its profits earned in the United States
   e) The U.S. government pays interest to a bondholder in Canada

5. Match each concept in Column A with a definition or example in Column B.

Column A		Column B	
a.	Tariff	1.	Makes international incomes comparable, by accounting for differences in the cost of living
b.	Current account	2.	A rise in the value of a currency in a floating exchange rate system
c.	Currency appreciation	3.	An organization charged with providing loans for development
d.	Purchasing power parity adjustment	4.	Investing in a foreign business
e.	Balance of payments crisis	5.	Tracks flows arising from trade, earnings, and transfers
f.	Quota	6.	A tax put on an internationally traded ite
g.	Non-tariff barriers to trade	7.	When a country runs short of foreign exchange
h.	World Bank	8.	A rise in the value of a currency, under a fixed exchange rate system

i.	International Monetary Fund	9.	Using measures such as standards and licensing to restrict trade
j.	Capital controls	10.	When a central bank buys or sells foreign exchange
k.	Revaluation	11.	A fall in the value of a currency under a floating exchange rate system
l.	Foreign Direct Investment	12.	Putting a quantity limit on imports or exports
m.	Currency depreciation	13.	Government intervention to reduce or eliminate international capital flows
n.	Foreign exchange market intervention	14.	An organization charged with overseeing international finance

APPENDIX: AN ALGEBRAIC APPROACH TO THE MULTIPLIER, IN A MODEL WITH TRADE

Just as we modified the multiplier in the appendix to Chapter 9 to take account of the impact of taxes, we can now go a step further to consider the effect of trade. Suppose that, in addition to consumption's depending on income, imports depend on income according to the equation $IM = mpim\ Y$, where $mpim$ is the marginal propensity to import (the proportion of additional income spent on imports). The $mpim$ is a fraction. Starting with the equation for aggregate expenditure with a proportional tax that we had derived in the appendix to Chapter 9, we can get an equation for aggregate expenditure in an economy including trade, as follows:

$$
\begin{aligned}
AE &= C + I_I + G + X - IM \\
&= \bar{C} + mpc(Y - tY + TR) + I_I + G + X - mpim\ Y \\
&= (\bar{C} + mpc\ TR + I_I + G + X) + \left[mpc(1-t) - mpim\right]Y
\end{aligned}
$$

The AE curve now has the intercept given by the first term in parentheses. Changes in exports shift the curve upward or downward. The new slope is given by the term in brackets. The slope is flatter, due to the subtraction of $mpim$.

Solving for Y (using the same method as in the appendix to Chapter 10—but leaving out some of the intermediate steps) yields:

$$
Y - mpc(1-t)Y + mpim\ Y = C + mpc\ TR + 1_I + G + X
$$

$$
Y = \left[\frac{1}{1 - mpc(1-t) + mpim}\right](\bar{C} + mpc\ TR + I_1 + G + X)
$$

545

The term in brackets is a new multiplier that includes both proportional taxes and imports that depend on domestic income. This multiplier here is even smaller than the previous two. For example, if *mpc* = 0.8, t = 0.2, and *mpim* = 0.1, the new multiplier is $1/(1 - 0.64 + 0.1)$ or $1/(0.46)$ or approximately 2.2. This is because any increase in Y now "leaks" not only into saving and taxes but also into increases in imports (which takes away from demand for domestic products).

NOTES

1   Farrer, 2021.
2   World Bank, 2020.
3   U.S. Census Bureau, 2020.
4   Radosavljevic, 2020.
5   Sharma, 2021.
6   Walsh and Phillips, 2020.
7   Sundaram, 2017.

REFERENCES

Farrer, Martin. 2021. "Global Supply Chain Crisis Could Last another Two Years, Warn Experts." *The Guardian*, December 18.

Radosavljevic, Zoran. 2020. "Africa Loses $89 Billion a Year to Illicit Capital Flight, UN Report Finds." *Euractiv Media Network*, September 28.

Sharma, Ruchir. 2021. "The Pandemic Stimulus Has Backfired in Emerging Markets." *Financial Times*, October 25.

Sundaram, Jomo Kwame. 2017. "1997 Asian Crisis Lessons Lost." *Inter Press Service News*, July 25.

U.S. Census Bureau. 2021. *Trade in Goods with China*. www.census.gov/foreign-trade/balance/c5700.html.

Walsh, Mary Williams and Matt Phillips. 2020. "Poor Countries Face a Debt Crisis 'Unlike Anything We Have Seen." *The New York Times*, June 1.

World Bank. 2020. *World Development Report*.

Part IV

Macroeconomic Issues and Applications

Chapter 14

Inequality: Economic and Social Perspectives

Addressing economic and social inequality has become one of the central challenges of the current era. Why has inequality been increasing in most parts of the world in the last few decades? What are the causes and consequences of inequality? What can we do to ensure a more equitable distribution of resources and opportunities among large parts of the population?

This chapter provides some insights into these complicated questions. We will begin with definitions and measurements of inequality and go on to examine trends in inequality in the United States and globally. We will then look at the causes and effects of inequality, especially at the macroeconomic level, and review policy measures for creating a more equitable—and therefore stronger and more sustainable—economic system.

1 DEFINING AND MEASURING INEQUALITY

Inequality is the state of not being equal, especially in status, rights, opportunities, and outcomes. While few desire a society in which everyone earns the exact same income or possesses the exact same amount of resources, huge disparities in income, wealth and economic opportunities reduce the productive capacity of economies and contribute to economic and social instability. In order to discuss how to achieve a good balance of income and wealth distribution, we first need some objective measures of inequality, to allow us to draw comparisons across time and across societies. We will first consider *what* we are measuring, and then *how* we measure it.

1.1 Different Perspectives on Inequality

Inequality is commonly measured in terms of income or wealth—with wealth inequality generally being significantly greater than income inequality. While these measures are central to the economic analysis of the topic, it is also important to recognize that inequality is a broader concept that extends beyond the realm of economics.

DOI: 10.4324/9781003251521-19

For example, vast inequality exists in the quality of health care across the world. Preventable or treatable diseases in numerous tropical developing countries (such as malaria, measles, and tuberculosis) cause average life expectancy to be significantly shorter than in richer countries. A 2019 study found that countries with a higher level of income inequality also report a higher rate of cardiovascular-related deaths.[1] There is also significant health inequality within many countries. According to a 2021 analysis, average life expectancy in the United States is about 13 years longer for those in the top 20 percent by income as compared to those in the bottom 20 percent—a gap that has increased over time.[2]

Education is another important area of inequality, both nationally and internationally. Children in Germany receive, on average, about 14 years of schooling—the most years compared to any country. Meanwhile, the average for children in the sub-Saharan countries of Ethiopia, Mali, Chad, and Guinea is less than three years of education.[3] Inequalities in education are partly due to income differences, but may also be accentuated by race and gender. In the United States, the difference in academic achievement between white and black students has decreased significantly in recent decades but still remains large. At the same time, the achievement gap between students from low- and high-income families in the United States has increased since the mid-1990s.[4]

There are mixed results for gender-based educational inequality across the world. By 2021, 37 countries had fully closed the educational attainment gap by gender, but in 26 countries girls still had less than 90 percent of the educational attainment of boys, including Afghanistan, Iraq, Niger, and Pakistan.[5]

Nobel laureate Amartya Sen has broadened the concept of inequality to include "capabilities." In Sen's analysis, money is only one dimension—albeit an important one—of an individual's "capability" to function in his or her economic environment. Other social and economic factors, such as discrimination and access to or isolation from social networks, can also be crucial. As Sen has pointed out, there is considerable inequality of capabilities throughout the world, not just in poor countries. Many of these inequalities have been exacerbated in the recent COVID-19 pandemic as the poor and the vulnerable population have been hit harder by the pandemic. (See Box 14.1.)

Inequality may also show up in environmental outcomes. Pollution levels are typically higher in low-income areas, which are also more likely to be the location for toxic waste facilities. This kind of inequality is even more pronounced in developing countries: for example, oil and gas development in Nigeria by international corporations has resulted in thousands of oil spills that have impoverished local residents due to reduced agricultural production, lower fish harvests, and polluted drinking water.[6] The impacts of climate change also accentuate global inequality, with poorer countries suffering the strongest effects while contributing the least to the causes of climate change.[7] A 2019 analysis

---

BOX 14.1 ECONOMIC INEQUALITY AND COVID-19

The COVID-19 pandemic has increased global inequality. The United Nations reports that in 2020 the pandemic pushed 119–124 million additional people into extreme poverty and increased the number of malnourished people by 70–161 million across the world.[10] During this same period, the collective wealth of billionaires in the United States increased from $3.4 trillion to $5.3 trillion, driven primarily by significant growth in stock valuations, thus increasing the economic gap between the world's richest and the poorest.[11]

Less developed countries are more likely to feel larger impacts of the COVID-19 crisis due to their weaker healthcare systems, poorer governance, and lack of financial capacity to address the crisis. Take, for instance, the disparity in access to vaccination across countries. While developed countries have invested heavily in vaccine development, have the capability to produce and distribute vaccines, and were able to vaccinate a large part of their populations relatively quickly, most of the rest of the world had to wait much longer to gain adequate access to vaccinations. According to data from the World Health Organization, as of September 2021, only 3 percent of people in low-income countries had been vaccinated with at least one dose, compared to the 60 percent vaccinated population in high-income countries.[12]

The pandemic has also exacerbated pre-existing racial and gender inequalities. For example, empirical research indicates that infection rates and mortality rates have been much higher for people from black and ethnic minority communities in the UK, and for African-Americans in the United States.[13] The pandemic has also had a gendered impact—while men are more vulnerable to COVID-19 infection, women face an overall higher risk of infection as they are more likely to be employed in the care industry. In addition, women have had to take on a disproportionate share of the increase in childcare and household work and also faced a higher incidence of violence during the pandemic. Job losses during the pandemic have also been higher for women globally—4.2 percent in 2020 compared to 3 percent for men. The UN predicts that the effects of the pandemic are likely to roll back decades of progress in the fight against gender inequality.[14]

---

by researchers at Stanford University concluded that the current GDP gap between the world's richest and poorest countries is 25 percent larger than it would have been without climate change.[8] Climate change is projected to lower crop yields, especially in Africa and other developing regions.[9] Richer countries also generally have much better resources for adaptation to climate change.

1.2 Measuring Inequality

One of the most common ways to measure inequality is by looking at the income share (percent of the total income) held by various groups ordered by income from the poorest to the richest, such as the bottom 20 percent, middle 20 percent, top 5 percent, etc. The U.S. Census Bureau measures incomes by summing up households' incomes from wages and salaries, rent, interest, and profits, and cash transfer payments received from government agencies.

Table 14.1 *Distribution of U.S. Household Income in 2020*

Group of households	Share of Income (%)	Annual Income Range
Poorest fifth	3.0	Below $27,026
Second fifth	8.1	$27,027 - $52,179
Middle fifth	14.0	$52,180 - $85,076
Fourth fifth	22.6	$85,077 – 141,110
Richest fifth	52.2	Above $141,110
Richest 5 percent	23.0	Above $273,739

Source: U.S. Census Bureau, Income Distribution Measures 2020, Table A-3, and Per-cent Distribution of Households by Selected Characteristics within Income Quintile and Top 5 Percent, Table HINC-05.

The distribution of U.S. household income for 2020 is presented in Table14.1. To understand this table, imagine dividing up U.S. households into five equal-size groups (called "quintiles"), with the poorest house-holds all in one group, then the next poorest in the next group, and so on. The last group to be formed has the richest one-fifth (or 20 percent) of households. The poorest quintile, with household incomes below $27,026, received only 3.0 percent of all the household income in the country. The richest quintile, those with incomes of $141,110 or more, received 52.2 percent—that is, more than half—of the income received in the United States. The table also shows that the top 5 percent of households receive nearly as much income as the bottom 60 percent.

Using these data, we can construct several measures of inequality based on the ratios of the income share of one group compared to another group. One common measure is the ratio of the income share of the richest fifth to that of the poorest fifth of the population; in this case, we obtain 52.2/3.0 = 17.4—that is, households in the richest quintile have over 17 times the income, on average, of households in the poorest quintile. In 1980 this ratio was only about 10, indicating a sig-nificant increase in the spread between the richest and poorest fifth of the population over a 40-year period. The U.S. Census Bureau publishes various ratios based on the incomes at different percentiles of the distri-bution, such as the 90th/10th ratio and 95th/20th ratio. These ratios can be tracked over time to determine how inequality has changed.

Economists generally prefer to use a more comprehensive measure to describe the pattern of inequality based on the **Lorenz curve**.* A Lorenz curve graphs the *cumulative* percentage of households lined up from left to right in order of increasing income on the horizontal axis. The vertical axis measures the *cumulative* percentage of total income received by different groups of households (the lowest 20 percent, the lowest 40 percent, etc.).

---

* Named after the statistician Max Lorenz, who first developed the technique.

Lorenz curve: a line used to portray an income distribution, drawn on a graph with percentiles of households on the horizontal axis and the cumulative percentage of income on the vertical axis

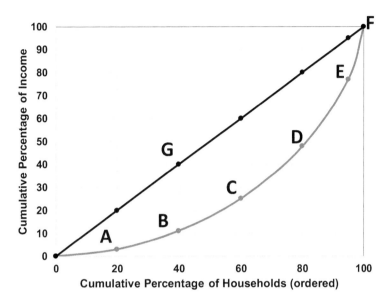

Figure 14.1 *Lorenz Curve for U.S. Household Income, 2020*

Source: U.S. Census Bureau, Historical Income Tables: Income Inequality, Table A-2.

The data shown in Table 14.1 can be used to construct the Lorenz curve for the U.S. shown in Figure 14.1. Point A represents the fact that the lowest 20 percent of households received 3.0 percent of total income. Point B shows that the cumulative percentage of income received by the bottom 40 percent is 11.1 percent of total income. Point C presents the cumulative percent of income received by the bottom 60 percent of households, which is 25.1 percent of total income. Similarly, point D shows that the income of the bottom 80 percent is 47.7 percent of all income. Finally, point E shows that the bottom 95 percent (everyone except the top 5 percent) received 77 percent of all income. The Lorenz curve always starts at the origin, at the lower left corner of the graph (because 0 percent of households have 0 percent of the total income) and ends at point F in the upper right corner (because 100 percent of households have 100 percent of the total income).

The Lorenz curve provides information about the degree of income inequality in a country. Note that the 45-degree line in Figure 14.1 represents a situation of absolute equality. If every household had the same exact income, then, for example, the "bottom" 40 percent of the households would receive 40 percent of all income. This is shown by point G in Figure 14.1. Imagine the other extreme—a situation in which one

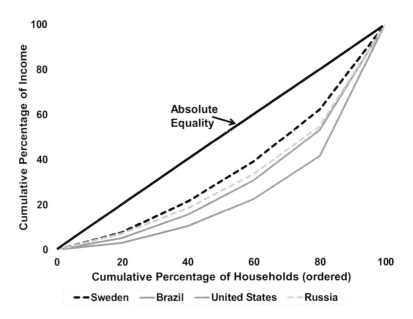

Figure 14.2 *Lorenz Curves for Sweden, Brazil, Russia, and the United States, 2018*

Source: World Bank, World Development Indicators database.

household received all the income in a country. In this case, the Lorenz curve would be a flat line along the horizontal axis at a value of zero until the very end, where it would suddenly shoot up to 100 percent of income (at point F).

Of course, these two extremes do not occur in reality, but they indicate that the closer a country's Lorenz curve is to the 45-degree line, the more equal its income distribution. This is illustrated in Figure 14.2, which shows the Lorenz curve for four countries: Sweden, Russia, Brazil, and the United States. Income is distributed relatively equally in Sweden; its Lorenz curve is closest to the 45-degree line of absolute equality. Brazil has one of the most unequal income distributions—we see that its Lorenz curve bows far from the line of equality. Inequality in Russia is higher than that in Sweden but lower than that in the United States.

Inequality, as shown by a Lorenz curve, can be measured by a **Gini ratio (or Gini coefficient)**. Referring to areas A and B in Figure 14.3, the Gini ratio is A/(A + B). The Gini ratio can vary from 0 for perfect equality (in which everyone receives the same income) to 1 for complete inequality (in which one individual receives all the income in the society, and everyone else gets none). According to the U.S. Census Bureau, the Gini ratio for U.S. household income in 2020 was 0.489. The U.S. has a higher Gini coefficient than all other major industrialized countries, signifying that the United States has the highest degree of income inequality in this group (as shown in Figure 0.11 in Chapter 0).

Note that the definition of income used for the data in Table 14.1 is pre-tax income. It also excludes the value of non-cash government

Gini ratio (or Gini coefficient): a measure of inequality, based on the Lorenz curve, that goes from 0 (perfect equality) to 1 (complete inequality). Greater inequality shows up as a larger area between the curved line and the diagonal

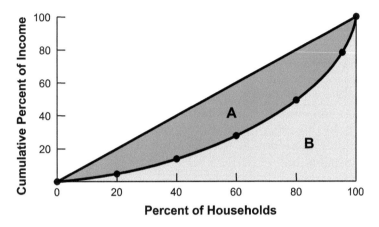

Figure 14.3 *Gini Ratio, A/(A + B)*

benefits such as food assistance and Medicare, and the value of employer-provided benefits such as health care. Including taxation and benefits can change the Gini coefficient.

The U.S. Census Bureau has developed different definitions of income to take these issues into account. Accounting for the effects of the tax system lowers relative income in the top groups. Adding the effects of non-cash government transfer programs, such as government-provided health benefits, also makes the income distribution somewhat less unequal. In general, the role of government moderates levels of inequality within a country. If we wish to consider the distribution of *well-being* rather than just the distribution of income, government provision of public goods, such as parks and public transit, as well as household production of goods and services such as childcare and cooking, should also be taken into account. Some of these goods may contribute to lessening inequality—for example, everyone, rich or poor, can enjoy a public park or use a public library. But if the distribution of these goods is uneven—for example, if pleasant parks are mainly in upper-income neighborhoods—they might increase inequality. (Recall that we have described some broader efforts to assess well-being that go beyond money incomes and GDP in Chapter 5.)

Discussion Questions

1. What do you think is the minimum level of income that an individual, or a small family, would need to live reasonably well in your community? (Think about the rent or mortgage on a one- or two-

bedroom residence, etc.) What does this mean about where the average level of income in your community fits into the U.S. income distribution shown in Table 14.1?

2. What are some of the differences between inequality of income and inequality of well-being? How are these two concepts related? Which one do you think deserves more attention from policymakers?

2 INEQUALITY TRENDS AND ISSUES IN THE UNITED STATES

We can also use inequality data to track how inequality has changed over time, and how it affects patterns of wealth and labor market outcomes. In this section, we explore income inequality trends in the United States, then look at wealth inequality and inequality resulting from discrimination.

2.1 Income Inequality over Time

Income inequality in the United States has increased in recent decades. We can see this in Figure 14.4, which shows the Gini coefficient in the United States from 1967 to 2020, based on data from the U.S. Census Bureau. The Gini reached a record low of 0.386 in 1968. After that, the Gini coefficient increased in 38 of the next 52 years.

Figure 14.5 presents an alternative way of looking at the increase in inequality in the United States by comparing the growth in income for people in different income percentiles for two time periods: 1946 to 1980

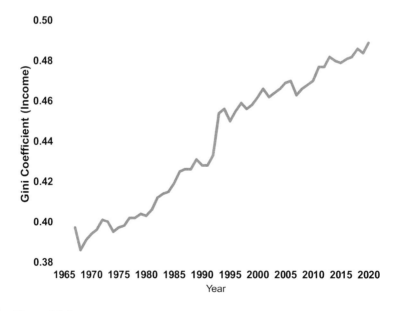

Figure 14.4 *Gini Coefficient in the United States, 1968–2020*

Source: U.S. Census Bureau, Historical Income Tables: Income Inequality, Table A-2.

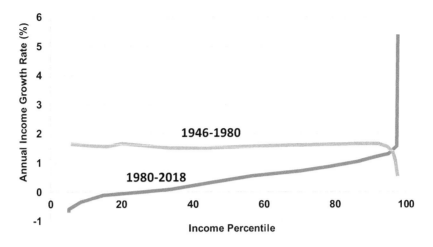

Figure 14.5 *Growth in Income by Percentile*
Source: Saez and Zucman, 2020.

(represented by the gray line) and 1980–2018 (represented by the blue line). Between 1946 and 1980, the average national income per capita rose by about 2 percent a year. This growth was widely shared among the population—only the richest 1 percent had a slightly lower growth than the average. But since the 1980s, the wealthiest people (mainly those in the top 1 percent) saw the largest income growth. The average annual growth rate during 1980–2018 was 1.4 percent, but for almost 90 percent of the population income growth was much below this average. In fact, the bottom 50 percent only saw a 0.2 percent increase in their pre-tax income. Thus, rising inequality over the last four decades has mostly resulted from the wealthiest accumulating a much greater share of the national income growth. We will consider some explanations for this trend toward higher inequality later in this chapter.

2.2 Wealth Inequality

The distribution of wealth (what people own in assets) tends to be much more unequal than the distribution of income (what people receive over a time period). The majority of the population own relatively little wealth, relying mainly on labor income or government, non-profit, or family transfers to support their expenditures. It is possible to have *negative* wealth when the value of a person's or family's debts (such as the amount they owe on their car, house, or credit cards) is greater than the value of their assets. For people in the middle class, the equity that they have in their house is often their most significant asset.

Wealth, and wealth inequality, can be harder to measure than income inequality. Much wealth is held in the form of **capital gains** on assets, such as shares in a company, land, or antiques. Capital gains refer to the increase in the value of such assets over time. It can be difficult to estimate the value of capital gains on assets unless the assets are actually sold. Additionally, a comprehensive report of asset holdings is not required by most governments making it harder to get data on wealth.

---

capital gain: an increase in the value of an asset over time

It is still possible to make approximate estimates of the U.S. Gini coefficient for wealth. One estimate from Credit Suisse suggests that the U.S. Gini coefficient for wealth for 2020 is 0.85—significantly higher than the income Gini coefficient of 0.49.[15] While the top 10 percent of U.S. households by income receive about 45 percent of all income, the top 10 percent by wealth own 70 percent of all wealth. The top 1 percent own 31 percent of all wealth, about the same as the bottom 90 percent combined. And the bottom half of Americans own very little of the national wealth—only about 2 percent (Figure 14.6).

Just as income inequality has been increasing in recent decades, so has wealth inequality. A plot of the wealth shares owned by the top groups in the United States over time looks much like the income shares in Figure 14.4. According to one study, the share of national wealth owned by the top 1 percent was over 50 percent prior to the Great Depression, declined to less than 25 percent by the late 1970s, but then steadily increased to around 45 percent after about 1980.[16]

The extent of wealth inequality suggests that many people in the lower half of the wealth distribution suffer significant loss of well-being due to the lack of any wealth "cushion", creating insecurity and lack of opportunity. In addition, the extreme concentration of wealth in the

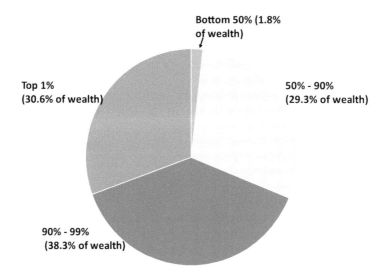

Figure 14.6 *The Distribution of Wealth in the United States, 2020*

Source: United States Federal Reserve, 2021.

top 1 percent confers on its owners both economic and political power. The owners of wealth may then use this power to maintain their position or to exacerbate existing inequalities.

2.3 Labor Market Discrimination

One aspect that is particularly important in understanding trends in inequality is the differences in labor market outcomes for individuals from different groups. In the United States, it is generally true that opportunities to have well-paid work, with good compensation, are greater for men than for women; for younger people than for older ones; for the more educated than for the less educated; and for white, native-born Americans than for immigrants or people of color.

We will now explore these realities by considering the role of **labor market discrimination**, which exists when, among similarly qualified people, some are treated disadvantageously in employment on the basis of race, sex, age, sexual preference, physical appearance, or disability. Workers who belong to disfavored groups may be paid less for the same work, may be denied promotions, or may simply be excluded from higher-paying and higher-status occupations.

---

labor market discrimination: a condition that exists when, among similarly qualified people, some are treated disadvantageously in employment on the basis of race, sex, age, sexual preference, physical appearance, or disability

---

2.3.1 Inequality by Race and Ethnicity

In Chapter 7, we looked at differences in unemployment rates by race and ethnicity and noted that unemployment rates for blacks and Hispanics have been significantly higher than those for whites and Asians. In 2021 the unemployment rate for whites was 3.4 percent compared to 6.7 percent among blacks, 4.9 percent among Hispanics, and 3.8 percent among Asians.

The higher unemployment among minority groups is at least partly due to discrimination in the labor market. Researchers studying racial discrimination have used creative experiments that explore, for example, how employers respond to job applicants with "minority-sounding" names. A 2017 paper that reviewed the results of 28 such studies found that applicants with white names like Emily and Greg receive, on average, 36 percent more callbacks than applicants with names like Lakisha and Jamal, and 24 percent more callbacks than applicants who appear to be Latinos.[17]

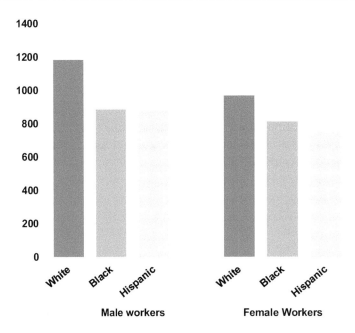

Figure 14.7 *Median Weekly Earnings, Select Groups of U.S. Workers, Age 25 and Over, 2021*

Source: U.S. Bureau of Labor Statistics, 2021.

Wide disparities in wages and income levels are also evident across different racial and ethnic groups. Figure 14.7 uses government data from 2021 to compare the median weekly earnings in the United States of full-time, year-round workers in various groups. We see that the median earnings of both black and Hispanic male workers were only about 75 percent of the earnings of their white male counterparts. Disparities in earnings also exist among female workers from different races and ethnicities, with women of color facing the most severe gender wage gap in the U.S. While white women earn 81 percent of the earnings of white men, the earnings of black women are only 68 percent of white male earnings and that of Hispanic or Latino women are about 63 percent of the earnings of white men.

Economists have used statistical studies to estimate how much of the difference in wages between workers of different races is due to various factors. A 2013 article finds that differences in formal education are important in explaining the gap, but at least one-third of the gap is due to discrimination.[18] The analysis also finds that black job seekers tend to be offered and accept lower wages than white workers. A 2016 analysis finds that the gap in wages between black and white workers in the U.S. narrowed in the 1990s due to low unemployment and minimum wage increases, but has increased since 2000 as black workers were more negatively impacted by the Great Recession of 2008 and the COVID-19 recession.[19]

Disadvantages in jobs and wages translate, of course, to disadvantages in income and wealth. The poverty rate for blacks has come down significantly from about 31 percent in the mid-1970s to 18.8 percent in 2019. However, blacks are still more than twice as likely as whites to be living in poverty. Also, 2019 Census data shows that women in all racial and ethnic groups were more likely than white, non-Hispanic men to be in poverty. Specifically, 22.5 percent of black women, 24.6 percent of native women, 19.4 percent of Hispanic women, and 10 percent of Asian women lived in poverty. In comparison, 9 percent of white women, and 7.1 percent of white men, were described as living in poverty.

2.3.2 Gender Wage Gap and Inequality

> **gender wage gap:** the difference in average wages between men and women; women are paid, on average, less than men

According to a comprehensive 2016 analysis, about half of the difference between men's and women's pay in the United States is associated with **occupational segregation**—the tendency of men and women to be employed in different industries and different occupations.[20] For example, in the United States, jobs like child-care worker, registered nurse, and preschool teacher are held overwhelmingly by women. Meanwhile, men dominate in occupations such as construction trades, truck driving, and engineering. Occupational segregation could be a result of differences in preferences, or it could reflect discrimination. For example, existing stereotypes may lead more women to become nurses while men receive more encouragement to become doctors. The jobs taken by men typically have higher wages than the jobs taken by women, resulting in the gender wage gap.

> **occupational segregation:** the tendency of men and women to be employed in different occupations

The study also concludes that workforce interruptions, such as taking time off to raise children or to care for family members, help explain why women earn less than men, on average.[21] But even after accounting for gender differences in education, experience, occupational choice, and other variables, about 40 percent of the gender pay gap remains unexplained. At least part of this unexplained difference can be attributed to discrimination. Notably, women are less likely than men to reach the highest-paying leadership and executive positions. For example, in 2021 only 8 percent of the Fortune 500 companies had female CEOs, and women held just 27 percent of the seats in U.S. Congress.[22]

In the U.S., the gender wage gap has narrowed over the years, especially as younger women have increased their education levels and taken up occupations traditionally dominated by men.[23] Additionally, the evolution in the overall structure of the U.S. economy to a more service-oriented and knowledge-based economy has benefited women. From 1990 to 2021, while overall non-farm employment increased just 33.3 percent,[24] employment growth in the United States more than doubled in the educational services and health care and social assistance sectors, which employ a greater proportion of women. At the same time, the largest portion of jobs that have been disappearing at an ever-faster rate in the last 30 years are those that are male-gendered, such as truck drivers, construction, and warehouse jobs, which face a higher risk of being replaced through automation.[25]

None of this indicates that the jobs picture for women is rosy. Immigrant women in particular are shunted into home health care and personal care positions; demand from the aging baby boomers' cohort is expected to require 1.2 million more workers in these roles in the decade from 2016 to 2026.[26] This industry is also in the midst of tremendous growth because of the increased demand for care due to the COVID-19 pandemic. Despite this high demand and the critical importance of home health aides to the well-being of tens of millions of Americans, nearly one in five aides live in poverty.[27] In 2020, the median annual wages for home health aides, over 85 percent of whom are women, was just $27,080. Other traditionally female-gendered care work professions are better paid: physical therapists assistants typically earn $46,938 annually, while physician assistants and nurse practitioners—roles that are increasingly attracting males—are likely to earn over $100,000.[28]

According to the International Labour Organization, women are paid about 16 percent less than men globally.[29] While data are not available for all countries, the gender wage gap is the highest, above 30 percent, in India, Pakistan, and South Korea. Developed countries with a comparatively low gender wage gap include Australia (13 percent), Italy (8 percent), and Belgium (7 percent). Women are paid more than men, on average, in more than a dozen countries including Argentina, Costa Rica, Thailand, Bangladesh, and the Philippines.

2.3.3 Age Discrimination

A 2016 study by economists at the University of California at Irvine and Tulane University found strong evidence of age discrimination in hiring, particularly for older women. The researchers sent out 40,000 fictitious job applications that included signals on the job seekers' ages, and found that the response rates for workers aged 49–51 years were 29 percent lower than younger workers, and 47 percent lower for workers aged 64 and over.[30] A field experiment in Sweden based on over 6,000 fictitious resumes sent to employers showed that the callback rates began to fall substantially for workers in their early 40s and became very low for workers close to retirement.[31]

Ever since the start of the Industrial Revolution, the kinds of work available have kept changing, creating new types of jobs and reducing or eliminating old ones. The rate of such change seems to be accelerating, requiring a substantial number of workers to seek jobs that are quite different from those they are used to. People who had developed valuable skills in one job may find that their labor commands a lower price in other types of work. Many displaced workers, particularly older ones, may never find the kind of pay and satisfaction that they had in their earlier occupations. Between 2007 and 2019, weekly earnings for workers aged 55–64 increased by only 0.8 percent after accounting for inflation, compared to a 4.7 percent increase in earnings for workers 35–54 years old during the same time period.[32] One study found that in 2021 over one-fifth of the 34 million American workers over the age of 55 earned so little that they qualified as working poor.[33]

Older displaced workers are also more likely than younger workers to stay unemployed for long periods or to exit the labor force.[34] In the fourth quarter of 2020, the long-term unemployment rates for workers in the age group 46–64, and 65 and over, were 45 percent and 42 percent, respectively—compared to long-term unemployment rates of 21 percent for workers ages 16–24, and 37 percent for workers ages 25–44.[35] The COVID-19 pandemic has also had a disproportionate impact on older workers as more adults aged 64 and older left the labor force in 2020 than in any year since 1948. Between February 2020 and February 2021, the labor force participation rate of people aged 65 and over dropped by 11.1 percent, compared to the drop of about 1–3 percent for workers aged 16–64.[36]

In spite of the lower wages and the difficulty in finding jobs among older workers, poverty in this group is less widespread than it was in the 1960s. This decline in poverty among older people is largely attributed to government programs such as Social Security, Supplemental Security Income benefits, Medicare, and Medicaid. Social Security is credited with lifting over 15 million seniors out of poverty; it is estimated that without Social Security benefits the poverty rate for elderly Americans would increase to 37.8 percent.[37] It is important to note, however, that this poverty measure does not consider health care costs. High and rising medical bills for the elderly can greatly reduce the income available to meet other basic needs. The U.S. Census Bureau also provides an alternative measure of poverty, known as the Supplemental Poverty Measure (SPM), that takes into consideration financial resources such as taxes, the value of in-kind benefits such as food assistance, and out-of-pocket medical expenses. In 2019, the SPM for Americans aged 65 and older showed a poverty rate of 12.8 percent, which was higher than the official poverty rate of 8.9 percent.[38]

2.3.4 The Role of Education

There is a significant connection between education, employment, and wages. Figure 14.8 shows the disparities in unemployment rates and median weekly earnings of full-time wage workers based on their educational attainment. In 2020, those with a professional or doctorate degree experienced the lowest unemployment rates, followed by those with master's or bachelor's degrees. The unemployment rate for those without a high school degree was more than twice the unemployment rate for those with a bachelor's degree and almost three times the unemployment rate of those with a master's degree.

In terms of wage differences, we see that in 2020 the median weekly earnings for workers with doctoral or professional degrees were more than three times greater than that of workers with less than a high school diploma. Median earnings for those without a high school diploma were 26 percent lower than those with high school diplomas and 52 percent lower than for those with an associate degree.

This disparity in the earnings of workers with different educational backgrounds has been widening in the last few decades. Since 1980 workers with at least four years of college have seen a much larger increase in their median incomes compared to other groups. Between 1980 and 2020 the median earning of a college-educated worker increased 35 percent, from $57,764 to $78,020. During the same period, the median income for workers who had not completed high school dropped from $33,442 to $27,510, a loss of 17.7 percent.[39]

The inequalities in labor market outcomes between people from different educational backgrounds have been exacerbated during the COVID-19 crisis. While the pandemic caused disruptions in employment for workers in all industries and occupations, those without a college degree experienced the most severe impact. For example, during

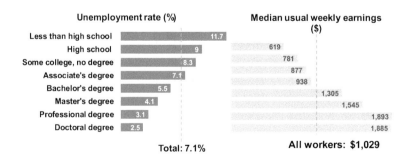

Figure 14.8 *Earnings and Unemployment Rates by Educational Attainment, 2020*

Source: U.S. Bureau of Labor Statistics, Current Population Survey.

the initial months of the pandemic (February to May 2020) when large-scale shelter-in-place policies were implemented, the unemployment rate for workers with a high school diploma or less increased to 12 percent compared to a 5.5 percent unemployment for those with at least a college degree. One factor that made workers with higher education less vulnerable to the crisis was the ability of these workers to work remotely. While almost 65 percent of the workers with a bachelor's degree reported working remotely during the pandemic, only 22 percent of those with high school or less were able to do the same.[40]

Economic inequality is also evident in the United States beyond the categories discussed above. For example, households with one or more disabled members (someone with ambulatory, vision, cognitive, or other difficulties) are more likely than other households to face income poverty and have over 40 percent less in household assets.[41] Also, individuals who identify as lesbian, gay, bisexual, or transgender (LGBT) are more likely to face income poverty and have lower assets than those who identify as straight. LGBT adults were twice as likely to report that they experienced discrimination in 2019 than non-LGBT adults.[42]

Discussion Questions

1. Does inequality have some useful functions in society? To what extent is inequality necessary, and to what extent does it damage social well-being? Is it possible to limit the negative consequences of inequality while still harnessing the positive aspects?
2. Is the data on the various kinds of inequalities presented in the section above surprising to you? Based on some of the data presented, discuss how discrimination in the labor market may limit the ability of individuals to enhance their well-being.

3 INTERNATIONAL DATA ON INEQUALITY

3.1 Cross-Country Comparisons

We next consider inequality in other countries throughout the world. Figure 14.9 shows the same data on national Gini coefficients that was presented in Figure 0.11 in Chapter 0. South Africa, with a Gini coefficient of 0.63, has the highest degree of income inequality of any country. Slovenia, with a Gini coefficient of 0.24, has the lowest level of income inequality among the 148 countries with available data. While some high-income countries such as Norway and Germany have low inequality, inequality is also relatively low in some poorer countries such as Afghanistan, Iraq, and Bangladesh (not shown in Figure 14.9).

Latin American countries tend to have relatively high degrees of inequality. Brazil, Colombia, Costa Rica, Guatemala, Honduras, and Panama all have Gini coefficients above 0.48. Asian countries are generally more economically equal, with Gini coefficients generally between

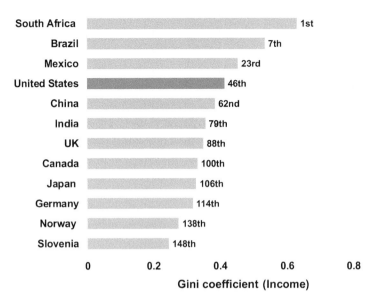

Figure 14.9 *Income Gini Coefficient for Select Countries*

Source: World Bank, World Development Indicators database. Data for the most recent year available, between 2011 and 2019.

0.3 and 0.4. African countries have the greatest variability, with Gini coefficients ranging from 0.33 (Tunisia) to 0.63 (South Africa).[43]

Income inequality is increasing in some countries and decreasing in others. Between 1990 and 2015 the Gini coefficient increased in each of the world's five most populous countries: China, India, the United States, Indonesia, and Pakistan.[44] In China, for example, the richest 10 percent received 41 percent of the income growth since 1980, compared to 13 percent received by the bottom half. Income inequality in Brazil, South Africa, and the Middle East, on the other hand, has remained relatively stable but extremely high, with the top 10 percent of the income earners capturing about 55–65 percent of the income growth while the bottom 50 percent received about 9–12 percent. Even in Europe, which is considered to be more egalitarian, the richest 10 percent got 37 percent of the income growth between 1980 and 2016, while the bottom half got 12 percent. Among the more unequal regions, such as the United States or Russia, income disparities have risen to levels not seen before in modern history, with the bottom half of Americans only receiving 3 percent of the growth since 1980, and the income of the bottom half in Russia actually shrinking.[45]

Income inequality is generally decreasing in Latin American countries, with 13 of 16 countries with comparable data experiencing a falling Gini coefficient from 1990 to 2015. In Asia inequality is generally increasing, while in Africa 15 out of 23 countries experienced a reduction in inequality between 1990 and 2015.[46]

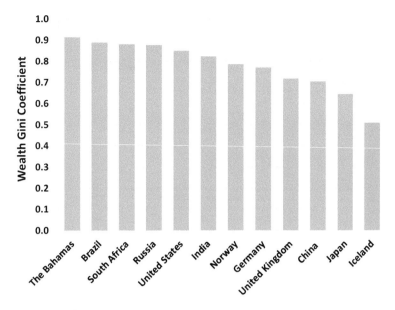

Figure 14.10 *Wealth Gini Coefficient for Select Countries*
Source: Credit Suisse, 2021.

Figure 14.10 presents the wealth Gini coefficients for selected countries. National wealth Gini coefficients, generally higher than income coefficients, range from 0.52 in Iceland to 0.91 in the Bahamas.

3.2 Global Inequality

We can also look at inequality in the world as a whole. In 2021, the richest 10 percent of the global population earned 52 percent of the global income, while the poorest half of the population only earned 8.5 percent.[47] Global wealth inequalities were even more pronounced, with the bottom half of the global population owning just 2 percent of the total wealth, while the richest 10 percent owned 76 percent of all wealth.[48]

Recent estimates on the global Gini coefficient for income range around 0.63–0.67.[49] Comparing this value to the values of Gini coefficients in Figure 14.9, we notice that the global Gini coefficient is higher than that for any individual country. This is because the global coefficient compares all global incomes, including both the very poorest and the very richest, while the income disparity within any given country tends to be smaller.

Despite the high levels of inequality, global inequality has been declining in recent decades. According to the 2022 "World Inequality Report," between 1980 and 2020, the gap between the average incomes of the richest 10 percent of countries and the poorest 50 percent has declined from around 50 times to less than 40 times. The global Gini

567

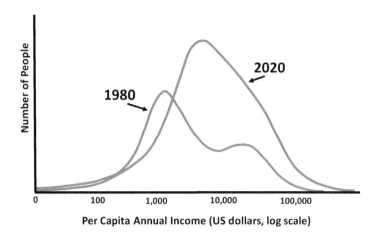

Figure 14.11 *Global Income Distribution, 1980 and 2020*

Source: Chancel et al., 2021.

Note: Income adjusted for inflation and purchasing power.

coefficient has also fallen from about 0.72 in 2000 to 0.67 in 2020.[50] This decline in inequality between countries is partly explained by the growth of the "global middle class" in countries such as China, which has reduced overall global inequality. This is shown in Figure 14.11, which shows the global distribution of income between 1980 and 2020. The peak of the 2020 distribution shows the large number of people now having "global middle class" levels of income. This replaces a peak at a much lower level in 1980 when many more people were at a low level of income. The number of people considered poor by global standards fell from 44 percent of the world's population in 1980 to less than 10 percent in 2020, according to the World Bank.[51]

The global wealth Gini coefficient, around 0.89, is higher than the global income Gini coefficient.[52] Global wealth inequality has declined somewhat in recent decades, once again reflecting the growth of the "global middle class" and a decline in extreme poverty. From 1995 to 2020, the wealth of the world's poorest 90 percent increased by 3.7 percent per year, while the wealth of the top 10 percent grew at a slightly lower rate of 3.0 percent per year. But there has been a more rapid increase among the very wealthy. The wealth of the world's top 0.1 percent grew by 4 percent per year, and the wealth of the top 0.01 percent by 5 percent per year.[53]

Figure 14.12 shows median wealth levels by country. Net worth per adult in developed countries ranges from about $80,000 to over $200,000. The median net worth in China of about $24,000 per adult has increased by a factor of twelve between 2000 and 2020, again reflecting middle-class growth. Over the same period, India's median wealth grew by a factor of four, to $800 per person. The median net worth in the world's poorest countries is generally less than $1,000 per person.

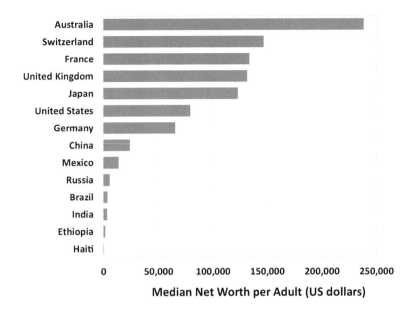

Figure 14.12 *Median Net Worth per Adult, Select Countries, 2020*
Source: Credit Suisse, 2021.

3.3 Inequality and Growth

The relationship between inequality and growth was articulated most famously by economist Simon Kuznets, in the **Kuznets curve hypothesis**. This hypothesis suggests an inverted-U relationship between economic growth and inequality—inequality first rises, then falls, with economic growth.[54] Kuznets proposed that during the initial stages of economic growth inequality would increase as investment opportunities created a wealthy class, while an influx of rural laborers into cities would keep wages low. Eventually, further industrialization would lead to democratization, widespread increases in education, and safety-net policies that would lead to lower inequality.

> Kuznets curve hypothesis: the theory that economic inequality first increases during the initial stages of economic development but then eventually decreases with further economic growth

Empirical evidence does not always support the Kuznets hypothesis. Some countries, such as Brazil, have remained highly unequal even as their per capita incomes have increased.[55] The Kuznets curve hypothesis implies that rising inequality might be tolerated during the initial stages of development, with long-run economic growth eventually

569

reducing inequality. But this is not a reliable guide to development policy. Extreme inequality can retard growth, or limit its benefits to a small rich class while the majority of the population remains excluded from the beneficial effects of development. When we broaden our scope to consider the well-being aspects of development, instead of just economic growth, the negative effects of inequality become more apparent.

It is also not clear that high inequality is important for economic growth. A 2014 study published by the International Monetary Fund found that high inequality can actually reduce economic growth and that "it would be a mistake to focus on growth and let inequality take care of itself, not only because inequality may be ethically undesirable but also because the resulting growth may be low and unsustainable."[56]

Discussion Questions

1. What are the main trends in global inequality? Do these seem to be positive or negative in terms of human well-being?
2. Is some degree of inequality necessary and even beneficial for development? Can inequality have a damaging effect on development?

4 THE CREATION OF AN UNEQUAL SOCIETY

The question of why inequality has been increasing in the United States, China, and many other countries is a source of much debate. We now consider several of the explanations proposed by economists, recognizing that rising inequality is something that cannot be attributed to a single cause. We focus on the case of the United States here, though some of these explanations also help understand the rise in inequality in other countries.

Some of the increase in inequality in the United States and many other industrialized nations is due to changing demographics. As people live longer on average, the proportion of the population that is elderly increases. As elderly people tend to have relatively low incomes, this demographic trend pushes incomes down on the low end.

Another trend increasing the share of the population with low incomes is an increase in the rate of single parenthood. Single-parent households in the United States are much more likely to have low incomes. At the other end of the income spectrum, the increasing number of women entering the labor force has helped boost the income of married-couple households.[57] Another factor increasing household inequality is the increase in "assortative mating"—the tendency of people to marry partners who have a similar earning potential to themselves.[58]

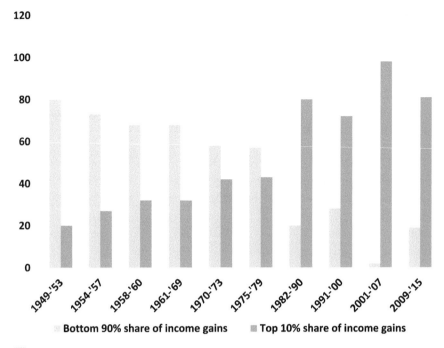

Figure 14.13 *Income Gains during U.S. Expansions for the Richest 10 Percent and the Bottom 90 Percent*

Source: Tcherneva, 2017, based on data from Thomas Piketty, Emmanuel Saez, and the National Bureau of Economic Research (NBER).

Demographic change, however, cannot explain the full extent of the increase in inequality in the United States. Figure 14.13 shows the dramatic shift in the distribution of income gains in recent decades. From the 1940s to the 1970s, income gains during economic expansions mostly went to people in the bottom 90 percent of the income distribution. Since then, a much larger share of income gains has gone to the richest 10 percent.

Between 1980 and 2019, the share of income going to the top 1 percent of income earners in the United States almost doubled from 10 percent to 19 percent, while the income share of the bottom 50 percent declined from about 21 percent to 11.5 percent.[59]

How can we explain this increasing income share of the wealthier population? Factors contributing to this shift include: rising wage inequality; a decline in the power of trade unions; a gradual shift in employment patterns away from long-term employment to part-time and temporary positions; the deregulation and privatization of business and finance; financialization of the economy; reduction in social spending; and tax cuts primarily benefiting the rich and major corporations.

4.1 Causes of Rising Income Inequality

A major factor that helps explain growing inequality is that the wage "share" of the income "pie" has diminished over time. The compensation received by workers, in exchange for their labor, in the form of wages, salaries, and fringe benefits makes up **labor income**, while rents, profits, and interest are called **capital income**. ("**Rent**," as economists use the term, refers not just to rent for housing but to payments for the use of any capital asset, such as machinery or an e-mail list.) The distribution of total income between capital and labor income determines how much income is received by each group.

In general, higher-income households receive a larger portion of their total income from capital income. Increases in wealth and income inequality are strongly related to patterns of capital ownership, with those who have little or no capital failing to capture economic gains.

---

labor income: payment to workers, including wages, salaries, and fringe benefits
capital income: rents, profits, and interest
rent: payments for the use of any capital

Most economists believe that there is a legitimate role for fair and reasonable profits and dividends, interest payments, and rents. But many economists also acknowledge that ill-gained or excessive capital incomes, often depriving workers of their fair share of labor income, do not serve the social good. Persistently high profits may be a sign that a company has excessive market power, indicating that a market is not competitive. Profits might not be a sign of economic health if the companies that earn them create significant negative social or environmental externalities in the process of obtaining them, for example, by exploiting labor or environmental resources.[60]

As shown in Figure 14.14, in the United States wages grew faster than corporate profits between 1966 and 1979. But since the 1980s, this trend has reversed, with annual growth in wages declining over time while corporate profits increased rapidly. Between 2000 and 2007, corporate profits grew at over 5 percent annually, while growth in wages remained below 1 percent. Between 2007 and 2017, as the economy recovered from the financial crisis, profits grew at around 2.5 percent, while wages hardly increased at all.

In the non-farm business sector (which accounts for roughly 74 percent of the output produced in the U.S. economy), labor's share of total income fluctuated around a long-run value of approximately 65 percent through about 1980. By 2019 it had decreased to 59.7 percent.[61] This trend of declining labor share of total income has also been observed in other developed countries since the 1970s.[62]

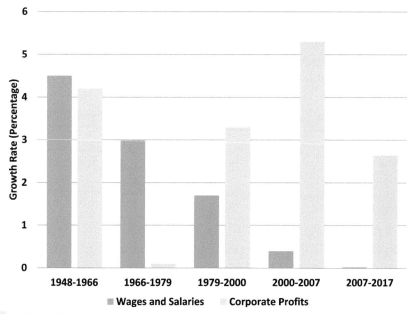

Figure 14.4 *Annual Growth Rates of Wages and Salaries and Corporate Profit, 1948–2017*

Source: *U.S. Bureau of Economic Analysis, NIPA Table 1.14, 1.1.4; Bureau of Labor Statistics (2017).*

One explanation for this could be a reduction in the growth of labor productivity—but statistics on average output per hour worked indicate that labor productivity has grown steadily, while wages have not kept up. Real median wages in the United States, for example, only grew by 11.6 percent from 1979 to 2018—that's not annual growth, but total growth over 40 years! Meanwhile, real productivity in the United States grew by 70 percent over this same time period.[63] This means that since the 1970s, the gap between productivity growth and real wage growth (**wage-productivity gap**) in the United States has been increasing (as shown in Chapter 7, Figure 7.7). With wage increases not keeping up with productivity growth, a growing share of the gains from productivity growth has been going into expanding profits rather than raising wages.

---

wage-productivity gap: the gap between the growth of labor productivity and the growth of hourly labor compensation

---

If the declining share of wage income is not explained by slower productivity growth, what are the causes? Some explanations for why wages have not kept up with productivity include:

4.1.1 The Decline of Unions

The decline in the bargaining power of unions in the United States is one obvious explanation for the widening wage-productivity gap. Workers have not had the power to insist that their wages keep up with the increasing value of their output. Union membership has declined from a high of about 25 percent of the work force in the 1950s to about 11 percent today. Over the period in question—approximately 1970 to the present—government policy has become decidedly less supportive of unions and of low-wage workers, and the rate of union participation has declined markedly.

Figure 14.15 illustrates that during periods with high union membership the share of income going to the rich was lower. Although the relation between union strength and income distribution is not simple, in general, it is likely that workers can push for higher wages when unions are stronger. It is also likely that when inequality is high, and unions are weak, the rich have more influence over the political process, and may be able to promote policies that further weaken unions.

Labor union membership has also been falling recently in Germany, Japan, Sweden, Australia, the UK, and most other wealthy nations.[64] A 2015 analysis by the International Monetary Fund finds that weaker unions increase income inequality, but more by fostering higher incomes at the top rather than depressing wages in the middle.[65] A 2021 study of European labor unions concludes that:

> Workers need strong collective mechanisms and bargaining power to countervail the bargaining power of employers, obtain a fair

Figure 14.15 *Union Membership and Income Inequality, 1917–2019*

Source: Shierholz, 2019.

wage share and limit wage inequality. … And if union density continues to decline in the great majority of EU countries and/or bargaining coverage continues to fall in an important number of them, inequality is bound to continue to increase.[66]

As discussed in Chapter 7, there has also been an increase in the proportion of workforce taking up contract-based secondary jobs, often associated with lower incomes, shorter-term projects, and no employment security. Workers in the secondary sector are likely to have lower bargaining power, which also contributes to inequality in wages and working conditions. One study exploring the relation between employment protection and inequality in 14 high-income countries in North America, Scandinavia, Continental and Eastern Europe, the Middle East, and East Asia, finds that earnings inequalities were higher in countries with weaker labor market protections.[67]

4.1.2 Globalization and Trade

Another common explanation for why workers have lost bargaining power is globalization, including globalization-related trade. One aspect of globalization is that employers have become accustomed to looking around the world for the cheapest labor. Jobs are lost when transnational corporations shift production facilities to developing countries to take advantage of low-cost labor. Globalization is often hypothesized to be responsible for both the loss of middle-class jobs and the stagnation of middle-class wages in developed nations.

Although trade can create many jobs in export industries and promote general economic growth, expanded trade can also put downward pressure on middle-class wages when producers in developed countries face greater competition from cheaper imports from developing countries, compelling domestic producers to either lower their prices (and therefore wages, too) or simply leave the business. Competition from imports has indeed eliminated many industrial jobs—in textiles and automobiles, for example—that formerly fell in the middle of the U.S. wage distribution. When people who had worked in these middle-income jobs move to lower-income service and retail jobs the "hollowing out of the middle" contributes to the increase in inequality.

4.1.3 Technology

Technology affects labor market outcomes in various ways. Technology has contributed to the upward trend in labor productivity over time, but it is also the cause of job losses in some sectors where there is potential for businesses to replace human labor with various mechanical substitutes, as discussed in Chapter 7. Technology can also affect wages and the distribution of wages across different types of workers.

One theory, referred to as **skill-biased technical change**, proposes that workers who possess the education and skills needed to use modern technologies will see relative increases in employment and wages. For example, workers who are able to use computers and other digital technologies may gain an advantage over workers who lack such skills. If these skilled workers are a minority of the workforce, they could obtain wage gains while most workers' wages stagnate. Note that *average* wages may increase while the *median* wage stays relatively constant if most of the gains accrue to those in the top half of the wage distribution.[†]

---

skill-biased technical change: the theory that relative wage gains will be the greatest for those workers who possess the education and skills to use modern technologies

---

Skill-biased technical change has been hypothesized to be one of the reasons for an overall increase in inequality in the United States, as the income of skilled workers who understand and use the new techniques and equipment has risen, leaving behind the less-skilled workers who remain in low-technology occupations. In 1979 those with a college degree in the United States earned 35 percent more than those with just a high school degree. But by 2021 this differential had risen to 67 percent.[68] This difference in wage gains is partly because skilled workers are relatively scarce. The less-skilled workers are, in contrast, relatively abundant, all the more so as technological change has allowed machines to replace human workers at the low-skill end of the spectrum, depressing their average wage.

As technological unemployment creeps up the skill ladder, evidence suggests that fewer workers are experiencing a net benefit from technology in recent years. A 2012 paper notes:

> It is hard ... to find the winners from technical change in the last ten years, as the wages of the bottom 70 per cent of college graduates have been flat or in decline. That would leave just 30 per cent of college graduates (6.6 per cent of the workforce) and the 11 per cent of workers with advanced degrees as the winners of technical change. It also seems unlikely that technical change has generated the upward trajectory of the top 1 per cent of wage earners.[69]

[†] The median wage is the wage received by workers at the exact middle of the wage distribution. Thus the median wage can remain constant or decline while wages in the top half of the distribution increase.

4.2 Financialization and Inequality

The increase in inequality in the past few decades in the United States has occurred concurrently with the expansion of the financial sector. Scholars studying the relation between the two mostly find that financialization has contributed to a rise in inequality. For example, a 2012 study on the impacts of financialization on growth, unemployment, and inequality in OECD countries finds that financialization has a negative impact on all three variables, with each percentage increase in financialization being associated with a 0.49 to 0.81 percent rise in inequality.[70] Another report from the International Labor Organization examining the causes of inequality finds that about 46 percent of the rise in inequality can be attributed to financialization—much greater than the impacts of globalization (19 percent), technological change (10 percent), and other institutional factors (25 percent).[71] So how does financialization contribute to inequality?

According to economist Gerald Epstein, as economies become more financialized a greater share of income generated goes to the owners of financial assets, who tend to be in the upper-income brackets in most countries (see Figure 14.16). Stock market indices are generally seen as a barometer for the economy, and gains in stock markets often generate consumer spending and job growth. But direct gains from rising stock prices go to those who own stocks—in the U.S. about 89 percent of stocks were held by the wealthiest 10 percent as of 2021.[72]

While just over half of Americans have at least one financial account tied to the market, wealthier people are far more likely to have larger

Figure 14.16 *Financialization and Inequality, 1929–2020*

Source: NIPA Tables 6.2A-6.2D, BEA; Saez and Zucman, 2020.

portfolios in these accounts than less affluent families.[73] Higher stock prices increase the value of retirement accounts, but only about half of the country has retirement accounts. In 2019, less than 40 percent of the families in the bottom half of the income distribution in the U.S. were in a retirement plan, compared with more than 80 percent of upper-middle income families.[74]

The impacts of the disparity in ownership of financial assets on inequality were evident during the pandemic when even as the country suffered a public health crisis the stock market surged. With the rise in stock prices during the pandemic, the richest 1 percent of the population gained $5.6 trillion in wealth, compared to a $1.2 trillion gain for the bottom 90 percent of the population. About 70 percent of this gain in wealth for the top 1 percent was estimated to be coming from the stock market.[75]

One of the other major aspects of financialization that has affected inequality is a shift in the focus of corporations from creating wealth by making productive investments to "maximizing shareholder value" by increasing stock prices, often by buying back their own stock. Between 2009 and 2018, S&P 500 companies spent $4.3 trillion—more than half of their income—on stock buybacks. While stock buybacks dropped sharply at the start of the COVID crisis, they have otherwise increased every quarter, reaching almost $200 billion in 2021 for the S&P 500.[76]

This focus on raising stock prices through buyback is partly motivated by the change in pay structure in large corporations. Until the 1990s, chief executive officers (CEOs) were generally paid a salary that would grow at a rate comparable to other employees. Since then, a larger proportion of executive pay has come in the form of stock options and bonuses, based on the idea that executive compensation should include performance incentives. But getting their pay as stock options also means that the executives benefit personally from raising stock prices. This was a significant factor in the development of the 2007–2008 financial crisis. From 2000 to 2007, Lehman Brothers and Bear Stearns paid their CEOs $61 million and $87 million respectively in bonuses, with both citing the rise in stock prices. These CEOs also earned $461 million and $289 million respectively from exercising their stock options during that time. By the time the game was up in 2007, and the share prices plummeted, the CEOs had already become immensely wealthy and were under no obligation to return the funds.

It may not be self-evident why shareholders would allow such a skewed incentive structure if it threatened their share values in the long term. However, shareholders in many companies do not possess much influence over CEOs. Even the board of directors, who historically acted on behalf of shareholders (at least in theory), have become more aligned with CEO interests, as CEOs often hold influence over board members' compensation and re-election prospects. Additionally, many

CEOs sit on boards of other corporations, providing ample opportunity for board members to cater to CEO interests, and vice versa.

One study finds that financialization could account for over half of the decline in workers' income share and about 10 percent of the growth in top executives' share. Corporations' increasing reliance on earnings through financial channels has excluded the general workforce from the revenue-generating and compensation-setting process, and reduced labor's share of income while increasing the top executives' share of income.[77]

Another aspect of financialization that has contributed to inequality is the difference between wages in the financial sector vs. the rest of the economy. The compensation of workers in the financial sector is usually higher than that of an average worker in other sectors, and about 14 percent of the top 1 percent of income earners are employed in finance. The average compensation in the financial sector has increased from about $20,000 per year per employee in 1980 to over $100,000 today.[78]

4.3 Macroeconomic Policies and Inequality

The increase in inequality has also been explained in terms of macroeconomic policies that, intentionally or unintentionally, have widened the gap between workers and those who receive their income from the ownership of various forms of capital, including production facilities such as factories, banks, or web-based systems, or ownership of stock in these companies.

4.3.1 Fiscal Policy

Over the last several decades, tax policies in the United States have become much less progressive than they used to be. The difference in effective tax rates paid by the rich and the poor has narrowed, with reductions in federal income tax rates on the highest income earners and declines in corporate taxes as a percentage of GDP, while payroll taxes on the working class have increased.[79] Since the 1980s, marginal tax rates for upper-income brackets, corporate tax rates, estate, and inheritance taxes, and capital gains tax rates have all declined. In 1986, for example, top marginal tax rates were reduced from 50 percent to 38.5 percent and corporate taxes fell from 46 percent to 34 percent.

These changes have generally been justified by the supply side argument that such tax cuts would result in investments that would expand job creation. Evidence on the impacts of these tax reforms, however, indicates that they have contributed more to inequality than to economic growth. A 2013 study by French economist, Thomas Piketty, looking at a set of industrialized countries from the 1970s to the years preceding the financial crisis, finds that "big tax cutters like the United States did not grow faster than countries like Denmark, which kept taxes high, but inequality in the United States grew much more sharply than in countries like France and Germany, where top tax rates changed little."[80]

One round of tax cuts (the "Bush tax cuts"), implemented in 2001–2003, included reductions in income taxes for almost everyone, but with the largest share going to the rich. According to a report by the Economic Policy Institute, by 2010 more than half of the benefits of these tax cuts went to the top 10 percent of income earners, those making over $170,000 a year, with 38 percent going to the top 1 percent of earners, making over $645,000. Meanwhile, the bottom 60 percent, making under $70,000 annually, received less than 20 percent of the benefits of the tax cuts. Some of this increased inequality was reversed during the Obama presidency when tax cuts benefiting low- and moderate-income workers were implemented, and some of the upper-income tax cuts were repealed. Together with expansion in health care and other programs benefiting the middle class, policies during the period 2009–2016 mitigated but did not reverse the increase in inequality.

Most tax cuts since the 1980s have focused on reducing income taxes, which only make up about half of the total taxes received by the federal government. About a third of the taxes collected comes from payroll taxes—which fund Social Security and Medicare—and these taxes have increased from just 2 percent of wage income at the end of World War II to 6 percent in 1960 and to 15.3 percent in 1990.[81] (Half of this 15.3 percent is nominally paid by the employer and half by the employee, but economic analyses indicate that the real burden falls mostly on the employee since employers can reduce wages to compensate for the tax.[82]) For 68 percent of households, the payroll tax is the largest tax that they pay. The payroll tax is capped at the income of $147,000 as of 2022, meaning that anyone earning more than $147,000 essentially pays the same amount as those earning $147,000. This makes payroll taxes **regressive**, as middle- and lower-income families pay a higher proportion of their income in payroll tax than higher-income families.[83]

---

regressive income tax: a tax in which a larger share of income is collected from households with lower incomes

---

Another major tax-cutting bill in 2017 (the "Trump tax cuts") included further tax reductions for upper-income earners, lowering the top marginal tax rate from 39.6 percent to 37 percent and reducing corporate taxes from 35 percent to 21 percent. The bill also cut income taxes for the middle class, but only modestly and temporarily, while the tax cuts benefiting the wealthy were much larger, and intended to be permanent. According to a report by Americans for Tax Fairness, the

Trump tax cuts have widened inequality between the rich and working-class families. The report estimates that in 2020 the richest 1 percent of taxpayers received an average tax cut of $50,000—75 times higher than the tax cut for the bottom 80 percent, which averaged just $645.[84]

Figure 14.17 shows the average tax rates, including all federal, state, and local taxes by income groups for 1950, 1980, and 2018. We see that for the bottom 90 percent of the population average tax rates were much lower in 1950 (around 10 percent) than in 1980 or 2018 (between 20 to 30 percent). The tax structure in 1950 was slightly progressive for the bottom 99 percent of the income distribution and highly progressive for the top 1 percent. But in 2018, the US tax system looks like a flat tax for the bottom 99 percent and regressive for the richest 1 percent. In fact, in 2018 the tax rate for the richest 0.1 percent was slightly lower than the tax rate for the bottom 50 percent.

In addition to tax policies, the various cash transfer programs run by the U.S. government to help households achieve income security also influence inequality outcomes. These programs can be categorized into two major types: social insurance programs and means-tested programs.

In the case of **social insurance programs**, transfers are designed to help people if certain specific events occur. Because people cannot predict how long into old age they will live or whether unfortunate events will befall them, it is difficult for workers to know just how much to save for retirement or "a rainy day." By coming together to create a pool of

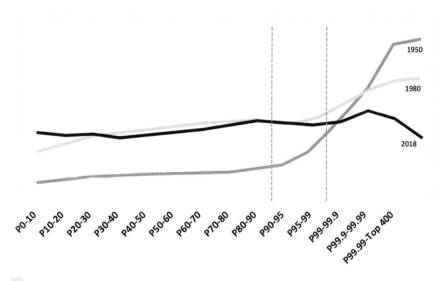

Figure 14.17 *Average Tax Rates by Income Group, Select Years*

Source: Saez and Zucman, 2020.

Note: P0-10 denotes the bottom 10 percent of the population, P10-20 the next 10 percent, etc. The figure depicts US average tax rates, including all federal, state, and local taxes.

social insurance, people can be ensured of basic provisioning even if their personal needs turn out to exceed their personal savings. At certain times in their lives, people contribute to these programs (through taxes), and at other times they receive benefits.

---

social insurance programs: programs designed to transfer income to recipients if and when certain events (like retirement or disability) occur

---

Social insurance programs in the United States include the federal Social Security and Medicare programs (mostly for retired persons) and programs at all levels of government that have been designed to help workers and their families should a worker suffer a disability or a period of unemployment. Eligibility for these programs generally depends on having a family member in the paid labor force for a period of time, but does not depend on the income or wealth of the recipient.

Means-tested programs, by contrast, are intended to help people who simply have insufficient resources. Unlike the beneficiaries of most social insurance programs, recipients of these programs do not need to have established a substantial history of market work in order to qualify for means-tested benefits, but they must demonstrate that their other means of support (income and resources) are very low. Examples of means-tested programs in the United States include food assistance, public housing, Medicaid, and Temporary Assistance for Needy Families. In recent years, access to means-tested programs in the United States has become increasingly restrictive, with many now limiting assistance to a certain number of months or requiring recipients to work a minimum number of hours per week to remain eligible.

---

means-tested programs: programs designed to transfer income to recipients based on need

---

There is ample evidence that these transfer programs help reduce inequality, as they are targeted to provide support to the poor. For example, one study from the Center on Budget and Policy Priorities finds that economic security programs are largely responsible for the decline in poverty in the United States over the last 50 years. Using the Supplemental Poverty Measure (SPM), the study estimates that the poverty rate has fallen from 26 percent in 1967 to about 14.4 percent in 2017 mainly due to the effectiveness of programs such as Social Security, food assistance, and tax credits for working families.[85]

Starting in the 1990s, however, there has been a reduction in the spending on welfare programs, with the phasing out of programs such

582

as Aid for Families with Dependent Children (AFDC), which has also contributed to the increase in inequality. Government outlays on affordable housing and public infrastructure as a share of GDP have also declined sharply. The federal minimum wage ($7.25 as of 2022) has fallen significantly behind inflation, lowering the purchasing power of the lowest-income workers.

In addition to directly reducing such support, the diminished availability of benefits also adversely affects workers' bargaining power, hence their wages. With less government benefits on which to rely, employees threatened with unemployment are more likely to accept a wage cut. Research has found that a strong public sector, including the effective provision of public goods, can reduce income inequalities.[86]

4.3.2 Monetary Policy

The impact of monetary policies on the rise of inequality in the last two decades is less clear. This is because monetary policies affect household income and wealth levels through different channels. An expansionary policy, on one hand, could reduce inequality by creating middle-income jobs and by generating more options for refinancing, which benefits those in lower quintiles of income distribution.[87] On the other hand, low interest rates tend to increase asset prices and thus benefit those in upper-income brackets. At the same time, middle-income savers lose returns on their savings when interest rates are low. Overall, expansionary monetary policy tends to increase capital income faster than labor income, and since it is usually the wealthier households that receive capital income, such policies could worsen inequality.

A 2017 report from the Federal Reserve argues that the evidence that unconventional monetary policies have led to increases in inequality is inconclusive and that the impact of monetary policy on inequality is moderate at best.[88] Another study on the subject, however, asserts that the dis-equalizing effects of expansionary monetary policy (through a rise in asset prices and loss in returns from saving) are greater than the equalizing effects (through refinancing and job creation).[89] The recent rise in wealth inequality, with dramatic increases in equity prices primarily benefiting the rich, indicates that the overall impacts of expansionary monetary policy on inequality may in fact be negative.

Discussion Questions

1. In a 1963 speech, President John F. Kennedy stated, "A rising tide lifts all boats," implying that everyone benefits from economic growth. Is this statement still true? Have periods of economic growth been equally beneficial to people from different income groups?
2. Which of the "causes" of inequality described in the text seem most important? What could be done to modify their impacts?

4 POLICIES TO PROMOTE GREATER EQUALITY

Inequality in the United States declined fairly steadily from the 1940s to the 1970s, as the country experienced fairly steady growth that "lifted all boats" and led to improved living standards. Economic reforms after the Great Depression (1929–1939) emphasized infrastructural development, creation of the welfare state, redistributive taxation, regulation of businesses and financial activities, increase in the provision of public goods, and strong trade unions. These all played an important role in lowering inequality during these years. In contrast, the shift toward pro-market policies, a less assertive government role, and a decline in labor market institutions since the 1970s have contributed to rising inequality. What kind of reforms might help to reverse this trend and achieve greater equality?

Some economists—mostly those following the "free-market" ideology—argue that deregulation and smaller government are the path to prosperity. To the extent this is true, however, we have seen that the benefits of prosperity have been distributed unevenly, with the main gains going to those who are already wealthy. Other economists propose that appropriate regulation could help with many of the current problems. The powerful trends that we have discussed—including globalization, automation, and financialization—suggest that regulation alone may not be sufficient to resolve issues such as the wage-productivity gap and shifts in corporate culture that promote greater inequality. Structural changes, as well as specific public policies to address such issues, are essential to achieving a more equal distribution of income and wealth, and a more stable economic system.

Specific policies to mitigate inequality could include:

- More progressive tax policies that involve shifting the overall tax burden to high-income households. A 2018 analysis by the International Monetary Fund documents an overall decline in tax progressivity in OECD countries, particularly in the 1980s and 1990s, that likely contributed to rising inequality in many countries. The authors conclude that "making a tax system more progressive does have a real impact on market economy outcomes by reducing inequality".[90]
- Instituting wealth taxes on high-asset households could help address wealth inequality. Four countries, Colombia, Norway, Spain, and Switzerland levy annual wealth taxes on high-asset households. For example, Norway's wealth tax rate is 0.85 percent assessed on net assets above about $180,000 for single individuals and $360,000 for married couples.[91] A 2019 analysis argues that wealth taxes can be particularly effective at reducing inequality and recommends spending the revenues from wealth taxes on productivity-enhancing investments such as infrastructure and human capital.[92]
- Expansion of transfer systems, and more public investment in areas with wide social benefit. Increased investment in social programs,

584

such as career skills training, housing assistance, or healthcare could enhance the well-being and productivity of workers. Research shows that redistributive policies can simultaneously reduce inequality and promote higher growth.[93]

- Increasing minimum wage rates. The current federal minimum wage rate in the United States of $7.25/hour has not kept up with inflation and is hardly sufficient to meet basic needs. In several U.S. states, "living wage" campaigns have advocated passing legislation at the state or municipal level that requires a minimum wage higher than the federal standard. About 30 states have a higher minimum wage than $7.25, the highest minimum wage as of 2022 being $14.49/hour in Washington state. Raising minimum wages would improve the well-being of most low-wage workers and reduce poverty.[94] While substantial increases in the minimum wage could result in increased unemployment, most evidence indicates that smaller phased increases have little negative impact on overall employment.[95] Minimum wages in other developed countries are generally higher than the minimum wage in the United States. For example, the minimum wage is about $12/hour in France, $11/hour in the UK, and $15/hour in Australia.[96]

- Investment in human capital through such programs as universal pre-kindergarten and more effective public school systems, together with increased public financing to make public colleges more affordable and community colleges more accessible, can reduce inequality by strengthening workers' skills and their bargaining power. Increased investment in workers through training programs could increase their productivity and wage-earning potential.

- Government policies that support the right to organize and the bargaining power of labor unions. Research by the IMF suggests that stronger labor unions may be able to reduce inequality.[97] Similarly, reducing the gap in job protection between regular and temporary workers contributes significantly to reducing inequality. [98]

- Investment in infrastructure, which can provide stable employment by hiring people to work on infrastructure projects such as roads, rail, water, and sewage systems, natural resource conservation, and other public projects. Such projects also provide general public benefits which improve the quality of life for all, including low-income workers.

- Direct income support for low-income workers. Expanding the current earned-income tax credit is one approach to providing direct income support. In the United States, the earned-income tax credit, which provides a tax benefit to lower-income workers, has proven to be effective in reducing poverty and inequality.[99] A 2020 analysis found the tax credit to be particularly effective at reducing child poverty in the United States.[100]

- Another, more radical, proposal is to institute a universal basic income, as discussed in Chapter 7 (Box 7.6). If set at a relatively low level, a guaranteed income for all workers could provide greater equity without undercutting the incentive to work. It could also increase flexibility as workers adjust to technological change in the workplace or attempt to make ends meet in the "gig economy."

- Fiscal and monetary policies that promote full employment. Low-income and minority workers suffer most when unemployment rises. As we saw in Chapter 12, there is often a tradeoff between unemployment and inflation, but so long as inflation is not a major threat, placing a priority on maintaining low unemployment will promote a more equitable labor market.[101]

- Restricting companies from buying back their stock, and rewarding them through the tax system for investing in their employees; linking executive pay to the productive performance of the company instead of share prices; adding worker representatives on corporate boards so their interests are represented when decisions are made.[102]

- Encouraging cooperative-based organizations, as discussed in Chapter 7, could also help create a stronger and more equitable economic system. Cooperatives have a motive to invest in the long-term viability of the company and improve the well-being of workers. Worker-owned companies, community development corporations, and credit unions tend to be locally oriented and resilient to economic fluctuations at the national level.

The economy of the future will be different from the economy of the past. But we can learn lessons from past experiences, about how to promote greater stability and equity, and avoid catastrophic crises. There is abundant evidence that greater equity is also conducive to economic stability and prosperity since an economy lacking the stabilizing impact of a prosperous middle class will also tend to be more unstable in terms of aggregate demand. The fiscal and monetary policy tools that we have learned about, together with other innovative approaches, will be required in the future in an effort to achieve the goal of an economy that works well for all.

Discussion Questions

1. What economic policies relating to government spending and regulation, taxes, wages, and interest rates have been in the news recently? What do you think about the impact of these policies on economic equity?

2. Do you think the spending priorities and tax policies of the government should be changed in order to reduce economic inequality? Beyond the suggestions in the text, can you think of any other ways that government spending and tax policies could be changed?

REVIEW QUESTIONS

1. In the United States, what share of aggregate income did each quintile of household receive in 2020?
2. What is a Lorenz curve? What does it measure?
3. What is the Gini coefficient (or ratio)? What does a higher value of the ratio signify?
4. What effect do taxes and transfer payments have on the distribution of U.S. household income?
5. What tends to be more unequal—the distribution of income or wealth? Why?
6. Has income inequality in the United States decreased or increased over recent decades? What are some of the reasons?
7. What is labor market discrimination?
8. How does income and employment vary by race or ethnicity?
9. What are some of the key causes of the gender wage gap?
10. What are some of the constraints faced by older Americans in the labor market?
11. How do income and employment vary by education levels?
12. How does economic inequality in the United States compare to other countries?
13. How has income inequality in some of the most populous countries such as India and China changed in recent decades?
14. How is it that the global Gini coefficient for income is higher than the Gini coefficient for any single country?
15. How is it that the global Gini coefficient is declining but the Gini coefficients in most countries are increasing?
16. What is the Kuznets curve hypothesis? Does the research generally support the theory?
17. What are some of the factors that have contributed to a rise in wage inequality in the past few decades?
18. In what ways has globalization affected inequality?
19. How has the rise of financialization influenced the level of inequality in the economy?
20. What macroeconomic policies have contributed to the rise in inequality since the 1980s?
21. What is the difference between means-tested and social insurance programs?
22. How can tax and transfer policies be used to reduce inequality?
23. How can government spending policies and other regulations impact inequality?
24. What kind of policy measures might help reduce inequality levels?

EXERCISES

1. Statistics from the World Bank indicate the household income distribution in Thailand for 2019 was:

Group of Households	Share of Aggregate Income (%)
Poorest quintile	7.7
Second quintile	11.5
Third quintile	15.7
Fourth quintile	22.3
Richest quintile	42.8

a) Create a carefully labeled Lorenz curve describing this distribution. (Be precise about the labels on the vertical axis.)

587

b) Compare this distribution to the distribution in the United States. Would you expect the Gini ratio for Thailand to be higher, lower, or about the same? Why?

2. You can access the World Bank's World Development Indicators database online to download income share data for various countries, and construct Lorenz curves. Choose two countries you are interested in and construct their Lorenz curves on the same graph. Note that the WDI database does not have data for all countries, or for the most recent years. Also, the database provides income shares for the top and bottom 10 percent, in addition to each quintile—include the data points for the top and bottom 10 percent in your graph. Which one of your two countries seems to have a more unequal distribution of income?

3. Match each concept in Column A with a definition or example in Column B.

Column A	Column B
a. Social insurance programs	1. A very unequal income distribution
b. Kuznets curve hypothesis	2. Wages, salaries, and fringe benefits
c. Capital gain	3. Individuals with similar qualifications receive different wages because of demographic characteristics, such as race, gender or age
d. Quintile	4. Payments for the use of an asset
e. Labor income	5. A very equal income distribution
f. A Gini ratio close to 1	6. A group containing 20 percent of the total
g. Skill-biased technical change	7. Programs designed to transfer income to recipients who are retired or disabled
h. A Gini ratio close to 0	8. An increase in the value of an asset at the time of sale
i. Rent	9. Inequality first increases, then decreases, with development
j. Labor market discrimination	10. the theory that relative wage gains will be the greatest for workers with skills to use modern technologies

NOTES

1 Dewan et al., 2019.
2 Congressional Research Service, 2021.
3 Data from the United Nations Development Programme, Human Development Reports database.
4 Dynarski and Michelmore, 2017.
5 World Economic Forum, 2021.
6 Godwin et al., 2016.
7 See, for example, Taconet et al., 2020.
8 Diffenbaugh and Burke, 2019.
9 Vidal, 2013.
10 UN Sustainable Development Goals Report, 2021.
11 Peterson-Withorn, 2021.

12 Data from World Health Organization, https://data.undp.org/vaccine-equity/.
13 Public Health England, 2020 and CDC 2020.
14 UNCTAD, 2021.
15 Credit Suisse, 2021.
16 Saez and Zucman, 2016.
17 Quillian et al., 2017.
18 Fryer et al., 2013.
19 Wilson and Rodgers, 2016.
20 Blau and Kahn, 2016.
21 Ibid.
22 Hinchliffe, 2021; Blazine and Desilver, 2021.
23 Dowell, 2022.
24 Based on data from Bureau of Labor Force, Workforce Statistics.
25 Molla, 2019.
26 BLS News Release, October 2017.
27 Donovan and Alarcon, 2021.
28 Based on data from Department of Labor: https://www.dol.gov/agencies/wb/data/
occupations.
29 ILO, 2018.
30 Neumark et al., 2015.
31 Carlsson and Eriksson, 2019.
32 Nova, 2019.
33 Ghilarducci and Schuster, 2021.
34 Koenig et al., 2015.
35 Bennett, 2021.
36 Johnson, 2021.
37 Romig, 2020.
38 Congressional Research Service, 2021.
39 Pew Research, October 2016 and Bureau of Labor Statistics, Occupational Employment and Wage Statistics.
40 Daly, Buckman, and Seitelman, 2020.
41 Prosperity Now, 2018.
42 Watson et al., 2021.
43 All Gini coefficients from World Development Indicatros database, World Bank.
44 Hasell, 2018.
45 Data sources: World Inequality Database (https://wid.world/data/).
46 Data source: World Development Indicators, World Bank.
47 World Inequality Report, 2022.
48 Human Rights Watch, 2022.
49 See, for example, Chancel et al., 2021; Milanovic, 2021.
50 Chancel et al., 2021.
51 World Bank, World Development Indicators database.
52 Credit Suisse, 2021.
53 Credit Suisse, 2016.
54 Kuznets, 1955.
55 Moran, 2005; Wade, 2011.
56 Ostry et al., 2014, p. 25.
57 Shrider et al., 2021, Table A-1.
58 Greenwood et al., 2014.
59 Kopczuk and Zwick, 2020; and York, 2022.
60 Bartz and Lawder, 2022.
61 Based on data from FRED Economic Data on Share of Labor Compensation in GDP
for the United States.
62 IMF, 2017.
63 Gould, 2020.

589

64 OECD online statistics, trade union density.
65 Jaumotte and Buitron, 2015.
66 Keune, 2021.
67 Tomaskovic-Devey et al., 2020.
68 BLS, 2021.
69 Mishel and Gee, 2012.
70 Assa, 2012.
71 ILO, 2012.
72 Woodward, 2021.
73 Gebeloff, 2021.
74 Federal Reserve Bulletin, 2020.
75 Woodward, 2021.
76 Americans for Financial Reform, 2021.
77 Tomaskovic-Dewey and Lin, 2013.
78 Gordon, 2014.
79 Piketty and Saez, 2007.
80 Porter 2017, based on findings from Piketty et al., 2013 NBER study.
81 Leonhart, 2017.
82 See CBO, 2006. "The Congressional Budget Office assumes — as do most economists — that employers' share of payroll taxes is passed on to employees in the form of lower wages than would otherwise be paid."
83 Bellafiore, 2019.
84 Americans for Tax Fairness, 2020.
85 Trisi and Saenz, 2019.
86 Obst, 2013.
87 Montecino and Epstein, 2015a.
88 Amaral, 2017.
89 Montecino and Epstein, 2015b.
90 Gerber et al., 2018.
91 Bunn, 2021.
92 Mattauch, 2019.
93 Ostry et al., 2014.
94 Dube, 2017.
95 Autor et al., 2016.
96 https://en.wikipedia.org/wiki/List_of_countries_by_minimum_wage.
97 Jaumotte and Buitron, 2015.
98 OECD, 2012.
99 Hoynes and Patel, 2018.
100 Rothstein and Zipperer, 2020.
101 Matthews, 2012.
102 Lazonick, 2012.

REFERENCES

Amaral, Pedro S. 2017. "Monetary Policy and Inequality." *Federal Reserve Bank of Cleveland*, January 10.

Americans for Financial Reform. 2021. "Tax Corporate Stock Buybacks that Enrich Executives and Worsen Inequality." November. https://ourfinancialsecurity.org/wp-content/uploads/2021/11/AFR-TOWS-buyback-tax-FS-11-21.pdf.

Americans for Tax Fairness. 2020. "Chartbook: Trump-GOP Tax Cuts Failing Workers and The Economy." Report. October 23. https://americansfortaxfairness.org/chartbook-trump-gop-tax-cuts-failing-workers-economy/

Assa, Jacob. 2012. "Financialization and its Consequences: the OECD Experience." *Finance Research, 1*(1), January.

Autor, David H., Alan Manning, and Christopher L. Smith. 2016. "The Contribution of the Minimum Wage to US Wage Inequality over Three Decades: A Reassessment" *American Economic Journal: Applied Economics, 8*(1): 58–99.

Bartz, Diane and David Lawder. 2022. "Corporate Power Keeps U.S. Wages 20% Lower Than They Should Be – White House." *Reuters,* March 7.

Bellafiore, Robert. 2019. "New Report Shows the Burdens of Payroll and Income Taxes." *Tax Foundation,* March 26. https://taxfoundation.org/payroll-income-tax-burden/.

Bennett, Jesse. 2021. "Long-term Unemployment has Risen Sharply in U.S. Amid the Pandemic, especially among Asian Americans." *Pew Research Center,* March 11.

Blau, Francine D., and Lawrence M. Kahn. 2016. "The Gender Wage Gap: Extent, Trends, and Explanations." *National Bureau of Economic Research,* Working Paper 21913, Washington, D.C., January.

Blazine, Carrie and Drew Desilver. 2021. "A Record Number of Women are Serving in the 117th Congress" *Pew Research Center.* January 15.

Brown, Anna, and Eileen Patten. 2017. "The Narrowing, but Persistent, Gender Gap in Pay." *Pew Research Center,* April 3.

Bureau of Economic Analysis (BEA). National Income and Product Accounts (NIPA) tables. https://apps.bea.gov/iTable/index_nipa.cfm

Bureau of Labor Statistics (BLS). 2017. "Projections of Occupational Employment, 2016–26." *BLS News Release,* October.

Bureau of Labor Statistics (BLS). 2021. Median usual weekly earnings of full-time wage and salary workers by age, race, Hispanic or Latino ethnicity, and sex 4th quarter 2021 averages. Economic News Release, Table 3.

Bunn, Daniel. 2021. "What the U.S. Can Learn from the Adoption (and Repeal) of Wealth Taxes in the OECD." Tax Foundation, February 5. https://taxfoundation.org/wealth-taxes-in-the-oecd/.

Carlsson, Magnus, and Stefan Eriksson. 2019. "Age Discrimination in Hiring Decisions: Evidence from a Field Experiment in the Labor Market." *Labour Economics, 59*: 173–183.

Centers for Disease Control and Prevention (CDC). 2020. "Coronavirus Disease 2019 (COVID-19) in the U.S. Centers for Disease Control and Prevention," April 20. https://www.cdc.gov/coronavirus/2019-ncov/cases-updates/cases-in-us.html. Accessed 15 Jun 2020.

Chancel, Lucas, Thomas Piketty, Emmanuel Saez, and Gabriel Zucman. 2021. *World Inequality Report 2022.* World Inequality Lab.

Congressional Budget Office (CBO). 2006. "Historical Effective Federal Tax Rates: 1979 to 2004." December 1. https://www.cbo.gov/publication/42871

Congressional Research Service. 2021. "Poverty among the Populations Aged 65 and Older." *Report R45791.* April 14.

Credit Suisse. 2016. *Global Wealth Report 2016.* Credit Suisse Research Institute, November 2016.

Credit Suisse. 2021. *Global Wealth Databook 2021.* Credit Suisse Research Institute, June.

Daly, Mary C., Shelby R. Buckman, and Lily M. Seitelman. 2020. "The Unequal Impact of Covid-19: Why Education Matters." *Federal Reserve Bank of San Francisco Economic Letter,* June 29.

Diffenbaugh, Noah S., and Marshall Burke. 2019. "Global Warming Has Increased Global Economic Inequality." *Proceedings of the National Academy of Sciences of the United States of America (PNAS), 116*(20): 9808–9813.

Donovan, Liz and Muriel Alarcon. 2021. "Long Hours, Low Pay, Loneliness and a Booming Industry." *The New York Times,* September 25.

Dube, Arindrajit. 2017. "Minimum Wages and the Distribution of Family Incomes." *Institute of Labor Economics, Discussion Paper Series.*

Dynarski, Susan, and Katherine Michelmore. 2017. "Income Differences in Education: The Gap within the Gap." *EconoFact, Education Policy*, April 20. https://econofact. org/income-differences-in-education-the-gap-within-the-gap.

Dowell, Earlene K.P. 2022. "Women Consistently Earn Less than Men" *U.S. Census Bureau*, January 27.

Federal Reserve Bulletin. 2020. "Changes in U.S. Family Finances from 2016 to 2019: Evidence from the Survey of Consumer Finances." *Board of Governors of the Federal Reserve System, 106*(5), September.

Fryer, Roland G., Jr., Devah Pager, and Jörg L. Spenkuch. 2013. "Racial Disparities in Job Finding and Offered Wages." *Journal of Law and Economics, 56*: 633–689.

Gebeloff, Robert. 2021. "Who Owns Stocks? Explaining the Rise in Inequality during the Pandemic." *The New York Times*, January 26.

Gerber, Claudia, Alexander Klemm, Li Liu, and Victor Mylonas. 2018. "Personal Income Tax Progressivity: Trends and Implications." *IMF Working Paper WP/18/246*.

Ghilarducci, Teresa and Barbara Schuster. 2021. "Working Longer Not a Panacea Considering the Number of Low-wage Work Options." *Generations Now, American Society on Aging*, November 16.

Godwin, Uyi Ojo, and Nosa Tokunbor. 2016. "Access to Environmental Justice in Nigeria: The Case for a Global Environmental Court of Justice." *Environmental Rights Action and Friends of the Earth*. https://www.foei.org/wp-content/uploads/2016/10/Environmental-Justice-Nigeria-Shell-English.pdf

Gould, Elise. 2020. *State of Working America Wages 2019*. Economic Policy Institute.

Greenwood, Jeremy, Nezih Guner, Georgi Kocharkov, and Cezar Santos. 2014. "Marry your Like: Assortive Mating and Income Inequality." National Bureau of Economic Research, NBER Working Paper 19829, January.

Hasell, Joe. 2018. "Is Income Inequality Rising around the World?" Our World in Data, November 19. https://ourworldindata.org/income-inequality-since-1990.

Hinchliffe, Emma. 2021. "The Female CEOs on This Year's Fortune 500 Just Broke Three All-Time Records." *Fortune*. June 2.

Hoynes, Hilary W., and Ankur J. Patel. 2018. "Effective Policy for Reducing Poverty and Inequality? The Earned Income Tax Credit and the Distribution of Income." *Journal of Human Resources, 53*: 859–890.

Human Rights Watch. 2022. "World Inequality Report 2022: Events of 2021", https:// www.hrw.org/sites/d.efault/files/media_2022/01/World%20Report%202022%20 web%20pdf_0.pdf

International Labor Organization (ILO). 2012. "*Global Wage Report 2012/13: Wages and Equitable Growth*." http://piketty.pse.ens.fr/files/ILO2012(GlobalWageReport). pdf

International Labour Organization (ILO). 2018. *Global Wage Report 2018/19: What Lies behind Gender Pay Gaps*. Geneva.

International Monetary Fund (IMF). 2017. "World Economic Outlook: Gaining Momentum?" April.

Jaumotte, Florence, and Carolina Osorio Buitron. 2015. "Inequality and Labor Market Institutions." *International Monetary Fund, IMF Discussion Note 15/14*, July.

Johnson, Richard W. 2021. "Will Older Adults Return to the Workforce?" *Urban Wire: The Blog of the Urban Institute*, March 12.

Keune, Maarten. 2021. "Inequality between Capital and Labour and among Wage-Earners: The Role of Collective Bargaining and Trade Unions." *Transfer, 27*(1): 29–46.

Koenig, Gary, Lori Trawinski, and Sara Rix. 2015. "The Long Road Back: Struggling to Find Work after Unemployment". AARP Public Policy Institute, March.

Kopczuk, Wojciech, and Eric Zwick. 2020 "Business Incomes at the Top." *Journal of Economic Perspectives, 34*(4): 27–51.

Kuznets, Simon. 1955. "Economic Growth and Income Inequality." *The American Economic Review, 45*(1): 1–28.

Lazonick, William. 2012. "How American Corporations Transformed From Producers to Predators." *HuffPost*, April 3.

Leonhart, David. 2017. "A Tax Plan to Turbocharge Inequality, in 3 Charts." *The New York Times*, December 17.

Matthews, Dylan. 2012. "Ten Ways to Reduce Inequality without Raising Tax Rates." *The Washington Post*, December 6.

Mattauch, Linus. 2019. "Reducing Wealth Inequality through Wealth Taxes without Compromising Economic Growth." Oxford Martin School, University of Oxford, January 31. https://www.oxfordmartin.ox.ac.uk/blog/reducing-wealth-inequality-through-wealth-taxes-without-compromising-economic-growth/.

Milanovic, Branko. 2021. "Notes on Global Income Inequality: A Non-technical Summary." *Global Policy*, May 20.

Mishel, Lawrence and Kar-Fai Gee. 2012. "Why Aren't Workers Benefiting from Labour Productivity Growth in the United States?" *International Productivity Monitor, 23*: 31–43.

Molla, Rano. 2012. "The Robot Revolution Will Be Worse for Men." *Vox*, December 12.

Montecino, Juan Antonia and Gerald Epstein. 2015a. "Banking From Financial Crisis to Dodd-Frank: Five Years On, How Much Has Changed?" July 21, 2015, *Political Economy Research Institute, Working Paper.*

Montecino, Juan Antonia and Gerald Epstein. 2015b. "Did Quantitative Easing Increase Income Inequality?" October, 2015, *Political Economic Research Institute, Working Paper Series Number 407.*

Moran, Timothy Patrick. 2005. "Kuznet's Inverted U-Curve Hypothesis: The Rise, Demise, and Continued Relevance of a Socioeconomic Law." *Sociological Forum, 20*(2): 209–244.

Neumark, David, Ian Burn, and Patrick Button. 2015. "Is It Harder for Older Workers to Find Jobs? New and Improved Evidence from a Field Experiment." National Bureau of Economic Research, Working Paper No. 21669.

Nova, Annie. 2019. "Older Workers Haven't Seen a Raise. Here's Why." *CNBC*, May 2.

Obst, Thomas. 2013. "Income Inequality and the Welfare State – How Redistributive Is the Public Sector?" *Institute for International Political Economy Berlin, Berlin School of Economics and Law, Working Paper No. 29/2013.*

Ostry, Jonathan D., Andrew Berg, and Charalambos G. Tsangarides. 2014. "Redistribution, Inequality, and Growth." IMF Staff Discussion Note 14/02, April.

Organisation for Economic Cooperation and Development (OECD). 2012. *Economic Policy Reforms: Going for Growth*. OECD Publishing, Paris.

Peterson-Withorn, Chase. 2021. "Led by Elon Musk's Crazy Gains, American Billionaires Have Added Nearly $2 Trillion to their Fortunes during the Pandemic." *Forbes*, November 7.

Piketty, Thomas, and Emmanuel Saez. 2007. "How Progressive Is the U.S. Federal Tax System? A Historical and International Perspective." *Journal of Economic Perspectives, 21*(1): 3–24.

Piketty, Thomas, Emmanuel Saez, and Stefanie Stantcheva. 2013. "Optimal Taxation of Top Labor Incomes: A Tale of Three Elasticities." *National Bureau of Economic Research Working Paper Series, Working Paper 17616*, March 2013.

Porter, Eduardo. 2017. "Tax Cuts, Sold as Fuel for Growth, Widen Gap between Rich and Poor." *The New York Times*, October 3, 2017.

Prosperity Now. 2018. *Financial Stability of People with Disabilities*. Prosperity Now Scorecard. https://prosperitynow.org/sites/default/files/resources/Financial-Stability-of-People-with-Disabilities.pdf.

Public Health England. (2020) Disparities in the risk and outcomes of COVID-19. Public Health England, London.

Quillian, Lincoln, Devah Pager, Ole Hexel, and Arnfinn H. Midtbøen. 2017. "Meta-analysis of Field Experiments Shows No Change in Racial Discrimination in Hiring over Time." *Proceedings of the National Academy of Sciences*, pre-publication online version.

Real World Macro. 2015. "From Boring Banking to Roaring Banking: How the Financial Sector Grew Out of Control, and How We Can Change It." *An Interview with Gerald Epstein, Real World Macro,* July/August 2015, Dollars and Sense.

Romig, Kathleen. 2020. "Social Security Lifts More Americans Above Poverty Than Any Other Program." *Center on Budget and Policy Priorities,* February 2020.

Rothstein, Jesse, and Ben Zipperer. 2020. *The EITC and Minimum Wage Work Together to Reduce Poverty and Raise Incomes.* Economic Policy Institute Report, Washington, DC, January 22.

Saez, Emmanuel, and Gabriel Zucman. 2016. "Wealth Inequality in the United States since 1913: Evidence from Capitalized Income Tax Data." *The Quarterly Journal of Economics, 131*(2): 519–578.

Saez, Emmanuel, and Gabriel Zucman. 2020. "The Rise of Income and Wealth Inequality in America: Evidence from Distributional Macroeconomic Accounts." *Journal of Economic Perspectives, 34*(4): 3–26.

Shierholz, Heidi. 2019. "Working People Have Been Thwarted in Their Efforts to Bargain for Better Wages by Attacks on Unions." *Economic Policy Institute,* August 27.

Shrider, Emily A., Melissa Kollar, Frances Chen, and Jessica Semega. 2021. *Income and Poverty in the United States: 2020.* U.S. Census Bureau, Current Population Reports, P60–273, September.

Taconet, Nicolas, Aurélie Méjean, and Céline Guivarch. 2020. "Influence of Climate Change Imacts and Mitigation Costs on Inequality between Countries." *Climate Change, 160*: 15–34.

Tcherneva, Pavlina. 2017. "Inequality Update: Who Gains When Income Grows?" *New Economic Perspectives,* March 29.

Tomaskovic-Dewey, Donald, and Ken-Hou Lin. 2013. "Financialization and U.S. Income Inequality, 1970–2008." *American Journal of Sociology, 118*(5): 1284–1329.

Tomaskovic-Dewey, Donald, Anthony Rainey, Dustin Avent-Holt, and Zaibu Tufail. 2020. "Rising Between-Workplace Inequalities in High-Income Countries." *Proceedings of the National Academy of Sciences (PNAS), 117*(17), April 13.

Trisi, Danilo, and Matt Saenz. 2019. "Economic Security Programs Cut Poverty nearly in Half Over Last 50 Years." *Center on Budget and Policy Priorities,* November 26. https://www.cbpp.org/sites/default/files/atoms/files/9-14-18pov.pdf

UN. Sustainable Development Goals Reports 2021.

UNCTAD. 2021 "COVID-19 Threatens Four 'Lost Decades' for Gender Equality." October 1. https://unctad.org/news/covid-19-threatens-four-lost-decades-gender-equality

United Nations Development Programme, Human Development Reports. 2020. https://hdr.undp.org/content/human-development-report-2020

Vidal, John. 2013. "Climate Change Will Hit Poor Countries Hardest, Study Shows." *The Guardian,* September 27.

Wade, Robert. 2011. "Global Trends in Income Inequality." *Challenge, 54*(5): 54–75.

Watson, Spencer, Oliver McNeil, and Bruce Broisman. 2021. *The Economic Well-Being of LGBT Adults in the U.S. in 2019.* Center for LGBTQ Economic Advancement & Research.

Wilson, Valerie, and William M. Rodgers III. 2016. "Black-White Wage Gaps Expand with Rising Wage Inequality." *Economic Policy Institute,* Washington, DC, September 19.

Woodward, Alex. 2021. "Wealthiest 10% of Americans Own Overwhelming Majority of all US stocks, Report Finds." *Independent,* October 18.

World Development Indicators, *World Bank.*

World Economic Forum. 2021. Gender Gap Report.

World Health Organization. https://data.undp.org/vaccine-equity/.

York, Erica. 2022. "Summary of the Latest Federal Income Tax Data, 2022 Update." *Tax Foundation,* January 20.

Chapter 15

Deficits and Debt

You may have seen the national debt clock in New York City that continually shows how much our debt is increasing by the second.* The total amount of the debt, which presently exceeds $30 trillion, seems very large. But what does it mean? Why does the country borrow so much money? To whom is all this money owed? Is it a serious problem? Is it possible for the United States to stop borrowing? This chapter goes into detail in answering these questions and examines the relationship between the national debt and the economy. But first, we provide some historical context to the notion of a national debt.

1 DEFICITS AND THE NATIONAL DEBT

Perhaps because the two terms sound so much alike, many people confuse the government's deficit with the government *debt*. But the two "D words" are very different. The deficit totaled $2.8 trillion in fiscal 2021, while total federal debt exceeded $30 trillion by early 2022. The reason the second number is much larger than the first is that the debt represents deficits accumulated over many years. In economists' terms, we can say that the government deficit is a *flow* variable while its debt is a *stock* variable. (See Chapter 1 for this distinction.) Large deficits following the COVID-19 recession of 2020 added to the total debt. While the size of the deficit declined significantly after the need for pandemic assistance ended, the debt is projected to continue increasing for the foreseeable future.†

In general, the government's debt rises when the government runs a deficit and falls when it runs a surplus.‡ Figure 15.1 shows how the

---

* The national debt clock can be seen at https://usdebtclock.org
† The federal fiscal year runs from October to September, so fiscal 2020 is October 2019 to September 2020, and fiscal 2021 is October 2020 to September 2021.
‡ Although the arithmetic requires that the debt rise when the government is in deficit—because the only way to finance a deficit is to borrow money—in the case of a surplus it is possible for the government to hold some funds in reserve, for example, to finance future expenditures. It is usually the case, however, that governments will use some of their surplus to reduce existing debt.

DOI: 10.4324/9781003251521-20   **595**

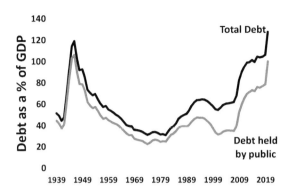

Figure 15.1 *U.S. National Debt as a Percentage of GDP, 1939–2020*

Source: Federal Reserve Bank of St. Louis. FRED Economic Database.

government's debt, measured as a percentage of GDP, has varied since 1939. (The total debt figures alone can be misleading since they do not take into account economic growth or inflation.) The two lines on the graph indicate the total government debt and the part of government debt held by the public (as opposed to debt held by government agencies, which is money that the government effectively owes to itself). After hitting a high of more than 100 percent of GDP during World War II, the debt generally declined as a percentage of GDP until 1980. It rose between 1980 and 1995, then declined again relative to GDP until 2001. Since 2001, the debt has mostly risen, with particularly sharp increases in the years following the 2007–2009 and 2020 recessions. As of 2020, the national debt as a percent of GDP was above its World War II peak.

What is the impact on the economy of government debt? One commonly expressed view of the government's debt is that it represents a burden on future generations of citizens. There is some truth to this assertion, but it is also somewhat misleading. It implicitly compares the government's debt to the debt of a private citizen. Certainly, if you personally accumulated a huge debt, it would not be good for your financial future. But government debt is different in some important ways.

First, about half of government debt held by the public is, directly or indirectly, owed to U.S. citizens. When people own Treasury bills (T-bills), Treasury notes, or Treasury bonds, they own government IOUs. From their point of view, the government debt is an asset, a form of wealth. If your grandmother gives you a U.S. Savings Bond, she is giving you a benefit, not a burden. These assets are some of the safest ones that you can own.

Second, government debt does not have to be paid off. Old debt can be "rolled over," that is, replaced by new debt. Provided that the size of the debt does not grow too quickly, the government's credit is good— there will always be people interested in buying and holding government bonds. Most economists use the rule of thumb that as long as the rate of increase in government's debt is not significantly greater than that of

GDP for several years in a row it does not represent a severe problem for the economy. As Figure 15.1 shows, following the 2007–2009 recession and the pandemic-induced downturn in 2020, persistently large deficits caused the debt to rise much more rapidly than GDP. But unless sustained, this is not in itself a problem. The rapid increase in debt relative to GDP during World War II was, after all, followed by nearly two decades of relative economic prosperity.

Third, the U.S. government pays interest in U.S. dollars. A country such as Argentina that owes money to other countries and must pay interest in a foreign currency (the U.S. dollar) can get into big trouble and eventually be forced to default on its debt. But it is much easier to manage a debt that is denominated in your own currency. Even if some of the debt is owed to foreigners, the United States does not have to obtain foreign currency to pay it. And so long as foreigners are willing to continue holding U.S. government bonds, it will not be necessary to pay it at all—instead, the debt can be rolled over as new bonds replace old ones.

None of this should encourage us to believe that government debt is never a concern. Rising debt creates several significant problems. First, interest must be paid on the debt. This means that a larger share of future budgets must be devoted to paying interest, leaving less for other needs. It is also true that the largest holders of government bonds tend to be wealthier people, so most of the interest paid by the government goes to better-off individuals. If this payment is not counteracted by changes in the tax system, it encourages increased income inequality—a growing concern, as discussed in the previous chapter.

Government debt also creates a problem of generational equity—future taxpayers will have to pay more interest because of government borrowing today. Thus, it is a burden on future generations in that debt finance detracts from other important functions that the government could be performing. The portion of tax receipts that goes to debt service (paying the interest, if not the principal, of the government's debt) is not available for other uses such as education, health, etc.

A second problem is that in recent years an increasing proportion of the debt has been borrowed from governments, corporations, and individuals in foreign countries. As evident from Figure 15.2, US debt to foreigners has increased considerably since 1970, both in absolute terms and as a fraction of total debt. The interest payments on this portion of the debt must therefore be made to others outside the country. That means that the United States must earn enough income from its exports and other sources to pay not only for its imports but also for interest payments to the rest of the world (as shown by the discussion of the balance of payments in Chapter 13). Alternatively, the country could borrow more, but it is best to avoid this solution since it would just make the overall foreign debt problem larger in the long run.

597

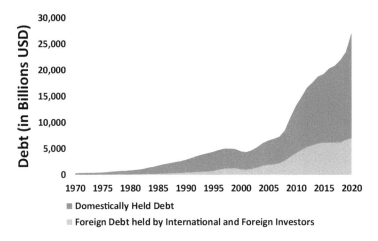

Figure 15.2 *Domestic and Foreign Holdings of U.S. Debt (billions of dollars), 1970–2020*

Source: Federal Reserve Bank of St. Louis. FRED Economic Database.

Large foreign holdings of debt also pose another problem—what if those foreign debt holders decided to sell the U.S. bonds that they own? In that case, the government might have trouble finding enough people who are willing to hold government bonds (that is, lend money to the government). This could cause interest rates to rise sharply, which in turn would push the government budget further into deficit and could tip the economy into recession.

The question "Is government debt worth it?" can be answered only if we consider what that debt is used to finance. In this respect, an analogy to personal or business debt is appropriate. Most people—including economists—do not reject consumer and corporate debt. Rather, our judgment about debt depends on the benefits received.

For example, if debt is accumulated for gambling, it is a bad idea. If the bet does not pay off, then it may be very difficult to pay the interest on the debt (not to mention the principal). But if the government borrows to pay for intelligently planned investment, it can be very beneficial. If the investment leads to economic growth, the government's ability to collect tax revenue is enhanced. This kind of borrowing can pay for itself, as long as the investment is not for wasteful spending, poorly planned or unnecessary projects, or unnecessary short-term consumption.

Even if the debt finances current spending, it can be justifiable if it is seen as necessary to maintain or protect valuable aspects of life. There was widespread support, for example, for the government borrowing undertaken to assist tens of millions of families adversely affected by the COVID-19 pandemic (although some felt the amounts were excessive). As of late 2021, Congress had spent more than $4 trillion on pandemic relief, and a significant portion of this sum will add to the national debt. Similarly, programs to provide relief for hurricane and wildfire damage in hard-hit communities are generally viewed as necessary spending. (Notably, even politicians who have opposed government disaster relief for other states have usually been quick to accept it for their own states.) The management of debt generally involves standard principles of wise stewardship of finances. But when we apply them to government deficits and debt, we must also weigh the economic costs and benefits of different spending and tax policies.

Discussion Questions

1. What is the difference between the deficit and the national debt? How are they related?
2. "The national debt is a huge burden on our economy." How would you evaluate this statement?

2 THE U.S. NATIONAL DEBT: A HISTORICAL PERSPECTIVE

2.1 Two Centuries of Deficits and Debt

Deficit financing has been part of U.S. history from the very beginning. The Continental Congress of 1776 put the country into debt in order to continue its fight for independence from Great Britain. As is done today, Congress issued bonds in order to finance the country's war effort. There was considerable controversy after the war regarding the role of the new federal government in absorbing the debts incurred by individual states. Alexander Hamilton, secretary of the Treasury under George Washington, was prominent among those who believed that, by introducing greater flexibility into the money supply, a national debt had the potential to strengthen the economy and the country. Despite opposition from other political leaders—John Adams and Thomas Jefferson among them—Hamilton helped set in motion a process through which the federal government regularly relied on debt to finance its operations.

After the United States became independent from Great Britain, its federal government generally repaid its debts fairly quickly. The War of 1812, however, proved very costly, and the national debt approached 15 percent of national income by 1816. In the nineteenth and early twentieth centuries, it was primarily wars that depleted the government's finances. The Civil War was especially costly—the debt approached 40 percent of total national income at its peak—but the Mexican-American and Spanish-American wars also added to the national debt. By 1900 the debt had fallen below 5 percent of total GDP, but budget deficits during World War I again pushed the national debt beyond 40 percent of GDP.

In terms of its effect on government finances, the Great Depression of the 1930s was truly a watershed. The economic crisis ultimately led to President Franklin D. Roosevelt's New Deal social programs. From

599

that point on, federal spending on social programs—in addition to military spending, which soared during World War II and remained high afterward—has figured prominently in the total debt figures. Consequently, since 1931 the U.S. federal budget has been in surplus for only seven years, compared with the years from independence until 1931, during which surpluses were twice as frequent as deficits. National debt in relation to income rose significantly during the 1930s, but World War II had an even greater impact. Because consumer goods were rationed, savings accumulated, and many people used them to purchase U.S. war bonds (a form of debt), which helped finance U.S. participation in World War II. After the war, the national debt totaled an unprecedented 122 percent of GDP.

2.2 "Supply-Side" Economics

After World War II, the debt generally declined as a percentage of GDP until 1980. The national debt was just over $900 billion in 1981 but rose by nearly $2 trillion during the next eight years. In other words, over those eight years, the country incurred twice as much debt as it had in its first 200 years! How did this happen?

Ronald Reagan's 1980 presidential campaign leaned heavily on the principles of "supply-side" economics, which promised that offering more benefits and incentives to the individuals and groups that held the most wealth and productive capital would stimulate rapid investment growth and job creation. According to this principle, tax cuts would pay for themselves through greater revenues from an expanding economy. This is consistent with the oft heard but controversial concept of "trickle-down" economics, which is the idea that benefits enjoyed by the well-off eventually percolate (i.e., trickle down) to everyone else.

The major policy experiment with supply-side economics was the Economic Recovery Act (ERA, 1981), which cut income and corporate tax rates, substantially reducing government revenues. At the same time, military spending increased in the 1980s. Consequently, the annual budget deficit, which had been 2.7 percent of GDP in 1980, grew to an annual average of about 4 percent during the Reagan presidency (see Chapter 9, Figure 9.5). A portion of the debt increase was due to cyclical factors, specifically an unusually deep recession in 1981–1982. Most of it, however, resulted from the failure of supply-side economics to produce the revenue growth that was needed to make up for the tax cut.

2.3 1989 to the Present

In absolute terms, the national debt continued to grow after Reagan left office, despite the fact that by then public awareness of the government's fiscal problems had grown. In an attempt to address persistent deficits, President George H.W. Bush raised tax rates slightly and signed a bill in 1990 requiring that all spending increases be matched by either decreases in spending in other areas or tax increases, in a system known as PAYGO ("pay as you go").

Despite the introduction of that system, another recession (1990–1991) and the first Iraq war kept deficits in the range of 4 percent of GDP annually. It also did not help matters that sizable sums had to be used to bail out many savings and loan banks that collapsed due to losses from risky and ill-conceived real estate investments (a precursor of the real estate bubble of the twenty-first century). In 1992 the national debt was $4 trillion.

Bush's PAYGO policy was continued under the administration of Bill Clinton. Congress again raised income tax rates, and the end of the Cold War allowed the federal government to lower military expenditures (although only relative to GDP, not in absolute terms), a side benefit often referred to as a "peace dividend." At the same time, the economy emerged from recession and began a period of sustained growth. The resulting movement from the trough to the peak of the business cycle from 1992 to 2000 generated surpluses in the overall federal budget from 1998 to 2001, a feat that had not been achieved since 1969. This period of budget surpluses, however, was short-lived.

During the presidency of George W. Bush (2001–2009), a combination of recession, tax cuts, and increased military expenditures pushed the budget back into deficit and caused the debt to increase further. By 2008, the debt totaled almost 70 percent of GDP. During the first Obama Administration (2009–2013), annual deficits averaged around 8 percent of GDP, and the national debt rose to just over 100 percent of GDP, as the government deployed an $800 billion fiscal policy package to keep the 2007–2009 recession from turning into a full-fledged depression. Tax revenue fell sharply, from $2.5 trillion in 2008 to $2.1 trillion in 2009 and, as is normal in a recession, expenditures increased due to automatic stabilizers (see Chapter 9, Figure 9.5). The combination of these factors with continued military expenses in Iraq and Afghanistan led to record deficits of more than $1 trillion.

After 2012 the annual deficit fell to a historically more normal level of around 2.5 to 4 percent of GDP, only rising again to 4.6 percent (or nearly $1 trillion) by 2019, as a result of the Trump tax cuts of 2017. The national debt remained at just over 100 percent of GDP. In 2020, however, government outlays jumped by 50 percent in response to the pandemic emergency, sending the deficit to 14.9 percent of GDP (over $3 trillion). By the end of 2020, the national debt had soared to almost 128 percent of GDP. The budget deficit declined in 2021, but remained high at $2.7 trillion. It was projected to decrease further in 2022, to about $1 trillion.

Discussion Questions

1. Has the U.S. federal government ever had a budget surplus? When was the last time? Was there ever a time that the government was not in debt?
2. What causes budget deficits? Are budget deficits necessarily a bad thing?

3 THE DEBT AND ITS LINKS TO FINANCE

3.1 Taxonomy of Debt Types

In the popular press, one encounters different estimates of the country's debt, which can vary considerably depending on whether it refers to government debt or all debt including government and private debt. Total U.S. debt, including both public and private debt, is now approaching 400 percent of GDP. Most of this, however, is household, financial, and business debt (Figure 15.3). Some confusion has been caused by differing terminology relating to the debt, so it may be helpful to distinguish between different categories.

The term "national debt" usually refers to the **gross federal debt**, which is actually the total debt outstanding for the federal government (Table 15.1). It is not, however, the same as the **debt held by the public**. The gross federal debt includes money that the federal government "borrows" from other government accounts. Prominent examples include Social Security and Medicare, which, as noted earlier, are classified as "off budget." Basically, when the government collects more in tax revenue for these programs than it pays out, it realizes an off-budget surplus. It is then in a position to "borrow" the surplus, or at least a portion of it, as an alternative to borrowing money from the public. So, it is the debt held by the public, not the gross federal debt, that is a direct consequence of federal budget deficits.

---

gross federal debt: the total amount owed by the federal government to all claimants, including foreigners, the public in the United States, and other government accounts

debt held by the public: the gross federal debt minus the debt owed to other government accounts

---

As discussed in Chapter 11, the Federal Reserve is an active participant in the market for U.S. bonds, as it buys and sells them to conduct its open market operations in hopes of influencing interest rates. So, the Fed also holds a significant share of the federal debt. Somewhat

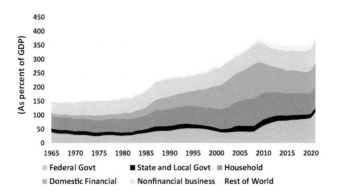

Figure 15.3 *Total U.S. Indebtedness as a Percentage of GDP, 1965–2021*
Source: Federal Reserve Bank of St. Louis, FRED Economic Database.

Table 15.1 *Debt Taxonomy*

	Debt type	Description
Government	Gross federal debt	Generally synonymous with the national debt; refers to the total amount of money owed by the federal government to all claimants
	Debt held by public	Gross federal debt minus debt held in government accounts
	Internal debt	The share of the gross federal debt owned by domestic individuals or groups
	External debt	The share of the gross federal debt owned by foreign individuals or groups
	State and local debt	The total value of all state and local bonds outstanding
Private	Households and not-for-profits	Includes mortgage debt, credit card debt, and bank loans
	Financial sector	Total of all corporate debt for the financial industry
	Nonfinancial business	All corporate debt and bank borrowing for nonfinancial business

confusingly, its share is also considered a part of the debt held by the public (since the Fed is not a government agency, but technically independent, as explained in Chapter 11).

One final distinction is between **internal debt** and **external debt**. The internal debt refers to the portion of the gross federal debt that is owned by individuals or groups within the country, and the external debt represents the portion held by foreigners or foreign groups.

> **internal debt:** the portion of the gross federal debt that is owed to individuals or groups within the country
>
> **external debt:** the portion of the gross federal debt that is owed to foreign individuals or groups

Like the federal government, state and municipal governments also often rely on borrowing to fund their operations. They issue a variety of bond instruments to acquire funds from the public, which in a sense add to the country's total indebtedness. This is also a point of frequent confusion. In its common usage, the term "national debt" refers only to the federal portion of the debt. This seems reasonable because it is the debt that is directly related to fiscal policy and how it affects the national economy. Yet if we speak of the total debt of the country, it appears misleading to exclude the state and local debt. And the picture becomes even more complicated because a complete accounting of debt would also include all household debt (e.g., mortgage and credit card), financial sector debt, and the debt of nonfinancial business, which includes both bank loans outstanding and corporate bonds issued to finance private debt.

If we add all the categories to represent the total indebtedness of the whole country, we find that, in 2021, it approached 400 percent of GDP and was more than double what it had been as recently as the1980 (Figure 15.3). Such an inclusive debt concept is not of great significance in ordinary times, since, as discussed in Chapter 10, most of the debt exists as an *asset* on someone else's balance sheet. During the run-up to the Great Recession of 2007–2008, however, the rapidly rising debt, especially notable in the financial sector, should have been setting off alarm bells, as it meant that the country as a whole had used up much of the leeway in terms of borrowing capacity that could have been drawn on to get out of a recession. Note that after the Great Recession, overall debt levels fell as a percent of GDP through 2019, with a particularly marked reduction in household debt.

While the level of total indebtedness might be misleading, *changes* in the level, especially as significant as those we've seen in recent years, could portend future difficulties. Although it is true that the United States owes most of the trillions of dollars in debt "to itself," the fact conceals two important details: inequality over to whom the debt is owed, and the fact that such sizable sums reflect a much greater degree of leverage (debt as related to personal or corporate assets) than in the past, which could signify greater economic instability in the future. As we can see in Figure 15.3, the US response to the global pandemic has sent total indebtedness soaring anew.

3.2 Federal Government Borrowing: Potential Problems

In earlier chapters, we saw that when the government borrows money, it issues bonds on which it must pay interest. The interest payments form part of the annual federal budget. Figure 15.4 shows how these payments as a percentage of federal spending have varied over time. Note that interest payments accounted for a much greater portion of the budget during the 1980s and 1990s than they do now. Considering that federal debt as a percentage of GDP has risen quite rapidly over the past decade, how can this be? The answer is that the unusually low interest rates that have prevailed over most of the past two decades make this possible.

If interest rates are lower throughout the economy, the Treasury can issue new debt (e.g., Treasury bonds) at a low interest rate. When it does so, it is effectively reducing the portion of the federal budget that must be set aside for debt service. The phenomenon is not unlike the low monthly payments a homeowner makes after obtaining a mortgage with a very low interest rate.

As of March 2022, the interest rate on a ten-year Treasury bond was about 1.8 percent. This is extremely low from a historical perspective (see Figure 15.5). The ten-year rate has been below 3 percent for virtually the entire time from 2011 to 2022, even falling to just over 0.5 percent in mid-2020.

One might think that at such low interest rates, borrowing was especially cheap, making it a good time for the government to run a budget deficit and accumulate debt. It is important to consider, however, that interest rates are likely to rise in the future, increasing the burden of servicing the debt. The argument for adding to federal debt seems stronger

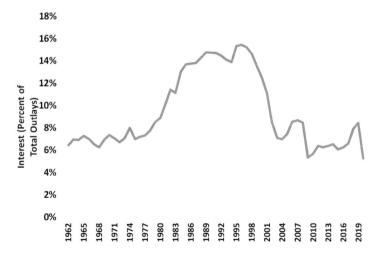

Figure 15.4 *Interest Payments as Percentage of Total Federal Outlays, 1962– 2020*

Source: Federal Reserve Bank of St. Louis, FRED Economic Database.

605

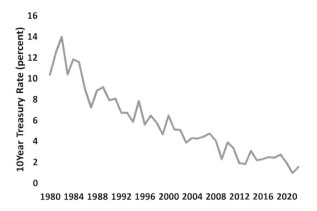

Figure 15.5 *The Interest Rate on Ten-Year Treasury Bonds, 1980–2022*

Source: Federal Reserve Bank of St. Louis, FRED Economic Database.

if the government spends on programs that produce a high multiplier effect (as discussed in Chapter 9). With low interest rates, the gain from the multiplier effect (in terms of the increase in aggregate demand) is potentially larger than the loss (in terms of adding to the debt burden), which would make the net gain positive.

It may be counterproductive, however, to allow the debt to grow if it is financing "low-multiplier" activities. An example is tax cuts for the wealthy, which, as we saw in Chapter 9, do not produce as much "bang for the buck" as tax cuts that benefit lower-income families and individuals, or new spending on constructive activities. A useful way of understanding the problem is to imagine the federal government as a private business. Would a business borrow money at an interest rate higher than its expected rate of return? Of course not. The government's situation is a bit more complicated because it needs to assess the projected "social return" on its expenditures (e.g., a more educated citizenry, better infrastructure). The problem is that it is seldom easy to express the social return in dollars.

Another concern with mounting debt is that if debt relative to GDP becomes sufficiently large, lenders might start to doubt the borrowers' ability to repay. If the doubt were severe and widespread, it could affect the bond market and, as a result, the national economy. Risk-averse investors would sell their bonds, driving bond prices down. When bond prices go down, bond yields (rates of return) go up (as noted in the Appendix to Chapter 11), because the amount that the government has to pay in interest on the bond becomes higher relative to the value of the bond. Any new bonds that are then issued will have to match this higher rate of return, meaning that the government will have to pay more in debt service costs in the future.

The greater the unease over the borrower's ability to pay, the higher the interest rate that the borrower must offer in order to attract lenders. In the summer of 2011 Standard and Poor's, one of the major rating agencies, downgraded U.S. government debt from AAA to AA+ as a result of a political impasse between the Obama Administration and the Republican Congress that created doubt about the reliability of government debt payments. Fortunately for the United States, even with this downgrade, its debt remained very much in demand.

A third potential problem with too much debt concerns exactly how it gets repaid. An indebted country must repay the principal on its debt and service it with interest payments. To do so, it must either engage in new borrowing, raise tax revenues, or, more likely, both. We have seen that increasing tax rates can reduce consumption and investment, affecting GDP growth and employment. New borrowing carries no such problems, though it does postpone repayment further into the future and increases the total size of the debt over time. It is also possible to finance a federal budget deficit with bonds that are purchased by the Fed from the Treasury.[§] If the Fed buys new bonds directly from the Treasury upon issuance, it is known as **monetizing the debt**. In effect, this action combines expansionary fiscal and monetary policy. If, on the other hand, the Fed buys Treasury bonds on the secondary market, it merely amounts to an expansionary monetary policy, as we saw in Chapter 11.

---

monetizing the debt: the purchase of new debt from the Treasury by the Federal Reserve

---

Monetizing the debt risks causing inflation, especially if the increase in the money supply is large and continues over a long period. If such inflation does occur, the bond markets would then demand higher interest rates on new debt to compensate for the anticipated loss from inflation. How serious is this danger? Some economists believe that a mild to moderate increase in inflation is not necessarily a problem, especially if it occurs in a depressed economy facing a looming threat of deflation. As we saw in Chapter 10, deflation would in most circumstances be more dangerous than inflation, while mild inflation has historically been associated with economic recoveries and gains in domestic employment. Severe inflation, however, would be very damaging to the economy, and other economists point to this as a possible long-term result of increasing government debt.

Even moderate inflation carries significant economic risk. The Federal Reserve is likely to respond to observed inflation by raising interest rates—as described in Chapters 11 and 12—thereby restraining economic activity and possibly pushing the economy into recession.

---

§ This process is often described – or depending on one's viewpoint, derided – as "printing money."

Discussion Questions

1. How many different "types" of debt can you think of? Which one do people usually mean when they speak about the "national debt"?
2. What are some potential problems with excessive federal debt? How can the debt be managed or repaid?

4 POLITICAL ECONOMY OF THE DEBT

4.1 Who Owns the Debt?

We have already seen that when the federal government goes into debt, it sells government bonds. But who buys these bonds? It might surprise you to see how ownership of the gross federal debt is divided up. Federal Reserve and U.S. government holdings account for over one-third of the debt (Figure 15.6). We might, in other words, say that the US government owes one-third of its debt to *itself*.

Social Security is the largest of the government accounts that hold federal debt. Among many other funds, the principal ones are the funds for federal employee retirement, federal hospital insurance, and federal disability insurance. State and local governments, perhaps surprisingly, account for another 2.9 percent of federal debt. States and municipalities with budget surpluses will often buy federal debt because it is considered mostly risk-free. The domestic private sector owns 15.7 percent of the federal debt in the form of bonds, which are found in a variety of locations: banks, insurance companies, and mutual funds, among others. Private and public pensions together account for another 5 percent of the total, and individuals, companies, and trusts hold 11.6 percent

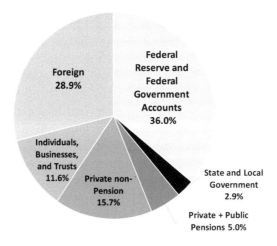

Figure 15.6 *Ownership of Gross Federal Debt, 2019*

Source: Treasury Department, 2021, Tables OFS-1; Distribution of Federal Securities by Class of Investors and Type of Issues, Table OFS-2; Estimated Ownership of US Treasury Securities and Table.

of Federal debt. Finally, foreigners own 28.9 percent of the debt —this is the U.S. external debt.

In 2021, Japan and China together owned more than 30 percent of the external U.S. debt (Figure 15.7), a reflection of the large trade surpluses that the two countries have had with the United States for several decades. As we saw in Chapter 13, when China and Japan export more to the United States than they import from us, they acquire a surplus of U.S. dollars, which they then use to buy U.S. federal debt. Why do they choose to hold U.S. government debt? For the same reason that domestic investors, state and local governments, and the Social Security trust fund trustees do: U.S. federal debt is widely perceived as returning risk-free income.

Eleven countries—the United Kingdom, Ireland, Luxembourg, Switzerland, the Cayman Islands, Brazil, Taiwan, France, Hong Kong, Belgium, and India—accounted for over 40 percent of the U.S. external debt. Other countries collectively owned 27.4 percent of the U.S. external debt as of 2021.

Although in absolute terms the U.S. debt is by far the highest in the world, it is a very different story if we look at total debt in relation to GDP. Japan's ratio of debt to GDP has risen since its economic slowdown started in the 1990s and is currently 256 percent of GDP (Figure 15.8). Nevertheless, Japanese bonds are still bought and traded on the secondary market, which may be a testament to the widespread belief in the stability of the Japanese economy. This is in contrast to Greece, which has had to raise interest rates on its bonds substantially to attract

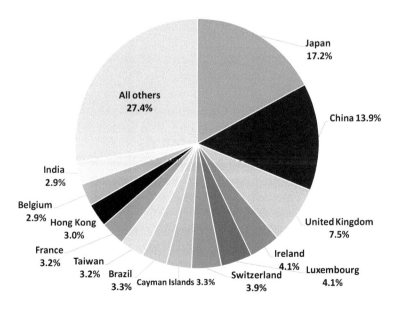

Figure 15.7 *Foreign Holders of Gross Federal Debt, 2021*

Source: *Treasury Department, 2021, Major Foreign Holders of Treasury Securities.*

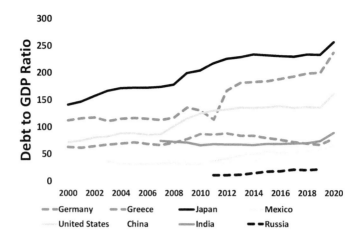

Figure 15.8 *Debt-GDP Ratios, an International Comparison, 2000–2020*

Source: OECD, General Government Debt, www.oecd.org

Note: U.S. debt figures include Federal, state, and local debt.

continued investors. Like Japan, Greece has a high debt to GDP ratio (237 percent) but is clearly considered less creditworthy.

Including state and local debt, the U.S. debt to GDP ratio more than doubled from 72 percent in 2000 to over 161 percent in 2020, impelled by tax cuts, the financial crisis, and the more recent global pandemic. Still, the U.S. situation continues to resemble Japan's, in that growing indebtedness has not noticeably altered investor confidence, allowing the U.S. bond yields to remain relatively low.

4.2 The Twin Deficits

As we have seen, the term "deficit" can refer either to a government's finances or to a country's trade balance. The fact that the two types of deficits are closely linked adds to the not infrequent confusion between the terms. Indeed, our debt to other countries as measured in terms of their ownership of our bonds is related *both* to our budget and trade deficits. Yet as we can see from Figure 15.9, the trend lines do not always move together.

Up until the early to mid-1970s, the trade balance in the United States was around 1 percent of GDP, a relatively insubstantial amount, and frequently changed from surplus to deficit and vice-versa. The federal budget, on the other hand, was consistently in deficit (with a brief exception in 1969), though mostly at less than 2 percent of GDP. Starting in the mid-1970s, however, both the federal budget and the trade balance turned sharply more negative. The United States has failed to run a trade surplus (i.e., exports greater than imports) since then, and its trade deficit has not been below 2 percent of GDP since 1998, reaching almost 6 percent in 2005 and 2006. The federal budget balance has

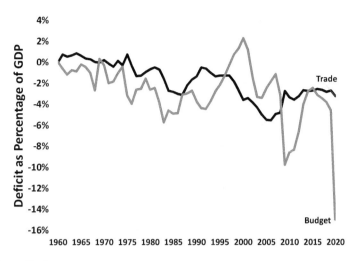

Figure 15.9 *United States Twin Deficits as Percent of GDP, 1960–2020*

Source: CBO and U.S. Census Bureau.

been even more volatile over this 40-year period, swinging from a surplus of more than 2 percent of GDP in the year 2000 (one of only four years since 1969 that the budget was in surplus) to a deficit of almost 15 percent most recently, in 2020.

As discussed in Chapter 13, if a country has positive net exports, it means that it will have a surplus of funds (foreign exchange) to lend to other countries. If, in contrast, a country has negative net exports, it typically must borrow from foreigners, essentially to pay for the difference. If the government budget is in deficit, as also discussed in Chapter 13, this tends to create or increase a trade deficit, unless it is financed by a surplus of domestic savings—which has generally not been the case for the United States. Thus, while the two deficits do not move together in lockstep, the **twin deficits hypothesis** states that they should usually broadly move in the same direction.

---

twin deficits hypothesis: the belief in a causal link between a country's budget balance and its trade balance

---

4.3 The Balanced Budget Debate

If balancing the budget were legally required, the United States could not have accumulated a national debt. Hoping to avoid uncontrolled debt dependence, many in the past have advocated legislation, or even an amendment to the Constitution, requiring that the budget be balanced. While this idea sounds attractive to many people, the economic consequences would be severe.

Most states have a balanced budget requirement that forces them to cut services and government employees during a recession. The federal government often provides aid to allow states to minimize cost cutting, in an attempt to prevent the economy from weakening further. States have no other recourse because, unlike the federal government, they are unable to create additional funds. In large part, this explains why, as discussed in Chapter 9, states (as well as municipalities) often practice "procyclical" instead of countercyclical policy, which tends to worsen rather than counteract recessions.

A balanced budget amendment would effectively make the federal government little different from the states in its budgetary constraints. Proponents argue that such a law would prevent the federal government from imprudently running deficits, potentially causing inflation, in good economic times. But there is a very serious downside, in that such an amendment would make the federal government powerless to use countercyclical policy to fight recessions.

In 1985, Congress passed the Balanced Budget and Emergency Deficit Control Act, more popularly known as the Gramm-Rudman-Hollings act (named after the senators who sponsored it). It required that a limit be set on the annual deficit and that the limit be reduced until a balanced budget was achieved in 1991. While less stringent than a constitutional requirement, the **deficit ceiling** was nevertheless strict. Not meeting it would require spending to be reduced automatically to the point where the deficit was no higher than the prescribed limit for that year. This proved too much for Congress, and even for the Supreme Court, which found the automatic reduction provision unconstitutional.

---

deficit ceiling: a congressionally mandated limit on the size of the federal budget deficit

---

Congress frequently has contentious debates over raising the **debt ceiling**. (This is different from a deficit ceiling. According to rules set by Congress, a vote of Congress is required to increase the debt beyond a set amount, called the debt ceiling.) As the debt approaches the mandated ceiling, the country confronts the prospect of not being able to borrow fresh funds to pay bonds that are coming due for payment. The risk of such a default would be a decline in the perceived creditworthiness of the United States. As noted earlier, in 2011 Standard and Poor's lowered the grade of U.S. Treasury bonds from AAA to AA+ as a result of a debt ceiling crisis, the first time in history that this had happened.

> **debt ceiling:** a congressionally mandated limit on the size of the gross federal debt

Following heated and partisan negotiations, Congress and the President struck a deal in 2011, allowing the debt ceiling to be raised (by about a trillion dollars). Since then, debt ceiling deadlines have become an issue every few years. The debt ceiling was suspended three times during the Trump presidency and recently increased under Biden. In October of 2021, Congress increased the debt ceiling by $480 billion, only to increase it by another $2.5 *trillion* in December of the same year.

The periodic focus on the debt ceiling is in many ways misleading. If Congress and the President want to avoid increasing the debt, they would have to agree on a balanced budget, in which case the debt ceiling would no longer be an issue. But that is a lot easier said than done. A balanced budget would either require drastic cutbacks in popular programs such as Social Security, or significant tax increases. In the long run, of course, it is important to keep debt levels under control, but it is a mistake to presume that the federal government should maintain zero debt. The ability to use deficits at appropriate times to generate a fiscal stimulus is what sets the federal government apart from the states and cities and possibly protects a weak economy from sinking deeper.

An alternative approach to balanced budgets is the principle of **functional finance**, which requires that national governments do their utmost to ensure that aggregate demand remains at a reasonable level, ideally achieving full employment. The assumption behind this principle is that the healthy economy that resulted would ensure that the government could sustainably finance its debt with greater tax revenue. A similar argument that it is more important to focus on current employment than debt levels is put forward by advocates of the Modern Monetary Theory (MMT) school, as discussed in Chapter 11. This point of view is in direct conflict with the perspective of deficit "hawks," who would maintain absolute limits on deficit and debt levels.

> **functional finance:** the idea that a sovereign government should finance current needs and provide for adequate aggregate demand to maintain employment levels

Who are the hawks? This is not a simple question. Republicans have traditionally claimed to be the party of fiscal "prudence" but in fact some of the biggest debt increases have come under Republican administrations. In recent years both Republicans and Democrats have found themselves on either side of the controversy. Those who strongly advocate reducing the deficit often disagree about whether this should be done through spending cuts or tax increases. There are also major differences among those not so concerned about deficits. Keynesians like economist Paul Krugman have long believed that the government should spend more in such areas as infrastructure investment. Most Republican members of Congress, in contrast, believe that the government should be taxing less. From the standpoint of fiscal balance, the two approaches are equivalent. But from an equity standpoint, they are very different. Federal government spending tends to benefit the broad population, while major tax cuts, including the Reagan tax cuts of the 1980s, the Bush tax cuts of the 2000s, and the Trump tax cuts of 2017, have disproportionately benefited the well-off.[1] As noted in Chapter 14, tax cuts that primarily benefit upper-income groups have contributed to the recent intensification of inequality in the United States.

Discussion Questions

1. Should there be a balanced budget amendment to the Constitution? What problems might such an amendment create?
2. What is the difference between the budget deficit and the trade deficit? Are they related? How?

5 DEFICIT PROJECTIONS AND POTENTIAL POLICY RESPONSES

5.1 Deficit Projections

The U.S. annual federal deficit declined from a peak of 10 percent of GDP in 2009 to 2.4 percent of GDP in fiscal 2015 (Figure 15.10). It then increased again, shooting up to nearly 15 percent of GDP in

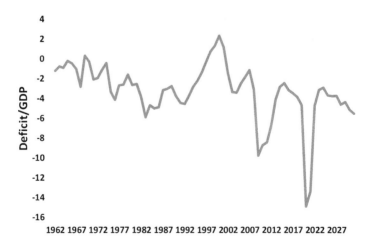

Figure 15.10 *Annual Deficit as a Percent of GDP, Actual and Projected 1962–2031*

Source: Congressional Budget Office, 2021.

Note: Data from 2020 to 2031 are projected.

614

response to the global pandemic. The Congressional Budget Office (CBO), which provides non-partisan economic analysis for Congress, expects the deficit to remain in double digits for 2021 and projects that the deficit will then drop sharply and remain at 3–5 percent of GDP for the remainder of the decade.[2] This is greater than the annual average of about 3.3 percent over the past 50 years, implying a continual increase in overall federal debt.[3]

Figure 15.11 *Federal Debt Held by the Public as a Percent of GDP, Actual and Projected 1962–2031*

Source: Congressional Budget Office, 2021.

Note: Data from 2020 to 2031 are projected.

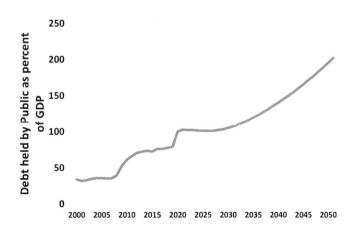

Figure 15.12 *Federal Debt Held by the Public a Percent of GDP, Long-Term Projection 2000–2051*

Source: Congressional Budget Office, 2021.

Note: Data from 2020 to 2050 are projected.

The federal debt held by the public is accordingly projected to increase slightly from about 100 percent of GDP in 2020 to about 106 percent by 2031 (Figure 15.11). But the longer-term outlook is more severe (see Figure 15.12). According to a CBO analysis conducted one year into the COVID-19 pandemic, "Federal debt held by the public will reach double the size of the economy, rising from 79 percent of GDP at the end of 2019 and 100 percent of GDP at the end of Fiscal Year FY 2020 to 202 percent of GDP by 2051. Projected debt in 2051 will be over 4.5 times the 50-year average of 44 percent of GDP and will be on track to double the previous record of 106 percent of GDP a few years later."

In addition to insufficient revenue—a problem aggravated by Trump's 2017 tax cuts (Box 15.1)—there are other factors contributing to the projections that deficits will remain at relatively high levels, causing a

---

BOX 15.1 TRUMP'S MOST ENDURING LEGACY?

The Trump tax cuts of 2017 have left a legacy of insufficient revenue that will seriously affect budgetary management for decades.

The growth in the annual deficit under Trump ranks as the third-biggest increase, relative to the size of the economy, of any US presidential administration, according to a calculation by Eugene Steuerle, cofounder of the Urban-Brookings Tax Policy Center. And unlike George W. Bush and Abraham Lincoln, who oversaw the larger relative increases in deficits, Trump did not launch two foreign conflicts or have to pay for a civil war.[4]

Federal finances under Trump had already deteriorated before the pandemic, as revenues fell as a percent of GDP following the tax cuts. Major spending increases in response to the pandemic then caused both the deficit and the debt to soar.

After he took office, Trump predicted that economic growth created by the 2017 tax cut, would help eliminate the budget deficit and let the United States begin to pay down its debt. On July 27, 2018, he told Fox News's Sean Hannity, 'We have $21 trillion in debt. When [the 2017 tax cut] really kicks in, we'll start paying off that debt like it's water.' That's not how it played out. Trump's tax cuts, especially the sharp reduction in the corporate tax rate to 21 percent from 35 percent, took a big bite out of federal revenue.

The actual amount of revenue collected in FY2018 was significantly lower than the Congressional Budget Office's (CBO) projection of FY2018 revenue made in January 2017—before the tax cuts were signed into law in December 2017. The shortfall was $275 billion, or 7.6% of revenues that were expected before the tax cuts took place.[5]

As of Dec. 31, 2020, the national debt had jumped to $27.75 trillion, up 39 percent from $19.95 trillion when Trump was sworn in ... about $23,500 in new federal debt for every person in the country.[6]

Analyses have also shown that the overall effects have largely benefited corporations and wealthy Americans more than middle-class and low-wage workers. The corporate tax cuts, in particular, failed to translate to the promised wage and economic growth.[7]

significant increase in total debt over time. First are the demographic pressures of an aging population. According to estimates from the US Census, 21 percent of the country's population will be 65 or older by 2030—compared to 17 percent today—after which the elderly population will only continue growing until at least 2060. What this means is that a smaller share of the US population will be working to support a greater share of retirees, putting further strain on government finances.

Second, US health care costs are projected to continue increasing. According to the Centers for Medicare and Medicaid Services, national health care spending is expected to grow at an average annual rate of 5.4 percent, significantly faster than projected GDP growth. The two factors are closely related and suggest that a focus on health care should be an important component of any significant long-term budgetary reforms in the United States. Social Security and Medicare taxes and outlays are, as we have seen, considered "off budget." In other words, Social Security taxes are dedicated to financing Social Security benefits, not military or social expenditures. One might, therefore, justifiably question whether old-age or health-related taxes and spending should be affected by the debate over the deficit.

The reality is, unfortunately, more complex. Since, as noted earlier, one of the many federal government creditors (i.e., buyers of Treasury bonds) is the Social Security trust fund itself, many of the hundreds of billions of dollars held in the fund are invested in government debt. Social Security recipients are therefore, in part, paid from the income as federal debt held by the Social Security system comes due. This reinforces concerns about the future sustainability of the deficit. As the number of retirees grows relative to the working age population (which contributes to Social Security taxes), full payment of Social Security benefits will require an additional contribution from the federal budget, increasing the size of the deficit. If nothing changed, the government could eventually face a choice between paying Social Security beneficiaries or other creditors (see Box 15.2).

BOX 15.2 HOW CAN THE UNITED STATES SALVAGE SOCIAL SECURITY?

In a 2016 report to Congress, the Social Security Board of Trustees projected that the [Social Security] program's funds will be depleted by 2034, after which only 79 percent of what was promised to American retirees will be paid out. The "crisis" of Social Security isn't that it's going bankrupt or that there won't be any benefits paid out after 2034. It's that the system may not be able to pay all of what retirees put in and were promised—an issue that, according to many polls, is very important to many Americans both young and elderly.

What can be done to put Social Security on a sounder basis before 2034? A number of possible solutions have been proposed:

- Raising the payroll tax by about 2 percent. This would be enough to make Social Security solvent for the next 75 years.[8]
- Raising or eliminating the cap on the Social Security payroll tax. The Social Security tax only applies to income earned below a certain threshold—$147,000 in 2022. It is thus regressive, taking a higher proportion of income from lower-income taxpayers. Eliminating the cap would make the tax less regressive by requiring more affluent taxpayers to contribute more.
- Raising the retirement age, which would reduce the amount of benefits paid out over the lifetime of recipients.
- Indexing benefits to inflation using techniques such as the chained CPI (discussed in Chapter 4) that yield a smaller annual increase in benefits.

There really are only two basic answers to the Social Security problem: increase revenue or reduce benefits. Any potential solution will thus run into political opposition from those who would pay higher taxes or receive lower benefits. To be politically feasible, any potential compromise needs to be perceived as fair as well as effective in preserving income security for everyone in the system. Measures such as raising the retirement age would disproportionately harm lower-income individuals, as they rely more heavily on Social Security benefits, and would therefore be likely to encounter significant political opposition.

Rejecting the idea of reducing benefits, Senator Elizabeth Warren has proposed an across-the-board *increase* in Social Security benefits and in Supplementary Security income for people with disabilities. She proposes to pay for this with a substantial increase in contributions from upper-income taxpayers:

a new 14.8 percent payroll tax on individuals who earn more than $250,000 a year, to be split by workers and their employers, and a 14.8 percent tax on investment income that would apply to the top 2 percent of earners.[9]

This would convert the Social Security tax from a regressive tax (with lower-income people paying a higher proportion of income in tax) to a progressive tax (with higher-income people paying a higher proportion).

The issues of meeting growing needs and diminishing tax revenues are linked. Assuming that the CBO projections on deficit increases are correct, lower tax receipts will aggravate problems such as the adequate funding of Social Security and health costs. Advocates of the 2017 tax cuts argued that the positive effect of the tax cuts on the economy would, over the long term, bring in higher revenues—essentially the "supply-side" argument discussed earlier. But the overall effect of the cuts has been shown to be higher, not lower, deficits.

In addition, it is broadly assumed that the historically low interest rates of the past decade are unsustainable. When rates *do* go up, a significant increase in interest payments on the federal debt is likely. Although the lending rate was only around 1 percent in 2020, the federal budget could eventually be hit with an annual interest charge several times what it currently pays. Such an event would make an already difficult debt problem that much more difficult to handle.

5.2 Future Policy Choices

Given these foreseeable issues with debt and deficits, the principle that the United States requires long-term budgetary reform is widely accepted. The basic math dictates that the choices are limited to revenue (i.e., tax) increases, spending cuts, or—most realistically—some combination of the two.

The controversial issues concern *which* taxes should be increased (and for whom), and *which* expenditures should be cut. The recent patterns of federal spending and revenues give some indications of what the options for the future may be. After generally declining in the two decades following 1980, federal spending increased from 17.7 percent of GDP in 2000 to 31.2 percent in 2020. The spike in federal spending in 2020 was pandemic-induced (the ratio was 21 percent in 2019), and the CBO expects the number to taper into the 21–23 percent range for the remainder of the decade. But this is still significantly higher than projected revenues, which are not expected to exceed about 18 percent of GDP.[10]

New challenges that will unquestionably be costly to address include climate change, future pandemics, and supporting an aging population. The United States will need to confront these challenges while trying to reduce—or at least stabilize—its debt as a percent of GDP. Therefore, as controversial as they are, revenue (i.e., tax) increases will likely be essential.

Experience has taught us that tax cuts tend to increase the deficit because they fail to promote sufficient growth to increase overall tax revenues. But we also know that tax increases have the potential to dampen economic activity. The main difficulty, then, will be to address the country's upcoming challenges while achieving fiscal stability.

Possible policies to consider can be summarized as follows:

- Increase revenues through growth-promoting policies. Of course, the *type* of growth matters. As noted in Chapter 9, responding to climate change is likely to require major "green" infrastructure changes, with the potential to create many new jobs. To lower deficits, this job creation must generate sufficient tax revenue to pay for them in the long term.
- Eliminating government subsidies for fossil-fuel and chemical-intensive industries would generate revenue, but there may be a case for moving these subsidies to sectors relying on renewable energy and environmentally efficient approaches. This would be an effective climate policy but might mean no net revenue increase.

619

- Tax reform, such as lowering rates for middle-class earners, while closing loopholes that allow the wealthy to avoid taxes and repealing tax cuts for upper-income individuals and large corporations.
- Instituting a general wealth tax as a reliable means of generating revenue. Another possibility is to introduce a tax on financially speculative transactions—such as futures and derivatives trading—as an indirect means of encouraging economically productive investment, while raising revenue.
- Increase revenue through environmentally oriented taxes such as taxes on carbon emissions or (federal) consumption taxes. These would require rebates or dividends for lower-income taxpayers in order to avoid a regressive impact (since the poor on average spend a greater percentage of their income).
- Reduce "mandatory" spending on programs such as Social Security, Medicare, Medicaid, and the Affordable Care Act. Cuts to these programs are likely to increase inequity, but spending reductions could be achieved through holding down health care costs, which has already been achieved to some extent in Medicare and through Affordable Care Act provisions.
- Increase efficiency of spending in health care and other areas, seeking more "bang for the buck" including state/federal and public/private collaboration initiatives. This is especially critical in anticipation of future pandemics and other health crises that experts predict.
- To the extent that any of these policies can be successful in reducing deficits and long-term growth of the debt, interest costs will also be reduced.
- While there is broad agreement that some combination of these policies will be needed to avoid a long-term increase in debt, the question of which policies to implement will remain controversial.

5.3 Debt and Deficits in Context

The debate over debts and deficits should be placed in a larger macroeconomic context as well as a social and environmental context. Given the strong negative impacts of wide inequalities on the social and economic health of a society, it makes sense that major federal policies, regarding both spending and taxing, should emphasize reducing inequality. Addressing environmental concerns and improving infrastructure are also important priorities.

Our review of the history of debt and deficits indicates that neither is inherently bad for the economy, and that deficits in times of recession are often essential to helping the economy recover. But some degree of balance is required. Deficits must be limited as a percent of GDP, and long-term increases in the debt burden should be avoided. Some combination of the policies we have discussed can promote both a healthy economy and a manageable debt.

620

Gaining sufficient political support for such policies will represent a major challenge, but perhaps not an insurmountable one since some aspects, such as greater tax equity and job-creating investment, may prove politically popular.

Discussion Questions

1. Do you think that we can reduce deficits while also avoiding an increase in tax rates? Why would political leaders consider tax hikes? Should everyone experience the same increase?
2. Are there tax policies that can reduce the deficit while also addressing social and environmental problems?

REVIEW QUESTIONS

1. What is the difference between the national debt and a deficit?
2. What years were debt/GDP levels the highest in the United States? What years were the lowest?
3. What was the role of the national debt in the early period of U.S. history? What was Hamilton's vision for the U.S national debt?
4. How did the national debt picture change with the New Deal and World War II?
5. What factors contributed to the federal surplus during the Clinton administration, and why did it turn into a deficit in the following Bush administration?
6. Summarize some of the potential problems with government debt.
7. What does it mean to monetize the debt?
8. How do European policies of austerity differ from U.S. policies reading debt and deficits?
9. What do we mean by "twin deficits"? How are the two types of deficits related?
10. What are the pros and cons of a balanced budget amendment? What are some other policies that could be used to limit the growth of national debt?

EXERCISES

1. Go to Federal Reserve Economic Database (https://fred.stlouisfed.org) and look in categories/national accounts for recent data on the U.S. national debt as a percent of GDP and recent figures on budget deficits. What does this tell you about recent trends? Compare the period 1990–2007 to more recent years. Do the figures indicate that we may be returning to a more "normal" situation regarding debt and deficits?
2. Search the internet and locate relatively recent debt/GDP data for European countries. Construct a table of Eurozone members and their debt/GDP ratios based on your search. Review the convergence criteria for participation in the Eurozone presented in this chapter. Don't forget to document your source(s)! What did you discover in this exercise? Explain your answer.
3. This chapter identifies and explains several reasons why it is inappropriate to compare the government debt to the debt of a private citizen. Which of these explanations are consistent with the presentation in this chapter?

a) Governments have the ability to "roll over" their debt more or less endlessly.
b) Governments cannot default on their debt obligations.
c) A significant portion of the government debt is owed to U.S. citizens.
d) The U.S. government pays interest on its debt in dollars that it prints.
e) Government debt is always used to finance investments.

4. This chapter identifies and explains several reasons why we are likely to observe relatively high deficits in the United States even as the economy stabilizes. Which of these explanations is consistent with this chapter's presentation?
a) Health care costs are expected to continue to increase.
b) Young adults are having too many children and that creates demographic pressures.
c) Federal subsidies for health care are expected to grow.
d) The rising costs of higher education will contribute to deficits.
e) Interest payments on the debt will likely increase in the future.

5. This chapter is very clear that it's dangerous to assume that "government debt is never a concern." Which of the following are reasons articulated in this chapter for why debt can be a concern?
a) Foreign holders of U.S. debt may decide to sell their bonds.
b) A larger share of future budgets must be devoted to interest payments.
c) It is always unwise for governments to get into debt
d) Interest payments to high-income individuals could exacerbate income inequality.
e) Deficit spending during a recession will only make the economic downturn worse.

6. Match each concept in Column A with a definition or example in Column B.

Column A		Column B
a. Debt	1.	The portion of the gross federal debt that is owed to individuals or groups within the country
b. Deficit	2.	A congressionally mandated limit on the size of the federal debt
c. Gross federal debt	3.	The portion of the gross federal debt that is owed to foreign individuals or groups
d. Debt held by the public	4.	A stock variable that represents the accumulation of deficits over many years
e. Internal debt	5.	The gross federal debt minus the debt owed to other government accounts such as Social Security and Medicare
f. External debt	6.	A policy of deficit cutting that reduces public expenditures and/ or raises taxes to balance the budget
g. Monetizing the debt	7.	A flow variable that measures the excess of spending over revenue collections
h. Debt ceiling	8.	The requirements that EU countries must satisfy as a condition for participating in the Eurozone
i. Austerity	9.	The purchase of new debt from the Treasury Department by the Federal Reserve
j. Convergence criteria	10.	Total amount owed by the federal government to all claimants, including foreigners, the public in the United States, and other government accounts

NOTES

1   See for example Croucher, 2019.
2   Congressional Budget Office, 2021.
3   Congressional Budget Office, 2021.
4   Sloan and Podkul, 2021.
5   Gale, 2020.
6   Sloan and Podkul, 2021.
7   Amadeo, 2021.
8   Lam, 2016.
9   Rappeport and Tankersley, 2019.
10   Congressional Budget Office, 2021.

REFERENCES

Amadeo, Kimberley. 2021. "How much Trump's tax cuts cost the government: tax cuts under the Trump Administration increased the deficit and debt." *The Balance*, November 19.

Congressional Budget Office. 2021. "The 2021 Long-term Budget Outlook." https://www.cbo.gov/publication/57038

Croucher, Shane. 2019. "Trump's 2017 Tax Cuts Helped Super-rich Pay Lower Rate Than Bottom 50 Percent" *Newsweek,* October 9.

Gale, William G. 2020. "Did the 2017 Tax Cut—the Tax Cuts and Jobs Act—Pay for Itself?" *Brookings Institute,* February 14.

Lam, Bouree. 2016. "How Can the U.S. Salvage Social Security? *The Atlantic,* April 5.

Rappeport, Alan, and Jim Tankersley. 2019. "Elizabeth Warren's Social Security Plan: Raise Benefits by $200 a Month." *New York Times,* September 12.

Sloan, Allan, and Podkul, Cezary. 2021. "Trump's Most Enduring Legacy Could Be the Historic Rise in the National Debt." *The Washington Post*, January 14.

Chapter 16

How Economies Grow and Develop

The median income in the world today is about equal to that of the United States in the early 1900s. Although billions of people still live in severe poverty, some formerly poor countries such as South Korea have achieved high levels of economic development, and others such as China and India have experienced rapid growth in the last few decades. Many others have experienced little economic progress. It is both interesting and important to evaluate how economies grow, and why some countries are very successful at promoting economic development, while others seem to be "stuck" at low levels of development.

Our discussion in this chapter is mainly focused on what are known as developing countries, where there is a clear need for improving people's access to basic needs for food, shelter, health care, and education. But it is worth noting that the term "development" can be used for *all* kinds of positive economic change and thus could also be applied to countries even after they have successfully achieved greater wealth and industrialization. That is an issue to which we return in Chapter 17, where we will take a look at the changes that will be required both in wealthier countries and in rapidly developing countries such as China if the global economy is to achieve a sustainable balance with its ecological context.

1 ECONOMIC GROWTH AND DEVELOPMENT

What do people mean by development? Standard economic models focus on GDP per capita as the key measure of economic progress. But as we have discussed extensively in Chapter 5, focusing only on GDP provides a very narrow measure of well-being, since it overlooks important aspects like quality of healthcare, education, housing, and environmental considerations, as well as overall life satisfaction, and inequalities among genders, classes, and regions. Growth in GDP may be best seen as an intermediate goal or a means to achieve the final goal of enhancing human well-being. Economists have increasingly recognized the need to consider broad-based human development, and to formulate development policies balancing the goal of GDP growth with the promotion of human development goals.

DOI: 10.4324/9781003251521-21

Such an approach has been championed by Nobel laureate Amartya Sen, for whom the relevant concept is not *economic development* but *human development*. The **human development** approach (introduced in Chapter 5) is geared toward meeting basic needs and also encompassing other dimensions of a worthwhile life. Sen defines development as the process of enlarging people's choices, whatever it is that people have reason to value. He has proposed that one's **capabilities**—that is, the opportunities that people have to be well-nourished, decently housed, have access to education, and in many other ways live lives that they find worthwhile—are more important than a simple income measure. This requires a multidimensional approach that focuses on adequate access to clean water, nutrition, shelter, health care, and education, along with issues such as environmental sustainability, economic equality, and gender equality.

---

human development: an approach to development that stresses the provision of basic needs such as food, shelter, and health care

capabilities: the opportunities that people have to pursue important aspects of well-being, such as being healthy and having access to education

---

We begin this section by looking at two of the most commonly used indicators of economic progress—economic growth and poverty. At least during the earlier stages of development, economic growth generally goes hand in hand with improvements in quality of life. In addition, measures of poverty can also help us understand how countries are doing in terms of general development. We will then discuss how these indicators relate to outcomes in inequality and other well-being indicators more broadly.

1.1 Standard Economic Growth Theory

Recall from our discussion in Chapter 4 that economic growth is defined as an increase in real GDP (i.e., GDP adjusted for inflation). Mathematically, it is expressed as the percentage change in real GDP from one year to the next. It is often more meaningful to focus on the growth rate of GDP *per capita*—that is, output *per person*—rather than simply on overall output, because GDP per capita growth indicates the actual increase in average income being experienced by the people of the country. Mathematically, GDP per capita is expressed as:

$$\text{GDP per capita} = \text{GDP/population}$$

625

The growth rates of GDP, population, and GDP per capita are related in the following way (where the sign $\approx$ means "approximately equals"):

$$\text{Growth rate of GDP} \approx \text{Growth rate of population} + \text{growth rate of GDP per capita}$$

or:

$$\text{Growth rate of GDP per capita} \approx \text{Growth rate of GDP} - \text{growth rate of population}$$

Thus, for example, an economy that has a GDP growth rate of 4 percent and a population growth rate of 2 percent would have a per capita GDP growth rate of approximately 2 percent. If a country had a 2 percent GDP growth rate, but a 3 percent population growth rate, its per capita GDP growth rate would actually be negative, at -1 percent. The people would on average be getting poorer each year, even though the overall economy is growing. Thus, for people's incomes on average to increase over time, the GDP growth rate must exceed the rate of population growth.

In terms of the aggregate supply and demand graphs that we used in Chapter 12, economic growth can be shown as a rightward shift of the aggregate supply (AS), increasing the economy's maximum capacity (Figure 16.1). If this kind of increase in aggregate supply took place without any shift in aggregate demand (AD), its effects would include growth in output and a declining rate of inflation. In practice, however, economic growth is almost always accompanied by, and is often caused at least in part by, an increase in aggregate demand. Thus, a more typical pattern for economic growth would be for *both* the AD and AS curves to shift to the right, as shown in Figure 16.1. In this case, output clearly rises, but the effect on inflation is ambiguous.

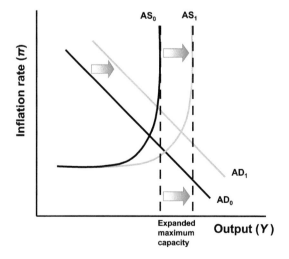

Figure 16.1 *Economic Growth in the AS/AD Model*

1.2 Experiences of Economic Growth around the World

Much of the economic development that has shaped the world we know today occurred during the twentieth century when real income in the United States rose about sevenfold, and world per capita economic output grew about fivefold. Figure 16.2 shows the record of global growth since 1971. Gross world product went up by a factor of 4.3 during this period (in inflation-adjusted terms). This was accompanied by increases in energy use and food production, both by a factor of about 3. Even though the world population more than doubled over the period 1971–2020, food production and living standards grew more rapidly than population, leading to a steady increase in per capita income.

This economic growth has been very unevenly distributed among countries, as well as among people within countries. Table 16.1 shows the per capita national incomes and rates of economic growth for selected countries and income category groups during 1990–2020. The table gives national income in purchasing power parity (PPP) terms, which compares countries based on the relative buying power of incomes.*

We see that some countries achieved less than 1 percent annual per capita economic growth, and others achieved more than 4 percent, with China in the lead at a sizzling 8.3 percent. Some already poor countries, such as Haiti and the Democratic Republic of Congo, are becoming even poorer. The average growth rate of the middle-income countries

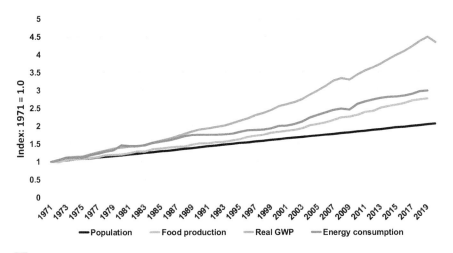

Figure 16.2 *Global Growth in Population, Food Production, Economic Production, and Energy Consumption, 1971–2020*

Sources: World Bank, World Development Indicators; BP, 2017; FAO, 2022.

Note: GWP is gross world product. All variables are indexed, with 1971 = 1.0

---

* As discussed in Chapter 13, purchasing power parity accounts for differences in purchasing power across countries based on the cost of living.

Table 16.1 *Income, Growth, and Population Comparisons of Selected Countries and Country Groups*

Country or Category	GDP per capita, 2020 (PPP, 2017, US$)	Percent growth in GDP per capita (annual average, 1990–2020)	Percent of the world population (2020)
High Income	48,028	1.4	15.7
Hong Kong	56,154	2.3	0.1
United States	60,287	1.3	4.2
Japan	40,232	0.8	1.6
France	42,313	0.8	0.9
South Korea	42,381	4.3	0.7
Middle Income	11,224	3.3	75.4
Russia	26,456	0.8	1.9
Turkey	28,393	3.0	1.1
Brazil	14,064	0.8	2.7
China	16,316	8.3	18.2
India	6,166	4.2	17.8
Low Income	1,988	0.5	8.6
Bangladesh	4,871	3.9	2.1
Nepal	3,800	2.9	0.4
Haiti	2,934	−0.6	0.1
Ethiopia	2,297	3.7	1.5
Congo, DR	1,082	−1.8	1.2

Source: World Bank, World Development Indicators Database, 2022.

appears to be well above that of either the high or low income. This is primarily a result of rapid growth in China and India, which together account for more than half the population of all middle-income countries.

Traditionally, many economists have argued that the economies of low- and middle-income countries should be expected to grow faster than those of high-income countries. One line of reasoning for this view is that poorer countries should be able to benefit from technologies and knowledge that have already been developed in wealthier countries and experience higher growth rates. Economic theory also suggests that a given increase in the manufactured capital stock should lead to a greater increase in output in a country that is capital-poor than in a country that is already capital-rich. Therefore, as developing countries build up their capital stocks, it should be just a matter of time until they "catch up" with the more developed countries. This idea that poorer countries are on a path to "catch up" is often referred to as **convergence**.

> **convergence** (in reference to economic growth): the idea that underlying economic forces will cause poorer countries and regions to "catch up" with richer ones

Some studies of GDP per capita growth rates, using data such as that in Table 16.1, emphasize that low-income countries have grown more rapidly, on average, than high-income ones. However, the average annual growth rate of real GDP per capita (PPP) from 1990–2020 was 0.5 percent in low-income countries, 3.3 percent in middle-income countries, and 1.4 percent in high-income countries—suggesting convergence between currently middle and high-income countries, but further divergence between low-income countries and others. It is also true that if a rich country and a poor one are experiencing the same *percentage* growth rate, this adds a great deal more income in the rich country than in the poor one, thus widening the gap between them in absolute terms. A recent study examining the growth records of 182 countries over the period 1950–2010 finds no evidence of convergence in growth between developed and developing countries.[1]

With their recent high growth rates, China and India represent the "good news" side of the development story. Although many people in these two very populous countries remain very poor, at least the trend is going in the right direction, with a large number of people being lifted out of poverty in recent decades. The countries of sub-Saharan Africa, which have been hit particularly hard by AIDS and war, account for a substantial proportion of the very low and negative growth rates. This is the "bad news" side of contemporary development. Far from "developing," countries such as Haiti and DR Congo have actually become poorer in recent decades. In addition, as discussed in Chapter 14, the gap between the rich and poor countries widened further during the COVID-19 pandemic, as the impacts of the pandemic fell disproportionately on the world's poorest.

1.3 Measures and Trends in Poverty

How do we determine whether someone is poor or not? One approach that is commonly used by development organizations and researchers working in villages in poor countries is to gather local people to collect information about housing conditions and access to basic resources and varying income levels. Known as **participatory rural assessment**, this approach usually provides researchers with a good understanding of community needs and helps them design poverty alleviation strategies. This approach to collecting data has some limitations. There may be biases in responses collected, for example, some people may be inclined to report themselves or their friends or family as being poor if they expect to benefit from poverty alleviation programs. Additionally, it is not feasible to use this approach to collect data at regional or national levels. Hence, we must consider some other poverty measures to gain a broader understanding of poverty trends and examine where economic growth is most needed and what role it plays in development.

> **participatory rural assessment:** an approach to identifying the poor by collecting information from local people about housing conditions, poverty levels, and access to resources

1.3.1 Headcount and Poverty line

One common approach is to define poverty as the percentage of the population below what is known as the **poverty line**. One international poverty line that is often used as a minimum standard to escape extreme poverty is US$1.90 per day. According to this measure, many developing countries have succeeded in reducing the incidence of poverty. For example, from 1981 to 2019, Brazil had an average annual growth rate in per capita GDP of only 1 percent, yet this was sufficient to reduce its poverty rate from 21.5 to 4.6 percent (Table 16.2). Countries with higher growth rates, such as China and India, have experienced even larger declines in poverty rates. But growth in GDP per capita does not guarantee a decline in poverty rates. For example, Zimbabwe actually saw an *increase* in poverty, despite an average growth in GDP of about 3 percent. This increase in poverty was mainly explained by the rising prices of food and fuel due to climatic shocks that have affected food production and hit the poor the hardest.[2]

> **poverty line:** the income threshold below which members of a population are classified as poor

This comparison among countries is made relatively easy through the use of a universal standard, such as the US$1.90-per-day threshold. This minimum poverty threshold is often explained as the cost of obtaining enough food to survive. While this measure draws attention to the poorest people in the world, it excludes the poor population in wealthier countries, who still struggle with meeting basic necessities such as food and housing. Hence, almost all countries also have their own (national) poverty line and calculate their national poverty rate based on it. The threshold for the United States, for example, is about US$26,500 per year for a family of four. According to the U.S. Census Bureau, an estimated 37.2 million (11.4 percent) Americans lived in poverty in 2020.

Table 16.2 *Growth Rates and Changes in Poverty Rates based on $1.90/day Poverty Line of Selected Countries*

	Period	Annual growth rate in per capita GDP (%)	Poverty rate at beginning of period (%)	Poverty rate at end of period (%)
Bangladesh	1991–2016	3.7	43.5	14.3
Brazil	1990–2019	1.0	21.5	4.6
China	1990–2016	8.8	66.3	0.5
Egypt	1990–2017	2.3	8.7	3.8
Ethiopia	1995–2015	4.9	69	30.8
India	1983–2011	4.1	56.4	22.5
Indonesia	1990-2019	3.5	54.9	2.7
Mexico	1992–2018	1.0	7.4	1.7
Philippines	2000–2018	3.6	13.7	2.7
Rwanda	2000–2016	5.1	78	56.5
South Africa	1993–2014	1.4	31.5	18.7
Thailand	1990–2019	3.6	9.2	0.1
Zimbabwe	2011–2019	2.9	5.2	13.4

Source: World Bank, World Development Indicators Database, 2022.

Note: The poverty rate is based on a poverty line of $1.90 per day (2011 PPP).

Both national and universal poverty lines are typically referred to as "headcount" measures since they simply require the "counting" of people who fall below the poverty line. One problem with using the headcount ratio to measure poverty is that it neglects people who are just above the poverty line but still struggle to meet basic needs. Additionally, policymakers focused on reducing the headcount ratio might have an incentive to give small amounts of money to those just below the poverty line to lift the maximum number of people out of poverty, rather than reaching out to the poorest of the poor. An alternative measure that addresses this issue is the poverty gap index, which measures the average income shortfall from the poverty line and focuses on the amount of resources needed to eliminate poverty. Measuring poverty based exclusively on income reflects only a small part of the poverty picture. More broad-based measures of poverty include other aspects of life as well, and we will examine these also.

1.3.2 The Multidimensional Poverty Index

The multidimensional poverty index (MPI) is based on Amartya Sen's capabilities approach. It was developed in 2010 by the Oxford Poverty and Human Development Initiative for the United Nations Development Programme's *Human Development Report*. The MPI considers several elements that are critical for a decent life, in the areas of physical living standards, education, and health.

Figure 16.3 illustrates how the MPI index of poverty is constructed. The three main dimensions of poverty—health, education, and living standards—each receives one-third of the weight, and each of these dimensions is measured by different indicators. Health outcomes are measured by nutrition levels and child mortality rate; education outcomes are measured by years of schooling and school attendance; and living standards are measured using six indicators of living conditions and asset values. The numbers in the parenthesis in Figure 16.3 represent the weight given to each indicator. A person is identified as multi-dimensionally poor if he or she is deprived of one-third or more of the ten weighted indicators included. Though the 10 indicators in the figure are not the only essentials, they are good proxies for essential categories of well-being.

According to a 2020 report from the Oxford Poverty and Human Development Initiative, a total of 1.3 billion people (22 percent of the population in 107 developing countries) are living in multidimensional poverty, meaning they are deprived in one-third or more of the 10 dimensions used in MPI. Among these, 41 percent live in South Asia and 43 percent in sub-Saharan Africa.

It is interesting to compare the data for poverty rates based on MPI with the "less than US$1.90 a day" (income-poor) approach (see Table 16.3). In most cases, the percentage of population that is "MPI poor" is greater than the percentage of population that is income poor. Only 26 out of 107 countries, including Brazil, Malawi, Rwanda, Zimbabwe, and Georgia, had more people living under US$1.90 a day than those counted as being in multidimensional poverty. Some of the largest

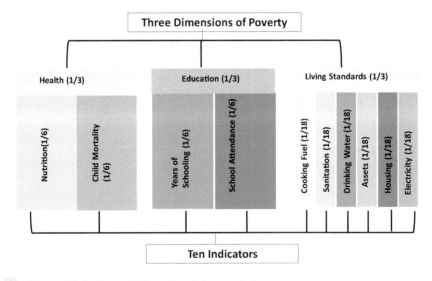

Figure 16.3 *The Multidimensional Poverty Index*

Source: Oxford Poverty and Human Development Initiative

Table 16.3 *Population in Multidimensional Poverty and Income Poverty*

Country	Year	Population in multidimensional Poverty (%)	Population living below income poverty line PPP $1.90 a day (%)
Bangladesh	2019	24.6	14.3
China	2014	3.9	0.5
Ethiopia	2019	68.7	30.8
Ghana	2017/18	24.6	12.7
Haiti	2016/17	41.3	24.5
India	2015/16	27.9	22.5
Mexico	2016	6.6	1.7
Nepal	2019	17.5	15
Niger	2012	91	45.4
Philippines	2017	5.8	2.7
Rwanda	2014/15	54.4	56.5
Vietnam	2013/14	3.9	3.1

Source: Multidimensional Poverty Index 2021 Statistical Data Table 1.

discrepancies between the levels of "income poor" and "MPI poor" were in African countries like Ethiopia, Niger, and Uganda. Such discrepancies reveal the limitations of relying exclusively on income-based poverty measures.

1.4 Income and Economic Well-Being

Countries with lower income levels generally perform more poorly on many well-being indicators. Take, for example, the effect of poverty on the health of the population in a country. Figure 16.4 plots one proxy for health—average life expectancies—against GDP per capita, with spheres proportional to the population of the country represented. A curve is drawn to fit the general pattern made by the data points. On the far left-hand side of the figure, we see that living in a very poor country, such as Nigeria, dramatically increases the chance that one will die prematurely, compared with living in a country with a somewhat higher GDP per capita, such as India or China. Life expectancy is even greater in countries with higher income including Japan, Germany, and the United States. However, at high-income levels, we see that the positive relationship between income and life expectancy essentially disappears as the curve flattens out.

At high incomes, in fact, inequality within countries—not income per capita—may be a more important factor in determining health and life expectancy. For example, the United States, which has one of the

633

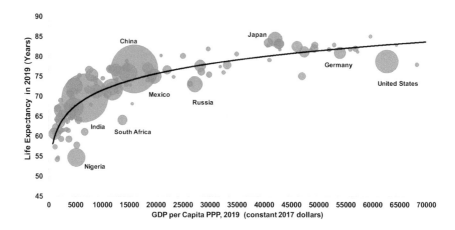

Figure 16.4 *The Relation Between Life Expectancy and Income, with Area Proportional to Population, 2019*

Source: World Bank, World Development Indicators Database, 2022.

highest inequality levels among the advanced countries, also has lower life expectancy and higher infant mortality rates than other advanced countries. Inequality is also positively associated with a range of negative social outcomes, including mental health and the incidence of violence.[3] A recent study based on survey data from 180,000 individuals from 51 countries over 24 years (1990–2014) finds that higher inequality is associated with lower life satisfaction and lower happiness levels for individuals in both high-income and low-income groups.[4]

All of this provides an overview of experiences of growth and poverty levels around the world. We will now use specific examples from the world today and from history to illustrate some ways that economic development may occur, and how effective it is in raising living standards and reducing poverty.

Discussion Questions

1. How important to you are your income goals, relative to your other goals? A recent survey, for example, asked respondents to say whether each of the following was absolutely necessary, very important, somewhat important, not very important, or not at all important "for you to consider your life as a success." How would you answer?

   Earning a lot of money
   Having an interesting job
   Seeing a lot of the world
   Helping other people who are in need
   Becoming well-educated
   Living a long time

Having a good marriage
Having good friends
Having a good relationship with your children
Having strong religious faith

2. Do you think the categories in the Multidimensional Index of Poverty do a good job of reflecting who is truly poor? If you were asked to add one item to this list, what would it be?

2 ECONOMIC DEVELOPMENT IN THE WORLD TODAY

2.1 Early Experiences and Theories of Development

The idea of economic development only became formalized in the mid-twentieth century, as the world's colonial empires began to break down and the more industrialized countries gradually took on a changed set of attitudes toward the parts of the world that had not experienced industrialization.[†]

During the period when European nations controlled colonies in the rest of the world—from the fifteenth century through the middle of the twentieth century—the economic relations between colonies and their rulers had been dominated by the desire of the ruling countries to enrich themselves. This was done first through the extraction of raw materials and, second, through the creation of markets for goods that they wished to export. By the mid-twentieth century, resistance to imperial domination and strong movements for independence had made it impossible for the ruling countries to maintain their control. Some scholars argue, however, that the former colonial powers have continued to use political and economic power to maintain their dominant position.

The United States and Europe had a head start in development, as early as the eighteenth and nineteenth centuries. This early phase of development was largely driven by the **Industrial Revolution**, involving a dramatic transformation in the nature of economic production through a process of rapid social, technological, and economic change. The Industrial Revolution began in Britain in the late eighteenth century, and by the nineteenth and early twentieth centuries, it was well along in much of Western Europe and the "early industrializing" countries, such as the United States, Canada, and Australia.

---

† In the first half of the twentieth century, a number of Western countries, including Britain, Germany, France, the Netherlands, Portugal, and Spain, were colonial powers, exerting control over many colonies in Africa, Asia, and South America. Japan was also a colonial power, ruling South Korea and, at various times, parts of China. Most of the colonies had become independent countries by the 1960s.

635

> **Industrial Revolution:** a process of social, technological, and economic change, beginning in Western Europe in the eighteenth century, that developed and applied new methods of production and work organization resulting in a great increase in output per worker

It is useful to understand the steps involved in creating the Industrial Revolution, taking Britain as the prime case and first mover. First, new agricultural techniques, along with new kinds of tools and machines, made agriculture more productive. Because farmers became more productive, fewer farm workers were needed to produce food for the whole population, and many migrated to the growing urban areas. Second, the invention and application of technologies using fossil-fuel energy (especially coal) contributed not only to the productivity gains in agriculture but also to the growth in the number of factory jobs and the development of transportation networks. Third, Britain's increasing reliance on other countries, including its extensive network of colonies, for supplies of raw materials and as markets for its goods, was critical in the development of its industrial sector. Britain imported cotton fiber from India, for example. It discouraged the further development of cotton manufacturing within India by putting high import tariffs on Indian-made cloth while requiring that India let British-made cloth come in without tariffs.

With this history in mind, the early models of economic development, formulated in the 1950s, assumed that a central feature of achieving development was an increase in the production of goods and services achieved through rising productivity, technological advances, and increased trade. The economic historian W.W. Rostow, for example, advanced the thesis that progress from "underdevelopment" to development invariably went through five stages. The first he referred to as "traditional, agrarian society," meaning a stagnant economy based on farming. In the second stage—"preconditions for take-off"—the economy possesses a critical mass of entrepreneurs and educated people, signifying the country's *potential* for development. The third stage was "take-off" (into self-sustaining growth), where the country realizes its development "potential" by achieving a sufficiently high level of *savings* to finance the *investment*—specifically, the accumulation of manufactured capital—necessary for growth. From there, growth and development were expected to sustain themselves. The fourth stage is the "drive to maturity," and the final stage, characteristic of rich countries, is the "age of high mass consumption."

The main conclusion from Rostow's theory is that after the necessary "preconditions" (education and entrepreneurship) are present, investment in manufactured capital and technology is sufficient to propel a country to a high living standard. A very similar conclusion was reached by the more mathematical Harrod-Domar model, named after the economists Roy Harrod and Evsey Domar.

636

Another theory, proposed by economist Sir Arthur Lewis (one of the earliest prominent black economists, born in St. Lucia, in the Caribbean), similarly describes development as a process of structural transformation from an agriculture-based economy to industrialization. Lewis anticipated that the higher productivity in the industrial sector would gradually attract workers from agriculture, without hurting rural productivity (because the labor being lost was "surplus"—more than was actually needed in the agricultural sector). As happened in the Industrial Revolution, this flow of labor into the industrial sector allows firms to expand production, increasing their profits and incentivizing further investment in production. According to this theory, the economy moves toward self-sustaining development through the continuation of this process of labor flows and increased investment and production.

This emphasis on the movement of labor from agriculture to industry as being the engine for growth meant that policymakers often focused on the development of the industrial sector and neglected agriculture. The development path taken by Russia, earlier in the twentieth century, could be interpreted as an extremely heartless version of such transformation from agriculture to industry; the number of Russian peasant deaths was appallingly high, as they were squeezed to transfer a hardly existing "surplus" into the nascent industrial economy. China, accepted into the communist/socialist camp in the cold war of the twentieth century, followed Russia in these respects, with even less industrialization to show for it until the late 1970s, when China's agricultural policies changed to allow the entrepreneurial spirit to flourish in the countryside. At that point, much of what Lewis described did occur, as the agricultural sector quickly developed a capacity to send surplus labor and capital into the cities.

Note that the vocabulary of referring to rich countries as "developed" and poorer countries as "developing" involves an implicit assumption that poorer countries are on a path of industrialization, on the road to perhaps eventually "catching up" with rich countries' lifestyles and levels of wealth. Early theories of development assumed that the lessons from industrialized economies simply needed to be applied to poorer countries so that they could follow a similar path of economic growth. But there is a danger, as this chapter will illustrate, in assuming that any one model of development can necessarily be transferred from a country where it has been successful to another set of circumstances. The history of colonization and the changing nature of the global economy results in a different set of conditions faced by developing countries today, as poorer countries are directly affected by their interactions with the rich countries. Based on such arguments, an alternative theory of development—referred to as **dependency theory**—originated from developing countries (primarily Latin America) in the late 1950s and gained prominence in the 60s and 70s.

637

Dependency theory was promoted by economists Raul Prebisch, Hans Singer, Paul Baran, Andre Gunder Frank, Samir Amin, and others. While there are some variations in the arguments made by these scholars, the theory mainly locates the roots of underdevelopment in the dominance of developed countries and the unequal trade relations between the developed and developing countries. It notes that the poor countries mostly export **primary goods**—goods derived directly from nature, such as metal ores, or lightly processed goods, such as timber or sugar cane. These tend to be traded for much lower prices as compared to the industrialized goods exported by the developed countries. Thus, trade was more beneficial to the rich countries.

The poor countries were dependent on the rich for capital and for exporting their goods but were unable to control the supply and prices of the exports. The **terms of trade**—defined as the price of exports relative to imports—between the developing and developed countries were unbalanced so that the value of what developing countries can sell on the world market was low relative to the value of what they want to import. Hence, the theory argues that developing countries need to protect and promote their own domestic industries, rather than importing so many manufactured goods.

---

dependency theory: the theory that underdevelopment in developing countries is caused by unequal trade relations, where developing countries export primary goods that are much cheaper than the industrial goods they import from the developed nations

primary goods: goods that are directly derived from nature, such as metal ores, or are lightly processed, such as timber or sugar cane

terms of trade: the price of exports relative to the price of imports

---

Based on this view, Latin American countries as well as several poor countries in Asia and Africa embarked on protectionist policies (as defined in Chapter 13) to promote import substitution and domestic industrialization. They also created common markets and trading blocs with other similarly situated countries, in hopes of securing greater advantages from their interactions with the developed world. Up to the 1970s, this model seemed to work, with real per capita income nearly doubling in many of these countries.

This approach to development ran into problems in the late 1970s. The oil price hikes of the 1970s increased the cost of importing oil and hurt many countries that were oil importers. Also, many of the countries adopting protectionist policies in the 1960s and 1970s had borrowed heavily from the rich countries to finance their development. When these rich countries—including the United States—increased interest rates in the early 1980s to fight inflationary pressures, the debt burden of developing countries rose sharply.[5]

The result, especially in many Latin American countries, was a debt crisis. The total outstanding debt of Latin American countries was US$29 billion at the end of 1979 but rose to US$327 billion by 1982.[6] In 1982, Mexico failed to service its US$80 billion debt, followed by the prospects of major loan defaults in 27 other developing countries, 16 of which were Latin American.[7] This was one of the worst economic crises in Latin America's history, with high unemployment and inflation and steep declines in income and growth. After this period, development strategies based on import substitution lost favor.

In contrast, developing countries such as Hong Kong, Singapore, Taiwan, and South Korea (known as the Asian Tigers) adopted an export-oriented development strategy. They were less focused on substituting domestically produced high-value products for their own populations, and more on policies designed to steer their industries away from exports of primary goods toward exports of manufactured goods. This approach, involving protective tariffs to help develop key industries, resulted in tremendous success for these countries, with rapid growth and improvements in the quality of life during the second half of the twentieth century.

But it has become increasingly hard for other countries to follow this model, especially as the high-income countries have increasingly insisted that poor countries follow "free trade" rules. In fact, countries that are now wealthy (including Britain and the United States) typically used protectionism—tariffs and quotas to limit trade—to foster the early development of their important domestic industries. Critics such as economist Ha-Joon Chang claim that such countries have "kicked away" the (protectionist) ladder that they used to ascend to higher living standards, sponsoring international trade rules that disallow the use of tariffs or quotas to protect industries in poor countries.

2.2 The Second Wave of Development Theory

By the 1980s dependency theory and import substitution industrialization policies were viewed as failed approaches to development. This supported the rise of a "neoliberal" ideology that promoted an export-oriented strategy of free trade and the abandonment of protectionist policies.‡ Developed countries like the United States took some responsibility for providing developing countries with foreign aid to help them raise their living standard; given the reality of the cold war, such aid was also designed to collect allies within the U.S. "sphere of influence". (Russia was similarly providing aid to countries that could be persuaded

---

‡ "Neoliberal" here refers to market-oriented development theory. It is derived from an older sense of the word "liberal," meaning freeing markets from government controls. This can be confusing since "liberal" in politics today often means using government action to help the poor.

to take their side.) Aid from the U.S. side increasingly came with the condition that the countries should engage in "structural reforms."

Multilateral institutions such as the International Monetary Fund (IMF) and the World Bank, which provided loans for development, or to assist countries in financial difficulties, began to insist that *all* recipient governments undertake a broad swath of policy changes to qualify for further loans. The set of favored policies came to be known as the "Washington Consensus." The main principles of the Washington Consensus were:

- *Fiscal discipline.* Developing countries were urged to end fiscal deficits and balance government budgets by developing reliable sources of tax revenue and limiting spending, including social services as well as subsidies for food or oil.
- *Market liberalization and privatization.* Abolition of government-controlled industries, price controls, and other forms of intervention in domestic markets along with widespread deregulation were seen as essential to promoting growth.
- *Trade liberalization and openness to foreign investment.* Countries were pressured to remove tariffs and other barriers to trade, as well as capital controls and other restrictions on foreign investment flows.

A new element that arrived with the Washington Consensus was a set of limits on the autonomy of developing country governments. The implicit promise was that if these policies were followed, the conditions for rapid growth would be created. The slogan "stabilize, privatize, and liberalize" governed the thinking of development policymakers during the 1980s and 1990s. The emphasis was on reforming the institutions in developing countries to make developing economies appealing and "safe" for foreign investment; also, the presumption was that the same guidelines applied to every developing country. These policies, however, often increased the debt burdens of borrowing countries (see Box 16.1).

BOX 16.1 JAMAICA'S EXPERIENCE WITH STRUCTURAL RE-FORMS

Until recently, Jamaica was among the most highly indebted countries in the world. The country's debt-to-GDP ratio hit a record high of 147 percent in 2013 but has since declined to about 94 percent in 2019. The country underwent various rounds of IMF structural reforms for over three decades but experienced weak economic performance including sluggish growth, high unemployment, and high crime rates. What explains the high debt levels and the poor economic outcomes in Jamaica despite the aid inflows?

Not long after the country's independence from Britain, in 1962, the Jamaican economy was hit by global economic problems. Faced by rising import prices due to the oil price hikes of the 1970s, the economy went into debt, forcing the country to sign its first agreement to borrow from the IMF in 1977. As interest rates rose in the 1980s, Jamaica's debts soared. Since then, in an effort to stabilize its economy, the Jamaican government signed on to billions of dollars in loans from the IMF, World Bank, and the Inter-American Development Bank.[8]

By 2013, the country had repaid more money ($19.8 billion) than it had borrowed (US$18.5 billion), and yet the government still owed US$7.8 billion due to huge interest payments.[9] The large debt burden crowded out public spending on development programs and stagnated growth, as most Jamaicans faced poverty and unemployment.

The imposition of Washington Consensus policies turned out to be a significant deterrent to growth in Jamaica. The lowering of import tariffs flooded the Jamaican markets with cheap foreign goods that destroyed local businesses. The agricultural sector was especially hurt, as imports of fruits, vegetables, meat, and milk replaced locally produced food. In addition, the imposition of austerity measures, to maintain a balanced budget, led to steep declines in public expenditures on health, education, and housing, and worsened the overall living standards in the country. Additionally, the IMF forced a devaluation of the Jamaican currency in order to achieve a more attractive international investment position. This, however, caused a decline in the worth of the Jamaican dollar and significantly added to its debt burden, as more Jamaican dollars were needed to pay the same debt.

Between 2013 and 2019, the country was able to ease its debt burden with six consecutive years of budget surpluses.[10] This was achieved through a series of reforms including debt restructuring with support from the IMF as well as reforms in tax and monetary policies, and the financial and public sector.[11] While both the IMF and the Jamaican government have touted this as a success story, others have criticized the extreme austerity measures taken to reduce the debt burden. With the recent pandemic, the government has run its first deficit in six years in 2020, and calls for further easing austerity measures have escalated.[12]

Recent growth performances seriously call into question the validity of these policy prescriptions. The region of the world most influenced by the Washington Consensus has been Latin America. As can be seen in Figure 16.5, the average growth rates in most Latin American countries were much higher between 1961 and 1980 than they have been since then. Since the 1980s the average growth rates of Latin American countries compare rather unfavorably to the average growth rate for middle-income countries as a whole (with few exceptions, Latin American countries are in the "middle-income" category). Only Chile had a higher average annual growth rate than the global average for middle-income countries between 1980 and 2000, while the entire Latin America and Caribbean region grew only 0.48 percent on average, compared to the average growth in middle-income countries which was close to 2 percent. Even in more recent decades (2001–2020), where countries such as Peru and Colombia have had over 2 percent growth rates, the average growth in Latin America has been less than 1 percent, compared to over 4 percent growth in middle-income countries on average. The poor performance of this region of the world is, to date, the strongest indictment of the Washington Consensus.

641

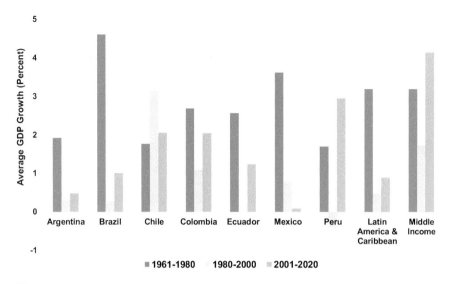

Figure 16.5 *Average Per Capita Annual Real GDP Growth, Selected Latin American Countries, 1961–2020 (Percent)*

Source: World Bank; World Development Indicators Database, 2022.

Some alternatives to neoliberal theory emerged in the 1990s. One, known as new growth theory, emphasized that sustained economic growth could be achieved through increasing returns to knowledge, rather than labor and capital, since knowledge and innovation can grow boundlessly without much additional cost. The policy recommendation from this theory was for governments to increase investment in human capital formation. This theory was criticized for ignoring the importance of social and institutional structures. Another proposal emphasizing the role of government investments came out of the theory of coordination failure, which argued that markets may fail to achieve coordination among complementary activities, requiring the government to solve this problem through public-led massive investment programs. Critics of this theory pointed out that government itself could be the problem when it pursued poor policies or was corrupt or inefficient.[13]

Discussion Questions

1. Do you think that the economic challenges faced by developing countries today are similar to those faced by industrialized countries when they were starting out? If not, how are they different?

2. Discuss how the Washington Consensus affected the development of the countries in Latin America and the Caribbean since the 1980s.

3 TWENTY-FIRST CENTURY RECONSIDERATIONS OF THE SOURCES OF ECONOMIC GROWTH

As shown in Figure 16.6, there are huge discrepancies in GDP per capita levels across countries. While countries such as the United States, along with Canada, most of Europe, Australia, Japan, and a few others, enjoy a per capita GDP of more than US$35,000, some of the poorest countries have income per capita below— sometimes much below—US$2,500. The countries whose economies have seen little growth are mostly in sub-Saharan Africa, including Burundi ($760), Somalia ($930); Mozambique ($1300); and Malawi ($1,400). Other countries that continue to struggle include Venezuela, Haiti, Pakistan, and Cambodia, all with per capita GDP between US$5,300 and US$3,000; and central Asian countries such as Afghanistan at US$2,400.

What are some of the ways in which poorer countries could achieve higher growth levels? In Chapter 1, we outlined five kinds of capital: natural, manufactured, human, social, and financial. An increase in these capital resources could push the production-possibility frontier out and increase the level of output produced (see Chapter 2).

In addition to increasing the quantity of inputs, there can also be significant increases in their quality. Human and social capital, in particular, may be increased through education, or through better laws, or improvements in social norms of honesty or collaboration. Technological advances and efficiency gains may also make it possible to increase output without increasing physical quantities of inputs. The

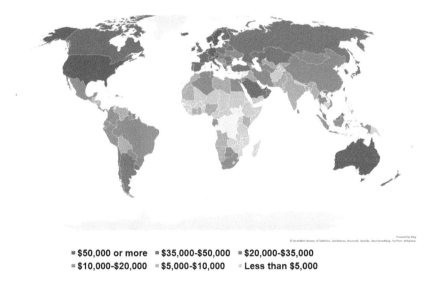

■ $50,000 or more ■ $35,000-$50,000 ■ $20,000-$35,000
■ $10,000-$20,000 ■ $5,000-$10,000 ■ Less than $5,000

Figure 16.6 *GDP per Capita in 2020 (PPP International Dollars per Capita)*

Source: World Economic Outlook Database 2021, IMF.

following observations summarize a range of possible sources of economic growth and development; their relevance varies from one situation to another.

3.1 Urbanization

Arthur Lewis, mentioned earlier, emphasized the process of moving people out of the countryside into urban industrial centers. Indeed, this process has continued apace, as we compare the urban/rural proportions of today, when 56.2 percent of the world population lives in cities, versus 1960, when it was 33 percent. This proportion is expected to rise to 68 percent by 2050.[14] The biggest change has been in Latin America and Caribbean, with 81.2 percent of the population now living in urban areas compared to 41.3 percent in 1950. The United Nations has projected that the overall growth of the world's population could add another 2.5 billion people to urban areas by 2050, with almost 90 percent of this increase taking place in Asia and Africa. This trend appears necessary, as advances in agricultural productivity (see Chapter 6) have continually lowered the number of people who can profitably work at farming. One caveat to this is the possibility that, as soils continue to be exhausted by industrial agriculture techniques, there will be at least a slight rise in the demand for farm labor due to the adoption of regenerative agriculture techniques that require more workers per acre.

3.2 Natural Resources

Often one of the first things that students of development think of is the role of natural resources. Indeed, large expanses of arable land, rich mineral and energy resources, good natural port facilities, and a healthy climate may make it easier for a country to prosper, while a poor natural endowment, such as a climate that makes a country prone to malaria or drought, can be a serious drag on development. But the historical record includes some surprises. Hong Kong and Singapore are among several examples of countries that have developed prosperous trade-based economies even though they have scant domestic resources, with little land and few energy sources of their own.

In fact, the overexploitation of natural resources can lead both to environmental degradation and to economic distortion. Countries such as Nigeria have found that oil reserves, seemingly a source of wealth, can easily be misappropriated with very damaging effects on development. Misdirected oil revenues can lead to massive corruption and waste, or other sectors of the economy may be starved of investment as available resources go primarily toward oil production. And because oil is an exhaustible resource, the country can eventually run out of

644

oil and find itself worse off than before. Nigeria's experience is symbolic of what many have referred to as the "resource curse" (the idea that countries endowed with abundant natural resources often do worse than countries with fewer resources).

3.3 Savings and Investment

Financial capital, which comes from savings, is essential for investment in manufactured capital as well as in agriculture in order to maintain and improve productivity in these sectors. Countries can also invest in human capital by improving their systems of education and health care. Workers who are skilled and healthy are more able to be productive.

Starting in the mid-twentieth century Japan and other "Asian Tigers," demonstrated a pattern of **virtuous cycles** in which high savings and investment lead to greater productivity, a competitive export industry, and growth of domestic industries. The resulting financial capital is then invested in machines, factories, and other equipment as well as in education and healthcare systems that can further enhance productivity—and the cycle begins again. As the economy grows, more resources are available to invest in both human and manufactured capital. It sounds simple and obvious—yet many countries have had great trouble in achieving such virtuous cycles.

---

virtuous cycles (in development): self-reinforcing patterns of high savings, investment, productivity growth, and economic expansion

---

Additions to capital do not automatically lead to growth. Technologies that are highly automated or "**capital intensive**" may sometimes be inappropriate in countries with much unemployment. In such countries, more appropriate investments might be made in technologies that make greater use of their abundant potential workers—in other words, technologies that are more "**labor intensive**." But goods produced by labor intensive processes tend to be less sophisticated, and therefore usually generate less export revenue than high-tech products. Indeed, one of the conflicts regularly confronted by developing countries is the need to balance economic diversification (especially into "higher-end" products) with the need to provide employment opportunities. There may also be a significant tension between producing more sophisticated products for export versus producing goods for domestic use. Cheaper domestic products may be squeezed out by more capital-intensive exports that are more profitable but too expensive for the local population.

645

> **capital intensive:** a process or procedure that makes use of more capital relative to other inputs such as labor
>
> **labor intensive:** a process or procedure that makes use of more labor relative to other inputs such as capital

3.4 Allocation of Investment

According to market theory, investors should be attracted to the most profitable opportunities. But market allocation of investment may ignore social priorities and will not necessarily contribute much to the development of infrastructure (things like roads, ports, railroads, and electronic networks). These and other public goods such as education, environmental quality, and water supplies require a public role in directing investment.

In addition to investing in public goods, governments have often played a role in planning other industrial investments. Known as **industrial policy**, this approach can involve promoting particular industries, using tariffs, subsidies, and other economic tools as needed, even when this implies active government modification of market outcomes. These tools may be applied to protect or subsidize industries that are not yet competitive, in the hope that they may become so over time; this is sometimes referred to as an **infant industry** policy.

> **industrial policy:** a set of government policies designed to enhance a country's ability to compete globally
>
> **infant industry:** an industry that is not yet globally competitive, but receives government support with the expectation that it may become so

Virtually all currently high-income countries used such policies in earlier stages of growth. Britain and the United States consciously formulated tariff policies to encourage domestic industries. Similar industrial policies employed by Japan and the Asian Tigers were essential to their rapid development between the 1960s and 1990s. A critical requirement for the working of industrial policy is a government that is oriented toward the economic success of the country, and that is capable of implementing its policies. It also needs to be able to take account of local differences, and find policies that can nurture productivity in a variety of modern settings.

The economic environment for industrial policy today is significantly different from that of the nineteenth and first half of the twentieth centuries. In Chapter 6, we described a transition in which the primary sector (especially agriculture) lost workers to manufacturing, while the services sector has continued to grow at the expense of these other two. That transition has occurred to a greater or lesser extent in almost every country, but it may no longer be the road to development that it once was.

For the manufacturing sector to be the basis for development required that it be able to employ a large number of low-skilled workers, giving them opportunities to increase their skills and knowledge, and hence their incomes. But manufacturing, over at least the last half-century, has drifted toward a global dualism, consisting of an informal sector, characterized by labor intensive production techniques, lower productivity, and lower wage, and a formal sector with capital intensive production, higher wages, and higher productivity.

Firms in the formal sector that have the capital and the know-how to use relatively high technology offer good jobs to skilled workers, but these firms are under constant pressure from globalized competition to reduce, not increase their labor/capital ratio. On the other hand, firms in the informal sector, comprised of small enterprises that lack the resources to increase their productivity, are growing more rapidly but creating low-wage jobs with limited potential for countries to experience the kinds of industrialization experienced by the developed countries in the nineteenth and early twentieth centuries. These enterprises (which may include small farms) are most prevalent in low-income countries but are also found in middle- and upper-income countries. This appears closely related to the declining income share of low-skilled workers, worldwide.

Given the trap of dualism in manufacturing, with large, productive, internationally competitive firms, and small stagnant ones, we might hope that services could pick up the role of absorbing low-skilled labor. But dualism also affects services, with relatively high-tech firms offering high wages in finance, IT, and related industries—especially those that are internationally traded—while the traditional service occupations such as cashiers, cleaners, food service workers, child care workers, hairdressers, and home health aides continue to be low tech, low skill, low status, and often poorly compensated.

As this dualism is increasingly recognized, along with a growing awareness of inequality generally, there is some movement to reconsider an older approach toward development called **appropriate technology**. This approach asks policymakers to consider directing investment toward the technologies that are appropriate to the existing and the wished-for mix of skills in the workforce, as well as to prevailing environmental and resource realities. As long as international competitiveness is a major determinant of the success of enterprises in any sector—agriculture, manufacturing, or services—there is little scope for diverting investment away from the capital-intensive, skill-intensive technologies that yield the highest profits. Renewed attention to appropriate technology and appropriate capital-labor ratios may only be possible with restraints on globalization in its present forms.

647

> **appropriate technology:** technologies that are appropriate to the skills in the workforce, as well as to prevailing environmental and resources realities

3.5 Foreign Sources of Financial Capital

If a country is not able to finance the investments it needs for development out of its own domestic savings, it generally seeks grants, loans, or investments from abroad. The sources of foreign capital can be either public or private. Public aid for development can take the form of either bilateral assistance or multilateral assistance. **Bilateral development assistance** consists of grants or loans made by a more affluent country's government to a poorer country. In recent decades, emerging economies, including China, the United Arab Emirates, Saudi Arabia, and Brazil, have also been increasingly providing aid to poorer countries. (See Box 16.2) Many developing countries also receive **multilateral development assistance** from institutions such as the World Bank and IMF, regional development banks such as the Inter-American Development Bank, and UN agencies such as the United Nations Development Programme (UNDP).

> **bilateral development assistance:** aid (or loans) given by one country to another to promote development
> **multilateral development assistance:** aid or loans provided by the World Bank, regional development banks, or UN agencies with the announced intention of promoting development

---

BOX 16.2 DEVELOPMENT ASSISTANCE FROM CHINA

While the discussion on aid often centers around aid from the OECD countries, emerging economies, such as China, Brazil, United Arab Emirates, and Saudi Arabia have been increasing their assistance to poorer countries and becoming major donors. At the head of this group of emerging donors is China, spending an average of $39.5 billion per year since 2000—similar to the amount of aid provided by the United States.[15] Between 2000 and 2014, Chinese funds went to more than 4,300 projects in 140 countries and territories, and China now outspends the U.S. on an annual basis.[16]

China's flagship project, the Belt and Road Initiative (BRI) launched in 2013, is one of the largest infrastructure projects, spanning 139 countries (as of 2021) in Asia, Europe, Africa, and Latin America. The project aims to improve regional integration and increase trade by providing countries with low interest loans to build infrastructure, including roads, ports, railways, airports, as well as telecommunication networks, and power plants. A 2019 World Bank study suggests that the BRI will promote global growth and reduce poverty by lowering trade costs and increasing foreign investments.[17]

There are, however, several concerns about aid from China. Because data on Chinese aid is often opaque, there are fears that it might be encouraging poor policies, lowering aid standards, or increasing the debt burdens of poor countries. China argues in response that its aid prioritizes the needs and sovereignty of receiving nations, and that it has provided debt relief to some highly indebted countries.[18]

Another concern is that the labor and environmental standards of Chinese-run infrastructure projects have been poor. This is a valid concern, and the Chinese government has made some efforts to address this. For example, China has committed to stop financing coal-fired plans and increase investment in renewables.[19] It created the China Internal Development Cooperation Agency (CIDCA) in 2018 to reform its aid program. Empirical evidence shows that China has been providing much needed assistance to poorer countries.[20] For example, aid from China has supported economic and social development in Africa by reducing bottlenecks in hard and soft infrastructure and promoting growth through increased trade.[21] As China's aid has become an alternative to Western aid, it has weakened the bargaining position of Western donors.

Total development aid reached a peak of US$170.9 billion in 2019—an increase of about 10 percent since 2015 and more than double its value in real terms in 2000.[22] In 2020, as countries around the world grappled with the COVID-19 crisis, foreign aid increased even further. The OECD reports a 3.5 percent increase in aid from OECD countries in 2020. The key recipients of aid from OECD countries were India, Turkey, and Afghanistan, and the largest donors were the United States, Germany, and the United Kingdom.[23]

While advocates of aid argue that it supports economic development by financing the gap in savings and raising human capital when it is directed toward health and education, critics argue that aid encourages dependency and creates perverse incentives for those in power.[24] Also, aid is often guided by the geopolitical interests of donors.[25]

The empirical evidence concerning the contribution of foreign aid to economic growth is mixed. Some of today's poorest countries have also been the heaviest recipients of concessional aid (meaning aid without any requirements for repayment). In some cases, aid went to corrupt leaders who spent it on their own luxurious lifestyles rather than on benefits for their people. In addition, most aid comes in the form of subsidized loans with conditions that are more favorable than private credit, rather than grants. Despite these concessionary conditions, many poor countries are now highly indebted and spend more on debt service (payment of principal and interest) than on health care for their population. For example, some African economies are spending five times more on debt repayments than on health care.[26]

Private foreign investment is carried out by private companies or individuals. Foreign direct investment (FDI) occurs when a company or individual acquires or creates assets for its own business operations in a foreign country (e.g., a German company building a factory to produce televisions in Mexico). FDI may or may not actually increase the capital stock in the recipient country, because it can include acquisitions of existing capital structures. Private flows also include loans from private banks.

Foreign investment can sometimes play an essential role in spurring development, but welcoming foreign businesses also can have a downside. When a large, powerful transnational corporation moves into a developing country, it may "crowd out" local initiatives, by competing with them for finance, inputs, or markets, sometimes in effect replacing a viable, though small-scale, local business sector with an international corporation producing for international sales. It may also be disruptive politically or culturally. Some of the most oppressive actions in development history (such as peasants being forced off their land or union organizers repressed with violence) have come about through alliances between large transnational corporations and corrupt governments.

3.6 Foreign Migration and Remittances

The high unemployment and poverty levels in developing countries have pushed many workers to pursue employment opportunities in other developed and developing countries. The remittances sent by these migrants to their families back home is an important source of livelihood for millions of poor households. In 2020, a total of US$651.1 billion was sent by international migrants to their families, with developing countries receiving US$548 billion. The largest recipients of remittances were India (US$83.2 billion), Mexico ($42.8 billion), the Philippines (US$34.9 billion), and Egypt (US$29.6 billion). Since total remittances received by developing countries are much larger than foreign aid, and remittance flows are more stable than FDI flows, remittances have become an important source of financial capital for developing countries.[27]

Research on the impacts of remittances shows positive effects on income levels along with better human development outcomes in terms of education and health.[28] In addition, remittances can ease credit constraints for poor rural households, facilitate investment in assets and in income-generating capital resources, and help reduce poverty levels. But remittances could also discourage members of the recipient households from working, and reduce domestic production. In addition, the loss of active labor force members who have migrated, along with dependence on foreign nations for continued employment, could pose serious challenges for the country's long-term development.[29]

3.7 Microfinance and Savings Groups

The poor often struggle to get loans because of their lack of assets for collateral, limited financial literacy, and the absence of financial

650

services in rural areas. Both microfinance and savings group programs are designed to address this issue by providing the poor with access to credit. Being able to take loans could help the poor meet their immediate consumption needs and also provide them with the financial capital to invest in some income-generating activity, such as starting a home-based enterprise or gaining skills to join the labor market. Such investments provide them with a source of income to sustain their livelihoods.

A traditional microfinance program requires borrowers to form small groups; loans are provided to group members, in turn, with the borrowing ability of each member being dependent on the loan repayment history of all the group members. Hence, social collateral in the form of peer pressure, instead of physical collateral, is used to ensure credit discipline.

In the past two decades, microfinance institutions have spread rapidly across the developing world. Evaluations on the effectiveness of such programs mostly show increases in household income, improvements in access to healthcare, education, and nutrition, and increased investment in small enterprises, among families receiving microfinance loans.[30]

Microfinance has some drawbacks. The poorest of the poor often have limited access to microfinance, as they are more likely to default on their loans and might find it difficult to get accepted into borrowing circles. There has also been some evidence of borrowers getting even poorer from having to sell their assets to pay off the debts, or getting trapped in vicious debt cycles from having to take new loans to pay off old ones.[31]

While microfinance may bring some gains, many developing economies have become saturated with informal microenterprises which are likely to fail if there is a lack of demand. Also, because microenterprises are unable to benefit from efficiencies of scale, some scholars have argued that directing resources toward small and medium enterprises, rather than to microfinance programs, may be a more effective development strategy.[32]

Savings groups, like microfinance programs, provide access to credit to the poor. The key difference between the two is that, instead of receiving loans from a bank or development agency, the funds for savings groups are generated by pooling the savings of group members, who normally create and run these programs in a truly grass-roots manner. Savings groups are seen by their advocates as an improvement over the microfinance model as they are extremely low cost and require minimal outside support.

Most studies evaluating the ability of savings groups to address poverty find positive outcomes. For example, a 2017 study on three African countries (Ghana, Malawi, and Uganda) finds that the promotion of savings groups has led to improvements in household incomes and women's empowerment.[33] Another study finds that savings groups in

651

Mozambique allowed households to close seasonal consumption food gaps, and meet cash needs during a crisis.[34] Savings groups are relatively easy to operate and have spread rapidly all across the developing world.

3.8 Cash Transfer Programs

Cash transfer programs involve providing a certain amount of cash grants to the poor to help improve their standards of living. In general, there are two types of cash transfer programs—conditional and unconditional. **Conditional cash transfer (CCT)** programs provide cash to the poor based on the condition that they make specific commitments, such as getting a regular health check-up or sending their children to school. **Unconditional cash transfer (UCT)** programs, on the other hand, involve a transfer of funds to individuals with no specific conditions on how the funds should be spent. Some such programs specify that the recipients show some evidence of need; others are distributed to all individuals above a certain age, or all households, regardless of need.

---

conditional cash transfer (CCT): programs providing cash to the poor based on the condition that they commit to spending it on specific things, such as children's education, food, or healthcare

unconditional cash transfer (UCT): programs providing cash to the poor with no specific conditions on how the funds should be spent

---

Evidence on the effectiveness of CCT programs shows that such transfers improve outcomes related to health, education, and nutrition.[35] For example, recipients of PROGRESA—a CCT program in Mexico conditioned on sending children to school and attending health clinics—are found to have greater school enrollment, lower incidence of illness in young children, and fewer sick days for adults.[36] Despite such achievements, CCT programs are often difficult to implement because of high administrative costs, and may not be effective if local educational or health facilities are poor. For example, an evaluation of the PROGRESA program showed increased enrollment but a decline in students' performances and increased workload for healthcare workers.[37] Finally, CCT programs are sometimes viewed as being demeaning to the poor, as the government imposes conditions on how the poor should spend the funds, irrespective of their preferences.

The UCT programs address many of these criticisms. Because they don't have to monitor how the recipients use the cash inflow, administrative costs are much lower. UCT programs are based on the idea that the poor are best equipped to decide how to use their money, and that not imposing specific conditions enables them to spend the cash inflow on things they deem most important to their well-being. Evaluation of UCT programs mostly finds positive outcomes. For example, a study led by Haushofer and Shapiro found that in Kenya unconditional cash transfers had increased household assets, consumption, food security, and psychological well-being.[38] (The Universal Basic Income, discussed in Chapter 7, is also an example of UCT).

3.9 Domestic Demand vs. Export Orientation

Because there would be little point in increasing production if what is made cannot find a market, the level of aggregate demand in an economy is also of great importance for growth. One reason that developing countries sometimes fail to achieve sustained growth is that, while production for export is emphasized, not enough is done to develop domestic markets. There are counterexamples to this statement: countries such as Japan and South Korea, which broke into the ranks of more advanced economies by developing powerful export industries, and China is now following this same path. But export dependence can become a trap that stifles economic development when countries depend on exporting products for which world demand is limited. Producers of agricultural exports, in particular, often suffer when world terms of trade turn against them, as discussed in the case of Latin America above.

3.10 Financial, Legal, and Regulatory Institutions

Financial, legal, and regulatory institutions (which fit into the category of social capital) play an important role in encouraging—or discouraging—growth. Very poor countries sometimes have banking and legal systems that do not reach very far into rural areas and provide credit only for the well-connected or well-to-do, making it difficult for small businesses and entrepreneurs to finance new or growing enterprises. According to the World Bank, secure land rights are central to reducing poverty, especially for women, indigenous groups, and other vulnerable communities that depend on their land for daily livelihood. But only about 30 percent of the world's population has a legally registered title to their land, partly due to limited legal infrastructure.[39]

Countries that have been successful in maintaining growth generally have effective systems of property rights and contract enforcement, which allow entrepreneurs to benefit from their investments, as well as effective corporate and bank regulation. Even in the case of property rights, however, the conventional wisdom does not always hold. China and Vietnam, for example, have been able to attract significant amounts of investment, even though, being at least nominally still communist countries, they do not have systems of private property rights. Nevertheless, they are able to assure firms that they will benefit from their investments by other means.

653

Some developing countries suffer from severe corruption, internal conflict, and other factors that make it difficult for effective institutions to take root. Political instability leads to economic inefficiency, difficulty in attracting foreign investment, and slow or no growth. This, in turn, means that less saving is available for future investment, reinforcing the problems. Breaking this vicious cycle is essential for development but can be very difficult to achieve.

Discussion Questions

1. Think of a poor country that you know something about. Considering the variety of sources of economic development, where would you propose starting to design a development plan for that country?
2. How would you balance the issue of human development with the issue of economic growth? What approaches do you think are best for promoting human development?

4 RECENT PERSPECTIVES AND SUSTAINABLE DEVELOPMENT GOALS

In September 2000, the member states of the United Nations unanimously declared their intention to try to reach a set of development objectives called the **Millennium Development Goals (MDGs)** by 2015. The MDG initiative included eight objectives:

- eradicating extreme poverty and hunger
- achieving universal primary education
- promoting gender equality and empowering women
- reducing child mortality
- improving maternal health
- combating HIV/AIDS, malaria, and other diseases
- ensuring environmental sustainability
- developing a global partnership for development based on fair trade, debt relief, and access to health and information technologies.

Millennium Development Goals (MDGs): a set of goals declared by the United Nations in 2000, emphasizing eradication of extreme poverty; promotion of education, gender equity, and health; environmental sustainability; and partnership between rich and poor countries

Between 2000 and 2015, many dimensions of human development improved much more quickly than in the 15 years prior to 2000. According to the United Nations, the goal of halving the proportion of people living on less than US$1.25 a day (the threshold in 2000) was

654

met three years *before* the target date. By 2015, the global poverty rate had decreased from 47 percent to 14 percent, and the proportion of undernourished people in developing countries had dropped from 23.3 percent to 12.9 percent. This progress was, however, very uneven, with regions such as South and East Asia (especially China and India) having seen considerable gains, while conditions in parts of sub-Saharan Africa have deteriorated.

Some scholars have criticized the MDGs, believing that the goals do not go far enough in addressing inequalities between rich and poor countries. Also, most developed countries did not fulfill their commitments to offer at least 0.7 percent of their GDP as aid. Little progress was made in opening up rich countries' markets to the products of poorer countries, and the technological gulf between rich and poor countries persisted. For several decades, the macroeconomic strategies employed by donor countries and multinational agencies were dominated by the "neoliberal" Washington Consensus (discussed earlier), which was poorly suited to achieving the MDGs because it only focused on economic and financial indicators, rather than prioritizing issues that are central to the concept of human development, such as care for children and the aged, inequality in general, or gender equity, including intra-household distribution of income and assets.

In 2015 the United Nations initiated a follow-up to the Millenium Development Goals, the so-called **Sustainable Development Goals (SDGs)**. These have replaced the eight MDGs with 17 "focus areas" (see Box 16.3). These focus areas are broader than the original MDGs. For example, the SDGs do not only address the conditions in developing countries but also living conditions in rich countries, including goals such as "reducing inequality" or promoting "just, peaceful and inclusive societies." The SDGs are further specified in targets, such as "by 2030, eradicate extreme poverty for all people everywhere" or "promote development-oriented policies that support productive activities, decent job creation, entrepreneurship, creativity and innovation."

Sustainable Development Goals (SDGs): a set of goals set forth by the United Nations in 2015, building on and expanding the MDGs, including goals such as battling inequality worldwide, promoting inclusive growth, and limiting climate change

---

BOX 16.3 THE SUSTAINABLE DEVELOPMENT GOALS

1. End poverty in all its forms everywhere
2. End hunger, achieve food security and improved nutrition, and promote sustainable agriculture
3. Ensure healthy lives and promote well-being for all at all ages

4. Ensure inclusive and equitable quality education and promote lifelong learning opportunities for all
5. Achieve gender equality and empower all women and girls
6. Ensure availability and sustainable management of water and sanitation for all
7. Ensure access to affordable, reliable, sustainable, and modern energy for all
8. Promote sustained, inclusive, and sustainable economic growth, full and productive employment, and decent work for all
9. Build resilient infrastructure, promote inclusive and sustainable industrialization, and foster innovation
10. Reduce inequality within and among countries
11. Make cities and human settlements inclusive, safe, resilient, and sustainable
12. Ensure sustainable consumption and production patterns
13. Take urgent action to combat climate change and its impacts
14. Conserve and sustainably use the oceans, seas, and marine resources for sustainable development
15. Protect, restore and promote sustainable use of terrestrial ecosystems, sustainably manage forests, combat desertification, and halt and reverse land degradation and halt biodiversity loss
16. Promote peaceful and inclusive societies for sustainable development, provide access to justice for all, and build effective, accountable and inclusive institutions at all levels
17. Strengthen the means of implementation and revitalize the global partnership for sustainable development.[40]

While this widening in focus and ambition clearly addresses dimensions neglected in the MDGs, some commentators have pointed out that the SDG's targets are formulated more vaguely than the MDGs', so monitoring progress is more difficult with SDGs.

Before the COVID-19 pandemic hit, some progress had been made in gender equality, poverty reduction, access to electricity, and maternal and child health. But much of this progress has either stalled or reversed since 2020. According to the 2021 Sustainable Development Goals report, global poverty rose for the first time in 2020, increasing the population in extreme poverty by over 120 million people. Additionally, over two decades of gains in education have been wiped out, domestic violence and gender inequality have increased, global hunger and child malnutrition have been exacerbated, and the concentration of major greenhouse gases has continued to rise in 2020. The pandemic has also added debt distress for developing countries, which have relied on aid to address the immediate health care needs of their citizens.

Despite these challenges, the 2021 SDG report presents an optimistic vision of the future, arguing that with global solidarity and leadership, along with efforts to reduce carbon emissions, create better jobs, advance gender equality, and tackle poverty and inequality, it is still possible to achieve the SDGs by 2030.[41]

Discussion Questions

1. What does the mixed success in achieving the Millennium Development Goals say about current development policies?
2. Do you think the Sustainable Development goals are realistic or achievable?

5 DIFFERENT KINDS OF ECONOMIES

In discussing the sources of growth, we talked about the importance of investment. This raises the question: Who decides what are the most important investments to make? Should investment decisions be left to private markets or controlled by the government, or some combination of the two? Historical experience offers a number of models.

The most extreme form of government control, represented by the experience of the Soviet Union from 1917 to 1989 and often referred to as a "command economy," has generally been discredited as an economic model. Its achievements in areas such as military production and some public goods (such as the Moscow subway system and elements of public education) came at a terrible human cost. Comparisons of Communist North Korea and East Germany with market-oriented South Korea and West Germany showed starkly that markets had a far better chance of achieving a more humane kind of development.

However, these alternatives are not the only possibilities. Indeed, there are not only differences between market and command economies, but within each of these categories there is more than one alternative—and relative development successes or failures do not all fall neatly into one place. We can categorize economic organizations according to *forms of ownership*, making a basic distinction between capitalist vs. socialist economies. Then we may further subdivide each of these.

Capitalism is a system characterized by predominantly *private ownership* of productive assets; owners may be either private individuals or businesses. Under **laissez-faire capitalism**, the role of the state is supposed to be relatively small; at least in theory, it is confined to maintaining a legal-institutional environment conducive to corporate ownership and market exchange. The United States and the UK are the two advanced countries that lie closest to this end of the spectrum. In contrast, **administrative capitalism** involves a more substantial amount of state activity alongside market-coordinated activity. Japan, France, and the Scandinavian countries fit this description. Canada, Australia, and New Zealand have tended to be somewhere in the middle, between these two varieties of capitalism.

---

laissez-faire capitalism: a national system characterized by private corporate ownership and a great reliance on exchange as a mode of coordination, with relatively little coordination by public administration

---

657

> **administrative capitalism:** a national system characterized by private corporate ownership and a substantial reliance on public administration (as well as exchange) as a mode of coordination

Socialism is a system that relies much more on *public ownership*, where the owners may be either government or various kinds of cooperatives. The former Soviet Union and North Korea exemplify **administrative socialism**, which centralizes a very large proportion of economic power in the government. In contrast, China and Vietnam have been experimenting with a hybrid—**market socialism**—that keeps *political* power centralized with state ownership predominating, but releases a growing amount of *economic* decision-making power to market forces.

> **administrative socialism:** a national system in which state ownership predominates and activity is coordinated primarily by public administration (command)
> **market socialism:** a national system in which state ownership predominates but much economic activity is coordinated through markets

Which of these systems is most conducive to development? To compare the success of various types of economies, review some of the data presented in Chapter 0. How do the laissez-faire economies of the United States and the UK perform compared to the administrative capitalist economics of Japan, France, and the Scandinavian countries? Or to the market socialism of China or Vietnam? Consider the economic categories of the growth rate of GDP per capita, net national savings, government debt, labor productivity, average annual hours worked, and unemployment rate, as well as the more well-being-related categories of income inequality, gender gap, educational performance, life expectancy; and subjective well-being. Finally, consider the last two categories, CO_2 emissions per capita and local air quality, which tell us about the hidden environmental and health costs of high levels of production and consumption.

Clearly, there is not a single winner. The United States does relatively well in some areas such as GDP per capita, and labor productivity, but performs poorly on some other measures such as savings rate, inequality, and carbon emissions. If you look at the ranking of the countries whose economies are described as administrative capitalism (e.g., Japan and the Scandinavian countries), you will find a different pattern—one that, to some people, looks appealing in terms of greater equality as well as health and educational measures.[42]

China, as an example of market socialism, is virtually in a class by itself. It has extraordinarily high savings and GDP growth rates, low debt, and a positive trade balance. But its income inequality, which used to be very low, has climbed to equal that of the United States. On the environmental front, as is well known, it has become a major

658

BOX 16.4 COMPARING INDIA AND CHINA IN HUMAN DEVELOPMENT

Both India and China have experienced rapid economic growth since 2000, but there are significant differences in their human development levels. A comparison of the human development indicators between India and China reveals that China is ahead of India in most aspects.[43] For example, in 2019 life expectancy in China was 76.9 years compared to 69.6 years in India, the infant mortality rate (per 1,000 live births) was 5.9 in China compared to 28.3 in India, and the maternal mortality ratio (per 100,000 live births) was 29 in China compared to 143 in India.[44] Nobel Prize winner Amartya Sen comments that the most significant gap between China and India is in the provision of essential public services:

> Inequality is high in both countries, but China has done far more than India to raise life expectancy, expand general education, and secure health care for its people. India has elite schools of varying degrees of excellence for the privileged, but among all Indians 7 or older, nearly one in five males and one in every three females are illiterate. . . The poor have to rely on low-quality—and sometimes exploitative—private medical care, because there isn't enough decent public care.[45]
>
> According to Sen, if India is to match China's economic record, it needs a "better-educated and healthier labor force at all levels of society," as well as "more knowledge and public discussion about the nature and huge extent of inequality and its damaging consequences for economic growth."[46]
>
> China's successes, however, must be balanced against the highly centralized and authoritarian nature of its government. This makes it possible to mobilize resources for specific goals, but it also conflicts with other goals of democratically oriented development.

---

emitter not only of greenhouse gases but also of other harmful pollutants. India, which has a form of mostly administrative capitalism, is compared to China in Box 16.4.

The debate on development continues. As the experience of development over the last century reveals, there is nothing "automatic" about achieving sustained growth and a high standard of living. Undoubtedly, a combination of market and government-led policies will be used as countries continue to strive to develop. The unsettled questions are how to determine the combination that will work best for a particular country, and how best to promote a combination of goals that include economic development and social well-being.

Discussion Questions

1. Which of the four economic systems discussed above do you think might be most conducive to achieving sustainable growth and economic equality? Explain why.
2. How do China and India compare as models for development? What are some problems and drawbacks in each country?

659

REVIEW QUESTIONS

1. What is the capabilities approach to development? How is this approach different from the traditional approach of defining development based on GDP per capita growth?
2. How evenly has economic growth been distributed among different countries in recent decades?
3. Which two variables can be added together to obtain the growth rate of GDP in a country?
4. How can economic growth be represented using the *AS/AD* graphs discussed in Chapter 12?
5. Define the participatory rural assessment, headcount, and Multidimensional Poverty Index measures of poverty.
6. What is the concept of convergence in economic growth?
7. What is the evidence for and against economic convergence?
8. What was the Industrial Revolution? What factors were essential in creating the Industrial Revolution?
9. What is the key argument of the dependency theory?
10. What, according to Rostow, are the five "stages of growth" through which all countries must pass in order to become developed?
11. What are the main principles of the Washington Consensus?
12. What is the evidence regarding the performance of the Washington Consensus recommendations?
13. What factors are generally considered responsible for GDP growth in developed countries? Have the factors responsible for growth been the same in all developed countries?
14. How can investment be used to promote economic development?
15. Is an abundance of natural capital a prerequisite for economic development?
16. How can export development both promote and threaten economic growth?
17. What do we mean by 'appropriate technology' approach to development?
18. In what different methods can foreign capital be provided to promote economic development?
19. Describe how microfinance and savings group programs could promote development.
20. What are the Sustainable Development Goals? Are we on track to achieve these goals by 2030?
21. What are the four kinds of economic systems discussed in the chapter? Explain the key differences between them.

EXERCISES

1. Suppose the real GDP of Macroland is US$1.367 trillion in Year 1 and US$1.428 trillion in Year 2. Also, assume that the population in Macroland grew from 128 million in Year 1 to 131 million in Year 2.
   a) What is the growth rate of real GDP in Macroland during this period?
   b) What is the growth rate of real GDP per capita in Macroland?
   c) What is real GDP per capita in Macroland in Year 2?
2. Using the data for each country in Table 16.1, create a graph similar to Figure 16.4 showing real GDP per capita in 2019 on the horizontal axis and the rate of real GDP per capita growth for 1990–2019 on the vertical axis (instead of life expectancy as shown in Figure 16.4). (You don't need to include the three country income groups.)

660

Draw each data point as a sphere approximately equal to the population of the country. Does your graph support economic convergence? Explain.

3. Match each concept in Column A with a definition or example in Column B:

Column A		Column B	
a.	Remittances	1.	Haiti
b.	A country that has shown significant economic convergence in recent decades	2.	Development assistance from one country to another
c.	Foreign direct investment	3.	Underdevelopment in developing countries is caused by unequal trade relations between developing and developed countries
d.	A country that has not shown economic convergence in recent decades	4.	Singapore
e.	Fiscal discipline	5.	A characteristic of the Industrial Revolution
f.	Dependency theory	6.	A European company purchases a factory in an African country
g.	Conditional cash transfer program	7.	Important source of financial capital for developing countries as they are larger than aid and more stable than FDI flows
h.	The use of technologies employing fossil fuel energy, especially coal	8.	A structural reform under the Washington Consensus
i.	Bilateral development assistance	9.	2 percent
j.	A country that has grown despite a lack of natural resources	10.	China
k.	High savings and investment rates	11.	Poverty alleviation programs that give funds to the poorest if they meet certain conditions
l.	Growth in GDP per capita if population grows by 2 percent and GDP grows by 4 percent	12.	A common factor in the economic development of the "Asian Tigers"

NOTES

1 Johnson and Papageorgiou, 2020.
2 Chingono, 2021.
3 Wilkinson and Pickett, 2010.
4 Ugur, 2021.
5 Arias and Restrepo-Echavarria, 2015.
6 FDIC, 1997.
7 Ibid., 1997.
8 Morais, 2014.
9 Dearden, 2013.

10   Wigglesworth, 2020.
11   Ibid., 2020.
12   Perry, 2019.
13   Pheng and Sui, 2015.
14   UN, 2018.
15   Qian, 2021.
16   Murphy, 2017.
17   Maliszewska, 2019.
18   Woods, 2008.
19   Jinping, 2021.
20   Qian, 2021.
21   See, for example, Zhicheng et al., 2020; Wang, 2021.
22   Based on data from the World Development Indicators, World Bank.
23   OECD database, 2021.
24   For more detailed discussion on this debate, see Miller, 2010.
25   Reinsberg, 2019.
26   Adegoke, 2020.
27   The World Bank, 2017a.
28   Ratha, 2013.
29   Amuendo-Dorantes, 2014.
30   For example, see, Imai et al. 2012.
31   Westover, 2008.
32   Bateman and Chang, 2012.
33   Karlan et al., 2017.
34   Brunie et al., 2017.
35   Son, 2008.
36   Gantner, 2007.
37   Ibid., 2007.
38   Haushofer and Shapiro, 2016.
39   The World Bank, 2017b.
40   United Nations, https://sdgs.un.org/goals
41   United Nations, 2021 (SDG report).
42   If you want to look into this further, you can go to the Web site www.bu.edu/eci/
     macro, which provides figures for all countries for which there are reliable statistics,
     not just those that are presented in Chapter 0.
43   Sen, 2011.
44   World Development Indicators database, World Bank. Data for maternal mortality
     rate is for 2017, while that for infant mortality and life expectancy is for 2019.
45   Sen, 2013.
46   Ibid., 2013.

REFERENCES

Adegoke, Yinka. 2020. "African Economies Are Spending up to Five Times Their Health
    Budgets on Debt Repayments." *Quartz Africa*, April 29.
Amuendo-Dorantes, Catalina. 2014. "The Good and the Bad in Remittance Flows." *IZA
    World of Labor,* 97:1-10. doi: 10.15185/izawol.97
Arias, Maria A., and Paulina Restrepo-Echavarria. 2015. "Sovereign Debt Crisis in
    Europe Recalls the Lost Decade in Latin America." *The Regional Economist, The Fed-
    eral Reserve Bank of St. Louis,* January 2015.
Bateman, Milford and Ha-Joon Chang. 2012. "Microfinance and the Illusion of Develop-
    ment: From Hubris to Nemesis in Thirty Years." *World Economic Review, 1*: 13–36.

BP. 2017. *Statistical Review of World Energy.* June 2017.

Brunie, Aurelie, Diana Rutherford, Emily B. Keyes, and Samuel Field. 2017. "Economic Benefits of Savings Groups in Rural Mozambique." *International Journal of Social Economics, 22*(12): 1988–2001, December 4.

Chingono, Nyasha. 2021. "Half of Zimbabweans Fell into Extreme Poverty during COVID." *The Guardian*, June 21.

Dang, Giang, and Low Sui Pheng. 2015. "Theories of Economic Development," Chapter 2 of *Infrastructure Investments in Developing Countries*.

Dearden, Nick. 2013. "Jamaica's Decades of Debt Are Damaging Its Future." *The Guardian*, April 16.

Federal Deposit Insurance Corporation (FDIC), Division of Research Statistics. 1997. "The LDC Debt Crisis." Chapter 5 in *History of the Eighties — Lessons for the Future, Volume I: An Examination of the Banking Crises of the 1980s and Early 1990s.* Washington, DC: FDIC.

Food and Agricultural Organization (FAO). 2022. Global Agricultural Production database. https://www.fao.org/faostat/en/#data/QI.

Gantner, Leigh. 2007. "PROGRESA: An Integrated Approach to Poverty Alleviation in Mexico." *Case Study #5-1 of the Program" Food Policy for Developing Countries: The Role of Government in the Global Food System.*

Haushofer, Johannes and Jeremy Shapiro. 2016. "The Short-Term Impact of Unconditional Cash Transfers to the Poor: Experimental Evidence from Kenya." *The Quarterly Journal of Economics, 131*(4): 1973–2042.

Imai, Katsushi S., Raghav V. Gaiha, Ganesh Thapa, and Samuel Kobina Annim. 2012. "Microfinance and Poverty — A Macro Perspective." *World Development, 40*(8): 1675–1689.

Jinping, Xi. 2021. "Bolstering Confidence and Jointly Overcoming Difficulties to Build a Better Worl." *Statement by H.E. Xi Jinping, at the General Debate of the 76th Session of The United Nations General Assembly*, September 21.

Johnson, Paul, and Chris Papageorgiuo. 2020. "What Remains of Cross-Country Convergence?" *Journal of Economic Literature, 58*(1): 129–175.

Karlan, Dean, Beniamino Savonitto, Bram Thuysbaert, and Christopher Udry. 2017. "Impact of Savings Groups on the Lives of the Poor," *Proceedings of the National Academy of Sciences, 114*(12), March 21, 2017.

Maliszewska, Maryla. 2019. "The Belt and Road Initiative: Economic, Poverty and Environmental Impacts." *Policy Research Working Paper,* The World Bank.

Miller, Daniel. 2010. "Sachs, Easterly and the Banality of the Aid Effectiveness Debate: Time to Move On." *Mapping Politics, 3*: 72–86.

Morais, Stephanie. 2014. "Jamaica – Skyrocketing Debt, Poverty and Even More Austerity." *The Upstream Journal*, May 2014.

Murphy, Tom. 2017. "Find Out Some (But Not All) The Secrets of China's Foreign Aid." *NPR*, October 31.

Perry, Keston. 2019. "Jamaica Is Using Bob Marley's Legacy to Market Austerity." *The Nation*, July 2.

Qian, Nancy. 2021. "The Case for Chinese Foreign Aid." *Project Syndicate*. November 8. https://www.project-syndicate.org/commentary/economic-benefits-of-chinese-foreign-aid-by-nancy-qian-1-2021-11?barrier=accesspaylog

Ratha, Dilip. 2013. "The Impact of Remittances on Economic Growth and Poverty Reduction." *Policy Brief No. 8*, Migration Policy Institute, September 2013.

Reinsberg, Bernhard. 2019. "Do Countries Use Foreign Aid to Buy Geopolitical Influence? Evidence from Dnoro Campaigns for Temporary UN Security Council Seats." *Politics and Governance, 7*(2): 127–154.

Sen, Amartya. 2011. "Quality of Life: India vs. China," *The New York Review of Books*, May 12.

Sen, Amartya. 2013. "Why India Trails China." *New York Times*, Op-Ed, June 19.

Son, Hyun Hwa. 2008. "Conditional Cash Transfer Programs: An Effective Toll for Poverty Alleviation." *Asian Development Bank*, July 2008.

The World Bank. 2017a. "Migration and Remittances: Recent Developments and Outlook." *Migration and Development Brief 27, World Bank*, April.

The World Bank. 2017b. "Why Secure Land Rights Matter." *Feature Story*, March 24.

Ugur, Zeynep B. 2021. "How Does Inequality Hamper Subjective Well-being? The Role of Fairness." *Social Indicators Research, 158*: 377–407.

United Nations (UN). 2018. "68% of the World Population Projected to Live in Urban Areas by 2050, Says, UN." *UN Department of Economic and Social Affairs*, May 16.

United Nations. 2021. "The Sustainable Development Goals Report." https://unstats.un.org/sdgs/report/2021/

Wang, Yan. 2021. "Africa and China – Development Cooperation for Structural Transformation." *Global Development Policy Center, Boston University*. https://www.bu.edu/gdp/2021/10/27/africa-and-china-development-cooperation-for-structural-transformation/

Weisbrot, Mark. 2011. "Jamaica's Crippling Debt Crisis Must Serve as a Warning to Greece." *The Guardian*, July 22, 2011.

Westover, Jonathan. 2008. "The Record of Microfinance: The Effectiveness/Ineffectiveness of Microfinance Programs as a Means of Alleviating Poverty." *Electronic Journal of Sociology*, 12: 1-8.

Wigglesworth, Robin. 2020. "Inside the IMF's Outrageous, Improbably Successful Jamaican Programme (pt. 1)." *Financial Times*, February 14.

Wilkinson, Richard, and Kate Pickett. 2010. *The Spirit Level*. Bloomsbury Press, New York.

Woods, Ngaire. 2008. "Whose Aid? Whose Influence? China, Emerging Donors and the Silent Revolution in Development Assistance." *International Affairs, 84*(6): 1205–1221.

Zhicheng, Xu, Yu Zhang, and Yang Sun. 2020. "Will Foreign Aid Foster Economic Development? Grid Panel Data Evidence from China's Aid to Africa. *Emerging Markets Finance and Trade, 56*(14): 3383–3404.

Growth and Sustainability in the Twenty-First Century

Over the last 50 years the size of the world economy, as measured by global GDP, has increased by a factor of about four in constant dollars (i.e. after adjusting for inflation). Global economic growth over this period has averaged about 3 percent real growth per year. Recent projections indicate that global economic growth will slow somewhat over the next 50 years, to between 2 and 3 percent, mainly due to slower population growth rates and longer life expectancies that reduce the share of the working-age population. But even with a 2 percent rate of real growth, the world economy would expand by a further factor of 2.7 over 50 years, and more than sevenfold over 100 years.[1] While this future economic expansion has the potential to increase human well-being in many ways, particularly for the nearly 1 billion people living in absolute poverty, it is important to address the question of whether such continued growth is environmentally sustainable.

In this final chapter, we consider the relationship between the global macroeconomy and the environment. We explore whether environmental factors, including the climate crisis and other issues such as availability of natural resources and accumulation of wastes and pollutants, pose a constraint to future economic growth. How do we assess potential tradeoffs between economic growth and environmental sustainability? How much future economic growth is actually desirable? And what policies are needed, nationally and internationally, to transition to a future that is both environmentally sustainable and allows all people to achieve high levels of well-being?

1 MACROECONOMICS AND SUSTAINABILITY

Debate over the ability of the earth's resources to sustain human populations can be traced back to 1798 when the British scholar Thomas Malthus wrote *An Essay on the Principle of Population*. Malthus predicted that unchecked human population growth would eventually outpace the growth in agricultural production, leading to widespread food scarcity and a resulting population crash. Malthus' prediction turned out to be inaccurate (at least so far). Technological advances during

DOI: 10.4324/9781003251521-22

the Industrial Revolution contributed to a significant increase in food production in the nineteenth and twentieth centuries, such that a much larger population could be supported at a higher level of average food consumption.

Similar dire predictions were common in the 1960s and 1970s. For example, Paul Ehrlich's 1968 book *The Population Bomb* foretold massive famines in the 1970s and 1980s due to overpopulation. *The Limits to Growth*, published in 1972, used computer modeling to conclude that without significant changes humanity would suffer from a significant decline in population and economic output in the twenty-first century due to excessive pollution and resource depletion. Other analyses focused on the limited supply of oil as the factor that would cause a major economic decline.[2]

So far, these predictions have also not come true. As we saw in the last chapter (Figure 16.1), economic growth, energy consumption, and food production have all outpaced population growth in recent decades. Higher per capita GDP and increases in food supply and energy consumption generally imply increased well-being. But recall from Chapter 5 that GDP fails to measure well-being in important ways. Similarly, the data in Figure 16.1 fail to show the unequal distribution of many natural and economic resources or the environmental impacts of increased economic activity. An increase in real GDP per capita might not produce an increase in average well-being if it is associated with greater inequality, pollution, and natural resource depletion.

One alternative indicator discussed in Chapter 5 was the Genuine Progress Indicator (GPI). As noted earlier, the long-term growth pattern of GPI looks different from that of GDP. In real terms, global GDP/capita increased by a factor of three between 1950 and 2005. Meanwhile, global GPI/capita doubled from 1950 to the mid-1970s, but then essentially leveled off for the next 30 years.[3] So while people are clearly, on average, better off economically than they were in the 1970s, it remains unclear whether overall human well-being has increased in recent decades when we consider a broader range of measures including pollution and natural resource degradation.

One of the reasons this book is titled *Macroeconomics in Context*, as we have noted earlier, is that the macroeconomy exists within a broader environmental context. Some economists, most notably Herman Daly, have emphasized that while the macroeconomy continually expands, the earth's biosphere, which provides resources and assimilates wastes and pollution, does not grow. Daly writes:

> [T]he economy is a subsystem of the finite biosphere that supports it. When the economy's expansion encroaches too much on its surrounding ecosystem, we will begin to sacrifice natural capital (such as fish, minerals, and fossil fuels) that is worth more than

the man-made capital (such as roads, factories, and appliances) added by the growth. We will then have what I call uneconomic growth, producing "bads" faster than goods – making us poorer, not richer.[4]

A determination of whether growth is "economic" or "uneconomic" can potentially be made by comparing the value of lost natural capital to the value of additional produced capital. Green GDP, discussed in Chapter 5, attempts to do this by monetizing the loss of natural capital and deducting it from GDP. Estimating all environmental impacts in monetary terms, however, is likely infeasible, and depends upon numerous normative assumptions.

Even if national accounting metrics such as the GPI and Green GDP are increasing, suggesting that increases in traditional economic production are more than offsetting the value of lost natural capital, this may be a short-run phenomenon. It doesn't necessarily mean that an economy can be considered ecologically sustainable in the long term.

In addition, we need to consider what it means to be "sustainable." Economists have different views on this. One economic perspective on sustainability, referred to as **weak sustainability**, assumes that natural capital and other types of capital (produced, human, or social) are substitutes. Thus, weak sustainability asserts that natural capital depreciation is justified as long as it is compensated for with adequate increases in other types of capital. So, for example, the destruction of a wetland in order to construct a new highway would be justified if the economic benefits of the highway exceeded the lost ecological value of the wetland.

Strong sustainability takes the perspective that sustainability should be defined solely in terms of natural capital. Under strong sustainability, natural and other types of capital are not substitutes. Strong sustainability doesn't mean that natural capital can never be degraded, but it requires that any degradation of a particular type of natural capital (such as the cutting of a forest for timber or the draining of a swamp) be compensated for with appropriate natural capital restoration (such as replanting trees or restoring wetlands).

> **weak sustainability:** an analytical perspective suggesting that natural capital depreciation is justified as long as it is compensated for with adequate increases in other types of capital
> **strong sustainability:** an analytical perspective suggesting that natural capital depreciation is justified only if it is compensated for with adequate restoration of other natural capital

667

Strong sustainability isn't necessarily "better" than weak sustainability, but it changes the metrics we would use to determine whether an economy is sustainable. For weak sustainability, we could use a metric such as the GPI or Green GPI which allows a direct comparison of natural capital with other types of capital, measured in monetary units. But if our objective was to pursue strong sustainability, we would probably use satellite accounts (discussed in Chapter 5) that assess the levels of various types of natural capital, such as a forest account, a greenhouse gas emissions account, etc.

One variant of strong sustainability would seek to maintain the overall aggregate value of natural capital in a society. This would require a metric that would allow different types of natural capital to be compared, which could use monetary values, but could also be non-monetary, based on the biological productivity of different ecosystems or the views of scientific experts.[5] Another variant of strong sustainability would seek to maintain the levels of individual types of natural capital, such as total forest cover, fish stock biomass, air quality, etc. This suggests using physical metrics, such as the volume of timber or the concentration of air pollutants, to measure progress toward sustainability.

Any attempt to monitor sustainability efforts should recognize that the biosphere is ultimately finite, as indicated in the Daly quote above. A related perspective on sustainability considers whether the overall scale of human environmental impacts is within the carrying capacity of the planet. This approach measures the human **ecological footprint**, which estimates the amount of biologically productive land (called "biocapacity") that is required, both to supply the natural resources a society uses and to assimilate the waste and pollution that results from economic activity. This is then compared with the amount of productive land available to the society, to determine whether impacts are within sustainable levels.

> **ecological footprint:** a measure of the human impact on the environment, measured as the productive land area required to supply a society's resources and assimilate its wastes and pollution

Measuring some environmental impacts in land area units (acres or hectares) is rather straightforward, such as the amount of land needed to grow crops or provide forestry products. Converting other impacts to a land area measure is less obvious. For example, carbon emissions are quantified in the ecological footprint measure as the land area of vegetation that would be needed to absorb a given amount of carbon.[6]

While the ecological footprint is subject to methodological critiques,[7] it provides a comprehensive measure to determine whether a nation, or all of humanity, is within ecologically sustainable limits. The global ecological footprint over time is presented in Figure 17.1. As only one

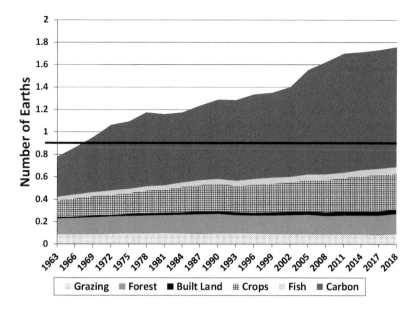

Figure 17.1 *Global Ecological Footprint, by Impact Type, 1965–2018*

Source: Global Footprint Network Public Data Set, https://www.footprintnetwork.org/resources/data/

earth is available to provide resources and assimilate wastes, we see that humanity reached a situation of "overshoot" starting around 1970. Currently, human impacts are exceeding the carrying capacity of the earth by about 70 percent.

Disaggregating the impacts, we observe that about 65 percent of humanity's ecological footprint is attributed to its carbon emissions. In order to bring the global system back to overall sustainability, carbon emissions would need to decline by 80 percent or more (as suggested by many scientists) to bring the total human ecological footprint back below the "one earth" level.[8]

Other human impacts on the environment, such as agriculture, forestry, and fisheries, while not so dramatic in absolute scale, may not be effectively captured simply by looking at the total productive land use required. In order to evaluate specific human impacts on the global environment, in the next section we turn to a discussion of several major environmental issues.

Discussion Questions

1. Explain the concepts of "economic" and "uneconomic" growth. Do you think that there is a danger that global growth is becoming "uneconomic"?
2. How would you define sustainability? Can you think of some examples in which the "weak" and "strong" versions of sustainability might imply different economic or environmental policies?

669

2 MAJOR ENVIRONMENTAL ISSUES

A number of environmental issues are closely related to macroeconomic growth and well-being at the national and international levels. In this section we summarize the data and the policy challenges for four major environmental issues:

1. Global population
2. Non-renewable resource availability
3. Renewable resources
4. Pollution and wastes

Then in the next section, we focus on the central global issue of climate change, and its implications for economic growth and macroeconomic policy.

2.1 Global Population

Economic and technological growth since the Industrial Revolution has fostered a dramatic increase in the world's population. The global population was approximately 1 billion in 1800, doubled to 2 billion by 1930, and reached 3 billion in 1960. Over the next 40 years, it doubled again, reaching 6 billion by 2000. As of 2022, it had reached 7.9 billion. Human population growth contributes to many environmental pressures. A larger total population creates a greater demand for food production and also translates to higher rates of resource depletion and more waste generation for a given level of technology. As mentioned previously, the intensification of food production so far has kept pace with population growth. The expanded scale of agricultural production, however, has led to significant costs in terms of land degradation, pollution from fertilizers and pesticides, and overtaxing of water supplies.

Although population growth rates have declined from 2.1 percent annually in the 1960s to approximately 1 percent today, as of 2021 the human population was still increasing by about 80 million people per year, equivalent to the population of Germany. The United Nations' global population projection published in 2022 indicates that the global population will reach 10 billion by 2060, and will then grow at a slower pace to reach 10.5 billion by about 2080, according to their "medium-variant" projection (see Figure 17.2).[9] The vast majority of population growth is expected to occur in developing countries, particularly in Africa.

Figure 17.2 shows, however, that there is considerable uncertainty in projecting population during the twenty-first century. Under the United Nation's high-variant projection, the global population reaches 15 billion by 2100. Under the low-variant projection, the global population peaks at 8.9 billion around 2050, and by 2100, it is expected to be lower than it is today.

670

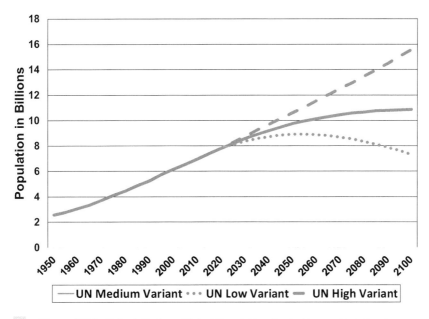

Figure 17.2 *United Nations Global Population Projections, 2020–2100*
Source: United Nations, World Population Prospects 2019.

The differences across variants are due to different assumptions about how quickly and how far fertility rates (the average number of children per woman) will decline during the twenty-first century. Declining population growth rates can be attributed to numerous factors including the widespread availability of birth control, higher costs associated with raising children, and, perhaps most importantly, a focus on educating girls. When women are educated and have employment opportunities, the opportunity cost of having children rises, leading to lower fertility rates.

Obviously, humanity's environmental impacts will be quite different in 2100 if only 7–8 billion humans are on the planet as opposed to 15 billion. Thus, the potential for a sustainable future may hinge upon what will happen to fertility rates around the world in the coming decades. Historical evidence generally suggests that the United Nations has underestimated how quickly fertility rates have fallen. One assumption that has been questioned for the medium-variant estimate in Figure 17.2 is that fertility rates will increase slightly for many developed nations, although so far this has not occurred. The low-range projection assumes a more rapid decline in fertility rates, which might be achieved by improved education, health care, and opportunities for women.[10]

2.2 Non-renewable Resource Availability

As noted in Chapters 6 and 16, depletion of important natural resources has typically accompanied economic growth. **Non-renewable resources** are those resources that do not regenerate through natural processes, at least on a human time scale, such as oil, coal, and mineral ores. While the global physical stock of a non-renewable resource is a fixed quantity, known reserves fluctuate as some resources are extracted while new reserves are discovered. Also, changes in technology and prices can determine whether particular reserves are economically viable to exploit.

> **non-renewable resources:** resources that do not regenerate through natural processes, at least on a human time scale, such as oil, coal, and mineral ores

Global stocks of key mineral resources, such as aluminum and copper, are for the most part not close to exhaustion, but as high-quality reserves are depleted recovery of lower-quality reserves tends to involve higher energy and environmental costs.[11] The environmental impacts of mining include pollution of rivers and lakes from mine runoff and air pollution from the processing of mineral ores. There are also significant social impacts, especially in developing countries, where poorer and indigenous communities may be devastated by these activities.

Factors that could contribute to the risk of disruptions in the supply of important minerals include the depletion of some physical stocks, the limited availability of substitutes, limits on the known possibilities for recycling, and overdependence on supplies from politically unstable countries. According to a 2015 analysis, the minerals with the greatest risk of global supply disruption include rare earth elements (mainly used in electronics), antimony (used in batteries and flame retardants), and bismuth (used in fuses and cosmetics).[12]

Global reserves of oil and natural gas are sufficient for over 50 years at current consumption rates and coal reserves for more than 100 years. Despite increasing consumption rates, known reserves of fossil fuels have actually been increasing in recent decades due to new discoveries and expanded recovery technologies. For example, known global oil reserves at the end of 2020 were about 60 percent higher than they were in the mid-1990s.[13] Thus, the evidence indicates that we will not exhaust the physical stock of fossil fuels in the foreseeable future.

While the availability of fossil fuels does not appear to be a constraint on economic development, their environmental impacts are extensive. The extraction of fossil fuels can cause significant local environmental damage, particularly as production shifts toward "unconventional" sources of oil and gas obtained through hydraulic fracturing or "fracking." The burning of fossil fuels has led to severe health damages from pollution in rapidly developing countries such as India and China as well as in coal-dependent areas such as Eastern Europe. An even greater concern is the impact of fossil fuel emissions on climate change. We will consider these impacts in Sections 2.4 and 3 of this chapter.

2.3 Renewable Resources

Renewable resources such as forests, fisheries, freshwater, and soil are regenerated over time through natural and biological processes. If renewable resources are used by humans at rates below the natural rate of regeneration, then sustained availability is possible. Excessive rates of use, however, can lead to depletion or degradation of renewable resources. For example, overfishing can rapidly deplete fish stocks, possibly causing their complete collapse. We will briefly consider the status of five types of renewable resources, all essential for economic systems: forests, fisheries, freshwater, soils, and biodiversity.

---

renewable resources: resources that are regenerated over time through natural and biological processes, such as forests, fisheries, and freshwater

---

2.3.1 Forests

Forests cover 31 percent of the world's land area. Forests provide us with numerous benefits including air purification, flood prevention, soil stabilization, and climate regulation. The global rate of deforestation has slowed somewhat since the 1990s, with annual net forest loss (area deforested minus area planted) declining from 7.8 million ha/year of forests during 1990–2000, and 5.7 million ha/year during 2000–2010, to an estimated 4.7 million hectares of net loss per year over the period 2010-2020. This is still a very high rate, especially for tropical forests, since the overall rate reflects a balance of loss of tropical forests with some gains in temperate forests.

Forest trends differ dramatically in different regions of the world. In Europe and North America, forests are expanding somewhat. Forest area is also increasing in Asia, primarily due to recent replanting efforts in China. But significant deforestation is occurring in Latin America (including the Amazon Forest in Brazil)—2.6 million ha/year— and Africa—3.9 million ha/year.[14]

2.3.2 Fisheries

Global fish consumption is at record levels, putting pressure on the health of many of the world's fisheries. The United Nations classifies fish stocks into three categories: underfished, fully fished, or overfished. The share of the world's fisheries classified as overfished has increased from less than 10 percent in the 1970s to more than 30 percent today. Another 60 percent of fish stocks are considered fully fished, indicating that sustainable harvest increases are possible on only about 10 percent of global fisheries.[15]

673

The increasing scarcity of most wild-caught fish has generated incentives for a rapid expansion of aquaculture (fish farming). But there are also adverse ecological impacts from aquaculture, especially with the farming of saltwater species, such as shrimp and salmon. Five pounds of wild-caught fish are used as feedstock in the production of each pound of farmed salmon, while shrimp farming has led to widespread destruction of coastal mangrove forests.

2.3.3 Freshwater

While freshwater is continually renewed through natural processes, only a limited amount is available for human use at one time. Global water use increased by more than a factor of five during the twentieth century and is projected to increase by another 55 percent between 2000 and 2050, with the largest increase in developing countries. The availability of freshwater varies significantly across the world—while water is abundant in some areas, it is quite scarce in others. About a billion people currently suffer from water scarcity—a number that is expected to increase due to supply depletion and climate change, which will reduce water availability further in many water-scarce regions.[16]

Many countries are becoming increasingly dependent upon groundwater, which is essentially a non-renewable resource with a limited supply. India extracts more groundwater than any other country (more than the next two countries, China and the U.S. combined), which has led to a national crisis as water tables fall in overexploited aquifers, leading to water shortages and increased contamination. In most places in the world groundwater is essentially unregulated; farmers and other water users can extract all they want at low cost and with little regard for environmental consequences. Agriculture is responsible for about 70 percent of global freshwater demand. In 2020 the World Economic Forum ranked the global water crisis as one of the top five most significant global risks, along with climate change, biodiversity loss, extreme weather, and weapons of mass destruction.[17]

2.3.4 Soils

Soil resources are in decline in much of the world, especially in the nearly 40 percent of the Earth's land area that is devoted to agriculture. According to the Food and Agriculture Organization of the United Nations (FAO), about a third of the world's soil has already been degraded. If population growth and current agricultural practices continue, the global amount of arable and productive land per person in 2050 will be only about a quarter of the level it was in 1960. As noted in Chapter 6 (Box 6.2), organic and regenerative agricultural techniques are needed to rebuild soils, including storing carbon in soils to reduce the impacts of climate change.

2.3.5 Biodiversity

One of the most significant environmental problems is the continuing loss of the world's biodiversity, meaning the abundance and variety of wild plant and animal species. Virtually all human environmental impacts—pollution, deforestation, agriculture, overfishing, climate change—are contributing to what many researchers conclude to be an ongoing extinction crisis on the same scale as previous mass extinctions, such as the one that killed off the dinosaurs 65 million years ago. According to the United Nations, "there is well-established evidence indicating an irrevocable and continuing decline of genetic and species diversity."[18] The most significant threats to vertebrate species are, in order: agriculture/aquaculture, logging, and urban development. In the future, these threats are likely to be overtaken by climate change. According to one analysis in the prestigious scientific journal *Nature*, under a mid-range scenario, 15–37 percent of all species would be "committed to extinction" by 2050.[19]

2.4 Pollution and Wastes

As discussed in Chapter 6, damage from pollution is not reflected in traditional national accounting measures, even though it clearly reduces welfare. A 2017 study presented a comprehensive analysis of the global health and economic costs of air, water, and soil pollution. The summary of the report indicates that:

> Diseases caused by pollution were responsible for an estimated 9 million premature deaths in 2015–16% of all deaths worldwide— three times more deaths than from AIDS, tuberculosis, and malaria combined and 15 times more than from all wars and other forms of violence . . . Pollution disproportionately kills the poor and the vulnerable. Nearly 92% of pollution-related deaths occur in low-income and middle-income countries and, in countries at every income level, disease caused by pollution is most prevalent among minorities and the marginalized.[20]

Of the 9 million deaths attributed to pollution, 6 million were linked to air pollution, 1.8 million to water pollution, and 0.8 million to workplace-related pollution. The global economic damages from pollution-related disease were estimated to be US$4.6 trillion annually, or more than 6 percent of global economic output.

Efforts to reduce pollution levels have generally been found to be cost-effective, and pollution in developed countries has generally declined in recent decades. For example, policies to reduce air pollution in the United States since the 1970s are estimated to have returned about $30 in benefits for every dollar spent.[21] Aggregate emissions of the most common air pollutants in the U.S. have declined by 78 percent

675

since the 1970s.[22] Meanwhile, pollution in developing countries has typically increased. As we see in Figure 17.3, air pollution levels in most major cities in developing nations exceed the World Health Organization's recommended level of 20 micrograms per cubic meter (μg/m^3) of particulate matter (PM_{10}), composed of suspended particles of dust, ash, and other harmful material.

In addition to pollution, economic production and consumption generate a significant amount of physical waste—over a billion tons per year. In general, as economic production and urbanization increase, a society produces more solid waste. People in wealthier countries produce at least twice as much waste per person, on average, as those in middle- and lower-income countries. Much of this waste, particularly plastic waste, ends up in the world's oceans where it poses a significant threat to marine life.[23] Global generation of solid waste is projected to increase by a factor of three by 2100, primarily due to population growth and income gains in developing countries.[24]

Toxic waste produced in developed countries is frequently exported for disposal in developing countries. A particular concern is the production and export of e-wastes, which often contain toxic chemicals such as mercury, lead, and arsenic, and are often disposed of in unregulated

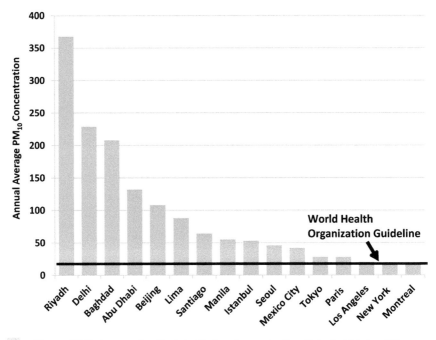

Figure 17.3 *Average Particulate Matter Concentration, Selected Major Cities*

Source: World Health Organization, Ambient Air Quality Database.

Notes: Particulate matter concentrations in μg/m^3; data vary by city, between 2012 and 2015.

conditions that cause significant environmental consequences and human health risks.[25] Rapid future development will mean that pollution and waste management problems, both domestic and trade-related, are likely to grow, despite efforts to control them with environmental regulations.

Discussion Questions

1   What are some recent trends in global population? Do you think that future population growth is likely to pose major problems, and what factors will affect the future course of population growth?
2   Which resource and environmental problems, other than climate change, do you think are the most pressing? What kinds of policies might be appropriate in responding to these problems?

3 CLIMATE CHANGE

The resource and environmental issues discussed above all pose serious problems. But perhaps the primary environmental challenge of the twenty-first century is global climate change. Global climate change combines issues of resource use and environmental impact and is strongly related to economic growth.

3.1 Climate Change Science, Data, and Impacts

The vast majority of scientists have concluded that human activity is changing the planet's climate, and that major impacts of climate change are already occurring.[26] Emissions of various greenhouse gases, particularly carbon dioxide (CO_2) and methane from the extraction and burning of fossil fuels, trap heat near the earth's surface, leading not only to a general warming trend but to sea-level rise, ecological disruption, and an increase in severe weather events, such as hurricanes, floods, droughts, and wildfires.

Climate change is expected to impact poor countries most heavily, as they tend to be located in tropical regions already exposed to severe weather events and also lack the financial and technological resources to adapt and respond to climate change. Climate change threatens to increase food insecurity, with the number of people at risk of hunger projected to increase by 10 percent to 20 percent by 2050. In a 2018 study, the World Bank estimated that climate change will cause the migration of over 100 million people in developing countries over the coming decades due to droughts, crop failures, and rising seas. According to one study, climate change "could fundamentally redraw the map of the planet, and where and how humans and other species can live."[27]

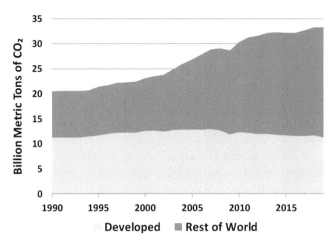

Figure 17.4 *Global Carbon Dioxide Emissions, 1965–2019, Developed and Developing Countries*

Source: International Energy Agency, https://www.iea.org/articles/global-co2-emissions-in-2019

Global emissions of carbon dioxide have generally been increasing in recent decades, as shown in Figure 17.4. The wealthier OECD nations[*] accounted for the majority of global emissions up to 2003, but by 2016 the non-OECD nations emitted over 60 percent of the world's carbon dioxide. China is currently the world's top emitter of carbon dioxide, followed by the United States, the European Union, India, and Russia.

While developing countries now emit more total carbon than developed countries, it is important to realize that emissions per capita are still much higher in richer nations. For example, annual CO_2 emissions per person are about 15.7 tons in the United States, 10 tons in Japan, 7.7 tons in China, 1.8 tons in India, and 0.5 tons in Nigeria.[28]

At the 2021 United Nations meeting in Glasgow, a target was adopted of limiting the eventual global temperature increase, relative to pre-industrial levels, to no more than 1.5° Celsius (2.7°F). In order to achieve this target, it is estimated that global CO_2 emissions will need to fall to near zero by 2050. Since temperatures have already risen by about 1.1°C, this is obviously a major global challenge, especially as global economic growth is now largely dependent on fossil fuels.[29]

Even if this ambitious target can be achieved, the world is still committed to further warming and other adverse impacts. Greenhouse gases persist for decades or even centuries in the earth's atmosphere. In addition, there is a lag between the time a gas is emitted and the time when its effects are fully realized.

Dramatically reducing, or eliminating, carbon emissions will require a transformation of how humans obtain energy.

---

[*] The Organization for Economic Cooperation and Development (OECD) is an organization of primarily developed countries aiming to promote economic progress, trade, democracy, and the market economy. https://www.oecd.org.

678

Currently, the world economy obtains over 80 percent of its energy from fossil fuels, roughly equally split between coal, oil, and natural gas.[30] The U.S. Energy Information Administration forecast in 2021 that under its "reference scenario" the world will still rely on fossil fuels for 58 percent of its energy in 2050—a path that would clearly make the 1.5°C target unattainable.[31] Fortunately, EIA forecasts have typically underestimated the growth rate of renewable energy sources such as wind and solar.[32]

Economic analysis has an important role to play in estimating the damages associated with climate change, and determining the cost, the benefits, and the feasibility of actions, such as investment in renewable energy and energy efficiency, intended to reduce its impacts. We consider these economic analyses next.

3.2 The Economics of Climate Change

Carbon dioxide emissions are an example of a negative externality. As discussed in Chapter 2, when externalities are present unregulated markets will not allocate resources efficiently because those involved in market transactions do not bear the costs. The solution to this problem, according to economic theory, is to introduce a tax or other market policy (such as a system of tradable pollution permits) so that current consumers and producers pay for the full social cost of their choices, including those that impact future generations. The economic basis for these policies, reflecting the estimated social damages from emitting CO_2 (normally one ton), is referred to as the **social cost of carbon**.

---

social cost of carbon: a monetary estimate of the discounted long-term damages from emitting a ton of CO_2 in a given year

---

As far back as the 1990s economists have widely recommended instituting carbon pricing as a policy response to climate change.[33] Economists have had differing estimates of the value of the social cost of carbon, however, leading to different recommendations for policy action. Early economic analyses of climate change generally recommended limited policy action based on a social cost of carbon of around $10 per ton of CO_2.[34] Applied to transportation, a social cost of carbon of $10 per ton of CO_2 translates to a tax on gasoline of about 10 cents per gallon. As the demand for gasoline is relatively inelastic, a 10-cent/gallon tax would only reduce the quantity demanded by perhaps about 1 or 2 percent. There would be similarly small effects in other areas of energy use such as heating and cooling.

679

A major economic analysis in 2006, funded by the British government, concluded that much more dramatic action was justified. The *Stern Review of the Economics of Climate Change*, written by former World Bank economist Nicholas Stern, estimated a social cost of carbon of \$85 per ton of CO_2. One of the differences between this and most previous analyses was the use of a lower **social discount rate** to weigh future costs and benefits (see Box 17.1). This approach placed a higher value on avoiding future damages, leading to much stronger policy recommendations.

> **social discount rate:** a discount rate that reflects social rather than the market valuation of future costs and benefits; usually lower than the market discount rate

The Stern Review estimated the damages from climate change in the twenty-first century to be between 5 percent and 20 percent of global GDP, while projecting that the most severe effects of climate change could be avoided at a cost of approximately 1 percent of GDP. Thus, the report concludes that the benefits of immediate action to minimize climate change significantly exceed the costs, and that ignoring climate change will eventually damage economic growth.

BOX 17.1 DISCOUNTING THE FUTURE

In economic theory, future costs and benefits are evaluated with a technique called discounting. The discount rate is defined as the annual percentage by which impacts are reduced compared to the current year. The further into the future an impact occurs, the more it will be discounted.

The choice of a discount rate is a critical component of an economic analysis of climate change. A relatively low discount rate of 1 percent would devalue impacts 50 years in the future by only 40 percent, while a high discount rate of 5 percent would reduce the estimated economic value of impacts by more than 90 percent over 50 years. A low discount rate would thus support significant present investments in mitigating climate change because the avoided damages are valued relatively highly. A high discount rate, on the other hand, would justify little action today, as the perceived future benefits would be negligible.

Most economic analyses use a discount rate higher than 3 percent, based on market conditions including, for example, the rate of return on government bonds. But in the Stern Review of the Economics of Climate Change, a discount rate of only 1.4 percent was chosen. This choice was based on the principle that each generation's well-being should be valued equally. Economists using a higher discount rate implicitly allocate a lower value to the well-being of future generations when issues such as climate change damages are evaluated. The deliberate choice of a lower rate represents the principle of social discounting—that evaluation of future well-being should be based on a principle of equity between generations, rather than on market conditions today.

According to the Stern Review:

> Our actions over the coming few decades could create risks of major disruption to economic and social activity, later in this century and in the next, on a scale similar to those associated with the great wars and the economic depression of the first half of the twentieth century. And it will be difficult or impossible to reverse these changes. Tackling climate change is the pro-growth strategy for the longer term, and it can be done in a way that does not cap the aspirations for growth of rich or poor countries.[35]

The Stern Review initiated a vigorous debate among economists about the appropriate discount rate, the social cost of carbon, and climate policies. A 2015 survey of economists working on the topic found a strong trend toward favoring more aggressive policy actions (see Box 17.2). A 2019 statement by over 3,000 economists, including 28 Nobel laureates, 15 former chairs of the Council of Economic Advisers, and four former Federal Reserve chairs, stated that "global climate change is a serious problem calling for immediate national action."[36]

BOX 17.2 ECONOMISTS' VIEWS ON CLIMATE CHANGE

A 2015 study collected the views of 365 economists who have published articles on climate change economics in peer-reviewed academic journals. The results revealed that economists are much more concerned about the impacts of climate change than the American public. For example, half of the surveyed economists indicated that "immediate and drastic action is necessary" compared to just 23 percent of the American public.

The vast majority of economists feel that climate change will have significant negative effects on the economy. Seventy-eight percent responded that climate change would be "extremely likely" or "likely" to have a negative impact on the growth rate of the global economy. A similar percentage (77 percent) indicated that the United States should commit to reducing its greenhouse gas emissions regardless of the actions of other countries.

The survey also asked opinions about the social cost of carbon used by the U.S. government at the time, $37 per ton of CO_2. Over 50 percent thought the value should be higher, 18 percent thought it was somewhat accurate, and only 8 percent thought it should be lower (some respondents expressed no opinion). The study concludes:

> that the [economic] models used to calculate the social cost of carbon are likely underestimating climate damages. There is clear consensus among economic experts that climate change poses major risks to the economy and that significant policy responses will be needed to avoid large economic damages.[37]

3.3 Climate Change Policy

As mentioned above, economists tend to favor responding to the negative externalities associated with climate change by instituting market-based policies. The two most prominent proposals are carbon taxes and a system of tradable permits. A carbon tax would charge large emitters of CO_2, such as electricity producers, gasoline refineries, and factories, a per-ton fee, effectively "internalizing" the externality. The individual emitters would choose their pollution level by comparing the tax against the cost of actions to reduce emissions. In other words, as long as reducing emissions was cheaper than paying the tax, companies would reduce their emissions. The tax, or the cost of emissions control, would then, to some extent, get passed on to consumers in terms of higher prices.

Revenues raised by such a tax could be used to fund the transition to renewable energy. Rather than an overall tax increase, carbon taxes could be offset by lowering other taxes, such as income or social insurance taxes, as part of a revenue-neutral tax shift. A carbon tax would encourage the reduction of fossil-fuel-based energy use, as well as investment in renewable technologies (which would mostly avoid taxation).

The most serious disadvantage to a carbon tax is that it would fall more heavily on lower-income households. The U.S. Bureau of Labor Statistics reports that households in the lowest income decile allocate 9 percent of their spending on utilities and 4 percent on gasoline, while households in the highest income decile only spend about half as much, as a percent of income, on these products.[38] There are, however, several ways to respond to this, the most straightforward being a direct rebate of some of the tax revenues, which could leave lower-income consumers with no net loss, or even a gain.

With a system of tradable carbon permits, the government requires large CO_2 emitters to obtain permits for each ton they desired to emit, with the permits either auctioned to the highest bidders or freely distributed according to some criterion, such as historical emissions. Permits can then be traded among firms, with firms holding unneeded permits offering those for sale to other companies that find they need additional permits, with the permit price freely set by the market.

Permits create many of the same incentives as taxes—encouraging businesses and consumers to shift away from fossil fuels, fostering investment in renewable energy, and even raising government revenue if the permits are auctioned. The main advantage of permits is that the government effectively controls the overall level of emissions. With a tax, the effect on emissions is indirect, depending on the behavioral response by businesses and consumers. In other words, the greater the elasticity of demand for the products taxed, the more emissions would decline. With a permit system, uncertainty about the resulting emissions level is removed, which is particularly important in achieving emissions targets. On the other hand, a permit system creates uncertainty about the permit price, which may make it difficult for firms and households to determine whether energy efficiency investments will prove worthwhile. With a carbon tax, such long-term investment planning is expedited since the price impact of the tax is known in advance.

Both carbon taxes and permit systems have been used by a number of countries. Carbon taxes have been implemented in India, Japan, South Africa, Canada, and Costa Rica, among other places. The most extensive permit system is the European Union's Emissions Trading System, which has been in place since 2005. The system covers about 11,000 power stations and manufacturing plants, covering nearly half of all greenhouse gas emissions in the EU.[39] The price of permits in the EU system has varied significantly, and as of 2022 had reached €90/ton following an EU announcement of a goal of a 55 percent cut in carbon emissions by 2030. California has also instituted a carbon trading system and has partnered with Canadian provinces to expand the system. In 2021 China implemented a nationwide carbon permit system, effectively doubling the proportion of the world's carbon that is subject to pricing.[40]

Since climate change is a global problem, international cooperation is critical in mounting an adequate response. The first international treaty to address climate change, the 1997 Kyoto Protocol, specified emissions targets only for richer nations, with penalties enforced on those that failed to meet their targets. When the treaty expired in 2012, some countries had achieved their targets while others had not (the United States never ratified the treaty), but no penalties were ever enforced.

In order to bring nearly all nations into the process, the 2015 Paris Climate Agreement let each country set its own targets on a voluntary basis, without enforceable penalties. It is left to each country what national policies they will enact in order to meet their targets, whether these policies be taxes, permits, or other regulations. As of 2022, 197 nations are signatories to the treaty, and their commitments were updated at the 2021 Glasgow conference.[41] Each country's targets, referred to as their National Determined Contribution (NDCs), will be re-evaluated every year, with the goal of making the targets successively more stringent. An independent assessment of each country's NDC finds that only 8 out of 368 countries assessed are rated "almost sufficient", with the majority being rated "insufficient" or "highly insufficient."[42] The hope is that these commitments will be strengthened in future rounds of negotiation.

An overall evaluation of the status of the Paris Climate Agreement and NDCs is shown in Figure 17.5. We see that under current national policies, global emissions would continue to rise until at least the middle of the twenty-first century, and a temperature increase of 2.5–2.9°C relative to pre-industrial levels. The Glasgow NDCs collectively reduce the expected temperature increase to 2.4°C. More ambitious long-term

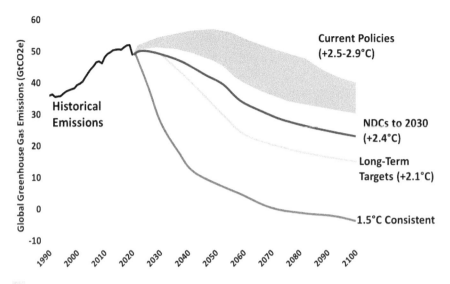

Figure 17.5 *Global Greenhouse Gas Emissions under Alternative Scenarios*

Source: Climate Action Tracker, http://climateactiontracker.org/global.html.

Note: Emissions data include carbon dioxide and other greenhouse gases converted to carbon dioxide equivalents.

targets agreed to at Glasgow—but not yet included in national pledges—would hold the temperature rise to 2.1°C. In order to achieve a 1.5°C target, emissions would need to begin to decline essentially immediately, rapidly fall to close to zero by 2050, and actually decline below zero by 2070 (meaning net absorption of CO_2 from the atmosphere either by technical or natural means).

A crucial set of policies to fill the gap between current reductions plans and a 1.5°C target is carbon sequestration in forests, soils, and wetlands. This would involve modified techniques for agricultural production and forestry. This important area has only just begun to receive attention in national policy and international negotiations.[†]

Discussion Questions

1 How do you think we should evaluate the economic impacts of climate change? What kinds of economic analysis are involved, and what accounts for the differences in various evaluations of the issue?

2 What do you think should be done by the United States and other countries in response to global climate change? Can you think of specific policies that would reduce carbon emissions without resulting in significant economic disruption?

---

† An evaluation of numerous policy solutions including emissions reduction and carbon sequestration can be found at https://www.drawdown.org/.

4 ECONOMIC GROWTH AND THE ENVIRONMENT

This section will consider three topics that explore the relationship between economic growth and the environment:

1. How does economic growth tend to affect environmental quality?
2. Does protecting the environment harm employment and economic growth?
3. How have economists envisioned the transition to a sustainable economy?

4.1 The Environmental Kuznets Curve Hypothesis

Some researchers have suggested that, in the long run, economic development reduces per capita environmental damages. The logic behind this assertion is that sufficient wealth and technology allow countries to adopt clean production methods and move to a service-based economy. Further, environmental quality is generally considered a "normal good," meaning that people will demand more of it as they become wealthier.

The **environmental Kuznets curve (EKC) hypothesis** posits an inverted U-shaped relationship between economic development and environmental damages.[‡] It states that environmental damage per capita increases in the early stages of economic development as a country transitions away from an agricultural-based economy to an economy with more manufacturing, energy use, transportation network, and higher consumption. Eventually, however, damages reach a maximum and then diminish as a country attains even higher levels of income, allowing it to invest in cleaner production methods. This hypothesis implies that policies that foster macroeconomic growth will eventually promote a cleaner environment as well. But is it supported by the evidence?

---

environmental Kuznets curve (EKC) hypothesis: the theory that as a country develops economically environmental damages per capita initially increase, then peak, and eventually decrease

---

The EKC relationship does seem to hold for some pollutants. Figure 17.6 shows the findings of a study that estimated the relationship between the average particulate matter (PM_{10}) concentration in a country and a country's per capita income. At very low levels of income,

---

[‡] This hypothesis was not devised by Simon Kuznets but is similar to his hypothesis, discussed in Chapter 16, that inequality first increases, then decreases with growing national wealth.

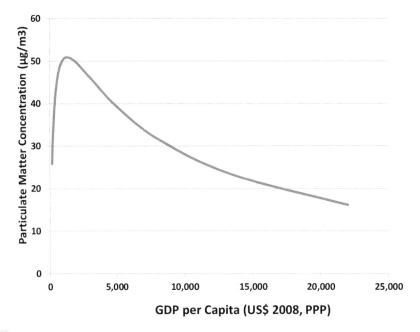

Figure 17.6 *Environmental Kuznets Curve for Particulate Matter*

Source: Mazurek, 2011.

the expected PM_{10} concentration tends to rise quickly as a country develops economically. But the PM_{10} concentration peaks when a country reaches an average income of around US$1,300 per person. Air pollution levels then fall steadily with further economic advancement. As noted earlier in the chapter, the World Health Organization has recommended that PM_{10} levels be below 20 µg/m³. On average, countries achieve this standard when income per person rises above US$17,000 per person. Evidence supporting the EKC hypothesis has also been found for municipal solid waste and other air pollutants such as sulfur dioxide and carbon monoxide.[43]

The EKC relationship, however, does not appear to hold for all environmental problems. Perhaps most importantly, CO_2 emissions show a positive relationship with average income, as shown in Figure 17.7. A simple statistical test to fit an inverted-U curve through the data in Figure 17.7 finds that there is no turning point—per-capita CO_2 emissions continue to rise as GDP/capita increases. A more sophisticated analysis in 2015 reached a similar conclusion, that "rising income is associated with an increase in [CO_2] emissions. No income turning points are found for the observed sample of countries."[44] Thus, promoting economic growth does not appear to be an effective means to address the issue of global climate change.

The relationship between economic growth and the environment is, in reality, more complex than implied by the EKC hypothesis. As one analysis of various Kuznets curve studies concludes:

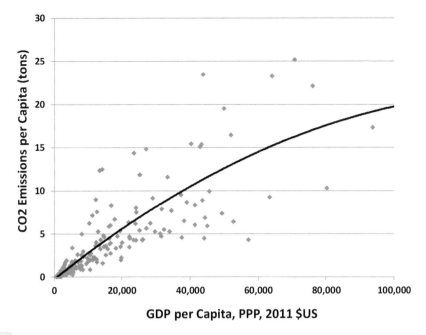

Figure 17.7 *Relationship between Carbon Dioxide Emissions and GDP per Capita*
Source: World Bank, World Development Indicators database.

it would be misleading to follow the policy of polluting first and cleaning later as espoused by proponents of EKC. It does not make much sense to "do nothing" and wait for the magic-wand of economic growth to cure environmental problems. Proactive policies and measures are required to mitigate the problem.[45]

4.2 Does Protecting the Environment Harm Employment and Economic Growth?

Policies that increase environmental protections are sometimes criticized for causing decreases in employment or harming economic growth. What is the evidence on this subject?

Several research studies have explored the relationship between employment and environmental regulation. The overall conclusion is that while increased environmental spending leads to the loss of certain jobs, it creates other jobs. These effects may cancel out or actually result in a net gain of jobs. One study estimating the impact of environmental spending and regulation on employment in various industries found that:

> contrary to conventional wisdom, [environmental protection (EP)], economic growth, and jobs creation are complementary and compatible: Investments in EP create jobs and displace jobs, but the net effect on employment is positive.[46]

687

Another study reached the conclusion that strong environmental policies will change the distribution of jobs in society but will have little effect on the overall level of employment. Focused on Europe, the study found that well-designed environmental policies can sometimes result in net job gains. For example, the additional revenue from higher environmental taxes could be used to reduce the taxes on labor, thus reducing the cost of hiring workers and leading to higher overall employment.[47]

A similar conclusion was reached by a 2016 analysis of policies to reduce carbon emissions in the United States. Job losses in "dirty" sectors such as coal mining were essentially offset by job gains in cleaner sectors such as renewable energy. The authors concluded that the "overall effects on unemployment should not be a substantial factor in the evaluation of environmental policy" because the net effects are likely to be quite small.[48]

Another study found that shifting to renewable energy provides a net employment benefit. Public investments in clean energy sources in the United States create about three times as many jobs as similar spending on fossil fuel energy sources, according to a 2012 study. The reasons are that clean energy sources tend to be more labor intensive, and the money invested is more likely to be spent domestically as opposed to funding imports. Worldwide, renewable energy sources employed nearly 10 million people in 2016—more than 1 million each in solar photovoltaics, liquid biofuels, and wind energy. More than half of these jobs are in low- and middle-income countries, mainly China and India. Solar and wind technologies have advanced rapidly, making these sources economically competitive with fossil fuels for new power installation.[49]

Another criticism of environmental protection based on the results of some studies is that environmental regulations reduce GDP growth rates. For example, a comprehensive analysis of the Clean Air Act in the United States estimated that GNP in 1990 was about 1 percent lower than it would have been without the policy. The aggregate macroeconomic loss from the Act over the period 1973–1990 was estimated to be about $1 trillion. Analysis of the economic impact of major environmental regulations in Europe suggests an aggregate economic loss of about 0.2 percent of GDP.[50]

But these macroeconomic costs must be assessed against the benefits of the regulations. When an estimate of the Clean Air Act benefits was made, it was found that the central estimate of the 1973–1990 benefits was $22 trillion, giving a benefit-cost ratio of 22:1. So while there appears to be a slightly negative impact of environmental regulation on economic growth as traditionally measured, we need a more complete analysis to determine its effect on social welfare. As we saw in Chapter 5, GDP was never intended to measure overall well-being, and economists have developed alternative national accounting approaches to supplement or replace GDP. These alternatives may present a better framework for fully assessing the impacts of environmental regulations since

688

they take into account not just consumption levels but also improvement in the quality of life.

4.3 Economic Perspectives on the Transition to a Sustainable Economy

We now consider a broader question: Is continued macroeconomic growth compatible with a sustainable national or global economy? Some economists studying this topic believe that, at least for the foreseeable future, further economic growth is acceptable or desirable as we transition to a more sustainable economy. Other economists, who believe that we have already exceeded the planet's carrying capacity, advocate for a transition to a "no growth" economy, perhaps requiring a period of degrowth (negative growth) during that transition.

Among those economists favoring "greener" growth rather than no growth or degrowth is Nicholas Stern, whom we discussed above. While Stern believes significant policy changes are required to address climate change, he argues that "… the economic opportunities of the transition to the low or zero carbon economy are real and very attractive: it is a story of sustainable growth."[51]

Another proponent of this perspective is the United Nations. The United Nations' Green Economy Initiative, launched in 2008, seeks to promote an economy that "results in improved human well-being and social equity, while significantly reducing environmental risks and ecological scarcities." The Initiative proposed an annual investment of 2 percent of global GDP over the period 2010–2050 to fund sustainable technologies and practices. The United Nations developed a macroeconomic model to estimate the short-term and long-term effects of this investment, relative to a business-as-usual (BAU) scenario. Their results found that while in the first few years the additional investment reduced global GDP/capita by about 1 percent, by 2030 global GDP/capita would be 2 percent higher in the Green Economy scenario. And by 2050, global GDP/capita would be 14 percent higher as a result of sustainable investments.[52]

Further, the Green Economy scenario resulted in dramatic reductions in environmental impacts. Relative to the BAU scenario, by 2050 global energy demand is reduced by 40 percent, water demand is reduced by 22 percent, total forested land increases by 21 percent, and the global ecological footprint is reduced by 48 percent.

Economist Robert Pollin, in his 2015 book *Greening the Global Economy*, also advocates for an investment of 1.5 percent of global GDP in renewable energy and energy efficiency to fund a transition to a sustainable, low-carbon economy. His analysis concludes that green investments expand employment and economic growth, as jobs in renewable energy and energy efficiency tend to be more labor-intensive than jobs in the fossil fuel sector, as shown in Figure 17.8. In each country, investments in green energy result in higher job creation, yielding 75–135 percent more jobs per dollar than fossil fuel investments, with the greatest job gains in developing

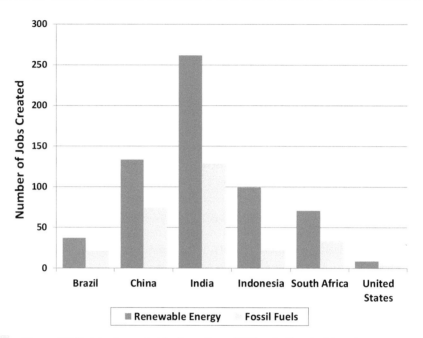

Figure 17.8 *Jobs Generated by Investing 1 Million Dollars in Clean Energy versus Fossil Fuel Production, Selected Countries*

Source: Pollin, 2015.

nations. To assist displaced fossil-fuel industry workers, Pollin argues for job retraining programs and policies promoting full employment.[53]

Analyses such as Pollin's book and the United Nations' Green Economy Initiative suggest that sustainability is compatible with economic growth, and green investments can even *increase* rates of economic growth. But other economists argue that continual economic growth is incompatible with long-term sustainability. As we saw earlier in this chapter, economist Herman Daly has noted that indefinite expansion of the macroeconomy within a finite biosphere is physically impossible. Since the 1970s, Daly has advocated for a transition to a **steady-state economy** in which population and the stock of physical capital are held constant.[§]

> **steady-state economy:** an economy in which population and the stock of physical capital are held constant, but things such as technology, information, fairness, and wisdom can continue to grow

A steady-state economy would not hold human well-being constant, as things such as technology, information, fairness, and wisdom could continue to improve. Also, activities that do not involve resource consumption, and are environmentally neutral or environmentally friendly,

---

§ Daly's perspective is promoted today by the Center for the Advancement of the Steady-State Economy (CASSE), https://steadystate.org

could continue to grow. Such activities could include services, arts, communication, and education. But Daly maintains that consumption levels should be kept "sufficient" but not extravagant. After basic needs are met and reasonable levels of consumption achieved, the concept of a steady-state economy implies that economic development should be increasingly oriented toward these kinds of inherently "sustainable" activities. Thus, Daly distinguishes between growth and development—the steady-state economy "develops but does not grow, just as the planet earth, of which it is a subsystem, develops without growing."[54]

A similar viewpoint is espoused in Tim Jackson's book *Prosperity Without Growth*. Jackson calls for an ecological macroeconomics that maintains economic stability without reliance on traditional growth. He proposes that three macroeconomic interventions are necessary to transition to a sustainable economy:

1. A structural transition toward service-based activities. Like Daly, Jackson advocates for a shift of economic activity away from resource-intensive goods toward "dematerialized" services such as education and the arts.
2. Investment in ecological assets. Jackson notes that the definition of a "productive" investment would need to change under ecological macroeconomics. Ecological investments may provide lower financial returns, as traditionally measured, but can provide greater social value due to increases in resource efficiency and the enhancement of ecological functions.
3. A working time policy to maintain employment levels. Given that in a no-growth scenario total hours worked would likely fall, Jackson proposes that working hours per week (or per job) decline to prevent unemployment, leaving people more leisure time. Labor productivity could continue to increase due to improvements in technology, potentially further reducing working hours per week.[55]

A macroeconomic simulation model developed by Canadian economist Peter Victor explores how a national economy would perform during a transition to a sustainable, low- or zero-growth future. A conventional economic growth scenario is compared to two scenarios with specific policies for greenhouse gas reduction and "sustainable prosperity." These scenarios include:

- A "greenhouse gas reduction" scenario, in which the Canadian government is assumed to introduce a tax on greenhouse gas (GHG) emissions, creating incentives to switch from high GHG energy sources to low-carbon sources, making energy in general more expensive (at least in the short term) and encouraging conservation, efficiency, and electrification of transport. The revenues from the GHG tax are used to reduce other taxes so that the net effect on government revenues is zero.

691

■ A broader "sustainable prosperity" scenario, in which there is an additional focus on "green" investment, reduction of inequality and poverty, a shorter work week, and a lower rate of population growth.

In both of these scenarios GDP growth is reduced as compared with the standard case—in the "sustainable prosperity" scenario it is reduced to zero. But using a Sustainable Prosperity Index (similar to the Genuine Progress Indicator discussed in Chapter 5), both scenarios perform substantially better than the standard case, in which Sustainable Prosperity actually declines.[56]

Those who believe that we have already "overshot" the level of population and consumption that can be sustained by the available natural resource base, known as **carrying capacity**, argue that a period of **degrowth** will be needed before a stable steady-state economy can be achieved. This is shown in Figure 17.9. As this hypothetical economy (blue line) exceeds its carrying capacity (gray line) it is forced to reduce its overall size until it stabilizes at a new, somewhat reduced, carrying capacity. This transition could be based on deliberate policy choices, or it could occur due to an "overshoot-collapse" syndrome similar to that predicted by the original *Limits to Growth* report mentioned in Section 1 of this chapter.

---

carrying capacity: the level of population and consumption that can be sustained by the available natural resource base

degrowth: a policy of reducing the level of economic activity to promote environmental sustainability

---

Regardless of whether we believe that "green growth", steady-state, or degrowth scenarios are likely, it seems evident that much stronger policies for long-term sustainability are required. We now turn to an examination of such policies.

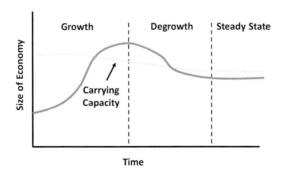

Figure 17.9 *The Degrowth Transition to a Steady-State Economy*
Source: Adapted from O'Neill, 2012.

Discussion Questions

1   What is the principle of the Environmental Kuznets Curve (EKC)? In what areas does it seem applicable, and in what ways could it be inaccurate or misleading? What are some policy implications that can be drawn from an analysis of the evidence reading the EKC?

2   The promotion of economic growth is often seen as a major policy goal. What do you think is the feasibility of a model that stresses alternative goals such as ecological sustainability and well-being? How would you compare the Green Economy, steady-state economy, and degrowth concepts?

5 POLICIES FOR SUSTAINABLE DEVELOPMENT

Much of macroeconomic theory and policy is currently oriented toward promoting continuous economic growth. But an over-emphasis on policies that promote growth can result in outcomes that severely degrade natural resources and lead to environmental problems such as global climate change. What kind of policies would be required to promote ecological sustainability, whether defined as weak or strong sustainability? How can these policies be designed such that they also enhance well-being and promote human development?

5.1 Rethinking Employment and Production

Designing macroeconomic policies that are compatible with sustainability requires some fundamental rethinking about economic goals. Specifically, what do we want from employment and production?

The macroeconomic models we developed starting in Chapter 8 have implicitly assumed that more employment is better. There is no doubt that employment contributes to people's well-being, and not only as a source of income. People's satisfaction with their jobs is an important predictor of their overall life satisfaction, while unemployment is a significant cause of family stress and other problems. About one in five suicides are linked to unemployment, and suicide rates increase during recessions.[57]

Thus, maintaining employment levels is important, but people also benefit from the time that they spend away from paid employment, to do unpaid work, including family care, and pursuing leisure activities. As we saw in the previous section, working time policies have been proposed to maintain employment levels, while providing workers with more time for leisure and other activities.

Several European countries have instituted labor policies that mandate comparatively short working weeks for most employees. France instituted a maximum 35-hour working week in 2000, and most German workers also have a standard 35-hour working week. In 2018, workers in Germany's largest labor union won the right to work a 28-hour working week for up to two years.[58]

693

Research suggests that policies mandating shorter working weeks are not necessarily effective at reducing unemployment rates. But two positive effects have been identified. First, people working shorter weeks tend to be more productive per hour. Based on a sample of OECD countries, GDP per hour worked declines as the hours worked per worker increases. Second, shorter working weeks tend to be correlated with lower GHG emissions. According to one study, policies to reduce annual work hours by 0.5 percent per year could mitigate one-quarter to one-half of future global warming.[59]

Traditional macroeconomic models also assume that more production is always preferable. The model that we developed in earlier chapters focuses only on the *level* of output, *Y*, and says nothing about the *composition* of output. From a sustainability perspective, however, the composition of output makes a very big difference. Some things that we produce require relatively little use of material and energy inputs. Eating locally grown produce, taking a bike ride with friends, or engaging in educational and cultural activities, for example, puts little stress on the natural environment. Other activities, such as heating and furnishing a very large house, driving an SUV, or maintaining a perfect lawn using chemical fertilizer, have more negative impacts. Shifting away from producing goods and services that are most damaging to ecological systems and toward producing goods and services that are less destructive—or even environmentally beneficial—could allow an economy to maintain consumption, investment, and employment in a less environmentally damaging way.

Rethinking employment and production for a sustainable economy means that traditional macroeconomic indicators, such as the unemployment rate and GDP growth rate, are no longer sufficient. We would want to measure the *quality,* not just the quantity, of employment and consumption. The OECD has developed a framework for assessing job quality in a country by considering three dimensions: earnings, labor market security, and the quality of the working environment.[60] And of course, we would want to adjust GDP to account for resource degradation and pollution, as discussed in Chapter 5.

5.2 Reforming Tax and Subsidy Policies

5.2.1 Green Taxes

Fiscal policy affects economic behavior by setting taxes that discourage certain actions and subsidies that encourage other choices. Taxes have traditionally been placed on income and profits, an approach which is criticized by some economists for creating a disincentive for employment and entrepreneurism, and consequently reducing productivity. An alternative is to shift taxation away from income and profits in favor of higher taxes on negative externalities such as pollution.

"Green" taxes make it more expensive to undertake activities that deplete important natural resources or contribute to environmental degradation. They discourage energy- and material-intensive economic activities while favoring the provision of services and labor-intensive industries. One example of a green tax, as discussed above, is a tax on carbon emissions, favoring renewables and efficiency over carbon-based fuels. Another is a tax on the extraction of virgin resources, which encourages resource conservation and recycling.

All countries have implemented environmentally based taxes to some extent. As shown in Figure 17.10, environmental taxes in industrialized countries can range from less than 3 percent of total tax revenues (in the United States) to around 10 percent (in South Korea). Environmental taxes in developing countries range even more widely, from less than 1 percent in Nigeria to about 18 percent in India. A shift toward higher reliance on environmental taxes does not seem to be occurring, with the OECD average remaining around 6 percent of all tax revenues since the mid-1990s.[61]

Green taxes are strongly supported by economic theory as a means of internalizing negative externalities. When a negative externality such as pollution exists, an unregulated market will result in an inefficient allocation (as discussed in Chapter 3). Because all taxes, in addition to raising revenue, discourage the "taxed" activity, it is economically and socially desirable to discourage "bads" such as environmental pollution and natural resource depletion by placing taxes on them, rather than on positive economic activities like investment and the earning of income.

Two common objections to green taxes frequently arise. First, it is likely that green taxes would fall disproportionately on lower-income

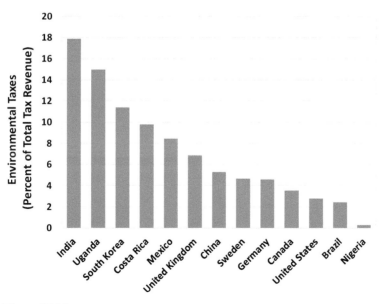

Figure 17.10 *Environmental Taxes, as a Percent of Total Tax Revenues, Selected Countries*

Source: OECD, OECD.Stat, "Environmentally related tax revenue," 2019.

households. But as noted earlier with respect to carbon taxes, a rebate or credit to these households could be implemented to avoid making green taxes regressive. The other criticism is that green taxes are politically unpopular—no one wants higher taxes. Increases in green taxes can be offset, however, by reductions in other taxes (such as income taxes) so that the tax burden on a typical household remains unchanged. Also, households and businesses would have the option to lower the amount of green taxes they pay by undertaking energy conservation measures and other environmentally friendly practices, which is not the case with income or business taxes.

5.2.2 Eliminating Damaging Subsidies

While subsidies for renewable energy can encourage a transition to a more sustainable economy, many current subsidies actually increase environmental damages. Agricultural and energy subsidies that encourage the overuse of energy, fertilizer, pesticides, and irrigation water could be reduced or eliminated. This would reduce government expenditures, and the money saved could be used to lower taxes or to promote more sustainable agricultural systems that rely on the recycling of nutrients, crop diversification, the use of natural pest controls, and minimizing the use of artificial chemicals and fertilizer. Such systems also tend to be more labor-intensive, so they also have the potential to boost employment.

The fossil fuel industry receives the largest share of perverse subsidies. According to a 2017 journal article, fossil fuel subsidies amount to about 6.5 percent of global GDP. This not only includes direct payments by governments to fossil fuel companies but also the implicit subsidy when negative externalities are not included in market prices. This mispricing of goods and services effectively permits producers to transfer the costs of environmental damage onto society. A broader estimate of the global environmental externalities imposed on society from economic activity is about 11 percent of global GDP. These damages are expected to increase to 18 percent of world GDP in 2050.[62]

5.3 Greening Macroeconomic Policy

As discussed in previous chapters, Keynesian economics focuses on using monetary and fiscal policy to spur aggregate demand during economic downturns. Stimulus packages passed in many countries in response to the 2007–2009 and 2020 recessions included significant public investment in green projects. For example, over 10 percent of the 2009 stimulus package passed in the United States (the American Recovery and Reinvestment Act) was directed toward investment in energy efficiency, renewable energy, and other kinds of green spending. Green stimulus government spending in China was even higher, at over US$200 billion.[63] The $1.2 trillion Biden administration Infrastructure Investment and Jobs Act of 2021 included about $300 billion in specifically green investments such as electrical vehicle fleets and charging systems, zero-emissions public transit, bicycle infrastructure, expanding renewables and modernizing the electric grid, upgrading water systems, and climate resilience and weatherization. The Inflation Reduction Act of 2022 included a further $369 billion in spending on investments related to renewable energy and climate change.

Some critics have argued that there is a contradiction between the "green Keynesian" goals of economic growth and environmental protection.[64] But it is possible to direct policies toward different kinds of growth. Instead of just thinking of consumption (C), investment (I), and government spending (G), we can divide each of these terms into environmentally harmful and environmentally positive activities. Thus, it should be possible to achieve growth in employment and well-being) while reducing **throughput**—the flow of material and energy inputs into the economy and outputs of wastes and pollution. According to one "green Keynesian" analysis:

> we can distinguish between those macroeconomic aggregates that should be strictly limited—resource-intensive consumption and investment, and energy-intensive infrastructure—and those that can expand over time without negative environmental consequences. The latter would include large areas of health, education, cultural activity, and resource- and energy-conserving investment. . . there is plenty of scope for growth in economic activity concentrated in these categories, without growth in resource throughput, and with a significant decline in the most damaging throughput, that of carbon-intensive fuels.[65]

---

throughput: the flow of raw materials and energy through the economy, leading to outputs of waste

---

DISCUSSION QUESTIONS

1   What specific economic incentives and policies would you recommend for promoting sustainability? Have you heard of any policy examples from the news recently that you think were good ideas?

2   Can you identify areas in which "green Keynesian" economic growth would be desirable and areas in which economic growth is more destructive to the environment? In what ways would a "green" economy look different from our current economy?

697

6 CONCLUDING THOUGHTS

Throughout the twentieth century, the main objective of macroeconomics was steady, strong economic growth. Considering the social and environmental challenges that we face in the twenty-first century, macroeconomics will need to adapt to new realities. Employment, price stability, and GDP growth will continue to be issues of great importance—not as ends in themselves but as means to the broader goals of human development and sustainability. Keeping ultimate well-being goals in mind, macroeconomics must look beyond the experience of the past and ask new questions.

A fundamental question confronting macroeconomics in the twenty-first century is how the majority of people in the world, currently at relatively low standards of living, can improve their well-being. The issues of "human development" discussed in Chapter 16 involve a combination of traditional economic growth and new approaches that are more oriented toward dealing with problems of poverty, inequality, and ecological sustainability.

Economic analysis needs to take into account the need for technologies that can provide energy, food, and other materials for human consumption in ways that are ecologically sound, and that help remedy past damages. The transition to a more sustainable economy will have economic costs, but also significant benefits, such as increased employment and improved quality of life.

If the true goal of economics is to enhance well-being, then we need to realize that the economic goals and policies of the future may differ significantly from those of the past. This was recognized by John Maynard Keynes nearly a century ago. Even during the Great Depression in the 1930s, Keynes looked into the future and imagined a world of relative affluence, where humanity's "economic problem may be solved," creating little need for traditional economics, and where people will instead be able to focus on how to live "wisely and agreeably and well." (See Box 17.3.)

BOX 17.3 ECONOMIC POSSIBILITIES FOR OUR GRANDCHILDREN

Looking beyond the dire conditions during the Great Depression, John Maynard Keynes imagined what the world, and economics, might be like 100 years into the future (in 2030). Considering what would be the "economic possibilities for our grandchildren", Keynes' main conclusion was that as people's needs and goals changed with further affluence, so should economics. Writing in 1930, Keynes suggested that:

> a point may soon be reached, much sooner perhaps than we are all of us aware of, when [basic] needs are satisfied in the sense that we prefer to

---

> devote our further energies to non-economic purposes. . . This means that the economic problem is not—if we look into the future—the permanent problem of the human race.
>
> When the accumulation of wealth is no longer of high social importance, there will be great changes in the code of morals. . . All kinds of social customs and economic practices, affecting the distribution of wealth and of economic rewards and penalties, which we now maintain at all costs, however distasteful and unjust they may be in themselves, because they are tremendously useful in promoting the accumulation of capital, we shall then be free, at last, to discard.
>
> While Keynes did not specifically emphasize environmental issues, his comments foreshadow a situation in which policies to promote the maintenance of a sustainable and equitable world could replace a preoccupation with economic growth.[66]

Macroeconomics can be compatible with the goal of sustainability. Policies are available to address all the major environmental problems discussed in this chapter. These will need to be combined with our earlier analyses of issues concerning national income, fiscal and monetary policy, unemployment and inflation, and economic development. This effort can generate new macroeconomic theory and policy capable of responding to the challenges of our current era.

Discussion Questions

1. How can we reconcile the need for global economic development with the problems of environmental limits? In what ways will established models of economic development have to be modified to deal with new realities?
2. Do you agree with Keynes's belief that industrialized countries can reach a point where needs will be "satisfied in the sense that we prefer to devote our further energies to non-economic purposes"? Do you think that we are any closer to this point than in 1930 when Keynes wrote his essay? Do you see any evidence that this is starting to occur?

REVIEW QUESTIONS

1. What are some of the environmental issues related to economic growth?
2. What can we expect in terms of future global population growth?
3. Are we running out of non-renewable resources? What are the major problems regarding these resources?
4. How well are we managing renewable resources? What are some of the major areas in which these resources are being depleted?
5. What are some of the projected effects of future climate change?
6. What are some policies that could be effective in responding to climate change?

7. What are some of the goals of recent international climate negotiations? How well are countries doing in meeting the targets set by the Paris 2015 and Glasgow 2021 conferences?

8. What is the environmental Kuznets curve (EKC) hypothesis? What is the evidence regarding this hypothesis?

9. What are "green" taxes?

10. What are tradable permit systems?

11. What are "green Keynesian" policies? Give some examples.

12. What is a steady-state economy? What is degrowth and how is it related to the steady-state economy?

EXERCISES

1 Issues of environmental sustainability can sometimes be a bit abstract. This exercise is designed to bring them to an individual level. Start at https://www.footprintnetwork.org/ and familiarize yourself with the notion of "ecological footprints," then take the quiz to discover what your personal footprint looks like. What did you learn that was new information to you? What specifically can you do about this new information?

2 Go to https://data.footprintnetwork.org/ and access data for a number of different countries. For each country answer the following questions:
   a) What was the per capita ecological footprint of consumption?
   b) What was the per capita biocapacity?
   c) Explain the meaning of the two numbers you just located. What are the implications?

3 Match each concept in Column A with a definition or example in Column B:

Column A		Column B	
a.	"Green" taxes	1.	The perspective that natural capital depreciation should be compensated for with restoration of other natural capital
b.	Tradable permit systems	2.	An inverted U-shaped relationship between economic development and environmental damages
c.	Strong sustainability	3.	A situation where population and the use of raw materials and energy have stabilized
d.	Throughput	4.	Based on the principle that a process of pollution reduction may be most efficiently achieved if businesses have choices
e.	Social discount rate	5.	Designed to discourage pollution and natural resource depletion by making them more expensive
f.	Environmental Kuznets Curve	6.	Reflects social rather than market valuation of future costs and benefits
g.	Steady-state economy	7.	The flow of raw materials and energy into the economic system, and the flow of wastes from the system

NOTES

1 World Bank's World Development Indicators database; OECD, 2012; Manyika et al., 2015.
2 See, for example, Ruppert, 2009.
3 Kubiszewski et al., 2013. More recent global GPI data are not available, but data for individual countries and regions show a similar pattern for recent years.
4 Daly, 2005, p. 100.
5 See, for example, Kelemen et al., 2016.
6 See Lin et al., 2016, for a description of the ecological footprint calculations.
7 See, for example, Giampietro and Saltelli, 2014; Harris, 2019.
8 See, for example, Fischer, 2009.
9 United Nations, 2022.
10 Worstall, 2017; International Institute for Applied Systems Analysis (IIASA), 2014.
11 Tanquintic-Misa, 2012.
12 British Geological Survey, 2015.
13 Our World in Data, "Oil Reserves, 1980 to 2020."
14 FAO, 2020a; UNEP, 2019.
15 FAO, 2020b.
16 UNEP, 2008; UN Water, http://www.unwater.org/water-facts/scarcity/.
17 Biswas and Hartley, 2017; Khokhar, 2017; WEF, 2020.
18 UNEP, 2019.
19 Thomas et al., 2004.
20 Landrigan et al., 2017.
21 Ibid.
22 U.S. Environmental Protection Agency, 2021.
23 Lebreton et al., 2018.
24 Hoornweg and Bhada-Tata, 2012; Hoornweg et al., 2013.
25 Ajibo, 2016; Vidal, 2013a.
26 See, https://climate.nasa.gov/scientific-consensus/ and Intergovernmental Panel on Climate Change (IPCC), 2021.
27 Vidal, 2013b; Harvey, 2018; Fankhauser and Stern, 2016.
28 European Commission EDGAR Database for Global Atmospheric Research, 2020 (data for 2017 emissions).
29 United Nations, 2021.
30 International Energy Agency, Data and Statistics, "Total Energy Supply by Source," 2020.
31 U.S. EIA, 2021.
32 Harris and Roach, 2022, Chapter 11, pp. 306-307: "Consistent Inaccuracies in Renewable Energy Forecasts."
33 See https://en.wikipedia.org/wiki/Economists%27_Statement_on_Climate_Change.
34 Tol, 2008.
35 Stern, 2007, Executive Summary, p. 2.
36 www.econstatement,org, published in the *Wall Street Journal*, January 17, 2019.
37 Howard and Sylvan, 2015.
38 Data from the Consumer Expenditure Survey, for 2016.
39 European Commission, 2016.
40 Roberts, 2017.
41 United Nations, 2021.
42 Climate Action Tracker, http://climateactiontracker.org/countries.
43 Ichinose et al., 2015; Georgiev and Mihaylov, 2015.
44 Georgiev and Mihaylov, 2015.

45 Akpan and Abang, 2014, p. 16.
46 Bezdek et al., 2008.
47 Rayment et al., 2009.
48 Hafstead and Williams, 2016.
49 Pollin, 2012; IRENA, 2017; U.S. Energy Information Administration, 2017.
50 Commission of the European Communities, 2004.
51 Fankhauser and Stern, 2016, p. 22.
52 UNEP, 2011, https://www.unenvironment.org/explore-topics/green-economy/why-does-green-economy-matter/what-inclusive-green-economy.
53 Pollin, 2015.
54 Daly, 1973, p. 330.
55 Jackson, 2011.
56 Victor, 2019.
57 Unanue et al., 2017; Nordt et al., 2015.
58 Huggler, 2018.
59 Estevão et al., 2008; Anonymous, 2013; Rosnick, 2013.http://www.oecd.org/statistics/jobquality.htm.
60 OECD, Job Quality, http://www.oecd.org/statistics/job-quality.htm.
61 OECD Statistics Database (OECD.Stat), environmentally related tax revenue.
62 Coady et al., 2017; UNEP Finance Initiative and PRI, 2011.
63 Tienhaara, 2018; http://www.wri.org/resources/charts-graplis/green-stimulus-spending-country.
64 Blackwater, 2012.
65 Harris, 2013.
66 Keynes, 2009 [1930].

REFERENCES

Ajibo, Kenneth I. 2016. "Transboundary Hazardous Wastes and Environmental Justice." *Environmental Law Review, 18*(4): 267–283.

Akpan, Usenobong F., and Dominic E. Abang. 2014. "Environmental Quality and Economic Growth: A Panel Analysis of the 'U' in Kuznets." *MPRA Paper*, University Library of Munich, Germany, February 2014.

Anonymous. 2013. "Get a Life." *The Economist*, September 24.

Bezdek, Roger H., Robert M. Wendling, and Paula DiPerna. 2008. "Environmental Protection, the Economy, and Jobs: National and Regional Analyses." *Journal of Environmental Management, 86*: 63–79.

Biswas, Asit K., and Kris Hartley. 2017. "From Evidence to Policy in India's Groundwater Crisis." *The Diplomat*, July 22, 2017.

Blackwater, Bill. 2012. "The Contradictions of Environmental Keynesianism." *Climate & Capitalism*, June 14, 2012. http://climateandcapitalism.com/2012/06/14/the-contradictions-of-envi-ronmental-keynesianism/.

British Geological Survey. 2015. *Risk List 2015*. http://www.bgs.ac.uk/mineralsuk/statistics/risklist.html.

Coady, David, Ian Parry, Louis Sears, and Baoping Shang. 2017. "How Large Are Global Fossil Fuel Subsidies?" *World Development, 91*:11–27.

Commission of the European Communities. 2004. *The EU Economy: 2004 Review. EC-FIN (2004) REP 50455-EN*. Brussels.Daly, Herman. 1973. "The Steady-State Economy: Toward a Political Economy of Biophysical Equilibrium and Moral Growth." In *Toward a Steady-State Economy* (Herman Daly, ed.), Freeman, San Francisco.

Daly, Herman. 2005. "Economics in a Full World." *Scientific American*, September 2005: 100–107.

Estevão, Marcello, Filipa Sá, and Barbara Petrongolo. 2008. "The 35-Hour Workweek in France: Straightjacket or Welfare Improvement?" *Economic Policy, 23*(55):417–463.

European Commission. 2016. *The EU Emissions Trading System (EU ETS). Factsheet.* https://ec.europa.eu/clima/sites/clima/files/factsheet_ets_en.pdf.

Fankhauser, Samuel, and Nicholas Stern. 2016. "Climate Change, Development, Poverty and Economics." *Grantham Research Institute on Climate Change and the Environment,* May 2016.

Fischer, Douglas. 2009. "Even Deep Cuts in Greenhouse Gas Emissions Will Not Stop Global Warming." *Scientific American,* April 14, 2009.

Food and Agriculture Organization of the United Nations (FAO). 2020a. *The State of the World's Forests 2020.* Rome.

Food and Agriculture Organization of the United Nations (FAO). 2020b. "*The State of the World Fisheries and Aquaculture 2020.*" Rome.

Georgiev, Emil, and Emil Mihaylov. 2015. "Economic Growth and the Environment: Reassessing the Environmental Kuznets Curve for Air Pollution Emissions in OECD Countries." *Letters in Spatial and Resource Sciences,* 8(1):29–47.

Giampietro, Mario, and Andrea Saltelli. 2014. "Footprints to Nowhere." *Ecological Indicators,* 46:610–621.

Hafstead, Marc A.C., and Roberton C. Williams III. 2016. "Unemployment and Environmental Regulation in General Equilibrium." *Resources for the Future, Discussion Paper 15–11,* Washington, DC, May 2016.

Harris, Jonathan M. 2013. "Green Keynesianism: Beyond Standard Growth Paradigms." *In Building a Green Economy: Perspectives from Ecological Economics* (Robert B. Richardson, editor). Michigan State University Press, East Lansing, MI.

Harris, Jonathan M. 2019. "Responding to Economic and Ecological Deficits Tufts University Global Development and Environment Institute, Working Paper No. 19-01, https://sites.tufts.edu/gdae/working-papers/

Harris, Jonathan M., and Brian Roach. 2022. *Environmental and Natural Resource Economics, A Contemporary Approach.* Routledge, New York and Abingdon, UK.

Harvey, Fiona. 2018. "Climate Change Soon to Cause Movement of 140m People, World Bank Warns." *The Guardian,* March 19, 2018.

Hoornweg, Daniel, and Perinaz Bhada-Tata. 2012. "What a Waste: A Global Review of Solid Waste Management." *World Bank, Urban Development Series Knowledge Papers, No. 15,* March 2012.

Hoornweg, Daniel, Perinaz Bhada-Tata, and Chris Kennedy. 2013. "Environment: Waste Production Must Peak This Century." *Nature,* 502(7473).

Howard, Peter, and Derek Sylvan. 2015. *Expert Consensus on the Economics of Climate Change.* Institute for Policy Integrity, New York University School of Law. December 2015.

Huggler, Justin. 2018. "German Workers Win the Right to 28-Hour Working Week." *The Telegraph,* February 7.

Ichinose, Daisuke, Masashi Yamamoto, and Yuichiro Yoshida. 2015. "The Decoupling of Affluence and Waste Discharge under Spatial Correlation: Do Richer Communities Discharge More Waste?" *Environment and Development Economics,* 20: 161–184.

Intergovernmental Panel on Climate Change (IPCC). 2021. *Climate Change 2021: The Physical Science Basis.* https://www.ipcc.ch/report/ar6/wg1/.

International Institute for Applied Systems Analysis (IIASA). 2014. "*World Population Likely to Peak by 2070.*" October 23, 2014. http://www.iiasa.ac.at/web/home/about/news/20141023-population-9billion.html.

International Renewable Energy Agency (IRENA). 2017. *Renewable Energy and Jobs, Annual Review.*

Jackson, Tim. 2011. *Prosperity without Growth: Economics for a Finite Planet.* Routledge, London.

Kelemen, E., M. García-Llorente, G. Pataki, B. Martín-López, and E. Gómez-Baggethun. 2016. "Non-monetary Techniques for the Valuation of Ecosystem Service." *In OpenNESS Ecosystem Services Reference Book* (M. Potschin and K. Jax, eds). http://www.openness-project.eu/library/reference-book.

703

Keynes, John Maynard Keynes. 2009. "Economic Possibilities for Our Grandchildren." In *Essays in Persuasion*. Classic House Books, New York [original publication 1930].

Khokhar, Tariq. 2017. "Chart: Globally, 70% of Freshwater Is Used for Agriculture." *The World Bank, The Data Blog*, March 22, 2017. https://blogs.worldbank.org/opendata/chart-globally-70-freshwater-used-agriculture.

Kubiszewski, Ida, Robert Costanza, Carol Franco, Philip Lawn, John Talberth, Tim Jackson, and Camille Aylmer. 2013. "Beyond GDP: Measuring and Achieving Global Genuine Progress." *Ecological Economics, 93*:57–68.

Landrigan, Philip J., and 46 other authors. 2017. "The Lancet Commission on Pollution and Health." *The Lancet 391*:462–512.

Lebreton, L., and 16 other authors. 2018. "Evidence that the Great Pacific Garbage Patch is Rapidly Accumulating Plastic." *Nature, Scientific Reports* 8:4666.

Lin, D., L. Hanscom, J. Martindill, M. Borucke, L. Cohen, A. Galli, E. Lazarus, G. Zokai, K. Iha, D. Eaton, and M. Wackernagel. 2016. "*Working Guidebook to the National Footprint Accounts*: 2016 Edition." Global Footprint Network, Oakland.

Manyika, James, Jonathan Woetzel, Richard Dobbs, Jaana Remes, Eric Labaye, and Andrew Jordan. 2012. "*Global Growth: Can Productivity Save the Day in an Aging World?*" McKinsey Global Institute.

Mazurek, Jiri. 2011. "Environmental Kuznets Curve: A Tie between Environmental Quality and Economic Prosperity." *E+M Ekonomie a Management, 14*(4):22–31.

Nordt, Carlos, Ingeborg Warnke, Erich Seifritz, and Wolfram Kawohl. 2015. "Modelling Suicide and Unemployment: A Longitudinal Analysis Covering 63 Countries, 2000–11." *The Lancet, 2*(*3*):239–245.

O'Neill, D.W. 2012. "Measuring progress in the degrowth transition to a steady state economy," *Ecological Economics*, 84:221-231.

Organisation for Economic Co-operation and Development (OECD). 2012. Looking to 2060: Long-Term Global Growth Prospects." *OECD Economic Policy Papers, No. 03*.

Pollin, Robert. 2015. *Greening the Global Economy*. The MIT Press, Cambridge, MA.

Pollin, Robert. 2012. "Getting Real on Jobs and the Environment: Pipelines, Fracking, or Clean Energy?" *New Labor Forum, 21*(3): 84–87.

Rayment, Matt, Elke Pirgmaier, Griet De Ceuster, Friedrich Hinterberger, Onno Kuik, Henry Leveson Gower, Christine Polzin, and Adarsh Varma. 2009. "The Economic Benefits of Environmental Policy." *Report ENV.G.1/FRA/2006/007,* Institute for Environmental Studies, Vrije University, The Netherlands. November 2009.

Roberts, David. 2017. "40 Countries Are Making Polluters Pay for Carbon Pollution. Guess Who's Not." *Vox*, June 15, 2017. https://www.vox.com/energy-and-environment/2017/6/15/15796202/map-carbon-pricing-across-the-globe.

Rosnick, David. 2013. "*Reduced Work Hours as a Means of Slowing Climate Change*." Center for Economic and Policy Research, February 2013.

Ruppert, Michael C. 2009. *Confronting Collapse: The Crisis of Energy and Money in a Post Peak Oil World*. Chelsea Green Publishing, White River Junction, Vermont.

Stern, Nicholas. 2007. *Stern Review: The Economics of Climate Change*. Cambridge University Press. https://webarchive.nationalarchives.gov.uk/ukgwa/20100407172811/https://www.hm-treasury.gov.uk/stern_review_report.htm

Tanquintic-Misa, Esther. 2012. "*Global Mining to Get Costly as Quality Mineral Reserves Decline*." Nasdaq.com, April 19, 2012.

Thomas, Chris D., Alison Cameron, Rhys E. Green, Michel Bakkenes, Linda J. Beaumont, Yvonne C. Collingham, Barend F. N. Erasmus, Marinez Ferreira de Siqueira, Alan Grainger, Lee Hannah, Lesley Hughes, Brian Huntley, Albert S. van Jaarsveld, Guy F. Midgley, Lera Miles, Miguel A. Ortega-Huerta, A. Townsend Peterson, Oliver L. Phillips, and Stephen E. William. 2004. "Extinction Risk from Climate Change," *Nature 427*:145–148.

Tienhaara, Kyla. 2018. *Green Keynesianism and the Global Financial Crisis*. Routledge, London.

704

Tol, Richard. 2008. "The Social Cost of Carbon: Trends, Outliers, and Catastrophes." *Economics: The Open-Access, Open-Assessment E-Journal*, vol. *2*, 2008–2025.

Unanue, Wenceslao, Marcos E. Gómez, Diego Cortez, Juan C. Oyanedel, and Andrés Mendiburo-Seguel. 2017. "Revisiting the Link between Job Satisfaction and Life Satisfaction: The Role of Basic Psychological Needs." *Frontiers in Psychology, 8*:1–17.

United Nations. 2019. "*World Population Prospects, Volume 1*." Department of Economic and Social Affairs, Population Division, New York.

United Nations. 2021. COP26: A Snapshot of the Agreement." https://unric.org/en/cop26-a-snapshot-of-the-agreement/

United Nations. 2022. "*World Population Prospects.* Department of Economic and Social Affairs, Population Division, New York https://population.un.org/wpp/

United Nations Environment Programme (UNEP). 2008. *Vital Water Graphics: An Overview of the State of the World's Fresh and Marine Waters,* Second Edition. Nairobi, Kenya.

United Nations Environment Programme (UNEP). 2011. *Towards a Green Economy: Pathways to Sustainable Development and Poverty Eradication, A Synthesis for Policymakers.*

United Nations Environment Programme (UNEP). 2019. *Global Environmental Outlook 6: Healthy Planet, Healthy People,* https://www.unenvironment.org/resources/global-environment-outlook-6

United Nations Environment Programme (UNEP) Finance Initiative and Principles for Responsible Investment (PRI). 2011. *Universal Ownership: Why Environmental Externalities Matter to Institutional Investors.*

U.S. Energy Information Administration (EIA). 2021. *International Energy Outlook 2021.* Washington, DC.

U.S. Environmental Protection Agency. 2021. *Our Nation's Air: Trends Through 2020.* Washington, DC.

Victor, Peter. 2019. *Managing Without Growth: Slower by Design, Not Disaster* (Second Edition). Edward Elgar, Northampton, MA.

Vidal, John. 2013a. "Toxic 'e-waste' Dumped in Poor Nations, says United Nations." *The Guardian,* December 14, 2013.

Vidal, John. 2013b. "Climate Change Will Hit Poor Countries Hardest, Study Shows." *The Guardian,* September 27, 2013.

World Economic Forum (WEF). 2017. *The Global Risks Report 2020*. Geneva. https://www.weforum.org/reports/the-global-risks-report-2020

Worstall, Tim. 2017. "The Problematic Assumption in the UN's 9.8 Billion People Projection." *Forbes,* June 22, 2017.

Glossary

Numbers in parentheses indicate the chapter number of occurrence.

abundance resources are abundant to the extent that they exist in plentiful supply for meeting various goals (2)

accelerator principle the idea that high GDP growth leads to increasing investment, and low or negative GDP growth leads to declining investment (11)

accommodating monetary policy loose or expansionary monetary policy intended to counteract recessionary tendencies in the economy (11)

accounting identity an equation that is true by definition, regardless of the value of its variables (8)

adjusted net saving a national accounting indicator which aims to measure how much a country is actually saving for its future (5)

administrative capitalism a national system characterized by private corporate ownership and a substantial reliance on public administration (as well as exchange) as a mode of coordination (16)

administrative socialism a national system in which state ownership predominates and activity is coordinated primarily by public administration (command) (16)

aggregate demand (AD) curve graph showing the relationship between the rate of inflation and the total quantity of goods and services demanded by households, businesses, government, and the international sector (12)

aggregate demand the total demand for all goods and services in a national economy (1,7)

aggregate expenditure (AE) (in a simple model without government or foreign trade) what households and firms *intend* to spend on consumption and investment (8)

aggregate supply (AS) curve graph representing the relationship between the rate of inflation and the total goods and services producers are willing to supply, given the reality of capacity constraints (12)

appropriate technology technologies that are appropriate to the skills in the workforce, as well as to prevailing environmental and resources realities (16)

appropriation (of federal funds) Congressional approval of funds for a particular purpose (9)

assets property owned by an individual or company (1)

austerity a policy of deficit cutting that reduces public expenditures or raises taxes to balance the budget (15)

automatic stabilizers tax and spending institutions that tend to increase government revenues and lower government spending during economic expansions but lower revenues and raise government spending during economic recessions (9)

balance of payments (BOP) account the national account that tracks inflows and outflows arising from international trade, earnings, transfers, and transactions in assets (13)

balance of payments crisis when a country gets precariously close to running out of foreign exchange and is therefore unable to purchase imports or service its existing debt (13)

balanced budget multiplier the impact on equilibrium output of simultaneous increases of equal size in government spending and taxes (9)

bank reserves funds not lent out or invested by a private bank but kept as vault cash or on deposit at the Federal Reserve (10)

barter exchange of goods, services, or assets directly for other goods, services, or assets, without the use of money (10)

base year (in the constant-dollar method of estimating GDP) the year whose prices are chosen for evaluating production in all years. Normally real and nominal GDP are equal only in the base year (4)

basic neoclassical model a model that portrays the economy as a collection of profit-maximizing firms and utility-maximizing households interacting in perfectly competitive markets (2)

behavioral equation in contrast to an accounting identity, a behavioral equation reflects a theory about the behavior of one or more economic agents or sectors. The variables in the equation may or may not be observable (8)

Better Life Index (BLI) an index developed by the OECD to measure national welfare using 11 well-being dimensions (5)

bilateral development assistance aid (or loans) given by one country to another to promote development (16)

bond a financial instrument that pays a fixed amount each year (the coupon amount) as well as repaying the amount of principal (the face value) on a particular date (the maturity date) (11)

Bretton Woods system a system of fixed exchange rates established after World War II, lasting until 1972 (13)

budget deficit an excess of total government outlays over total government tax revenues (9)

budget surplus an excess of total government tax revenues over total government outlays (9)

Bureau of Economic Analysis (BEA) the agency in the United States in charge of compiling and publishing the national accounts (4)

Bureau of Labor Statistics (BLS) in the United States, the government agency that compiles and publishes employment and unemployment statistics (7)

business cycle (trade cycle) recurrent fluctuations in the level of national production, with alternating periods of recession and boom (1)

708

business sphere firms that produce goods and services for profitable sale (2)

capabilities the opportunities that people have to pursue important aspects of well-being, such as being healthy and having access to education (16)

capital account (in the BOP account) the account that tracks flows arising from international transactions in assets (13)

capital controls the regulation or taxation of international transactions involving assets (13)

capital flight rapid movement of capital assets out of a country (13)

capital gain an increase in the value of an asset over time (14)

capital income rents, profits, and interest (14)

capital intensive a process or procedure that makes use of more capital relative to other inputs such as labor (16)

capital stock any resource that is valued for its potential economic contributions (1)

capitalists those who own capital goods used in production, hire wage workers, and sell the products to make profits (1)

carrying capacity the level of population and consumption that can be sustained by the available natural resource base (17)

ceteris paribus a Latin phrase meaning "other things equal" or "all else constant" (2)

chain-type quantity index an index comparing real production in the current year to the reference year, calculated using a series of year-to-year Fisher quantity indexes (4)

change in demand a shift of the demand curve in response to some determinant other than the item's price (3)

change in quantity demanded movement along a demand curve in response to a price change (3)

change in quantity supplied movement along a supply curve in response to a price change (3)

change in supply a shift of the supply curve in response to some determinant other than the item's price (3)

civilian non-institutional population (BLS definition) persons 16 years or older who do not live in institutions (for example, correctional facilities, nursing homes, or long-term care hospitals) and who are not on active duty in the Armed Forces (7)

classical economics the school of economics, originating in the eighteenth century, that stressed issues of growth and distribution, based on an image of smoothly functioning markets (1)

closed economy an economy with no foreign sector (4)

collective investment vehicle or pooled fund an investment vehicle that pools investments from many different sources, making investment decisions for them all as a group (10)

commodity money a good used as money that is also valuable in itself (10)

common market a group of countries forming a customs union and additionally permitting free movement of labor and capital between participating countries (13)

common property ownership of assets by government or particular subsections of society (2)

complementary good a good that is used along with another good (3)

conditional cash transfer (CCT) programs providing cash to the poor based on the condition that they commit to spending it on specific things, such as children's education, food, or healthcare (16)

conscious consumption being aware of the costs of consumption on others and on the planet, and making consumption decisions responsibly to minimize waste and achieve a more sustainable lifestyle (1)

consumer durable goods consumer purchases that are expected to last longer than three years. These generally include equipment, such as vehicles and appliances, used by households to produce goods and services for their own use (4)

consumer price index (CPI) an index measuring changes in the prices of goods and services bought by households (4)

consumption the final use of a good or service to satisfy current wants or needs (1)

contextual economics economic analysis that takes into account the social and environmental realities within which the economic system operates (1)

contractionary fiscal policy reductions in government spending or transfer payments or increases in taxes, leading to a lower level of economic activity (9)

contractionary monetary policy the use of monetary policy tools to limit the money supply, raise interest rates, and encourage a leveling off or reduction in economic activity (11)

convergence (in reference to economic growth) the idea that underlying economic forces will cause poorer countries and regions to "catch up" with richer ones (16)

convergence criteria the requirements that EU member countries must satisfy as a condition of participating in the Eurozone (15)

core sphere households, families, and communities (2)

cost-push inflation inflation primarily caused by supply restrictions and bottlenecks (12)

countercyclical policy fiscal policy in which taxes are lowered and expenditure is raised when the economy is weak, and the opposite occurs when the economy is strong (9)

credit rationing when banks deny loans to some potential borrowers, in the interest of maintaining their own profitability (11)

cross-sectional data observations on a variable for different subjects at one point in time (2)

crowding in the process in which government spending leads to more favorable expectations for the economy, thereby inducing greater private investment (9)

crowding out a reduction in the availability of private capital resulting from federal government borrowing to finance budget deficits (9)

currency appreciation when a currency becomes more valuable, for example, when increased demand for a country's exports causes an increase in demand for its currency (13)

currency depreciation when a currency becomes less valuable, for example, due to a decrease in demand for a country's exports or an increase in its demand for imports (13)

current account (in the BOP account) the national account that tracks inflows and outflows arising from international trade, earnings, and transfers (13)

customs union A group of countries that have abolished tariffs and quotas among themselves, and have introduced a common external tariff (13)

cyclical deficit (surplus) the portion of the deficit (or surplus) that is caused by fluctuations in the business cycle (9)

cyclical unemployment unemployment caused by a drop in aggregate demand (normally associated with a recession) (7)

damage-cost approach assigning a monetary value to an environmental service that is equal to the actual damage done when the service is withdrawn (5)

debt ceiling a congressionally mandated limit on the size of the gross federal debt (15)

debt held by the public the gross federal debt minus the debt owed to other government accounts (15)

defensive expenditures money spent to counteract economic activities that have caused harm to human or environmental health (5)

deficit ceiling a congressionally mandated limit on the size of the federal budget deficit (15)

deficit spending government spending in excess of tax revenues collected (9)

deflation when the aggregate price level falls (10)

degrowth a policy of reducing the level of economic activity to promote environmental sustainability (17)

demand curve a curve indicating the quantities that buyers are ready to purchase at various prices (3)

demand the willingness and ability of purchasers to buy goods or services (3)

demand-pull inflation inflation primarily caused by excessive aggregate demand (12)

dependency needs the need to receive care, shelter, or food from others when one is unable to provide these for oneself (1)

dependency theory the theory that underdevelopment in developing countries is caused by unequal trade relations, where developing countries export primary goods that are much cheaper than the industrial goods they import from the developed nations (16)

depreciation a decrease in the quantity or quality of a stock of capital (1, 4)

devaluation lowering an exchange rate within a fixed exchange rate system (13)

direct public provision the supply of goods or services from government or nonprofit institutions (2)

discount rate the interest rate at which banks can borrow reserves at the Fed discount window (11)

discouraged workers people who want employment but have given up looking because they believe that there are no jobs available for them (7)

discretionary fiscal policy changes in government spending and taxation resulting from deliberate policy decisions (9)

disinflation a decline in the rate of inflation (12)

disposable income income remaining for consumption or saving after subtracting taxes and adding transfer payments (9)

distribution the allocation of products and resources among people (1)

division of labor an approach to production in which a process is broken down into smaller tasks, with each worker assigned only one or a few tasks (1)

domestic content requirement laws requiring traded goods to contain a certain percentage of goods produced by domestic companies (13)

dual labor market theory a theory according to which workers tend to get slotted into either a "primary sector" of good jobs, or a "secondary sector" where workers are taken on essentially an "as needed" basis (7)

dynamic analysis analysis that takes into account the passage of time (2)

ecological footprint a measure of the human impact on the environment, measured as the productive land area required to supply a society's resources and assimilate its wastes and pollution (17)

economic actor (economic agent) an individual, group, or organization that is involved in economic activities (1)

economic and monetary union an economic union in which participating countries share a single currency (13)

economic development the process of moving from a situation of poverty and deprivation to a situation of increased production and plenty, through investments and changes in the organization of work (1)

economic growth increases in the level of marketed production in a country or region (1)

economic liability anything that one economic actor owes to another (10)

economic union a group of countries forming a common market and additionally adopting a common set of economic policies (13)

economics the study of how people manage their resources to meet their needs and enhance their well-being. (1)

efficiency wage theory the theory that an employer can motivate workers to put forth more effort by paying them somewhat more than they could get elsewhere (7)

efficiency the use of resources in a way that does not waste any inputs (2)

empirical investigation observation and recording of the specific phenomena of concern (2)

environmental Kuznets curve (EKC) hypothesis the theory that as a country develops economically environmental damages per capita initially increase, then peak and eventually decrease (17)

excess reserves the portion of bank reserves that banks are permitted to lend to their customers (17)

exchange rate the number of units of one currency that can be exchanged for one unit of another currency (13)

exchange value value that corresponds to the value of goods or services for which the item can be exchanged (10)

exchange trading one thing for another (1)

expansionary fiscal policy the use of government spending, transfer payments, or tax cuts to stimulate a higher level of economic activity (9)

expansionary monetary policy the use of monetary policy tools to increase the money supply, lower interest rates, and stimulate a higher level of economic activity (11)

expected real interest rate the nominal interest rate minus expected inflation, $r_e = i - \pi_e$ (11)

explicit contract a formal, often written, agreement that states the terms of exchange and may be enforceable through a legal system (2)

external debt the portion of the gross federal debt that is owed to foreign individuals or groups (15)

externalities spillover effects of market activities on parties who are not participating in the activity (2)

factor markets markets for the services of land, labor, and capital (2)

federal funds rate the interest rate determined in the private market for overnight loans of reserves among banks (11)

Federal Open Market Committee (FOMC) the committee that oversees open market operations. It is composed of the Fed Board of Governors and 5 of the 12 regional Fed presidents (11)

fiat money a medium of exchange that is used as money because a government says it has value, and that is accepted by the people using it (10)

final goal a goal that requires no further justification; it is an end in itself (1)

final good a good that is ready for use, needing no further processing (4)

financial assets a variety of holdings in which wealth can be invested with an expectation of future return (6)

financial capital funds of purchasing power available to facilitate economic activity (1)

financial institution any institution that collects money and holds it as financial assets (6)

financial intermediary an institution such as a bank, savings and loan association, or life insurance company that accepts funds from savers and makes loans to borrowers (10)

financialization a process in which the financial sector of the economy is increasingly able to generate and circulate profits that are not closely related to the real economy (6)

fiscal capacity public revenues that can be spent within a given jurisdiction (13)

fiscal policy government spending and tax policy (9)

Fisher quantity index an index that measures production in one year relative to an adjacent year by using an average of the ratios that would be found by using first one year and then the other as the source of prices at which production is valued (4)

fixed assets structures, equipment, and intellectual property products owned by businesses and governments (4)

fixed exchange rate system a system in which currencies are traded at fixed ratios (13)

flexible (floating) exchange rate system a system in which exchange rates are determined by the market forces of supply and demand (13)

flow something whose quantity can be measured over a period of time (1)

foreign direct investment (FDI) investment in a business in a foreign country (13)

foreign exchange market intervention an action by central banks to buy or sell foreign exchange reserves in order to keep exchange rates at desired levels (13)

foreign exchange the class of currencies that is broadly acceptable by foreigners in commercial or investment transactions. Generally limited to three currencies—the dollar, the euro, and the yen (13)

foreign trade zone a designated area of a country within which foreign-owned manufacturers can operate free of many taxes, tariffs, and regulations (13)

fractional reserve system a banking system in which banks are required to keep only a fraction of the total value of their deposits on reserve (11)

free riders people who seek to enjoy the benefit of a good without paying for it (2)

free trade area a group of countries that have abolished tariffs and quotas for goods produced in the area and traded between these countries (13)

frictional unemployment unemployment that arises as people are in transition between jobs (7)

full employment a situation in which those who wish to work at the prevailing wages are able to find it readily (7)

full-employment output (Y*) for modeling purposes, a level of output that is assumed to correspond to a case of no excessive or burdensome unemployment, but the likely existence of at least some transitory unemployment (8)

functional finance the idea that a sovereign government should finance current needs and provide for adequate aggregate demand to maintain employment levels (15)

GDP deflator price index for measuring the general level of prices and defined as the ratio of nominal GDP to real GDP (4)

GDP growth rate of change in GDP showing how fast the economy is expanding or contracting (4)

gender wage gap the difference in average wages between men and women; women are paid, on average, less than men (14)

Gini ratio (or Gini coefficient) a measure of inequality, based on the Lorenz curve, that goes from 0 (perfect equality) to 1 (complete inequality). Greater inequality shows up as a larger area between the curved line and the diagonal (14)

global economy the system of economic rules, norms, and interactions by which economic actors and actions in different parts of the world are connected to one another (1)

global supply chain a network of countries directed at transforming resource inputs into finished products for delivery to the consumer (13)

government bond an interest-bearing security constituting a promise to pay at a specified future time (9)

government outlays total government expenditures, including spending on goods and services and transfer payments (9)

government spending (G) the component of GDP that represents spending on goods and services by federal, state, and local governments (9)

Green GDP GDP less depreciation of both manufactured and natural capital (5)

gross domestic product (GDP) (BEA definition) a measure of the total market value of final goods and services newly produced within a country's borders over a period of time (usually one year) (4)

gross federal debt the total amount owed by the federal government to all claimants, including foreigners, the public in the United States, and other government accounts (15)

gross investment all flows into the capital stock over a period of time (4)

Gross National Income (GNI) the total amount of money earned by a nation's people and its businesses (4)

hedge fund a type of pooled fund that often engages in highly speculative investments and to which access is generally restricted to wealthy clients (10)

historical investigation study of past events (2)

human capital people's capacity for work and their individual knowledge and skills (1)

Human Development Index (HDI) a national accounting measure developed by the United Nations, based on three factors: GNI per capita level, education, and life expectancy (5)

human development an approach to development that stresses the provision of basic needs such as food, shelter, and health care (16)

implicit contract an informal agreement about the terms of exchange, based on verbal discussions and on common norms, traditions, and expectations (2)

import substitution the policy of subsidizing domestic producers to make products that can be used in place of imported goods (13)

imputation a procedure in which values are assigned for a category of products, usually using values of related products or inputs (4)

index number a figure that measures the change in magnitude of a variable, such as a quantity or a price, compared to another period (4)

industrial policy a set of government policies designed to enhance a country's ability to compete globally (16)

Industrial Revolution a process of social, technological, and economic change, beginning in Western Europe in the eighteenth century, that developed and applied new methods of production and work organization resulting in a great increase in output per worker (16)

infant industry an industry that is not yet globally competitive, but receives government support with the expectation that it may become so (16)

inflation a rise in the general level of prices (1)

informal sphere businesses, usually small in scale, operating outside government oversight and regulation. In less industrialized countries, it may constitute the majority of economic activity (2)

in-kind transfers transfers of goods or services (1)

inputs resources that go into production (1)

institutions ways of structuring interactions between individuals and groups, including both formally constituted establishments and patterns of organization embodied in customs, habits, and laws (2)

insurance company a company that pays to cover all or part of the cost of specific risks against which individuals and companies chose to insure themselves (10)

intermediate goal a goal that is primarily desirable because its achievement will bring you closer to your final goal(s) (1)

intermediate good a good that will undergo further processing (4)

internal debt the portion of the gross federal debt that is owed to individuals or groups within the country (15)

International Monetary Fund (IMF) an international agency charged with overseeing international finance, including exchange rates, international payments, and balance of payments management (13)

intrinsic value value related to the tangible or physical properties of the object (10)

inventories stocks of raw materials or manufactured goods held until they can be used or sold (4)

investment goods goods such as machines and computers that aid in further production (1)

investment actions taken to increase the quantity or quality of a resource now, in order to make benefits possible in the future (1)

Keynesian economics a school of thought, named after John Maynard Keynes, that argues for an active government involvement in the economy, to keep aggregate demand high and employment rates up, through changes in government spending and taxation (1)

Kuznets curve hypothesis the theory that economic inequality first increases during the initial stages of economic development but then eventually decreases with further economic growth (14)

labor force (BLS definition) people who are employed or unemployed (7)

labor force participation (LFP) rate the percentage of potential workers either with a job or actively seeking a job or the labor force as a percentage of the civilian non-institutional population (7)

labor income payment to workers, including wages, salaries, and fringe benefits (14)

labor intensive a process or procedure that makes use of more labor relative to other inputs such as capital (16)

labor market discrimination a condition that exists when, among similarly qualified people, some are treated disadvantageously in employment on the basis of race, sex, age, sexual preference, physical appearance, or disability (14)

labor productivity the level of output that can be produced per worker per hour (1, 6)

laissez-faire capitalism a national system characterized by private corporate ownership and a great reliance on exchange as a mode of coordination, with relatively little coordination by public administration (16)

laissez-faire economy an economy with little government regulation (1)

leverage the use of debt to increase the potential rate of return of one's investment (at greater risk) (10)

liquidity trap a situation in which interest rates are so low that the central bank finds it impossible to reduce them further (11)

liquidity the ease of use of an asset as a medium of exchange (10)

living standards growth improvements in people's diet, housing, medical care, education, working conditions, and access to transportation, communication, entertainment, and other amenities (1)

Lorenz curve a line used to portray an income distribution, drawn on a graph with percentiles of households on the horizontal axis and the cumulative percentage of income on the vertical axis (14)

M1 a measure of the money supply that includes currency, checkable deposits, and other liquid accounts like savings, shares, and money market accounts (10)

M2 a measure of the money supply that includes all of M1 plus, small certificates of deposit and retail money market funds (10)

macroeconomics the study of how economic activities at all levels create a national (and global) economic environment (1)

macroeconomy an economic system whose boundaries are normally understood to be the boundaries of a country (1)

maintenance-cost approach assigning a monetary value to an environmental service that is equal to what it would cost to maintain the same standard of services using an alternative method (5)

manufactured capital physical assets generated by applying human productive activities to natural capital (1)

manufacturing productivity an index of the value of the goods produced per hour of labor in the manufacturing sector (6)

marginal propensity to consume the number of additional dollars of consumption for every additional dollar of income (typically a fraction between zero and one) (8)

marginal propensity to save the number of additional dollars saved for each additional dollar of income (typically a fraction between zero and one) (8)

marginally attached workers people who want employment and have looked for work in the past 12 months but not in the past 4 weeks (7)

market (first meaning) a physical place or web location where there is an expectation of finding both buyers and sellers for the same product or service (2)

market (second meaning) an institution that brings buyers and sellers into communication with each other, structuring and coordinating their actions (2)

market (third meaning) an economic system (a "market economy") that relies on market institutions to conduct many economic activities (2)

market disequilibrium a situation of either shortage or surplus (3)

market equilibrium a situation in which the quantity supplied equals the quantity demanded, and thus there is no pressure for change in price or quantity bought or sold (3)

market failure a situation in which markets yield inefficient or inappropriate outcomes (2)

market power the ability to control, or significantly affect, the terms and conditions of the exchanges in which one participates (2)

market socialism a national system in which state ownership predominates but much economic activity is coordinated through markets (16)

maximum capacity output the level of output an economy would produce if every resource in the economy were fully utilized (12)

means-tested programs programs designed to transfer income to recipients based on need (14)

menu costs the costs to a supplier of changing prices listed on order forms, brochures, menus, and the like (3)

microeconomics the study of the economic activities and interactions of individuals, households, businesses, and other groups at the subnational level (1)

migration controls restrictions on the flow of people into and out of a country (13)

Millennium Development Goals (MDGs) a set of goals declared by the United Nations in 2000, emphasizing the eradication of extreme poverty; promotion of education, gender equity, and health; environmental sustainability; and partnership between rich and poor countries (16)

model an analytical tool that highlights some aspects of reality while ignoring others (2)

modern monetary theory the belief that fiscal expenditure and taxes determine output and price levels, while money is supplied or withheld merely in response to fiscal policy (11)

monetarism a school of economic thought that argues that governments should aim for steadiness in the money supply rather than playing an active role (1, 11)

monetary base (or high-powered money) the sum of total currency plus bank reserves (11)

monetary neutrality the idea that changes in the money supply may affect only prices while leaving output unchanged (11)

monetary policy the use of tools controlled by the central bank, such as interest rates on funds commercial banks borrow from the central bank, or the purchase of government bonds by the central bank to affect the levels of interest rates, credit, and money supply (10)

monetizing the debt the purchase of new debt from the Treasury by the Federal Reserve (15)

monetizing the deficit when a central bank buys government debt as it is issued (equivalent to "running the printing presses") (11)

money multiplier as the ratio of the money supply to the monetary base, it tells by how much the money supply will change for a given change in high-powered money (11)

money supply rule committing to letting the money supply grow at a fixed rate per year (11)

moral hazard the creation of perverse incentives that encourage excessive risk-taking because of protections against losses from that risk (10)

mortgage broker an agent who assists in identifying a lender for prospective homeowners looking to borrow money for their purchase (10)

multilateral development assistance aid or loans provided by the World Bank, regional development banks, or UN agencies with the announced intention of promoting development (16)

national accounting conventions practices adopted by government agencies in order to make national accounts as standardized and comparable across different countries and time periods as possible (4)

national income (NI) a measure of all domestic incomes earned in production (4)

National Income and Product Accounts (NIPA) a set of statistics compiled by the BEA concerning production, income, spending, prices, and employment (4)

natural capital physical assets provided by nature (1)

negative (or inverse) relationship the relationship between two variables if an increase in one variable is associated with a decrease in the other variable (or vice versa) (2)

neoclassical synthesis a combination of classical and Keynesian perspectives (12)

net domestic product (NDP) a measure of national production in excess of that needed to replace worn-out manufactured capital, calculated by subtracting depreciation from GDP (4)

net exports the value of exports less the value of imports (4)

net investment gross investment minus an adjustment for depreciation of the capital stock (4)

net taxes taxes minus transfer payments (9)

New Keynesian macroeconomics a school of thought that bases its analysis on micro-level market behavior, but which justifies activist macroeconomic policies by assuming that markets have "imperfections" that can create or prolong recessions (12)

nominal (current dollar) GDP the dollar value of all final goods and services produced in a year in that year's prices (4)

non-bank financial institution a financial institution that performs a number of services similar to those offered by banks but that is not a licensed bank and is not subject to banking regulations (10)

non-excludable good a good whose benefits are freely available to all (2)

non-renewable resources resources that cannot be reproduced on a human time-scale, so that their stock diminishes with use, such as oil, coal, and mineral ores (17)

non-rival good a good whose use by one person does not reduce the quantity available to others (2)

non-tariff barriers to trade use of licensing or other requirements to limit the volume of trade (13)

normative questions questions about how things should be (1)

"not in the labor force" (BLS definition) the classification given to people who are neither "employed" nor "unemployed" (7)

occupational segregation the tendency of men and women to be employed in different occupations (14)

off-budget expenditures government-funded programs that are exempted from the normal budgeting process because the taxes that fund them cannot be used for budgetary items that are subject to congressional appropriations (9)

official reserve account the account reflecting the foreign exchange market operations of a country's central bank (13)

Okun's "law" an empirical inverse relationship between the unemployment rate and real GDP growth (8)

on-budget expenditures all federal expenditures that rely on general tax revenue subject to congressional approval each year (9)

open economy an economy with a foreign sector (4)

open market operations sales or purchases of U.S. Treasury bonds by the Fed (11)

opportunity cost the value of the best alternative that is forgone when a choice is made (2)

opportunity-cost method (for estimating the value of household production) valuing hours at the amount that the unpaid worker could have earned at a paid job (5)

output sectors divisions of a macroeconomy based on what is being produced (6)

outputs the goods and services that result from production (1)

paradox of thrift the phenomenon that an increase in intended savings can lead, through a decline in equilibrium income, to lower total savings (8)

participatory rural assessment an approach to identifying the poor by collecting information from local people about housing conditions, poverty levels, and access to resources (16)

path dependence the idea that the state of a system such as the economy is strongly dependent on its past history (12)

pension fund a fund with the exclusive purpose of paying retirement benefits to employees (10)

perfectly competitive market a market in which there are many buyers and sellers, all units of the good are identical, and there is free entry and exit and perfect information (3)

physical infrastructure the equipment, buildings, physical communication lines, roads, and other tangible structures that provide the foundation for economic activity (2)

portfolio investment the purchase of financial assets such as stocks and bonds; in international finance, investment in stocks or bonds of a foreign country or company (10, 13)

positive (or direct) relationship the relationship between two variables if an increase in one variable is associated with an increase in the other variable (2)

positive questions questions about how things are (1)

post-Keynesian macroeconomics a school of thought that stresses the importance of history and uncertainty in determining macroeconomic outcomes (12)

poverty line the income threshold below which members of a population are classified as poor (16)

precautionary demand the demand for money to pay for contingencies (11)

precautionary principle the principle that we should err on the side of caution when facing a significant possibility of severe damage to human health or the natural environment (1)

price elasticity of demand a measure of the responsiveness of quantity demanded to changes in price (3)

price elasticity of supply a measure of the responsiveness of quantity supplied to changes in price (3)

price elasticity a measure of the sensitivity or responsiveness of quantity supplied or demanded to changes in price (3)

primary goods goods that are directly derived from nature, such as metal ores, or lightly processed, such as timber or sugar cane (16)

primary sector the sector of the economy that involves the harvesting and extraction of natural resources and simple processing of these raw materials into products that are generally sold to manufacturers as inputs (6)

prime rate the interest rate that banks charge their most creditworthy commercial borrowers (11)

private property ownership of assets by non-government economic actors (2)

procyclical policy fiscal policy in which taxes are lowered and expenditure is raised when the economy is strong, and the opposite is done when the economy is weak (9)

product markets markets for newly produced goods and services (2)

production the conversion of resources to goods and services (1)

production-possibilities frontier (PPF) a curve showing the maximum amounts of two outputs that society could produce from given resources, over a certain time period (2)

progressive income tax a tax in which a larger share of income is collected from those with higher incomes (9)

proportional income tax a tax in which the same share of income is collected from households, irrespective of income level (9)

protectionism the practice of limiting the extent of trade with other countries through direct policy intervention (13)

public good a good whose benefits are freely available to anyone, and whose use by one person does not diminish its usefulness to others (2)

public purpose sphere governments and other local, national, and international organizations established for a public purpose beyond individual or family self-interest and not operating with the goal of making a profit (2)

purchasing power parity (PPP) adjustments adjustments to international income statistics to take into account the differences in the cost of living across countries (13)

purchasing power parity (PPP) the theory that exchange rates should reflect differences in purchasing power among countries (13)

quantitative easing (QE) the purchase of financial assets including long-term bonds by the Fed, creating more monetary reserves and expanding the money supply (13)

quantity adjustments a response by suppliers in which they react to unexpectedly low sales of their goods primarily by reducing production levels rather than by reducing the price and to unexpectedly high sales by increasing production rather than raising the price (3)

quantity equation $M \times V = P \times Y$, where M is the money supply, V is the velocity of money, P is the price level, and Y is real output (11)

quantity index an index measuring changes in levels of quantities produced (4)

quantity theory of money the theory that money supply is directly related to nominal GDP, according to the equation $M \times V = P \times Y$ (11)

rational expectations theory the theory that people's expectations about Federal Reserve policy cause predictable monetary policies to be ineffective in changing output levels (12)

real business cycle theory the theory that changes in employment levels are caused by a change in technological capacities or people's preferences concerning work (12)

real exchange rate the exchange rate between two currencies, adjusted for inflation in each country (13)

real GDP a measure of gross domestic product that seeks to reflect the actual value of goods and services produced, by removing the effect of changes in prices over time (4)

real interest rate nominal interest rate minus inflation, $r = i - \pi$ (11)

real money supply the nominal money supply divided by the general price level (as measured by a price index), expressed as M/P (12)

real wealth effect the tendency of consumers to increase or decrease their consumption based on their perceived level of wealth (12)

recession a downturn in economic activity, usually defined as lasting for two consecutive calendar quarters or more (1)

regressive income tax a tax in which a larger share of income is collected from households with lower incomes (14)

regulation setting standards or laws to govern behavior (2)

renewable resources resources that are regenerated over time through natural and biological processes, such as forests, fisheries, and freshwater (17)

rent payments for the use of any capital asset (14)

replacement-cost method (for estimating the value of household production) valuing hours at the amount it would be necessary to pay someone to do the work (5)

required reserves the portion of bank reserves that banks must keep on reserve (10)

resource management the management of capital stocks so that their productivity is sustained or improved (1)

restorative development economic progress that restores economic, financial, social, or ecological systems that have been degraded and are no longer adequately supportive of human well-being in the present and the future (1)

revaluation raising an exchange rate within a fixed exchange rate system (13)

rule of 72 a shorthand calculation that states that dividing 72 by an annual growth rate yields approximately the number of years it will take for an amount to double (4)

satellite accounts additional or parallel accounting systems that provide measures of social and environmental factors in physical terms, without necessarily including monetary valuation (5)

saving refraining from consumption in the current period (1)

Say's Law the classical belief that "supply creates its own demand" (1)

scarcity limits on resources such that that they are not sufficient to meet various different goals at once (2)

secondary sector the sector of the economy that involves converting the outputs of the primary sector into products suitable for use or consumption. It includes manufacturing, construction, and utilities (6)

securities broker an agent responsible for finding a buyer for sellers of different securities, thereby offering enhanced liquidity to the seller (10)

securitization the process of pooling various kinds of loans, slicing and sorting them according to their risk levels, and repackaging them into financial instruments (10)

self-correcting market a market that automatically adjusts to any imbalances between sellers (supply) and buyers (demand) (3)

shadow bank credit intermediation that involves entities and activities outside the regular banking system (10)

shortage a situation in which the quantity demanded at a particular price exceeds the quantity that sellers are willing to supply (3)

skill-biased technical change the theory that relative wage gains will be the greatest for those workers who possess the education and skills to use modern technologies (14)

social capital the institutions and the stock of trust, mutual understanding, shared values, and socially held knowledge that facilitates the social coordination of economic activity (1)

social cost of carbon a monetary estimate of the discounted long-term damages from emitting a ton of CO_2 in a given year (17)

social discount rate a discount rate that reflects social rather than market valuation of future costs and benefits; usually lower than the market discount rate (17)

social insurance programs programs designed to transfer income to recipients if and when certain events (like retirement or disability) occur (14)

sovereign debt government debt, especially debt denominated in a currency that the government does not control (15)

specialization in production, a system of organization in which each worker performs only one type of task (1)

speculation buying and selling assets with the expectation of profiting from appreciation or depreciation in their value (3)

speculative bubble the situation that occurs when mutually reinforcing investor optimism raises the value of an asset far above what can be justified by fundamental value (3)

speculative demand the demand for money to exploit new expectations of changes in asset prices (11)

stagflation a combination of rising inflation and economic stagnation (12)

static analysis analysis that does not take into account the passage of time (2)

"sticky wage" theories theories about why wages may stay at above-equilibrium levels, even when a labor surplus exists (7)

stock something whose quantity can be measured at a point in time (1)

stock-flow diagram an illustration of how stocks can be changed, over time, by flows (1)

strong sustainability an analytical perspective suggesting that natural capital depreciation is justified only if it is compensated for with adequate restoration of other natural capital (17)

structural deficit (surplus) the portion of the deficit (or surplus) that results from tax and spending policy dictated by the President and Congress at their discretion (9)

structural unemployment unemployment that arises because people's skills, experience, education, or location do not match what employers need (7)

subjective wellbeing a measure of welfare based on survey questions asking people about their own degree of life satisfaction (5)

subprime mortgage a mortgage given to someone with poor credit (3, 10)

substitute good a good that can be used in place of another (3)

supply curve a curve indicating the quantities that sellers are willing to supply at various prices (3)

supply shock a change in the productive capacity of an economy (12)

supply-side economics an economic theory that emphasizes policies to stimulate production, such as lower taxes. The theory predicts that such incentives stimulate greater economic effort, saving, and investment, thereby increasing overall economic output and tax revenues (9)

supply the willingness of producers and merchandisers to provide goods and services (3)

surplus a situation in which the quantity that sellers wish to sell at the stated price is greater than the quantity that buyers will buy at that price (3)

Sustainable Development Goals (SDGs) a set of goals set forth by the United Nations in 2015, building on and expanding the MDGs, including goals such as battling inequality worldwide, promoting inclusive growth and limiting climate change (16)

tariffs taxes on imports or exports (13)

tax multiplier the impact of a change in a lump sum tax on economic equilibrium expressed mathematically as $\Delta Y / \Delta \bar{T}$ *(mult) (mpc)* (9)

technological progress the development of new products and new, more efficient, methods of production (1)

technological unemployment unemployment caused by reduced demand for workers because technology has increased the productivity of those who have jobs (7)

terms of trade the price of exports relative to the price of imports (16)

tertiary sector the sector of the economy that involves the provision of services rather than tangible goods (6)

theoretical investigation analysis based on abstract thought (2)

theory of market adjustment the theory that market forces will tend to make shortages and surpluses disappear (3)

throughput the flow of raw materials and energy through the economy, leading to outputs of waste (17)

time lags the time that elapses between the formulation of an economic policy and its actual effects on the economy (9)

time-series data observations of how a numerical variable changes over time (2)

trade account (part of the current account) the portion of the current account that tracks inflows and outflows arising exclusively from international trade in goods and services (13)

trade deficit an excess of imports over exports, causing net exports to be negative (13)

trade quota a restriction on the quantity of a good that can be imported or exported (13)

trade-related subsidies payments given by governments to producers to encourage more production, either for export or as a substitute for imports (13)

transaction costs the costs of arranging economic activities (2)

transactions demand the demand for money to pay for the goods and services that satisfy our day-to-day needs (11)

transfer payments payments by government to individuals or firms, including Social Security payments, unemployment compensation, interest payments, and subsidies (9)

transfer the giving of something with nothing specific expected in return (1)

transnational corporation a company that produces goods or services in more than one country (13)

twin deficits hypothesis the belief in a causal link between a country's budget balance and its trade balance (15)

unconditional cash transfer (UCT) programs providing cash to the poor, with no specific conditions on how the funds should be spent (16)

underemployment working fewer hours than desired or at a job that does not match one's skills (7)

unemployed person (BLS definition) a person who is not employed but who is actively seeking a job and is immediately available for work (7)

unemployment rate the percentage of the labor force made up of people who do not have paid jobs but are immediately available and actively looking for paid jobs (7)

unemployment a situation in which people seek a paying job, but cannot obtain one (1)

universal basic income (UBI) a periodic cash payment to all citizens (or all adult citizens) regardless of means-test or work requirements so that people can at least cover basic expenses such as housing, food, and healthcare (7)

utility the level of usefulness or satisfaction gained from a particular activity such as the consumption of a good or service (2)

value-added the value of what a producer sells, less the value of the intermediate inputs it uses, except labor. This is equal to the wages paid out by the producer plus its profits (4)

velocity of money the number of times that a dollar would have to change hands during a year to support nominal GDP, calculated as $V = (P \times Y)/M$ (11)

virtuous cycles (in development) self-reinforcing patterns of high savings, investment, productivity growth, and economic expansion (16)

wage and price controls government regulations setting limits on wages and prices or on the rates at which they are permitted to increase (12)

wage-price spiral when upward pressure on wages creates upward pressure on prices and, as a result, further upward pressure on wages (12)

wage-productivity gap the gap between the growth of labor productivity and the growth of hourly labor compensation (14)

Washington Consensus specific economic policy prescriptions used by the IMF and World Bank with a goal of helping developing countries to avoid crises and maintain stability. They include openness to trade and investment (liberalization), privatization, budget austerity, and deregulation (13)

waste products outputs that are not used either for consumption or in a further production process (1)

weak sustainability an analytical perspective suggesting that natural capital depreciation is justified as long as it is compensated for with adequate increases in other types of capital (17)

well-being a term used to describe the overall quality of life (1)

World Bank an international agency charged with promoting economic development, through loans and other programs (13)

World Trade Organization an international organization that conducts negotiations aimed at lowering trade barriers, and mediates trade disputes between countries (13)

Index

733